THE CAMBRIDGE HIST
OF TWENTIETH-CENTURY
POLITICAL THOUGHT

This major work of academic reference provides a comprehensive overview of the development of political thought from the late nineteenth century to the end of the twentieth century. Written by a distinguished team of international contributors, this Cambridge History covers the rise of the welfare state and subsequent reactions to it, the fascist and communist critiques of and attempted alternatives to liberal democracy, the novel forms of political organisation occasioned by the rise of a mass electorate and new social movements, the various intellectual traditions from positivism to post-modernism that have shaped the study of politics, the interaction between Western and non-Western traditions of political thought, and the challenge posed to the state by globalisation. Every major theme in twentieth-century political thought is covered in a series of essays at once scholarly and accessible, of interest and relevance to students and scholars of politics at all levels, from beginning undergraduate upwards.

TERENCE BALL is Professor of Political Science at Arizona State University. He taught for many years at the University of Minnesota, and has held visiting professorships at the universities of Oxford and California-San Diego. Professor Ball has edited the political writings of James Mill and *The Federalist* for the Cambridge Texts series, co-edited (with Joyce Appleby) the writings of Thomas Jefferson for the same series, and his own books include *Transforming Political Discourse*, *Reappraising Political Theory* and *Rousseau's Ghost: A Novel*, in addition to numerous edited and co-edited works.

RICHARD BELLAMY is Professor of Government at the University of Essex and Academic Director of the European Consortium for Political Research (ECPR). He has previously held chairs at the universities of East Anglia and Reading. Professor Bellamy has edited the writings of Beccaria and Gramsci for the Cambridge Texts series, and his own books include *Modern Italian Social Theory, Liberalism and Modern Society, Liberalism and Pluralism* and *Rethinking Liberalism*, in addition to numerous edited and co-edited works.

THE CAMBRIDGE HISTORY OF TWENTIETH-CENTURY POLITICAL THOUGHT

EDITED BY

TERENCE BALL

Arizona State University

AND

RICHARD BELLAMY

University of Essex

CAMBRIDGE UNIVERSITY PRESS
Cambridge, New York, Melbourne, Madrid, Cape Town, Singapore, São Paulo,
Delhi, Dubai, Tokyo

Cambridge University Press
The Edinburgh Building, Cambridge CB2 8RU, UK

Published in the United States of America by Cambridge University Press, New York

www.cambridge.org
Information on this title: www.cambridge.org/9780521691628

First published 2003
Third printing 2010

Printed in the United Kingdom at the University Press, Cambridge

A catalogue record for this publication is available from the British Library

ISBN 978-0-521-56354-3 hardback
ISBN 978-0-521-69162-8 paperback

Contents

Contributors

WALTER L. ADAMSON
Samuel C. Dobbs Professor of History, Emory University

TERENCE BALL
Professor of Political Science, Arizona State University

RICHARD BELLAMY
Professor of Government, University of Essex

MARIO CACIAGLI
Professor of Political Science, University of Florence

MARTIN CEADEL
Professor of Politics, University of Oxford, and Fellow of New College

RICHARD DAGGER
Professor of Political Science and Director of the Philosophy, Politics and Law Program in the Barrett Honors College, Arizona State University

PETER DEWS
Professor of Philosophy, University of Essex

JAMES FARR
Professor of Political Science, University of Minnesota

MICHAEL FREEDEN
Professor of Politics, University of Oxford, and Fellow of Mansfield College, Oxford

DICK GEARY
Professor of Modern History and Director of the Humanities Research Centre at the University of Nottingham

ROBERT E. GOODIN
Professor of Social and Political Theory and of Philosophy in the Research School of Social Sciences, Australian National University

List of contributors

NEIL HARDING
Professor of Government, University of Wales, Swansea, and Professor of Political Science, University of Michigan, Ann Arbor.

JEFFREY C. ISAAC
James H. Rudy Professor of Political Science, Indiana University, Bloomington

SALWA ISMAIL
Senior Lecturer in Middle East Politics, University of Exeter

SUSAN JAMES
Professor of Philosophy, Birkbeck College, University of London

SUNIL KHILNANI
Professor of Politics and Director of South Asia Studies at the Nitze School of Advanced International Studies, Johns Hopkins University, Washington D.C.

MELISSA LANE
University Lecturer in History, Cambridge University, and Fellow of King's College, Cambridge

STEVEN LUKES
Professor of Sociology, New York University, and Visiting Centennial Professor of Sociology, London School of Economics

DAVID McLELLAN
Professor of Political Theory, Goldsmiths College, University of London

JAMES MAYALL
Sir Patrick Sheehy Professor of International Relations, University of Cambridge

DAVID MILLER
Professor of Political Theory at the University of Oxford and Official Fellow in Social and Political Theory, Nuffield College, Oxford

NOËL O'SULLIVAN
Professor of Political Philosophy, University of Hull

ANTONINO PALUMBO
A Ricercatore, University of Palermo

BHIKHU PAREKH
Centennial Professor, London School of Economics

WAYNE PARSONS
Professor of Public Policy, Queen Mary and Westfield College, University of London

STANLEY G. PAYNE
Hilldale-Jaume Vicens Vives Professor of History, University of Wisconsin-Madison

PAUL ROAZEN
Professor Emeritus, Social and Political Science, York University, Toronto

ALAN SCOTT
Professor of Sociology, University of Innsbruck

JAMES TULLY
Henry N. R. Jackman Distinguished Professor of Philosophical Studies, University of Toronto

Preface

This is the capstone volume in the now-monumental Cambridge Histories of Political Thought. Conceived and planned in 1993, the present volume has been a long time in the making. Our greatest debts are of course owed to our contributors, whose patience is as great as this book is long. Many must have wondered if it would ever appear at all. We are scarcely less indebted to Richard Fisher, our editor at the Cambridge University Press, who first approached us about editing this volume, and later prodded and cajoled us even as we prodded and cajoled our contributors. That we are all still on speaking terms attests to our shared and strong sense of civility and mutual respect.

We owe a great deal to Ciarán O'Kelly for able assistance in the final stages of revising and editing the present volume, to the external readers who commented on various chapters, to Frances Nugent for conscientious copy-editing and to Judith Ball for preparing the index and, with assistance from Michelle Tolman, correcting page proofs. Finally, though not least, each of the editors wishes to thank the other for the pleasure of the collaboration.

Terence Ball and Richard Bellamy

Editors' introduction

This, the final volume of the Cambridge History of Political Thought, attempts to provide an overview of the main currents of twentieth-century social and political thinking. It is difficult to narrate the history of political thought in any period; but to attempt to survey the history of twentieth-century political theorising in all its variety and diversity presents particular difficulties, if only because the century just ended was marked by a pervasive scepticism about the ways in which histories are narrated and an acute awareness of the many and alternative ways in which they may be constructed. The influence of Marx and Freud, amongst other theorists, has fostered 'the hermeneutics of suspicion', according to which nothing is ever as it appears to be, and this suspicion extends to the writing of histories, including the present one. For a start, suspicions about ideological bias are bound to arise, and these are only compounded because our contributors are narrating the history of their own time. Questions may also be asked about why some topics and thinkers are included and others excluded. And, not least, there is the ever-present question of method: why narrate from one orientation rather than another? Why employ this method (or methodology) instead of that?

These are difficult questions for which we confess we have no fully satisfactory answers. But several disclaimers may be in order. First, the editors of and contributors to the present volume doubtless do have their own political preferences and ideological biases, and these doubtless influence what we write about and how we go about doing that. Happily, however, we do not all share the same political preferences or subscribe to a single ideology. Quite the contrary; we believe that the reader will be struck not only by the variety of topics treated here, but (we hope) by the diverse and even-handed, if not invariably 'objective', ways in which they are treated. Unfortunately, but inevitably, some thinkers and topics are treated at greater length than others, while many are excluded entirely. This selectiveness is an unavoidable consequence of our being bound by a word limit that we have come perilously close to exceeding. We have attempted to be as inclusive as possible in our choice of thinkers and themes, and to detect and mitigate overt ideological bias. And finally, as regards method, we should note that the present volume is not wedded to or inspired by any particular methodology. Rather, we have thought it best to be eclectic, adopting a variety of approaches according to the thinkers, problems and themes addressed in individual chapters. The chapters are primarily thematic, generally chronological and occasionally focused on a particular theorist. In the main, each chapter explores a theme throughout the whole of the period covered by this volume. Exceptions arise when a particular theorist is notably associated with a given idea or school of thought; or when a theme is of sufficient importance to merit treatment in more than one chapter, either because of the longevity, centrality and pervasiveness of its influence, or because, although short-lived, it produced a particularly rich literature.

Nevertheless, we admit the very enterprise of writing a history of political thought produces certain inherent distortions. Though we have aimed to be as ecumenical as possible, devising the table of contents and setting word limits obliged us to make some hard, certainly contentious, and occasionally no doubt arbitrary choices. Because it is a history, we have tried to avoid making presentist judgements concerning which ideas are of the most relevance or importance for us today, instead taking our cue from their significance in their own time. Because our concern is political thought rather than practice, we have often given more weight to theories that have had greater resonance in the world of ideal rather than in that of real politics – though the two are closely connected, with all contributors exploring the links between them. Above all, because our focus is on political ideas rather than intellectual history more generally, we, like the editors of earlier volumes in this series, have been faced with difficulties in delineating the range and identity of the subject matter.

These problems are particularly acute in the twentieth century, when the scope of 'the political' was hotly contested and frequently extended to make the variety of themes, thinkers and topics enormous. Our starting point has been that the twentieth century was pre-eminently an age of ideologies, and these formed the main languages of political thought. As modes of political thinking, however, they can hardly be explored in isolation from the political events they helped to shape and were in turn shaped by. Similarly and relatedly, the identity of political thought during this period has become fractured and further complicated by the ever-increasing scope and complexity of phenomena that can be regarded as political. In an age of globalisation, the state, long the central focus of political thought, is now widely regarded as one actor among many others, including NGOs (non-governmental organisations), international corporations, regional and global trade regimes, human-rights monitoring agencies, international relief organisations, and transnational political movements of women, environmentalists and other groups. Thus, what is (and is not) regarded as 'political' restricts or extends the range of 'political thought', whose identity is open to question in its turn. Issues of immigration, international trade, environmental protection, human rights, terrorism, cultural identity, the evolving languages of the social sciences and aesthetics, new social movements, the changing constitution of states and societies – these and other developments have helped define the character of modern (and arguably 'post-modern') political thought. In consequence, we have considered the emergence of the environmental and women's movements, an anti-Western and anti-liberal backlash in Islamic movements and states, the development of the discipline of political science, and the impact of modernism in art and literature and Freudian psychology on political thought. This degree of diversity is unprecedented and well-nigh unmanageable in editorial if not in political terms. Finally, like its predecessors, this volume deals primarily with 'Western' political thought. Even so, the expansion of the West and the processes of globalisation, which greatly increased during this period and have enhanced the interaction and mutual influence of Western and non-Western political languages and tradition, have put the adjective 'Western' into question. Instances of transnational and cross-cultural fertilisation include the influence of Henry David Thoreau on Gandhi, and Gandhi on Martin Luther King and the environmental movement, of Marx and Lenin on Mao, and Mao on ultra-leftist movements in Europe and South America. We have accordingly looked at instances in which Western political thinking has been either appropriated or criticised by non-Western traditions, as with Mao and Gandhi on the one hand and anti-colonial and Islamic movements on the other.

In order to dovetail with its predecessor volume, the present history has in several instances picked up where that volume left off and has in others (and perhaps unavoidably) trespassed into the territory of the nineteenth century. There are two rather obvious reasons for this. The first is that a century is a chronological convention, not a hermetically sealed capsule into which everything fits without remainder or overlap; consequently any division of the history of political thought (or indeed of anything else) is largely artificial. A second reason for reaching back into the nineteenth century is that many of the agendas of twentieth-century political thinking were to a very considerable extent set in the latter part of the preceding century. Thus we begin roughly in 1880, when the major European states had been largely established and the era of liberal regimes begun. This was also the period of imperial consolidation, the socialist critique of liberal-capitalist society, the rise of modern mass democracies, the women's suffrage movement, and the search for a social democratic middle way, as found for example in the modern welfare state. The next main chronological divide within our period comes with the First World War, mass military mobilisation, the Russian Revolution, the rise of totalitarianism, and the economic chaos of the Great Depression, and culminates with the Holocaust and the Second World War. The next great divide comes with the Cold War, decolonisation and the end of the European empires, a much-vaunted (and greatly exaggerated) 'end of ideology', followed by the end of the end of ideology with the rise of new social movements, the demise of communism, a resurgent conservatism, the onset of a new tribalism (often linked to a revival of religious fundamentalism), and the crisis of the welfare state as it comes under pressure from both internal and external social, economic and ideological forces.

In taking our history up to the present, we do not wish in any way to advocate a Whiggish (and still less a Hegelian) account of twentieth-century political thinking. Very few indeed would wish to claim that the history of the twentieth century – and of twentieth-century political thinking – is a story of progress. Quite the contrary. The twentieth century was a time of turmoil, of mass movements and mass murder, of holocausts and hydrogen bombs. As the Russian revolutionary leader Leon Trotsky observed with uncharacteristic understatement, 'Anyone wishing to live a quiet life has done badly to be born in the twentieth century.' Whether, or to what extent, the twenty-first century and the new millennium will be any quieter or less violent remains an open question. If the terrorist attacks of 11 September 2001 and the subsequent 'war on terrorism' are any indication, the prognosis is far from promising.

Part I
The changing fortunes of liberal democracy

I
The coming of the welfare state

MICHAEL FREEDEN

The welfare state – the overriding objective of domestic politics in most developed Western states during the first half of the twentieth century – was a product of fundamental changes in the conceptualisation both of welfare and of the state. Evolving accounts of human nature and of the interdependence between individual and society were supplemented by structural experimentation with various measures intended to secure the realisation of those understandings. They were also accompanied by competing ethical and conceptual interpretations of rights, duties, responsibilities and agency. Moreover, they were nourished within opposing ideological families that sought to be sharply distinguished from one another, yet displayed overlapping and complex configurations of ideas. Variations in time and space account for some important differences of emphasis, but also demonstrate that shared pools of ideas were drawn upon from which these local divergences emanated.

Ideological disparities

At its zenith in the mid-twentieth century, the welfare state was frequently defined as one in which the power of a democratic state is deliberately used to regulate and modify the free play of economic and political forces in order to effect a redistribution of income (Schottland 1967, p. 10). This definition, like any other, conveys a particular interpretation, in this case one that presupposes a state-instigated deviation from a market norm, as well as the absence of 'modification' or intervention in earlier welfare arrangements – both highly contestable assumptions. It also fails to differentiate between the practices of welfare as insurance and as assistance, or between welfare as the guaranteeing of minimal material conditions and welfare as human flourishing in broad, even optimal senses.[1] Nor does it offer a comparative distinction between 'welfare state', 'l'état providence' and 'Wohlfahrtsstaat', or furnish the historical perspective without which twentieth-century welfare-state thinking is unintelligible. Ultimately, that economistic and materialist definition constitutes an impoverished representation of the more extensive political ends and ideals welfare thinkers were hoping to realise, even those thinkers who themselves resorted to economic argument. For many, a democratic underpinning of the welfare state was a requisite of welfare, even though its conceptualisations emerged from undemocratic origins. Moreover, in line with more focused and functional thinking about the state, it was proffered as a vital instrument in securing further social and human ends such as flourishing, community, equality, dignity, responsibility, free self-development, participation, and productive and satisfying labour, in many of their multiple forms.

But even at the level of historical explanation difficulties abound. Conventionally, the welfare state has been portrayed as emerging from a collectivist assault on the principles of individualism; or – not at all the same thing – from a struggle between rival liberal and socialist viewpoints; or even, as in the German case, between rival conservative and socialist ones; or as a paternalist or, conversely, mutualist impulse derived from charitable practice in the private sector. Such frames of reference no longer seem the most fruitful interpretative devices to apply, if offered as monolithic causes. The richness of the ideational composite of welfare thinking defies earlier simplistic categorisations that saw social reform as the 'golden mean' between laissez-faire and socialism (Fine 1956), a view predominant particularly in the less nuanced world of the American ideological spectrum. Rather, welfare thinking is both shaped by, and the shaper of, a multitude of factors. These include modern theories and practices of citizenship, physical and psychological notions of human well-being, the growth of bureaucracies, new understandings of the ends of politics and the uses to which state power may be put, objectives of modernisation and nation-building, perceptions of changing equilibria among social forces and classes involving the encouragement of democratic participation, developing technologies of social security, alternative economic bases to the rationales for the redistribution of wealth, contesting views concerning social justice, competing allocations of ethical and social responsibility to diverse social agencies, emerging future-oriented attitudes towards time and its mastery, reassessment of risk,

1. For the replacement of the minimum with the optimum see Briggs (1961).

and novel means of effecting social control and social order. Nor was there any simple correlation among all these factors: their manifold permutations reflected the fecundity and flexibility of the ideological packages in which they were presented. For those who expected ideologies to be highly structured and visible, such as the Swedish welfare theorist Gunnar Myrdal, this state of affairs was confusing, causing him to complain in the 1950s about 'the remarkable absence of any adequate positive and realistic ideology of the Welfare State' (Myrdal 1965, p. 59). A broader understanding would regard the loose system of political ideas attached to the welfare state, referred to here as welfarism, as a house of many mansions, though its pivotal permeation by liberal principles is unmistakable.[2]

Any account of twentieth-century welfare thinking has to begin at the end of the nineteenth; even then, while the direction of some welfare solutions was becoming apparent, there remained a large number of contested areas of principle, and further issues were being introduced. Nevertheless, welfare-state thinking in Europe did not progress seamlessly. It erupted in particular during two bridging periods:[3] the turn of the century and mid-century. The emergence of society as a significant, possibly predominant, actor in its own right, and the acceptance of the state as a prime organiser, even initiator, of domestic public policy, with the concomitant of state intervention as normal and perennial rather than exceptional and temporary, were two of the most salient legacies bequeathed by the progressive ideologies of the fading nineteenth century to its successor. Both feared and welcomed, these understandings prevailed across the spectrum of political ideologies. In Britain, those developments accompanied a late resurgence of utilitarianism now wedded to the exciting messages of social evolution. The two schools of thought were employed to confront the growing realisation of the social costs of the industrial revolution and, moreover, of the avoidability of many of those costs. British idealist thought merged with late-Victorian conceptions of progress and with new social theories to proclaim the importance of social wholes and, by implication, of group membership.[4] Independently of socialist teachings, the abstract individual – who had thrived only amidst the powerful myths of laissez-faire axioms, while absent in social practices – was replaced with an appreciation of the interdependence of individuals

2. See Ashford (1986, p. 13): 'one of the major misperceptions about the political development of welfare states cultivated by a short historical perspective is that the rise of social policy to prominence was a socialist accomplishment'.
3. The phrase relates to Reinhart Koselleck's *Sattelzeit*: an epoch of consequential change that both links and separates two periods (Koselleck 1972, p. xv).
4. For a critical view of such welfare theories of progress see O'Brien and Penna (1998, pp. 210–12).

and the indispensable blessings of social cooperation. In parallel, France witnessed the advance of ideas on social solidarity which, though deriving from slightly different starting points, emphasised state support for individual responsibility and foresight, conjointly with their partial replacement by social insurance, as a matter of national interest. Security and liberty were bonded together by perceived sociological necessities of social life. Germany, at the time, was combining a form of state paternalism with the social duty to produce organisational efficiency. Sweden was pushing the twin notions of individual liberty and social equality with a highlighted democratic tint. Only the United States was treading a more tentative path in which limited and decentralised private welfare arrangements were preferred to heavy state intervention. All these themes, however, were evident in major or minor keys in every one of those countries.

Pauperism, poverty and work

The development of twentieth-century welfare thinking requires interpretation against a complex backdrop. To begin with, aid to the needy was associated primarily with poverty, especially in its specific form of pauperism: the extreme and often irredeemable poverty associated with idleness, inefficiency, destitution, weak character and, on another level, social destabilisation. Pauperism entailed a quadruple set of perspectives. First, it was attached to a moral stigma, signifying an individual lapse in terms of expected standards of conduct, if not criminal then blatantly anti-social. Second, pauperism was to be treated through local rather than national initiatives. Third, it upheld the ascendancy of the voluntarist principle, in which either charity (the good will of the donor) or self-help through mutual benefit societies (the prescient will of the recipient) played a major, if not exclusive, role. Fourth, it was sustained as a conceptual category by the belief in the virtues of the free market, however much economic practice deviated from it. Prior to 1914, the view of poverty as pauperism competed for recognition and legitimacy with two other conceptualisations. For some – in Britain notably Charles Booth and B. Seebohm Rowntree, whose social surveys of London and York respectively provided path-breaking insights into the incidence of penury – poverty denoted a non-judgemental characterisation of disadvantaged individuals located beneath a specified point on a quantitative scale of income or means at their disposal. But this understanding was augmented by a fuller view, according to which poverty referred to a spectrum of non-monetary and non-material indicators, the absence of which removed certain individuals from a wide range of benefits a society had to offer. That alienation was often imposed by the very arrangements set up to cope with pauperism.

The intellectual paradigms conjoined with these last two conceptualisations reacted against older beliefs about poverty, deemed to be insufficient in tackling the dehumanising effects of industrialisation. They were abetted by the vital part played by new social theories concerning the identifiably distinct nature of society, the path of social evolution and the breadth of human needs. But the voluntarist principle undoubtedly provided a more subtle foundation than is often acknowledged, legitimating not only philanthropy but the sharing of risk through a reciprocal expression of responsibility, recognising the importance of groups through this mutual aid, and fostering civil participation in planned responses to economic distress. Hence 'voluntarism was not a social ideal associated with a specific political ideology' but could even be assimilated into socialist understandings of cooperation (Davies 1997, p. 59; Kropotkin 1972), and its continuing presence was a significant libertarian, extra-statist, ingredient of later welfarism. Nonetheless, it too offered no comprehensive solution to the problems of poverty.

Added to poverty was a key cost of the industrial revolution: unemployment. The partial depersonalisation of employer–employee relationships and the growing fluidity of the labour market loosened the tie between workers and work: mass production created mass unemployment. Again, different themes united under that umbrella: unemployment as a reflection of individual inefficiency and weak character; unemployment as a structural fragility of certain industries and hence both located within the domain of employer responsibility and, more generally, invoking the public accountability incumbent upon a deeper social malorganisation; unemployment as an affront to human dignity, implying a definition of human worth based primarily on respectability. That last definition emanated from the individualist conservative tradition – for which property ownership was the guarantee of individual standing and security – and it transformed into a duty to eschew, through work, financial dependence on others. Indeed, for the propertyless work offered the sole channel to security and respectability. Hence, the redistribution of security necessitated some infringement of the property rights formerly deemed sufficient to provide security (Holmes 1988, p. 93). Work was also central to the socialist tradition, exalted as an essential of human nature. While capitalism secured for individuals the right to property, it allowed them to be deprived of work (Hatzfeld 1971, p. 29). Thus for socialists the right to work became paramount. Non-socialist progressives, however, retained marked residues of the older nineteenth-century ideological traditions. These regarded work almost exclusively as an activity with moral undertones, through which survival, and possibly material comfort, were purchased. Concurrently, the duties of citizens were redefined in terms of obligations to promote the community's welfare, one route towards which was the investment of one's labour in the collective enterprise. As the mid-twentieth-century ideologist of welfare T. H. Marshall noted, the duty to work became explicit when contract made way for obligations occasioned by communal interdependence, since contract entailed the liberty not to work (Marshall 1965, p. 129). That argument resonated with the social functionalism that R. H. Tawney had ascribed to work (Tawney 1945, pp. 7–8). But it also consolidated the link between social security and full employment.

The socialisation of virtue

At the beginning of the twentieth century all major ideologies drew on three categories in developing welfare measures. The first related to virtue and its reward; it deemed social policy as a return on valuable individual conduct. But there were quasi-contingent occupiers of this general grouping. It could refer to thrift – to practices under which individuals conscientiously avoided burdening society by engaging in private foresight, thus discharging themselves from the concern of others (Fraser 1973, pp. 91–101). It could involve mutual societies, pledged to reciprocal assistance within a locally or occupationally exclusive group and nourishing internal solidarity and a restricted pooling of risks (Beveridge 1948, pp. 21–117). Both these versions were contractual, located in the domain of civil society. They sustained the classical liberal model of conditional social relationships, including individual opt-outs, underpinned by legal arrangements. As just noted, however, this category could also sanction socially useful work, by rewarding not the voluntarism of individuals and groups, but the duty incurred in social membership and the activity embedded in one of the core attributes of a social personality – labour as beneficial to *others*. Diverse welfare ideologies could thus retain the ethical dimension of aid to others by upholding virtue in discrete ideational contexts. By mid-century the third version had been elevated into a central feature of welfarism. As Richard Titmuss, one of the prime post-1945 theorists of welfare, observed, social policy could not be reduced to economic policy, to a 'set of income transfers' (Mead 1997, p. 197), because 'the most unsordid act of British social policy in the

20th century has allowed and encouraged sentiments of altruism, reciprocity and social duty to express themselves' (Titmuss 1973, p. 254). The concept of virtue migrated continuously between its privatisation, its anchorage in voluntary communalisation while poised between the private and public spheres, and its nationalisation.

The normalisation of risk

The second category related to chance and its cognitive rationalisation: risk. Originally, at its most basic level, this was a question of security: of protection against or, more likely, compensation for, the abnormal. That excluded one major form of welfare policy, old-age pensions, inasmuch as old age was both predictable and normal. Accordingly, pensions were one of the least controversial welfare measures to be adopted, as on one understanding they concerned the deserving poor who had now entered a category over which they had absolutely no control, and on another overlapping interpretation they signified a recompense for a life of toil from a grateful community (Freeden 1990, pp. 57–9). But illness, accidents, unemployment and destitution were unpredictable and seemingly random, and insurance as risk management offered the best social technology to compensate for their onset. Insurance appeared as the reciprocal virtue incorporated in mutualism; but additionally it constituted a pooling device that had some appeal for collectivists as well as individualists. Particularly in France, social as distinct from private insurance constituted a response to the determinate legal duties of mutualism. The burdens of increasingly industrialised societies necessitated the development of additional means of creating general, possibly limitless, obligations in a world of permanent uncertainty, by shifting them away from the reciprocal individual relationships of civil society and assigning them to communal responsibility: the collectivisation of risk. A legally indeterminate group – society as a whole – could be saddled with legally indeterminate duties (Ewald 1986, p. 60 and *passim*), especially if human interdependence was regarded as an inevitable social fact.

Specifically, social insurance was presented as an expression of equality of treatment. That denoted equality of opportunity and respect rather than equalising incomes, accompanied by child support as a means to guarantee the integrity of the family – always close to the heart of French ideologues. In that sense, security preceded equality (Ambler 1991, p. 12). Social insurance could also be comprehended as a rationalist and 'scientific' legacy of French positivism, renouncing the uncertainty and high costs of the laws of the market for individuals and groups who lost out in competition; it could be interpreted as conferring public status on employers, now charged with social duties backed up by the state; and it also comprised a social duty attached, for instance, to life insurance (Ewald 1986, p. 148). Most interestingly, it neutralised the misadventures of employers and workers by regarding them as objective facts of life (Rosanvallon 2000, p. 15), thus eliminating at a stroke the problems of virtue and altruism by refusing either to penalise personal irresponsibility or to reward responsibility, and consequently reducing benefits to an impersonal legal minimum. Risk had become normal. In general, the category of risk served in France as an organising conceptual principle through which to advance both private and public insurance. It constituted an ideological counterpoint to the implied predictability of the world of individual thrift and collaborative mutualist foresight (*prévoyance*), not least because it avoided the treatment of poverty separately from other forms of individual misfortune (Ashford 1991, p. 36) and because it attempted to sever or reduce the link between morality and foresight asserted by promoters of individual liberty and will (Rimlinger 1971, p. 62). Alongside such neutralisation came the novel notion of compensation for events for which no-one was responsible: a *risque professionnel* as articulated in the French law on industrial accident insurance in 1898, which, however, drew the line at universality and compulsion (Stone 1985, p. 104). Finally, social and industrial change had highlighted the unpredictability of the future, so that planning for contingencies offered an alternative notion of controlled and anticipated time. Thus Pierre Laroque, one of the prime architects of French social security, saw the menace of future misery suspended over the working class as a powerful spur to demanding social security and removing that uncertainty (Laroque 1953, pp. 49–51).

More broadly, these developments signalled a decisive shift in the conceptualisation of human nature and relationships, by reducing the component of individual autonomy associated with prudence, strength of character and self-control – and their obverse, subjective fault – with respect to both employers and employees. The departure from interpreting harm as necessarily deliberate and culpable was brought on by a common interest in the decency, and mutability, of human conduct and conditions. Human nature was henceforth not a static attribute of individuals, but a malleable feature of individuals in society. Rather than regarding politics as a series of necessary if unfortunate constraints on individual action, it was reconceptualised as a process that promoted the collective 'good life'. Hence a new function was bestowed on the state. 'Interference' or 'intervention' were replaced by 'regulating' or 'enabling', for reasons of humanism, efficiency or political expediency. Tolerable conditions were provided through arranging for compensation when individual liability for harm could not be established, initially most obvious in work accidents, which dispensed with the need to demonstrate negligence (Dawson 1912, p. 9 and *passim*). Put differently, social insurance applied probabilities or, in Winston Churchill's words, the 'magic of averages', to the government of society, a conception that introduced a new, albeit technical and anonymous, equality of all in the eyes of the insurer, the state (Freeden 1978, p. 237; Ewald 1986, p. 247). Insurance identified social groups that were no longer located in specific time or space, thus reducing (and abstracting) social divisions between present and future generations, and among classes and regions. From these understandings there emerged a telling reformulation of equality: a specific conception of equality of treatment in the form of social compensation – seen by some as the 'logic of the welfare state' (Luhmann 1990, p. 22) – for crucial and dehumanising lacunae in the human condition, whether through social inequity or personal handicap, which could deny individuals access to vital goods irrespective of their efforts or merit. In Titmuss' stark phrasing, compensation was due to 'the people who are compelled to pay – as diswelfares – part of the costs of other people's progress in a dynamic and changing society' (Titmuss 1976, p. 63). Unsurprisingly, with this ideological baggage in potential trail, early twentieth-century American businessmen refused to recognise workmen's accident compensation as social insurance, basing it 'not upon the duty of society, but upon the duty of the industry to the worker'[5] and dismissing the discourse of social rights.

However, virtue and its traditional corollary, individual responsibility, still played a salient role in many versions of insurance. The principle of social insurance continued to exhibit the perennial tension it contained between liberty and security. Whereas Bismarckian Germany had opted decisively for the latter, French and British theorists sought a balance between the two. In the French tradition of political thought it was not uncommon to deem the state and its laws as the definers and guarantors of public morality, so that the virtue of foresight could be a duty imposed by the state on individuals. It was therefore a minor ideational and linguistic transformation, as the solidarists were to demonstrate, to replace social obligation with calls for compulsory social assistance and, unlike the pioneering German welfare ideology, to refer to a communal rather than a legalistic, authoritarian ethic of obligation.

5. Quoted in Rimlinger (1971, p. 77).

Schismatically opposed was a French liberalism that parted only reluctantly with private and communal welfare arrangements, being far more market-oriented and politically right-of-centre than its British counterpart (Logue 1983). In the latter, the role of compulsion had a more complex pedigree, evolving from an idealist reassessment of the relationship between liberty and constraint, yet hampered by the contention that morality could never be imposed (Green 1941, pp. 221–2), as well as by a cultural reluctance to accord the state too powerful a regulatory role.[6]

But if private insurance pooling could be egoistic and commercial, social insurance habitually failed to satisfy the new social technology of actuarial science intended to facilitate it (Shapiro 1997, p. 116). The promoters of social insurance appealed instead to a combination of *social* self-interest and *collective* virtue, both goods that now adopted the form of socialising risk.[7] And social insurance now divorced the legal right to income from the market value of the claimant (Marshall 1965, p. 106), opening up new avenues for a citizenship that applied simultaneously to the dual spheres of civil society and the state. Virtue was rediscovered in the ethos of public service in state bureaucracies, in the active participation of large sections of society in designing their own well-being alongside that of others, and in the pulling together of social resources in the tripartite compact between worker, employer and the state preferred by the British unemployment insurance programme of 1911. The involvement of the state created additional value neatly encapsulated in Lloyd George's slogan 'ninepence for fourpence', but it also acknowledged the state as partner to families and civil society in the goal of attaining the prized goods of a civilised standard of life, rather than as a superimposed network of power relationships.

The legitimisation of need

The third category employed in developing principles of welfare policy related to the identification of need as a fundamental human and social attribute. Neither the categories of virtue nor of risk invoked the principle endemic to the objectification of need – the redistribution of scarce resources as a constant of social policy. This took welfarism into new territory. Initially, need-cum-poverty had been perceived as an aberrant claim on the social resources of a capitalist economy, its satisfaction to be attained, at best, through

6. See Hennock (1986, pp. 63–94) on the unwillingness to make accident insurance compulsory.
7. For an American argument on these lines see Hook (1967, p. 168).

the minimal eradication of the anomaly. In the early twentieth century, need was frequently reinterpreted through the austere filter of personal and national efficiency, and incorporated into scientific understandings of welfare. Thus Rowntree explored both private and state-financed minima requisite to physical and mental efficiency (Rowntree 1919, pp. 50, 144). His classification anticipated the Beveridge Report: human needs were the basis for fixing a minimum wage, but the market value of services would determine wages above that minimum (Rowntree 1937, p. 15). More broadly, welfare theory began to encompass redistribution as the linchpin of an ethical assault on dehumanising socio-economic differences among people, which had to be mitigated through concerted action. Social reformers regarded this as the rationale behind policy measures that included social insurance, assistance, graduated taxation and direct fiscal state management of the welfare of the needy (Freeden 1978, pp. 117–69). However, much of the development of welfare-state theory revolved around the transmutation of such minima into an optimum, though the emergence of new conceptions does not suggest that welfare practice was unequivocally unilinear.

The movement may be epitomised by contrasting Churchill at the beginning of the century, who wished to 'draw a line below which we will not allow persons to live and labour, yet above which they may compete with all the strength of their manhood' (Churchill 1909, p. 82), with Marshall at mid-century. For Marshall – associating the growth of welfare with the rise of citizenship – a major shift had incorporated economic and material conceptions of welfare into an extended and unconditional 'right to share to the full in the social heritage and to live the life of a civilized being according to the standards prevailing in a society' (Marshall 1965, p. 78). That rider consciously recognised the space- and time-bound limits of welfare. Contrary, however, to Marshall's postulation of a development from civil through political to social rights in the domain of social legislation, the 'claim for a share in life'[8] as a development in social thought had occurred not sequentially but in tandem with the minimalist approach to need.

Once social theorists subscribed to the notion of optimal human development, they had to extend it to all members of a society and to replace selectivity with universalism. Hence, no matter how pivotal redistribution became to theories of social reform, it intermeshed with a further element. As the liberal theorist L. T. Hobhouse explained: 'The true aim of social progress is not so much to make one class richer, as to purify and brighten the

8. Thus the title of an article in the new liberal *Nation*, 28 September 1912.

life of the whole community' (Hobhouse 1899, p. 211). Titmuss later contended that welfare ceased to be mainly redistributive, aiming at reducing the gross inequalities from which the marginalised suffered, and began instead to emphasise social solidarity and integration by detecting commonalities of well-being that overrode the legitimacy of customary differences (Titmuss 1976, p. 191). It also advanced the typical British liberal non-sectionalism, often mistaken for radical collectivism, which endeavoured to release individuals from dependence on any particular social group (Freeden 1978, pp. 150–8; Titmuss 1976, p. 242). This involved a rejection of judgemental discrimination among groups, not only among individuals, as irrelevant to the identification and treatment of need (Deacon 1996, pp. 199–201).

Put differently, the notion of human need as flourishing became central to conceptions of human nature, and to the *raison d'être* of social organisation. Human purpose and conduct were no longer confined to an unstructured space safeguarded by an external authority. Rather, they constituted a temporal process of maturation, as much expressive as instrumental, directed towards the optimal enjoyment of one's faculties within reasonable social constraints. Needs were extended into non-material areas: the assertion of one's beneficial intellectual, emotional and spiritual properties, singularly and jointly. From the minimalist perspective, such benefits had been 'superfluous', because removed from considerations of the economic worth or physical survival of the recipient and applied irrespective of individual merit. Now, they related to the recipient's status as citizen: a member of a polity fully entitled to a portion of whatever goods that polity produced.

Consequently, the static notion of citizenship as occupying a respectable position in one's society, primarily through property ownership, made space for citizenship as a dynamic cluster of social interactions. Virtue was attached not to desert but relocated to participation and self-development in a communal, and indeed national, context, facilitating new forms of human expression. In tandem, crucially, these understandings merged with the French 'normalisation' of the notions of risk and uncertainty. The outcome was the novel location of vulnerability at the core of human nature. Individuals were not just bundles of ability-oriented needs that had to be satisfied to gain full human realisation, underpinning liberalism's fully functional and autonomous individual, capable of perfectibility or at least of purposive improvability. They were also existentially precarious and interdependent entities, incapable of fully controlling their own lives and futures, who required continual mutual support. What had in the past been ascribed to personal weaknesses became reconceptualised, eliciting the concern and empathy that came of a universal human condition. If older theories often saw human weakness as shaped by natural, extra-human forces – a core conservative argument – and therefore irredeemable, or eliminable only through strength of character, a new naturalism of human fragility now emerged. Hence the provision of care was identified as a necessary norm, rather than an act of contingent and sporadic private kindness. Moreover, the sociability ingredient itself became a need: a catalyst through which changes in individual circumstances, even in individual virtue, could always be attained. Titmuss vigorously reflected this movement of ideas, going so far as to base altruism on a biological need to help, and reformulating the network of social obligations with his extraordinary phrase 'the right to give' (Titmuss 1973, p. 272). It was a right individuals could only waive at considerable cost to themselves, just as for J. S. Mill individuals could choose not to develop, but would consequently impoverish themselves and society. Titmuss linked altruism to social compensation for the vagaries of human misfortunes, certain only in their uncertainty. As he argued:

> All collectively provided services are deliberately designed to meet certain socially recognised 'needs'; they are manifestations, first, of society's will to survive as an organic whole and, secondly, of the expressed wish of all the people to assist the survival of some people. 'Needs' may therefore be thought of as 'social' and 'individual'; as inter-dependent, mutually related essentials for the continued existence of the parts and the whole' (Titmuss 1958, p. 39; Titmuss 1973, p. 223).

Those ideational developments incurred a lengthy rethinking of welfare. Nor were they ever disentangled from each other, as major welfare theorists engaged all three categories of virtue, risk and need. The categories of both virtue and risk recognised the importance of group support and thus contained the germs of collectivism: the one through acknowledging socially desirable conduct; the other through sharing life's uncertainties. That permeability of the categories, rather than their exclusiveness, was crucial to the morphology of the winning welfare ideologies throughout. The concepts and practices they invoked – responsibility, uncertainty, redistribution, solidarity and flourishing – had different intellectual roots but intermeshed imaginatively. Individualists could recognise material need and regard charity as a moral duty and virtue, but they could also accommodate insurance as a sign of thrift. Collectivists – whether socialist or (liberal) social democratic – might oppose insurance and prefer universal benefits out of general taxation as a fundamental social responsibility, but they could also endorse social insurance as a form of mutualism. However, in the absence of unadulterated human altruism, the gap between voluntarism and universalism would have to be spanned by compulsion. And if one adopts a different decontestation, conservatives could extol security and appeal to a common good, as long as a virtuous society was one that upheld social order and controllable change, but they would also sanction inequality and difference, above accepted minima, as would liberals. Liberals, however, were more ready to accept planned social reform, while acknowledging the importance of individual choice, development and participation as human needs in themselves, catered to by welfare measures or, at least, procedural necessities without which mutual aid could not be considered legitimate.

Humanising the state: liberal organicism and social rights

One of the most striking developments in the political thought accompanying the evolution of welfarism was the conjoining of welfare and state, with the emphasis on the state. A critical contest among competing understandings of the state was occurring. It was gradually accruing further roles, from a legal, rational and power organisation wielding sovereign authority, to overseeing and executing some central economic functions, to providing emotional as well as physical sustenance, while constituting a focus of affective loyalty for its members. The latter was fostered not only through the discourse of nationalism but through assuming tasks of care traditionally discharged by families and voluntary organisations. Because the classic liberal state had been viewed as the supreme underwriter of constant and rational policy procedures, practitioners of the welfare state faced the challenge of transferring that understanding to the more diffuse spheres of human well-being. That proved problematic, mainly because state action now began to penetrate walks of life that had been customarily excluded by previously rigid boundaries. By the beginning of the twentieth century, the state, as the rising principal source of the authoritative policy and the necessary means to attend to poverty, had begun to impose national (and thus general, if not universal) patterns on hitherto limited and uncoordinated measures to alleviate extreme distress. The state was becoming humanised and tamed, in its goals if not in its continual adherence to power as gentle persuasiveness. It was also civilised through being drawn into the realm of the familiar, both in the sense of being less distanciated from individual experiences, and as arrogating, albeit clumsily and mechanically, some of the traditionally altruistic and nourishing functions of the family. This reflected the state's immense growth, not only as institution but as central political concept, with its attendant categories of organisation, comprehensiveness and 'scientific' planning, and its search for new sources of legitimacy via popular approval. But there was a price to pay, for it also required the diminution and channelling of the ideas contained in the more inventive visions of welfare theorists.

Much of the impetus for state-directed welfare came from Bismarckian Germany, in which a controlling but modernising bureaucracy was enhanced by a widespread respect for the *Rechtsstaat* as the source of enlightened justice. The state demonstrated a patriarchal 'positive duty of promoting the welfare of all its members', with an emphasis on the nation rather than on separate individuals. It engaged in strong forms of social control while rejecting liberal voluntarist solutions to welfare problems. Throughout the 1880s the state established patterns of care for the victims of industrial accidents, and the poor, unfortunate and destitute. It was driven partly by a desire to maintain a political edge over a growing socialist radicalism through locking the working class into a client relationship with the state, and partly by a desire for a protectionist investment in a competitive industrial advantage. This was couched in the conservative language of serving 'one of the highest obligations of every community based on the ethical foundations of a Christian national life'.[9] Irrespective of that multiple motivation, and with due adjustments for local ideologies, the German experiments in compulsory social insurance excited great interest in more liberal European regimes, not least in Britain (Hennock 1986, pp. 168–79).

The initial stages of the growth of liberal-social thought from the 1890s onwards were characterised by a reduction of the tension between welfare and state, achieved neither by the superimposition of a powerful state nor by its subordination to civil society, but by harnessing the state as a major partner in coordinated social activity and as a facilitator of newly expanded human ends. Narrow mid-nineteenth-century utilitarian renderings of human happiness as pleasure had given way to J. S. Mill's more intricate idea of well-being. Though both retained a subjectivist and personal assessment of individual good, they were in turn beginning to be replaced by attempts at more 'objective' standards – hence the shift to welfare. A prime mover in this process was the progressive idealist philosopher David G. Ritchie, who subtly established the parameters of welfare thought. First, he unpacked the

9. Dawson (1912, pp. 14, 17, 234). Dawson reported a conversation with Bismarck in which the latter's idea was 'to bribe the working classes, or, if you like, to win them over to regard the state as a social institution existing for their sake and interested in their welfare' (p. 11). See also Rimlinger (1971, pp. 100–2, 107, 116).

emerging concepts of welfare or well-being – notions which included 'the element of right conduct, virtuous action, *well-doing*, and the element of favourable environment, pleasure, or, as we can say in English, of *doing well* in the sense of faring well'. Advancing beyond Mill, Ritchie insisted that the happiness of its citizens, which was among the ends of government, covered a spectrum of understandings, comprising either 'directly removing obstacles to physical health, to intellectual and moral development', including the use of compulsion, or indirectly encouraging individuals to make free choices that furthered such well-being (Ritchie 1895, pp. 273–5). Second, he reassigned the hitherto individualist and aggregative concept of utility to a new unit: society itself. That was what 'proved most permanently valuable in Utilitarianism . . . Right and wrong appear now as what help or hinder the good of the society.' Hence morality was 'the conscious and deliberate adoption of those feelings and acts and habits which are advantageous to the welfare of the community' (Ritchie 1893, pp. 62–3).

Third, Ritchie viewed society as an interconnected organism, capable of purposive self-control. Moreover, 'it is as a State, i.e. as an ordered political society, that a social organism becomes most distinctly conscious of its existence as an organism and consequently most capable of regulating the tendencies, which if left to themselves, would make its history a merely natural process' (Ritchie 1887, p. 6). And, fourth, he harnessed the established discourse of rights language to new purposes. From a static defence of individual action, the pursuit of human rights evolved into an active furtherance of human and social flourishing. Inverting the traditional approach to natural rights, Ritchie maintained that 'certain mutual claims which cannot be ignored without detriment to the well-being and, in the last resort, to the very being of a community' were the true fundamental or natural rights. 'They represent a minimum of security and advantage which a community must guarantee to its members' (Ritchie 1895, p. 87). The defining feature of these radical intellectual developments was a new appraisal of the state as a contributor to individual and national health.[10] Even at the level of metaphor, the state was intimately associated with nourishing human vigour and promoting human growth. This approach anticipated the pivotal significance that health was to be accorded in twentieth-century welfare ideology, encapsulated in British social legislation in 1911 and 1946.

10. Though of course in small increments the state was already intervening in the standards of living of the very poor, stigmatised as paupers.

Ritchie's arguments were resolutely advanced by Britain's two most prominent liberal welfare theorists: L. T. Hobhouse and J. A. Hobson. Hobhouse's famous reformulation of liberal principles elevated mutual aid to co-equal status with mutual forbearance, based on an elaboration of T. H. Green's conception of a common good to which rational and ethically minded individuals would subscribe. Well-being implied human and social growth, but also the realisation of collective ends which, on an evolutionary scale, constituted a higher harmony. The state had increased responsibility for human welfare, but within a constraining paradigm that still retained a liberal notion of contract, now devoid of forensic immediacy and exact quid pro quo. Instead, a new interrelationship was posited. The individual had the personal responsibility of industriously working for himself and his family and, more innovatively, the duty to respect enlightened norms of human decency within the family: 'not to exploit the labour of his young children, but to submit to the public requirements for their education, health, cleanliness and general well-being'. The state in turn owed the individual 'the means of maintaining a civilized standard of life' and of winning 'full civic efficiency' for normal healthy citizens through their own efforts. It also exercised an 'overlordship', moderated by democratic control, on matters of economic justice (Hobhouse 1911, pp. 158, 164, 173–4, 210). Hobhouse epitomised the trend to intertwine arguments from efficiency with those from social justice so typical of welfarism. Welfare, however, was placed at the heart of the political enterprise, indeed of the rationale of social life. It was interpreted as the central aim of organised human existence, seeking to encompass the full range of human potential. It was also buttressed by empirical findings that reinforced sociological preoccupations with synthesis and holism (Harris 1992, pp. 123–5).

In order to alleviate the plight of the disadvantaged, Hobhouse expanded Ritchie's conception of rights: 'The "right to work" and the right to a "living wage" are just as valid as the rights of person or property . . . they are integral conditions of a good social order' (Hobhouse 1911, p. 159). An extended scope of rights was commensurate with an extended notion of state responsibility, and was designed to end the conflict between individual claims and communal duties. Hobhouse, like many reformers, reacted against the Poor Law principles, which excluded paupers and the destitute from the circle of full civic rights by making them 'less eligible' to receive not only material benefits but social goods such as liberty. Instead, the elimination of poverty, and the 'prevention of suffering from the actual lack of adequate physical comforts' was essential to the common good. To this was attached a further argument developed by Fabians and other socialists, namely, that every social function 'must receive the reward that is sufficient to stimulate and maintain it through the life of the individual' (Hobhouse 1911, pp. 184–6, 203–4). Need was tempered by desert, and both were constrained by their contribution to social well-being.

Hobson was the most important and perceptive of the British liberal welfare theorists. Arguing that society was an organism with a life and purposes of its own, alongside individual rights and needs, he contended that society, as a maker of values, could claim its own property rights. Those rights safeguarded the needs essential to supporting the 'full healthy progressive life of the community' (Hobson 1901, pp. 148–9). As a liberal Hobson advocated the realisation of equal opportunities for individual self-development. But 'to this individual standpoint must be joined a just apprehension of the social, viz., the insistence that these claims or rights of self-development be adjusted to the sovereignty of social welfare' (Hobson 1909, p. xii). If happiness was evolving into well-being, it was also, in the words of the French socialist politician Alexandre Millerand, 'social happiness'.[11]

Hobson's distinctive liberal organicism maintained not that the whole was superior to the parts, but that the liberty and development of the parts were indispensable to the health of the collective life. Social ends could be both directly attained by social action and realised in individuals; however, it was incumbent upon society, through the government, to conserve individual rights and interests (Hobson 1914, p. 304). The 'interdependence and interaction of individual character and social character [were] expressed in social environment' because poverty represented a deficiency 'in the moral force of the community' which the community had to remedy by applying that force to the reform of economic structure. Anticipating Keynes, Hobson legitimated redistributionary state expenditure for social policy purposes as a means to stimulate demand. Notwithstanding, he cautioned that state action would not in itself cure poverty, but would rather 'enable poverty to cure itself by securing liberty for all to use their powers to the best advantage for their own gain and for the common good'. The power of the state was always at the disposal of the welfare of its citizens. From that viewpoint, poverty simply constituted the absence of equal access to the requisites for the development of one's full human potential, which the generation of Millite liberal theorists had seen as the purpose of rational individual conduct, and which a later liberal generation also regarded as essential to

11. Quoted in Scott (1951, p. 180).

communal flourishing (Hobson 1909, pp. 171–2, 207, 217). In a clear shift away from idealist argument, the active moralisation of individual behaviour declined in importance.

In his mature work, Hobson confronted the issue of welfare directly, as a concept uniting ethical and economic values. Welfare embraced physical needs; the protection of the evolutionary process which 'presents a continually increasing surplus of organic energy over and above the requirements for specific survival'; the catering for psychological and emotional needs under effective rational control; and the conscious satisfaction of civilised interests, intellectual and spiritual. Crucially for the development of twentieth-century welfarism, Hobson portrayed this as 'a New Utilitarianism in which physical, intellectual, and moral satisfactions will rank in their due places', qualitatively rather than quantitatively, building on his earlier endorsement of John Ruskin's famous adage 'there is no wealth but life' (Hobson 1929, pp. 11, 13–16). To this perspective was added a conception of social welfare based on an organic interpretation of a nation's personality and purposiveness, which acknowledged that some organisations, too, produced values which contributed to individual and general welfare. The challenge, as many welfare theorists knew, was to control the tendency of the state – the agent centrally charged with promoting socially determined values – to appeal to experts when imposing standards of food, housing, hygiene and industrial conditions. The emerging universalist ethos of the liberal welfare state drew on the distinction between personal and common elements of welfare. 'For the organized economic society is mainly concerned with the common elements of welfare and only indirectly, though not unimportantly, with strictly personal values' (Hobson 1929, pp. 32, 36, 39–40, 68).

The new liberal approach to social welfare encapsulated the realisation that welfare had caught up with liberty as a prime indication of human development and a key value of social life. It both conceptually constrained, and enriched, liberty by holding it proximate to welfare. It stretched welfare into a holistic construct. It redeployed rights discourse to encompass the protection of human capacities, specifically through prioritising the sharing and consumption of available social resources that catered to human needs. It recognised the anchoring of individuals in a purposive community subject to an evolutionary law of increasing rational self-regulation. It identified a series of functions required of the newly defined guarantor state, far removed from the Prussian authoritarian overseer and locked instead into the accountable defence of democratic and egalitarian ends. It emphasised citizenship not just as the formal membership of a polity but as an unconditional entitlement to 'a certain share in the social inheritance', as a charge on the social surplus, to safeguard individuals from misfortune, sickness and unemployment (Hobhouse 1911, p. 208); and, beyond that, to enable citizens to participate in the symbolic as well as the material goods of civilised life simply by dint of their status as social entities. Notwithstanding, it also continued to identify the voluntary pursuit of individual ends as crucial to the flourishing of part and whole alike, while realising that traditional liberal organisational voluntarism had been beached on the shores of a conservative individualism. It attested to the importance of economic productivity. And it signalled that responsible individual conduct, now expressed through contributions to social health, would attract social rewards.

Ultimately, this constituted a universalisation of the particular. Differential life experiences, including deprivation or disadvantage, no longer reflected private, individual pathologies. They were experiences human beings shared in common. But those very experiences were predominantly the product of failures of human understanding and activity, generating in turn deficient social conditions resulting in an uneven satisfaction of human needs. Their rectification required acknowledging the mutual interdependence between individual and individual, and individual and community.

These beliefs brought with them a burst of philosophical and ideological creativity. But the intellectual, and partial political, success of such developments must also be understood within the multiple semantic fields that constituted the ideological map of welfare thought. A mixture of sensitivity to the human costs of the industrial revolution, of a consciousness of the inclusion of new groups in the political arena, and of deference to expert advice had created a complex compound of beliefs and values. It is inaccurate to speak of a liberal, or socialist, theory of the welfare state as if these were hermetically sealed variants rather than the continuously changing outcome of the interplay between competing and complementary views. The dominant liberal version in Britain already contained many components of rival positions. It was a complex and imbricated ideology. Moreover, though by the end of the nineteenth century state intervention had occurred in a small number of specific intolerable social evils, civil society had in tandem provided throughout Europe extensive communal security of its own, through mutual benefit societies and trade unions. This corresponding strand of social interdependence transcended to a considerable extent the older economic and moral edicts of individualistic self-reliance.

The impact of social and institutional practice on ideology was also considerable. For example, the labour exchange system institutionalised by

Churchill in 1909 integrally linked its job-placement function with the provision of unemployment insurance. This arrangement shaped a constrained but at the time approved ideological position, so that when the climate supporting state-instigated insurance changed in the 1930s the exchange system was in turn delegitimated through the absence of ideological flexibility (King and Rothstein 1993).

Social democracy: the appeal to science and the pitfalls of universalism

The intellectual development of progressive ideologies also occurred against a backdrop of an increased scientisation and compartmentalisation of welfare, accompanied by an inevitable elitism of knowledge, evident particularly in the visions of socialist thinkers such as the British Fabians. Though British socialism drew partly from continental thinking, its concentration on bread-and-butter issues was embodied in a concern for the techniques and minutiae of policies designed to abolish poverty and ensure greater participation in the social arena, rather than focusing on macro-visions of the good life. This conception of welfare found its most trenchant expression in the *Minority Report of the Royal Commission on the Poor Laws and the Relief of Distress*, 1905–9, largely penned by Beatrice Webb, a member of the Commission, and Sidney Webb. The *Minority Report* reflected Fabian views which related welfare to physical well-being, though not exclusively so, and anticipated the sufficient and responsible reproduction of the human race (or, more specifically, the British people) through the endowment of motherhood and eugenic methods. The individual as the basic unit was jettisoned in favour of a new positivism that classified social ills in categories. Consequently, people could be made to attain external standards of existence through institutional structures. That controversial methodology of welfare encouraged the fragmentation of citizenship, advancing policies under the banner of the break-up of the Poor Law, while eliminating the class of paupers and the destitute as a separate stigmatised group. Poverty was also to be eliminated in fact, as the Webbs were among the main proponents of a state-established national minimum income (McBriar 1987, p. 303).

In parallel, the Webbs appealed to a sense of collective morality, institutionalised by means of national uniform standards, though issues of individual morality, even pauperism itself, were not entirely factored out by liberals and socialists alike (Kidd 1996, pp. 189–205). Progressives had effectively transmuted the stark distinction between pauperism and poverty into a similarly dubious divide between morality and science, with Hobhouse calling for 'a scientific conception of the social bond'.[12] Beatrice Webb in particular wished to retain some modicum of deterrence directed at habitual idleness, vagrancy and mendicity: 'the grant from the community to the individual, beyond what it does for all, ought to be conditional upon better conduct'. Hence she objected to compulsory state unemployment insurance, which suffered from the 'fatal defect that the state got nothing for its money – that the persons felt they had a right to their allowance whatever their conduct' (Webb 1948, p. 417). That puritan sense of duty, common in socialist ideology, was accompanied in Fabian proposals by its frequent concomitant, the notion of enforced welfare, applied to recipients as well as providers. This, however, distinguished many Fabians from their New Liberal counterparts, for whom the compulsion of recipients was restricted to pooling risks, rather than imposing happiness on workers.

'Scientific' welfarism was also inspired by notions of national efficiency with their curious combination of expecting the nation to be a well-run enterprise, yet an enterprise in which communal thriving was paramount. Even New Liberal politicians such as Lloyd George dressed up their moral concerns in the language of a 'business proposition', their arguments coalescing with the longer-standing self-interest of business circles in welfare (Freeden 1978, p. 242; Hay 1981, p. 109). In Sweden, too, arguments from efficiency emanated from the progressive left (Tilton 1990, p. 164; Myrdal and Myrdal 1941). Here, reason, science, community and planning all combined to launch this new social morality. But ideological advances towards the welfare state diverged from such socialist aspirations (McBriar 1962, p. 278), if by socialism was meant a universal, compulsory, uniform, state-underpinned and state-financed welfare system. Even the *Minority Report* pulled back from that posture, advocating the retention of friendly societies and trade unions for compulsory health insurance (S. and B. Webb 1909a, p. 591), partly because their circumvention would constitute an impossible burden on a state they wished to succeed in its guardianship of the people (McBriar 1962, pp. 275–6). The Webbs desired 'complete state responsibility with a view of prevention' (Webb 1948, p. 476), but were often prepared to settle for second best.

The principled objection raised by continental socialists to reforms within capitalism made many of them initially unreceptive to most forms of social insurance and to the path that led to the welfare state (Rimlinger 1971,

12. See [L. T. Hobhouse], *Manchester Guardian*, 10 April 1908; S. and B. Webb (1909b, pp. 333–4).

pp. 124–6). That principled stance was destined to fail. For when social democratic forces prevailed, as they did for a while in the Weimar Republic, the rudiments of a welfare state materialised in a recognition of social rights within a capitalist structure. The Weimar constitution drew up a state insurance system, though social democrats considered welfare legislation to be but one means to solve the social problem, together with other forms of economic democracy. The mitigation of class conflict was a German and French welfare goal absent in Britain and the USA (Crew 1998, pp. 16–18, 23, 29, 47, 55, 155–6, 199–200; Miller and Potthoff 1986, pp. 76–7). By the late 1920s, understandably, German social democrats and trade unions came to support universal state unemployment insurance as the central plank of any welfare policy to counter social risk (Weisbrod 1981, pp. 189, 197). Notably, German welfare practices combined comprehensive state treatment, municipalisation, trade union welfare and private organisation. Even German liberalism exhibited a patently social element. Already by the turn of the century its left-wing variant had developed a tradition of social service at the municipal level, precisely in order to counter the authoritarian and conservative aspects of centralised state welfare (Langewiesche 1990, pp. 230–5).

This hybrid configuration became an ideological focal point of secular and religious tensions, statist and individualist frictions, and mass versus bourgeois culture. By the 1920s socialist communitarianism in particular was counterposed to the traditional extolling of the family as the unit of nurture. In addition, German welfarism had been nourished on an ethos of public responsibility overseeing a myriad of self-sustaining administrative organisations (Zöllner 1982, pp. 23, 28). From the beginning of the century, the notion of 'Fürsorge' with its connotation of specifically targeted care both differed from and converged upon the re-emerging term 'Wohlfahrt', the latter vacillating between a broader economic well-being and narrower support functions, both public and private (Rassem 1992, pp. 632–5; Crew 1998, p. 11). The expression 'social security' was adopted in German discourse only in the 1950s, and 'Wohlfahrt' was phased out and replaced by the seemingly more neutral 'Sozialhilfe' (Rassem 1992, p. 636; Zöllner 1982, p. 61). Its continued survival in the concept 'Wohlfahrtsstaat' is infused with a *mélange* of the above meanings.

Implicit in these debates were further competing notions of universality. Equality could indicate universality not only in scope, regard, access or treatment, but in the shape of uniform state-delivered arrangements and benefits or, at least, entitlement to benefits. However, liberals who transcended a narrow and unsentimental contractarianism[13] were wedded to promoting pluralism and variety, and the ideas of both a minimum and an optimum were compatible with their individualism and open-ended developmental ethos. As they had discovered, the universality of rights did not imply their uniformity. But the practice of compulsion remained prevalent in most welfare systems, even liberal ones. The perceived alternative to a state-imposed uniformity were the risk-pooling procedures of social insurance that required state compulsion in order to attain solvency through universality of scope,[14] at least by recruiting all those who could afford to pay. Selectivity reappeared in the form of means-testing, or the distinction between insurance and assistance.[15] An equality wedded to universalism and voluntarism, while evident in the ideals of some welfare theorists, seemed too chimerical a conceptual configuration. Ultimately, both the individual and the mutual society had to give way in the ideological battle.

French republicanism and solidarism

The French experience of welfare measures emerged from a somewhat different background. Local administration and funding were part of a vibrant communal tradition, with hospitals providing for the sick and destitute, and welfare bureaux operating as 'autonomous, public, communal establishments, having an independent civil personality'.[16] The strength of the conservative agricultural sector and the underdeveloped nature of industry also precluded rapid movement towards a state welfare system. Reliance on philanthropy, and a preference for encouraging welfare recipients to look to their own efforts side by side with assistance, reflected the hold of individualism and thwarted the possibility of compulsory relief provisions, while building up problems of coordination between public assistance and private charity. The liberal tradition in France – despite the presence in its midst of Charles Dupont-White who had favoured early forms of state intervention to better the condition of workers and the poor (Hazareesingh 1997) – was resolutely anti-statist towards the end of the nineteenth century, with key figures such as Paul Leroy-Beaulieu resisting increased state aid to the dispossessed (Leroy-Beaulieu 1891). Nevertheless, public and private

13. For an example of that unsentimental contractarianism, see Sumner (1883, p. 74).
14. See Irving Fisher, quoted in Rimlinger (1971, p. 69).
15. For some of these interlocking problems see Esping-Andersen (1990, pp. 11–34).
16. Quoted in Weiss (1983, p. 49).

interests were not proffered as alternative polarities. Indeed, the importance of *mutualité* generally relegated social insurance to a residual category, once voluntarist channels had been exhausted (Ashford 1991, pp. 34–5). But statist undertones and a sense of public duty and fraternity, while not matching the radicalism voiced during the French Revolution as a demand for the right to subsistence (Rimlinger 1971, p. 30), were nonetheless noticeable within the broad ambit of the republican tradition (Hazareesingh 1994, pp. 80–9). The first compulsory poor relief legislation in the 1890s was significantly described as a revolution introducing 'if not a new right, the right of those judged worthy of aid to receive it, at least a new obligation for the state, department, and commune' (Weiss 1983, pp. 60, 63). In a manner characteristic of French political discourse, public bodies were seen to assert their supremacy in organising welfare without quite formulating that role in terms of citizen status, and the state habitually slipped into the role of *état providence*, not entirely bereft of its own 'Bismarckian' paternalism. The process was a slow one, though. The practical advent of public assistance, a compromise between individualist and organicist views, such as the law of 1905 concerning the aged, the infirm and the incurable, preceded the much later introduction of social insurance, still strongly opposed by conservatives, free market liberals and independent entrepreneurs (Merrien 1997, pp. 19–20).

The hostility of the French version of liberal ideology to state-directed social reform and to the attendant compulsion that only the state could deliver, and its persistent support of mutualism and localism, distinguished it from its more radical British counterpart, whose views would not have been recognised in France as internal to liberalism. The tightly packed spectrum of ideological movements in France, with liberalism bounded on the left by solidarism as well as by a plethora of socialist positions, contrasted notably with British liberalism, able at an early stage in the development of welfarism to adopt communitarian and statist ideas, owing to the lack of clear-cut contenders for that ideological space. French welfarism was pervaded by the clash between liberal and socialist arguments (Ashford 1986, p. 32). Straddling that divide, solidarism was the movement whose political thought was closest to the nascent welfare state and that provided the ideological resources required to further the cause of social reform. Its radicalism was advanced, among others, through Charles Renouvier's identification of the state as the prime social association assigned to promote social justice, assuming the interrelationship of social groups; through Alfred Fouillée's assertion of an organicism similar to that of the British New Liberals – one of reciprocity and mutual dependence (Fouillée 1880; Hayward 1963, pp. 211–12); and through Leon Bourgeois's re-prioritising of the Republic's motto as 'solidarity, equality, liberty' (Hayward 1961, p. 27; Freeden 1996, pp. 215–16). Natural interdependence had to be reaffirmed and raised to the level of consciousness through a moral, willed and voluntary social act: a 'contractual organism' (Scott 1951, p. 164). This adjoined the prevailing welfare theme of voluntarism with the newer one of identifying natural need, and paved the way for their reconciliation, not as an act of intellectual eclecticism but as the central feature of the laws of advanced human evolution, an insight Hobhouse was to formulate independently and more meticulously. For solidarists, however, catering to need served the broader aim of restoring individual initiative (Mitchell 1991, p. 234), while the New Liberals did not prioritise liberty over welfare, regarding them as partially overlapping concepts.

If for French reformers *l'état providence* was the culmination of an existential condition comprising the inevitability of association which the state eventually came to regulate, for their British equivalents the welfare state was a planned act of social self-direction that arose at a specific historical moment. Although the French republican tradition of the state enabled it to glide more easily into its role as initiator of social policy, this did not necessarily entail a strong collectivism. On the level of practical policy recommendations, British social reformers were more willing to appeal to direct state intervention and compulsion, while French solidarists had to frame proposals that satisfied a broad cultural preference for private property ownership (Stone 1985, pp. 162–3). That propensity was spurred on by the less radical nature of French liberal thought, and it influenced the continuing struggle, via economic liberalism, over social versus private insurance between the wars (Ashford 1986, pp. 86, 91, 150). Hence the French conceptions of liberty were torn between liberal and solidarist interpretations, wedded to security on the one hand, and to a supportive social environment on the other. As Paul Pic, an expert on labour legislation, argued, the means to ensure the maximum individual liberty resided 'in association, in laws based on *solidarité*'.[17] This contrasted with the British Millite attachment of liberty to self-development (Freeden 1996, pp. 144–54). Yet positivist and empirical understandings of science intermeshed in both cultures, and proceeded

17. Quoted in Stone (1985, p. 163).

to portray welfare as their necessary outcome. Significantly, the solidarists endorsed the biological and evolutionary cooperation the New Liberals had claimed to corroborate.[18]

By emphasising that interdependence of individuals, Bourgeois – directly influenced by Fouillée – sanctioned a conscious and scientifically inspired social responsibility for social evils. 'This gave rise to a social duty that was wider than the traditional conception of justice but more precise, rigorous, and obligatory than charity', linked instead to asserting the social debt of the wealthy. Human solidarity was seen as a superior and supra-individual replacement for Christian charity, and justice was, in Bourgeois's own words, 'the means of establishing an equilibrium between moral and social data' (Hayward 1961, pp. 25–7; Scott 1951, p. 175). Subsequently, Emile Durkheim – himself an advocate of the blend of mutually regulating centralised statism and decentralised associationalism endemic to French political culture – trod a similar path between social fact and moral prescription. Weaving theories of social solidarity and interdependence into a complex analysis of modern society, he proffered a scientifically based social morality for which French social reformers mustered considerable appeal (Stone 1985, p. 30), and from which later welfare theorists such as Titmuss were to draw. Justice and well-being were associated with acknowledging the limits imposed on increased individual autonomy by a desirable and necessary social association. For Durkheim, this was the outcome of a gradual increase in moral sentiment. His functionalism, too, was reflected in an established ratio between contribution to society and reward. Beyond that, human sympathy – charity in its true, obligatory meaning – would recognise the inequity in rewarding natural talents as if they were meritorious: 'It is society', he wrote, 'that is coming to exercise complete dominion over nature, to lay down the law for it and to set this moral equality over physical inequality which in fact is inherent in things.' The appreciation that social fact could override physical fact and thus drive a new social morality was a landmark on the route to welfarism (Durkheim 1992 [1950], pp. 219–20; Lukes 1973, p. 157).

By the beginning of the twentieth century compulsory state social insurance had become the logical corollary of such arguments. It was vitally informed by a conception of temporal solidarity, including the redistribution of security across generations (Shapiro 1997, p. 137). It was driven by

18. On the appeal to patriotism see Stone (1985, p. 46); on organicism and evolution see Freeden (1996, pp. 218–22).

Fouillée's conception of reparative justice which legitimated compensation and indemnification as a social duty. And mirroring a well-established theme of French political theory, running from Montesquieu through Rousseau and Saint-Simon, liberty was squarely located within communal life. In that sense the French mutual societies, offering health insurance based on self-help, blended into the solidarist assertion of group responsibility, though without the universalism that only the state could provide (Mitchell 1991, p. 249). Finally, it was underpinned by a notion of 'quasi-contract' linking liberal discourse to an as yet non-vocal community of equal access to social goods, expressed in bills on social welfare 'often couched in Bourgeois' own phraseology'. Due to the solidarist requirement to share the social heritage among all, this entailed more than satisfying minimum standards of life, though areas of individual activity and private wealth accumulation were not ruled out (Hayward 1961, pp. 29–30, 36–7; Scott 1951, pp. 166–7, 171, 176). Insurance was still designed to reinforce an individual's will to achieve the kind of security that only personal property could provide (Stone 1985, pp. 34–5, 101).

Unlike the British experience, French political thinking on welfare was moulded in particular within the field of two further ideological constraints: Marxism and Catholicism. Despite the emergence of a sophisticated theory of social insurance, divisions abounded even within the French left, following debates in the Marxist camp between those who refused to shore up capitalism through small injections of humanist social reform and those who preferred evolutionary socialism. This was compounded by the power of mutualism within liberal welfare ideologies, often wedded to an employer-paternalism that clashed with socialist views of class (Saint-Jours 1982, p. 115). Centralised state apparatuses, to the contrary, were necessary to justify socialist and Marxist conceptions of power and social unity-cum-equality. Yet the French sensitivity to class divisions – for which Marxism had only revolutionary solutions – enhanced the appeal of communal arguments for social harmony, now that such harmony was also conceptually attainable via the route of welfare rather than free trade or blatant nationalism. Moreover, socialists – as in Britain – notably employed a discourse of individual rights when insisting on universal state-provided subsistence (Rimlinger 1971, p. 62).

Social Catholicism, later in the century amalgamating with (social) Christian democracy, encouraged the protection of the family and the traditional role of women. This merged into support for family allowances, famously expressed in Leo XIII's 1891 papal encyclical *Rerum novarum*, which set out a public social policy as an alternative to liberal and socialist doctrines based on a just wage. The endorsement of family allowances by different ideological families placed the former in a linchpin position in French welfare policy, sustained by long-standing fears about French depopulation. Liberal social Catholicism surfaced in the ideas of Frederick Le Play about social harmony as the aim of the state (Ashford 1986, pp. 83, 85; Le Play 1982). It eventually detached itself from right-wing French clericalism, and re-emerged within the Mouvement Républicain Populaire to assist in defining the features of the post-1945 welfare state, particularly through an emphasis on decentralisation and the protection of individuals from the ravages of market forces (Hazareesingh 1994, pp. 219–20). Compulsory social insurance for wage-earners was only inaugurated in France in 1928 and 1930. Because it established voluntary insurance above a minimal level, and was associated with mutualist organisations, it was a non-universalist scheme of public assistance rather than a full embodiment of solidarist ideals (Saint-Jours 1982, p. 95). But the recognition of social obligation, both at the level of civil society and of the state, had become ingrained, prompting a merger between the welfare norms of the two levels (Rosanvallon 1990, pp. 191, 194; Ashford 1986, pp. 138–9). Though republican-solidarist principles still represented an ideological position much opposed in the inter-war years by the French economic liberals – who contested the offering of family allowances as a reward for need rather than for work – they were gaining the upper hand over resistance from both right and left. Laroque reflected this transformation in his organicist emphasis on the advantages public welfare services would bring to the entire community (Ewald 1986, p. 402) and in his strong preference for social insurance – as a socially integrating measure that would eradicate working-class exclusion and inferiority – over the demoralising effects of public assistance (Merrien 1994, pp. 128–30, 135; Laroque 1953, pp. 12, 55–6). The syndicalist tradition, in which class autonomy overrode the now legally established acknowledgement of the state as engine and regulator of social progress, was relinquished. In the area of unemployment insurance, however, France lagged behind other countries until 1958 (Rosanvallon 1990, pp. 179–81; Rosanvallon 1992, p. 155). More significantly, *l'état providence* is both an accurate and an imprecise epithet. Though the state managed the discharge of central social welfare functions, it was not catapulted into the position of their main supplier except as a reaction to anomie (Merrien 1997, pp. 9–11). Contrary to British new liberalism, it was unnecessary to provide social solidarity through the state while those ties were furnished by intermediary bodies.

American exceptionalism? The diluting of progressivism

To talk about American exceptionalism in the realm of social welfare would be exaggerated, as none of its specific features were alien to its European counterparts (Rodgers 1998, pp. 255–8 and *passim*). Nonetheless, the sum total of American welfarism constituted a case apart in terms of the internal balance of its components. Ostensibly mirroring typical nineteenth-century tensions between individualism and collectivism, it displayed a sharp divide between theory and practice, a pronounced division of labour between localism and federalism which skirted around the principle of universalism, a reluctance to move beyond a modest interpretation of welfare, even when provided by the state, and a high degree of activity on the part of business, gradually subsumed into – rather than replaced by – governmental regulation and intervention. Despite its former openness to imported European ideologies, on issues of social policy the USA proffered less fertile soil. Thinkers within the progressive liberal tradition, especially from among the Progressive movement and the ranks of social scientists (Hofstadter 1955a) – however eloquent their voice – enjoyed only short periods of political influence, unlike many of their European counterparts. Social democratic ideologies were anathema to a political culture nourished on individual effort and on social divisions in which ethnicity overshadowed both class and collectivist community. By contrast, welfare systems in the old world had not designed redistributive systems in which ethnicity signalled a criterion of social vulnerability. It was not until mid-century, for example, that non-discriminatory services relating to race were recognised in Britain as of equal importance to the redistribution of resources in constituting the ideology of welfare (Titmuss 1976, p. 191).

The absence in the USA of strong national bureaucracies and of a centralised state tradition necessitated an appeal to the abstract and partly mythical attributes of a constitution providing the impartiality and unifying focus which were unavailable at the fissiparous concrete political level. But the constitution infiltrated notions of social policy through its legal formalism, with the courts actively engaging in the formulation of welfare policy. They condoned a minimalist equality of opportunity embedded in ideas of due process (Skocpol 1995, pp. 11, 24–5, 96), and preferred the bestowal of rights on the basis of contract over that of need. The inability of this notional universalism to drive federal social policies in the first part of the twentieth century shifted the balance towards the uneven localism of social policy, municipal reform (Faulkner 1931, pp. 124–9), and the sporadic attempts by businesses to offer particularist solutions to the welfare of their workers,[19] inspired by their search for greater efficiency and a self-interested desire to reduce waste (Rimlinger 1971, pp. 67, 73). Unlike America's major European equivalents, this institutional and geographical separation helped prevent an integrated ideology of welfare. Bereft of a strong sense of a central state, the appeal of federalism encouraged the organisation of welfare mainly on the basis of the individual states (Skocpol 1995, p. 11).

Initially welfare was relatively uncontroversial, as long as it was narrowly aimed at war pensioners in the nineteenth century, at the elderly ex-employed in the early twentieth century, and at mothers' pensions and the protection of women workers, devoid of the dependency connotations which later undermined its good standing (Berkowitz 1991, pp. ix, 3, 92, 95; Skocpol 1995, pp. 7, 76–8, 96).[20] Notably, even trade unionists such as Samuel Gompers, the president of the American Federation of Labor, were suspicious of government, with its business connections. The AFL's leadership vacillated between opposing and supporting a national system of social insurance (Patterson 1994, p. 33; Skocpol 1995, pp. 101, 110–12).

In its more ambitious forms, welfare thinking was frequently considered to be socialist, as was the case with one of the most important theoreticians of American welfarism, I. M. Rubinow. In effect, his ideas were close to European social reformism in the mould of J. A. Hobson, with whose works he was familiar. Rubinow saw social insurance as 'the substitution of social effort for individual effort', relating centrally to the distribution of loss under conditions of hazard. That was 'the concern of the modern progressive state', encompassing the broader aim of eradicating poverty and ensuring an equitable return for one's labour. Tellingly, his conception of welfare incorporated the benefits of modern civilisation and industrial development, including art, poetry and music. Social insurance meant readjusting 'the distribution of the national product more equitably . . . in accordance . . . with those standards which due consideration for national vitality makes immediately imperative' (Rubinow 1916, pp. 3, 5, 10, 481, 491). In a similar vein Abraham Epstein, secretary of the American Association of Social Security and credited with originating the phrase 'social security', chose the term to transcend the class limitation of support for workers alone. 'Social insurance' unacceptably echoed Bismarck's compulsory savings, and 'economic

19. On the interaction between welfare capitalism and the welfare state in the USA see Berkowitz and McQuaid (1992).
20. Skocpol (1995, p. 72) refers to experiments with a 'maternalist welfare state'.

security' overlooked welfare for society as a whole (Haber and Cohen 1948, pp. 39–40).

Such views had an intellectual resonance in American culture. In particular, the progressive social philosopher John Dewey resurrected the notion of the pursuit of the common good as offering the opportunity for the full realisation of individual potential, underpinned by a restructuring of economic organisation (Dewey 1935, pp. 25–6, 51, 88). From another standpoint the reformers and intellectuals clustered around *The New Republic*, Herbert Croly, Walter Weyl and Walter Lippmann, had during the First World War directed that progressive publication to advocate a redistributionary fund to provide the resources for compensating for workers' accidents, for disability, or for old-age insurance (Seideman 1986, p. 35). Croly had conceived of 'social welfare ... as an end which must be consciously willed by society and efficiently realized', for society was 'a whole, with certain permanent needs and interests'. His view of the promise of American life comprised a new nationalism in which the public and fraternal interest was furthered by the active state, while such activity would still promote individual liberty, and it was taken up in Theodore Roosevelt's 1912 electoral campaign (Croly 1909, pp. 186–90, 207–8; Croly 1915, pp. 148–9, 188–97; Rimlinger 1971, p. 64). Lippmann increasingly reflected the early twentieth-century mixture of social (or in Britain, national) efficiency focused on a eugenic concern for the quality of human stock and interdependent human improvement. His was a liberalism that would 'insure and indemnify against its own progressive development'. With unusual insight into the nature of welfare liberalism and unencumbered by the ideological constraints operating on British liberals, especially their greater suspicion of the market, Lippmann proclaimed: 'Liberalism is radical in relation to the social order but conservative in relation to the division of labour in a market economy' (Lippmann 1956, pp. 213, 224, 236).

However, these views of welfare – mainly British-inspired but with a local capitalist twist, combining a social holism with individual effort – lost out in the American ideological competition, for even that balance of individual and social input was seen as too broad. The USA did not produce a critical mass of welfare theorists who could capture the public imagination and fashion a dominant body of social thought, as happened in Britain. The institutional solutions produced by government did not necessarily reflect Progressive theories of welfare – a point made by Dewey – and many of its policies did not emerge from coherent and well-established ideological positions of the kind available in Europe (Young 1996, pp. 169–70). To the contrary, Herbert Spencer, who had portrayed welfare measures as undermining the survival of a fit society, still exercised a powerful impact in America. His American disciple W. G. Sumner had asserted that the social order 'was fixed by laws of nature precisely analogous to the physical order. The most that man can do is by ignorance and self-conceit to mar the operation of social laws' (Spencer 1969; Sumner 1914, p. 37; Taylor 1992; Hofstadter 1955b; Rimlinger 1971, pp. 48–9). The curtailing of welfare was notably linguistic as well as operational; the term was sharply delimited from 'social security', tending to be reserved for handouts for the poor, and designed as conditional gratuities – a phrase that was ideologically *non grata* – that came from general revenues. This pivotal distinction limited the notion of social security, and accompanied its unconditional material relief with conditional social approval (King 1999, pp. 150, 270; Patterson 1994, p. 76). That disparity had been central to Beatrice Webb's reluctance to adopt social insurance in the first place, precisely because it would perpetuate the stigmatised distinction between insurance and assistance (McBriar 1962, p. 276).

The ideology sustaining social policy frequently replaced the social contract of equal citizens with a socio-economic contract in which social support had to be purchased through good behaviour. In the words of an official report in 1936, the distinct American system of welfare 'does not offer the individual a life of security. It grants him an opportunity and imposes upon him the obligation to find security for himself... and for opportunity the individual must look to private enterprise.'[21] American welfare thought was permeated by an individualism that privileged personal responsibility for one's financial well-being – for Franklin D. Roosevelt, pensions were the 'natural profits of their years of labor and insurance' (Rimlinger 1971, p. 214) – but that incurred communal censure when individuals failed to live up to those expectations. The central state merely facilitated the discharge of that responsibility, the expression of which could only be realised as a set of private transactions, not as a manifestation of integrated social solidarity or organicism. Social insurance protected 'that spirit of independence' regarded as 'the essence of Americanism'.[22] It was a far cry from the French normalisation of risk.

The emphasis on obligations ran headlong into a discourse in which (natural) rights had been predominant, exposing a major fissure in American

21. 'Security for a People', First Annual Report of the Social Security Board, 1936 [1937], in Haber and Cohen (1948, p. 75).

22. The Ohio Unemployment Insurance Commission, quoted in Rimlinger (1971, p. 216).

political thought between a constitutional ideology of procedural equality, and claims for individual protection, and a social ideology in which a conservative communitarianism adopted republican language and symbols that severely constricted such individualism. The latter prevailed in the sphere of social policy, which in other Western societies had become the defining arena of the transformation of state–individual relationships. In the USA, a social welfare system could only maintain its dignity and legitimacy through the ethical chain of work–provision–security, while welfare narrowly construed was tainted precisely through its direct association with a statist redistributionism linked to need rather than earned through effort. 'The new concept of the state as the instrument of organized collective action' (Rubinow 1916, p. 500) found no adherents even among New Dealers. Although the practices of European welfare states also fell short of the objectives of their own theoreticians, American practices reflected an ideology far more parsimonious in its conceptions of radical reform.

The salience of the market in American welfarism, whether in the role of businesses, the purchase of welfare, or the appeal to private interests, was, however, evident in Europe as well. In the emerging Federal Republic of Germany after 1949 the term 'social market economy' became prominent as a symbol of welfare on a staunchly capitalist base, while in France reliance on a mixture of public and private arrangements was integral to conceptualisations of welfare. Even the acclaimed Beveridge Report did not depart from a heavy reliance on the market, and in so doing revealed itself as part of the complex web of British welfare thinking. As Marshall rightly observed, that web contained influencing, interfering with *and* superseding the free play of market forces (Marshall 1965, p. 308).

Social insurance and a liberal social democracy

The 1942 Beveridge Report serves as an apposite marker for the condition of progressive welfarism in all its mid-century complexity and diversity. Its recognition of the interplay of social units was staunchly liberal, mirroring the 1911 insurance partnership between state, individual and employers (Beveridge 1942, pp. 109–10). In addition assistance, designed as less socially and economically attractive, was mooted for those outside the arena of social insurance. Its view of social life was organic, stressing the communitarian and non-sectional nature of British society (Beveridge 1942, pp. 6, 155). Its conception of the state was directive and centralising, though far from all-encompassing, and bolstered by the infusion of Keynesian economics into public debate. Through planned compulsory welfare measures, and through accentuating the obligation of citizens to seek work (Beveridge 1942, pp. 57–8), the force of the state was wielded alongside the acknowledgement that liberty was a supreme indication of that very welfare. Liberty was significantly located entirely within the domain of individual initiative, the goods which it could attain being beyond the responsibility of the state to provide or enable, but dependent on the state's discharge of non-libertarian measures (Beveridge 1942, p. 170). However, Beveridge believed that the freedom to spend benefits as one wished was essential to the principle of insurance (Harris 1977, p. 399). Totalitarian models, looming large at the time, were firmly rejected.

The report's understanding of human nature was entrepreneurial, extolling the individual's capacity for 'incentive, opportunity, responsibility'. Its ethical sweep was ostensibly universal and non-stigmatised in scope, expressed in measures for free health care, yet suffused with arguments from social efficiency. Its ideas of citizenship were a compound of universality (a social security scheme – at subsistence level – protecting all individuals from want and addressed to 'every citizen of working age'), conditionality ('benefits in return for contributions, rather than free allowances from the State, is what the people of Britain desire'), contract (simple egalitarian flat rates of benefit for flat rates of contribution) and national particularism, levelled at the survival of the 'British race' and its 'national unity' (Beveridge 1942, pp. 7, 170, 11, 9, 154, 172). It was male-oriented, identifying men as bread-winners and women as wives and mothers (Lewis 1992, p. 163). Its view of welfare was both generous and modest. On the one hand, it nodded in the direction of human vulnerability and concomitant care, at least with respect to children, by introducing a long-anticipated but nevertheless highly innovative and redistributionary family allowances system, advocated among others by Eleanor Rathbone in the inter-war years, and reiterating the cross-cultural respect for the family in Western welfare solutions. On the other hand, it focused on welfare primarily as an aspect of smoothing out the practice of work (Parker 1998, p. 146), which Beveridge regarded as essential to self-esteem (Deacon 1996, p. 196). In effect, the report's concentration on want, social security and social insurance became the linchpin of a modern welfare policy, though its ideological caution removed it from the forefront of welfarism. Yet that very caution was embraced by British Labour circles, who adopted the report as their own despite its centralising tendencies to which, unlike many of their continental counterparts, they had been opposed (Freeden 1986; Harris 1981, pp. 254–5). British Progressives continued to be divided between welfare theories of conditional reciprocity and unconditional thriving, social efficiency and humanism, civil responsibility and universal altruism.

Among British welfare theorists, Marshall recognised the inegalitarian implications of modern welfarism. The right to pursue and receive welfare under conditions of equal opportunity meant an equal chance to reveal differences, even superiorities, though always within the organic constraints of social needs (Marshall 1965, pp. 259–60, 266). Titmuss evinced a stronger sense of liberty than Beveridge, inherited and modified from the new liberalism, with intimations of its strong social underpinning in French welfarism. He was vociferous in warning against the new authoritarianism that medical and welfare technologies could generate. In particular, the professional solidarities which had been at the centre of Durkheim's social analyses required counter-measures. Doctors needed encouragement to act as free agents while patients, as consumers of care, had rights and needed to exercise choice. Contra Durkheim and the solidarists, those essential freedoms could only be secured through releasing individuals from unalterable dependence on any particular social group (Titmuss 1958, pp. 141, 183, 187–8, 195, 201–2; Titmuss 1976, p. 242). Never before had choice been so prominently associated with physical welfare, and not since the New Liberals had health been so emphatically allied to an organic view of society that fostered democratic social integration.

Only Swedish welfarism struck similar notes, though it emerged more specifically out of a social democratic political tradition than its other European counterparts. Even more so than in Germany, where Eduard Bernstein had begun to point the way, the Swedish tradition was fully cognisant of the major roles of liberty, choice and participation in the flourishing of a society's citizens (Heclo 1974, pp. 179–81). When one of its major theoreticians, Ernst Wigforss, elaborated on the cluster of concepts that ought to direct the path to social democracy, he included specific versions of equality, liberty, democracy, security, efficiency and community in a mutually constraining configuration. Constant awareness of other West European welfare policies and theories was later reflected in the impact of the Beveridge Report (Tilton 1990, pp. 116–18), but Wigforss himself was not content to rest with the state guarantee of a minimum, to be exceeded through individual effort. Like many left-wing Swedish voices he saw social insurance as part of a broader conception of welfare that included cooperation and solidarity.

Overlapping configurations and precarious boundaries

Marshall's characterisation of the welfare state as centrally extending civil and political participatory rights into the social sphere underplays two crucial dimensions. First, the rise to prominence of modern social policy reflected a paradigm shift in the conceptualisation of human nature and the consequent nexus of institutions, practices, responsibilities and goods these entailed. Hence two notions of state activity vied with each other: a formalistic and legal conception of universalism, with the state as the impartial meter out of justice – defined as the access of rational, purposive agents to public decision-making – confronted an alternative understanding of the political based on human needs, vulnerability and risk, all held within a socially interdependent structure. The extent to which the two meshed, with varying degrees of success, intensity and compatibility, is the diverse story of different Western welfare ideologies. Importantly, this was bolstered by two other fluctuating distinctions. The one, the continuing tension between specific and holistic interpretations of welfare, was far more evident in Europe than in the United States. The other was that of contractual versus unconditional entitlement to welfare goods, but the unconditional dispensing of goods was infused at the very least with a residual contractualism (White 2000, pp. 507–32). The reciprocity of services between individuals and social agencies was salient both in new liberal and socialist theory. Beveridge was not atypical in preferring a 'social service state' to a 'welfare state', taking the former to imply duties as well as rights (Harris 1977, p. 459). The innovative aspects of progressive welfare theories lie not in their eradication of the concept of contract, but in their expanded understandings of human capacities, human precariousness and social dependence. These identified additional impediments to the ability to discharge contractual and quasi-contractual obligations.

Second, extension was accompanied by both inclusion and exclusion. Conceptions of citizenship fed on notions of nationhood as the locus of social rights, alongside the decline of the hitherto pivotal role of localities and associations in defining human identity and administering the means to maintaining it. The development of civil society had to be constrained by state regulation for the sake of greater equality, security and liberty; as well as due to the formulation of national, integrating projects that demanded implementation. This implicit and moderately benign nationalism, surplus to intended meaning, often masqueraded as a universalism that stopped at the boundaries of the state. But some internal boundaries continued to exist in the socio-political thought of the period. Women, other than as mothers, rarely figured as a focus of state welfarism, despite their indispensable shaping of its conditions and ends. And though inroads were made into the distinction between workers and non-workers by reclassifying both categories as vulnerable and needy, another distinction was retained in the eugenist thinking that pervaded all the countries under consideration here, significantly across the ideological spectrum. On one level, eugenics introduced a determinism into the relationships between social groups that dictated the marginalisation of some beneficiaries of welfare. On a second level, progressives argued that social reform should always include physical as well as economic, ethical and cultural improvement, a theme present in the radical social thinking of the Myrdals in inter-war Sweden (Myrdal and Myrdal 1941, pp. 115–16, 213–16), and among British liberals and socialists (Freeden 1979, pp. 645–71). On a third level, even progressive and liberal reformers practised exclusionist policies designed to remove certain categories from the full circle of citizenship (King 1999, pp. 51–134). Physical and mental defects were depersonalised by detaching them from individual fault, but at the expense of denying those hapless members of society the possibility of voluntary self-improvement, or of benefiting from social assistance. To that extent, their social exclusion was harsher than that meted out to paupers. Ultimately, this was an atypical political language, but it nonetheless penetrated the modes of discourse not only of conservatives but of liberals and socialists.

If there is one lesson to be learnt about welfare thought in the first half of the twentieth century, it is that no neat categorisations, dichotomies or boxes can express the complexity, overlap and multi-layering of its configurations. Of course, regional tendencies and evolving themes were in evidence, but they were fluid. Constantly shifting internal priorities within a range of competing positions were discernible not only among welfare theorists and across ideological groupings, but were voiced simultaneously by the same individuals and groups. Concurrently, comprehensive welfarism addressed issues that necessarily contained contradictions and were pulling in different directions. That ideological indeterminism matched the new uncertainties of individual lives that had restructured the concerns of the welfare state. Yet even in, and perhaps because of, its indeterminism, welfare thought provided one of the most powerful and appealing intellectual and political constructs to grace the twentieth century.

2
Politics and markets: Keynes and his critics

WAYNE PARSONS

Introduction

John Maynard Keynes (1883–1946) is one of that small group of social scientists who may be said to have had a profound influence on the development of their subject as well as on the conduct of political argument and public policy. His work is accorded the singular accolade of having an entire branch of economics named after him, and his impact on the theory and practice of politics and public policy is such that we speak of 'the Keynesian revolution' and 'the age of Keynes'. 'Keynesianism' came to prominence in the 1940s, 1950s and 1960s as an approach to economic policy which focused on the management of the demand side of the economy so as to secure full employment. However, by the 1970s, the dominance of Keynesian economics in government and academia faded in the face of persistent high inflation and unemployment ('stagflation', as it became known). James Callaghan famously confessed to the annual conference of the Labour Party in September 1976 that the option of 'spending your way out of recession' no longer existed. By the 1980s, as Robert Skidelsky observed, 'Keynes, who was praised for having saved the world from Marxism, had joined Marx as the God that failed' (Skidelsky 1996, p. 107). This chapter shows that Keynes, despite becoming an 'ism', was not as dogmatic a thinker as those in the vanguard of the counter-revolution against 'Keynesian' economics chose to depict him. Rather he fashioned his theories from his philosophy and beliefs in response to events and problems of the day. His name has been closely associated with one book, *The General Theory of Employment, Interest and Money* (1936), which revolutionised both economic analysis and economic policy in Britain, the USA and in many other countries. It is on the influence of this landmark book that so much commentary and scholarship has been focused (Blaug 1991, p. xv). However, in the closing decades of the twentieth century, Keynes's contribution to the theory and practice of political economy has been rightly re-evaluated in terms of understanding the development of his thought, life and 'vision' (Fitzgibbons 1988) as a whole.

The making of a political economist

The greatest influence on the young Keynes was unquestionably the philosopher G. E. Moore. In later life he was to reflect on the impact of Moore in an essay on 'My Early Beliefs'. It was a 'religion' in which, he notes: 'Nothing mattered except states of mind, our own and other people's of course, but chiefly our own' (Keynes 1971–89, vol. X, p. 436). It was a religion preoccupied with human relationships, personal friendship, love and the contemplation of beauty and truth and an intuitive belief in what is good and it gave Keynes and his fellow 'Apostles' a licence to ignore Victorian moral conventions and rules in their pursuit of the 'good' as a state of mind. For all its faults, Keynes remained convinced that Moore's philosophy was 'nearer to truth than any other' (Keynes 1971–89, vol. X, p. 442). Civilisation, he came to realise after the First World War, was altogether more fragile a 'crust' than the young disciples of Moore had believed. For Keynes it was the 1914–18 war and the peace that followed which exposed the shortcomings of his Mooreite religion, but he never really lost the faith and in particular his faith in the power of ideas. Politically he was inclined towards the pragmatic and anti-ideological philosophy of Edmund Burke. His undergraduate essay on Burke offers much insight into Keynes's attitude towards uncertainty, moral risk, the 'long run' and his belief in the virtues of expediency and a profound distrust of abstract theorising (Helburn 1991; Skidelsky 1992, pp. 61–4). In terms of his economics, Keynes was first and foremost schooled in Marshall's *Principles of Economics* and in the idea of economics as a *moral* science. However, although Marshall's economics was a vital influence, his knowledge of economic theory came, as Skidelsky notes, 'not from reading about it as from working out the problems for himself, and discussing them with others' (Skidelsky 1983 p. 206).

On graduating, Keynes opted for a career in the civil service, and spent a few years at the India Office (1906–9). He was, however, a most reluctant civil servant and was far more preoccupied with working on a fellowship dissertation than the tedious routine of the civil service. After a failed first attempt, the dissertation (*A Treatise on Probability*) eventually managed to secure Keynes an exit from the civil service and a re-entry into academic life. For many years this dissertation was neglected by scholars but it is now recognised as absolutely central to understanding Keynes's philosophy as a *whole* (Carabelli 1988; Fitzgibbons 1988; O'Donnell 1989). It argued, to use Fitzgibbons' succinct summation, that: 'our state of knowledge in practical affairs is not sufficient, except in trivial instances such as structured games, to estimate the future of events with quantitative precision. Nevertheless, we can anticipate the future by seeing, in an artistic but rational way, that there is a pattern to the facts' (Fitzgibbons 1988, p. 130). This issue of decision-making in conditions of uncertainty and the limits to rational calculation is a core aspect of his later political economy, and is the key theme of the *General Theory*.

His return to Cambridge, however, was not as a philosopher or a mathematician, but as the protégé of Alfred Marshall. Whilst being utterly conventional in his economic teaching, Keynes lived a highly unconventional life as a member of the Bloomsbury set and this radical, avant-garde aspect of his life is not to be discounted in understanding his political economy (Crabtree and Thirlwall 1980; Skidelsky 1983; Hession 1984; Parsons 1997). His philosophy of life and his approach to economic theory and policy-making were wholly intertwined (Mini 1991; 1994). After 1919 Keynes criticised conventional nineteenth-century economic wisdom in public just as he had earlier challenged prevailing Victorian morality in his private life.

Taking time off from preparing his *Treatise on Probability* for publication, Keynes became involved in the future of Indian currency and banking. This led to the publication of his first book, *Indian Currency and Finance* (1913). His concern with money and economic institutions was to remain central to his writings thereafter. His expertise on the subject of Indian currency resulted in the 29-year-old Keynes being appointed to a Royal Commission to investigate Indian finance and currency. This early experience was to set a pattern for the rest of his life: he was from then on an economist focused on *policy* and *institutions* rather than theory for its own sake. He was interested in solutions to problems and issues of the moment, rather than pursuing an academic research agenda per se. Inevitably, given his concern to understand contemporary problems and advance policy recommendations, the outbreak of war in 1914 was to focus Keynes's mind on the issue of war finances. The preparation of the *Treatise on Probability* for publication was put aside and he joined the Treasury in 1915. At first he was involved in food prices, but was soon drawn into other areas of internal and external finance. By 1916 he had become a leading figure in financial negotiations between the Allies and neutral countries. In due course, Keynes found himself as the Treasury's man at the Versailles peace negotiations. This was really the turning point in his career. Keynes was astonished and dismayed at the attempts by the Allies to impose a massive reparations bill on Germany. To show his disgust he resigned and published an indictment of the peace settlement which was to make him a world figure: *The Economic Consequences of the Peace* (1919).

The First World War and after

In *The Economic Consequences of the Peace* Keynes was still working very much within the framework of the conventional economics of the day, but this adherence to prevailing economic orthodoxy sat uneasily alongside his analysis of an economic, political and social order which had been utterly transformed by the war. It showed how the moral, economic and political ideas and assumptions of the Victorian era had ceased to be appropriate to understanding a changing and uncertain world haunted by the threat of monetary instability and Malthusian overpopulation. The book exposed the fragility and instability of the old order, and made a powerfully argued case for abandoning the belief that the mechanisms which maintained a 'complicated and artificial' system would continue to work and deliver the economic prosperity which was so vital to the continued existence of liberal democracy. He became a prolific journalist, campaigning for a monetary policy which was not reliant on the maintenance of the gold standard, and in 1923 he put the case in a *Tract on Monetary Reform*. Like his *Economic Consequences of the Peace*, the *Tract* was to stress the dangers of inflation to capitalism and democracy, and the consequences of fluctuations in the value of money. The *Tract* contains one of his most memorable phrases: 'But the *long run* is a misleading guide to current affairs. In the long run we are all dead' (Keynes 1971–89, vol. IV, p. 65). The key theme of the *Tract* was that rather than seeking the dubious certainty of a fixed gold standard, government should recognise that stable prices require the acceptance of on-going *management* responsibilities. However, in 1925 Churchill rejected the advice of Keynes and others and returned Britain to the gold standard at a parity of $4.86. For Keynes, this represented the height of folly and he promptly told Churchill so in a pamphlet whose title echoed his best-selling book on the peace: *The Economic Consequences of Mr Churchill*. The 'faith' in 'automatic adjustments' (such as the use of deflation to force wages down) and 'pure chance' was, he predicted, bound to fail and cost much waste and human misery. The government, he argued, had to radically change its way of thinking about how the apparently automatic processes of a laissez-faire economy worked – in reality as opposed to in theory. In the next few years he developed his critique of laissez-faire capitalism in a number of pieces including: 'The End of Laissez Faire' (1926); 'Am I a Liberal?' (1925); and 'Liberalism and Labour' (1926). In the first of these he shows how laissez-faire ideas gained currency, and challenged the assumptions which underpinned a way of thinking which he believed was increasingly anachronistic. It did not follow, he argued, that individuals striving to maximise their own advantage will produce the greatest aggregate of wealth. Keynes was not persuaded by the doctrine of laissez-faire, as either an explanation of how the real world worked *or* as a theory of how it *ought* to work.

It is *not* true that individuals possess a prescriptive 'natural liberty' in their economic activities. There is *no* 'compact' conferring perpetual rights on those who Have and those who Acquire. The world is *not* so governed from above that private and social interest always coincide. It is *not* so managed here below that in practice they coincide. It is not a correct deduction from the principles of economics that enlightened self-interest always operates in the public interest. Nor is it true that self-interest generally *is* enlightened; more often individuals acting separately to promote their own ends are too ignorant or too weak to attain these. Experience does *not* show that individuals, when they make up a social unit, are always less clear sighted then when they act separately (Keynes 1971–89, vol. IX, pp. 287–8).

As Burke had argued, the issue of deciding what should be on the governmental agenda could not be determined in a 'theoretical' or 'abstract' way (Keynes 1971–89, vol. IX, p. 288). Defining the relationship between the state and the economy was a matter of *expediency*, and *experiment* and organic change rather than doctrine. Socialism and laissez-faire economics were simply 'dusty' plans fifty years out of date: capitalism had moved on and Keynes's aim was to show which ways of thinking about economic problems were more appropriate in the context of the institutional evolution of the capitalist system. In practice this meant that government should aim to provide a new institutional environment which could *facilitate* the growth of individualism and free markets.

Many of the greatest economic evils of our time are the fruits of risk, uncertainty and ignorance . . . Yet the cure lies outside the operations of individuals; it may even be to the interest of individuals to aggravate the disease. I believe that the cure for these things is partly to be sought in the deliberate control of the currency and of credit by a central institution, and partly in the collection and dissemination on a great scale of data relating to the business situation, including the full publicity, by law if necessary, of all business facts which it is useful to know. These measures would involve society in exercising directive intelligence through some appropriate organ of action over many of the inner intricacies of private business, yet it would leave private initiative and enterprise unhindered (Keynes 1971–89, vol. IX, p. 292).

There was, he thought, nothing in his proposals which was 'seriously incompatible' with the essentials of free market capitalism: 'namely the dependence upon an intense appeal to the money-making and money-loving instincts of individuals as the main motive force of the economic machine' (Keynes 1971–89, vol. IX, p. 293). In which case, Keynes thought the main task facing liberal democratic societies was 'to work out a social organisation which shall be as efficient as possible without offending our notions of a satisfactory way of life' (Keynes 1971–89, vol. IX, p. 294).

In his essays 'Am I a Liberal?' (1925), and 'Liberalism and Labour' (1926) Keynes comes closest to expressing where he stood in relation to the party political ideologies of his day. They reveal someone who was ill at ease with democracy and had a definite preference for elite control over the formulation of policy:

I believe that in the future, more than ever, questions about the economic framework of society will be far and away the most important of political issues. I believe that the right solution will involve intellectual and scientific elements which must be above the heads of the vast mass of more or less illiterate voters (Keynes 1971–89, vol. IX, p. 295).

In respect of party organisation, therefore, he admitted to a preference for the Conservative Party, rather than the more democratic arrangements of the Labour and Liberal parties. But the Tory Party offered him 'neither food nor drink – intellectual nor spiritual consolation' (Keynes 1971–89, vol. IX, p. 296–7). The Conservatives also stood condemned by Keynes as the party which defended the hereditary principle: something which Keynes thought was in large part responsible for the decay and decline of so much of the energy and enterprise of British capitalism. As for Labour, it was a class party, and it was not his class. The revolution would find him on the side of 'the educated bourgeoisie' (Keynes 1971–89, vol. IX, p. 297). Keynes believed that the great task for liberalism in the twentieth century was to facilitate a transition from laissez-faire individualism and 'economic anarchy' to a 'regime which deliberately aims at controlling and directing economic forces in the interests of social justice and social stability' (Keynes 1971–89, vol. IX, p. 305). This required a new understanding of how capitalism had changed in the twentieth century: a 'new wisdom for a new age'. But working out the practical details of policy and reform could not be accomplished in an abstract way. Policies would have to be devised in the context of 'actual events'. A party policy – and one might add Keynes's political economy itself – could not be defined 'beforehand, except in the most general terms' (Keynes 1971–89, vol. IX, p. 306).

Keynes and the 'new liberalism'

Keynes was an important figure in the Liberal Party between the two world wars. He had become editor of the *Nation* in 1923 and used the weekly journal to advance his views on the issues of the day. From 1924 to 1929 Keynes took a prominent part in shaping the ideas and policies of the Liberal Party and it is important to place the development and dissemination of his political economy in the context of this political involvement (Freeden 1986; Clarke 1983; 1978). Keynes was advancing his ideas against the background of the so-called 'new liberalism' which had emerged before the First World War associated with the writings of people such as T. H. Green and L. T. Hobhouse (Freeden 1976; Bentley 1977). This 'new liberalism' stressed the importance of social reform and the role of the state in actively promoting a fairer, more democratic society. Where Keynes's own brand of liberalism stands in relation to this 'new liberalism' is problematic. On the one hand, Keynes may be viewed as advancing ideas which are broadly continuous with the new liberalism (Clarke 1983, p. 175). On the other, Keynes may be viewed as having little sympathy with new liberalism's regard for positive freedom and democracy (Skidelsky 1992, pp. 134, 223). Keynes's concept of liberty was undoubtedly more negative than positive: in this regard he had more in common with later 'classical' liberals such as Hayek than the New Liberals. He was not disposed to use the state as an instrument of social justice, except when it was expedient so to do. His interest in social justice was expressed negatively, rather than positively; that is, he gave instances of how people had been badly or unfairly treated, rather than how they *ought* to be treated. He was concerned about inequalities, but did not believe in using public policy to create a more egalitarian society. Keynes was therefore out of step with the egalitarian and democratic tendency of new liberalism: at heart he was an intellectual elitist who believed that the solutions to economic problems were best left to the philosopher kings (and preferably King's graduates) than ignorant politicians and voters. Above all, Keynes did not feel the need to increase or extend democracy as did the exponents of the new liberalism. His aim was to preserve the kind of liberalism to be found in Hayek's *The Road to Serfdom*. The central argument, which runs through his writings from the 1920s to the *General Theory* and after, was the fear that unless the role of the state in relation to the economy was adjusted, liberalism and the cause of individual freedom (as Hayek expressed it) would not survive. In this sense, as Maurice Cranston notes, Keynes was not seeking to transform or modernise the philosophy of liberalism as were Green and Hobhouse, so much as 'to preserve the essential core of classical liberalism by attaching to it certain practical policies which he chose to call socialistic' (Cranston 1978, p. 111). Keynes, he argues, wanted to 'go straight back to the simple liberalism of Locke and not in any way to subscribe to the idealistic and metaphysical philosophy of radical liberalism which emerged after J. S. Mill' (Cranston 1978, p. 111).

Keynes's liberalism can therefore be read as either saving liberal democracy or destroying it; as promoting a highly technocratic and managerial way of thinking about the role of the state in economic and social life; or as a political philosophy working within the traditions of Burke and Locke. In a sense all contain aspects of the truth: Keynes was indeed a *radical conservative* who was concerned to defend parliamentary democracy but not to extend it, and was mindful of the social injustice which capitalism inevitably generated, but did not wish to go beyond the creation of full employment as a way of remedying injustice and inequality. He supported the existing order and wanted to defend it (from stupidity and muddle) in the short run. In his mission to persuade, Keynes was seeking to build a new, broadly based consensus of opinion, he was not too troubled with precise definitions, language and ideological positioning. He had the gift, as Skidelsky puts it, of 'talking right and left at the same time' (Skidelsky 1992, p. 493). In 'Liberalism and Labour' Keynes beautifully encapsulated what place on the political spectrum he occupied: 'The republic of my imagination lies on the extreme left of celestial space. Yet – all the same – I feel that my true home, so long as they offer me a roof and a floor, is still with the Liberals' (Keynes 1971–89, vol. IX, p. 309). He was, as Victoria Chick puts it: 'profoundly revolutionary and profoundly conservative: in his life as in his writing there is both tradition and dissent, continuity and revolution, at almost every stage' (Chick 1992, p. 310). It is when we read his essay on the 'Economic Possibilities for our Grandchildren' that we see that the whole point of liberal democracy and capitalism for Keynes was that it contained many *possibilities*. His liberal vision was, perhaps, (Whitehall) conservative in the short run, but far more (Bloomsbury) radical in the long run. Technological advances and capital accumulation, he thought, meant that 'in the long run mankind is solving its economic problems' (Keynes 1971–89, vol. IX, p. 325). He envisaged a possible future for liberal democratic civilisation in which basic human ('absolute') needs would be met. For a while, he suggested, we have to pretend that 'fair is foul and foul is fair'. The money-makers might yet lead us out into a world in which 'for the first time since his creation man will be faced with his real, his permanent problem – how to use his freedom from pressing economic cares, how . . . to live wisely and agreeably and well' (Keynes 1971–89, vol. IX, p. 328).

In 1929 he entered the election debates by backing Lloyd George's plans to reduce unemployment through a programme of public spending. The previous year he had contributed to the so-called Liberal 'Yellow Book' by putting the case for public works (Keynes 1971–89, vol. XX, p. 731). This line of argument continued in *Can Lloyd George Do It?* – which he wrote with Hubert Henderson. By 1930 Henderson and Keynes were to part company on the issue of the continued relevance of public works (Clarke 1983, pp. 179–80). Baldwin was castigated for appealing to abstract, unintelligible economic theory and the 'Abara cadabra' of Treasury orthodoxy to justify keeping millions of men unemployed. There was no need, he argued, for a socialist revolution to solve the problem of mass unemployment, but if capitalism were to survive there had to be a radical change in the way institutions thought. The revolution as such was in how we 'feel': capitalism had to be saved from itself by defeating the timidity and obstructiveness of a 'sinking administrative vitality' (Keynes 1971–89, vol. IX, p. 125). The problems of capitalism were, in a sense, all in the mind: in the assumptions, feelings, expectations, fears, ideas and psychological dispositions which held sway in institutions. If capitalism were to collapse and liberal democracy were to fall to communism or fascism it would be due to 'stupidity' and 'muddle' (Keynes 1971–89, vol. IX, p. 126), rather than rampant self-interest and wickedness. There was another dimension to this muddle – the international situation. If a depression were to be avoided a new way of thinking about economic problems had to emerge which took account of the need for new *international* institutional arrangements. This was a primary concern of his political economy, which culminated in his work on the Bretton Woods agreement shortly before his death.

Towards the *General Theory*

Keynes eventually turned his mind to the challenge of bringing about a change in academic as well as public opinion and in 1930 he published two volumes (the *Treatise on Money*): *The Pure Theory of Money* and *The Applied*

Theory of Money. Typically, given his predisposition towards the analysis of current events and problems, by the time of its publication Keynes had already moved on (Keynes 1971–89, vol. XIII, p. 176). These volumes develop the arguments about the relationship between savings and investments which had been set out earlier in the *Tract on Monetary Reform*. Theoretically the *Treatise on Money* showed how the link between savings and investment ($S = I$) was no longer automatic, as the classical theory of money supposed and as policy-makers assumed. It showed that savings do not always translate directly into investment. Thrift did not necessarily result in investment and enterprise (Keynes 1971–89, vol. VI, p. 132). Although Keynes challenges the relationship between savings, investment, interest, prices and employment, the model which emerges from the *Treatise on Money* was hardly a radical departure from the classical theory. Where Keynes does depart from the classical position is with regard to the notion that the interplay of the various variables will produce (left to themselves) equilibrium. The problem was that it would attain a balance, but in the long run. The *Treatise* gave rise to an argument between Keynes and Hayek in the pages of *Economica* in 1931, which saw Hayek attack Keynes's rejection of the theory that markets can automatically adjust to sustain $S = I$. Keynes was at a loss to understand why Hayek could not see his point of view and reasoned that it was all too symptomatic of what happens when a 'remorseless logician' ends up in a 'muddle' (Skidelsky 1992, pp. 456–7). Between the publication of the *Treatise on Money* and the *General Theory* Keynes continued to develop his thinking in a very public way. Indeed, this was a vital part of his strategy: he wanted to bring opinion-formers (and his fellow economists) along with him and allow them to enter as fully as possible into his way of thinking: as witnessed by his evidence to the Macmillan Committee in 1930 (Keynes 1971–89, vol. XX). The activities of theorising and persuasion were essentially one and the same for Keynes. An important intermediate statement – 'The Means to Prosperity' (1933), in which he introduces the idea of the 'Multiplier' – is indicative of his belief that economic problems were fundamentally to do with the way in which ideas and states of mind get jammed or stuck, with the result that, as he put in 1928, there is a: 'failure of our ideas, our conventions, our prejudices to keep up with the pace of our material change' (Keynes 1971–89, vol. IX, p. 316). Prosperity, he believed, depended on un-jamming and getting policy makers to rethink. The problems facing capitalism came 'from the failure in the immaterial devices of the mind' and 'nothing is required and nothing will avail, except a little clear thinking' (Keynes 1971–89, vol. IX, p. 355). The economic problem was one which involved political economy, that is: 'a blend of economic theory and the art of statesmanship' (Keynes 1971–89, vol. IX, p. 336).

The Keynesian revolution and the *General Theory*

In January 1935 Keynes confided to George Bernard Shaw that he believed he was 'writing a book on economic theory, which will largely revolutionise – not, I suppose, at once but in the course of the next ten years – the way the world thinks about economic problems' (Keynes 1971–89, vol. XXVIII, p. 42). Few books published in the twentieth century may be said to have had the kind of impact which *The General Theory of Employment, Interest and Money* was to enjoy. The *General Theory* brought about a 'revolution' in economic theory, and changed the way which even those who disagreed with him thought about economics (Pigou 1949, p. 21). The theory was to provide a language and a way of thinking about the economy as a whole in terms of the relationship between aggregate demand and supply. It was at this analytical level that the 'Keynesian revolution' was most complete (Johnson 1978). The *General Theory* was quickly translated into textbook economics through the work of John Hicks, Alvin Hansen and Paul Samuelson. However, Keynes's economics underwent considerable distortion in the hands of his intellectual heirs ('bastard' and otherwise) – not least in respect of the way in which his theories were translated into mathematics, notwithstanding Keynes's deep distrust of mathematical economics (Keynes 1971–89, vol. XIV, pp. 319–2, 299–300, 310).

The *General Theory* also played an important part in changing the way in which the policy-makers in Britain, America and elsewhere sought to manage economies to secure high levels of employment through counter-cyclical demand policies (Hall 1989a; Przeworski 1984; Worswick and Trevithick 1984; Hirschman 1989). Exactly what the nature of this revolution in policy was, however, is the subject of extensive scholarly debate. At first the 'Keynesian revolution' was taken to be the story of how Keynes's theories changed policy: a revolution in British Treasury orthodoxy, for example, that culminated in the 1944 White Paper on employment which committed the government to the goal of full employment (Stewart 1967; Winch 1969) and in America in the Employment Act of 1946 (Galbraith 1975). This view of the Keynesian revolution owed much to the accounts offered by economists themselves, which emphasised the role of economists in government and the spread of ideas and theories. However, with the release of documents from the Public Records Office, and the publication of the *Collected Writings*, scholars began to question this somewhat simplistic account of the revolution in the 1970s and 1980s (Howson 1975; Skidelsky 1975; Howson and Winch 1977; Hutchison 1978; Peden 1980; 1983; Booth 1983; 1985; Rollings 1985; Weir and Skocpol 1985). This literature explored the relationship between Keynes and Keynesian theories and changes which had taken place in the context of institutional and policy processes. As far as America is concerned, although one can say that Keynes's ideas shaped the climate of opinion in the 1930s and 1940s, there is little evidence that Keynes's theories had much influence on either Roosevelt's New Deal, or on the Truman administration (Stein 1969; Heller 1966). The theoretical influence of Keynes has, therefore, to be set in the context of 'practical' and 'administrative' (Rollings 1985) influences within which economic policy-making evolved in the 1930s and 1940s. Others have sought to explain the Keynesian revolution less in terms of the spread of ideas or institutional and administrative change than in how Keynes's theories attracted – or failed to attract – broader 'coalitions' of support between policy-makers, politicians and social and economic interest groups (Gourevitch 1984; 1986). Whilst the influence of the *General Theory* on the development of economic analysis was undeniably 'revolutionary', the impact of his ideas on practical policy and politics is far more problematic (Hall 1989b). Indeed, some have argued that what did take place was hardly a *Keynesian* revolution at all (Tomlinson 1981; Hutton 1986), and that the Keynesian revolution 'still remains to be made, both in teaching economic theory and in forming economic policy' (Robinson 1975, p. 131).

For Keynes, the *General Theory* provided the missing component to the *Treatise on Money* – the idea that unemployment could be the outcome of a shortfall in demand and that the classical view of the economy was a 'special case' – and expanded on the significance of expectations, ignorance and uncertainty in a market economy. Policy-makers no longer needed to be held captive by the trade cycle, with all its dismal promise of recovery in the long run. Through *counter-cyclical* policies it was possible to even out the booms and busts so as to sustain an economy operating at high levels of employment. The book concludes with 'notes on the social philosophy towards which the general theory might lead'. Chapter 24 of the *General Theory* is, perhaps, the clearest exposition of Keynes's political and social philosophy. It begins by identifying the main fault of capitalism as its inability to provide for full employment and its 'arbitrary and inequitable distribution of wealth and income'. For Keynes, however, the issue was not *inequality* as such, so much as the existence of 'large disparities'. He concedes that the desire to make money and own private wealth have their uses, but that the 'stakes' of the game should not be so high:

dangerous human proclivities can be canalised into comparatively harmless channels by the existence of opportunities for money making and private wealth, which, if they cannot be satisfied in this way, may find their outlet in cruelty, the reckless pursuit of personal power and authority, and other forms of self-aggrandisement... But it is not necessary for the stimulation of these activities and the satisfaction of these proclivities that the game should be played for such high stakes as at present. Much lower stakes will serve the purpose equally well, as soon as the players are accustomed to them. The task of transmuting human nature must not be confused with the task of managing it. Though in the ideal commonwealth men may have been taught or inspired or bred to take no interest in the stakes, it may still be wise and prudent statesmanship to allow the game to be played, subject to rules and limitations, as long as the average man, or even a significant section of the community, is in fact strongly addicted to the money making passion (Keynes 1971–89, vol. VII, p. 374).

Given that he shows the importance of the propensity to consume and of the level of aggregate demand to the output of the economy as a whole, the use of high interest rates to promote high savings and thence investment is no longer necessary. The *rentier* phase of capitalism, he predicted, was coming to an end, and in its place would emerge a more interventionist approach whereby the state itself would assume the responsibility of managing the inducement to invest and the propensity to consume:

I conceive, therefore, that a somewhat comprehensive socialisation of investment will prove the only means of securing an approximation to full employment; though this need not exclude all manner of compromises and devices by which public authority will co-operate with private initiative. But beyond this no obvious case is made out for a system of State Socialism which would embrace most of the economic life of the community. It is not the ownership of the instruments of production which it is important for the State to assume. If the State is able to determine the aggregate amount of resources devoted to augmenting the instruments and the basic rate of reward to those who own them, it will have accomplished all that is necessary. Moreover, the necessary measures of socialisation can be introduced gradually and without a break in the general traditions of society (Keynes 1971–89, vol. VII, p. 378).

Apart from the state taking responsibility for determining the level of output consistent with full employment, by adjusting the relationship between the propensity to consume and the inducement to invest, there will 'be no more reason to socialise economic life than there was before'. The aim of the *General Theory* was not to dispose of classical theory, but to show what kind of institutional environment was necessary for the 'free play of market forces' to realise their 'full potentialities'. As such he believed that his approach 'purges' individualistic capitalism of its 'defects' and 'abuses', whilst holding fast to the principles of personal liberty and freedom of choice. Keynes thus advanced his plan as a way of ensuring the survival of liberal democratic institutions and values. Change was necessary in order not to change:

> The authoritarian state systems of to-day seem to solve the problem of unemployment at the expense of efficiency and of freedom. It is certain that the world will no longer tolerate the unemployment which, apart from brief intervals of excitement, is associated – and in my opinion, inevitably associated – with present day capitalistic individualism. But it may be possible by a right analysis of the problem to cure the disease whilst preserving efficiency and freedom (Keynes 1971–89, vol. VII, p. 381).

In addition to this, having learnt how to 'provide themselves with full employment by their domestic policy', the economic causes of war based on the competitive struggle for markets could be lessened – provided of course the ominous warnings of the Reverend Malthus were heeded. By way of conclusion Keynes proclaims his belief in the ultimate power of ideas:

> The ideas of economists and political philosophers, both when they are right and when they are wrong, are more powerful than is commonly understood. Indeed, the world is ruled by little else ... I am sure that the power of vested interests is vastly exaggerated compared to the gradual encroachment of ideas (Keynes 1971–89, vol. VII, pp. 383–4).

This famous and oft-cited passage expresses much about Keynes's political philosophy and political economy. This is the Platonist, the disciple of Moore speaking: all that mattered were states of mind. Ideas do far more good or ill than vested interests. These comments were, of course, to initiate a debate which has gone on ever since as to the relationship between ideas and the policy process (Hall 1989a; Parsons 1983; Gamble *et al.* 1989) and (as we see below) were viewed by some of his critics as indicative of his serious underestimation of the power of bureaucratic and group interests to capture institutions. Significantly Hayek, perhaps his greatest critic, was in complete agreement with Keynes's argument about the power of ideas – if with little else (Hayek 1948, p. 108).

Paying for the war and preparing for the peace

The coming of the Second World War made the policy recommendations of the *General Theory* rather irrelevant as the onset of war quickly remedied mass unemployment. Realising that an economy with full employment would soon face the problem of inflation, Keynes set his mind to finding solutions to new problems. The result was 'How to Pay for the War' (1940). As in the *General Theory*, the theme is finding a balance between the apparently contradictory demands of freedom and democracy, the state and market forces. In 'How to Pay for the War' it is a problem of 'how best to reconcile the demands of war and the claims of private consumption' (Keynes 1971–89, vol. IX, p. 367), and how to enlarge social justice whilst restricting and diminishing individual choice in order to curb inflation. Keynes proposed a way of restricting spending and consumption in conditions where the 'size of the cake is fixed' (Keynes 1971–89, vol. IX, p. 375) which would not undermine liberal democracy. Planning could promote freedom only when it was mindful of the need to distribute the cake fairly (Keynes 1971–89, vol. IX, pp. 375–7). His solution was to propose a savings scheme which would work through deferring a proportion of everyone's earnings until after the war. The effect of this would, he argued, be to reduce the levels of consumption to the levels of output, thus controlling price rises. This kind of democratic planning was akin to 'rules of the road' (Keynes 1971–89, vol. IX, p. 381) and was wholly consistent with free markets and freedom of choice (Bateman and Davis 1991). As he put it in a letter to *The Times*: 'I am seizing an opportunity to introduce a principle of policy which may come to be thought of as marking the line of division between the totalitarian and the free economy' (Keynes 1971–89, vol. XXII, p. 123). His aim was 'social: to prevent the social evils of inflation now and later; to do this in a way which satisfies the popular sense of social justice; whilst maintaining adequate incentives to work and autonomy' (Keynes 1971–89, vol. XXIII, p. 218). In other words, Keynes wanted to institute a system of financial planning which served to advance social justice while at the same time allowing individual freedom of choice. One of the most important aspects of his war work was his involvement in negotiating a US loan and his leading role in the Bretton Woods agreement. He was determined that the lessons of Versailles should be learnt (Keynes 1971–89, vol. XXV, p. 11) and he worked tirelessly to ensure that economic reconstruction was given the highest of priorities. Keynes's ideas for an International Clearing Union failed to secure US support and in the end the IMF and the World Bank were shaped more by American interests than Keynes's ideas (Van Dormael 1978).

Hayek contra Keynes

Friedrich von Hayek was born in 1899 and died in 1992. Having been swamped by the 'Keynesian avalanche' in the 1950s and 1960s, Hayek was to come into his own in the 1970s and 1980s as the favoured economist of the 'New Right' (McCormick 1992). Hayek was thus to dominate the debate on the relationship between politics and markets in the closing decades of the twentieth century, as Keynes had dominated it during the inter-war and post-war decades. In Keynes's own lifetime Hayek was always one of his severest critics. And yet in so many respects Keynes and Hayek were arguing on parallel lines. Central to both of them was the idea that human beings faced a world full of uncertainty and ignorance. Both were passionately committed to the freedom of the individual and both rejected the simplistic assumptions of neo-classical economics. Both wanted to see the continuation of democratic civilisation and both believed that the preservation of capitalism was vital if freedom were to survive and thrive. Both were influenced by the political philosophy of Edmund Burke (Hayek 1948, pp. 13, 24). Both were sceptical about the use made by economists of mathematics and the positivistic disposition of so much economic theory. The issues which separated them were, in many ways, to do with means rather than ends. Even so, the differences between the two were profound and significant. The reasons for these differences derive in great part from the intellectual environments or traditions within which the two men worked (Caldwell and Hayek 1995). Keynes's political economy was the outcome of the Cambridge school of economics, Alfred Marshall and the philosophy of G. E. Moore, whilst Hayek's ideas were shaped by the 'Austrian school' of Karl Menger (1840–1921), F. von Wieser (1851–1926) and L. von Mises (1881–1973) (Gray 1984, pp. 16–21). For Keynes the turning point in his intellectual life came with reading Moore's *Principia Ethica*, whereas for Hayek it was the publication of Mises's *Die Gemeinwirtschaft* (*Socialism*) in 1922 (Mises 1981), which marks a transformation in his way of thinking about how the market economy and the price system worked, and alerted him to the dangers of socialism and planning (Hayek 1956, p. 133). Mises's *Die Gemeinwirtschaft* provided Hayek with a 'Gospel' (*sic*) as Moore's *Principia Ethica* had given Keynes a new 'religion'. (Neither man, however, remained wholly faithful to his early conversion.) Rooted in this Austrian tradition

Hayek was to be opposed to any notion that we could understand economic problems in an objective way, or that economic, political and social orders could be designed or constructed.

Hayek had the privilege and good fortune of being able to have the last word, if not the last laugh, and was at pains to set up Keynes as the man who took a major part in the corruption of liberalism, the subversion of free-market capitalism and the growth of big government (Hayek 1978, p. 192). Hayek fundamentally disagreed with Keynes's analysis of the economic problems of the 1920s and 1930s and proposed radically different policy solutions. Whilst at the London School of Economics, Hayek – with Lionel Robbins – took Keynes to task for trying to promote the view that the slump was the result of underinvestment and urged government to pursue a course of deflation so as to lower prices and wages. Of course, they argued, there would be higher unemployment and other adjustments, but there was no alternative to the policy of allowing market forces and economic cycles to work themselves out. Government-led expansion and investment might bring about short-term benefits, but in the long run they would do immense damage and make matters far worse. Keynes, however, could not accept either that there was no alternative or that we could take the risk of letting unrestrained economic forces rip society apart. What was needed, Keynes believed, was English pragmatism and good judgement, rather than abstract Austrian economic theory.

Where Hayek and Keynes fundamentally part company is with regard to how they saw the capacity of markets to generate order or equilibrium. Hayek argued that, from an epistemological point of view, as the social order cannot be understood in an objective way, and as that order is so very complex and unknowable, only free markets could serve to distribute information efficiently. Knowledge is highly fragmented and tacit, and as a consequence the idea that it could be aggregated so as to enable politicians and bureaucrats to direct or plan it to some end was, for Hayek, nonsensical and dangerous. For Hayek, this also meant that the attempt to understand the economy in 'macro'-economic terms was also misguided. Indeed, it was Keynes's attempt to formulate a macro-economic model which Hayek later argued was the main reason why he did not respond to the *General Theory* (Hayek 1978, p. 284). Hayek maintained that the price system was the most efficient planning system: for only the price system could coordinate all the dispersed localised knowledge in a complex economy (Hayek 1948). Hence, centralised planning of whatever kind was doomed to failure, and any attempt to interfere in the free flow of market forces would invariably do more harm than good. Knowledge of the kind that Keynes believed possible was far too fragmented and divided ever to be possessed by a 'directive intelligence' – whether composed of people like Keynes or Stalin (Hayek 1945). There could and should be no conscious control of what he termed the '*catallaxy*' of social and informational exchange which gives rise to '*spontaneous*' forms of human order.

An important episode which well illustrates the differences between the two was Keynes's response to Hayek's *The Road to Serfdom*. In a letter to Hayek written in 1944, Keynes argued that it was a 'grand book' and at a moral and a philosophical level he was 'virtually' in complete agreement with Hayek (Keynes 1971–89, vol. XXVII, pp. 386–8). He disagreed with Hayek, however, on the practical and economic aspects and consequences of his book. Given the optimistic view which Keynes had about the post-war period, he begins his critique by taking Hayek to task for rejecting the view that there was 'plenty just around the corner'. Second, he disagrees with Hayek as to the intractability or difficulty of solving the 'economic problem' and of giving the economic problem far too much emphasis. This argument is then followed by two significant points of agreement which put his later main criticism into context. To begin with, Keynes endorses Hayek's stress on the profit motive and risk-taking. Planning should not, from Keynes's standpoint, lead to a society in which risk-taking is discouraged – far from it. Keynes was firmly in support of enterprise, and saw no harm in speculation provided it did not replace enterprise as the primary business motivation. The main difference between Hayek and Keynes is not about the profit motive, and the importance of risk, but what conditions can best provide the environment in which enterprise can be released and be made most productive. Planning cannot be a substitute for risk-taking, but the state can seek to create an environment in which the creative 'animal spirits' of capitalism are liberated. Whereas Hayek and Keynes both address the issues of uncertainty and ignorance, they arrive at different conclusions as to what to do about them. For Keynes, uncertainty and ignorance did not mean that we can do nothing, whereas for Hayek uncertainty and lack of knowledge mean that it is best if we do nothing and let order emerge out of complexity. As Keynes neatly put it earlier in 1925: 'the only hope lies in the possibility that in this world, where so little can be foreseen, something may turn up – which leads to my alternative suggestions. Could we not *help* something turn up?' (Keynes 1971–89, vol. IX, p. 226).

Helping something to turn up when we 'do not know what the future holds' and we are 'forced to act' (Keynes 1971–89, vol. XIV, p. 124) involves recognising the limits of rational knowledge. Though Keynes argues, from the *Treatise on Probability* onwards, that we know very little, he was able to see the role which human intuition and intelligence can play in responding to and shaping an uncertain and changing world. Policy-making had to be pragmatic and *unprincipled* (in a Burkean sense) *because* the world was so uncertain and changing, and our knowledge so very inadequate, but it *also* had to be open to the 'unrealised possibilities' and be wary of conventional or ruling opinion. Planning *did* carry risks, but Keynes believed that the alternative of doing nothing posed far more risk to the future of the very liberal values which *The Road to Serfdom* expounded. Planning, therefore, was not really the issue, but the morality of the community engaged in planning: 'Dangerous acts can be done safely in a community which thinks and feels rightly, which would be the road to hell if they were executed by those who think and feel wrongly' (Keynes 1971–89, vol. XXVII, pp. 387–8).

Although it is reasonable to suggest that Hayek and Keynes disagreed in terms of means rather than ends – that is, on where to draw the line and exercise 'practical judgement' in how to *avoid* the road to serfdom (Gamble 1996, p. 161) – it is important to stress that Hayek and Keynes saw capitalism in two utterly contrasting ways. For Keynes, capitalism was a necessary evil which was driven by a rather distasteful human urge: the love of money. Keynes frequently demonstrated a very low opinion of capitalism. He tolerated it and hoped that it would, in due course, evolve to the point that the money motive – the driving force behind capitalism – would no longer predominate. When once the 'economic problem' had been 'solved' and 'absolute' needs could be met, mankind would be able to focus on the 'arts of life'. Money love could finally be recognised for what it was: 'a somewhat disgusting morbidity, one of those semi-criminal semi-pathological propensities which one hands over with a shudder to the specialists in mental disease' (Keynes 1971–89, vol. IX, pp. 326–9). Although Keynes was not too concerned about the role of the state in the distribution of welfare, (as were to be many of his disciples) he was appalled by what human misery free markets could produce if left unchecked. Keynes's case against laissez-faire was as much a moral and aesthetic argument as it was an economic or political one. Keynes, Joan Robinson once observed, 'hated unemployment because it was stupid and poverty was ugly. He was disgusted by the commercialism of modern life' (Robinson 1975, p. 128). For Hayek, however, capitalism was an economic order in which the price system provided a powerful and efficient *informational* system which facilitated production and exchange. It was neither good nor bad. Morality or aesthetics did not enter into it. However, Hayek was very critical of Keynes's morals. He was particularly dismayed by Keynes's confession that, under the influence of Moore, he and his friends thought themselves free from the 'constraint to obey general rules' (as he argued in his essay on 'My Early Beliefs'). Later on, when he became aware of Keynes's sexual orientation, he concluded that it went some way to explain why Keynes was so disposed to reject ruling morals and conventions (Hayek 1978, p. 16).

Intellectually the two men were divided by two very different world views. First of all, Keynes did not see equilibrium as being *automatic*, spontaneous or self-generating. Perhaps it could be in the long run, but 'in the long run, we are all dead' – as he put it in the *Tract on Monetary Reform* (Keynes 1971–89, vol. IV, p. 65). If left to itself, the modern economy could remain in a slump for very long periods. Second, for Hayek, who *was* prepared to wait for the long run, even if this did mean prolonging unemployment, and who did not believe in the concept of economic equilibrium, this remark struck at a key difference between the two men. Keynes, Hayek once argued,

> believed that he was fundamentally still a classical English liberal and wasn't quite aware of how far he had moved away from it. His basic ideas were still those of individual freedom. He did not think systematically enough to see the conflicts. He was, in a sense, corrupted by political necessity. His famous phrase about, 'in the long run we're all dead', is a very good illustration of being constrained by what is now politically possible. He stopped thinking about what, in the long run, is desirable (Hayek 1977, p. 3).

However, Keynes did not consider the long run as *politically* problematic, as Hayek maintained (Hayek 1978, p. 57), so much as *morally* unacceptable. It was morally wrong for policy-makers to risk the continuation of human misery and revolution in the belief that all would be well in the future if we left things alone. Hayek – and other critics – read this attitude towards the short run as being illustrative of Keynes's preoccupation with 'political necessity' and the politically possible. For Hayek, Keynes wrote *tracts*, to influence opinion, rather than economic theory. Hence, Keynes was quite capable of changing his mind, if it was expedient so to do. Hayek takes this intellectual expediency as symptomatic of what Keynes was really all about:

> he was always concerned for expediency for the moment. In the last conversation I had with him . . . I asked him if he wasn't getting alarmed about what some of his pupils were doing with his ideas. And he said, 'Oh, they're just fools. These ideas

were frightfully important in the 1930s, but if these ideas ever become dangerous, you can trust me – I'm going to turn public opinion around like this.' And he would have done it. I'm sure that in the post-war period Keynes would have become one of the great fighters against inflation (Hayek 1977, p. 3).

It was Hayek himself who was to take up the challenge of turning around public opinion when inflation was to overtake unemployment as the predominant concern of economic policy-makers in the 1970s and 1980s. He campaigned for 'sound money' and focused his attack on the role of trade unions, interest groups and institutions in subverting market forces and fuelling inflation and big government, all of which was supportive of the arguments of those on the 'New Right' for free market capitalism and reducing the role of government.

Monetarist and public choice critiques of Keynes

Two other sources of anti-Keynesian, if not anti-Keynes, critiques, which came to prominence in the twilight of the Keynesian era and the dawn of the new age of markets, were monetarism and public choice theory. Unlike the arguments of Hayek, however, the criticisms of Keynes which emerged from monetarism and public choice were predicated on a highly positivistic approach to political economy: specifically both relied upon constructing scientific, predictive macro-economic models deriving from neo-classical economic assumptions. Although their names tend to be linked together, Hayek was never a monetarist. In the 1970s Milton Friedman, who was the pre-eminent exponent of the monetarist critique, campaigned effectively (using macro-economics) to demonstrate that the Keynesian model lay at the bottom of so much of the economic misery and failure of that decade. The charge was simple enough: Keynes had just not considered how important the money supply was, and had given too much attention to fiscal policy at the cost of neglecting monetary policy. Monetarists focused their attention on the monetary causes of inflation; in particular they urged a return to the quantity theory of money – the very theory which had been Keynes's point of departure from orthodoxy. The economy was, Friedman argued, far more stable than the Keynesian model assumed. He demonstrated this in a number of important theoretical ideas: the 'permanent income hypothesis', the 'stable demand for money function' and the 'natural rate of unemployment'. The attempt by governments to regulate the economic cycle through Keynesian techniques was doomed to failure and pushed up inflation and unemployment. Friedman was especially critical of the influence Keynes had on politics. His ideas, he argued, were responsible for 'the proliferation of overgrown governments, increasingly concerned with every aspect of the daily lives of their citizens' (Friedman 1986, p. 47). Keynes's great mistake, he suggested, was not paying more attention to the chapter in *The Road to Serfdom* on 'Why the Worst Get to the Top'. That is, Keynes stands condemned for the way in which he ignored the problem of how the interests of civil servants and politicians do not always equate with the 'public interest':

> Keynes believed that economists and others could best contribute to the improvement of society by investigating how to manipulate the levers actually or potentially under control of political authorities so as to achieve ends they deemed desirable, and then persuading the supposedly benevolent civil servants and elected officials to follow their advice. The role of voters is to elect persons of the 'right' moral values to office and let them run the country (Friedman 1986, p. 51).

Keynes's faith in the ruling elite to govern in the public interest, Friedman maintained, is suspect and flies in the face of actual experience – especially in the USA. This theme of Keynes's belief in an elite who were 'rightly orientated in their own minds' to make policy in the public interest was also to be the main focus of the critique advanced by the public choice school. Buchanan and Wagner, for example, challenged Keynes's assumptions about the relationship between bureaucrats, politicians, voters and budgets. In *Democracy in Deficit: The Political Legacy of Lord Keynes* (1977) and (with John Burton) *The Consequences of Mr Keynes* (1978) they sought to expose the naïveté of his belief in the benevolent rule of politicians and bureaucrats. This critique of the so-called 'presuppositions of Harvey Road', which assumed that 'the government of Britain was and would continue to be in the hands of an intellectual aristocracy using the methods of persuasion' (Harrod 1966, pp. 192–3) was also advanced by theorists such as Tullock (1965; 1976) and Niskanen (1971). For the public choice school the rhetoric of 'the public interest' deployed by both politicians and bureaucrats simply obscured the fact that policy-making operated to secure the maximisation of political and bureaucratic interests and to the detriment of the public interest. Public choice approaches to explaining the predisposition of liberal democratic government to bigger bureaux and ever larger budget deficits and 'throwing money' at problems formed a powerful component of the attack on the Keynesian consensus during the closing decades of the twentieth century. However, Keynes did not discount the role of self-interest, but simply believed ideas embodied in institutional conventions and expectations had the far greater capacity for 'good or ill'. Keynes's focus was not on how interests can capture institutions so much as how *ideas* capture institutions, and in turn shape how those institutions think and respond to risk, uncertainty and ignorance. Perhaps his greatest fault was not his insistence that ideas matter and his account of policy-making which tended to downplay the role of interests, but his profound and arrogant conceit (as Hayek recounted) in believing in his own creative capacities to change the way in which the world thought about economics.

Conclusion

Post-Keynesians, New Keynesians and others have attempted to refine Keynesian theory in order to provide a viable alternative to what Joan Robinson (1975) termed 'bastard' Keynesianism and the free market consensus which dominated the political agenda from the late 1970s onwards. Post-Keynesians have emphasised the importance of time and historical process; the role of expectations in an uncertain world; and the impact of political and economic institutions in shaping economic events (Davidson 1981). The New Keynesians have also sought to refashion Keynesian economics in order to make it more relevant to policy-making by focusing on issues such as wage and price rigidity, information and 'menu' costs (Hutton 1995, pp. 245–7). This latter version of Keynesian economics informed the return of Keynesianism to the British Treasury under Gordon Brown in New Labour's second term of office. Labour's new Keynesianism, he explained in a lecture to the Royal Economic Society in the summer of 2000, aimed to reject the crudities of the past and 'draw on the best of Keynes's insights about political economy and put a modern Keynesian approach into practice' (Brown 2001, p. 37). As Larry Elliot commented on this twenty-first-century revival of Keynes:

> There was a time, not so long ago, when a Keynesian was as rare as an Englishman in Chelsea's back four. There were a few devotees of the General Theory knocking about in the lower divisions, but the real stars were the monetarists and the neo-classicists. According to the Thatcherites, Keynesianism was responsible for everything that was wrong with Britain – inflation, unemployment, tower blocks, welfare scroungers, the permissive society, single mothers, modern art. You name it. Now Keynes is being rehabilitated (Elliot 2000).

With perfect timing, Macmillan published the third and final volume of Robert Skidelsky's monumental study of Keynes in November 2000

(Skidelsky 2000). A leading post-Keynesian, Paul Davidson, in criticising the New Keynesian orientation in British policy-making, suggested that Gordon Brown read the book, since: 'Unfortunately, Keynes' argument for remedying the serious flaws of our entrepreneurial economy without destroying the spirit of enterprise or the promotion of a civilised society is not well understood by the Bank of England or the Treasury' (Davidson 2000). In the closing years of the twentieth century Skidelsky looked forward to the prospect of Keynes returning from the dead (Skidelsky 1997). By the beginning of the twenty-first century, however, it looked as if Keynes was indeed back from the grave, haunting the corridors of Whitehall and Washington and putting to flight the various shades of monetarism and laissez-faire political economy which had taken up residency in the 1970s. As Lord Skidelsky noted in August 2001:

> The Bank of England cut interest rates this month by a quarter point in response to growing fears of recession. In the US, President George W. Bush's recently enacted package front loaded tax reductions for the same reason. All of this sounds rather Keynesian. Yet we are told *ad nauseam* that Keynes is dead: that economies are inherently stable; that governments should stick to clear rules to avoid monkeying around with the economy as they did in the bad old days. So what exactly is macroeconomic policy trying to achieve nowadays? Officially, one thing only: price stability . . . Yet consider what Sir Edward George . . . told the House of Lords committee on economic affairs: 'What we are trying to do all the time is to balance the aggregate demand with aggregate underlying supply in the economy'. According to Donald Brash, governor of the Reserve Bank of New Zealand, monetary policy should aim at 'regulating the level of demand'. This all sounds pretty Keynesian to me (Skidelsky 2001).

With the return to 'depression economics' (Krugman, 2000), in which old fears about inflation gave way to new fears about deflation and slump, and in the aftermath of the terrorist attacks of 11 September 2001, *The Economist* could report that: 'After a decade of budgetary prudence, Keynes is back in fashion' (*The Economist*, 2001). The renewed fashionability of Keynes in this period was also to be much in evidence amongst a variety of groups who campaigned against the 'Washington consensus' and for radical reforms to the Bretton Woods institutions and tighter regulation of the international financial system to reduce what Keynes had called 'casino capitalism' (Rowbotham 2000; Ellwood 2001).

In the light of these attempts to make Keynes's ideas more relevant for the twenty-first century it is well to keep in mind the fact that his political economy was constantly evolving to fit the problems and issues of the day:

for he was above all an economist for whom abstract (mathematical) theorising and fixity of thought were anathema. As Lord Kahn recorded: 'Keynes often used to remark to me that he enjoyed the advantage of waking up every morning like a new born babe, entirely uncommitted to what he had thought or advocated previously' (Kahn 1974, p. 32). As so much Keynesian scholarship emphasised from the 1980s onwards, it is only when we place his political economy and his approach to policy-making in the context of the *problems* which he endeavoured to solve and of his life and philosophy (or vision) as a whole that we come to a fuller appreciation of his contribution to the history of ideas in the twentieth century. Keynes thought of himself as a Cassandra, whose daily task it was to 'pluck the day, fling pamphlets to the wind, write *sub specie temporis* and achieve immortality by accident, if at all' (Keynes 1971–89, vol. X, p. 199). Keynes's quest was less to do with devising economic policies and theories per se than with the problem of finding a middle way between the extremes of a centrally planned economy and a free market economy. The defining challenge for liberalism in the twentieth century was to develop appropriate governmental and financial institutions for managing, over time, the relationship between money, knowledge and uncertainty. This was the unifying theme running throughout his approach to economic theory and policy. The fact that his name became associated with 'big government', 'fine tuning', 'acceptable levels of inflation', 'the Phillips curve', 'the welfare state', 'spending your way out of recession' and 'wages and incomes' policy would have amused and annoyed him greatly. That the particular diagnosis and remedies he advanced for dealing with the particular problems of the 1920s and 1930s continued to be applied and misapplied in the very different political and economic circumstances of the second half of the twentieth century would, no doubt, have served to confirm his belief in the power of academic scribblers to influence mad men – and women – in authority and to freeze the way institutions think long after their ideas had ceased to be relevant as a guide to policy in an uncertain and changing world.

3
The advent of the masses and the making of the modern theory of democracy

RICHARD BELLAMY

'There are in fact no masses; there are only ways of seeing people as masses' (Williams 1971 [1958], p. 289).

The gradual extension of the suffrage to all adult men and ultimately women too during the late nineteenth and early twentieth centuries transformed the politics of Western Europe and North America. Many contemporary theorists attributed these reforms not to any improvement in ordinary people's political judgement because of better education and higher living standards, nor to a progressive appreciation of the right of all adults to be considered full citizens, but to a new social and economic reality having made such measures unavoidable. Quite simply, within a mass society political power could only be exercised with mass support. In spite of the inevitability of a widened franchise, many theorists believed deep tensions existed between the concepts of the 'mass' and 'democracy', rendering a 'mass democracy' almost a contradiction in terms. For the ideas of the 'masses' and 'mass society' were embedded within accounts of social organisation and behaviour that challenged the models of individual agency and rationality traditionally associated with democratic decision-making. Consequently, even democratically minded thinkers found that a coherent conception of mass democracy required a radical rethinking of the norms and forms of the democratic process (Femia 2001). This chapter traces the development of the new sociological and psychological languages of mass politics and their deployment in the construction of a modern theory of democracy. As we shall see, though still widely accepted, this theory incorporates empirical and normative assumptions arising from contentious and anachronistic views of human nature and society few would wish to espouse today.

The 'masses' and 'mass society'

Originating in counter-revolutionary analyses of the French Revolution, the concepts of 'the masses' and of 'mass society' became part of the new 'scientific' approaches to politics developed by pioneering political sociologists and social psychologists from the 1890s onwards (Bramson 1961, ch. 2). Underlying these concepts were more general theories of social disorganisation, disorientation and anomie occasioned by the break-up of the allegedly homogeneous and hierarchical communities typical of agrarian societies, and their replacement by the quite different social relations of large-scale industrial societies (Pick 1989; for examples see Mill 1977 [1836], Tönnies 2001 [1887], pp. 17–21; Durkheim 1984 [1893], pp. 292, 304, 311; Le Bon 1926 [1895], p. 14; Ortega y Gasset 1961 [1930]). On the one hand, industrialisation was said to have fostered greater interconnectedness between a wider circle of people through better communications, the growth of cities and large factories, a more extensive division of labour and so on. On the other hand, these new relations were believed to be less close-knit and more compartmentalised than the organic ties of the extended families and local communities they had supplanted. Instead of possessing a clear status with known rights and obligations within a fixed social hierarchy, the increasingly mobile individual had to assume a multiplicity of often transient roles within an ever-changing social environment. In the process, individuals lost both the coherent sense of self and the unified set of values that came though living within a more integrated society. Lacking either a stable moral framework or a strong identity, the individual had become an anonymous member of an amorphous mass (Bramson 1961, pp. 32–4).

Three features of this mass condition attracted the attention of contemporary social theorists (Hawthorn 1976; Hughes 1958). First, they highlighted the psychological aspects of involvement in the mass. Masses, they contended, were motivated by passion rather than reason. Being part of a mass made people a prey to their emotions. They became open to suggestion, highly malleable, impulsive, instinctive and even bestial. Mass behaviour was described in pathological terms and linked to various types of moral and social deviance – from supposedly abnormally high rates of crime to drunkenness, suicide, lunacy and sexual perversion. Second, theorists associated mass society with new forms of social organisation. The state had expanded vastly, overseeing economic and social behaviour ever more closely, while the economy was dominated by huge corporations and industries. Bureaucratic methods suited to the efficient administration of complex tasks by large departments and businesses had swept through the private and public sectors. As a result, the mass individual was subject to increasing managerial regulation in all spheres of his or her life. Finally, and largely as a result of these two features, traditional elites – intellectuals, the clergy and social superiors – had been displaced by demagogues and technocratic managers.

All three features were held to typify the new mass political actor – the urban and increasingly organised proletariat (Williams 1971 [1958], pp. 287–8). Uprooted from rural communities and massed into the expanding industrial towns, they were prone to strikes, riots and other forms of 'deviant' and 'emotive' behaviour, only being contained by the discipline of factory routines and mass organisations – be they unions or parties. Meanwhile, mass production and consumption had displaced high culture with popular culture and the mass media. Educated elites had given way as the shapers of opinion and taste to populist, rabble-rousing politicians, their journalistic supporters, manufacturers and advertisers. Socialism and organised labour became symptoms of the psychological and structural malaise afflicting modern societies, prompting even liberals to reconceptualise both liberalism and democracy via the new psychological and sociological political categories (Femia 2001). Reasoned deliberation to reach a consensus on the common good became an impossible ideal within a mass society. Instead, agreement had to be manufactured through controlling the masses and improving the quality of leadership.

Thus, all three features of the social theory of mass society came to be incorporated into a reworking of democracy in mass terms. In what follows, we shall trace the development of the resulting new language of democratic politics. The next section explores how social psychologists extended their analysis of mass crowd behaviour to the electorate more generally, giving both the attributes of a mob. The third section then examines an early analysis of political parties as the new mass political organisations. In each case, individual political judgement and action were claimed to have been curtailed – in the first by absorption into the irrational collective consciousness of the group, in the second by the discipline of party bureaucracy. The fourth section reveals how scope was nonetheless believed to exist for elites to manipulate both popular passions and the party machine. The fifth section then traces how these three theses were brought together to produce a denial of the very possibility of mass (or indeed any) democracy in the strict sense, thereby forcing its rethinking as a mechanism for selecting between party elites and leaders, who compete to win the people's vote by exploiting the tools of mass persuasion and organisational superiority.

Two general themes emerge from this analysis. The first notes how, rather than being scientific discoveries, each of these theses involved national variations on the more general historical experiences and intellectual trends of the time, in which a certain political culture shaped the various ideological preferences of the individual thinkers, making some theoretical moves more accessible and plausible than others. Thus, crowd theory reflected reactions within France to the French revolutionary tradition, whereby popular sovereignty frequently took the form of direct action or the plebiscitary populism of Bonapartism, as refracted through a predominantly positivist psychological approach. Elite theory was shaped by Italian clientalistic politics as perceived by a similarly positivistic social science tradition, whilst the bureaucratisation of the state and parties in Germany rendered organisation theory particularly compelling to German theorists, even if a more historical methodology enabled it to be interpreted in more socially contingent terms than were allowed by the behaviourist explanations favoured elsewhere. Significantly, the one analysis to see mass movements as enriching and even spreading democracy drew on Britain and America, where revolutionary mass movements were lacking, though its conclusions were subsequently systematically misread by others.

These different emphases did not prevent theorists drawing upon each other's work, making national comparisons, or – in certain cases – eventually forging a synthesis. Indeed, this became all the easier as the various arguments became codified as elements of a scientific political sociology. The second theme enters here. For this codification made later political scientists prisoners of a supposedly 'scientific' discourse, the true assumptions of which few knew and most would have rejected (see chapter 21). Theorists were led by the pseudo-scientific logic of their arguments to conclusions at variance with their own ideological commitments, forcing them into either incoherent reworkings of their beliefs, pessimism or a volte-face. This tendency was especially true of those theorists who emphasised psychological rather than structural and organisational laws to account for mass behaviour. In their eyes, altering social structures had little purpose so long as human nature appeared unreformable and unchanging.

From crowds to mass electorates

Since classical times, theorists have criticised democracy for being less rational and efficient, whilst more prejudiced, parochial and intolerant, than rule by an enlightened elite. Neither genius nor difference could survive the democratic desire to level everything down to the same lowest common denominator. These criticisms were standardly linked to descriptions of the anarchy, destructive violence and irrationality of the mob (McClelland 1989). The French Revolution reinforced such views among conservatives and liberals alike, from Burke and de Maistre, de Tocqueville and J. S. Mill, onwards. However, later theorists now saw the character of crowds as determined by human psychology and their growing dominance as the product of social development. Consequently, they generalised the analysis of crowd behaviour to cover all activity within a mass society – from the operations of elected assemblies and the influence of the popular press, to the nature of religious worship and political activism, and the production and marketing of everyday commodities. As Gustav Le Bon dramatically put it: 'The age we are about to enter will in truth be the ERA OF CROWDS ... The divine right of the masses is about to replace the divine right of kings' (Le Bon 1926 [1895], pp. 15, 17).[1]

Le Bon's *Psychology of Crowds* is by far the best-known work in the field. A huge success when published, it was rapidly translated into English and German and remains in print in several languages. Fundamental for later thinkers as diverse as Sigmund Freud (1953–74 [1921], pp. 23–4), Robert Michels (1959 [1911], pp. 159, 206) and Graham Wallas (1908, p. 53), it became a touchstone for the whole discipline of social psychology. If his conclusions have been remarkably little challenged, however, they rested on assumptions that are highly contestable, amounting as they do to little more than the prejudices of the day. A brilliant and prolific populariser, Le Bon simply synthesised the ideas of contemporary French and, to a lesser extent, Italian authors – notably Victor-Alfred Espinas, Henry Fournial, Gabriel Tarde and Scipio Sighele (Barrows 1981; Nye 1975). Few had undertaken much empirical research, though empiricist assertion and pseudo-scientific psychological speculation characterised their arguments. Rather, their views reflected the *fin-de-siècle* preoccupations with the social disorder of mass societies outlined earlier. As Susanna Barrows (1981, p. 5) has remarked, these views provided the often 'distorting mirror' through which theorists reflected on the growing political presence of 'the popular classes', particularly organised labour.

1. Mass had been in use since the late seventeenth century but began to replace multitude and mob from the 1830s. It only took on a definite class connotation from the 1880s (Briggs 1979). Crowd was regularly used either interchangeably with mass or as a special category of it. For example, the 1908 German translation of Le Bon's book called *Psychologie der Massen* (Baehr 1990).

In the early 1880s the Third Republic had loosened restrictions on the freedoms of association, speech and assembly, but became subject to what were perceived as unprecedented levels of popular protest at the corruption of its parliamentary system. Many French intellectuals saw echoes of 1789 and the Paris Commune of 1871 in these demonstrations – both the object of an influential analysis of crowds by Hyppolite Taine (1962 [1887–8]). Two events in particular became symbols of the susceptibility of contemporary democracy to popular uprisings and violence: the meteoric career of General Boulanger in the late 1880s, and the Decazeville miners' strike of 1886 (Barrows 1981, ch. 1). Boulanger had capitalised on disaffection with the Third Republic amongst both conservatives and workers, inspiring huge popular demonstrations in Paris in 1886 and 1887. Appointed minister of war in 1885 because of his supposed radical sympathies, his army reforms won him great popularity and led a nervous government to remove him from office in 1887 and send him into unofficial exile from Paris. Growing discontent with the government following the Wilson affair, when the president's son-in-law Daniel Wilson was revealed to have been trafficking in bribes, encouraged Boulanger to enter a series of by-elections in 1888 with outstanding success, including winning Paris where a gathering of 30–100,000 Parisians celebrated his victory. For the French theorists, Boulanger's power to galvanise crowds exemplified the capacity of a charismatic figure to harness mass support. Le Bon even credited him with the capacity to inspire an almost religious fervour (Le Bon 1926 [1895], p. 85). Yet the return to Bonapartism that different groups either feared or hoped for failed to materialise. Urged to storm the Elysée rather than wait for the general election, Boulanger lost his nerve and, fearing prosecution, fled abroad where he committed suicide two years later. The Decazeville strike, by contrast, was seen as an example of the destructive impulses of the leaderless, spontaneous crowd. Made famous by Emile Zola's fictional account in *Germinal* (1885; Barrows 1981, ch. 4), Decazeville had given rise to the murder of a company official. Like Boulangism, however, it was a singular event. Despite the rising strike rate throughout the 1880s and the dramatic growth in union membership amongst industrial workers, less than 4 per cent of strikes involved violent acts and only a tenth public demonstrations. Though these strikes did become increasingly political in character, recent research has stressed their well-organised and strategically rational character (Shorter and Tilly 1974). Nonetheless, just as the Boulanger affair eclipsed the relative stability of

Third Republic politics, so this isolated episode also captured the crowd psychologists' imaginations and conjured up the spectre of proletarian violence against private property and the capitalist system.

Rightly interpreted as expressions of disaffection, these examples of popular protest became transformed into aspects of a broader social malaise brought about by the 'new conditions of existence' associated with industrial and urban life and 'the destruction of those religious, political beliefs in which all the elements of our civilisation are rooted' (Le Bon 1926 [1895], p. 14). Crowds resulted from the deracination associated with modern cities, the break-up of family and the forcing together of the masses into a single area (e.g. Tarde 1912 [1890], pp. 325–6). Seen as typical products of a transitionary period between an old and a new social and moral order, they took on the same characteristics as certain other forms of supposedly 'pathological' and 'anomic' behaviour studied at the time (e.g. Tarde 1912 [1890], pp. 323–4). Significantly, criminologists were key pioneers of crowd psychology, with Sighele and Tarde the most prominent (McLellan 1989, ch. 6; Barrows 1981, chs. 5 and 6).

Sighele's *The Criminal Crowd* (1892 [1891]) was indebted to both the Italian criminal anthropologists Cesare Lombroso and Enrico Ferri, under whom he studied, and French writers such as Taine, Espinas and Tarde (Barrows 1981, p. 126). Sighele sought to guide the sentencing of individuals involved in destructive riots. Following Ferri, he argued that the law should distinguish between the behaviour of 'born criminals', organised criminal 'sects', such as the Mafia, which they often formed, and those who were so influenced by the internal dynamics of crowds that they performed criminal acts. Only the first two categories deserved the severest penalties. Though certain crowds could be made up of 'born criminals', his example being the Decazeville strikers, he thought the majority consisted of normally lawful citizens and should be treated more leniently (Sighele 1892 [1891], pp. 117–22). Sighele explained crowd behaviour by reference to French theories of hypnotism. Hypnotism had fascinated medical researchers from the eighteenth century, but in the late nineteenth century it became enmeshed in both criminal psychology and sociology via the notion of 'suggestibility'. Following the Salpêtrière school, Sighele viewed the propensity to hypnotic suggestion as indicating various degrees of moral 'weakness'. In keeping with his distinctions between different sorts of crowds, he contended that only the 'criminaloid' could be influenced to commit terrible crimes (Barrows 1981, pp. 128–9; Sighele 1892 [1891], pp. 137–44). However, he was vague about the mechanisms whereby crowds induced their hypnotic effect. These were more fully elaborated by Tarde.

A provincial magistrate, Tarde belonged to Sighele's target audience. However, he had also acquired a formidable reputation as a social scientist and criminologist. Tarde saw hypnotism as the 'experimental junction point' between psychology and sociology (Tarde 1912 [1890], p. 193). Developing this thesis in his *The Laws of Imitation* (1890), he argued that all social behaviour resulted from mutual suggestibility or 'imitation', which induced 'a kind of somnambulism'. Indeed, he contended 'the social, like the hypnotic state, is only a form of dream' (Tarde 1890, pp. 77, 87). In his *Penal Philosophy* of the same year he had begun to apply this thesis to the study of crowds. Crowds were simply extreme forms of this imitative effect, all the more potent when they involved members of a similar social group – notably workers. Spurred by Sighele's work, he now developed this aspect further. Though the two agreed on many points, Tarde was apt to think any individual would fall under the spell of the crowd. Like hypnotic subjects, crowds acted 'unconsciously', with only the 'spinal cord' rather than the brain (Tarde 1892, pp. 354–5, 359). Thus, 'a spark of passion' could turn 'a gathering of heterogeneous elements, unknown to one another', into a cohesive, homogeneous mass 'which marches towards its goal with an irresistible finality' (Tarde 1912 [1890], p. 323). People lost all sense of personal responsibility, acting in a quite different manner from how they would have done as individuals. Even if the majority in a crowd 'assembled out of pure curiosity', 'the fever of some of them soon reached the minds of all, and in all of them there arose a delirium. The very man who had come running to oppose the murder of an innocent person is one of the first to be seized with the homicidal contagion' (Tarde 1912 [1890], p. 323).

By reference to descriptions of mob violence such as Taine's (Tarde 1912 [1890], pp. 323–4), Tarde and his contemporaries gradually mixed the hypnotic metaphor with others stressing how crowds induced a diseased and disordered mental and physical state. So crowds were not only prone to drunkenness, they acted in many respects like alcoholics – mentally inebriated and deprived of their reason by the heady atmosphere, they were subject to 'hallucinations' and delusions of grandeur. As a result, they lacked all restraints, giving way to pure 'instinctual' behaviour involving sexual excesses and murder. Like alcohol, membership of a crowd could 'poison' an individual, driving him temporarily 'insane'. Crowd behaviour was also compared to a group sickness or an 'epidemic' – individuals were 'infected' by the collective consciousness of the crowd, which spread 'contagiously' throughout all its members until they found themselves in a mental 'fever' or 'delirium' (for all of the above, see Tarde 1892, pp. 359–60). Finally, crowds were 'savage' and 'bestial' – atavistic throwbacks to a 'primitive' evolutionary stage – 'the human animal [*la bête humaine*]' (Fournial 1892, p. 109; Tarde 1892, p. 358).

In these ways, crowds became portrayed as the exact opposite of the classical ideal of citizenship and democratic deliberation. Whereas citizens were traditionally characterised by such supposedly 'masculine' virtues as courage and fortitude, their discussions directed by reason, all the pathological symptoms associated with crowds, with the inconvenient exception of alcoholism, were traditionally dubbed as 'feminine' traits. Like women, crowds were 'cowardly', 'instinctive', moved by 'feelings' and 'passions' rather than reason, inconstant and unpredictable, prone to hysteria, at once highly open to suggestion and alluring to others. As Gabriel Tarde observed: 'By its whimsy, its revolting docility, its credulity, its nervousness, its brusque psychological leaps from fury to tenderness, from exasperation to laughter, the crowd is feminine, even when it is composed, as is usually the case, of males' (Tarde, quoted in Barrows 1981, p. 47). Civilisation, like reason, being male, the violence of crowds was akin to that of 'a female savage or a female faun, worse than that, an impulsive and maniacal plaything of its instincts and its mechanical habits, often an animal of the lower orders, an invertebrate, a monstrous worm whose sensibility is diffuse' (Tarde 1892, p. 358).

Le Bon both summarised and simplified the work of these authors, turning discussion of the crowd's 'collective mind' (Le Bon 1926 [1895], pp. 29–30) into 'the *law of the mental unity of crowds*' (Le Bon 1926 [1895], p. 26). Likewise, he drew out in typically brazen fashion the misogynistic and racist prejudices informing these ideas, blithely asserting ('its demonstration being outside the scope of this work') how those 'special characteristics of crowds – such as impulsiveness, irritability, incapacity to reason, the absence of judgement and of the critical spirit, the exaggeration of the sentiments, and others besides . . . are almost always observed in beings belonging to inferior forms of evolution – in women, savages and children, for instance' (Le Bon 1926 [1895], p. 40). His own contribution lay in treating crowds no longer as aberrations that threatened the prevailing social and political order, but as typifying mass behaviour within modern societies – not least the new popular democracy. Crowds, he argued, did not 'always involve the simultaneous presence of a number of individuals on one spot'. 'Thousands of individuals', including 'an entire nation', could, when 'under the influence of certain violent emotions', acquire the characteristics of a 'psychological crowd' (Le Bon 1926 [1895], pp. 26–7). Indeed, the detachment and isolation of the individual from traditional hierarchical structures and loyalties had turned the populations of mass societies into 'an agglomeration of individualities lacking cohesion' and rendered them particularly susceptible to acting as a crowd (Le Bon 1926 [1895], pp. 238–9).

Meanwhile, it was beside the point to talk of protecting juries and parliamentary assemblies from crowds because they operated largely in a like manner (Le Bon 1926 [1895], pp. 36, 215). Tarde had lamented how 'Our political constitutions are primitive mechanisms compared to our own organisms, and the collective spirit called a parliament or congress is never equal in sure rapid functioning, in profound and far-reaching deliberation, in inspired intuition or decision, to the *esprit* of the most mediocre of its members' (Tarde 1892, p. 358). Le Bon went further – political institutions had no independent influence on behaviour. They were only effective when attuned to the nation's sentiments. Character and custom rather than law and government were the determining factors in how a people were ruled, an argument Le Bon increasingly associated with race.

Within a mass society, the masses had to be accommodated. Democracy may have had no intrinsic worth, and notions of the general will or consent might be illusory because no agglomeration of people was capable of rational deliberation (Le Bon 1926 [1895], p. 210), but the prevailing democratic dogma held that truth and numerical superiority went hand in hand (Le Bon 1926 [1895], p. 211). Though 'stupidity', 'not mother wit', was accumulated in crowds, mass approval and assent were necessary for any regime's legitimacy (Le Bon 1926 [1895], p. 32). Fortunately, however, the masses could be manipulated, with crowd psychology offering statesmen a scientific guide to how to do it (Le Bon 1926 [1895], p. 21). If Decazeville revealed the dangerous destructiveness of crowds, Boulanger had indicated their malleability. 'Primitive' and 'suggestible', crowds were highly susceptible to the arts of oratory and charisma. Unable to think for themselves, crowds were always controlled by a few leaders. Needless to say, crowds did not respond to 'pure reason' or 'ideas' but, like women, had to be 'seduced' by exaggerated appeals to their 'sentiments'. Moreover, they had no opinions of their own but only those that were 'impressed' upon them (Le Bon 1926 [1895], pp. 21–2, 56–9). The key to political power lay in the ability to stir the popular imagination and to inspire an almost religious devotion amongst one's followers. The allure of socialism, like all successful ideologies, was in this respect fundamentally religious in character (Le Bon 1926 [1895], pp. 77–80, 82–5).

'Electoral crowds' resembled other crowds in possessing 'but slight aptitude for reasoning, the absence of critical spirit, irritability, credulity and simplicity' (Le Bon 1926 [1895], p. 201). Nor was there any point in restricting the electorate, given that 'in a crowd men always tend to the same level and, on general questions, a vote recorded by forty academicians is no better than of forty water-carriers' (Le Bon 1926 [1895], pp. 211–12). However, the electorate was as easy to manipulate as other crowds, swayed by the 'prestige' of a leader and rhetorical skills that by 'affirmation' and 'repetition' could appeal to sentiments and create a groundswell of support by the contagious effects of suggestibility (Le Bon 1926 [1895], pp. 141–59, 202–4). Drawing a parallel that would become a cliché amongst his successors, Le Bon noted how 'statesmen called upon to defend a political cause' used the same techniques as 'commercial men pushing the sale of their products by means of advertising'. Just as 'when we have read that X's chocolate is the best, we imagine we have heard it said in many quarters, and we end by acquiring the certitude that such is the fact', so 'if we read in the same papers that A is an arrant scamp and B a most honest man, we finish by being convinced that this is the truth, unless, indeed, we are given to reading another paper of the contrary opinion, in which the two qualifications are reversed' (Le Bon 1926 [1895], pp. 142–3). The power of 'imitation' was such that any notion pushed with sufficient vigour would soon pass amongst the populace as a received truth.

Much the same tactics also allowed leaders to dominate parliamentary assemblies (Le Bon 1926 [1895], p. 215). Again, like later theorists, Le Bon noted that a cost of needing to constantly woo the masses was the gradual extension of government. The result was financial waste as different parts of the electorate were bought off, and the gradual restriction of liberty as taxes were raised to pay for these measures. The consequent growth of the state also augmented the number and authority of the bureaucracy – the latter's power being all the greater because it was impersonal, permanent and without responsibility (Le Bon 1926 [1895], pp. 231–5). Mass politics thereby reinforced that other feature of mass societies, the introduction of mass production methods into government as well as industry. Though this development drew ideological support from socialism, Le Bon maintained that it would ultimately provoke a popular reaction. Citizens would become dismayed at the corruption of politicians embroiled in bribing their local constituencies to win support. The state would become increasingly mechanical and despotic (Le Bon 1926 [1895], pp. 235–6). It was in these circumstances that the destructiveness of crowds became a creative force, especially when controlled by a charismatic leader possessing sufficient prestige to harness their spontaneity and energy (Le Bon 1926 [1895], pp. 237–9, 150–1).

Reactionary and racist, Le Bon's views would find a natural audience with the far right. As the power of organised labour grew, Le Bon was to become increasingly opposed to parliamentary democracy and turn to nationalism and charismatic leadership as the means to control the masses (see Geiger 1977 – who notes a parallel change in Sighele's thinking). However, his approach proved just as influential amongst both radical (Wallas 1908) and conservative (Lippmann 1965 [1922], p. 127) liberals. Though these later thinkers would no longer have subscribed to Le Bon's or Tarde's explanations of the actual hallucinatory effects of crowds, or even the sexist let alone racist assumptions on which they often relied, they were captivated by the metaphors and pseudo-social laws to which these theories gave rise. In addition, these theorists had access to a further dimension absent from Le Bon – namely the psychological influence of party organisation on the masses, politicians and their leaders.

The rise of party organisation

Much as the origins of crowd psychology are associated with Le Bon, so the study of political parties as mass organisations can be traced to Moisei Ostrogorski and his *Democracy and the Organisation of Political Parties* of 1902. Once again, this linkage distorts as much as it illuminates (Barker and Howard-Johnston 1975; Pombeni 1994a, pp. 163–9; Quagliariello 1996). Ostrogorski was outside many of the historical experiences that shaped the new science of politics. A Russian Jew who studied with Emile Boutmy at the Ecoles Libres des Sciences Politiques, Ostrogorski was influenced by the nineteenth-century French historical school and its British followers and shared their anglophile liberal sympathies. Thus, he was broadly Tocquevillian in seeing democracy as a social and moral phenomenon (Quagliariello 1996, ch. 2), with de Tocqueville's famous call for 'a new political science for a new world' providing the epigraph for his book (see too Ostrogorski 1902, vol. II, pp. 633–4). Rather than the constant tendencies of human nature or social structure, he emphasised ideas or 'mental tendencies' and the 'working of wills' of the main political actors, noting how these 'forces' were both shaped by and helped to shape responses to changing social and political conditions (Ostrogorski 1902, vol. I, pp. li–lii).

Ostrogorski's decision to compare political parties in Britain and America was inspired by the contemporary British debate over whether Britain was succumbing to the 'American model' of 'machine politics' described by James Bryce in *The American Commonwealth* (1888) (Quagliariello 1996, ch. 3). Hence the book's appearance in English translation, with a preface by Bryce who had encouraged his project, prior to publication of the French original (Pombeni 1994b; 1994a, pp. 162–3). Ostrogorski's argument that British politics had been 'Americanised' was taken by many commentators as confirming a general trend towards the domination of party organisation. However, his analysis was much more nuanced and ultimately rooted in earlier debates about the extension of the franchise, most particularly the views of J. S. Mill.

A Millean liberal, Ostrogorski shared his fear that that 'the general tendency of things' within commercial societies was towards 'mediocrity' – a process he associated with the growing influence of 'the masses' as 'the only power deserving the name' (Mill 1977 [1836], p. 121; Mill 1991b [1859], p. 73). Like Mill, though, he saw the danger as stemming less from democracy per se than from the social pressures to conform to the lowest common denominator. As a result, the public were increasingly guided only by people like themselves. Mass parties both reflected and exacerbated this trend. The worry was that 'persons of genius' would be unable to thrive and society would stagnate in consequence. For he shared Mill's belief that 'the initiation of all wise or noble things comes and must come from individuals'. Yet Ostrogorski also followed Mill in optimistically thinking that 'the honour and glory of the average man' lay in being 'capable of following that initiative' (Mill 1991b [1859], p. 74). Again picking up on Mill's lead (Mill 1991a [1861]), he argued that the solution lay in devising institutional mechanisms for preserving individuality and ensuring that exceptional persons could voice their views and be heard. So long as they could be, the mass of people would follow.

Consequently, Ostrogorski did not accept the inevitability of mass parties. Alternative forms of democratic organisation could and should be promoted. Like many British liberals of the time, he saw Gladstone's remarkable ability to harness popular support to the Liberal Party through moral campaigns as revealing how parties could both galvanise and elevate their popular supporters though a combination of inspired leadership and a focus on crucial issues of rights and justice (Vincent 1966, ch. 3; Harvie 1990). Parties could thereby obtain some of the ethical force of earlier campaigning organisations, such as the Anti-Corn Law League. His aim was to advocate a return to this model against the new forms of party organisation being promoted by Chamberlain in Birmingham.

In these respects, Ostrogorski's analysis reflected both British liberal political culture, with its optimistic faith in social and moral progress (Bradley 1980; Bellamy 1992, ch. 1), and the absence in Britain of a significant revolutionary socialist party or movement. Yet Ostrogorski's work has been consistently misread. Contemporaries plundered his study for examples which they then reinterpreted according to their own theories. Later commentators have followed their lead, praising him as a pioneering 'behaviourist' political scientist (Butler 1958, p. 44), but regarding his reform proposals as a bafflingly 'absurd' (Butler 1958, p. 44) 'fantasy' (Runciman 1963, p. 71) – totally at variance with his analysis of modern party politics. However, his importance in this story lies in his *not* being 'one of the most important originators . . . of political sociology' (Lipset 1964, p. xiv). His recruitment to that role derived from the triumph of a given intellectual paradigm that he had stood outside, sharing neither its methodological nor its experiential assumptions: a position that allowed him to evaluate democracy's prospects quite differently.

Though Ostrogorski linked the rise of mass parties to certain features of modern societies and a related climate of ideas, he avoided both structural and psychological determinism. Social structures and ideas were independent variables, albeit with a mutual influence on each other, which developed in historically contingent ways. Ostrogorski believed the nature of both British and American parties arose from the social and economic changes that had created a mass society having been accompanied by an individualistic ethos. This combination had different origins in the two countries, but in Britain had resulted from the linking of the industrial revolution with a Benthamite ideology (Ostrogorski 1902, vol. I, p. 39). Initially a genuinely radical doctrine, which expressed the entrepreneurial bourgeoisie's struggle for the extension of civil liberties and a more meritocratic society, diffusion amongst the masses had transformed Benthamism into a levelling and materialist creed (Ostrogorski 1902, vol. I, pp. 48, 580–1, 587). As a result, the organic social ties of duty and deference of the aristocratic social order were replaced by the bonds of economic interest between buyers and sellers. When these cultural attitudes were accompanied by the decline of supportive social structures, individuals became isolated atoms who were attracted to being part of a homogeneous mass. It was these circumstances rather than human psychology per se that was 'forcing individuals to dissolve into crowds' (Ostrogorski 1902, vol. I, pp. 48–50) and explained their subsequent behaviour. Just as mass production offered people generalised tastes, habits, culture and ready-made opinions that spared them from having to make up their own minds, so mass organisations gave individuals a sense of solidarity and collective purpose they seemed unable to provide for themselves. He saw the spread of evangelical religion as exemplifying this trend.

Mass parties simply mirrored this more general social transformation. Ostrogorski regarded the ideal nature of parties to be the Burkean one of being 'a body of men united, for promoting by their joint endeavours the national interest, upon some particular principle in which they are all agreed' (quoted at Ostrogorski 1902, vol. II, p. 652). This view reflected the early stages of a more individualistic society, in which notions of organic unity had given way to a conscious union between individuals (cf. Ball 1989). However, the extension of the franchise had turned parties into mere electoral machines to organise the mass vote. Ostrogorski associated this change with the 'caucus' system developed by Joseph Chamberlain in Birmingham, which paralleled similar organisations in the United States, such as the infamous Tammany Hall. These new types of parties reflected the ethos of the age. Popular election of leaders and officials had produced politicians who followed rather than challenged the mass mediocrity around them. Professional politicians rather than public-spirited citizens, they saw politics as a trade from which they sought a living (Ostrogorski 1902, vol. I, p. 593). The parties were 'businesses', with electioneering and the pursuit of office ends in themselves, rather than the means to realising certain desirable policies (Ostrogorski 1902, vol. II, p. 651). Though not necessarily corrupt in the sense of seeking kick-backs, they were willing to do anything to win electoral success and hence secure their position (Ostrogorski 1902, vol. II, pp. 656–7). Requiring considerable funds to maintain the party machine, they became a prey to sectional interests, happy to exchange favours – from honours to public works contracts – for finance and support from business, unions or particular communities. A tendency particularly prevalent in the United States, especially in municipal elections, it led parties back into factionalism, albeit of a new kind.

The worst aspect of this new form of politics was in the realm of ideas. Ostrogorski related the Burkean notion of party to an extremely radical neo-Rousseauean idea of the social contract, in which support for any government had to be constantly negotiated by debating every single issue so as build a rational union of wills on policies of genuinely common interest (Ostrogorski 1902, vol. II, pp. 671–81). Ostrogorski's ideal was not '*a* social contract' but multiple 'social contracts, which follow each other in an indefinite succession' (Ostrogorski 1902, vol. II, p. 680). By contrast, the new parties wanted a permanent presence that allowed them to win and hold onto power – hence their need for professionals and a permanent organisation (Ostrogorski 1902, vol. II, p. 656). Consequently, they wished to speak for the majority on any matter that might arise. To do so, they abandoned the notion of a rational union of principle for a passive uniformity derived from peddling 'wholesale' opinions that would appeal to the lowest common denominator on any topic – no matter how incoherent the result (Ostrogorski 1902, vol. I, pp. 588–9). Rather than being vehicles of civic education, such parties pandered to conventional ideas and self-interest (Ostrogorski 1902, vol. I, p. 594). Independent views posed a constant threat to party ascendancy (Ostrogorski 1902, vol. II, p. 656), so appeal was made 'not so much to reason, which analyses and distinguishes, as to feeling; by stirring up emotions which confuse the judgement and make a prisoner of the will' (Ostrogorski 1902, vol. I, p. 585). Citizens and politicians alike were 'demoralised' in the process (Ostrogorski 1902, vol. I, p. 585; vol. II, p. 635), with the latter especially becoming 'timorous' conformists unwilling to say anything that might offend a potential supporter or paymaster (Ostrogorski 1902, vol. II, pp. 632, 635–6). Democracy had ceased to have the substantive purpose of deliberating on the common good, and had become a purely formal and mechanical procedure of popular endorsement (Ostrogorski 1902, vol. II, pp. 638–9, 650–1). Indeed the organisation mentality had infected all public duties, with personal rule and responsibility replaced by an empty 'mechanical' formalism and a deference to conventional views and practices (Ostrogorski 1902, vol. II, p. 643).

Ostrogorski regarded such 'organisation' parties as 'the negation of democracy' (Ostrogorski 1902, vol. II, p. 622), removing any sense of civic duty from citizens or politicians even to form an opinion of their own, let alone actively to participate in the democratic process. Yet he believed their days were numbered (Ostrogorski 1902, vol. II, p. 687). Parties had begun to break up as their members, alienated by their corrupt tendencies and essentially anti-political character, rebelled against the necessarily anodyne character of a common programme and began to militate for the various issues that interested them. A chief flaw of permanent parties was that they impeded the formation of new associations by crystallising opinion and preventing the evolution of ideas (Ostrogorski 1902, vol. II, p. 637–8).

He believed the solution lay in returning to a situation of temporary parties consisting 'of a combination of citizens formed specially for a particular issue' (Ostrogorski 1902, vol. II, p. 658). Such parties would be ad hoc and prevent the formation of a permanent cadre. Citizens would be forced to weigh up the merits of particular questions rather than accepting a ready-made package that often involved the log-rolling of inconsistent positions. Parties would have to take on an educative role of winning citizens around to a particular cause. Democracy would return to its ideal form of constructing social unity around the general will.

Ostrogorski believed his proposed 'league system' of temporary issue-based parties was 'suited to the conditions of a complex society with a multiplicity of interests', where citizens only became enthused about particular issues but found the concerns of the whole community hard to conceive of or identify with (Ostrogorski 1902, vol. II, p. 681). However, he also suggested a number of institutional devices for promoting this scheme, from a state-organised preliminary poll to select candidates, in which all could vote and from which party affiliations were excluded, to proportional representation for the election itself. He claimed that the resulting legislature would reflect the degree of concern people felt for particular issues of the day. Like modern political pluralists, he argued that society contained 'majorit*ies* and minorit*ies*, whose constituent elements change continually with circumstances', so that tyrannical majorities were unlikely (Ostrogorski 1902, vol. II, p. 678). Laws would 'no longer be the imperious decisions of a dominant majority' but 'a continual series of compromises, settled by majorities whose composition may vary from one question to another, but which will in each case present a genuine reflection of the views and feelings of the true, of the only majority that can have been constituted on the basis of the particular question' (Ostrogorski 1902, vol. II, p. 715).

Needless to say, for Ostrogorski the 'decisive battle' was in the realm of ideas – 'the *habeas animum*' (Ostrogorski 1902, vol. II, p. 728). Electors had to regain the moral will to employ their judgement. Crucial to this task was the revival of the political class, for 'equality of rights' could never 'make up for the natural inequality of brains and character' (Ostrogorski 1902, vol. II, p. 640). Ostrogorski believed his scheme would encourage men of merit and principle to come forward because, by contrast to the party system, moral conviction and the power of reason would once again become electoral assets rather than liabilities. Yet he admitted this could not be counted on. Indeed, hardly any of his contemporaries believed it possible. Though Bryce thought his analysis of the Americanisation of the British system exaggerated (preface to Ostrogorski 1902, vol. I, p. xliii), almost all other commentators believed he had not gone nearly far enough. In a telling analogy, Graham Wallas likened his analysis to 'a series of conscientious observations of the Copernican heavens by a loyal but saddened believer in the Ptolemaic astronomy' (Wallas 1908, p. 125). Paradoxically, the only theorist who took ideas seriously was unable to get his arguments a considered hearing because they belonged to a political language that contemporaries and most later commentators regarded as at best anachronistic, at worst incoherent, and for many incomprehensible. Wallas believed Ostrogorski had failed to grasp the lessons of the new social psychology and hence had totally unrealistic expectations of the electorate. Robert Michels was to add that he had also overlooked the historical necessity for organisation (Michels 1959 [1915], p. 361). In particular, he had not seen how psychological and organisational factors combined not to undermine elites but to change their nature and give them ever more power. Instead of serving to revive democracy, therefore, Ostrogorski found himself recruited to the service of those wishing either to declare its impossibility (e.g. Mosca 1939 [1923] p. 389)[2] or to argue that it was only possible in the very form he sought to criticise and change (e.g. Weber 1994c [1919], p. 340).

The persistence of elites

The thesis that democratic arrangements promoted rather than counteracted the rule of elites was to provide the third element of the modern theory of democracy. The notion that elites always rule was not itself novel. Indeed, as such it amounts to no more than the truism that rulers will almost always be fewer than the ruled, whatever the form of government. The originality of the democratic elite theorists arose from their reference to the new social psychology and the role of organisations, especially parties, to explain the character and basis of elite power, and from their contention that the elite were not only unaccountable to the electorate but manipulated them. They differed from the traditional elitism of a figure such as Ortega y Gasset, who saw the rise of the masses as a populist 'tyranny of the majority' which promoted a general levelling down to the lowest common denominator that replaced culture with barbarism (Ortega y Gasset, 1961 [1930], pp. 13–14).

2. Mosca (1939) is a translation of the first (1895) and some of the second (1923) editions of his *Elements of Political Science*, and is somewhat misleadingly given the English title of *The Ruling Class*. The two Italian editions were in fact two different books. The dates in brackets indicate the edition from which the reference derives.

Their contention was that elites still ruled, though their character and the sources of their power had indeed changed.

If the analysis of crowds drew on an account of French politics and the theory of parties on Britain and America, elite theory elaborated certain characteristics of Italian political life, with its chief proponents being Vilfredo Pareto and Gaetano Mosca. Pareto and Mosca quarrelled over who had originated elite theory throughout their careers. Though both aspired to producing a 'scientific' theory based on the social 'uniformities' (Pareto 1916, para. 69) and 'constant laws or tendencies that determine the political organisation of human societies' (Mosca 1939 [1895], p. 6), shared a positivist disregard for metaphysics, and employed their thesis to deflate and unmask the pretensions of democrats and socialists alike, their approach to and conception of elitism was very different. Pareto made his name as a free market political economist. He regarded economic and political liberalism as logical entailments of a rational actor model of human agency. Yet he found this belief confounded during the 1890s (Bellamy 1987, ch. 2; 1990). Rather than pursuing free trade and a limited state, liberal politicians had practised 'bourgeois socialism' by employing protectionism and state monopolies to benefit certain industrial and agricultural supporters (Pareto 1974 [1891], pp. 378–9). Pareto condemned Marxism as utopian and unworkable, but was initially sympathetic to 'popular socialism' as an understandable reaction to government corruption and the failings of its economic policies (Pareto 1966 [1893], p. 70). However, the bourgeoisie had not returned to liberal ways to reconcile the workers to the advantages of the market. Instead, they had bought them off by resorting to state welfare. Since the free market remained the optimal system, the explanation for this strategy could not lie in either changes in the nature of capitalism or flaws in liberal political economy. The answer had to reside in the psychological appeal of 'non-logical' irrational ideas to the masses and the ability of elites to exploit them to win power (Pareto 1902, vol. I, p. 125). His sociology simply elaborated this diagnosis of the nature of Italian transformist politics. By contrast, Mosca was a constitutional lawyer and parliamentarian (Bellamy 1987, ch. 3). A member of the very bourgeois liberal class Pareto came to vilify, Mosca remained convinced of their civic virtues and sought to revive their ethos and position. Like Ostrogorski, whose political attitudes and background he largely shared, he believed their decline and corruption arose from social and structural changes – particularly the extension of the franchise and a blurring of the separation of powers once the legislature came to predominate (Mosca 1958 [1884], pp. 310–26). However, unlike Ostrogorski he saw these developments as exemplifying sociological laws and so much harder to combat.

Pareto first outlined his theory in the early 1900s with his analysis of *Socialist Systems* (Pareto 1902). Elite theory clearly emerges from this work as both an alternative to Marxism and a critique and explanation of its appeal. Class struggle is replaced by the circulation of elites, the proletariat with the mass, and a future without domination is declared illusory because exploitative rule by an elite occurs under all systems, private property being but one source of power and authority. Like Le Bon, Pareto saw socialism's attraction as akin to millenarian religion: emotional rather than intellectual. Notions such as the 'general will', the 'common good' or 'popular sovereignty' were in themselves incoherent. They simply offered a spurious legitimacy for the replacement of a capitalist by a socialist elite. Subsequent writings, culminating in the massive *Treatise of General Sociology* of 1916, outlined the socio-psychological mechanisms involved.

Pareto argued that humans were moved by a number of basic emotional 'residues'. These could then be manipulated by certain sorts of argumentation, which he called 'derivations'. Though he enumerated some fifty-two residues, the most important were the 'instinct of combinations' and the 'persistence of aggregates'. Adapting Machiavelli, Pareto divided political elites into 'foxes' and 'lions', depending on which of these two residues they operated upon. The first favoured the 'cunning' of those who ruled via consent (Pareto 1916, para. 889); the second was a conservative tendency that was more inclined to employ force (Pareto 1916, para. 888). These two types of political elite obtained power by recruiting support from coalitions of much more heterogeneous social and economic groups possessing the parallel characteristics associated with innovative 'speculators' and investing '*rentiers*' respectively. Pareto argued there was a cyclical 'circulation' of elites which went hand in hand with socio-economic cycles. Thus, foxes wooed speculators by either tacitly or actively helping them to 'despoil' the *rentiers* – be they small petit-bourgeois savers or major shareholders. Initially, rising prosperity would be accompanied by a calling into question of traditional morality and a consumer boom. However, both the government and the populace would begin to go into debt due to over-consumption based on credit, whilst a scarcity of capital and a lack of productive investment would lead the economy to contract. The need for restraint and saving would become apparent, and a more conservative government of lions would come to the fore backed by a *rentier* economic class full of class 2 residues. Eventually, though, the economy would start to stagnate and people would begin to tire of leonine austerity, thereby precipitating the rise of foxes and speculators again and the start of a new cycle (Pareto 1916, paras. 2053–9, 2223–36).

Pareto claimed to be describing a universal phenomenon and mainly employed examples drawn from ancient history to demonstrate his theory's objectivity. However, the Italian context emerges as all important once he applies it to democracy in both the final chapters of the *Treatise* and the various articles written after the war, especially those later collected as *The Transformation of Democracy* (Pareto 1980 [1921]). Italy, he argued, was in the grip of a pluto-democracy. Parliamentary democracy offered the perfect instrument for foxish politicians to build up a clientalistic network of 'speculators'. To a certain degree, workers had common cause with the plutocrats. If the one desired increased wages and social benefits, the other wanted bigger bonuses and state subsidies. Both wished to expropriate the *rentiers*' surplus and raise taxes for an expanding state. However, at a certain point their paths were bound to diverge. He now feared democracy was likely to get the upper hand over plutocracy. Clientalism encouraged centripetal tendencies that dispersed state power, creating what he regarded as a new feudalism of warring barons, exemplified by the conflict between organised labour and fascists. Yet economic and social instability was encouraging centrifugal forces calling for a return to authority. Initially, he had anticipated a socialist seizure of power on the Bolshevik model, but he was equally happy to greet the rise of Mussolini as confirming 'splendidly the predictions of my *Sociology* and many of my articles' (Pareto 1975 [1922]). In fact, Pareto's theory was but an *ex post facto* elaboration of his jaundiced interpretation of the Italian situation, whereby he redescribed these events in terms of the categories of his theory and then read them back into all other past events as universal laws of human behaviour. However, though anti-democratic, he was not a fascist. He regarded the state as an instrument of 'spoliation' whoever ran it. Had he lived, he would undoubtedly have regarded Mussolini's regime as an archetypal 'demagogic plutocracy'. His difficulty was that he had ruled out the very possibility of realising the regime he most desired – a free market economy combined with a liberal state.

Mosca also criticised the transformist politics of the pre- and post-war liberal administrations, but his analysis was quite different. He attributed elite power to societal and organisational rather than purely psychological factors. A ruling class dominated not only because they possessed the personal qualities necessary for leadership in a given society, but also, and 'more important and less observed', because 'an organised minority, which acts in a co-ordinated manner, always triumphs over a disorganised minority, which has neither will, nor impulse, nor action in common' (Mosca 1958 [1884], p. 34; see too 1939 [1896], pp. 50–3). The problem with mass electoral politics was not elitism per se but its favouring a certain kind of elite.

Mosca believed in the traditional liberal parliamentary ideal of impartial, reasoned debate amongst independent, educated representatives. Unlike Le Bon, he denied that parliaments necessarily operated with the logic of the crowd. Far from being 'a "mob", in the sense of a haphazard inorganic assemblage of human beings', 'they contain many men of long experience of public affairs, who are thereby safeguarded against any harm that might result to less well-balanced brains from an overardent or ravishing eloquence' (Mosca 1939 [1896], p. 257). The difficulty was ensuring that such 'men' were indeed represented. Hitherto, this system had relied on a particular political class, the landed gentry. In his view, they had possessed both the intellectual qualities needed to administer a modern state and, most crucially, sufficient economic independence to devote themselves to public service out of a sense of duty rather than as a living (Mosca 1939 [1896], p. 144). Somewhat naïvely, he assumed they had no sectional interests of their own to promote that might conflict with those of the public at large. Yet they were a declining group, and he looked to the professional middle classes as a potential replacement. It was a role he adopted personally, combining an academic with a political career as a deputy from 1909 to 1919 and a senator thereafter, including serving as under-secretary in the Colonial Office from 1914 to 1916. He was nonetheless all too conscious that his fellow politicians rarely lived up to his high ideals (Mosca 1939 [1896], pp. 269–70). Thus, his aim was to identify the reasons for the poor quality of the contemporary elite and to seek possible remedies that might motivate them in ways he saw as more appropriate.

Mosca believed a major obstacle to reform arose from misconceptions about the nature of democracy. He argued that elites could not rule by force alone. They needed the moral legitimacy provided by a 'political formula', such as the divine right of kings or popular sovereignty, to obtain the willing cooperation of the ruled (Mosca 1939 [1896], pp. 70–2). Formulae did not require any 'scientific' basis; they merely had to be accepted. However, unlike Pareto, Mosca regarded the roots of such acceptance to be social rather than psychological. Formulae had to be appropriate to the social context in which they were employed, but were not socially determined. More than one formula might be viable in any society, though not all formulae would be. In a mass society, democracy and socialism had great appeal since they offered the prospect of government by and for the people. Mosca hoped to weaken their attraction to bourgeois intellectuals in particular by providing a 'positivist' analysis of these two 'metaphysical' systems that revealed how they enhanced rather than limited elite power (Mosca 1939 [1896], pp. 325–8).

Mosca observed how in mass democracies 'the electors do not elect the Deputy, but usually the Deputy has himself elected by the electors' (Mosca 1958 [1884], p. 275; 1939 [1896], p. 154). Universal suffrage favoured the prime factor fostering elite domination: the superiority of an organised minority over a mass of isolated individuals. Voters could not pick candidates at will from amongst themselves or propose whatever policies they pleased; within a mass electorate individual efforts were insufficient to obtain a hearing or galvanise support. As a result, the political agenda, including who might stand for election, was set by groups possessing an organisational and positional advantage: particularly parties and other political organisations, and influential individuals – especially the very wealthy (what Mosca called 'Grand Electors') and incumbent governments and their appointees (Mosca 1939 [1896], p. 155). Instead of being constrained by popular democracy, powerful interest groups were favoured by it. The result was a clientalistic political system concerned with the trading of favours rather than disinterested deliberation on the common good. Political success now called for 'moral cowardice, lack of a sense of justice, cunning, intrigue' rather than 'independence of character, boldness and impartiality' (Mosca 1958 [1884], p. 284).

Mosca had initially thought the best remedy for these failings was to limit democracy. He opposed the extensions of the franchise to all adult men and women in 1912, and suggested that the Senate and executive be royal appointees in order to weaken the power of the legislature. However, he regretfully acknowledged that these measures were unlikely to command much support. Consequently, he turned to how democracy might limit itself. This possibility arose from his doctrine of 'juridical defence', which he began developing as early as the first edition of his *Elements of Political Science* (1896). 'Juridical defence' consisted of the mechanisms which promoted the 'moral discipline' of people's selfish interests and hence their respect for government by law (Mosca 1939 [1896], p. 126). Such discipline originated from 'the reciprocal restraint of human individuals' making people 'better, not by destroying their wicked instincts, but by accustoming the individual to tame them' (Mosca 1939 [1896], p. 127). Mosca thought the ruling class was broader than simply the rulers – it consisted of all politically active and capable individuals. An effective form of 'juridical defence' not only established checks and balances between the governed and the governing class but also (and most crucially) between the various levels and sections of the ruling class. This system involved more than the establishment of legal constitutional constraints. Social and political power had to be dispersed in such a way that no one group monopolised them all. As he put it, the most important (and only practical) demand 'to make of a political system is that all social values shall have a part in it, and that it shall find a place for all who possess any of the qualities which determine what prestige and what influence an individual, or a class, is to have' (Mosca 1939 [1896], p. 258). To preserve liberty and obtain the rule of those best suited to any given task, no single political principle or class should dominate and dictate access to all sources of influence. He believed this pluralist argument provided the rationale not only for the separation of church and state, but also for a division between polity and economy and, within the state, between the bureaucracy and the government, as well as a measure of decentralisation.

A pure or ideal democracy tended to ignore the need for 'juridical defence', centralising all power in the hands of an elite chosen by the single method of popular sovereignty. He criticised socialism as leading to just this situation. He thought it natural for people to believe the remedy for democracy alone not producing political equality lay with introducing economic equality via the collective ownership of the means of production. Yet, as he presciently saw, this measure could only lead to despotism. For it gave the party elite a monopoly of both economic and political (including ideological and military) power (Mosca 1939 [1896], p. 144). However, within a social system in which there were many sources of influence, democracy could be redefined as a mechanism for fostering 'reciprocal restraint'. The key was to obtain a mix of different social classes and levels of political power, whilst improving the calibre of representatives. Whereas 'pure' democracy suggested rule by whoever obtained the support of the majority, he suggested that democratic procedures might be compatible with different electoral systems for the Senate and the lower house. Together with strong local government, these mechanisms would create counter-weights to the power of the executive with its base in the Chamber of Deputies. He developed this thesis in the second edition of the *Elements* published in 1923, the year after Mussolini's March on Rome. He maintained that social and political institutions should be designed to secure a balance between the 'aristocratic' and 'democratic' 'tendencies' within society, creating a ruling class open to below yet reasonably secure and able to perpetuate itself. Likewise, government should combine 'liberal' and 'autocratic' 'principles' to allow effective yet limited rule. The present danger lay in the combination of the democratic tendency with autocratic principles, whereby a popularly elected leader could claim absolute power.

Thus Mosca moved from being a critic of mass democracy to defending liberal against socialist democracy. In certain respects a precursor of contemporary pluralist as well as elite theories of democracy, he was ultimately pessimistic about the former being realised in ways that might moderate the malign effects of the latter. He recognised that the mechanisms he associated with 'juridical defence' would only work in propitious social conditions. In particular, he thought it necessary to have a middle class that was large enough to provide a check on both the masses and the wealthy, and which could supply rivals for office who would check each other. Yet this very stratum had been decimated by the First World War and economically impoverished by the slump that had followed. That left the mass vulnerable to plutocrats and demagogues. As an opponent of fascism, Mosca saw Mussolini as the epitome of democratic autocracy.

Democratic autocracy or competitive elite democracy

Mosca's dilemma was that the contemporary critique of mass democracy appeared to make democratic autocracy inevitable. To defend democracy in the terms established by the new science of politics, the elite manipulation of the masses had somehow to be made a virtue rather than a fatal flaw. This quandary is clear in the contrast between the political writings of Robert Michels and Max Weber. Both thinkers offered brilliant syntheses of the three components of mass democracy explored above – the view of the mass as an irrational crowd, the account of parties as electoral machines, and the theory of elites, in their case with Germany joining Italy, France, Britain and America as the backdrop to their reasoning. Notwithstanding their common reference points and mutual influence, however, they diverged over whether democracy was futile or had to be radically rethought. Once again, these differences not only reflect contrasting ideological standpoints but also indicate how narrowly scientific and psychological approaches provided less room for rethinking democracy than more historical and organisational analyses.

By contrast to the thinkers surveyed so far, Michels began as a socialist and a committed democrat. As a syndicalist activist in Germany, he had been critical of the SPD's preoccupation with 'organisation for its own sake' and its leaders' tendency to treat the party as a means to secure their own position rather than to further the revolutionary cause. However, he attributed this trend to German conditions, notably the SPD's fear of being disbanded and Germany's military and bureaucratic culture, and had not despaired of radicalising the party. His conversion to elite theory occurred after 1907 when, having been refused his *Habilitation* in Germany because of his socialist sympathies, Weber helped him obtain a post in Turin. Mosca had moved there four years earlier, and was to exert an important influence over his new colleague. Michels now came to regard the shortcomings of German social democracy as exemplifying a more universal process of elite circulation and the propensity of organisations to reinforce oligarchy (Beetham 1977a).

In developing this thesis in his classic study of *Political Parties* (1911, first English translation 1915), Michels drew on and synthesised various aspects of all the theories examined thus far (Beetham 1981, p. 82). From Pareto he took the argument that beliefs reflect certain basic 'sentiments'. He dropped both his earlier faith in the power of rational argument in favour of the socialist cause, and the Marxist view that ideologies and political forms could be related to changes in the economic structure. Instead, he focused on regularities of human behaviour that were allegedly the same at all times and places. However, he also went back to Sighele, Tarde and Le Bon (who published the French edition of his book) to argue that these psychological traits reflected differences between the masses and their leaders, with the one being subject to suggestion in the manner of a crowd and the other able to influence them through their eloquence, energy and boldness (Michels 1959 [1915], pp. 24–5). From Mosca he took the thesis that party organisation fostered the growth of an elite capable of running it. As he pithily put it: 'Who says organisation says oligarchy' (Michels 1959 [1911], pp. 401, 32). Moreover, organisation was inevitable. Weber had encouraged Michels to read Bryce on American 'machine' politics (Scaff 1981, p. 1279), a source he supplemented with Ostrogorski's volumes. Developing certain of Weber's views on bureaucracy, Michels argued that large groups of people needed organising if their activities were to be coordinated, especially when they performed the diverse tasks involved in modern societies characterised by the division of labour. Yet running an organisation was itself a specialised task that required technical expertise, separating the leaders from the mass. Organisations also fostered conservatism and the more general tendency for new groups to assimilate to and rejuvenate existing elites, rather than simply replacing them. Whilst Pareto and Mosca had feared the ousting of the bourgeoisie by a revolutionary elite, Michels argued that a revolutionary oligarchy proved a contradiction in terms, for it grew out of the creation of an organisation that would necessarily move the leadership away from their socialist principles.

Michels now thought democracy not so much a sham as vain. The psychological and organisational elements of his argument reinforced each other. However idealistic, leaders would find themselves unable to overcome either the 'profound need' of the masses 'to prostrate themselves' before some outstanding figure (Michels 1959 [1911], p. 67), or the manner in which power begets power (Michels 1959 [1911], pp. 205–9). Neither oligarchy nor the subjection of the masses could be overcome – 'The formation of oligarchies within the various forms of democracy is the outcome of organic necessity'; 'the objective immaturity of the mass is not a mere transitory phenomenon which will disappear with the progress of democratisation . . . it derives from the very nature of the mass as mass . . . because the mass *per se* is amorphous, and therefore needs division of labour, specialisation, and guidance' (Michels 1959 [1911], pp. 402, 404).

In *Political Parties* Michels hoped that the very striving to realise the ideal of democracy, while doomed to failure, might still serve the useful purpose of enhancing the criticism and control of elites, seeing the 'great task' of social education as the raising of 'the intellectual level of the masses' to enable them 'within the limits of what is possible, to counteract the oligarchical tendencies of the working class movement' (Michels 1959 [1911], p. 407). Ultimately, though, Michels found it impossible to follow Mosca in rethinking democracy as a mechanism for selecting and controlling elites. He remained true to his revolutionary past in regarding anything but a radically participatory form of democracy as no democracy. Residual left-wing prejudices also partly explain his overestimation of the established elites' capacity to absorb outsiders and his assumption that organisation must always produce conservative results (Michels 1959 [1911], pp. 304–7). The collapse of the old order with the First World War and the Bolshevik Revolution of 1917 were to explode both these beliefs, with Lenin and especially Gramsci drawing very different conclusions from the elitist literature to argue that organisation and elite leadership were crucial to a revolutionary party's success (Lenin 1963 [1902]; Gramsci 1977, pp. 1733–4; Bellamy and Schecter 1993, pp. 132–3). Of course, Michels could not be expected to foresee these developments, though Pareto for one had acknowledged they were likely if social circumstances meant that elite replacement could only occur through revolutionary action (Pareto 1902, pp. 34–41). Radical biases apart, what inhibited his contemplating such scenarios as even logical possibilities were the psychological qualities he attributed to leaders and masses, whereby the leaders' sense of their own superiority and desire to dominate were reinforced by not only organisational factors but also the apathy and susceptibility of the masses to emotional manipulation (Michels 1959 [1911], pp. 205–14). In this account, the mass played no independent role apart from the elites who controlled them. Believing that only charismatic leadership could transcend organisational conservatism and mobilise the masses, Michels ended up supporting Mussolini (Michels 1927). Thus elite theory transformed Michels' socialist critique into an argument for fascism as a 'scientific' necessity (Beetham 1977b).

Weber had encouraged Michels' study of the SPD (Scaff 1981; Mommsen 1989, ch. 6). Though Weber shared many of Michels' prejudices about the masses, however, he evaluated the role played by elites and organisations in controlling them quite differently. Like Michels' analysis, Weber's can also be viewed as a synthesis of the theorists examined earlier (Beetham 1987). But unlike his younger compatriot, Weber was not a disillusioned democrat. His concern was with the broader issue of power and its legitimation, effective use and control. Meanwhile, he regarded Michels' psychological emphasis as unsociological, turning his attention to the role of socially produced organisational factors. Both these differences can partly be related to Weber's desire for a 'scientific' account, purged of the researcher's ideological assumptions (Scaff 1981, pp. 1275–8). Yet it would be wrong to infer from these criticisms of Michels that he aimed at a 'value-free' and purely 'descriptive' account of mass democracy – merely that fact and value had to be clearly distinguished. Values might simply be matters of personal choice rather than fact, but the likelihood of their being realised could be empirically assessed. Weber's own interest was in the 'human type' a particular set of social relations gave rise to (Weber 1949 [1917], p. 27). Taking both elite rule and mass democracy as inevitable, his focus centred on the type of leadership different sorts of democratic organisation of the masses were likely to promote (Bellamy 1992, pp. 194–216).

Weber followed Le Bon in seeing the masses as a feature of modern societies and the social levelling produced by the spread of markets, industrialisation and bureaucracy (Beetham 1985, pp. 103–5; Weber 1978a, pp. 983–4). Even autocratic Germany had become a mass state, responsive to mass social and welfare concerns and the need for mass armies, for example. He denounced the Prussian three-class suffrage as not only socially untenable but politically so, given that modern state institutions presupposed equality of status – not least for military service. Indeed, he saw political equality as offering an all-important counter-weight to market-produced social inequalities and a source of national unity (Weber 1994a [1917], pp. 87, 103–6). However, Weber also shared Le Bon's view of the mass as irrational and as such incapable of social action (Baehr 1990; Weber 1978b [1918], pp. 1459–60). Moreover, the mass was not a social class but a condition of many members of modern societies. Emotional and imitative, concerned only with the short term, the mass were passive unless stirred up by outside stimuli. As such, they were easily swayed by demagogues. Reinforcing this tendency to demagogy was the elitist theory of the 'law of the small number', with which Weber also agreed. Yet, unlike many of the other theorists examined so far, Weber did not see these trends as necessarily destructive of democracy so long as they were linked to certain forms of party organisation. For, he argued, mob rule and the 'democracy of the streets' were products of 'the unorganised mass', 'strongest in countries with either a powerless or a politically discredited parliament, that means above all, in countries without *rationally organised parties*' (Weber 1978b [1918], p. 1460). Far from undermining democracy, party organisation made it possible.

In elaborating this thesis, Weber proceeded to reverse Ostrogorski's argument. In a mass age, machine politics was inevitable (Weber 1994c [1919], pp. 318–22, 338–48). Individuals no longer had the resources to wage election campaigns. Professionals were needed to raise the funds and provide the bureaucratic support needed for mass electioneering. Yet a consequence of the growth of parties was to organise the mass, constraining their mob tendencies, and to enhance not just the influence but potentially also the qualities of political leaders. Weber agreed with Ostrogorski that modern campaigning required different political skills from the notable politics of the eighteenth and early nineteenth centuries. As Ostrogorski had noted, politicians and party workers now lived 'off' rather than 'for' politics. Party bosses placed electoral success above principle and effective propaganda and campaign finance before a good argument, while party leaders had to be charismatic crowd-pleasers rather than public-spirited and independent (Weber 1978b [1918], pp. 1450, 1459; Weber 1994c [1919], pp. 342–3). However, he noted how the new politics nonetheless gave the mass an indirect influence on decision-making that ensured their interests were taken into account. Like Mosca, Weber argued that the mass, being passive and unorganised, were recruited by politicians rather than the other way round. But to win the support of the mass, parties had to respond to their concerns. The mass might not know which economic policies were best for the country, but they could feel the effects of bad policies and had the negative power to reject poor governments (Weber 1978b [1918], pp. 1456–7). In addition to being charismatic, therefore, leaders had to be decisive and effective.

The crucial element behind Weber's argument was that there should be party competition. Since Weber was preoccupied with domination rather than democracy per se, he wished to ensure that there were countervailing sources of power. Just as the efficiency and prevention of monopolies within the economy depended on market competition between firms and the entrepreneurs and managers who ran them, so the political system required the electoral contest between parties to ensure that only those politicians with a capacity for charismatic and effective leadership rose to the top (Weber 1978a, p. 288). Though Weber never cited Mosca's work, even if one can presume he knew of it – if only indirectly through Michels – he shared the Italian's view of democracy as a system of checks and balances. For example, he believed the average MP operated as little more than lobby fodder, yet he saw parliament – especially the committee system – as capable of forcing both leaders and the administration to justify their policies through debate, curbing executive authority in the process (Weber 1978b [1918], pp. 1452–3; Weber 1994c [1919], p. 343). Likewise, he saw the political system as itself a counter-balance to both the economy and bureaucracy, similarly regarding the danger of socialism as being the party's monopoly of economic and bureaucratic power (Weber 1994b [1918].

Weber's engagement with contemporary German politics runs through his analysis. Indeed, much of his argument emerged from a discussion of 'Parliament and Government in a Reconstructed Germany' (Weber 1978b [1918]). He compared German leaders unfavourably to the British during the First World War, and thought the political immaturity of the German middle class, the over-bureaucratisation of the state, the cartelisation of the German economy, and the mob-like interventions of the German masses could be explained in part by the absence under the Kaiser's regime of either a genuine electoral contest for power or effective parliamentary scrutiny of the executive. As he put it: 'In Germany we have *demagoguery* and the pressure of the rabble *without democracy*, or rather *because of the absence* of an orderly democracy' (Weber 1978b [1918], p. 1451). Nevertheless, some commentators have seen his emphasis on leadership as having unwittingly prepared the ground for Hitler's democratic seizure of power, aligning him in this and other respects with Carl Schmitt (Mommsen 1967, ch. 10). Yet Weber did not share Schmitt's decisionism or his anti-parliamentarism (Schmitt 1976; 1985; Bellamy 2000, ch. 4). Though he regarded the liberal democratic virtues of rational and responsible decision-making as historically contingent practices that could never be exercised by the masses, his aim was to provide an environment in which elites would adopt them in ways that benefited the populace at large. Leadership involved 'a feeling of responsibility and a sense of proportion' as well as charisma and 'passion'; the 'ethic of responsibility' as well as the 'ethics of conviction' (Weber 1994c [1919], pp. 352–3, 357–68). However, his reworking of democracy and liberalism deprived them of any intrinsic substantive value. In Weber's view, democracy does not promote the popular formulation of and allegiance to the public interest. Rather, it offers a mechanism whereby elites can manipulate the masses and, through competing with each other for their support, provide mutual checks that promote the selection of suitable political leaders. By allowing rulers to be popularly removed when they fail, electoral competition ensured they responded, at least indirectly, to the interests of the ruled. Liberalism no longer concerns the equal rights of individuals so much as responsible leadership that guides, but does not subvert, efficient administration and the due process of law.

Epilogue

The rethinking of democracy that culminated in Weber essentially reversed the priorities of classical democratic theory, turning the democratic process from a means whereby the ruled control their rulers into a mechanism for legitimating and improving the quality of control exercised by rulers over the ruled. As we have seen, the crucial factor was electoral competition between elites to win the right to rule. To quote Joseph Schumpeter's celebrated redefinition, democracy was now 'that institutional arrangement for arriving at political decisions by means of a competitive struggle for the people's vote' (1976 [1942], p. 269 and see more generally chapters 21–2). With various elaborations, Schumpeter's popularisation of Weber's synthesis was to be accepted for the next twenty years by a majority of American and European political scientists and theorists as a realistic account of what liberal democracy could attain in mass conditions (Bachrach, 1967; Parry 1969).

In effect, the social attitudes and historical conditions of the 1890s–1930s had become scientifically codified so as to circumscribe the normative and practical scope of democracy (Bellamy 2000, ch. 5). Post-war analysts of the democratic process simply took as read all three elements of the 'modern theory of democracy' traced above – from the nature of the masses to the role of parties and elites in organising and directing them. Thus the chief constraint upon and danger to democracy was deemed to be the mass character of modern society. The rise of totalitarian regimes was attributed to the pathological characteristics of unorganised, amorphous masses and their susceptibility to the extremist and emotive rhetoric of charismatic leaders (Mannheim 1943, p. 1; Arendt 1951, pp. 310–11; Kornhauser 1959, pp. 14–15; Lipset 1960, p. 109). Consequently, the insulation of elites from mass pressure was deemed crucial to avoiding the temptations of populist demagoguery (Kornhauser 1959, pp. 59–60, 64, 99; Sartori 1962, p. 119). Democratic stability depended on keeping voters passive and even indifferent to politics by organising them within the party system (Berelson *et al.* 1954, pp. 25–6).

Theorists now put their efforts into developing the democratic elitism of Mosca, Weber and Schumpeter in order to explain what incentives existed for elites to compete effectively in the absence of an informed and active electorate (Plamenatz 1958). This new generation of democratic elitists argued that the 'mass' tendencies of modern societies could be counterposed by 'pluralist' tendencies originating from the enhanced differentiation and diversity accompanying the spread of the division of labour (Kornhauser 1959, p. 13; Dahl 1961, pp. 85–6). As a result, there was a plurality of elites whose power rested on different social sources, such as wealth, technical expertise and community following, and who could influence different sorts of issues and sections of society. Consequently, no single elite could monopolise all forms of power and so dominate society (Dahl 1961, p. 228). Provided all adults possessed a vote and there were regularly held, free and fair elections, elites would be forced to compete for support from amongst a plurality of groups holding a variety of different sorts of interests. Rather than appealing through populist rhetoric to a mass majority, they would have to construct a coalition of different minorities. Elites would be obliged to bargain and collaborate with each other, with the public interest emerging from mutually beneficial compromises. Such bargaining was further facilitated by most people belonging to more than one group, mixing with different sets of people at work, in their church, with their families and so on. These cross-cutting cleavages prevented societies from becoming polarised between different classes or sectional interests, allowing a consensus around certain core democratic values to emerge. Though these pluralist theorists granted that political resources are unevenly distributed, so that certain elites and interests can mobilise more easily and effectively than others, they tended to downplay the effects of this inequality for the political agenda and remained unconcerned by low levels of political involvement or interest (Dahl 1961, pp. 280–1). Mass mobilisation was 'unnecessary' given that elite competition was sufficient to ensure minorities obtained a hearing (Polsby 1963, pp. 118–20).

However, critics noted how Pareto often seemed a better guide than Mosca to the dynamics of elite rivalry and the sorts of interests elites were likely to promote and attend to (Bachrach 1967; Parry 1969). For example, significant economic interest groups have decided advantages in accessing elites. They can employ professional lobbyists, offer financial support at elections and exercise various indirect kinds of influence – such as threatening to invest elsewhere in the case of business, or to hold a strike in the case of unions. As Pareto noted, such groups may employ public-interest rhetoric but it often covers self-interested activity of a rent-seeking kind, as when businesses justify incentive-giving tax cuts on the grounds that the economy as a whole will benefit. Because such groups frequently use intermediaries, their role in decision-making may not be immediately evident. Far from fostering democracy, however, their activities can profoundly distort the political agenda in ways that undermine it. By contrast, other kinds of minority interest may not be considered by competing leaders if political elites fear that courting them will alienate other groups or if they lack the standing or finances to gain entry to the political establishment (Bachrach and Baratz 1962). In these cases, the apathy of voters may signify not satisfaction with the system but alienation from it and difficulties in organising themselves in ways suited to exploiting the established channels. Their only alternative may be mass mobilisation and forms of protest that take them outside the formal political process, as occurred with the civil rights, anti-Vietnam, feminist and other movements from the 1960s.

These new social movements, discussed in part IV, inspired some theorists to argue against the elite democracy thesis for the possibility of more participatory forms of politics (Duncan and Lukes 1963; Bachrach 1967). They revealed the mass to operate in a more strategic and rational manner than the elite theorists had allowed, while being quite different from ordinary interest groups (Dalton and Küchler 1990; Clarke and Rempel 1997). Even when focused on a single issue, as with the peace and green movements, or a particular group, as with the feminist and civil rights movements, their arguments have been generally framed in terms of universal principles, such as human rights, equality or some public good, rather than private interests. Instead of relying solely on professional lobbying, with ordinary members being largely passive funders of such activities, these movements have engaged in more participatory activities, such as demonstrations, as well. In so doing, they have challenged both the prevailing political consensus and the existing boundaries of institutional politics, drawing attention to the issues and groups they exclude (Offe 1987). Conservative critics raised fears that such 'unconventional' political activism produces 'excessive' demands that risk 'overloading' and over-extending government. They enlisted the standard critiques of mass politics to condemn these movements as 'deviant' and 'unreasonable', reinvoking the elite theory of democracy as a solution to the ensuing 'crisis' (Crozier *et al.* 1975; Huntington 1975). However, this negative characterisation has found little if any support in studies of the new politics. Like earlier elite theorists, these critics have overlooked, or in some cases have been positively antagonistic to, the ways mass movements of this kind have worked to promote democracy. For example, they were responsible in the late nineteenth and early twentieth centuries for the political inclusion and continued involvement of both workers and women, and in the late twentieth century for addressing the limitations of state-based politics with regard to tackling issues of global justice. Indeed, scholars have shown how even violent protests by so-called mobs are frequently calculated, reasonable, organised, free from demagogic manipulation and motivated by democratic ideals (Canetti 1978 [1960]; Rudé 1981 [1964]; Thompson 1971; Tilly 1979). Far from threatening democracy, therefore, the various forms of non-institutional politics have often indicated a frustration with the democratic limitations of the party political elites – a disillusionment reflected in the generally declining party membership and growing dissatisfaction with politicians found within advanced industrial societies (Dalton 1996; 1999).

The loss of a mass base deprives parties of a vital source of democratic idealism. Without it, they risk developing many of the failings anti-democratic elite theorists feared, becoming increasingly dominated by professional managers and reliant on the support of well-organised and financed pressure groups and individuals, without acquiring the capacity for leading public opinion or framing the public interest hoped for by the democratic elitists. Therefore, in stressing the need for formal politics to connect to the campaigning and more participatory mass movements most relevant to people's lives, Ostrogorski, the outsider within this chapter's story, may well prove to be not a nostalgic throwback to the nineteenth century so much as a model for how politics needs to evolve in the twenty-first.

4
Nationalism and imperialism

JAMES MAYALL

The twentieth century witnessed the birth of the first global order the world has known. Few would dispute that the forces of imperialism and nationalism have played a major part in bringing this world into existence. The role played by political ideas about these concepts is more contentious, if only because there has seldom been agreement about what they mean, let alone their practical importance. It is the purpose of this chapter to suggest some of the ways in which ideas and events have interacted in the making and breaking of modern empires and nation states.

In outline, the story is quickly told. At the end of the nineteenth century the world was dominated by a few major powers, whose governments were engaged in territorial, economic and ideological expansion. In the United States and Russia, expansion involved consolidating their control of the North American and Eurasian continents respectively, without significant opposition, at least until the Russians were stopped in their tracks by Japan in 1904. Elsewhere, imperial competition brought the great powers to the verge of war, although in the end they drew back from the brink, most famously in the case of Africa, where the continent was divided at the 1884 Congress of Berlin, in the interests of preserving the balance of power and European peace. This phase of international history ended with the First World War. For the previous century, however, European energies were engaged in every corner of the globe, with little regard for the interests or cultural sensitivities of the local inhabitants. Its end saw the dismemberment of the Hapsburg, Hohenzollern, Ottoman and Romanov empires, and the creation in their place of numerous, allegedly, nation states.

European overseas empires were not immediately affected by the Paris peace settlement. Indeed, from one point of view, they were strengthened by the addition of the German and Ottoman possessions granted to them under the League of Nations Mandates System. But, viewed with hindsight, they were fatally weakened. In the face of American isolationism and the Bolshevik Revolution of 1917, the European great powers continued to dominate world politics between 1919 and 1939, but the basis of their power was under constant attack. Nationalist movements, first in Asia, then in Africa, argued that if the doctrine of national self-determination meant anything, it should apply to them as well as the successor states of Europe's dynastic empires.

Success for Asian and African nationalists followed the end of the Second World War. The British quit India in 1947; the Dutch were forced out of Indonesia in 1949; the Vietnamese defeated the French in 1954. The climax of the campaign came in 1960 with the passage at the United Nations of General Assembly Resolution 1514. This held, amongst other things, that lack of preparation for self-government was not a reason for denying a colonial people their independence.

The attempt to proscribe empire did not take hold immediately. Namibia, the last colony, only became independent in 1993. The delay was largely the result of the Cold War, which subordinated local politics to the vagaries of superpower competition. Once it was over, the Soviet government co-operated with the Western powers in bringing the age of imperialism to an end, a process that involved putting the Soviet Union itself into liquidation. In 1960, those who opposed imperialism had seldom included the Soviet Union amongst their targets, despite the fact that the Bolsheviks had taken over the Romanov Empire after the Russian Revolution. But, from 1991, the Russians withdrew from the territories they had inherited from the tsars and whose ethnic characteristics they had in the meantime reinforced (Bremmer 1993, pp. 3–11).

The imperial age was one of high drama. From an ideological point of view, the story can be reduced to a struggle of the few to dominate and of the many to resist. But those involved seldom viewed the conflict in these terms. Nor was it often perceived as a story with a single plot. The rise of imperialism, and the reaction against it, involved numerous debates, and were accompanied by a clamour of discordant voices. In the remainder of this chapter, we shall consider three of the most influential: liberal imperialism; the socialist critique; and the contrasting ideas of liberal and ethnic nationalists. Before turning to these themes, we should consider two issues that arise in relation to them all.

The first is the problem of definition. The concept of an empire – a system of territorially extended rule from a single centre – is easily grasped. The problem arises with the doctrine of imperialism: that is, the systematic attempt to justify or explain the establishment and maintenance of empires. This had not traditionally been considered necessary. From the seventeenth century, the European state had required theoretical support – hence the development of the various forms of social contract theory – but the acquisition of territory beyond the borders of the state did not call for any further justification.

Ultimately, it was the universal appeal of the American Declaration of Independence and the French Declaration of the Rights of Man and the Citizen that created the need to justify power wherever it was exercised. During the nineteenth century two kinds of theories evolved. The first sought to justify alien rule on historicist grounds. Sometimes, as in Hegel's philosophy, the mechanism by which some peoples earned the right to dominate others was made explicit (Hegel 1979 [1821], pp. 218–19). Sometimes, as in the writings of the English liberal John Stuart Mill, a process of social evolution, separating the civilised goats from the barbarian or savage sheep, was simply assumed to have happened in the past, so that a belief in universal rights was imminent, rather than realisable everywhere simultaneously (Mill 1972 [1861], pp. 359–66). Karl Marx advanced an alternative view. It denied the legitimacy of any existing state, and explained states and empires as instruments of capitalist exploitation and phases in a teleological history. This would eventually realise itself with the overthrow of world capitalism and its replacement by a communist society.

Twentieth-century adaptations of these theories were populist rather than substantive. Social Darwinian ideas about the survival of the fittest, and notions of a civilising mission and the white man's burden, were grafted onto liberal theories. Similarly, a loosely Marxian analysis of imperialism was used to underpin many Asian and African nationalist movements. Most twentieth-century Marxist accounts of imperialism ignored Marx's inconvenient argument that capitalism was a necessary stage of historical development, and hence, as in India, that imperialism might be historically progressive (Marx and Engels 1959 [1853], pp. 35–41). For most of the century, the term imperialism was used by those on the left as a form of political abuse, a way of delegitimising the most powerful interests and states.

In the case of nationalism, it was not the doctrine that was contested but the phenomenon it evoked. As Eli Kedourie described it, 'nationalism is a doctrine invented in Europe at the beginning of the nineteenth century ... to supply a criterion for the determination of the unit of population proper to enjoy a government exclusively its own, for the legitimate exercise of power in the state, and for the right organisation of a society of states'

(Kedourie 1960, p. 9). But what is a nation? The original idea drew on the ideas of government and community created by the French and American revolutions: that is, of free political communities defined externally by their independence of other powers and internally by citizenship. A common culture may have been assumed, but it was not a requirement of nationalist doctrine. Nor was common ancestry. In countries where political liberty came late, a more exclusive idea of the nation as an ethnic community took root. On this view, those who were not members of the majority community could not expect equal treatment and indeed might consider themselves lucky if they escaped expulsion from their homes or worse.

During the Cold War, the national question receded from view. In the West, the commitment of governments to democracy led them to identify nationalism with its pathological form, namely fascism and National Socialism. Democratic nationalism was assumed to be benign, and therefore not nationalism. In the East, the nationalist aspirations of the East Europeans were kept in check by the presence of the Soviet army and, for most of the time, by the loyalty to Moscow of the local communist rulers. Within the Soviet Union, the formula 'national in form, socialist in content' domesticated the subversive appeal of nationalist ideas, at least until the late 1980s (Connor 1984, pp. 45–61). The Soviet Republics were ethnically based and endowed with the outward trappings of cultural autonomy, but their political class was co-opted into the central party apparatus, which controlled all access to power. Amongst the ruling elites in the successor states to the European overseas empires, there was no inclination to challenge the interpretation of national self-determination that gained currency after 1945. This was that it meant decolonisation within the borders drawn by the former colonial powers (Mayall 1990, pp. 55–7).

The idea that the national question had been resolved was an illusion. The end of the Cold War was followed by a resurgence of nationalist claims and counter-claims, which were generally advanced with overwhelming democratic support. The restoration of democratic government was frequently accompanied by an upsurge of ethnic violence. This would not have surprised John Stuart Mill, who had argued in the 1860s that, in deeply divided societies, democracy could only be preserved by partition (Mill 1972 [1861], pp. 359–66). But, in the 1990s, no-one was prepared to draw this conclusion, at least publicly. Indeed, few new arguments were advanced, although the Georgian political theorist, Ghia Nodia, robustly defended the reconciliation of ethnic nationalism and democracy. He argued that any democratic constitution, however rational its arrangements, rested on a prior, and pre-rational, assertion of independence by a historically formed community. In many cases, he argued, this could only be an ethnic community (Nodia 1992).

The second problem is the relationship of the two concepts. As experienced by nationalists and imperialists, they were opposites: for nationalists, imperialism was the enemy to be overthrown; for imperialists, nationalism was the false creed of a small group of political agitators. Nonetheless, analytically, they are opposite sides of the same coin. Traditional empires needed no special justification – they were regarded as the rightful patrimony of the great dynastic families that ruled them. By contrast, Italian and German unification, the nineteenth-century expansion of the British and French empires, and the break-up of the European dynastic empires after 1918, were all major national projects. They differed in scale and direction, but not in their underlying rationale. Whether the policies that produced these outcomes were national or imperial, they were pursued in the name of the people, and consequently required ideological support.

In the early years of the nationalist era, Herder had viewed the division of the world into nations as a necessary first step towards a universal humanity. This benign vision did not last. By the turn of the twentieth century, as the German historian Karl Dietrich Bracher observed: 'Currents of a mission-inspired national imperialism surfaced in nearly all contemporary states from Pan-Slavism via a French and British sense of mission all the way to the American expansionist ideology of a "manifest destiny"' (Bracher 1982, p. 102).

The modern world was integrated into a global order by two opposing forces. Cognitively and intellectually, it was united by liberal ideology, geo-politically and economically by imperialism. Liberalism purports to be an anti-imperial philosophy; yet its universal values were spread around the world by national empires. To unravel the paradox, it is necessary to view the relationship of imperialism and nationalism in the wider context of international liberalism.

Liberalism, nationalism and imperial expansion

Few imperialists were political liberals. In Britain and France, the leading advocates of imperial expansion belonged on the political right, and the authoritarian leaders who rose to power in Europe after 1918 often endorsed irrationalist doctrines, which were the antithesis of liberal values. But they all lived within a world that had been transformed by the values they abhorred.

Ortega y Gasset, the minister of culture in the Spanish Republic, described the process in *The Revolt of the Masses*, published in 1930 (Ortega y Gasset 1963, pp. 224–5):

> In the eighteenth century certain minority groups discovered that every human being, by the mere fact of birth, and without requiring any special qualification whatsoever, possessed certain fundamental political rights, the so-called 'rights of man'; and further that, strictly speaking, these rights, common to all, are the only ones that exist . . . This was at first a mere theory, the idea of a few men; then those few began to put the idea into practice, to impose it and insist upon it. Nevertheless, during the whole of the 19th Century, the mass, while gradually become enthusiastic to these rights as an ideal, did not feel them as rights . . . the people . . . had learned that it was sovereign but did not believe it. Today the ideal has been changed into a reality; not only in legislation, which is the mere framework of public life, but in the heart of every individual, whatever his ideas might be, and even if he be a reactionary in his ideas, *that is to say even when he attacks and castigates institutions by which those rights are sanctioned*.

A belief in fundamental rights does not sit easily with the claims of either individuals or families to retain their privileges or of a whole people to superiority over others. Human beings are seldom consistent, however. A combination of developments drove European expansion. Perhaps the most spectacular were the scientific discoveries, which opened the world through exploration and facilitated long-distance trade and communication. These were accompanied by the spread of Western education, a proselytising Christianity and a restless competitive drive for supplies of raw materials to feed European industry and for markets to absorb European manufactured products.

Liberal economic theory is by implication anti-imperialist. Adam Smith argued against the direct involvement of the state in economic affairs, except in times of national emergency (Smith 1923 [1766], vol. II, pp. 29–52). The core of the liberal argument is that intervention raises costs and stifles enterprise, whereas free competition encourages efficiency, provides the consumer with the widest possible choice, and maximises public welfare over the long run. Liberal economic theory was also implicitly anti-national, because it was based on the assumption of individual sovereignty. Some twentieth-century economic liberals, such as Ludwig von Mises, believed with almost Cobdenite passion in the virtues of the liberal economy. On their view, the acquisition of territory was unnecessary and dangerous (Mises 1983 [1919], p. 94). Most, however, overcame their objections to both imperialism and nationalism. The essential reason was that while they were suspicious of power, and wished to restrict the state's functions, they had no interest in challenging its authority.

Britain and France, the two countries with the most substantial overseas possessions, had already been centralised in the pre-nationalist era. Little more was required, in Ernest Gellner's phrase, than 'a kind of *ex post* rationalisation' (Gellner 1994, p. 133). In other words, while the doctrine of popular sovereignty was held to require the extension of the franchise to all male members of the community, the political arguments that produced these results took place within historically named and bounded countries. Moreover, the national citizenry took over established states that already had extensive colonial possessions which had been acquired during the mercantilist wars of the seventeenth and eighteenth centuries.

Many liberals opposed the acquisition of new territories but seldom challenged the right of the state to retain its overseas possessions. For the most part, they appear to have taken over the mercantilist view of the outside world as an exploitable resource. As democrats, they insisted that those responsible for colonial administration should be held accountable at home, and that they should regard their role in the colonies as one of extending the principles of an enlightened government to other parts of the world. It was only with the emergence of local nationalist movements, demanding the right of self-determination for themselves, that liberal opinion transformed itself into a kind of sympathetic anti-imperial fifth column on their behalf (Owen 1999, pp. 188–211).

There were two other reasons why liberal nationalists supported imperialism in the first half of the twentieth century, before turning against it in the second. The first was economic. It was hardly accidental that liberal economic theory was developed in Britain at the time when its industrial and commercial supremacy was undisputed. Britain favoured open markets because it had most to gain from them. The fact that the internationalisation of the British economy was dependent on the *Pax Britannica* was not acknowledged by the theory, which took the institutional and legal framework of policy for granted (Polanyi 1957 [1944], pp. 1–19). But conservatives, who were mostly in favour of the empire, did not take it for granted at all. As Britain's economic hegemony was eroded by competition from Germany and the United States, opinion swung behind the view that the empire was an asset, which should be strengthened.

In both Germany and the USA, liberal economic theory had been nationalised to overcome the alleged disadvantages of being late industrialisers. In arguing for what later came to be known as 'infant industry protection',

Alexander Hamilton (Earle 1986, pp. 233–7) and Friedrich List (1904, pp. 97–107) were merely making the case that free trade worked to everyone's advantage only if all were at a comparable stage of economic development. After 1945, their arguments were echoed by third world nationalists who regarded the ideal of free trade as itself a form of imperialism, or at least as the mercantilism of the rich and powerful (Mayall 1990, pp. 133–9).

The campaign for imperial protection began in the 1890s, when, to quote Dennis Austin, 'Joseph Chamberlain began to talk of the need for imperial preference – a pan-imperial *Zollverein* – to ring fence the empire' (Austin 1998, p. 431). Despite his advocacy, Britain did not finally abandon free trade until 1932. By this time, at the height of the Great Depression, even Maynard Keynes supported national protection (Keynes 1934, pp. 755–69). Simultaneously, the British also established a parallel system of imperial and commonwealth preferences. For liberal ideologues, particularly in the United States, these were anathema. For many in Britain, the Dominions, and its overseas possessions, however, preferences were regarded not as a second-best solution to free trade, but as the economic defences of a free association of nations – the salvageable part of the proposals for an imperial federation, which surfaced periodically in the period before 1914.

The rapid development of the world economy, and the logic of the Cold War, undermined the vision of the European empires as an alternative framework for a liberal economy. Perhaps it was always a fantasy, and its demise, therefore, was both inevitable and quickly forgotten. But for some time it attracted support across the British political spectrum. For those on the right, the empire belonged to the natural order. Either it had to be strengthened or it would succumb to a new and more powerful imperial force. For others in the liberal centre and on the left, the empire, metamorphosed after 1945 into the multi-racial Commonwealth, held out the promise of a softer and more socially responsible form of internationalism than that offered by the rapacious world market (Austin 1988).

The two sides joined forces in their suspicion of the United States. It required the powerful advocacy of Maynard Keynes to persuade the British parliament that the country should join the IMF and the World Bank. The trouble was that the dilution of Keynes's proposals for these institutions – particularly the demonetisation of gold and the arrangements for providing credit to countries in balance-of-payments difficulties – convinced many that the United States had imperial ambitions of its own (Gardener 1980 [1956]). For socialists this was a self-evident truth, the inevitable consequence of

American dominance of world capitalism. However, the idea of a new post-colonial imperialism was not confined to socialists. In 1973, the French sociologist and philosopher Raymond Aron published a book about the United States under the title *The Imperial Republic*, describing the Bretton Woods institutions and the dollar exchange standard as the economic infrastructure of the new imperial order (Aron 1973, pp. 159–256).

The second reason why liberal nationalists inclined towards imperialism was in response to a predominantly French conception of geo-politics. The decision to partition Africa amongst the great powers was largely driven by the logic of competitive power politics. The French sought compensation in Africa for their defeat by Prussia in 1871, and the other powers responded. French liberals had been schooled in a different tradition from their British counterparts and did not face the same problem of reconciling a belief in individual freedom with territorial expansion. To quote the American historian Rupert Emerson, 'the ideal of the French colonial vocation is to bring less fortunate peoples within the fold of French culture and a single all-embracing France' (Emerson 1962 [1960], p. 69). Nor did Frenchmen, of any political persuasion, generally see any contradiction between the universalist values on which the state was built and an economy in which France *outre-mer* was deliberately integrated with, and managed by, the metropole.

The difference between the two versions of national imperialism was one of style more than substance. Most Europeans believed that they were justified in ruling over the rest of the world, even after their confidence had been shaken by the catastrophe of the First World War. Indeed, in the short run, the war may even have strengthened their resolve to find reasons for hanging onto their overseas possessions. The most fundamental reason continued to be that Asia and Africa were regarded as backward, a view in which claims to moral authority and economics were conjoined. Superimposed on this attitude of cultural, and often racial, superiority, was the idea that the world could only prosper if all its resources were tapped. 'This form of imperialism', wrote A. Sarraut in 1931,

> is merely the extreme expression of an idea and a need which are in principle justified absolutely but which, taken to excess, become intolerable . . . Nature has distributed unequally across our planet a wealth and variety of raw materials; and while she has located in this continental extremity which is called Europe, the inventive genius of the white races and the technical expertise with which to exploit natural resources, she has concentrated the most abundant reserves of these materials in Africa, tropical Asia and equatorial Oceania, towards which the developed countries in their need to live and create, are directing their impetus and drive . . . Must these

immense expanses of land . . . be allowed to lie fallow, abandoned to the thickets of indifference, ignorance and incompetence? (Grimal 1965, pp. 111–12).

The British colonial administrator, Lord Lugard, advanced a similar argument:

When Great Britain undertook the control of great regions in tropical Africa, she not only gave to her commercial rivals the same opportunities as were enjoyed by her own nationals . . . She secured to their inhabitants an unrestricted market for their products . . . She recognised that the custodians of the tropics are . . . 'trustees of civilisation for the commerce of the world'; that their raw materials and foodstuffs – without which civilisation cannot exist – must be developed alike in the interests of the natives and of the world at large . . . The tropics are the heritage of mankind, and neither, on the one hand, has the suzerain Power a right to their exclusive exploitation, nor, on the other, have the races which inhabit them a right to deny their bounties to those who need them (Lugard 1965 [1922], pp. 60–1).

This liberal defence of empire contained the seeds of its own destruction. Once it was conceded that the European empires were held in trust for the people, local nationalists were eventually bound to claim a right of self-determination. Of the two versions of liberalism, the British, with its theoretical separation of the public and private spheres and its scepticism about the concept of an imperial citizenship, was probably better placed to make concessions. The republican tradition faced French governments with the impossible task of converting their colonial subjects into Frenchmen. In a book published in 1903, A. Girault wrote:

The man whom we prevent from being first in his own country on account of its colonial status, must be offered in exchange the possibility of becoming first in ours. We must instil in those to whom we deny any local patriotism, the love of a common mother country, a cult of the Empire (Grimal 1965, p. 59).

Looking back, it seems a hopeless task, but it continued, not always completely unsuccessfully, right down to the short-lived Franco-African federal community, established under the 1958 constitution. Its failure had less to do with nationalism in francophone Africa – all but one of the francophone African leaders supported it – than with the effects of decolonisation elsewhere, and the fact that competition between the two superpowers for influence in the third world allowed the socialist critique of imperialism to have a direct impact on events in the former colonies.

The socialist critique

Imperialism, and the prospects of its downfall, had been passionately debated within the international socialist movement, but the imperial powers had been largely successful in quarantining their colonial subjects against what they regarded as the baleful effects of socialist doctrine. Ironically, the socialist critique of imperialism owed much to the work of the liberal internationalist, J. A. Hobson, whose book on the subject was published in 1902 and influenced Lenin. Hobson detected in contemporary imperialism a qualitatively different character from the earlier mercantile expansion of the European powers. At the heart of his theory was the concept of a generalised under-consumption in the advanced countries.

> The system prevailing in all developed countries for the production and distribution of wealth has reached a stage in which its productive powers are held in leash by its inequalities of distribution; the excessive share that goes to profits, rents and other surpluses impelling a chronic endeavour to oversave in the sense of trying to provide an increased productive power without a corresponding outlet in the purchase of consumable goods (Hobson 1988 [1902], pp. 51–2).

It was this condition – and the consequent desire to monopolise control of markets and outlets for surplus capital – which had driven European nations to the pathological behaviour that he identified as the new imperialism. The similarity with Lenin's pamphlet, *Imperialism: The Highest Stage of Capitalism*, first published in 1916, is indeed striking. But, as David Long has pointed out, there is a crucial distinction between the two accounts. For Hobson, imperialism was a policy pursued by capitalists, which could be remedied by government action. The paradox of Lenin's position was his denial of human agency, at least so long as the agents were capitalists. 'He suggested that it was the system of capitalism that was to blame and that nothing short of its overthrow would rid the world of the scourge of imperialism' (Long 1996, p. 218, note 37).

Much of Lenin's argument was taken up with a feud within the international socialist movement. His aim was to show that a correct analysis of the economic causes of imperialism would demonstrate that imperialism could never be reformed, as Bauer and Kautsky had allegedly claimed. In the preface to the German and French editions of the pamphlet, published after the revolution in 1920, he asks what is the explanation of the social democratic tendency, which had split the working-class movement. He proceeds to answer his own question (Lenin 1920, pp. 16–17):

Precisely the parasitism and decay of capitalism which are characteristic of its highest historical stage of development, i.e., imperialism . . . Capitalism has now singled out a handful of exceptionally rich and powerful states which plunder the whole world simply by 'clipping coupons'. Capital exports yield an income of eight to ten billion francs per annum . . . Obviously out of such enormous *super profits it is possible to bribe* the labour leaders and the upper stratum of the labour aristocracy . . . Unless the economic roots of this phenomenon are understood . . . not a step can be taken towards the solution of the practical problems of the Communist movement and of the impending social revolution. Imperialism is the eve of the social revolution of the proletariat. This has been confirmed since 1917 on a worldwide scale.

Events were to prove Lenin wrong, at least as far as the timing of the revolution of the proletariat was concerned! It was a characteristic of the international communist movement that its members took ideological disputes extremely seriously. It was not, however, the details of the argument that made *Imperialism* so influential, but the fact that it signalled to the capitalist enemy, and to nationalists in the colonies, that the Bolsheviks had identified imperialism as the Achilles heel of world capitalism. The argument was that by eliminating the enormous profits made in the colonies by the European bourgeoisie and their ability to corrupt the working classes, revolt in the colonies would lead to revolution in Europe. After the revolution, this belief led Soviet theorists to contemplate an accommodation with nationalism, which Marxists had originally discounted as a form of false consciousness, an opiate of the people, like religion.

The Bolsheviks were forced into their marriage of convenience with nationalism for tactical rather than theoretical reasons. Faced with a civil war at home, and encircled by hostile capitalist countries, they needed allies. The fiercest opponents of tsarist Russia had been the 'oppressed' nationalities, whose leaders were attracted to the package of liberal values on which the American president Woodrow Wilson had based his peace strategy. Lenin responded by offering the peoples of the former tsarist Empire a right of self-determination, up to and including secession. The right was later inscribed in the 1922 Soviet constitution, where it remained until the demise of the Soviet Union in 1991. Notoriously, it was honoured in the breach rather than the observance.

Civic and ethnic nationalism

The idea that each nation should be independent and self-governing was originally advanced without much attention to questions of definition. Such apparent carelessness should not surprise us. Enlightenment thinkers wanted the transfer of the national patrimony from a hereditary monarch and ruling caste to the people. The identity of nations was taken for granted. In as far as nineteenth-century thinkers such as Ernest Renan addressed the question, they started from the simple premise that the nation was a self-governing community of citizens (Renan 1882, pp. 26–9). It was only after 1918, with the equation of nation and state, that the definition of the nation became politically significant.

During the inter-war period, many nationalists were inspired by an alternative, anti-Enlightenment tradition of thought. Following Mazzini and Herder, they viewed the nation as a natural, organic and historically specific cultural community. Mazzini had predicted that the map of Europe would be redrawn along national lines, which, conveniently, he found had been inscribed by nature.

> The divine design will infallibly be fulfilled. Natural divisions . . . will replace the arbitrary divisions sanctioned by bad governments. The map of Europe will be remade. The Countries of the People will rise, defined by the voice of the free, upon the ruins of the Countries of Kings and privileged castes. Between these Countries there will be harmony and brotherhood . . . You should have no joy or repose as long as a portion of the territory upon which your language is spoken is separated from the Nation (Beales 1966, pp. 151–2).

The revolt against cosmopolitanism reached its climax in Germany. Its most distinguished exponent was the philosopher J. G. Herder. But, while his 'belief in the value of belonging to a group or a culture', like Mazzini's, was to have tragic political consequences in the twentieth century, as Isaiah Berlin pointed out, Herder's view of the cultural linguistic community was not political, and was indeed 'anti-political, different from and even opposed to nationalism' (Berlin 1976, p. 153).

By contrast, the twentieth-century quest for an objective definition of the nation has a clear political objective. It was a response to the collapse of the European dynastic empires. It was no longer obvious on what basis the political map of Europe was to be redrawn. Mazzini's belief in a divinely ordered natural design did not even work for Italy, where the exclusion of the Italian-speaking cantons of Switzerland and provinces of the Austro-Hungarian Empire added a new term – irredentism – to the political vocabulary of nationalism. Elsewhere, it proved impossible to redraw the political map without creating entrapped minorities in the process.

Woodrow Wilson had hoped that the principle of national self-determination could be applied by the use of plebiscites. The difficulty with this idea was the false assumption that the identity of the constituent people was unproblematic. As Ivor Jennings put it when the idea was revived after the Second World War in the context of decolonisation, 'on the surface it seemed reasonable: Let the People decide. It was in fact ridiculous because the people cannot decide until someone decides who are the people' (Jennings 1956, p. 56). In Europe after 1918, it would not have been ridiculous had a democratic culture already existed in the liberated territories. If citizenship alone had been accepted as the criterion for defining the nation, arguments about ethnic exclusion or discrimination need not have arisen. Unhappily this was not the case, with the result that liberals were forced to confront the problem of national minorities.

Wilson initially tried to include in the League Covenant a provision (Article 10) for peaceful territorial adjustments in the event of changes 'in present racial conditions and aspirations or present social and political relationships' (Cobban 1945, p. 28). So flagrant an assault on the principle of territorial integrity failed to convince even the American delegation to the Paris Peace Conference. The final version of the Article offered no such hostage to fortune, although the successor states of the Hapsburg Empire were subsequently made to sign treaties guaranteeing the rights of minorities as a condition of entry into the League. Since the major powers were not themselves similarly bound, an impression of double standards was created, causing resentment (Jackson Preece 1998, pp. 67–94). The fact that Nazi Germany used the presence of German minorities as a pretext for justifying its eastward expansion further damaged the liberal attempt to accommodate ethnic nationalism. Consequently, in 1945 the protection of national minorities virtually disappeared from the list of background ideas on which the United Nations Charter and the Universal Declaration of Human Rights were based. It was not revived until the 1990s.

The failure of liberal internationalists to establish the civic ideal of the nation state left the field open for those who believed that the problem could be resolved by identifying 'genuine' nations. In the West, historians and sociologists took up the debate. Unlike political theorists, they were not concerned to justify a particular social and political order, but to understand the conditions that had given rise to the phenomenon of nationalism itself. Max Weber's definition of the nation is worth quoting in this context because it begs the questions that many other academic writers have attempted to answer:

Insofar as there is at all a common object lying behind the obviously ambiguous term 'single nation', it is apparently located in the field of politics. One might well define the concept of a nation in the following way: a nation is a community of sentiment which would adequately manifest itself in a state of its own; hence, a nation is a community which normally tends to produce a state of its own (Weber 1948, p. 179).

What gives rise to a community of sentiment requiring a state of its own and what is the process by which such communities acquire statehood? Those seeking an answer to the first question mostly fall into one of two camps. For some, such as Walker Connor (1978, pp. 379–98) or Anthony Smith (1991), the answer is the re-emergence of an earlier pre-political ethnic sentiment, based on shared memories, myths and symbols. For others, such as Eli Kedourie (1960), Ernest Gellner (1983) or Benedict Anderson (1983), the rise of nationalism – including where necessary the invention of nations where they did not previously exist – is part of the process of modernisation. They differ over the causal links between nationalism and other aspects of modernity, but they are all sceptical of the ancestral claims of ethnic nationalists, and are not inclined to take nationalist arguments seriously in their own terms.

The issue is not susceptible to proof, but the writings of both groups are important for anyone trying to understand the way in which nationalism has shaped the modern world. However, they do not constitute political thought as generally understood – that is, a tradition of speculation about the basis of political organisation, and the justification for the exercise of authority and its limits. For this reason, they will not be considered further here. Max Weber's second question is empirical. There have been few attempts to provide a generalised theoretical answer, although Meinecke came closer than most with his distinction between culture-nations and state-nations from which he further derived a series of hybrid forms (Meinecke 1922, p. 15).

Isaiah Berlin rightly pointed out that, after 1945, the liberal world had mistakenly ignored the continuing influence of nationalist ideas (Berlin 1979 [1972], pp. 333–5). Western countries seldom examined their own national credentials. Nationalism was widely understood in terms of the extreme and pathological variants that had led the world into war. In Europe, nationalism was equated with failure, whereas in the colonial world it continued to be regarded as a doctrine of liberation. The ideas underlying the nationalist revolt against the West in Asia and Africa are covered elsewhere in this volume, as are communism, fascism and National Socialism. It is nonetheless necessary briefly to examine the contributions of these latter movements to nationalist political thought because they refined and promoted the ethnic idea of the nation, which was revived, often with dire consequences, after 1989.

This idea played an important, if subordinate, part in the development of communist ideology and was central to fascism between the two world wars. For the communists the problem was how to acknowledge it as legitimate in a cultural and administrative sense without allowing it to attack the integrity of the Soviet state. The task was given to Stalin, who aimed at an objective definition from which any echoes of liberal voluntarism had been purged:

> A nation is a historically constituted, stable community of people, formed on the basis of a common language, territory, economic life, and psychological make-up, manifested in a common culture . . . It must be emphasised that none of the above characteristics taken separately is sufficient to define a nation. More than that, it is sufficient for a single one of these characteristics to be lacking and the nation ceases to be a nation (Stalin 1973, p. 61).

There was nothing intrinsically absurd in this definition – indeed, it had much in common with those employed by liberal positivists. In Stalin's hands, however, it was used to provide the Soviet Republics with the trappings of autonomy while denying them the reality.

Fascists drew inspiration from many sources other than those that inspired earlier national thinkers. But they, unlike liberals or socialists, had no problems reconciling their beliefs with the idea of the nation. Indeed, to quote Roger Griffin, 'fascism is a genus of political ideology whose mythic core in its various permutations is a palingenetic form of populist ultra-nationalism' (Griffin 1993, p. 2). In other words, whatever else it was, fascism was a theory of the nation.

In the inter-war period a large number of fascist and proto-fascist regimes came to power, apart from the Italian movement, which gave the ideology its name, and German National Socialism, which developed the totalitarian logic to its ghastly and absurd conclusion. Not all these regimes rested their claims to power on an explicit theory of biological or racial superiority. Nor did they all regard violence as a cathartic principle of regeneration and liberation, although many did. But they all viewed the nation as prone to crisis and decay, but also capable of, and waiting for, salvation. They conceived of it as an organic whole, equally far removed from the liberal idea of a political community of citizens and the cultural community that the Bolsheviks finally conceded might constitute a staging post en route to the classless society.

Fascists saw themselves as shock troops, whose central task was to restore the nation to its lost greatness through an act of will. As a statement of the organic conception of the nation, it is hard to improve on the Nationalist Blueprint for a New Italy, published in 1920 by the Italian Nationalist Association, the precursor of the Fascists, with whom they merged in 1923:

> The fundamental thesis of Nationalism, which places the Nationalist doctrine in a special relationship with all other political doctrines, is that the various societies existing on earth are true organisms endowed with a life that transcends individuals and is maintained for centuries and millennia.
>
> Thus the Italian nation does not merely contain the 36 million Italians alive now, but all the hundreds of millions of Italian who will live in future centuries, and who are conceived as components of a single whole. In this conception each generation and every individual within a generation is but a transient and infinitesimal part of the nation, and is the cell of the national organism. Just as cells are born, live and die, while the organism remains the same, so individuals are born, live and die, while the nation continues to live out its millennial existence . . .
>
> Nationalism considers the expansion of Italy's power in the world . . . above all as a duty. It is a moral law which calls upon a people destined for geographic, historical and demographic reasons, either to perish or to expand and dominate, to embrace its destiny and be unflinching in the struggle with competing nations, a struggle which will be hard, but with victory assured, also glorious (Griffin 1995, pp. 37–8).

Ultra-nationalism was the pathological heir of that strand in European Romanticism that rejected the universalism of the French Enlightenment and the rationalism of British political economy. Fascists and Nazis were not interested in what they shared with the rest of humanity, but in what distinguished them and placed them on a higher plane. Their defeat in the Second World War fatally weakened the appeal of fascist theories of the nation. A few anti-imperial nationalist movements – for example Subhas Chandra Bose's Indian National Army or the Afrikaner National Party in South Africa – had supported the Axis powers on the ancient principle of making a friend of the enemy's enemies. Frantz Fanon, the leading ideologue of the Algerian revolt, developed the idea of revolutionary violence in a colonial context (Fanon 1965). The majority of anti-colonial movements also borrowed, although seldom consciously, the charismatic style of leadership that the fascists had cultivated. But in other respects few of them had anything in common with the cultivated irrationalism that was the trademark of European fascism.

On the contrary, most anti-colonial movements enthusiastically accepted the idea of a single humanity and universal values. Nehru caught the optimistic mood in 1947 when he urged his parliamentary colleagues to 'take the pledge of dedication to the service of India and her people and the still larger cause of humanity' (Nehru 1962, pp. 94–5). It was not until the 1990s that the challenge of ethnic nationalism re-surfaced, when the international community faced the contradictory pressures of globalisation and political fragmentation.

The theoretical problem was not new. It had arisen in the aftermath of both world wars. On what basis could a social group claim a right to a state of its own? On neither occasion had it been resolved. The search for a new answer came, as so often in this area, in reaction to events rather than because of a philosophical breakthrough. With the break-up of the Soviet Union and the widespread pursuit of economic de-regulation, people began to move across frontiers on a scale that had been impossible during the Cold War. Simultaneously, democratisation, proclaimed in the West as the solution to the problems of divided societies, often failed altogether, or was accompanied by inter-communal violence and the systematic violation of fundamental rights by state authorities. In some cases, the state ceased to function.

The need to respond to these challenges led to a revival of interest in the theory of self-determination. An old philosophical divide re-opened within liberalism, between those who argued for a system of cosmopolitan justice based on a more rigorous enforcement and extension of the Universal Declaration of Human Rights, and those who insisted that the foundation of ethics was to be found in the community. The founding father of the modern cosmopolitan camp was John Rawls. His *Theory of Justice* (Rawls 1971), underlies the work of a whole generation of cosmopolitan thinkers such as Charles Beitz (1979) and Brian Barry (1988). The communitarian response to the idea of an 'original position', the device on which Rawls based his theory, is more recent and is associated primarily with such writers as the American philosopher Michael Walzer (1985) and the British political theorist David Miller (1995).

Communitarians believe that human values are inextricably bound up with the communities in which we live, rather than grounded on a theory of abstract rights and obligations. For the cosmopolitan, the boundaries of nation and state are ultimately of secondary importance: what matters is what goes on inside them. For the communitarian, boundaries are an essential part of identity: they need not necessarily license a double standard in behaviour – towards insiders and outsiders – but unless they are properly drawn, the nation will not be able to function as an ethical community. No doubt this is a caricature of the two positions, but it helps to identify why it is so difficult to reach consensus on such issues as immigration and asylum policy, and on the question of whether there should be, and under what circumstances, a secessionist right to self-determination.

It is generally difficult to tell at what point a theory begins to influence practice. For example, there is no evidence that the writings of Buchanan (1991) or Beran (1987) on secession have had any impact on state practice. In his *Agenda for Peace* (1992), the then United Nations secretary general, Boutros Boutros-Ghali, stated that while the UN had not closed its doors to new members, if every dissatisfied group was to claim a right of self-determination, the result would be chaos and a loss of global welfare (Boutros-Ghali 1992, paras. 17 and 18). This did little more than indicate that the post-1945 consensus on the principle of self-determination – that it was synonymous with European decolonisation – was under pressure. The development of international law on the issue suggests a similarly modest conclusion. When in 1974 the International Court of Justice was asked for an opinion on the status of Morocco's claim to Mauritania, it ruled that, while there were 'loyalties of allegiance' between Morocco and some tribes living in the territory, this could not be used to deny the former French colony the right to self-determination. In other words the Court endorsed the prevailing political consensus. In 1996, the Canadian Supreme Court sought the advice of two eminent lawyers on whether Quebec had the right of unilateral secession. They responded that 'there may be developments in the principle of self determination according to which not only colonialism but flagrant violations of human rights or undemocratic regimes could lead to a right of unilateral secession', conditions that did not apply to Quebec (Mayall 1999, p. 70). At the end of the century, it did not seem that nationalism had followed imperialism into eclipse, let alone that either had been replaced by a new cosmopolitanism.

5
Fascism and racism

STANLEY G. PAYNE

The analysis of fascist political thought is a difficult task for several reasons. The political genus of fascism is itself poorly defined, and the conclusion has sometimes been advanced that fascism primarily represented a form of praxis, inherently non-ideological and without formal thought or programme. Moreover, as early as 1923 there developed a growing tendency to generalise beyond the initial Italian example and apply the term 'fascism' or 'fascist' to any form of right-wing authoritarian movement or system. More broadly yet, Soviet Stalinists began to apply the term, usually hyphenated with some additional adjective, to any and all rivals. By the 1930s fascist had sometimes become little more than a term of denigration applied to political foes, and this usage as a very broad and vague pejorative has continued to the present day.

A limited consensus has nonetheless emerged among some of the leading scholars in the study of fascism, who use the term to refer to a group of revolutionary nationalist movements in Europe between the two world wars, first in the cases of the Italian Fascist and German National Socialist parties and then in the cases of their clearest counterparts in other European countries. This limited consensus tends to agree that specific movements bearing all or nearly all of the same common characteristics did not exist prior to 1919 and have not appeared in significant form in areas outside Europe or in the period after 1945 (Griffin 1998, pp. 1–16). Nonetheless, disagreement persists among scholars as to whether the various reputedly fascist movements of inter-war Europe can be firmly linked together as a common and generic phenomenon, or whether they so differed among themselves that they can accurately be discussed only as individual phenomena. The weight of opinion generally tends to fall on the side of the former argument, though with important qualifications. Thus the term fascist is employed by scholars to define an ideal type of general model of a political movement, with the understanding that the various organisations referred to shared basic common characteristics but also sometimes differed considerably among themselves and did not all adhere to one single common programme. On this basis fascism may be defined as a form of organic revolutionary ultra-nationalism seeking national rebirth, based on a primarily vitalist and non-rationalist philosophy, structured on a seemingly contradictory combination of extreme elitism and mass mobilisation, emphasising hierarchy and the leadership principle, positively valuing violence to some extent as end as well as means, and tending to normalise war and/or military virtues (Griffin 1991, pp. 26–52; Payne 1995, pp. 3–19).

The genealogy of fascist ideas already had a history in political, social and philosophical thought prior to the founding of the Italian movement in 1919, though such ideas had never before been brought together in the service of one clear-cut political organisation. The distant origin of some of these ideas lay first in the major intellectual changes wrought by the Enlightenment in the second half of the eighteenth century and, second in the cultural and intellectual Romanticism of the late eighteenth and early nineteenth centuries (Nolte 1966; Wippermann 1989). This is little appreciated in so far as fascism categorically rejected basic principles of the Enlightenment, such as liberalism, rationalism, materialism and universalism. The intellectual transformation of the eighteenth century was, however, broad and multi-faceted and involved many different aspects of thought and culture. Fascism in fact drew on several distinct strands of Enlightenment thought, beginning with the replacement of orthodox Christianity with a naturalistic and impersonal deist concept of God, and the replacement of the traditionally sacred with a completely secular natural law, together with new concepts of nature, society and the nation. The idea of the nation and/or the people was fundamental to fascist thought, as was the concept of a new hierarchy of the enlightened, artistically advanced and culturally superior – strains of thought which in the Enlightenment had co-existed with universalism. Faith in secular progress and rebirth, a secular optimism, stemmed from the same sources, as did the orientation toward a 'higher humanity' based on secular natural law. The doctrines of the Enlightenment tended to posit the need for elitist guidance and rule, the dominance of human voluntarism and the triumph of a new cultural and reformist will, while distinguishing between productive and unproductive sectors of society. This sometimes took the guise of highly authoritarian reform, and in its most extreme manifestations emphasised drastic revolutionary change effected by violence, affecting broad areas of political, social, cultural and economic life, with the goal of achieving unity and a new uniformism within the nation. The French Revolution provided the first example of the introduction of a radical new civic religion to replace traditional culture, accompanied by a new public theatre and political liturgy with which to inculcate the masses. Finally, it was the Enlightenment which began the practice of classifying mankind racially, drawing distinctions between races which subsequently in the nineteenth century would become sharp racial hierarchies. All these aspects of Enlightenment thought would be drawn on by fascists, even as they rejected some of the most dominant Enlightenment doctrines (Birken 1995).

Equally or even more important in the initial genealogy of fascism were the anti-liberal cultural and political aspects of Romanticism. Romanticism rejected liberalism, rationalism and materialism in favour of emotion and idealism, and also tended to emphasise historic, ethnic or mystical identities and values in opposition to universalism. One major current of Romantic thinking stressed the centrality of the nation, not as a civic or legal constitution but as an exclusive and unique cultural and ethnic entity. In much of Romantic thought popular sovereignty was not derived from the electorate but from the people as a cultural and ethnic unity. Liberty in this approach was not represented by the civil rights of the individual but by the self-realisation of the nation – the perfection of the virtues of an ethnic community which might involve the sacrifice or the self-sacrifice of the individual.

These approaches to politics and society were then refashioned with specific new content between the 1880s and 1914 by what some historians call the cultural crisis or intellectual revolution of the 1890s or, variantly, the *fin de siècle*. Whereas the predominant political, social and philosophical trends of the main part of the nineteenth century had espoused liberalism, rationalism and materialism, these formerly dominant principles were challenged by new ideas and priorities among some of the cultural and intellectual elite in the latter part of the century (Sternhell 1978).

In formal philosophy and some aspects of literature, neo-idealism gained a vogue. Newer currents of thought emphasised non-rationalism and vitalist or action-oriented philosophy. Canons of truth were challenged and theoretically reconstructed by the German philosopher Friedrich Nietzsche (Aschheim 1992). In place of individualism, there developed a new tendency toward biological analogies and holistic and organic concepts (Mosse 1964). New research in anthropology and social psychology seemed to reveal broad cultural and moral differences within human society and to encourage moral and intellectual relativism, as well as demonstrating the dominance of the emotional, the non-rational and the subjective in social groups. Political sociologists such as Gaetano Mosca and Vilfredo Pareto wrote of a natural and inevitable tendency towards elitist dominance, rather than democratic or majority rule, in political and social groups. Social Darwinists sought to apply Darwinian biological and zoological concepts to human society, stressing the desirability, indeed the inevitability, of unremitting competition and the survival of the fittest. This was applied to international relations as well, to encourage national and imperial competition and even war (Kelley 1981). By the beginning of the twentieth century, there were many new calls to violence by revolutionary class leaders, national militarists and radical theorists. The French ideologue Georges Sorel, in his *Reflections on Violence* (1908), concluded that violence was not only a necessary evil or a reluctant means toward a greater good, but was positively constructive and desirable in itself. Sorel held that violence purified a social group, being the surest means – if conducted in the proper way – of eliciting such positive values as seriousness, idealism, unity, commitment and self-sacrifice, thus uplifting and ennobling its practitioners.

Particularly sinister in this regard was the rise of modern racial thought. Human beings have been conscious of certain racial differences, primarily with regard to skin colour, for many centuries, but in traditional Christian thought such differences were deemed entirely secondary to the common humanity of mankind. The main exception, from the fifteenth century on, had to do with the systematic enslavement of black Africans, but during the late eighteenth and nineteenth centuries this was increasingly challenged, until slavery was completely abolished throughout Europe, the Americas and the European colonies, though not in all Islamic societies of Africa and the Middle East.

The detailed categorisation of human society in terms of distinct races was first developed during the eighteenth century. Such analysis was initially descriptive and relatively disinterested, not formulated in terms of invidious hierarchies of races or pejorative distinctions. Racial thinking expanded steadily during the century which followed, leading eventually to the development of a 'scientific racism' which sought to record and classify physiological and other characteristics of many different ethnic and racial groups, and by the last years of the nineteenth century was reflected in the highly influential work of the Italian Jewish criminologist Cesare Lombroso, who defined the inherently 'criminal type' of human being in terms of head and facial physical characteristics. For several decades even a handful of Jewish scholars promoted 'Jewish race science' to define the specific 'racial' characteristics of Jews. By the end of the century commentators in many different countries expressed concern about the danger of social, cultural and racial decline, the most dramatic statement of which was the book *Degeneration* (1892) by the German-Jewish writer Max Nordau.

During the second half of the century, racial thinking became ever more elaborate, intolerant and invidious, with an increasing tendency to seek to define distinctions and hierarchies. Since all this classification was conducted by white Europeans and Americans, and since European society was increasingly dominating the world, white Europeans and their ethnic relatives elsewhere were placed at the top of such hierarchies. The writer who first succeeded in broadly diffusing the concept of the superiority of the white race was the elitist French aristocrat comte Arthur de Gobineau, whose *Essay on the Inequality of the Human Races* was published in 1853. Elaborating a terminology developed in the preceding half-century, Gobineau termed the superior white race 'Aryans', who were held to be inherently above other races but also doomed to inevitable decline through the destructive effects of miscegenation (Biddiss 1970; Bainton 1985).

Racial hierarchies were subsequently defined not merely for *Homo sapiens* as a whole, but in terms of distinct racial differences even among different groups of white Europeans. George L. Mosse, one of the leading historians of European racism, has aptly termed this 'mystical racism' – mystical in the sense that the differences posited between white Europeans were not physically visible in such characteristics as skin colour or shape of eyes but were simply verbally or conceptually imputed, defined in historical, cultural or linguistic terms, and were declared to be 'in the blood' even if not apparent to the eye. Such mystical racism was increasingly associated with extremist nationalism by the late nineteenth century (Mosse 1978, pp. 94–112).

Although it had proponents in various countries, the greatest concentration was found in Germany and Austria. There Aryans were made synonymous with Nordics, described as usually tall, blond and blue-eyed, who were identified with Germans and certain other peoples of northern and north-western Europe, and their relatives overseas. An increasing number of writers and publicists expounded the German Aryan racial concept, which was also espoused by the most prominent German composer of the period, Richard Wagner. Arguably the greatest publicist of Aryanism, however, was the English ideologue Houston Stewart Chamberlain, who moved to Germany and published in 1899 a lengthy work entitled *Foundations of the Nineteenth Century*. For Chamberlain the Germanic peoples were racially distinct and superior, possessing an 'Aryan race soul' and embodying all higher virtues. They were gravely threatened, however, by the surrounding tide of racial inferiority and must not hesitate to engage in race war to preserve themselves and win the triumph of their race (Poliakov 1971; Field 1981). Chamberlain became one of Adolf Hitler's favourite authors.

The propagation of such ideas in Germany at the close of the century was in some respects assisted by rapid social and cultural change and the secularisation of life in rapidly growing cities, which lessened resistance to new mystic ideas about nation and race. Before the close of the century there were even those who favoured adoption of a 'German religion' that sought to fuse race, nation and a perverted Lutheranism. By the beginning of the twentieth century it was thus becoming more common for the most vehement German nationalists to espouse racial doctrines.

A counterpart of the new mystical racism was the growth in many parts of Europe during the late nineteenth century of a new anti-Semitism. Modern racial anti-Semitism is distinct from traditional hostility towards Jews in so far as the latter was grounded in religious principles and might be reconciled by religious conversion, whereas the former is grounded in a perceived racial antipathy which does not admit the physical possibility of any reconciliation. Whereas traditionally Jews were denounced as the killers of Christ and the bearers of false religious ideas, the new racial anti-Semitism was based on the concept of the Jews as a separate malevolent race, a special 'anti-race' dedicated to the subversion of other societies and races. Such a doctrine held Jews to be inherently destructive by their very nature, a racial nature totally characterised by greed, materialism and the incapacity for altruism and love. Even a major scientific breakthrough such as the germ theory of disease provided a convenient metaphor – the new anti-Semitism deemed Jews to be equivalent to microbes which infected host bodies or societies as naturally and easily as disease-bearing bacteria.

The new anti-Semitism (the term had been coined in the 1860s) soon expressed itself in politics, the most extreme manifestations appearing in France, Russia and Romania. Outside of Russia and Romania, however, political anti-Semitism usually went down to defeat. The first attempts to create strongly anti-Semitic new political organisations in Germany, for example, ended in failure. Only after the trauma of the First World War did anti-Semitic forces begin to gain new momentum in central Europe, though not in France.

One of the most important new doctrines of radical nationalism which began to develop from the 1880s was a small but growing orientation toward expanding the appeal of nationalism by incorporating aspects of economic socialism to create a new formula of national socialism. This was expressed in a variety of different ways, and the initial appeals to a national socialism were not very successful. The first two German groups failed completely and disappeared, as did several tiny French entities seeking to raise the same banner between 1885 and 1905. The only national socialist parties to survive were separate democratic worker organisations for Czech and German workers in the lands of what would nearly a century later become the Czech Republic.

Thus the new concepts of revolutionary nationalism, non-rationalism, violence and racism failed to coalesce in any major new political forces prior to the First World War, but all the individual doctrines that would later make up fascism had already been voiced by ideologues and theorists prior to 1914. The impact of what was the most destructive conflict in world history to that time would be necessary to destabilise the political and social order sufficiently to permit the combination and crystallisation of most of these ideas in the first successful genuine fascist movement (Sternhell 1978).

In the history of political ideas and the classification of new forces, it is important to understand that even before the direct birth of fascism two other forms of authoritarian non-communist politics had already appeared, which may be described as the new radical right and the moderate authoritarian right. The other new forms of authoritarian politics also had nineteenth-century origins, the radical right first emerging in the neo-traditionalist and legitimist movements in France and Spain, and then in extremist nationalist movements in Austria and Russia, and later in Italy and elsewhere. The various forms of the radical right differed from fascism not so much in authoritarianism per se, or even in violence and international bellicosity, as in their social elitism, limited capacity for mass mobilisation and rejection of a revolutionary nationalism. The radical right emphasised much more the old elites, and in most cases – though not all – grounded itself in religion rather than in a radical new modern culture. Though in some respects transformative, it proposed to maintain most of the existing social and economic hierarchy and lacked the broadly revolutionary thrust of early twentieth-century fascism.

The moderate authoritarian right of early twentieth-century Europe differed from both fascism and the radical right in its aversion to violence and any new extreme of authoritarianism. Its two main sources lay in the search for a more controlled, elitist and authoritarian liberalism and in Catholic corporatism (as in the new corporatist movements in Catholic countries).

Semi-authoritarian 'neo-liberalism' had a long genealogy, going back to early and mid-nineteenth-century France and Spain, and was represented in most European countries by the early twentieth century. The moderate authoritarians or authoritarian liberals proposed only comparatively limited changes in constitutional structure to reinforce authority, often combining a more authoritarian liberalism with new corporatist proposals as well. They always proposed to give their new systems a formal legalist and constitutionalist structure, and to maintain considerable semi-pluralism. Nonetheless, it sometimes became difficult analytically to draw a dividing line between some forms of authoritarian liberalism and the less extreme expressions of the radical right, for there might be considerable potential for overlap (Payne 1995, pp. 14–19, 35–70).

Italian fascism

The term 'fascist' stems from the Italian *fasci*, meaning 'bundle' or 'union', which had often been used in the names of various radical or patriotic new Italian organisations of the late nineteenth and early twentieth centuries. The political group which eventually became the historic Fascist Party was an entity originally called the Fasci Italiani di Combattimento (Italian Combat Leagues), formed in Milan in March 1919 and made up of some 300 members who stemmed primarily from the left: former revolutionary syndicalists, former socialists led by Benito Mussolini, anarchists, a few republicans, members of the avant-garde Futurist art movement and veterans of the Arditi, the black-uniformed elite commando units of the Italian army.

The most coherent doctrine in pristine Italian fascist political thought stemmed from former revolutionary syndicalists who had come to embrace national syndicalism. They had begun to revise their original Marxist revolutionary doctrines as early as 1908, differentiating themselves more and more from the orthodox Socialist Party. Some revolutionary syndicalists had begun to take the position that a 'positive revolution' could not be carried out by the proletariat alone. Before the First World War they had begun to emphasise the importance of ethics, ideas, symbols and attention to social psychology rather than a relatively mechanical classist materialism. The syndicalists also stressed voluntarism rather than economic determinism, and the key role of an elite as revolutionary vanguard. They began to conclude that political mobilisation must be broadly cross-class and popular instead of being restricted to urban workers. Several of their theorists suggested that all productive Italians – including the hard-working middle classes – should be viewed as constituting a 'proletarian nation', discriminated against as an entire people by the existing international division of wealth and power. Thus, at least for the short term, productive industrialists were not the prime enemies of Italian workers, because they developed the nation's resources and generated employment. The real enemy was the liberal political establishment which repressed the growth of all classes. The key to positive revolution therefore lay in the people as a whole, rather than in a single class, in the nation conceived as a 'proletarian nation', and would require direct action, violence and heroic deeds (Roberts 1979, pp. 3–128; Sternhell *et al.* 1994).

After the First World War began, some revolutionary syndicalist leaders and theorists called for Italian entry into the conflict as a 'national revolutionary war', thereby achieving the first broad popular mobilisation of the nation and serving as a direct prelude to post-war domestic revolution. By the end of the fighting, some of the revolutionary syndicalists had become nationalist syndicalists, or national syndicalists for short, propounding the combination of nationalism with a broad cross-class system of national syndicalism to lead the workers and guide the economy, and to replace the liberal state. The national syndicalists were never able to dominate the subsequent fascist movement, but they would form a persistent core of 'left fascism', which, though little implemented in practice, would remain one of the two principal ideological poles of the movement (the other being the right-wing Nationalist Association group) (Gentile 1975; Gregor 1974).

Benito Mussolini, a principal pre-war leader of the ultra-revolutionary wing of the Socialist Party, had together with a few followers broken with internationalist socialism in October 1914, for reasons similar to those of the pro-war syndicalists. By the close of the conflict he had become a sort of nationalist or national socialist, though he did not use that specific label. Although he was sometimes influenced by the syndicalists, Mussolini's position had become more moderate and more opportunist, and was also influenced by the policies of patriotic socialists in France and Germany who had strongly supported their nation's war effort and had accepted a kind of national corporative structure for labour and economic relations (Gregor 1979; Milza 1999, pp. 163–217).

Unlike German National Socialism, Italian fascism had difficulty developing a clear-cut political doctrine and theory, its norms shifting and revealing considerable plasticity in the early years. The new 'ism' of fascism only began to take shape late in 1920 and in 1921, as the Fasci expanded into a mass movement in response to the apparent threat of a revolutionary and anti-nationalist socialism in Italy. By the time that the National Fascist Party (PNF) was officially organised in October 1921, the movement had changed many of its leaders and a number of its doctrines. Two months later, on 1 December, Mussolini declared in parliament that 'the Fascist programme is not a theory of dogmas about which no discussion is tolerated'. The new party officially defined itself as 'a revolutionary militia placed at the service of the nation. It follows a policy based on three principles: order, discipline, hierarchy' (Gentile 1989, p. 102). Fascists defined themselves as a new elite called to lead Italy; in economic issues they stood for 'productivism' as opposed to distributionism or collectivism and came out strongly for military and imperial expansion (De Felice 1966; Gentile 1989).

After Mussolini became constitutional prime minister of a coalition party government in October 1922, the lack of a clear-cut theory was one of the obstacles to converting this government into an organised dictatorship, which only began in January 1925. During the interim the party had incorporated the small Italian Nationalist Association, an elitist group of right radicals who espoused the doctrine of the authoritarian 'corporate state', as defined by the law professor Alfredo Rocco. Rocco and the Nationalists sought to discipline and structure aspects of fascist thought, and to eliminate leftist residues, though their success was no more than partial. Later, as minister of justice under the dictatorship, Rocco was the chief author of the so-called *leggi fascistissime* (ultra-fascist laws), which created key institutions of the new regime (Ungari 1963).

The key doctrine of the new system became that of the authoritarian corporate state, which attempted, not altogether successfully, to fuse the thinking of the national syndicalists with the right-wing authoritarian corporatism of the former Nationalists. The goal was to replace political and economic liberalism with an organic and authoritarian new structure. Thirteen national syndicates were organised under state aegis to represent and channel both capital and labour. In theory they were to be administered by a new ministry of corporations, and were later transformed into twenty-two national corporations in 1934. During 1928–9 the elected parliament was replaced by a corporative chamber whose members were in theory chosen indirectly by the party, the syndicates and other leading national institutions (Lyttleton 1973, pp. 308–424).

As early as 1925 the Fascist state was declared to be 'totalitarian', adopting a new term that had first been coined in the preceding year by one of the leaders of the liberal opposition, who had warned of the danger of a total dictatorship. This pejorative concept was soon turned into a positive one by Mussolini and certain other Fascist theorists – most notably the leading philosopher Giovanni Gentile – who invoked the doctrine of 'totalitarianism' to justify the extension of state authority over all political life and to some extent over other spheres as well (Gentile 1915; 1946). This doctrine did not propose total control of all institutions, but had an aggressive and absolutist character that might imply extension of further institutional controls in the future (Gregor 1969).

More than syndicate or corporative structure, it was the strength and potential of the 'new state' itself which became the dominant single political myth of fascism. Though different sectors of the party might have widely varying ideas about how to structure syndicates or corporations, Mussolini above all emphasised the role and character of the authoritarian national state – 'totalitarian' in the Italian terminology – which would complete the unfinished work of Italian unification and direct the construction of a powerful modern Italy, a new citizenry of Fascist Italians and finally a great new Italian empire. With the myth of the New State there soon developed a parallel cult of *Romanità*, of Fascist Italy as the third Rome to follow the splendours of the ancient empire and of the Renaissance, to become in the mid-twentieth century a modern equivalent of imperial Rome. The final myth to cap and lead the entire enterprise was the myth of the *Duce*: of Mussolini as the charismatic leader of genius whose extraordinary qualities would make it possible to guide fascism and its New State to empire and to world-historical glory.

Though the goal was to build a materially modern and powerful Italy, materialism was categorically rejected as a dominant value or goal for Italians. The 'new man' would be melded instead by Fascist ideals which would inculcate a new spirituality, a heroic idealism and a sense of mysticism which alone would make possible complete courage, self-sacrifice and heroic conquest. To implement this goal, in 1929 the regime inaugurated a School of Fascist Mysticism.

Fascism sought to cultivate this sense of the ideal and the spiritual through art, culture and education, and through elaborate public ceremonies and rituals of civic religion. It stressed even more than the Soviet Union a new style of public pageantry and performance, of politics as ritual, ceremony and theatricality, to imbue the heroic spirit, discipline and myths of fascism. Thus it inaugurated a politics of myth-making, with education, propaganda and elaborate ceremonials designed as the vehicles for implanting and expanding the Fascist spirit, while the relationship to reality tended to grow ever fainter (Gentile 1996).

Military action and nationalist violence were enshrined as not merely necessary to maintain national security, but as ultimately the highest and most ideal forms of national life. War was defined as not merely necessary to build a great new empire but as an inherent requirement both of the state and of the health of the Italian people. War was termed the truest test of any nation, without which the Italian 'new man' could not be born, and in the absence of which decadence and decline would be inevitable.

Despite the elaborate public myths and ambitions of the regime, during its first decade Mussolini's government was not especially aggressive in foreign affairs, while the 'totalitarian' corporate state in fact rested on a series of semi-pluralist compromises with the monarchy and other institutions in which the king remained head of state and broad autonomy was retained by the church, the military, the judiciary, economic institutions and even the world of art and culture. Fascist theory nonetheless posited a full 'revolution', and young Fascists eventually grew restive, calling for the *seconda ondata* (second wave) of Fascist dynamism that would produce the full fascistisation of Italian institutions, together with sweeping economic changes. A few left-wing Fascists urged that a process of economic nationalisation be initiated through the corporations.

Mussolini privately recognised some validity to these complaints, but held that full fascistisation could be brought about only through a combination of pedagogy and conquest: that is, that most Italians would only become genuine Fascists after an entire generation had been brought up under Fascist education and propaganda, and only after the martial triumph of fascism had been made complete by imperial conquest. Prior to that point a more direct takeover of Italian institutions might be successfully thwarted by conservative forces.

Roughly speaking, there were three different schools of Fascist economic thought, which, for the sake of convenience, may be termed left, right and centre. The left Fascists were to a large extent national syndicalists who advocated *sindacalismo integrato*, a complete or integral syndicalisation for representation and channelling of the economy in national syndicates to achieve not merely greater efficiency and production, but also higher income and greater social justice. This would theoretically lead to a broad transformation of the economy (though not to state collectivism), as well as providing a new syndical basis for the state. Rightist Fascists, led by Rocco and others, propounded the corporate state as a system of guidance and control to encourage greater production and national strength, but enhanced rewards for workers would depend exclusively on increased productivity. The centrists, who were moderate or 'revisionist' Fascists, took positions either of a kind of authoritarian liberalism or of a modernist technocratic corporatism. The authoritarian liberals held that the function of fascism was to create a strong nationalist state to encourage the economy but not to interfere overmuch with economic forces. The technocratic corporatists, led by Giuseppe Bottai, sought a corporatism led by experts rather than politicians, demagogues or ideologues, avoiding extreme authoritarianism or demagogy in the interest of an enlightened technocracy to maximise modernisation.

None of these programmes were consistently adopted by Mussolini, though ultimately that of Rocco enjoyed the greatest influence. During his first years in power Mussolini followed the 'liberal fascism' of the moderates, repressing leftist trade unions but otherwise interfering little with economic forces. The regime veered toward a more statist approach in 1926, but the subsequent creation of national syndicates adopted only the terminology of left fascism while rejecting 'integral syndicalism' in practice. Even after the constitution of the twenty-two corporations in 1934, Confindustria, the organisation of Italian industrialists, retained its own structure and autonomy, leading Bottai to term the system 'corporations without corporatism'.

The economic impact of the Depression after 1930 required further initiatives, but greater use of the corporations was generally shunned. The main response was direct state initiative for greater regulation and for the injection of large amounts of state investment in faltering industrial and financial institutions, until nearly 20 per cent of industrial and financial shares were owned (though not directly administered) by the state – the largest percentage anywhere in the world outside the Soviet Union.

The unsettling of the European power balance by Hitler after 1933 for the first time gave Mussolini an opportunity for what Fascist doctrine enshrined as the highest form of state achievement – imperial conquest. The seizure of Ethiopia in 1935–6 was accompanied by further expansion of state activity and regulation, threatening a closer approximation of the 'totalitarian state'. Yet, though by the late 1930s the extension of state power and institutions was greater than ten years earlier, 'totalitarianism' continued to remain more an unclear doctrine than a reality. There was no drive for total mobilisation and the established conservative institutions still enjoyed partial autonomy, though not quite so broadly as earlier.

German National Socialism

The variety, uncertain evolution and relative inspecificity of some major doctrines in Italian fascism had no counterpart in German National Socialism. Adolf Hitler provided the firm ideological leadership that Mussolini was never able to provide, so that it is little exaggeration to say that National Socialist political thought consisted essentially of the doctrines of Hitler. These had taken clear shape by 1925, when Hitler published his memoir *Mein Kampf* (*My Battle*), outlining most though not all aspects of his political thinking. Hitlerian National Socialism was grounded in the Aryan racism and international Social Darwinism of the most extreme form of German nationalism of the early twentieth century, further radicalised by the bitter experience of the First World War and its aftermath, with social and economic doctrines added by such German ideologues of the immediate post-war years as Dietrich Eckart and Gottfried Feder.

The two major categories of Hitler's thought were race and space. He held that the Aryan or Nordic race was in every way categorically superior to all other European 'races' and all those elsewhere. Because of their inherent differences and mutual competitiveness, races could no longer peacefully co-exist but inevitably strove for dominance. Thus Hitler maintained that all history was the history of racial conflict and struggle. This was not a matter of preference but simply a reflection of the natural facts of human life, as ordained throughout nature by 'God'. Hitler's concept of the deity was essentially that of a remote deism, in which the order of nature – red in tooth and claw – had been established by a remote first natural cause, and thus, so deistically construed, proper racial doctrine obeyed the 'will of God' (Ceicel 1972).

For proof of the validity of racial doctrine Hitler referred to history and to general human experience, where, he claimed, racial conflict was constantly present. The superiority of the Aryan race was amply demonstrated by the historical and cultural achievements of Aryans, whose principal incarnation was the German people. (In this regard it should be understood that Hitler was not a German nationalist in the narrow sense, for he recognised that there were numerous members of the Aryan race among other northern European peoples and privately admitted that the Germans were not racially pure. The Aryan principle was ultimately racial rather than national and thus transcended Germany, though the Germans were its primary representatives.)

The other polarity of Hitler's thought concerned space, for he held that all history ultimately involved competition between races for territory. In modern times, as all parts of the world entered into mutual competition, the Aryan race was confined primarily to the limited territory of Germany and other parts of northern Europe. Germany must thus acquire more space or *Lebensraum* (territory for living) in which to expand and from which ultimately to dominate the world, or else experience irremediable decline and destruction. The simple, vast categories of Hitler's doctrines in this respect reflected the vision of the most radical German expansionists of the First World War: *Weltmacht oder Niedergang* (world power or collapse).

Lebensraum must be achieved through conquest, since no other means were feasible. Germany must not shrink from such a task, because the alternative was its own destruction, while the superiority of the 'master race' would reveal itself in greater will power, discipline, determination and military prowess. Aryans produced the greatest artists and also the greatest warriors, but the warrior qualities of the race must be carefully cultivated and ever maintained at the highest level. Since all life was inevitably struggle, the practice of systematic violence was necessary to sustain the very qualities of racial superiority. It would be Hitler's responsibility to lead this battle, guiding Germans from one struggle to the next until the major immediate prize – dominance of most of Europe and conquest of all Soviet Eastern Europe for *Lebensraum* – had been accomplished. Ideally this should be achieved through war on only one front at a time (Jaeckel 1972).

Though all lesser races, particularly the masses of Slavs in Eastern Europe, tended to be rivals and enemies of the Aryans, one special mortal enemy existed in the form of the Jews. Hitler espoused the most extreme form of late nineteenth and early twentieth-century anti-Semitism, denouncing Jews as a special demonic anti-race, the only race whose only goal in existence was to pollute and corrupt other races. In Hitler's thinking, Jews could not be defined in normal human terms but were a sub-human form of corruption and disease equivalent to bacteria, responsible for Germany's defeat in 1918 and for the rise of communism. Hence they must be eradicated from the life of Germany and that of other lands as well, though Hitler never explained just how this was to be brought about.

The National Socialist German Workers Party was organised in Munich at the beginning of 1919 but only came to power under Hitler fourteen years later at the end of January 1933. The triumph of Nazism has often been attributed to the most extreme electoral demagogy, using the myth of the Jews as universal scapegoat and making the most exaggerated promises to counter the disastrous effects of the Depression in Germany. There is some truth to this, though in fact during the major electoral campaigns extreme anti-Semitism had to be toned down to avoid frightening voters, while the social and economic programme of National Socialism was carefully calculated to appeal to large cross-sections of the public. The Nazis inherited a tradition of German statist economics, some of whose concepts they applied vigorously to pump capital into the economy, control inflation and expand production and employment. Hitler, like most fascists, strongly upheld the principle of private property, but even more strongly employed the state to direct and channel economic activity through controls, regulations and contracts under an increasingly self-contained nationalist autarchy. Nazis sometimes called this a system of *Zwangswirtschaft*, or 'compulsion economy' (Kershaw 1985; Zitelmann 1987; Prinz and Zitelmann 1991).

Central to National Socialist doctrine was the *Führerprinzip*, or leadership principle, which recognised the complete and unconditional personal command of Hitler to lead the people, impart justice and guide the nation to greatness. The *Führerprinzip* was extended through all institutions, with the goal of creating internally strong subordinate leaders throughout – a 'nation of leaders'. German society was theoretically reconstructed as a *Volksgemeinschaft*, a 'people's community' of equal racial status but differentiated functions, under the common slogan *Gemeinnutz geht vor Eigennutz* (the common need before individual needs) (Burleigh and Wippermann 1991). A carefully cultivated policy of mass propaganda and regulation of all arts and entertainment implemented these doctrines (Voegelin 1986). Hitler was not a systematic thinker and never prepared an exact blueprint for government, so that some Nazi programmes developed rather haphazardly, but he was nonetheless able to proceed much more rapidly and thoroughly than Mussolini, because the general character of his policies had already been conceived by the time that he took over, while the extent of political crisis and fragmentation was actually much worse in Germany in 1933 than in Italy in 1922, limiting potential resistance.

However extravagant his racial theories might have seemed to non-Germans, they assisted Hitler's consolidation of power and even helped to generate broader support for expansion and conquest. Hitler's views were supplemented by those of other Nazi ideologues including Gottfried Neese and Alfred Rosenberg. Rosenberg's popular *Der Mythus des zwanzigsten*

Jahrhunderts (*The Myth of the Twentieth Century*, 1933) extolled the 'myth of the blood' and Aryan racial purity and supremacy. The ultimate goal of Nazi ideology – never explained in full detail to the German public – was the most unique of all revolutionary schemes of the century: a racial revolution to expand and purify the Aryan race in northern and eastern Europe. Hitler developed no specific blueprint or timetable for his grand campaigns of conquest, nor did he formally articulate in exact detail the planning for the most lethal of all his policies, which eventually became known as the *endgültige Auslösung* – the Final Solution, a systematic slaughter of nearly six million Jews, virtually all those to be found in what by 1942 had become Nazi-occupied Europe. This was nonetheless implied in the doctrine of all-out race war (particularly as applied in eastern Europe) which lay at the core of his thinking, as well as in his publicly expressed determination to end the 'Jewish problem' once and for all. Though Nazi theory might conceivably have permitted the mass expulsion of all Jews to other continents – a possibility briefly toyed with – Hitler's 'contagion theory' of Jewry always implied a policy of complete ruthlessness, even though the practical details had to be filled in on the march between 1939 and 1942 (Schleunes 1970; Ackermann 1970).

Italian fascism and German National Socialism shared a common 'fascist minimum' of basic principles and characteristics, which included fundamental opposition to the existing political left, right and centre (though willing temporarily to ally with sectors of the right to gain power); extreme authoritarianism; statist domination of the economy; a vitalist, non-rationalist and anti-materialist philosophy and culture; a theoretically highly positive evaluation of violence; eager espousal of war and expansion; an organic multi-class social policy; mass mobilisation and creation of a 'party army' of militia; extreme emphasis on 'virilism' or masculinity; a concept of charismatic leadership; exaltation of youth over other phases of life; and an elaborate development of ultra-nationalist civic religion and political theatre.

There were also deep differences, as well as great dissimilarity in the manner and extent to which they applied their common principles (Bessel 1996). The Italian regime was in some respects a relatively moderate form of authoritarianism which permitted varying degrees of institutional semi-pluralism (despite its abstract theory of totalitarianism), and prior to the Second World War had only carried out nine political executions, while the German regime was more extreme in every respect. Above all, Italian fascism did not espouse mystical racism and was not formally anti-Semitic. In every phase of the party's development down to 1938, the very small proportion of

Fascist Jews in the party was greater than the even tinier percentage of Jews in Italian society as a whole. In this sense Italian fascism was 'disproportionately Jewish', something for which the Nazis derided them.

When he decided in 1938 that Nazi Germany was becoming the strongest power in the world and that alliance with it was desirable, Mussolini also concluded that Italian Fascist doctrine must be adjusted to accommodate itself to the Nazi New Order. One consequence was a new 'Manifesto of Fascist Racism', which declared that because of their biological heredity and the melding of their environment and culture Italians constituted a distinct and superior race, a definition which differed from Hitlerism in giving an important place to history and education. Anti-Semitic legislation was also introduced, though never carried to the extremes of Nazi Germany.

Hungary and Romania

The other country in which a large fascist movement developed doctrines and principles most similar to those of Italy and Germany was Hungary. This land had suffered more severely from the peace settlement of 1919 than any other in Europe, and nowhere was frustrated nationalism stronger. Nowhere else were there as many fascist-type parties by the 1930s, and only in Hungary did the fascist parties approach the same high percentage of the popular vote (35 per cent or more in 1939) won by the Nazis in Germany in 1932.

Since most fascist-type parties in Hungary called themselves 'national socialists', there were eventually a half-dozen different organisations which employed that term in their titles in varying ways. The only one which became a major mass movement by the late 1930s was the Hungarist or Arrow Cross movement organised by a general staff officer, Ferenc Szalasi. Szalasi took over much but not all of Nazi doctrine, preaching the primacy of a superior Hungarian race (Szalasi was descended from an eighteenth-century Armenian immigrant named Salosian) for which he sought elaborate skull measurements, authoritarianism, militarism, charismatic leadership, an idealist-vitalist philosophy and an economic framework of statist national socialism.

There were also notable differences. While espousing nearly all the common doctrines of Italian fascism and German National Socialism, Szalasi propounded a radical and economically collectivist version of national socialism that would carry out a revolution in the ownership and distribution of wealth. The Szalasi movement was the most economically 'leftist' of all the larger fascist parties. It was also more moderate in terms of violence and anti-Semitism. Szalasi sought to recreate a Hungarian empire, if possible without war, though he offered staunch support for what he termed Hitler's 'Weltanschauung War' against the Soviet Union. Though Jews were frequently violently assaulted by the Arrow Cross, Szalasi proposed merely to expel them all from Hungary (Nagy-Talavera 2001, pp. 75–266; Szöllösi-Janze 1989, pp. 101–282).

By 1939 the Arrow Cross had become a major threat to the right-wing Hungarian government, but since the latter was quasi-authoritarian, it repressed the movement by force. Only later, at the very close of 1944, did Hitler install Szalasi as puppet dictator in the part of Hungary not yet occupied by the Red Army, but the radical national socialist decrees of the short-lived puppet regime remained largely on paper.

The only other fascist movements to develop significant strength were typologically more marginal ones which sought in contradictory ways to combine fascism with the dominant national religion – Orthodoxy in Romania and Catholicism in Spain and Croatia. The Legion of the Archangel Michael, organised in Romania by Corneliu Zelea Codreanu in 1927, was the most singular of the lesser fascist movements. The Legionary movement – later known from the name of its militia as the Iron Guard – was inspired in large measure by National Socialism and fascism and accepted virtually every single one of their common principles. It nonetheless presented a somewhat different concept of the revolutionary *Omul nou*, or 'new man', the title of the party's main periodical. Whereas the Nazi new man was a product of race and that of Italian fascism the result of Fascist pedagogy and revolution, the new man of the Romanian Legionaries would enjoy spiritual rebirth through Legionary doctrine and action and through the teachings and spirituality of the Romanian Orthodox church. Codreanu emphasised that all evil and troubles originate in the heart and that the primary goal must be spiritual regeneration, to achieve ultimately the eternal salvation of all Romanians living or dead. All regular Legionary meetings began with a brief religious service, which was not merely a formality.

The Legionaries murdered several of their leading opponents, assaulted and killed Jews, and were taught by Codreanu that life was unending struggle requiring violence and war, though the latter was not justified on quite the same terms as in Italy and Germany. Codreanu and other Legionary theorists sought to resolve the contradiction of a sort of 'Christian fascism' by reference to the sinful and debauched character of the present dispensation, full of cruelty and sometimes necessary violence, as contrasted with a world ultimately redeemed by Christ. The political thought and deeds of the Legion were largely governed by the former, even though the ultimate goal was theoretically the latter. Individual Legionary assassins sometimes sought to resolve this contradiction by voluntarily surrendering to the authorities for their own imprisonment and execution. A few, at least, recognised that the systematic violence of the Legion could never be justified by Christian doctrine, but contended that it was required for the present temporal rebirth of the Romanian nation. They might then profess that their love and self-sacrifice for the cause of the people was so great that they were willing to suffer eternal damnation as the ineluctable price of destroying the enemies of Romania, an absolutely indispensable task (Heinen 1986, pp. 127–414).

In Romania as in Hungary the fascist movement was forcibly repressed by an authoritarian government. As large mobilised multi-class nationalist organisations that could only be developed within the culture and institutions of a modern European polity, fascist movements had little opportunity to gain power by armed force or insurrection, as in the case of communist movements in less-developed lands or amid disturbed wartime conditions. Fascist movements of the inter-war period required freedom to mobilise political support and win allies for taking power within democratic or semi-democratic systems, and thus were usually foiled by the authoritarian non-fascist governments of eastern and southern Europe.

Only when the Romanian polity collapsed under the weight of German expansion in 1940 did the Legion have the opportunity to enter government as the junior partner of the new military dictator, Marshal Antonescu. By this time Codreanu had been murdered by the preceding regime, and the Legion revealed an absence of leadership combined with the most extreme and incoherent behaviour. In Romania there was no Hitler or Mussolini, and the Legion's tendency towards the most intense non-rationalism prevented the development of functional policies. Gaining the reluctant approval of a Hitler who primarily sought in Romania a reliable military ally, Antonescu soon rejected the Legion as irrational and destructive, crushing it in an attempted uprising of January 1941 (Nagy-Talavera 2001, pp. 431–76).

Fascism outside Europe

By the 1930s efforts were made to imitate fascism or Nazism in almost every single European country, in much of Latin America, in several regions of the Middle East and in South Africa. Elsewhere, those conditions which encouraged fascism in Italy, Germany and Hungary were lacking. In the stable democracies of northern Europe, in particular, fascist parties were a complete failure. This was also the case in Latin America, where twentieth-century mass mobilisation had not yet developed, nationalism was less intense and there was little sense of direct international threat or competition. The impact of fascism was somewhat stronger in South Africa, borne by racial doctrine and also encouraged by the fact that approximately one-sixth of the white population was of German origin. Nonetheless, two different parties patterned on European fascism failed, and the system of racial apartheid (separation) developed after the Second World War was led by the Afrikaner National Party, which maintained a 'racial democracy' for the white population, guaranteeing for them constitutionalism and direct elections. Though undoubtedly influenced by European racism, the South African system created a unique hybrid model of its own which lacked most of the features of generic fascism.

The non-European power which in the thinking of most observers most nearly approximated European fascism during the era of the Second World War was Imperial Japan. It developed its own form of Japanese ethno-racism, extreme military and imperial ambitions, and a political culture which fostered discipline and unity for aggressive war. A number of small Japanese extremist groups were strongly influenced by European fascism – more by Germany than by Italy – and sometimes used concepts of 'national socialism'. Yet none of the petty proto-fascist groups gained the slightest degree of political power in Japan, which in the 1930s had scarcely attained the level of political modernisation of the Germany of twenty years earlier. Thus the Japan of the Second World War in many respects resembled a more radical version of the Imperial Germany of the First World War. Rather than undergoing a fascist revolution, Imperial Japan was grounded in a radicalised neo-traditionalism of emperor worship that was increasingly dominated by the military (like Germany after 1914). No new political system was introduced, though all the non-left parties were combined in an umbrella grouping in 1940. Regular competitive elections were maintained on the national level, however, and the opposition registered a large minority of the vote in the balloting of 1942. Japan lacked the preconditions for full fascism in terms of social, cultural, economic and political development, although, even without an equivalent ideology or a new political regime, it did provide the nearest functional equivalent to a fascist system outside Europe (Payne 1995, pp. 328–54).

The Second World War

The Second World War was in large measure unleashed by the European fascist powers, and brought both the climax and the destruction of fascism. Germany's great military triumphs between 1939 and 1942 produced a sympathetic and opportunist trend toward some degree of fascistisation in a number of other countries, a trend which waxed and waned according to the military situation. As long as this lasted, it also produced a desire on the part of a certain minority of Europeans to align themselves with the Nazi racial hierarchy as well, but, as in the cases of the pre-war movements, this took distinct forms in different countries. In France, for example, neo-fascist parties maintained a somewhat more moderate approach (Milza 1987).

This trend was momentarily encouraged by certain ideological modifications of German policy and propaganda as the war became more difficult. The German aggression had originally been presented as a revolutionary struggle for a racial and anti-Semitic New Order, though this had had the effect of limiting support in other countries. By 1941, the Nazi cause was being presented as the leader of Europe in a struggle for European civilisation against the twin menaces of Soviet communism and Asian barbarism on the one hand and Anglo-American materialist plutocracy on the other. Such an approach gained sympathy for a time in certain religious and conservative quarters. It also paralleled but did not coincide with the approach articulated by Italian Fascist theorists in 1941, as they worked out schemes of Fascist leadership of a new international hierarchy in the Mediterranean and part of the Middle East that could embrace Arab society as well.

Meanwhile an elaborate network of satellite and occupation puppet regimes had been formed by Hitler. The first satellite state, nominally independent Slovakia, harboured an active fascist minority but was led by the Catholic Slovak People's Party, which kept domestic fascism under control. Similarly, the most important of the new satellite states, Vichy France under Marshal Pétain, was authoritarian and corporative in structure, but only late in the day gave limited representation in the government to any of the new French fascist parties. Nor were fascist parties normally given power in territories under direct military occupation, with the principal exception of Vidkun Quisling's Nasjonal Samling (National Assembly), after Quisling was made minister-president of Norway, still under direct German military occupation, on 1 February 1942.

The only satellite regime in which a fascist-type party was directly handed state power on an autonomous basis was in the new Independent State of

Croatia, created under the Ustashi government of May 1941. 'Ustasha' stands for 'insurgent', the Ustashi movement having been founded in 1929 by a lawyer, Ante Pavelic, as the most extreme sector of Croatian nationalism. Though Croats were oppressed under the authoritarian pre-war Yugoslav system that had been dominated by Serbs, the clandestine, terrorist Ustashi had gained little support and for some years had not developed a very elaborate ideology.

After receiving power from Hitler following his destruction of Yugoslavia, Pavelic and the Ustashi installed a set of policies inspired in part by Nazi Germany. They accommodated themselves to Nazi racism by defining a new identity for Croatians as a 'Gothic' race of Aryans, different from and superior to Slavic peoples. The Ustashi state failed to develop a fully conceptualised and developed system, but attained the gruesome distinction of being the only non-German regime to approach that of the Nazis in genocidal potential, carrying out mass slaughters of Serbs, Jews and Gypsies, more sadistic in practical execution than the operations of the SS. There may have been as many as 300,000 victims.

After Fascist Italy collapsed under military defeat in 1943, Hitler installed Mussolini as head of a new puppet Fascist regime in German-occupied northern Italy. During this final phase, the Duce and his Fascist diehards sought to recapture some of the pristine radicalism of the earliest years of the movement. Their new state was entitled the Italian Social Republic, and fascism was defined once more as a revolutionary people's movement which had been subverted by Italian conservatism and the bourgeoisie. New worker legislation was established to create elaborate workers' councils and profit-sharing in industry, but German occupation authorities completely ignored such measures in practice.

Unlike in Nazi Germany, fascism was generally rejected by the bulk of the population, but the rump Fascist state did maintain minority support among a sector of Italian society. During 1943–4 a vicious civil war was waged in northern Italy between the Resistance bands and the Fascist paramilitary. The third puppet fascist regime in occupied Europe, the Arrow Cross state in western Hungary that was mentioned earlier, was even more short-lived and artificial.

Ultimately, only the anti-communist aspect of the Europeanist myth projected by the Nazi imperium had much appeal, and even this declined with the waning of German military power. After the complete military destruction of Nazism and fascism, only an ideological residue of a kind of extremist 'Europeanist nationalism' was left behind, which would later be invoked by some of the neo-fascist organisations of the second half of the twentieth century.

The Spanish Falange

The most long-lived of the marginal fascisms was the Falange Española (Spanish Phalanx), organised by José Antonio Primo de Rivera in 1933. A charismatic young lawyer and aristocrat, José Antonio, as he generally became known, was the eldest son of the military dictator who had governed Spain from 1923 to 1930. The regime of the latter, the country's first military dictatorship, had been a failure, among other things because it had lacked an organised programme and ideology. Young José Antonio was obsessed by the desire to vindicate the work of his father, and became convinced that the appropriate vehicle and doctrine was a fascist-type movement modelled on that of Italy.

The new party was also at first a failure, for the preconditions for fascism prominent in Italy, Germany and Hungary were lacking in Spain. Spain had prospered from its neutrality in the First World War and was not threatened or aggrieved by any foreign power. Spanish nationalism ranged from weak to non-existent, and the country lacked imperial ambition. Its society was not as secularised as that of central Europe, so that most of the reaction to the left was monopolised by political Catholicism, leaving very little space for a secular fascist force. Conversely, in a land of weak nationalism it proved impossible to nationalise any part of the left, while even the impact of the Depression was more moderate, and the unemployment which did develop was exploited almost exclusively by the left. In the elections of 1936 the Falange drew only 0.7 per cent of the popular vote, one of the weakest showings of any fascist party in Europe.

What saved the movement was the outbreak of the Spanish Civil War in July 1936, a revolutionary/counter-revolutionary conflict marked by numerous political executions and escalating radicalism on both sides. Total civil war discredited moderate and democratic politics, enabling the extremist Falange to become a mass movement for the first time. Even more important, however, was the fact that in such a conflict the leadership of the right had been seized by the military, while nearly all the original leaders of the Falange had been executed by the left. The new dictator of the rightist or Nationalist zone, General Francisco Franco, thus held undisputed power, not to be challenged by a civilian political movement. He was determined to build an enduring new authoritarian regime that would avoid the ideological and political vacuum of what he termed 'the Primo de Rivera mistake'. In need of a political organisation, he found one in the large but amorphous and semi-leaderless Falange. Seizing control of it in April 1937, Franco merged it with extreme right-wing forces and presented the eclectic results as the new official single state party of Spain.

Throughout his life Franco held to basic political principles of nationalism, authoritarianism, imperialism, right-wing Catholicism and cultural traditionalism, shedding only the imperialism in his later years. Not a revolutionary fascist, he appreciated the examples of the new German and Italian states and what he perceived as the mobilising and indoctrinating potential of fascism, which he sought to utilise. The Twenty-Six Points of the Falange, largely modelled on Italian fascism, became the official political programme of the new Spanish state, though Franco made it clear at the outset that he considered some aspects of political doctrine to be subject to modification. The semi-fascist identity of the new regime was thus somewhat ambiguous, resting as it did on a coalition formed mainly by non-fascist right-wing elements. The main spiritual force behind the Nationalist regime was not Falangist mysticism but neo-traditionalist Catholicism, to which the government emphasised its full dedication. This created an ideological bipolarity and tension that at first could not be resolved. On the one hand, ideologues and propagandists of the regime declared that all political thought and doctrine was grounded in Catholicism, just as the Falangists of the new state party proclaimed total Catholic orthodoxy, but the latter often privately criticised what they considered the clericalism of the regime and a few even proposed a schismatic 'national Catholicism' somewhat similar to the 'German Christianity' of certain Nazis. So long as German military power remained predominant, Falangists proclaimed the inevitability of the 'national syndicalist revolution' and some of them looked towards the full fascistisation of Spain.

These issues were decided by the course of the Second World War in Europe, during the main part of which Spain was an official 'non-belligerent' (not technically 'neutral') and clearly tilted toward the Axis. Falangists, if not all sectors of the regime, hoped to participate fully in a new fascist Europe. The first strong sign that this was never likely to take shape was the collapse of Fascist Italy – always considered a sort of big brother by the Spanish regime – in July 1943, after which Franco's government began to institute a limited political and ideological defascistisation (Payne 1999).

In 1945 the Spanish system attempted to carry out a political metamorphosis, relying primarily on its Catholic polarity to replace most of its fascist polarity. It was proclaimed a regime of Catholic corporatism based on papal religious and social teaching, resting on religion, state syndicates, intermediate institutions and the Catholic church, a regime that had never embraced fascism and had never contemplated becoming a military ally of Nazi Germany. The Falangist state party was not dissolved but was downgraded and rebaptised the 'National Movement', an abstract and ambiguous label. The regime was slowly but steadily defascistised, though the fascistic Twenty-Six Points were never replaced as official doctrine until 1958, when new 'Principles of the National Movement' were adopted, eliminating most fascist residues and embracing religion, unity, international peace, the family and constructive social institutions. The semi-fascist past of the Franco regime was never forgotten by social democratic western Europe, making it impossible for Spain to join NATO or the European Common Market. In its later years, the regime emphasised rapid economic development and steadily liberalised its domestic policies, until in the final decade before the Generalissimo's death in 1975 it had become an increasingly depoliticised bureaucratic authoritarianism which sought to justify itself more and more by its achievements in social and economic development (Payne 1987).

Neo-fascism: the sequelae of fascist thought and politics

No ideology in modern political thought and discourse has been so rapidly and thoroughly discredited as that of fascism after 1945. This was due to revulsion at the crimes committed by fascists, particularly those by German Nazis, by the guilt imputed to them for the immeasurable destruction wrought by the Second World War, and finally by their complete defeat and obliteration at the close of that conflict. Fascists had proclaimed war as the highest test of a polity and a culture, and had failed completely at their own test.

Though fascism ceased to exist as a historical force, certain fascist ideas and goals survived in the political thinking of small minorities, to the extent that neo-fascism was a permanent, if completely marginal, feature of the political landscape in the late twentieth century and probably will be in the early twenty-first century as well. Neo-fascism has, however, been completely unable to escape the 'neo-fascist contradiction', which is simply that to the degree to which any neo-fascist party, cult or splinter group hopes to become a genuine political force as distinct from a lunatic fringe, it must to an almost equivalent degree defascistise itself, at least to a certain extent. Genuine hardcore neo-fascist grouplets which maintain the pristine ideology have been doomed to total isolation; conversely, those movements which have neared or broken the 5 per cent electoral barrier have always adopted somewhat more moderate and post-fascist doctrines.

Political groups often called neo-fascist can be broadly divided into two general categories. The first consists of the more or less genuine neo-fascists or neo-Nazis, who subscribe to all or almost all of the original ideologies and exist as small sects in almost every country of the world. There have been literally hundreds of them in the late twentieth century, and the general rule is that the greater the number of individual sects, the less significant they are as a whole, splintering into tiny mutually anathematising rivals. The other and much more important category consists of the right-wing nationalist parties which propose corporatist or other hardline changes in policies and procedures of a greater or lesser confrontational or authoritarian character, but have dropped any categorical fascist minimum so as to attract broader support.

One feature of a significant number of neo-fascist groups has been their espousal of a broader Europeanist identity in distinction from the intense individual chauvinism of the historical movements. Most have not embraced a mystical racism similar to that of the former central European parties, though a minority have done so. Neo-fascist thought has not developed any major body of new doctrine or any noteworthy new political thinkers. Its concepts have been drawn either directly from the historical movements or reflect pragmatic adaptations to later developments (Bardeche 1961). Some neo-fascists preach a 'left' fascism of social radicalism or revolution and semi-collectivism, though most maintain the principle of private property with a greater or lesser degree of state intervention.

Though the historic example of fascism and certain aspects of fascist doctrine continue to attract small numbers of extremists, it has been impossible to propagate the doctrines of fascism to any significant extent since 1945 because their form and content are severely dated and have had very little appeal in the drastically altered cultural context of the later twentieth century. In the atomic era fascist concepts of violence and war simply made no sense, while the philosophy of vitalism and anti-materialism lacked broad appeal during the great era of economic expansion which followed the Second World War. The climate of culture and society turned toward ever greater individualism, short-circuiting any possible attraction to fascist principles of group and racial identity and self-sacrifice. Knowledge of the Second World War and of the era of fascism also served as a significant source of inoculation.

Some of the specific individual ideas of fascism have lived on, and will perhaps be of some individual importance in the early twentieth-first century as well. These include such principles as extreme nationalism, charismatic leadership, political authoritarianism and statist economics, which, however discredited in most of Europe and the Americas, live on in certain other parts of the world. In no case, however, do non-Western movements and regimes simply mimic the complete ideology and systems of the classic fascist movements, for in every instance those individual features and doctrines which overlap with fascism are combined with more recent and indigenous characteristics, which in every case produce distinct morphologies.

The historic fascist movements were an epochal phenomenon of early twentieth-century Europe and cannot be specifically reproduced several generations later, for history never repeats itself exactly. There will be new authoritarian regimes, but they will not have all or even most of the unique characteristics of European fascism. Fascism was a product particularly of the nationalist-imperialist conflicts of early twentieth-century Europe and of the ambitions of the newer states or powers formed during the third quarter of the nineteenth century. Its ideas had a clear genealogy, stemming remotely from aspects of the Enlightenment and of Romanticism but drawing their specific form and content from the ideas and doctrines of the cultural crisis of the *fin de siècle*, catalysed by the consequences of the First World War and of the Great Depression. Though most early twentieth-century Europeans were not susceptible to fascism, it was shaped by influences and attitudes found primarily in the culture of Europe during the era of the world wars, and generated the most violent political forces of that singular age of conflict which produced both domestic and international tensions of unique intensity. It is unlikely that such a combined political and cultural constellation will reappear. The new forces of political violence and oppression of the twenty-first century will probably use some of the ideas of fascism, but will be unable to reproduce its full pattern, even should they so desire.

6
Conservatism

NOËL O'SULLIVAN

Although conservatism in the twentieth century has yielded a diverse body of literature, it is unified by a common object of hostility: namely, the progressive view of humankind and society. The main conservative objection to this view is that it vastly exaggerates the directive power of human reason, on the one hand, and the creative power of human will, on the other. Reason, as the British conservative Michael Oakeshott maintained, is always parasitic on tradition, which it can only ever 'abridge' (Oakeshott 1991 [1962]). So far as the relative impotence of human will is concerned, the American thinker John P. East strikes a characteristically conservative note when he writes (in the course of a sympathetic exposition of the thought of Leo Strauss) that: 'man is not the Creator, he is the creature; he is not the potter, he is the clay. It is then man who adapts to creation, not creation to man – to propose the latter is to propose perverting the natural order of things' (East 1988, p. 265).

This critique of rationalism and voluntarism is supported by the conviction that twentieth-century politics is dominated by a conception of human nature which mistakenly implies that humans are malleable and perhaps perfectible creatures of infinite possibilities. Such a view permits any existing social order to be portrayed as a system of oppression, regardless of the fact that a majority of its members may support it.

If conservatives generally agree on what they reject, they are less united on what they support. Traditionally, they have favoured an organic theory of society, in which individual reason and will do not construct but are produced by the social order. As soon as they develop the organic ideal in more detail, however, conflicting opinions emerge – to such an extent, as will become apparent, that in some forms of conservatism the organic ideal all but disappears. These conflicting options correspond to five distinct schools of conservative political thought, each of which is considered below.

The first three may be termed the reactionary, the radical and the moderate schools respectively. In the case of a fourth school, the New Right group of thinkers which became influential in the late 1960s, the organic theme is often only vestigial, whilst a fifth presents a postmodern and wholly 'post-organic' form of conservatism.

Varieties of conservatism

Reactionary conservatism

The central theme of reactionary conservatism has remained constant throughout the nineteenth and twentieth centuries. It is that political order is impossible without broader spiritual and cultural foundations which arrest the corrosive effect of rationalism by acknowledging the irrational side of human nature, the existence of natural inequality, the pervasive character of evil, and the inescapable place of the hierarchical principle in society. Since modern democratic states lack these foundations, they are regarded as inherently self-destructive.

During the first half of the twentieth century, Maurice Barrès and Charles Maurras gave the reactionary tradition a new lease of life by abandoning the tendency of earlier thinkers such as Joseph de Maistre and the Vicomte de Bonald to idealise the *ancien régime* (de Maistre 1884; Lively 1965; McClelland 1970, pp. 37–60; de Bonald 1864; Menczer 1952, pp. 87–95). Instead, Barrès invoked a mystical nationalism which anticipated the restoration of *La France* by a charismatic leader with an authority of purely democratic origin (Barrès 1925; McClelland 1970, pp. 143–211). Using a somewhat different strategy, Maurras attempted to adapt reactionary philosophy to the secular world of the twentieth century by abandoning the theological perspective adopted by earlier thinkers in favour of a scientific one based on an empirical study of the objective laws of history (Maurras 1954; McClelland 1970, pp. 213–304). No amount of intellectual ingenuity, however, could save him from the danger of political marginality which is the predicament to which the wholesale rejection of mass society typically condemns reactionary thinkers at large. Of particular interest here are the five main responses of reactionaries to this predicament.

The first has been to embrace the revolutionary cause, albeit in a somewhat half-hearted way. It was this response which led a number of reactionaries into the fascist camp during the inter-war era. A good example is the rather unenthusiastic support given to the Nazi Party by Oswald Spengler in 1932, when he voted for Hitler. 'Hitler is a fool', Spengler declared, 'but one must support the movement' (Hamilton 1971). Spengler's support may be traced back to *The Decline of the West*, in which he declared that the modern West was faced by an era of cultural and political decline from which only 'Caesarism' could save it (Spengler 1926). What he naïvely failed to recognise was that Hitler's demagogic determination to base Nazism on the perpetual mobilisation of the masses meant that it had no kinship at all with the essentially static kind of conservatism represented by the 'Caesars' (such as Frederick the Great of Prussia) whom he admired.

A second, closely related, reactionary response has been to advocate the use of violent, extra-constitutional political techniques whilst nevertheless trying to avoid the slide into fascism. This was the tightrope walked by, for example, Maurras and the Action Française, which Maurras helped to found in 1899 as the principal means for promoting a royalist and Catholic version of French nationalism. Maurras's balancing act, however, did not prevent his advocacy of violence discrediting him to such an extent that he was eventually disowned by both the church and the Pretender (the comte de Paris) – by those, that is, whose cause he supported (Weber 1962; Curtis 1959).

A third response has permitted greater accommodation to mass democracy: it consists of support for a charismatic leader who claims to represent his nation in a more profound way than mere constitutional representatives can. As Barrès in particular has maintained, what validates this claim is the ability of the true leader to penetrate directly to the inner, unchanging mystical unity of the nation that is always waiting to be reawakened, but lies buried at times beneath the corrupting pursuit of selfish interests that is prone to dominate mass democratic politics (Curtis 1959). By focusing on the need for charismatic leadership, Barrès was able to detach the reactionary ideal of spiritual unity from a past golden age and present it instead as one to be achieved in a future political condition. In a form still compatible with constitutional politics, echoes of this mode of thinking served to bolster the French Gaullist Party in the post-Second World War decades. In inter-war Germany, however, the cult of charismatic leadership shaded over into the wholly demagogic, completely anti-constitutional, conception of leadership found in fascist ideology.

Fourthly, the reactionary may seek consolation for his marginality by defiantly resorting to a variety of dangerous pursuits that display contempt for the spiritual mediocrity of modern mass society. These pursuits have often reflected a heroic cult of Nietzschean paganism, in marked contrast with the Christian values generally favoured by reactionary thinkers during the nineteenth century. Thus Henri de Montherlant turned to bull-fighting (Montherlant 1927; 1960, pp. 7–11), while Curzio Malaparte favoured duelling (Hamilton 1971, pp. 73–4). Despite this cult of the 'existential moment' – that is, of the encounter with death – the life expectancy of twentieth-century reactionaries appears to have been remarkably long.

Finally, the reactionary may adopt a policy of inner exile, withdrawing into a cult of literary, aesthetic and spiritual excellence that enables him to achieve maximum distance from the spiritual vulgarity by which he deems himself to be surrounded. In England, for example, the poet T. S. Eliot combined learning, aestheticism and religiosity in a vision of contemporary mass society as a spiritual wasteland in which the decline of Christianity combines with universal materialism to make Western democracies almost indistinguishable from the totalitarian regimes. Indeed, totalitarian states may even claim to be spiritually superior, since they have shown 'a steadiness of purpose not always found in democracies' in 'providing their national life with a foundation for morality – the wrong kind, perhaps, but a good deal more of it' (Eliot 1939). The authoritarian leanings evident in Eliot's sympathy for the 'spirituality' of totalitarianism also led him to express admiration for the ideas of Maurras (Eliot 1928) and accounts for his indifference to constitutional limits on power in his portrait of a Christian society (Eliot 1939). Similar authoritarian leanings were generated by, for example, the aesthetic elitism of the Spanish philosopher Ortega y Gasset, who castigated the 'dehumanisation' he found in modern mass society but could do no more than retreat in face of it into a simplistic dream of a world reorganised 'into two orders or ranks: the illustrious and the vulgar' (Ortega y Gasset 1968 [1925]; Ortega y Gasset 1963 [1930]). Perhaps the most viable consolation was found by the Japanese reactionary, Yukio Mishima, who opted for swimming (Sprawson 1992, pp. 294–9).

Radical conservatism

Diametrically opposed to the static, hierarchical reactionary vision of organic order stands a school of thought which offers a radical solution to the principal problem of conservatism in the twentieth century – the problem, that is, of deciding on a realistic response to an age in which tradition appears to be dying and regard for authority, individual excellence, personal discipline and selfless patriotism has no place. This school found its earliest and most impressive representatives in inter-war Germany, where thinkers such as Moeller van den Bruck, Ernst Jünger, Carl Schmitt and other opponents of the Weimar Republic sought to re-establish conservatism on a new, revolutionary foundation (Moeller van den Bruck 1971 [1923]; Jünger 1981 [1932]; Schmitt 1976 [1927]). Although some of these thinkers were associated with Nazism, the Cold War era saw the advent of a new generation of revolutionary conservatives who insisted that their movement had no connection with fascism of any kind. In Italy, for example, a form of radical conservatism inspired the *Nuovo Destra* (Eatwell 1996, pp. 195–215), while in France (Johnson 1995) it was associated in particular with Alain de Benoist and the *Nouvelle Droite* (Benoist 1980).

In order to distinguish themselves from fascists, the post-Second World War radical conservatives rejected such concepts as the leader principle (in its individualised form, at least) and racist doctrine (see chapter 5). They tended in addition to adopt a supranational ideal of European unity in order to offer effective opposition to the USA and the USSR. Finally, they forswore the use of extra-constitutional action, favouring instead the revolutionary strategy of the Gramscian left, on the ground, as a leading apologist for Germany's *Neue Recht* Pierre Krebs observed, that Gramsci was the first to understand that 'In order to exist at all, political power is . . . dependent on a cultural power diffused within the masses' (Krebs 1982, pp. 82–6).

Even if the fascist label is successfully avoided, however, it is difficult for radical conservatism to avoid the charge of demagogy. That accusation is elicited, in particular, by Carl Schmitt, for whom the distinction of friend and enemy is the essence of political existence (Schmitt 1976 [1927]). Since the enemy may be an entirely imaginary one, the claim to offer a 'realist' version of the organic ideal is difficult to distinguish from demagogic scapegoating.

Moderate conservatism

The primary concern of moderate conservatism is to reconcile the potential conflict between the requirements of the limited state and the interventionism necessitated by modern industrial society. Since the balance may be struck in many different ways, moderate conservatism is no more homogeneous than the two schools already considered. In practice, however, two forms have been especially influential.

One of these is Michael Oakeshott's endeavour in *On Human Conduct* (1975) to extricate the classical ideal of civil association from its long connection with liberal contractualism and rationalism. The principal feature of Oakeshott's revised model is its emphasis on the formal, non-purposive nature of the civil ideal. Since this formal emphasis means that no particular religious, moral, political or other substantive beliefs have to be held as a condition of citizenship, Oakeshott's conservatism is sufficiently flexible to accommodate the high degree of social diversity that characterises contemporary Western states. The chief difficulty, however, is his optimistic tendency to assume the existence of an organic, largely self-sustaining pluralist society.

A similar optimism is also evident in, for example, the version of the civil model developed in France by Oakeshott's contemporary, Raymond Aron, who explained that what it entails is

> Not universal suffrage, a belated and disputable political institution, [nor] the parliamentary system, which is one democratic procedure among others, but . . . the freedom whose historical conditions have been the duality of temporal and spiritual power, the limitation of State authority and the autonomy of [such institutions as] the universities (Aron 1957, p. 269).

After the Second World War a self-sustaining organic social order could not be taken for granted. This led to the second form of moderate conservatism, which is the 'middle way' compromise with collectivism that dominated Western European politics for some three decades after 1945.

In the British case, four considerations explain the conservative shift in a collectivist direction. One was the Tory tradition of paternalism, which looked favourably on socialist policies in so far as they appeared to promote its own 'one-nation' ideal. A second was the apparent success of wartime controls in ending the mass unemployment of the 1930s, a success which encouraged an uncritical post-war belief in the political efficacy of large-scale economic planning. A third was the work of Maynard Keynes in legitimating deficit finance. The fourth, purely pragmatic, consideration was the effectiveness of the 'middle way' compromise in securing electoral success. The price of that success, however, was a deepening crisis of conservative identity, as opinion polls revealed that voters could no longer distinguish between conservatism and moderate socialism. The result was a split between conservative intellectuals, who called for a major rethinking of the principles and practice of conservatism on libertarian lines (Blake and Patten 1976), and those who continued to defend the collectivist compromise (Gilmour 1977). To present this as imitating Labour, Gilmour insisted, was a gross error because 'The Conservatives could not imitate Labour even if they wished. They are not a class party. Even in the October 1974 election, when they secured only 35 per cent of the vote, the Conservatives had a wider base of support and were a far more national party than Labour' (Gilmour 1977, p. 257). Only the collectivist compromise, he maintained, could preserve the 'national' basis of conservatism. His view, however, did not give confidence to those who believed that conservatism had lost its way during the three post-war decades.

On the continent, similar misgivings appeared about the ideal of a social market economy to those that emerged in Britain about the middle way (Friedrich 1955; Peacock and Willgerodt 1989). Notable defenders of that ideal included German thinkers such as Walter Eucken and Franz Böhm (see chapter 7) and the influential Swiss thinker Wilhelm Röpke. Quite early in the post-war era, however, Röpke had emphasised the tension at the heart of it when he wrote that it was impossible to 'have political and spiritual liberty without also choosing liberty in the economic field and rejecting the necessarily unfree collectivist economic order' (Röpke n.d. [1958], p. 105). Despite reservations of this kind, the practical success of the collectivist compromise meant that widespread criticism did not emerge until the late 1960s, when the so-called New Right gave voice to growing concern about rising public expenditure, inflation and new social problems.

The New Right

Members of the heterogeneous group of thinkers and publicists to which the New Right label was applied in the Anglo-American world were distinguished from supporters of the more radical, culturally oriented *Nouvelle Droite*, *Nuovo Destra* and *Neue Recht* mentioned above by their narrower concern with defending the limited state. For the New Right, the meaning of that commitment may be summarised in the proposition that liberty is indivisible – in other words, that liberal democracy and a free market order are inseparable. This doctrine was defended, in particular, by invoking Hayek's theory of the free market as more than a mere device for organising supply and demand (Hayek 1976 [1960]). For him, it exemplifies the spontaneous, undesigned type of social order which has been destroyed by modern constructivist rationalism, with its faith in planning – the faith, Hayek believes, which gave birth to totalitarianism. Liberty cannot flourish until we recapture the wisdom of such eighteenth-century thinkers as Hume, Adam Smith, Adam Ferguson and Burke, who appreciated that reason cannot function independently of the unconscious process of cumulative growth of the institutions and practices in which it is always embedded (Hayek 1976

[1960], p. 57). Although reason may become conscious of the limits thus intrinsic to it, it can never render them transparent and convert them into the conscious knowledge which would permit rational central planning of the social order.

Although the anti-rationalist character of Hayek's concept of spontaneous order links him to conservatism, he rejected the label, partly because conservatism does not share 'the faith in the spontaneous forces of adjustment which makes the liberal accept changes without apprehension' (Hayek 1976 [1960], p. 400), and partly because conservatism shares with constructivist rationalism the belief that order is 'the result of the continuous attention of authority' (Hayek 1976 [1960], p. 401). Conservative critics, in turn, have rejected Hayek's tendency to subordinate social and political issues to the goal of economic progress, and have also maintained that Hayek fails to appreciate the destructive impact of the spontaneous market order on moral and civil values (Gray 1993, pp. 32–9; Kristol 1970).

Although the economic strand in New Right thought was the most influential, three other (potentially conflicting) ones were also significant. One derived from the libertarian theory of the minimal state developed in the USA in contractual form by Nozick (1974), and in more Nietzschean form by the Russian émigré Ayn Rand (1961). A second drew on research which purported to show that welfare legislation had unwittingly produced a dependency culture that perpetuated the very evils it set out to remedy. A third reasserted the dependence of political unity on the maintenance of a homogeneous national identity, an especially controversial position at a time of increasing cultural diversity (Scruton 1990).

Although the New Right mounted a powerful challenge to the middle way version of moderate conservatism (see chapter 2), the various strands of thought it deployed did not provide either an intellectually coherent or an electorally viable conservative alternative to it. Since the quest for such an alternative has been pursued with especial rigour in the USA, it is the American debate that must now be considered (Dunn and Woodard 1996; Gottfried 1993). Before doing so, however, it is necessary to consider briefly the view that the American political tradition is wholly unique, and therefore irrelevant to European concerns.

Emphasis on the 'exceptionalist' character of American experience is central, for example, to Frank S. Meyer's *What is Conservatism?* (1964). Meyer, who had been converted from communism to conservatism after reading Hayek's *The Road to Serfdom* (Hayek 1944; first US edn 1956), attempted to draw a clear distinction between the American conservative tradition and the old world one (Meyer 1996, p. 13). Meyer described the uniqueness of the American conservative achievement as follows:

> As Americans . . . we have a great tradition to draw upon, in which the division, the bifurcation, of European thought between the emphasis on virtue and value and order and the emphasis on freedom and the integrity of the individual person was overcome, and a harmonious unity of the tensed poles of Western thought was achieved in political theory and practice as never before or since (Meyer 1996, p. 28).

This optimistic faith in the uniquely 'fusionist' character of American conservatism is not, however, vindicated by a closer examination of the diverse elements within the American tradition. In practice, the project of constructing an American conservatism has been neither as unique nor as successful as Meyer suggests, and similarities with European experience are indeed at least as marked as the supposedly uniquely American ones which Meyer stressed (Hartz 1955; Brinkley 1996).

The American project began during the decade after the Second World War as a belated response to the 'liberal' politics inaugurated by Roosevelt's New Deal. A major division was immediately apparent between those such as Milton Friedman (1962), mainly concerned with the defence of the free market against state intervention, and those who felt the whole future of American culture was in danger. It was the latter concern which gave rise to the New Conservatism represented by writers such as Richard Weaver (1948), Peter Viereck (1949), Clinton Rossiter (1955), Robert A. Nisbet (1953), Walter Lippmann (1956) and, perhaps above all, Russell Kirk (1953).

The main characteristic of the New Conservatism was the attempt to apply old world political concepts to new world realities. The result was an American equivalent of the European reactionary tradition, condemned from the start, like its European counterpart, to political impotence. Thus Kirk, an admirer of Burke, found it hard to avoid turning his back on American capitalism (Kirk 1953), while Viereck sought refuge from democratic politics through sympathy for Metternich (Nash 1976).

If the attempt to introduce European political categories condemned the New Conservatism to political marginality, the appeal to the ancient Greek ideal of virtue found in two influential émigré German thinkers, Eric Voegelin and Leo Strauss (Voegelin 1952; Strauss 1989), seemed to be an even less appropriate basis for a conservative response to modern American society. This did not, however, prevent them influencing post-Second World

War intellectuals, such as Frank S. Meyer in Voegelin's case, and in Strauss's Allan Bloom (1989) and Thomas Pangle (1992). What unites these thinkers is their hostility to relativism, well expressed by, for example, Pangle's desire to ground liberal democracy in a concept of 'foundational reason' which unites Enlightenment universalism with the ancient Greek concept of virtue in a 'conception of humanity that does justice to the whole range of the human problem and the human potential' (Pangle 1992, p. 7). Since there is little agreement on what 'the human problem and the human potential' are in the first place, the prospect of finding a 'conception of humanity' that offers an adequate response to them seems somewhat ambitious.

A more determined effort to come to terms with the realities of American life was made during the 1960s and 1970s by a group of disillusioned radical and liberal intellectuals who came to be known (often in face of their own resistance) as neo-conservatives. Their target was neither the collectivist ideals which the New Conservatives had attacked, nor the deficiencies of modern culture at large which the German émigrés had focused upon. It was, rather, the dominant American liberal tradition itself.

Neo-conservative suspicion of liberalism was above all a response to the counter-culture of the 1960s. Specifically, neo-conservatives were convinced that the liberal idealism which nurtured the counter-culture was not only destroying the ability of the USA to protect its national interest effectively against the USSR but had also fostered a welfare system which produced a dependency culture and a new underclass (Murray 1984). These concerns found expression in, for example, the journal *The Public Interest*, founded by Daniel Bell and Irving Kristol; in *Commentary*, during the long editorship of Norman Podhoretz; and in such works as Bell's *The Cultural Contradictions of Capitalism* (1979) and Kristol's *Two Cheers for Capitalism* (1978).

Although neo-conservatives attempted to get close to the realities of American life by combining a qualified commitment to capitalism with a qualified acceptance of limited state welfare provision, they were charged by some with being little more than a mouthpiece for large corporate economic interests, and by others with vastly exaggerating the nihilistic propensities of contemporary American society. This was the basis of, for example, the critique mounted by Louis A. Coser and Irving Howe in their anthology, *The New Conservatives: A Critique from the Left* (1976). More generally, it was difficult to avoid the impression that neo-conservatives were themselves prone at times to the idealism which they belaboured in the politics of their liberal enemy. The result was that their teaching had little appeal beyond an elite circle of intellectuals.

Two conditions had to be satisfied by an American conservatism aspiring to a broader appeal than that achieved by the versions so far discussed. The first was to abandon the sustained hostility towards mass society which characterised the tradition of cultural critique inaugurated by the New Conservatives and perpetuated by émigré intellectuals and neo-conservatives. Acknowledgement of this need unites an otherwise disparate group of thinkers which includes defenders of the free market like Milton Friedman, rational choice opponents of state provision like James Buchanan (1975), and thinkers sympathetic to both the market and religion like William Buckley Jr. (1958), founding editor of the *National Review*. This group failed, however, to win mass support for their ideas because they failed to satisfy a second condition, which was the need to tap the vein of religiosity that permeates the American political tradition. That condition has been met by the most recent wave of post-war conservatism.

Paleo-conservatism, as it is sometimes called, goes much further in rejecting liberal orthodoxy than neo-conservatism (Woltermann 1993; Whitaker 1982). Its characteristic demand is for toughness, expressed above all in a desire for 'workfare' rather than welfare; in tough treatment for single mothers receiving social security benefits; tough treatment of prisoners; a tough stand on immigration; a tough stand on positive discrimination; and tough protectionist measures. As this programme suggests, the paleo-conservative attitude to the state is somewhat ambiguous, veering between unqualified hostility at one extreme and willingness to invoke draconian state intervention at the other.

Although they have not produced any impressive theorising, at the practical political level paleo-conservatives have succeeded in forging a broad coalition of those opposed to political and economic liberalism on the one hand, and those opposed to the whole ideal of the permissive society on the other. Thus critics of welfare interventionism, for example, have found common ground with Christians outraged by such Supreme Court decisions as *Roe* v. *Wade* (1973), which declared a right to abortion on demand constitutional on the ground that it was entailed by the right to privacy; with secular defenders of 'family values' and the 're-moralisation' of American society; with defenders of film censorship; and with opponents of the legalisation of homosexuality and the decriminalisation of drugs.

Linking these disparate groups is, in particular, the common conviction that key educational and judicial institutions have been hijacked by a liberal elite which is unrepresentative of the nation at large. In this vein, a symposium on 'The End of Democracy?' in the journal *First Things* (1996), led by Father Richard Neuhaus, even went so far as to question the legitimacy of the contemporary American democratic system. Not surprisingly, critics of paleo-conservatism see it as little more than an inherently fragile fusion of radically disparate kinds of conservatism by means of the time-honoured techniques of conspiracy theory. In particular, they maintain, this strategy entails a dangerous attempt to exploit economic problems by a simplistic analysis attributing them to immigration and lack of protectionist measures in the face of globalisation.

If any general lesson is to be learned from the American quest for a conservatism which combines moderation with mass appeal, it is perhaps that such a union cannot aspire to much intellectual coherence, amounting as it does to little more than a pragmatic union of constantly shifting interests. This, at least, appears to be the lesson drawn towards the end of the century by one leading neo-conservative, Irving Kristol, who maintains that what distinguished American conservatism in the 1990s was that it had become 'a popular movement, not a faction within any political party'. Since this movement was largely 'issue-oriented', Kristol notes, it would accordingly 'happily combine with the Republicans if the party is "right" on the issues. If not, it will walk away' (Kristol 1996). Although Kristol himself seems content with this situation, a pragmatic conservatism of this kind may easily slide into an unprincipled opportunism. Since that danger is not confined to the contemporary American context, it must be considered in more detail.

Postmodern conservatism

The end of the twentieth century has brought with it a faltering of the Enlightenment faith in the existence of a political or social remedy for every human ill that has inspired European politics for the past two centuries. In the wake of the liberal triumphalism which flowered briefly following the collapse of the Soviet Union, the new mood of disillusion is aptly expressed in a couplet by Dr Johnson (in Podhoretz 1996):

> How small, of all that human hearts endure,
> That part, which laws or kings can cause or cure!

As was mentioned above, the challenge confronting conservatism in face of this sombre mood is to avoid disintegrating into unprincipled pragmatism.

Neither reactionary nor radical conservatism is well placed to meet this challenge, the former because it takes for granted a hierarchical concept of society which no longer corresponds to the facts of modern life, and the latter because it slides too easily into demagogy. Likewise, the market ideology of the New Right displays undue optimism about the ability of capitalism to sustain what many conservatives regard as a civilised level of social existence. In this situation, it is the moderate school of conservatism that seems to many to be most applicable to advanced industrial democracies. As American experience has indicated, however, to determine what a viable form of moderate conservatism involves is not easy, especially at a time when the socialist enemy against which it was until recently defined has disappeared and when, more generally, tradition appears to have little relevance.

Some thinkers believe the most viable form of moderate conservatism in this situation is one that grasps the nettle and jettisons the remnants of the organic ideal, opting instead for a 'thin', more narrowly political concept of conservative identity as the focal point of a looser, more diversified type of social integration (Gray 1995). At the most general level, such a conservatism might take a feather out of the postmodern cap by acknowledging that conservatism cannot enunciate timeless truths from some privileged supra-political vantage point, whether conceived in religious, cosmological or social terms. The most it can do is, rather, to seek an underpinning in a historically based philosophical anthropology – in an analysis, that is, of the inescapable tensions which have come to constitute the heritage of our civilisation and to which our institutions must be adapted if their basis is to be non-coercive. In this respect, it is perhaps from a revisionist reading of Hegel's *Philosophy of Spirit*, extricating the portrait of the modern Western psyche from the metaphysics of *Geist*, that conservatives have most to learn (Kedourie 1995).

If pressed about what such a post-traditional conservatism should conserve, the moderate answer might elaborate upon the ideal of constitutional government by situating it within the broader western European ideal of civil association. The aim of this 'civic' ideal of conservatism, which must allow for pragmatic government intervention where that is required in order to maintain the social conditions of civil existence itself, is to avoid both the Scylla of neo-liberal market dogmatism and the Charybdis of big government without merely returning to the shifting sands of a middle way (Willetts 1994, p. 27).

To disengage the civil ideal from submergence in the market, or the nation state, or some organic ideal of community, is then the central task of a post-traditional form of moderate conservatism. Although that project is unlikely to satisfy the old organic aspirations of conservatism, it might nevertheless provide a viable, distinctively conservative mode of political association appropriate to increasing social diversity, and in particular to the concomitant growth of the 'politics of identity' which is a principal feature of contemporary European life.

7
Christian democracy

MARIO CACIAGLI

'Christian democracy' can generally be understood as the strategy whereby practising Christians, the majority of them Catholic, met both the challenges and opportunities presented by contemporary political societies and states. During its initial phase, Christian democracy constituted the Catholic church's response to the advent of mass politics and the secular and socialist collectivist movements that first raised the 'social question'. Then it came more or less to coincide with the branch of Catholic political thought that sought to reconcile Catholicism to the pluralist and democratic state. Finally, Christian democracy turned into the dominant, and successful, form of political Catholicism – the doctrine chosen by those Catholics who accepted that there should be a free competition for power, and sought to defend their ideas and interests and ensure the implementation of their programmes.

The experience of participating in various types of associations and trade unions led Catholics to organise themselves into political parties which both attracted an increasingly broad consensus and became ever more powerful. The exercise of power meant their initial purpose of winning back both state and society for Catholicism gradually gave way to the pragmatic management of the prevailing problems, especially among those parties that ruled certain European countries for long periods. Despite becoming more secular and habitually adopting a centre-right stance, Christian Democratic parties nevertheless remained faithful to certain aspects of their original programmes. These allegiances differentiated them from the various conservative parties, even if, like them, Christian Democrats opposed leftist or socialist parties.[1]

1. After many years of neglect, historians and political scientists are again showing interest in the phenomenon of Christian democracy (see Hanley 1994; Durand 1995; Kalyvas 1996).

In sum, for a century Christian democracy has encompassed a series of phenomena – a body of thought, a certain ideology, policies, strategies, forms of organisation and ways of managing power – that were inextricably linked, yet also, and most importantly, able to adapt to changing historical circumstances. Therefore, the true tradition of Christian democratic thought is found less in classic texts by a few key authors, and more in the constant debates resulting from its being a political movement.

The forerunners

The term Christian democracy first appeared on the European political scene at the end of the nineteenth century. However, predecessors of both its theory and political practice had always been acknowledged. It could even be argued that one of its founding fathers was the French abbot Félicité-Robert de Lamennais, who was excommunicated by the Pope because of his ideas. Lamennais was not only the first representative of a social Christian form of radicalism, but also the first to propose a political rather than a theological interpretation of New Testament Christianity that pointed in a democratic, social and revolutionary direction (Zanfarino 1994). In *Paroles d'un croyant* of 1833, and especially *Livre du peuple* of 1837 (both in Lamennais 1946), Lamennais gave the people a central role within politics, acknowledged the supreme value of democracy and identified the source of political legitimacy in popular sovereignty. Suffrage reform was the precondition for all to organise and participate in free political competition (Weill 1979).

The first direct involvement of Catholics in politics to have an important impact as a precursor of Christian democracy were the *Volksvereine* (Maier 1973),[2] a close network of associations that, together with the Catholic unions, operated in Germany from the 1860s organising the religious interests of all social groups, particularly in the agricultural and craft sectors (Ritter 1856). Its central figure was the Catholic bishop of Mainz, Wilhelm Emmanuel von Ketteler. Through his pastoral activity, he contributed to the first systemisation of Christian social doctrine, his article on the workers' question, *Die Arbeiterfrage und das Christentum*[3] (Ketteler 1864) becoming especially famous. Ketteler did not limit himself to arguing that society,

2. Catholics entered politics for the first time in Belgium just after the creation of the new state. However, this important precedent of a Catholic secular organisation that engaged in political and electoral competition (it was formally to become a party in 1882) was extremely conservative compared to what was to become Christian democracy.
3. 'The Workers' Question and Christianity.'

including the economy, should be based on the principles of religious ethics and the duties of charity and philanthropy, he also addressed political and institutional problems and urged Catholics to accept the modern world and its state institutions.[4] According to Ketteler, the state, even while respecting the autonomy of individuals and associations, had to become the guarantor of a social peace based on faith and solidarity between social classes (Morsey 1977).

Ketteler also participated in the creation of the Zentrum, the Catholic party destined to play a central role in the political struggles of the Second Reich and the Weimar Republic. German Catholics openly accepted, much earlier than their Italian and French counterparts, the need to participate in political life and to address the process leading to the involvement of the masses in a political system that had already been partly constitutionalised (Lönne 1986). The Zentrum combined an uncompromising defence of Catholic principles with political autonomy from Rome. Ludwig Windhorst, who led the party until his death in 1889, turned the Zentrum into a non-church, parliamentary and constitutional party for the social integration of those classes that had been excluded from the liberal system. Windhorst was not a true theorist, but his political creation was to be a model for the Christian democratic parties of the twentieth century.

The German Zentrum's pragmatism and cooperation with parties of different ideologies anticipated later Christian-inspired politics. Its programme included equality for all religious groups, the safeguarding of Catholic values and institutions, and in particular a strongly federalist decentralisation of the state. Most importantly, it also proposed solving the social question by balancing the interests of capitalists, landowners and workers, and protecting the bourgeois middle class and peasants whose concerns were dear to all future Christian democratic parties (Fattorini 1997). During the Wilhelmine period, the Zentrum did not participate in any government, but with almost one hundred deputies, it formed part of the political system. It accepted the social model and offered 'national cooperation' and support for foreign policy matters. When it later became a key player in the Weimar Republic, the Zentrum would lose part of the political and theoretical baggage of the Wilhelmine era. It would be the staunchest supporter of the Republic, participating in all government coalitions and obtaining the government presidency nine times out of twenty. In playing this role, it would of course

4. Ketteler wrote a book about this theme: *Die Katholiken im Deutschen Reich* ('Catholics in the German Reich') (Ketteler 1871).

defend the interests of the Catholic church (autonomy from the state, religious schools, the safeguarding of the family), but it would also undertake the difficult tasks of managing the precarious equilibrium of the new system and defending democracy. Its electoral strength would always be fairly significant: going from a maximum of 19.7 per cent in 1919 to a minimum of 11.2 per cent in 1933.

Pope Leo XIII and the birth of Christian democracy

Having rejected and condemned for decades all the ideological, institutional and political innovations of the century, the Catholic church took a new turn in the 1890s. Under the leadership of Pope Leo XIII, the door was opened to a flourishing of ideas and initiatives that were brought together under the label of Christian democracy. The teachings of Leo XIII provided the 'social doctrine' of the church. The encyclical *Rerum novarum* of 1891 became the manifesto of social Catholicism. It marked the shift from the papal condemnation of socialism and liberalism to a positive attitude towards the workers' question. The encyclical indicated the social function of property and assigned the state the task of promoting, when necessary, public and private prosperity. It condemned class struggle, but recognised that workers had the right to organise themselves, affirming the value of work and the principle of a basic wage. The encyclical took up and legitimised all the positions that had emerged from the various strands of so-called 'social Catholicism', identifying a third way between liberalism and socialism.[5] The papal doctrine paved the way for a social order based on natural law. However, the rationalist thesis of popular sovereignty was excluded from Catholic acceptance of the principle of democracy and self-government. The rediscovery of the Thomistic tradition, which was later also to be important for Christian democratic thinkers, allowed the Pope and his aides to recognise the varied and historical nature of forms of government and, thus, the possibility of abandoning authoritarian regimes and accepting democracy.

Leo XIII's teachings allowed for two differing interpretations, one built around *social democracy*, the other around *political democracy*. In the public stances which he was to take (in particular in the encyclical *Graves de communi*

5. As has been rightly observed, it was very important that the Pope wanted 'the presence of the Church in society to be based not on an alliance with governments, but on the support of the people; accepting democracy and the recognition of the rights of workers were preconditions for the new attitude'. This quotation comes from Scoppola (1972, p. 117), an essay to which I owe a lot for this and the following paragraph.

re of 1901) the Pope deliberately stressed the 'social' aspect of democracy, which represented an ideal order of justice and not a form of government. By contrast, the first movements that had started to call themselves Christian democratic stressed the 'political' nature of democracy and claimed that Catholics had the right to participate in political life. The social doctrine of the church would continue to influence the views of Catholics, but it would always be something different from a truly Christian democratic political theory. Although remaining within the framework of Christian values and papal teaching, Christian democrats aimed to give Catholics ever more autonomy in their choice of policy objectives, organisational forms and strategies, so long as these choices were compatible with democracy.

In practice, two different movements developed, even if their personnel and activities often overlapped. The so-called 'social Catholicism' followed the papal line and remained an essentially social and ethical movement, focused on raising the level of the working classes; the political movement, via a series of not always easy experiences, went down the road of political struggle in all its forms. It is the latter that has most often been called 'Christian democracy'.

Social Catholicism gave a significant boost to Catholic unionism in countries like Belgium, Holland, Austria, Germany and Switzerland. Its most important exponent at a theoretical level was, perhaps, Giuseppe Toniolo. A renowned economist, he tried to document the historical influence of religious and ethical factors on the economy. A critic of the pagan egoism of the modern world, he took as a model the economic theories of the scholastics and the medieval guild system, based on a solid hierarchy of social organisms. Thus Toniolo thought that democracy was not a form of political regime but an ethical and social order, in which all social, legal and economic partners cooperate for the common good and the benefit of the lower classes.[6]

Theory and practice before and after the First World War

Far from feeling nostalgia for the past, the movements of 'political' Christian democracy were open to the thought and praxis of contemporary reality. For these Catholics, democracy became the only possible way of organising power, not only because it was a means for advancing the people's interests,

6. See, especially, his essay 'Il concetto cristiano della democrazia' ('The Christian Concept of Democracy') of 1900 (now in Toniolo 1980).

but also because it was the best expression of the Christian ethic. This position often led to arguments between the Pope and the main representatives of the Christian democratic movement. Despite the strength and coherence of the principles they stood for, they were more men of action than theorists (Scoppola 1972).

In France, the crisis of positivist culture and the spiritualist renaissance, together with Leo XIII's appeal for a *ralliement* with the institutions of the Third Republic, promoted the growth of Christian democracy. The programmes of all the various groups strongly condemned bourgeois individualism and modern society. However, they clearly accepted political democracy in all its forms and content (freedom of assembly, universal suffrage and the decentralisation of power). The most significant legacy of these turn-of-the-century debates was the work of Marc Sangnier and *Sillon* ('The Furrow').

Sillon was the journal of the movement of the same name founded by Sangnier. Its ideology was based on the notion of a Christian-inspired participatory democracy. It had a strong educational orientation and a few mystical elements, and viewed democracy as a form of 'community' which tends to raise everyone's conscience and civic responsibility to the maximum extent. Only the moral transformation of workers, made possible by the influence of religion, would allow them to take control of their own destiny. Sangnier could imagine a non-church-based, democratic and popular movement, ready to participate in elections, such as he began to outline in his essay *L'esprit démocratique* (Sangnier 1905). This very proposal, together with the idea that equality and justice are necessarily linked to political democracy, provoked the Pope's condemnation.[7] Sangnier bowed to papal authority, but some years later, in 1924, he managed to create the Parti Démocrate Populaire. His work greatly influenced French political Catholicism right up to the contribution it made to both the Resistance movement and the creation of a Christian democrat-inspired party during the post-war period, the Mouvement Républicain Populaire (MRP).

A person who never bowed to the authority of the Pope was the priest Romolo Murri, the most important figure in Italian Christian democracy at the end of the nineteenth century. As early as 1899, the various Christian democrat groups had already started to make political demands for such policies as the introduction of proportional representation in municipal elections (the only elections in which the church, which had opposed Italian unification because of the loss of the papal states, then allowed Italian Catholics to

7. On the *Sillon* movement, see Caron (1967).

participate), the use of referenda and administrative decentralisation. Murri, thanks to his journal *La cultura sociale*, became the most authoritative representative of the movement. Educated as a Thomist, and so in agreement with the teachings of Leo XIII, Murri had also learned something of Marxism from Antonio Labriola. According to Murri, the work of renewal proposed by the Pope could be brought about through the strength and unity of the proletariat, who had to be organised according to democratic rules. He accepted Italian unification and, through a vigorous propaganda campaign and the writings collected in *Battaglie d'oggi: il programma politico della democrazia* (Murri 1901–4), he sought to demonstrate to Italian Catholics the necessity of participating in politics and elections to work against the liberal and bourgeois state for not just the political, but also the religious and cultural, reconstruction of Italian society. In the course of his activity and thinking, Murri soon came to conceive of democracy not as an instrument to achieve a theocratic restoration, but as valuable in itself. This view led to the creation of a democratic Lega (League) and the publication of the essays found in *Democrazia e cristianesimo*, and ultimately to his expulsion from the church in 1905.

Despite the excommunication of Murri, his ideas and movement were crucial for the future of Catholics in the Italian political system. His former aides, who united to form a new Lega Democratica Cristiana in 1911, tried to abandon the theoretical attempt to reconcile Catholicism and democracy and instead concentrated on the practical problem of the role of Catholics in the development of Italian democracy. This approach formed the premise of the Partito Popolare Italiano (PPI), a party created by another priest, Luigi Sturzo, in 1919.

From his youth, Sturzo had been both close to Murri and a committed activist within the associations and local government of his native Sicily. This twofold experience gave him the democratic ideas and policies for both a critique of the Italian state and the direct involvement of Catholics. Sturzo, who was also more of a politician than a theorist, drew from Christian democracy the ideas of sociality, pluralism and the independence of political action from the church. According to Sturzo, the principles of respect for human beings, of individual freedom and juridical equality, on which the new modern constitutional state is based, do not run counter to religious aspirations. On the contrary, they are 'permeated by Christianity' (Sturzo 1979). His work in municipal administration, where he had to confront the problems created by centralised power and the backwardness of the Mezzogiorno, inspired him to map out a programme for the renewal of the Italian state (De Rosa 1977; Vecchio 1997). By 1905, Sturzo had already launched a project for 'a nation and people's' party of Catholics. Democratic and autonomous from the ecclesiastic hierarchy, the PPI would have to turn even religious or ecclesiastic issues into political questions.

Shortly after its creation, the PPI achieved considerable success in the first election held in Italy following the First World War. With 20.6 per cent of the vote, it became the second largest party in Italy after the Socialist Party. This electoral success (100 seats in the Italian lower chamber) led to the PPI becoming part of a number of coalition governments, in which it was forced to cooperate with liberal and moderate parties. A large number of its voters were peasants: thus agricultural reform, aimed at strengthening or widening the class of small farm owners, was the first point on Sturzo's agenda, though he did not succeed in putting it into practice. Nevertheless, during the years prior to the Fascist dictatorship, when Sturzo was forced into exile, the PPI was conditioned by the policies of the church of Rome (which did nothing to save it from repression by the Fascists). Still, it remained different from that other component of its electoral base, which reflected the nationalistic and conservative Catholic world, which had little time for democracy and could even be regarded as anti-democratic (Malgeri 1993).

Christian democratic thought and the dictatorships

The need to confront nationalist ideologies, and in particular the tragic experience of the dictatorships that resulted from them, had important consequences for the political thinking of Catholics between the two world wars. The authoritarianism of the right and of the regimes that resulted from it attracted the sympathy of part of the Catholic community and even the church. In Italy, the so-called 'reconciliation' between state and church, after their break in 1870, was sealed by the *Patti Lateranensi* (the Lateran Treaties) of 1929 between Mussolini's regime and the Vatican, which brought the papacy, the ecclesiastic hierarchies and the majority of Catholics closer to fascism. The papacy and the Spanish church supported Franco before and after the Spanish Civil War (among politically organised Spanish Catholics, only the Basques were opposed to him). The Vatican maintained an ambiguous attitude towards Nazism for a very long time.

The heirs of the Christian democratic parties rejected these regimes, mainly silently, with only a few people openly opposing them or going into exile. Nevertheless, the tragic events of the 1930s and the Nazi–fascist threat led a significant number of European Catholic intellectuals to defend democracy. A minority of them developed a critique of capitalism which dropped any nostalgia for the corporatist order and drew instead on elements from the Marxist left.

During the 1930s, French Catholic culture was the most responsive to the problems of social equality and political liberty which contemporary events in Europe had brought tragically to the fore. That culture gave rise to a political theory which was not only relevant to the times, but also probably the most important expressed by Catholicism during the twentieth century. Amongst the numerous journals and clubs that flourished in this period, two names stand out – Emmanuel Mounier and Jacques Maritain, who had a close and fruitful relationship.

Mounier's personalism was not meant to be a systematic philosophy, but rather the identification of a method for the realisation of the historical destiny of man and his transcendent purpose.[8] In the programme of the journal *Esprit*, published from 1932, Mounier and his colleagues committed themselves to the separation of the spiritual from the political, and in particular from every conservative policy. They denounced the limits of liberal democracy and condemned capitalism and wealth, which they saw as obstacles to the liberation of man. Mounier, who was concerned about social justice, tried to find a way to reconcile Catholicism and socialism. The 'person', unlike the bourgeois individual, realises himself in the community. Mounier proposed cooperation between people on the basis of a social life and economy planned according not only to metaphysical values but also the lessons of history. Nevertheless, the state cannot be the only watchdog of the common good: pluralism and decentralisation are essential conditions for communitarianism. Mounier collected his articles in *La révolution personnaliste et communautaire* (Mounier 1934) and in *Manifeste au service du personnalisme* (Mounier 1936). His thought influenced the generation of Catholics who, on the eve of and during the Second World War, while awaiting the collapse of the dictatorships, prepared to return to organised forms of political struggle.

Humanisme intégral was another book published in the same atmosphere and during the same period (1936) which had a great influence on the political culture of anti-fascist Catholics. It remains the best-known work of Jacques Maritain, a Thomist theologian and philosopher who advocated, even more vehemently than Mounier, the ideas of keeping political action independent of the church and of cooperation between people of different

8. For this aspect, Boyer (1981) is the most useful recent work on Mounier.

religions in order to build the 'earthly city'. Political society cannot take on the task of guiding men to perfection. However, it has to be concerned with all the conditions that can lead to a moral and material lifestyle conducive to both the common good and social peace. The most important elements in Maritain's political thought are: a political society conceived as the free organisation of people from the bottom up, the common good and natural law. They are inspired by an evangelical message of which the democratic ethos is the historical and civil translation. For Maritain, modern democracy has a fundamentally Christian value. He developed this argument in his other important political essay, *Christianisme et démocratie* published in 1943 (now in Maritain 1986–95), where Christianity is conceived as not only the route to eternal life, but also the yeast of civic life. Democracy cannot thrive on rules alone; it must be based on values. A society organised according to the principles of a complete humanism cannot tolerate any form of statism. For Maritain, the state is not everything; it is not 'a sort of collective superman', it is only 'a specialised part working in the interests of all' – an institution that must serve collective order and well-being (Bars 1961).

Maritain was the major source of inspiration for Christian democratic parties in Europe and Latin America. There has been no other Catholic political thinker with such a high profile since. Maritain particularly influenced democratic Catholicism in Italy. The invitation to engage with historical reality was welcomed by the new generation and those who, like Alcide De Gasperi, had been committed to political action before the advent of fascism. Mounier and Maritain's Christian democracy belongs to the sphere of political philosophy, while Alcide De Gasperi's, like that of other important figures from the post-war period, belongs to the sphere of political praxis. Theory gives way to the commitment to provide programmes and the willingness to put them into practice through political struggle.

During his exile in the Vatican, De Gasperi had time to reflect on the Christian democrat movement and express his ideas and future programmes in writings that were collected and published after his death.[9] A subject and then a member of parliament of the Habsburg Empire, De Gasperi had remained aloof from the problems and fraught relations between Catholics and the Italian state; but he also distanced himself from Austrian social Catholicism, which, like other Catholic movements of the time, was marked by a culture of authoritarianism and revolt inspired by the myth of the Christian

9. De Gasperi propounded his ideas in a series of articles published between 1928 and 1929 in the magazine *Rivista Internazionale di Scienze Sociali e di Discipline Ausiliari*. These works were collected almost thirty years later in De Gasperi (1955).

middle ages. Following the experience of the PPI (he had been the last party secretary), and during the Fascist dictatorship, De Gasperi developed the plan of involving the Catholic masses in the democratic state rather than merely mobilising a few Catholic 'heretics' in support of freedom. Christian democracy, as the underground party that De Gasperi founded in 1942 was called, must be a 'national' party: that is, a party able once and for all to incorporate Catholics within the democratic state and make them guarantors of a tolerant and pluralist political life. For De Gasperi, French Catholic thought, Maritain included, seemed to insist too much on the primacy of religion over politics, and to be too remote from the concrete reality of contemporary society. Instead of the idea of a group of 'separate' intellectuals that could influence the masses from above, De Gasperi was more concerned about the masses, who needed to be shown, often with 'simple formulas', how Christian principles enshrined the solution to the social and economic crisis. When drawing on the historical experience of Christian democracy, De Gasperi preferred to take as models those countries where the Catholic social movement was closely linked to liberal and democratic political positions (Giovagnoli 1991).

After 1945: Christian democracy in power

Both during and after the war, Christian democratic parties had to cope not only with an authoritarian and conservative Catholic mindset that was compromised by its links to the fascist regimes, but also with progressive Catholic groups who were sympathetic to Marxist ideas. However, the need to fight against communists brought them closer to the conservatives, and in coalitions with conservatives they sometimes became the pivotal element. This happened to the two major Christian democratic parties: the Italian DC and the German CDU/CSU, both of which came to power after the war. Indeed, the CDU (which together with the Bavarian CSU constitutes the so-called 'Union') and the DC were to became the principal parties of their respective political systems during the second half of the twentieth century.

From the point of view of electoral support, the DC was, without interruption, the major party in Italy from 1946 to 1992: its percentage of the vote varied between 35 per cent and 38 per cent for decades, from the high of 48 per cent in 1948 (the year of the great clash with the Popular Front) to the low point of 29.7 per cent in 1992, the crisis year which led to the disappearance of the party, and which followed a slow decline during the 1980s. Likewise, the CDU/CSU has always been the major party in Germany – with the sole exceptions of 1972, 1998 and 2000; its percentage of the vote has varied between 42 per cent and 48 per cent, though it obtained an absolute majority of 50.2 per cent in 1957. The DC remained in government, without interruption, from 1945 to 1993; the CDU/CSU from 1949 to 1998 – with a thirteen-year interruption (1969–82) during which a social democrat–liberal coalition was in power. Both parties always formed coalition governments, even when they had the majority of seats in parliament.

The two parties became mass parties. From the 1960s onwards, membership of the DC equalled and overtook the PCI (Italian Communist Party), reaching a figure of around 1,800,000. Despite having a different tradition of party activism, the CDU attained the 700,000 mark in the 1980s, and the CSU has always had around 200,000 members. Both the Italian and German Christian democratic parties were the architects of the reconstruction of their respective countries. They promoted economic recovery, the strengthening of democratic institutions and the accession of their countries into the international community following the nationalist tragedy of Nazism and fascism.

The tradition of Christian democratic thought undoubtedly contributed to a qualified rather than full acceptance of the capitalist model of development. The CDU/CSU extended and strengthened the welfare state from as early as the 1950s. Indeed, in Italy the welfare state was expanded to such an extent that it degenerated into a system of handouts characterised by clientelism. The DC resumed the practice of state intervention in the economy, extending the presence of the state in Italian industry begun under the fascist regime. The CDU/CSU was more respectful of the autonomy of large enterprises, even if many large German companies remained under public control. Both the CDU/CSU and the DC determined the destiny of their countries with their choices in the field of international politics: the choice of the West, the alliance with the USA which was confirmed by the accession to the Atlantic Pact (strongly opposed by the left-wing opposition in both countries), and the choice of Europe, with the creation as early as 1952 of the European Coal and Steel Community, which was the first step on the way to the present European Union. The CDU/CSU and the DC have remained consistently and steadfastly loyal to these choices of their founders.

The Frenchman Robert Schuman is usually placed alongside the Italian Alcide De Gasperi and the German Konrad Adenauer, as one of the initiators of the European Community. Schuman was a member of the other important Christian democratic party of the post-war period, the MRP. By contrast to the other parties, the MRP, whose vote fell steadily from 28 per cent in 1946 to 10 per cent in 1956, played an ever-diminishing role within the French Fourth Republic, disappearing when the Republic did (during the Fifth Republic, Christian Democrats only formed small parties within the ambit of the centre-right alliance led by the Gaullists). The MRP was the party which remained most faithful to Christian democratic doctrine. This was perhaps why it placed itself on the centre-left of the party spectrum – a stance too left-wing to achieve the support of all French Catholics.

The DC and CDU/CSU always claimed to be parties of the centre, not only an alternative to the socialist or communist left, but also in strong opposition to the right. Both fought against the extreme right and tried to erode its electoral base. The large and heterogeneous electorate of the centre contributed to changing the original Christian democratic approach; its innovative and reformist ambitions gave way in the face of conservative ideas. The support of the secular and moderate middle classes in Italy, and the participation, even if only of a minority, of Protestants in Germany, allowed the Christian democratic parties to achieve a greater degree of autonomy from the Catholic church. The increasing affluence of society further diluted their original ideas: these religious parties became concerned with mere economic innovation and mass consumption, accepting individualism and rejecting the communitarianism of their tradition. Thus the possession of political power deterred the Christian democratic parties from developing the ability to formulate an original political theory. It could be argued that the definitive and enduring entry of Catholic organisations into the sphere of political practice led to the decline of Christian democratic theory.

The contribution of Christian democratic governments to the strengthening and development of the welfare state achieved some of the objectives of that tradition of thought; but the promotion of neo-capitalism and of the related consumer society led Christian democratic parties to veer away from the ideals of their forerunners, who had wanted to build a new Christianity.[10] A Catholic historian has critically observed that: 'The great forces that were mobilised to build Christianity, have to a large extent served the development of neocapitalism' (Scoppola, 1986, p. 14). With more realism, a secular political scientist has observed that even if Christian democratic parties have

10. On the action and the characteristics of Christian Democratic parties during the decades following the Second World War, see Irving (1979), Mayeur (1980) and the texts that I refer to in note 1.

separated themselves almost completely from religious institutions, they have nevertheless remained consistent: they have stayed loyal to Christian principles concerning moral issues (such as abortion, divorce, the contents of school curricula); they have also supported state intervention in the area of social policy in the name of solidarity and subsidiarity (some have even remained in favour of state intervention in the management of the economy); and, finally, they prefer institutions promoting decentralisation and federalism (Beyme 1983).

Within Italian Christian democracy, the only figure to whom a political theory of some sort can be attributed is Giuseppe Dossetti. After he became vice-secretary of the party, he abandoned political life to become a monk in the mid-1950s. Dossetti, whose political reputation was formed during the fight against fascism, wanted a democracy based on freedom and solidarity. Catholics had to contribute to the democratic renewal of Italy and to the foundation of a new political system in which the Christian-inspired concept of 'the person' was crucial to the distinction between church and state. The Christianisation of society needed to go hand in hand with the reform of capitalism or even the transition to a post-capitalist society. By contrast to traditional Catholic thought, Dossetti envisioned a strong state with a planned economy, even in opposition to the right to property: a state which was able to reform and harmonise society for 'the achievement of happiness for all' (Dossetti 1995).[11] Some of these ideas formed the basis of the Italian constitution of 1947, to which Dossetti contributed a great deal by managing to develop a dialogue with socialists and communists. Thanks to Dossetti's efforts, the Italian constitution enshrines not only the primacy of the human person as part of a social union that is as much spiritual as it is economic, but also the principle of freedom as a responsibility. Dossetti also fought for certain religious policies (such as the indissolubility of marriage, the defence of Catholic schools and, above all, for the inclusion of the Lateran Pacts in the Italian constitution) (Dossetti 1994).

The other great Christian democratic party, the German CDU, developed the doctrine of 'the social market economy'. This policy proved both realistic and highly effective practically and still forms part of the party's ideological heritage. According to the Christian democratic tradition, the 'social market economy' was supposed to represent a 'third way' between laissez-faire capitalism and a socialist planned economy. The origins of this conception can be

11. Dossetti set out his political programme in articles published in the journal *Cronache Sociali*, of which he was the *spiritus rector* from 1947 to 1952. On Dossetti's role during the first phase of the DC, see Baget-Bozzo (1974).

found in the neo-liberal economic doctrines re-elaborated in the so-called 'Ordo-Liberalism' of the Freiburg school. Walter Eucken, the most important representative of this school, viewed the free market as the sole solution to social problems and identified it with the democratic order guaranteed by the state. Following Eucken, the CDU economist Alfred Müller-Armack both formulated the strategy of the social market economy and created its name. Müller-Armack became the official economic theorist of the CDU when, having gained power under the leadership of Konrad Adenauer, it had rapidly distanced itself from the dreams of a 'Christian socialism' that had characterised the difficult early years of the post-war period (the Programme of Ahlen 1947). The economic minister Ludwig Erhard, who was schooled in liberalism, implemented monetary reform and became the father of the German economic miracle of the 1950s by applying the strategic guidelines of the social market economy. However, it was the secretary of state of his ministry, namely Müller-Armack, who, with his theory, really guided the German economy until the beginning of the 1960s.

By contrast to neo-liberal ideas, Müller-Armack underlined the social responsibilities of entrepreneurs, the need for political intervention in the economic cycle and, above all, the commitment of the state in the area of social policy. For Müller-Armack, the social market economy reconciles free enterprise with social progress, which in turn would be ensured by the performance of the free market which must aim, with the active cooperation of the state, for increasing prosperity and full employment (Müller-Armack 1956). The term 'social' was to indicate how the market, when production is regulated according to the requirements of the consumer, offers a social service, and by creating wealth allows the state to redistribute to ensure social equality. Such redistribution was achieved through social security and insurance policies, the pension system and benefits for individuals and families (health care, education, housing). Müller-Armack's economic programme follows the tradition of Christian democratic thought precisely because it takes up important elements of Catholic social doctrine and stresses the role of the state.

The social market economy can be considered the last important contribution of Christian democracy to European political thought. Christian democrats have been unable to develop an original political theory, not only because of the aforementioned assumption of power by the parties, but also because of the formation of a new type of political class, the secularisation of society and the parallel disengagement of the church from any direct involvement in politics. Consequently, one can only find some remnants of

Christian democratic thought where political and social conflicts still catalyse ideas. In this context, it is worth recalling the theorist Jaime Castillo, who continues to enjoy great intellectual prestige and moral respect in Latin America (where people call him 'the master'). The Chilean editor-in-chief of the journal *Política y Espiritu*, his book *Las fuentes de la democracia cristiana* (1963) describes all the various developments within Christian democratic theory from the end of the nineteenth century, and asserts their continued relevance, without adding anything new to them. Like European Christian democrats, Castillo's problem was to fight against Marxism and remove the working class from its influence towards an alternative conception of freedom and an 'avant-garde' outlook. Castillo defined Christian democracy precisely as an 'avant-garde' party, in order to avoid its inclusion in the rigid right/left spectrum.

In the conflictual, contradictory and centrifugal society of Western Europe at the end of the twentieth century and the beginning of the twenty-first, there is little if any room for a renewal of Christian democratic thought. The parties that still bear that name or claim to refer to that cultural tradition must adjust to the characteristics of modern politics which is marked by pragmatism, secularism and the rejection of all ideologies.

8
Critics of totalitarianism

JEFFREY C. ISAAC

Introduction

It is common among intellectual historians to conceive of distinct historical periods in terms of the values or world views to which these periods seem to give expression. Thus the eighteenth century is sometimes called the Age of Reason or Enlightenment, and the nineteenth the Age of Ideology or the Age of History. Raymond Aron, in a book of the same name, dubbed the twentieth century the Century of Total War (Aron 1955). Like all historical generalisations, this one seeks to capture what is fundamental – in this case, the organisation of prodigious violence and destructiveness – at the expense of developments deemed less than fundamental, however important they may be. Of course this involves certain judgements of significance. Aron was far from being alone in his assessment of what distinguishes the twentieth century.

The twentieth century has seen the perfection of revolutionary new technologies – petrochemicals, electronics, nuclear power, a 'world wide web' of computer networks. It has seen the emancipation of women in many parts of the world; the rise and fall of empires, the organisation of national independence movements and wars of 'national liberation'; the rise and fall of communism in Russia and Eastern Europe; the establishment of the United Nations; the creation of the modern welfare state; and the emergence of a 'third wave' of liberal democratic transformation in Asia, Africa and Latin America. In the face of all of these developments, many of them undoubtedly beneficial, all of them consequential, why think of the century as a century of total war?

Perhaps because the twentieth is the century in which the entire *world* was shattered and convulsed by waves of extraordinary and extraordinarily well-organised destructiveness, and because many of the more 'beneficial' developments cited above were unleashed by such destructiveness. Millions of people were killed, and millions more wounded, during the First World War. In the wake of this calamity the Russian, Prussian, Hapsburg and Ottoman monarchies fell, setting off a protracted process of decolonisation with global ramifications, and creating hundreds of thousands of stateless and homeless people. The Second World War exceeded its predecessor in its destructiveness, perfecting such technologies of death as saturation aerial bombing, the atomic bomb and, perhaps even more emblematic, the gas chamber and the death camp.

Even more devastating than the loss of human life was the loss of humanity, as peoples and cultures were swept away in a tidal wave of barbarism. The two world wars saw the development of propaganda into a science, as governments strove to vilify their enemies and to mobilise entire populations behind the war efforts. As Simone Weil put it: 'We seem to have lost the very rudiments of intelligence, the notions of measure, standard, and degree; of proportion and relation; of affinity and consequence... we people our political world with monsters and myths; we recognise nothing but entities, absolutes, finalities' (Weil 1946).

The First World War was but the inaugural episode in a series of traumatic political events – the Russian Revolution and the transformation of revolutionary dictatorship into Stalinism; the ascendancy of fascism in Italy; the implosion of the Weimar Republic and the rise of the Nazis to power; the fratricidal suppression of popular radicalism and revolutionary activism by the communists in Spain, leading to the victory of Franco; the Moscow show trials of 1936–8; the Hitler–Stalin pact of 1939; the outbreak of the Second World War and the Nazi genocide in Europe; the Soviet massacres at Katyn and Warsaw, and the deliverance of Eastern Europe from Nazi to communist dictatorship; and the bombings of Hiroshima and Nagasaki. Each of these events was the occasion of extraordinary propaganda and deceit; each involved prodigious amounts of violence and coercion. And these events followed one another with a convulsive rapidity that exacerbated the sense that history was out of control.

The power of such events and processes is what Aron meant to call attention to in calling the century the age of total war. Integral to the prosecution of such totalising warfare, and precipitated by the crises of the inter-war period alluded to above, was a novel and unanticipated form of regime, and of a novel political idea that signified this regime – *totalitarianism*. The idea of totalitarianism is without doubt the signal contribution of the twentieth century to the history of political thought. While many other important twentieth-century ideas – like Bolshevism, fascism, national liberation, liberal democracy or the welfare state – can be seen as extensions of earlier political ideas and concerns, the idea of totalitarianism is *sui generis*, and marks an unprecedented form of political domination and murderousness.

Like all political ideas or concepts, 'totalitarianism' has a rich and complex history. It has been used in a variety of ways: sometimes, surprising as it may seem, as an ideal, but most often as a form of criticism. But even in criticism the idea has served different constituencies and purposes, from European émigré intellectuals to Cold War academics and policy advisers, to central European anti-communist dissidents. In this chapter I will sketch out some of these different uses of 'totalitarianism', underscoring throughout how powerful this idea has been. If there is a moral to the brief story that I will tell, it is that while the discourse of 'totalitarianism' contains unifying themes and preoccupations, this discourse has shifted in subtle but important ways over time, and that these shifts have significant intellectual as well as political implications.

The emergence of an idea

Totalitarianism emerged as a political concept against the backdrop of the unprecedented mass mobilisation of the First World War and the political upheaval in Europe that followed its uncertain conclusion (Bracher 1981). In his recent study *Totalitarianism*, Abbott Gleason reports that the term was first used in 1923 by Giovanni Amendola, an anti-fascist journalist and politician, in reference to Mussolini's anti-liberalism and disregard for the principles of legality. Amendola wrote that 'the most salient characteristic of the fascist movement remains its totalitarian spirit. This spirit will not allow any new day to dawn that has not rendered the fascist salute, just as it does not allow the present era to know a conscience that has not bowed the knee and confessed: "I believe".' Gleason points out that the term quickly became common among the anti-fascist opposition to Mussolini's concentration of political power, quoting a socialist activist: 'All the organs of state, the crown, Parliament, the law . . . the armed forces . . . are becoming instruments of a single party that makes itself the interpreter of the people's will, or undifferentiated totalitarianism' (Gleason 1995, p. 15).

The term seems quickly to have been reappropriated by the Fascists themselves. The Italian Hegelian philosopher Giovanni Gentile wrote at length about the new 'totalitarian spirit' of the Fascist state that had extended its influence into all spheres of social life. In a 1932 article on 'The Doctrine of Fascism' ghost-written by Gentile, Mussolini himself declared that 'the armed party leads to the totalitarian regime...A party that governs totalitarianly a new nation is a new fact in history' (quoted in Curtis 1969, p. 59; see also the discussion in Linz 1975, p. 127). Mussolini went on: 'the fascist conception of the state is all-embracing; outside of it no human or spiritual values can exist, much less have value. Thus understood, fascism is totalitarian, and yet the fascist state...interprets, develops and potentiates the whole life of a people' (Gleason 1995, p. 19). Most commentators agree that these uses of the term antedate the full emergence of what came to be called 'totalitarianism' in Nazi Germany and Stalinist Russia and that, while Italian fascism clearly prefigured these developments, the Italian fascist notion of totalitarianism does not fully anticipate the extreme concentration and murderous exercise of power characteristic of the Hitler and Stalin regimes.

The same could even be said of the term's early uses in Germany, although German neo-fascist writers endowed the idea with a more activist, and racialist and anti-Semitic, character. Ernst Jünger's *Die totale Mobilmachung* (1930), Carl Schmitt's *Die Wendung zum totalen Staat* (1931), Ernst Fosthoff's *Der totale Staat* (1933) and General Erich von Luddendorf's *Der totale Krieg* (1935) all articulated anti-parliamentarist themes, prescribing a strong German state to mobilise military, industrial, and political will in the name of national renewal. Many of these texts, and others like them, frighteningly prefigure the full-fledged development of Nazi genocide in the 1940s. Schmitt, for example, in his *Crisis of Parliamentary Democracy* (1923), condemns liberalism and calls for a form of 'dictatorial and Caesaristic' rule that expresses the 'will' of a homogenous people (*Volk*) and that promotes 'the elimination or eradication of heterogeneity' (Schmitt 1985, pp. 14–17). Yet if Hans Mommsen is correct, these works reflected more the hopes of Hitler's conservative allies than they did the aims of the National Socialist movement itself (see Mommsen 1981 and Greiffenhagen 1981; also Wolin 1992 and Scheuerman 1994).

Within the communist movement, it is possible to trace the development of a political vision, rooted in Lenin's ideas of the 'vanguard party' and 'the dictatorship of the proletariat', that was similarly Manichean and militantly anti-liberal. Such a 'totalitarian' Marxism reached its apotheosis in the Stalinist conception of the Communist Party as the 'advanced detachment' and 'directing force' of the working class, for which all other institutions and organisations were seen as 'levers' and 'transmission belts'. As Stalin wrote in his 'Concerning Questions of Leninism':

> What are these 'transmission belts' or 'levers' in the system of the dictatorship of the proletariat? What is this 'directing force'? Why are they needed? The levers or transmission belts are those very mass organisations of the proletariat without the aid of which the dictatorship cannot be realised. The directing force is the most advanced detachment of the proletariat, its vanguard, which is the main guiding force of the dictatorship of the proletariat (Stalin, quoted in Leonhard 1974, p. 105).

While within the communist movement the Stalinist conception of the party was not without challengers, and while the idea of 'totalitarianism' never retained the generalised positive valence that it had achieved among fascist ideologues in Italy and Germany, both the vanguard party and the dictatorship of the proletariat were foundations of communist ideology. Indeed Antonio Gramsci, in his essays on the Communist Party as a 'Modern Prince', did write favourably about the 'totalitarian' party, by which he seems to have meant an 'all-embracing and unifying' political formation to which the communists aspired. In his words:

> A totalitarian policy is aimed precisely: 1. at ensuring that the members of a particular party find in that party all the satisfactions that they formerly found in a multiplicity of organisations, i.e., at breaking all the threads that bind these members to extraneous cultural organisms; 2. at destroying all other organisations or at incorporating them into a system of which the party is the sole regulator. This occurs: 1. when the given party is the bearer of a new culture – then one has a progressive phase; 2. when the given party wishes to prevent another force, bearer of a new culture, from becoming itself 'totalitarian' then one has an objectively regressive and reactionary phase, even if that reaction (as invariably happens) does not avow itself, and seeks itself to appear as the bearer of a new culture (see Gramsci 1971, pp. 147–8, 335).

The image of the mass party as all-absorbing, and of all other affiliations as 'extraneous' and eliminable, represents a striking parallel to the imagery of Stalin. Even more striking is the idea, also developed by Carl Schmitt, that the central historical conflict at present is the conflict between left and right, 'progressive' and 'regressive', forms of totalitarianism. As late as 1947 Maurice Merleau-Ponty, in his apologetic *Humanism and Terror*, made a similar argument, distinguishing between the Marxist 'idea of totality' and the 'so-called "totalitarian" ideology' of fascism in terms of the 'progressive' character of the former. While both ideologies reject liberalism and its legal 'formalism', only Marxism does so authentically. As he writes:

The opponents of Marxism never fail to compare this 'totalitarian' method with the Fascist ideology which also pretends to go from the formal to the actual, from the contractual to the organic. But the comparison is in bad faith. For fascism is nothing but a mimicry of Bolshevism. A single Party, propaganda, the justice of the state, the truth of the state – fascism retains everything of Bolshevism except what is essential, namely, the theory of the proletariat. For if the proletariat is the force on which revolutionary society is based and if the proletariat is that 'universal class' we have described from Marx, then the interests of this class bring human values into history and the proletariat's power is the power of humanity. Fascist violence, by contrast, is not the violence of a universal class, it is the violence of a 'race' or late-starting nation; it does not follow the course of things, but pushes against them (Merleau-Ponty 1969, pp. 123–4).[1]

Merleau-Ponty makes clear through this very justification of communist violence that what distinguishes communist from fascist forms of 'totalitarianism' is not the means that they employ but merely the ends that such means serve. While there is a rich literature on the relationship between this mode of thinking and the writings of Marx and the tradition of Marxism more generally, there can be no doubt that the Manichean thinking of many communists of the 1920s and 1930s mirrored that of their fascist antagonists, and that this ideological opposition between left- and right-wing versions of anti-liberalism presaged the bloody decades to follow.[2]

By the mid-1930s 'totalitarianism' had moved beyond the phase of praxiology as the communist regime in Russia and the fascist regime in Germany – regimes that had seemed ideologically and politically antithetical to one another, each justifying its power by vilifying the other – converged on what increasingly came to be seen as a new form of rule. European political writers and social theorists, many of them forced into exile by these developments, similarly converged on the concept of 'totalitarianism' or 'totalitarian dictatorship' as a way of signifying this disturbing political innovation. As George Orwell remarked in 1941: 'One development of the last ten years has been the appearance of the "political book," a sort of enlarged pamphlet combining history with political criticism... [Of] the best writers in this line... nearly all of them have been renegades from one or another extremist party, who have seen totalitarianism at close quarters and known the meaning of exile and persecution' (Orwell 1968b, p. 142).

1. Merleau-Ponty later abandoned this justification of communism. See his 1955 book *Adventures of the Dialectic* (Merleau-Ponty 1973) and the fine discussion of this evolution in Whiteside (1988).
2. On the relationships between Marxism and Stalinism, see especially Kolakowski (1985); Lukes (1985); and Jay (1984).

Hans Kohn and Sigmund Neumann made early efforts to note the similarities between Nazism and Stalinism, focusing on the mass mobilisational and 'total' character of state power in these regimes (Kohn 1935; Neumann 1942). Elie Halévy's *The Era of Tyrannies* (1966 [1936]) also emphasised the importance of war mobilisation, maintaining that as a consequence 'on the one hand, a complete socialism is moving towards a kind of nationalism. On the other hand, an integral nationalism is moving towards a kind of socialism'. Raymond Aron took up similar themes, supporting Halévy's thesis regarding the symmetry between Stalinism and fascism:

> Political freedom: the plebiscites only represent the derisory symbol of the delegation by the people of its sovereignty to absolute masters. Personal freedom: against abuses of power, neither the German citizen, nor the Italian citizen, nor the Russian citizen, have any means of recourse; the bureaucrat and the member of the Communist party, the local *fuhrer* and the secretary of the *fascio*, are the slaves of their superiors, but objects of fear to private individuals. Intellectual freedom, freedom of the press, freedom of speech and scientific freedom – all the freedoms have disappeared. If, in English democratic practice, opposition is, as an admirable phrase has it, a public service, in the totalitarian states opposition is a crime (quoted in Colquhoun 1986, p. iii).

These early efforts were accompanied by numerous books on the dangers posed by totalitarian regimes. While such books address these dangers from diverse political perspectives, their authors shared a commitment to opposing totalitarianism in the name of freedom. Some, like Aron, Karl Mannheim, Karl Popper and Emil Lederer, articulated a liberalism indebted to Montesquieu and Tocqueville, focusing on the despotic concentration of political power and the evisceration of intermediate associations and political pluralism. Others, like Ludwig von Mises and Friedrich Hayek, advocated a straightforward market liberalism, focusing on the corporatism of the totalitarian regimes, on their abrogation of legality and on their monopolistic claims to knowledge about the social good.[3]

On the non-communist Marxist left, scholars associated with the Frankfurt school sought to blend elements of the official communist theory of monopoly state capitalism with a more innovative approach that was attentive to the distinctively ideological features of the new totalitarian

3. The most influential of these works included Borkenau (1940); Mannheim (1940); Lederer (1940); Reimann (1941); Burnham (1941); Fraenkel (1941); Mises (1944); and Hayek (1944). In a class by themselves are the writings of Hermann Rauschning, the former Nazi who published a steady stream of books denouncing Nazism and highlighting its similarities with Stalinism (see especially Rauschning 1939 and 1941).

regimes. Herbert Marcuse's 'The Struggle Against Liberalism in the Totalitarian View of the State' (1934) was an early effort, though it focused only on emergent Nazism and relied heavily on correspondence between Nazism and 'the monopoly stage of capitalism'. Max Horkheimer's 'The Authoritarian State' (1940) emphasised the parallels between Nazism and 'state socialism', labelling both 'authoritarian' and 'repressive' and identifying 'permanent mobilisation', 'arbitrariness' and concentration camps as signal features of both right and left versions of totalitarianism. Friedrich Pollock's 'State Capitalism: Its Possibilities and Limitations' (1941) developed similar arguments, distinguishing between the attenuated 'democratic state capitalism' characteristic of the United States and Great Britain, and the 'totalitarian state capitalism' characteristic of both Nazi Germany and Stalinist Russia, a regime which 'offers the solution of economic problems at the price of totalitarian oppression'. And Franz Neumann's *Behemoth* (1942) was among the most formidable and systematic studies to explore 'the structure and practice of national socialism' and its establishment of a system of 'totalitarian monopoly capitalism'.[4] While in many ways Neumann's analysis remained wedded to the communist theory of monopoly capitalism, and thus to the notion that Nazism was a capitalist regime distinct from and antithetical to communism, in his appreciation for the distinctively dictatorial features of the Nazi regime, and in his emphasis on its repudiation of legality, his analysis is not far removed from his Frankfurt school colleagues who were increasingly taken with the convergence between the Hitler and Stalin regimes.

One can discern similar developments within the Trotskyist movement, despite the fact that Trotsky and those most loyal to him never abandoned their Leninist commitments nor their view of the Soviet Union as a 'deformed workers' state'. In 1937 Trotsky himself observed that 'Stalinism and fascism, in spite of a deep difference in social foundations, are symmetrical phenomena' (Trotsky 1937, p. 278). Trotsky's own writing during this period exhibits a creative effort to develop new theoretical categories within Marxism to account for this 'deadly similarity'. In his 1939 essay 'The USSR in War', he went so far as to suggest that the coming war, if it did not bring about a world revolution, would lead to the emergence in the Soviet Union of a 'totalitarian regime' heralding 'the eclipse of civilisation'. Should this occur, Trotsky maintained, 'a new minimum program would be required – for the defence of the interests of the slaves of the totalitarian bureaucratic

4. See also Jay (1973).

society'. (This essay is discussed in Macdonald 1946, pp. 97–115, 194–214.) His followers, most notably the American Max Schactman, extended the logic of this argument, contending that the Soviet Union, like Nazi Germany, was a 'bureaucratic collectivist' regime in which a new ruling class had emerged based on the monopolisation of political and economic power. Whereas Trotsky's position professed support for the Soviet system but opposition to its ruling elite, Schactman's entailed a thoroughgoing opposition to the Soviet system (Schactman 1962).[5] Similar arguments were developed by the American Marxist Sidney Hook and the Russian Marxist/anarchist Victor Serge, who had been imprisoned by Stalin and went on to become one of the most influential European critics of Stalinism.[6]

André Liebich has suggested that perhaps the most innovative Marxist thinking on the subject of totalitarianism was Rudolf Hilferding's 'State Capitalism or Totalitarian State Economy' (1940), published in the Paris-based Russian Menshevik journal *Sotsialisticheskii Vestnik*. In this essay Hilferding insisted that 'the controversy as to whether the economic system of the Soviet Union is "capitalist" or "socialist" seems to me rather pointless. It is neither. It represents a totalitarian state economy, i.e., a system to which the economies of Germany and Italy are drawing closer and closer' (Liebich 1987, pp. 239, 223).

It was from the independent, non- or ex-Marxist left that the most influential accounts of totalitarianism came. Ignazio Silone, a founder of the Italian Communist Party who broke with the party over its authoritarianism, penned a series of works on the bankruptcy of communism, its complicity in the rise of fascism, and the convergence of these movements on propaganda and violence, including *The School for Dictators* (1939) and his classic novel *Bread and Wine* (1937). Silone's contribution to the classic retrospective *The God That Failed* (1950) stands as one of the most penetrating accounts of the ethical vacuity of communism. Arthur Koestler's *Darkness at Noon* (1941) and *The Yogi and the Commissar* (1945) developed similar themes. Indeed the former surely stands, along with George Orwell's *Nineteen Eighty-Four*, as among the most influential dramatic accounts of the relentlessly ideological character of the totalitarian regimes (on these writers, see Walzer 1988).

Orwell is without doubt the most enduring of these critics of totalitarianism. As early as the mid-1930s, as a participant in and chronicler of the Spanish Civil War, Orwell had come to the conclusion that communism

5. On Schactman and his influence, see Isserman (1987, pp. 35–124) and Wald (1987).
6. On Hook, see his autobiography (Hook 1987); on Serge, see Serge (1937b). See also Ciliga (1940), first published in Paris in 1938, for an account of the author's experience of Stalinist repression.

was no different from the fascism it opposed in its mendacity and murderousness (see Orwell 1980). In his classic allegory *Animal Farm*, he depicted with sharp irony the transmutation of egalitarian ideals into dictatorial dogmas. In a series of book reviews and essays he condemned the relentless propagandising and nihilism of totalitarian regimes. He observed:

> The terrifying thing about the modern dictatorships is that they are entirely unprecedented. Their end cannot be foreseen. In the past every tyranny was sooner or later overthrown, or at least resisted, because of 'human nature,' which as a matter of course desired liberty. But we cannot be at all certain that 'human nature' is a constant. It may be just as possible to produce a breed of men who do not wish for liberty as to produce a breed of hornless cows. The Inquisition failed, but then the Inquisition had not the resources of the modern state. The radio, press-censorship, standardised education and the secret police have altered everything (Orwell 1968a, pp. 380–1).

In his most famous book, *Nineteen Eighty-Four*, Orwell brought such a nightmarish vision to life, dramatising a totalitarian dystopia where 'Big Brother' was ever present and individual freedom of action and even conscience were thoroughly extinguished (see the essays collected in Howe 1983).

In the early 1950s this anti-totalitarian literature was punctuated by the publication of four books that each expanded on the theme of the totalitarian extinction of freedom: Czeslaw Milosz's *The Captive Mind* (1953 [1951]), a brilliant account of the delusions of 'totalitarian thinking, whether of the left or the right'; Jacob Talmon's *The Origins of Totalitarian Democracy* (1970 [1952]), which traced the populist anti-liberalism of totalitarian ideologies to the political messianism of the French Revolution and its aftermath; Albert Camus's *The Rebel* (1956 [1951]), an essay on the project of mastery and 'totality' enacted by the Hitler and Stalin regimes; and Hannah Arendt's *Origins of Totalitarianism* (1951), a complex narrative of the rise of totalitarianism that culminated in an account of the death camp as the apotheosis of this horrifying regime. Of these the last was the most influential upon subsequent thinking about totalitarianism.

In many ways *Origins of Totalitarianism* is a synthetic work, drawing upon much of the earlier literature cited above, upon first-hand accounts by such writers as David Rousset, Boris Souvarine and Victor Serge, and upon Arendt's writings on the Jewish question from the 1940s. Yet in its scope and its delineation of the distinctive murderousness of the Hitler and Stalin regimes, *Origins* remains unsurpassed. The book links the emergence of totalitarianism to the history of European anti-Semitism and the crisis of European imperialism in the early part of the century that eventuated in the

First World War. Yet its most original parts go beyond historical narrative or empirical description, and present a striking account of the universe of the concentration camp, 'the true central institution of totalitarian organisational power'. She writes:

> The concentration and extermination camps of the totalitarian regimes serve as the laboratories in which the fundamental belief of totalitarianism that everything is possible is verified... The camps are meant not only to exterminate people and degrade human beings, but also to serve the ghastly experiment of eliminating... spontaneity itself as an expression of human behaviour and of transforming the human person into a mere thing, into something that even animals are not (Arendt 1951, p. 437–8).

In the penultimate and most dramatic section of the book, she likens the concentration camps, forced labour camps and extermination camps to Dante's three circles of Hell, where 'the human masses sealed off in them are treated as if they no longer existed, as if what happened to them were no longer of interest to anybody, as if they were already dead and some evil spirit gone mad were amusing himself by stopping them for a while between life and death before admitting them to eternal peace' (Arendt 1951, p. 445).

More than any of the other writers cited above, Arendt made the death camp the centre of her analysis. In her 1958 appendix to the second edition of *Origins*, entitled 'Ideology and Terror', she went further in exploring the connection between totalitarian terror, the destruction of all intermediate associations, the enforced atomisation and isolation of individuals, and the workings of ideology under totalitarianism:

> While the totalitarian regimes are thus resolutely and cynically emptying the world of the only thing that makes sense to the utilitarian expectations of common sense, they impose upon it at the same time a kind of supersense... The insanity of such systems lies not only in their first premise but in the very logicality with which they are constructed. The curious logicality of all isms, their simple-minded trust in the salvation value of stubborn devotion without regard for specific, varying factors, already harbours the first germs of totalitarian contempt for reality and facticity (Arendt 1951, p. 457).

For Arendt what distinguishes totalitarianism as much as its concentration of power and its bureaucratisation of violence is the spirit of unpredictability and fear that pervades both subjects of totalitarian power and their rulers, depriving individuals of any fixed rules, boundaries or expectations, and rendering human life utterly insecure.

The Cold War and its aftermath

Books like *Origins* and *The Captive Mind* still bear the imprint of the experience of resistance to totalitarianism undergone by post-war European intellectuals (see Wilkinson 1981). They are, in many ways, continuous with the 'political books' remarked upon by Orwell, composed by independent writers who had experienced persecution and displacement, and had emerged from the struggle against fascism traumatised by the horrifying convergence of fascism and communism. By the mid-1950s this discourse about totalitarianism had been subtly transformed by the onset of the Cold War. If in the earlier period anti-fascism had been a defining characteristic of the anti-totalitarian literature, even for those profoundly revolted by and opposed to Stalinism, by the 1950s it was *anti-communism* that became the virtually exclusive focus of concern about totalitarianism. If in the earlier period many of the principal writers about totalitarianism had been independent intellectuals – journalists, freelance writers or researchers, in many cases participants in Resistance activity of one sort or another – in the post-war period the theorisation of totalitarianism increasingly became linked to academic institutes of Soviet studies or Russian and East European affairs, heavily financed by the United States government, preoccupied with Soviet communism, its internal dynamics and its geo-political aspirations.

These changes are of course explicable in terms of post-war political developments – the expansion of Soviet military and political hegemony over what came to be called 'Eastern Europe'; the post-war military power of the United States, symbolised by its use of the atomic bomb against Japan, and the US projection of power in Europe associated with the organisation of the NATO alliance; the dramatic political crisis over the division of Berlin; the 1949 victory of the communists under the leadership of Mao Zedong in China, and the outbreak of the Korean War. In short, with the end of the Second World War and the triumph over fascism, Soviet communism seemed the only remaining obstacle to 'democracy', and the antagonism between 'Western freedom' and 'the Iron Curtain' in the 'East' assumed a new political, and intellectual, importance. In this new situation the discourse of totalitarianism shifted. The shift was subtle, both because its subject matter – totalitarian dictatorship – seemed to be the same, in spite of the shift in empirical concern, and because this sense of the continuity of concern seemed shared by many of the earlier writers. The works of Aron, Popper, Orwell and even Arendt continued to be cited and to exert influence on academic and political discussion, and many of these authors lent their imprimatur to the new exclusive focus on Soviet communism.[7]

Yet a shift, however subtle had occurred. In the words of Herbert Spiro and Benjamin Barber, the concept of totalitarianism had become a 'counterideological' weapon in the Cold War, a way of marking out the Soviet Union as what came later to be called an 'evil empire', and of identifying the US-led NATO alliance with the forces of light. As the German historian Hans Mommsen observed: 'the theory of totalitarianism . . . has assumed the features of an ideological syndrome . . . [A] heuristic model, originally fruitful in terms of the historical insights it yielded, was intellectually impoverished and transformed into an indirectly assertive ideology designed to preserve existing, liberal-parliamentary structures' (Mommsen 1981, p. 153).

The central work in this new discourse of totalitarianism was Karl Friedrich and Zbigniew Brzezinski's 1956 *Totalitarian Dictatorship and Autocracy*. In many ways this book represents a continuation, indeed a systematisation, of much of the earlier literature of the 1930s and 1940s. In roughly 400 pages its authors present a historically informed, synoptic theory of the distinctive character of totalitarian dictatorships – a theory intended to cover Nazi, fascist, and Russian and Chinese communist regimes. Their most famous formulation is the idea that a totalitarian regime is distinguished by a 'syndrome', or pattern, consisting of six interrelated traits: (1) an official, totalistic and messianic ideology; (2) a monopolistic mass party typically led by a single 'dictator' based upon a cult of personality; (3) a system of terror enforced by a secret police; (4) a monopoly of control over all means of mass communication; (5) a monopoly of control over the use of force; and (6) a command economy.

Totalitarian Dictatorship and Autocracy is a rich and informative book, distinguished less by any liberal or pro-American ideological agenda than by its taxonomic rigour and its social-scientific aspirations. Yet, as many commentators have pointed out, the 'end of ideology' posture of post-war American social science was not without ideological implications of its own, even when asserted in a way that purported to be 'non-ideological'. The bulk of Friedrich and Brzezinski's book is taken up with the dynamics of Soviet communism, and its unmistakeable conclusion is that this regime is monolithic, essentially unchanging and unchangeable, and imperialist in its global

7. Carl Friedrich and Zbigniew Brzezinski, for example, acknowledge the influence of Arendt, Sigmund Neumann and Franz Neumann in the preface to the first edition of *Totalitarian Dictatorship and Autocracy* (1956, p. xiii).

aspirations. They thus write, in their penultimate chapter on foreign policy, that:

> It is . . . quite evident that the possibility for peaceful coexistence of the nations peopling this world presupposes the disappearance of the totalitarian dictatorships. Since, according to their own loudly proclaimed professions, their systems must be made world-wide, those who reject the system have no alternative but to strive for its destruction. Any relaxation of the vigilance required to face such ideological imperialists as the totalitarians is likely to result in a disaster such as the Second World War, or worse.

This passage leaves little to the imagination regarding the ideological allegiances of its authors. 'The question remains', they conclude the chapter, 'who shall rule this world?' (Friedrich and Brzezinski 1956, pp. 365–6). Soviet totalitarianism or freedom. The choices are starkly posed.

It is this specific counter-position that most distinguishes the Cold War discourse of totalitarianism. On the one hand, numerous studies were published purporting to document the totalitarian dynamics of Soviet communism, the workings of Soviet ideology, the repression of political dissent, and the absence of leadership accountability and regular succession.[8] On the other hand, political scientists reacted to the danger of totalitarianism by developing an 'empirical democratic theory' designed to identify, and to solidify, those aspects of Western, capitalist, liberal democracies that stood opposed to communist totalitarianism. Authors such as Seymour Martin Lipset, Giovanni Sartori and Robert Dahl elaborated on the pluralism of Western democracies in contrast to the 'populism' of totalitarian mass mobilisation; the 'empirical', 'non-ideological' character of democratic political culture in contrast to the messianism and absolutism of communism; and the forms of political compromise that result from democratic political bargaining rather than from the dictates of a monopolistic regime.[9] In so doing they recapitulated Karl Popper's distinction between 'closed' and 'open' societies. Thus Merle Fainsod, one of most influential theorists of Soviet totalitarianism, titled his classic study *How Russia is Ruled*, while Robert Dahl's classic study of democracy in America was entitled *Who Governs?* (1961). Rulership, political domination and the subjection of individuals to political power were thus presented as something anathema to liberal democracy. In Russia people were ruled. In the United States they were governed; indeed they were

8. See Fainsod (1953); Brzezinski (1956); Schapiro (1959); Conquest (1961); Armstrong (1961); Bauer and Inkeles (1961); Wolfe (1961); Kassof (1964, pp. 558–75); and Schapiro (1972).
9. See Dahl (1956); Mayo (1960); Lipset (1963); and Sartori (1962). I have explored the politics of this democratic theory in Isaac (1998). See also Ball (1993).

self-governing. 'Empirical democratic theory' and 'totalitarian studies' were thus mutually reinforcing developments of the post-war period.

By the 1960s this conception of totalitarianism as the monolithic antithesis of 'the open society' was challenged in two directions. Politically, the emergence of the New Left in the United States – and indeed throughout Western Europe – engendered a powerful critique of the very picture of Western liberal democracy as the open society. Whether in connection with the civil rights movement, the anti-poverty struggles of the late 1960s, or the Vietnam War and the official secrecy that supported it, questions were raised about the openness and pluralism of liberal democratic politics in the United States. The popularity, and influence, of books such as Herbert Marcuse's *One-Dimensional Man* both reflected and nourished this new cast of mind. Anti-communism increasingly became seen by these activists as an ideology itself, a simplification of the world, and an excuse for deceit and militarism. The language of 'totalitarianism' came to be seen as a weapon in the prosecution of the Cold War and in the uncritical celebration of 'the West' (Spiro and Barber 1970, p. 21). Marcuse went one step further, maintaining that liberal democracy, far from representing 'the open society', was *itself* totalitarian (Marcuse 1964, p. 3).

At the same time, and partly in response to these events, the concept of totalitarianism was battered by changes taking place in the communist world that defied the picture of monolithic power originally suggested by Friedrich and Brzezinski and accepted by their many academic followers. The 'thaw' and de-Stalinisation accompanying Khrushchev's rise to power in the Soviet Union, and the beginnings of social criticism, symbolised by the officially sanctioned publication of Alexander Solzhenitsyn's *One Day in the Life of Ivan Denisovich*; policy debates about the limits of a command economy and the possibility of introducing market mechanisms; the development of currents of revisionist Marxism throughout the 'Soviet bloc', criticising political authoritarianism and bureaucratic inefficiency in the name of a more 'authentic' and libertarian communism; and the emergence of genuine dissident movements within Eastern European Communist parties themselves, most emblematically during the Prague Spring of 1968 – these developments called into question the idea that Soviet 'totalitarianism' was monolithic and relatively unchanging. 'Socialism with a human face' was of course in due haste crushed by Soviet tanks. But the very possibility of its emergence and ascendancy, however brief, raised questions about the adequacy of the concept of totalitarianism as a description of the organisation of political power in the communist countries. As a result, books and articles proliferated throughout the academy repudiating 'totalitarianism' as an explanatory concept and pointing to the 'pluralistic' aspects of power in Soviet-type societies.[10]

What had come to be called 'the totalitarian model' of Soviet studies and comparative communism was losing its scientific imprimatur, and came increasingly to be seen as itself an ideological construction: a political interpretation forced on events and processes that seemed increasingly to call the model into question.

The literature of revolt against communism

It is supremely ironic that just at the moment when the concept of 'totalitarianism' was losing its plausibility in the West, it was helping to fuel democratic activism in the East. If in the Western context the concept had lost whatever critical edge had characterised its original formulations in the 1930s and 1940s, and had become conscripted in the Cold War strategies of the 'free world colossus', in the East the concepts of totalitarianism and post-totalitarianism were crucial elements in the 'democratic toolbox' of the political opposition to the colossus that was Soviet-style communism.[11] In one sense of course the idea retained the same force in both contexts, as a 'tool' of anti-communism. But if in the West the struggle against communism was a geo-political struggle undertaken by a heavily armed military-industrial state at the head of numerous military alliances, in the East it was a struggle of beleaguered citizens acting on behalf of their own idea of freedom. If in the West the idea of 'totalitarianism' had come to legitimate a post-war liberalism that was increasingly corporatist and bureaucratised – and thus to narrow the boundaries of what was considered politically acceptable – in the East the idea contributed to a remarkable *opening* of political space.

This opening was prepared by the emergence and proliferation of a subterranean or *samizdat* idiom of anti-totalitarian writing and dissident activity traceable to earlier critiques such as Milosz's *The Captive Mind* (1953) and Milovan Djilas's *The New Class: An Analysis of the Communist System*, and to even earlier works such as Victor Serge's *From Lenin to Stalin* (1937a) and Boris Souvarine's *Stalin: A Critical Survey of Bolshevism* (1939). Much of this

10. See Skilling and Griffiths (1971); Cohen (1971); Hough (1972); and Bialer (1980). This more pluralistic approach to Soviet studies was in some ways pioneered by Brzezinski and Huntington (1964).
11. The term 'the free world colossus' comes from an influential New Left manifesto written by David Horowitz (1972). Hungarian writer George Konrad refers to the 'democratic tool box' in Konrad (1992, pp. 36–7).

samizdat literature was explicitly anti-Marxist. Among these texts none approached the influence of Alexander Solzhenitsyn's *The Gulag Archipelago*, a powerful description, informed by first-hand experience as a victim, of the Soviet concentration camp system, an account that sent shock waves throughout the Eastern bloc. In the Soviet Union a robust underground movement also sprang up around the dissident physicist Andrei Sakharov.[12] By the mid-1960s Marxist revisionism, sometimes referred to as Marxist or socialist 'humanism', had also developed into an increasingly vital genre of political criticism throughout Eastern Europe, as writers as diverse as Leszek Kolakowski in Poland, Karel Kosik in Czechoslovakia, the so-called Budapest school in Hungary and the *Praxis* school in Yugoslavia challenged the authoritarian features of Soviet-style communism.[13] The Soviet suppression of the Prague Spring in 1968 dashed the hopes of these self-styled Marxist humanists, and moved most of them away from Marxism and towards the more thoroughgoing critique of communist ideology presented in different ways by Solzhenitsyn and Sakharov.

It was out of this intellectual ferment that were born the democratic movements that would eventually fell Eastern European communism. Following Timothy Garton Ash, a number of recent commentators have charted the intellectual evolution of these movements, focusing on their convergence on a particular understanding of totalitarianism that in some ways recuperates the sensibility of the anti-totalitarian resistance of the 1930s and 1940s.[14] If much of the discourse about totalitarianism in the 1950s and 1960s had emphasised its implacable and demonic power, the literature of revolt that flourished in the post-1968 period is marked, perhaps ironically given the fate of the Prague Spring, by an emphasis on the power of the human spirit and by the ability of responsible individuals to make a dent in the totalitarian armour and to sustain islands of freedom amidst the sea of conformity and fear.

While this literature was voluminous, perhaps the most important contribution was Vaclav Havel's 1978 'The Power of the Powerless'. Havel's task was nothing less than an analysis of 'the spectre' that was 'haunting Eastern Europe' – the spectre of dissent. Havel argued that Soviet-style communism had ceased to work according to the terroristic principles of classical totalitarianism characteristic of the Stalin era. The regime, he argued, had become

12. Sakharov offers a detailed account of this movement in his *Memoirs* (1990). See also Babyonshev (1982).
13. For a superb summary of this Marxist revisionism, see Leonhard (1974).
14. See Garton Ash (1990); Tismaneanu (1992); Goldfarb (1989); and Isaac (1996, pp. 291–344).

'post-totalitarian', maintaining a monopoly on political power by inducing a more insidious form of complicity on the part of its subjects. If classical totalitarianism was characterised by fanatical ideological mobilisation, the 'post-totalitarian' regime was distinguished by its transparent ideological cynicism; if classical totalitarianism was rooted in a pervasive insecurity and fear, 'post-totalitarianism' survived because of the dependency it had induced in ordinary subjects. Post-totalitarianism, according to Havel, was a thoroughly *normalised* system of domination: one that worked according to what he called an 'auto-totality'. And yet, he argued, this system of power was profoundly vulnerable. Just as under this system all were complicitous in the 'auto-totality' of power, so too all were potentially rebels against this system. Each individual, as a moral agent, contained a seed of resistance. Havel proceeded to argue that the 'auto-totality' of the system was losing its momentum, and that as a result all kinds of independent activity were emerging, presaging the declining legitimacy, and the eventual decline itself, of the post-totalitarian system (Havel 1992).

Havel's essay was the most influential entry in the extensive pamphlet literature of the Charter '77 movement in Czechoslovakia (see Skilling 1981 and 1989; Skilling and Wilson 1991). The writings of Adam Michnik, especially his essays *The Church and the Left* (1992) and 'The New Evolutionism' (in Michnik 1985) played a similar role in Poland, as did the writings of George Konrad in Hungary (see Konrad 1984 and Konrad and Szelenyi 1979). These authors represented the tip of a swelling iceberg of intellectual and political opposition to the communist regimes of Eastern Europe (indeed, they increasingly insisted on calling this region central Europe or east central Europe to highlight its irreducibility to the terms of the Cold War). All set themselves against the 'totalitarian' features of the communist regimes, their insistence on one-party rule, their stifling suppression of civil liberties, and their reliance on propaganda and mendacity rather than on publicity. Yet they also recognised the 'post-totalitarian' character of these regimes: the declining significance of sheer terror, the dependence of political legitimacy upon the creation of kinds of consumerism that were both ethically vacuous and difficult to sustain in a command economy, the existence of systemic vulnerabilities that might afford spaces of freedom and even the possibility of strategic political manoeuvring on the part of democratic oppositionists. By 1989 these vulnerabilities became increasingly glaring, and the opposition that had been latent erupted into a tidal wave of opposition to communism that brought down the system, a development symbolised by the dramatic dismantling of the Berlin Wall.

The literature of revolt in Eastern Europe that helped to bring this about was resolutely anti-totalitarian. But many of its principal authors were committed to values of authenticity, truthfulness and civic initiative that remained in tension with the forms of liberal democracy and consumer capitalism that quickly overcame their societies with the collapse of communism. A profound historical irony resides in the fact that the moment of triumph for these activists was also the moment at which many of their most cherished ideals were rendered irrelevant. As Michnik noted in 1991: 'The time for people like myself to engage in politics has come to an end . . . today politics is becoming normal, and for those who did not treat politics as a game but as a way to defend basic values it is becoming difficult to find a space. It will become even harder in the future.'[15]

Antecedents and projections

If this brief survey of the discourse of totalitarianism has demonstrated anything, it is that this discourse, like all political discourses, is marked by both continuities and discontinuities. Since the 1930s the literature of totalitarianism has largely been a literature critical of the tyrannical features of a certain kind of political regime that was an invention of the twentieth century, a regime characterised by its concentration not simply of legal authority but effective political and ideological power, and by its exercise of this power in extraordinary, murderous ways. What has changed has been the nature of the criticism, in part explicable in terms of the changing object of criticism.

The critics of the 1930s and 1940s were largely political and existential exiles, traumatised by the convergence of the Hitler and Stalin regimes and by what this signified about the power of evil in the world. Many were independent leftists dispirited by the totalitarianisation of communism and seeking some political anchor amidst the turbulence of two decades characterised by political defeat and world war. The critics of the post-war period associated with the 'totalitarian model' of Soviet politics were singularly focused on the global 'threat' presented by a Soviet communism that was in control of half of Europe. Exhausted by the ideological fanaticisms of prior decades, secure amidst the power and plenty sustained by the post-war hegemony of the United States, yet anxious about the maintenance of this hegemony, these writers were critical of communism; but this singular focus

15. Paradowska (1991, pp. 95–6); see also Havel (1992); Tismaneanu (1994, pp. 130–42); Konrad (1995); and Garton Ash (1995).

of criticism rendered them less than critical of the injustices of capitalism, or of the deceit and violence mobilised by the 'free world' during the Cold War. This literature reached its apotheosis in the famous, perhaps infamous, disquisitions of Jeanne Kirkpatrick, chief ideologist of the Reagan administration, on the differences between 'authoritarian' and 'totalitarian' regimes, which among other things furnished a justification for why the United States should support brutal and murderous military regimes in Central America so as to counter revolutionary movements in El Salvador and Nicaragua that presented a purported 'totalitarian' threat (Kirkpatrick 1982).[16]

Central European critics like Havel, Michnik and Konrad shared the anti-communism of Cold War intellectuals, and indeed took some comfort in the hawkish foreign policy of the Reagan administration that was inspired by the hard 'anti-totalitarianism' of those like Kirkpatrick.[17] Indeed, during the 'dark years' after the Soviet crushing of the Prague Spring in 1968, many of those Westerners most interested in the Eastern European literature of revolt tended to be Cold Warriors.[18] Yet these central European critics of totalitarianism were not Cold Warriors. The thrust of their writings was to challenge bloc thinking of any kind, and to make space for an independent politics averse to totalitarianism but also in tension with the kinds of corporatism and bureaucracy characteristic of 'normal' liberal democracy. In many ways these writers hark back to precursors like Arendt, Orwell and Camus in the rebellious character of their thinking.

But they also hark back to earlier genres of modern political thought. Hannah Arendt, in the famous 1951 preface to *Origins of Totalitarianism*, maintained that the onset of totalitarianism had caused a radical caesura in history; previous political theory, she held, offered no guidance to the new phenomena associated with totalitarianism. But this judgement, however important in a cautionary sense, is no doubt exaggerated. It is true, as she insisted, that totalitarianism is a novel idea, associated with a novel form of political domination. And it is also undeniable that this novelty necessitated, and brought forth, new ways of thinking about politics. But the discourse of totalitarianism clearly drew, at least in part, from earlier

16. Gleason has a fine discussion of this in his *Totalitarianism* (1995, pp. 190–210).
17. For Havel's critique of the Western peace movement's opposition to such a foreign policy, see his 'Anatomy of a Reticence' (1985) in Havel (1992, pp. 291–322). See also Feher and Heller (1987 and 1990).
18. See, for example, the writings of the 'New Philosophers' in France: Revel (1977) and Levy (1979). There were, it bears noting, Western social democrats more inclined to hear these Eastern European voices. See Howe (1983), and the many issues of *Dissent* magazine containing translations of anti-communist dissidents.

idioms of political thought, especially the anti-despotic writings of such liberals as Montesquieu, Constant and Tocqueville, but also writers as diverse as Hobbes, Burke, Marx and Nietzsche. While the concept of totalitarianism was a novelty, this concept originally assumed importance amidst the ideological debates that took place between and among conservatives, libertarians, liberals, anarchists, socialists and communists of various stripes. The discourse of totalitarianism is of course not reducible to these ideological debates, which were dramatically transformed by the onset of totalitarianism in Stalinist Russia and Nazi Germany. Indeed, the most original participants in these political arguments, like Arendt, or the Frankfurt school theorists, were those who took the full measure of totalitarianism's novelty, and sought to move beyond nineteenth-century ideological categories. But there can be no doubt that these categories continued to exert their influence, and to shape the way in which totalitarianism has been seen since its emergence in the 1920s.

The idea of totalitarianism, and even more so the realities towards which this idea has pointed, has been at the centre of political controversy and at the heart of innovation in political theory since the 1930s. With the dramatic collapse of the Soviet imperium, and the triumph of liberalism that has been heralded in the East, it might appear that the literature of totalitarianism is a thing of the past, of merely antiquarian interest to intellectual historians. Yet appearances can deceive. 'Totalitarianism' is not yet extinguished, as witnessed by the Chinese, Cuban, Iraqi and North Korean regimes, and by the continued influence of Stalinism in Russia itself. But in any case we are still the heirs of the traumas caused by totalitarianism, just as we are the heirs of the courageous efforts of those who have struggled against them. As we embark upon a new century, the discourse of totalitarianism remains of continuing importance for those interested in the practice of freedom in the modern world.

9
The end of the welfare state?

ROBERT E. GOODIN

The halcyon days

The founders themselves would have been keenly sensitive to the diversity of motives and models underlying what we now know as 'the' welfare state. Bismarck's conservative corporatist version built on frankly neo-feudal foundations to buy social peace. Alva and Gunnar Myrdal's social democratic model aimed to generate more Swedish babies (Tilton 1990). The British welfare state was principally the product of two renegade Liberals, Lloyd George and Beveridge (Beveridge 1942). The American welfare state was a patrician Democrat's *noblesse oblige* response to the Great Depression, relieving distress among the old and disabled, the widowed and the chronically ill (Hofstadter 1948, ch. 12).

These distinctive trajectories are regularly revisited by theorists of the welfare state, some in search of typologies (Titmuss 1974, ch. 2; Esping-Andersen 1990; Goodin *et al.* 1999), others simply revelling in the utter uniqueness of their own country's distinctive history and particular programmes (Skocpol 1992; Castles 1985). As a matter of historical record, no doubt they are right. In terms of policy analysis likewise, causes and consequences of different welfare regimes sometimes clearly matter (Flora and Heidenheimer 1981).

Still, the received view of 'the welfare state' that has passed into contemporary political thought is of a much more unified phenomenon. In popular memory and broader political discourse 'the welfare state' was something born of shared wartime suffering and the Great Depression; it was animated by the desire to meet needs and promote social equality; and it operates on and through broadly capitalist economies managed along broadly Keynesian lines.

If Beveridge was the architect of Britain's post-war welfare state, Richard Titmuss was its chief theorist. Through his writings, and those who influenced him and who were influenced by him, a certain standard view of the welfare state phenomenon came to dominate post-war political thought (Titmuss 1950; 1971; 1973; 1974; 1987).

One plank of this paradigm was sociological. The welfare state is seen as a response to social dislocation occasioned by industrialisation. With the 'great transformation' wrought by industrialisation and the marketisation of the economy, people without access to market earnings became particularly vulnerable and in need of social protection (Polanyi 1957 [1944]; Wilensky and Lebeaux 1958). The welfare state thus conceived secured an income stream to those effectively excluded from the paid workforce, whether by reason of age (hence old-age pensions), family circumstance (family allowances; survivors' benefits), health status (work injury, sickness and disability insurance) or market conditions (unemployment insurance). Welfare states, like the economies they underpinned, were envisaged as progressing through 'stages of development', with ever-expanding ranges of such social protections being needed, and provided, as countries reached ever-higher levels of socio-economic development (Cutright 1965).

Programmatically, welfare states were seen as characteristically operating through systems of 'social insurance' (Atkinson 1995, ch. 11). Older programmes of 'general' (or 'social' or 'public') assistance – the old Poor Law and its successors – remained in force as well. But those older forms of social assistance were to be conceived (as in the official British terminology) merely as 'supplementary benefits', serving merely as a 'social safety net' to catch any needy cases which slipped through the welfare state's system of categorical benefits. In contrast to those old-style systems of discretionary, means-tested social assistance, the new and distinctively welfare state protections provided broadly the same level of benefit to everyone in specified categories, regardless of their financial means and, often, even of their prior earnings or contribution histories (tenBroek and Wilson 1954). Just as one's entitlement to a fire insurance payout if one's house burns down is unaffected by one's income or wealth or by how long one has been paying on the policy, so too with these insurance-style welfare state benefits.

Such programmes of social insurance were designed principally to provide income support. But the various other 'social services' designed to supplement them were organised broadly along similar lines. The three legs of the British welfare state were 'national insurance' (extended per Beveridge's plan, given statutory form in 1946), 'comprehensive education' (per Rab Butler's 1944 Act) and the National Health Service (per Nye Bevan's 1946 Act). Just as flat-rate benefits were to be provided to every pensioner, so too were uniform standards of medical care and schooling to be provided to all patients and students. Just as national insurance was to be paid without any test of financial means, so too was health care and education to be provided to everyone of an age or health status to qualify for it, regardless of their or their families' incomes or assets (Glennerster 1995, esp. chs. 2–3).

Ideologically, the characteristic catch-cries of such a welfare state echoed across most of the developed world through much of the post-war period. In contrast to the market, the welfare state was supposed to answer the call of social need rather than of effective demand (Doyal and Gough 1991; Braybrooke 1987; Plant 1988). In contrast to private charity or public poor relief, the welfare state's benefits were universal rather than selectively targeted on the poor alone (Titmuss 1967); and that was a crucial part of their strategy for reducing inequality across society as a whole rather than merely succouring the poor (Le Grand 1982, ch. 2; Ringen 1987). Welfare state benefits were meant to manifest and reinforce a diffuse sense of community, fraternity and social solidarity – what came to be called 'social citizenship' – through impersonal altruism on one side and claims 'as of right' on the other (Marshall 1965 [1949]; Titmuss 1971; 1973; 1974, postscript). Quibble though philosophers may over the coherence of all those propositions (Goodin 1988, chs. 2–4), in the popular imagination that package was a clear and cohesive one.

In its heyday, this construction came under challenge principally from the left. Radicals bemoaned its ameliorist orientation – its attempt to mitigate the effects of the market economy without in any way changing its basic structure (Cohen 1981). Others challenged its 'productivist' orientation – its attempt to provide income support for those suffering some interruption in their ordinary market earnings with scant regard for those not ordinarily in the market (Nelson 1990; Fraser 1994; Land 1994; Offe 1992).

'Poor people's movements' and 'poverty lobbies' more generally, however, took a less radical and more pragmatic tack (Piven and Cloward 1979). Observing that social welfare all too often served merely as a device for 'regulating the poor' (Piven and Cloward 1971), they lobbied for a reduction in administrative discretion and an increased scope for claimants' rights (Titmuss 1971b). Seeing that the relief of poverty stopped far short of providing the full range of resources that people needed to participate fully in their societies (Townsend 1962; 1979), and that providing equality of access fell far short of ensuring equality of outcomes (Le Grand 1982), they lobbied for increased sums to be spent in more directly redistributive ways.

Arguments over levels of benefits, always important, became increasingly so as the 'mean season' set in (Block *et al.* 1987). But arguments over the welfare state, in its heyday, were more arguments over the forms in which benefits were conferred. They focused much more on downplaying the disfavoured residual tier of 'social assistance' and on putting more and more social welfare benefits onto the more privileged, entitlement-based footing of 'social insurance'. These were, at root, arguments for 'completing the welfare state project' by phasing out the final remnants of the Poor Law (tenBroek and Wilson 1954; Nelson 1990).

Challenges/crises

In the wake of the oil shock of 1974, and of the economic downturn that it precipitated and the right-wing governments that it brought to power, there came a sea change in this familiar rhetorical construction (Hills 1993; Glennerster 1995, chs. 8–9). Public expenditures in general and social spending in particular came in for new questioning (Rose and Peters 1979; Ringen 1987, ch. 5; Lindbeck *et al.* 1994). As the 'growth of limits' (Flora 1986) began increasingly to bite, 'the welfare state in crisis' (OECD 1981) became an increasingly common refrain, taking the several more specific forms surveyed below.

Animating most of those more specific attacks was a New Right agenda composed of several strands (King 1987; Gray 1989). Whereas the Keynesian macro-economic orthodoxy called for governments to engage in demand management and pump-priming through counter-cyclical deficit spending, the New Right urged strict monetarist policies, reducing the public sector borrowing requirement, and balanced budgets (Friedman 1962; Friedman and Friedman 1980). Whereas progressives looked to government for solutions to social problems, the New Right opposed central government planning and instead urged reliance upon the 'spontaneous order' of self-regulating markets – in Hayek's case, for the regulation of money supply itself (Hayek 1976, 1979; see also Rhoads 1985; Self 1993).

While not denying the familiar flaws in market mechanisms, New Right theorists simply pointed to what they saw as greater flaws in non-market modes of social organisation (Wolf 1988). A government having power to issue authoritative edicts invites 'rent-seeking' on the part of those in a position to secure control over regulation and licensing, legislation and administration

(Buchanan, Tollison and Tullock 1980; Stigler 1988). Governmental edicts being enforced through hierarchical command and control structures invites 'principal–agent' slippage, allowing lower-level bureaucrats scope for pursuing goals of their own rather than those of their notional superiors (Niskanen 1971; Miller 1992).

Beyond its particular challenges to particular policies or mechanisms, the New Right attacked the notion of 'social justice' itself as a 'mirage' (Hayek 1979). Libertarians such as Nozick (1974) argued that redistribution as such was morally wrong: if you earned the money fair and square, you should be able to keep it and spend it as you wished; coercive taxation was akin to 'forced labour'. Free marketeers such as Hayek (1979) and Friedman (1962; Friedman and Friedman 1980) argued that central state planning, for social justice or anything else, will inevitably soon bump up against barriers imposed by the decentralisation of information in society.

Such critiques of the welfare state, influential in the 1970s and 1980s in the form of Thatcherism and Reaganomics, have themselves now been largely discredited. The 'spontaneous order' of the market has proven spectacularly disorderly, with the too easy movement of speculative capital wreaking havoc upon deregulated financial markets. The notion that the rich have obtained their riches fair and square has proved highly dubious where the rich get ever richer feeding on junk bond markets (Hutton 1995). Clearly there can be no return to the traditional mechanisms of state intervention and public subsidy: those mechanisms, too, have been discredited. But a return to those concerns pursued through some other mechanisms is now very much on the cards. I shall return to those themes, after first surveying the more particular forms such challenges to the welfare state have taken and the more specific responses they have evoked.

The affordability crisis

Talk of a looming 'affordability crisis' in the welfare state, long in the background, has suddenly gained new credence. One version of that story turns on demographics and the nature of pay-as-you-go pension systems. Private pension funds are 'vested', with pensioners basically just drawing out what they paid in during their working lives (and with those who live a little longer than expected being cross-subsidised at the margins by those who live less long than expected). Public old-age pensions, in contrast, characteristically pay present-day pensioners out of the contributions of present-day workers. The financial viability of such schemes then crucially turns on the so-called 'dependency ratio' – the number of dependants drawing social benefits compared to the number of workers supporting them. As baby boomers move toward retirement (and live increasingly long after retirement, to boot), fewer and fewer workers will have to pay for more and more state pensioners. Clearly, something will have to give: either social security taxes will have to increase, or pension levels will have to drop, or people will have to postpone taking up their pensions until later (OECD 1994; World Bank 1994).

Pay-as-you-go pensions are also said to undermine the 'affordability' of the welfare state by undermining saving and investment, thus inhibiting economic growth (World Bank 1994). Right-wing economists (Feldstein and Pellechio 1979) here join left-wing sociologists (O'Connor 1973; Gough 1979; Offe 1984; cf. Klein 1993) in emphasising the reliance of capitalist economies upon 'capital accumulation', with savings from current consumption forming the basis for subsequent investment and hence growth in the economy as a whole. Left-wing sociologists then point to the need of liberal democratic governments to spend rather than save, in order to buy political support; right-wing economists then point to the ways in which pay-as-you-go pensions supplant public or private savings that would otherwise occur as people (or their governments, under alternative 'vested' public pension schemes) salt away some of their current income for their retirement years. In both cases, though, 'capital formation' is inhibited and economic growth compromised.

The empirical evidence of these and other alleged 'incentive effects' of the welfare state (reducing work effort and increasing public dependency, and such like) is mixed at best (Danziger *et al.* 1981; Moffitt 1992). Cross-nationally, there is little evidence, and economically little logic, to support claims that welfare state expenditures impair economic growth overall (Atkinson 1995, ch. 6; 1999). But here, as elsewhere, public discourse is substantially impervious to econometric evidence. In the current climate of uncertain economic prospects or actual economic decline, it is a seemingly unshakeable article of conventional wisdom that we can simply 'no longer afford' the sort of large-scale social protections of earlier, richer eras.

The accountability crisis

A second strand in that New Right attack on the welfare state bemoans an 'accountability crisis'. The welfare state dispenses large sums of public monies, often in a highly discretionary manner at the point of provision, and in any case without any central accounting to ensure that this is the best way of getting 'value for money' in the welfare sector.

The notion of accounting at work here sometimes had more to do with accountancy than accountability in any genuinely political sense. 'Razor gangs' conducted 'efficiency audits' to prune 'unnecessary' public spending, in the welfare sector as elsewhere (Hood and Wright 1981; Power 1994). Early efficiency audits were characterised by imprecise instruments of measurement and blunt instruments of control. The focus on 'value for money' led to a fixation on financial measures, eclipsing all the less tangible or longer-term goals a policy might serve (Heald 1983). Global cuts to agency budgets have now given way to more targeted efforts at 'reinventing government', reshaping the organisation of government for the more effective discharge of agencies' missions and the more efficient delivery of services (Osborne and Gaebler 1993).

Beyond the narrow questions of financial accountability addressed by efficiency audits are larger questions of political accountability. On the face of it, that is assured by 'responsible government' of a perfectly ordinary sort. Spending programmes have been enacted by politicians electorally accountable to the public and implemented by civil servants accountable to them in turn (Day and Klein 1987). But the New Right's public choice critique of 'non-market decision-making' queries both halves of that model. On the one side, we cannot rely on vote-seeking politicians to promote the public interest: at best, there might be redistribution from both ends of the income scale toward the all-powerful median voter (Stigler 1970); at worst, the logic of collective action suggests that small groups with concentrated interests will be better organised, and better served politically, than large and diffuse interests (Olson 1965; Peltzman 1980; Pierson 1994). On the other side, bureaucrats have interests of their own in expanding their budget, staff and area of responsibility which gets in the way of their responding smoothly to the policy preferences of their elected masters (Niskanen 1971).

Those propositions are taken by the New Right to prove that public spending is always 'too high' in a democratically accountable polity, thus providing a theoretical warrant for their 'razor gangs' always looking for ways to cut public expenditure. In truth, however, the same arguments can equally well be used to show that in some respects public spending might be 'too low' in democracies (Downs 1960). The real implication of these arguments, in so far as they can be accepted at all (cf. Dunleavy 1991), is not that public spending is too high or too low, but rather that it is necessarily skewed, away from genuine public interests which are broadly shared across the community and toward narrow interests shared by only a few powerful sectors of society (Goodin 1982).

These early attempts to forge strong, necessary links between the New Right's critique of political accountability and its notions of financial accountability and overspending eventually gave way to more modulated claims of a more unexceptionable sort. Just as there are certain characteristic 'market failures' associated with public goods and externalities, so too are there certain characteristic 'non-market failures' associated with recognisable pathologies of public bureaucracies (Wolf 1988). Which on balance predominates in any given instance is an open question, and thus we have to decide on a more case-by-case (or sector-by-sector) basis whether market or non-market arrangements will better ensure greater efficiency or accountability to the wider public.

The New Right's preferred reform to the public sector is remarkably constant across all those modulations. Niskanen's (1971) original idea was that introducing market-like competitiveness within the state bureaucracy would promote efficiency, and hence accountability, of an implicitly financial or consumerist sort. Privatisation of many public enterprises, and the opening of others to competition from private providers, were justified in those terms. Where neither was practically or politically feasible, the preferred solution was to create 'internal quasi-markets' (Le Grand 1991). The model was the National Health Service reforms. In the old days, GPs seeking the best possible treatment for their patients had no particular motive for containing costs to the NHS, just as American GPs seeking to maximise the profits to their practice have no particular motive for containing costs passed on to their patients' insurance companies. Under the NHS reforms, GP 'fundholders' were given a notional 'budget' to spend on the patients on their lists, which they could use to 'purchase' whatever range of services from whatever providers they thought best. The effect of this 'purchaser/provider split' was to withdraw the blank cheque previously provided to GPs and to make them think harder about treatment priorities, efficiency and effectiveness.

GP fundholders clearly can in this way be made more accountable for what they do with the Exchequer's money, but it is much less clear that the accountability of the system overall is enhanced by these reforms. Overall responsibility is radically diffused. When asked why the NHS has set these priorities, all we can say is that those are the priorities that have emerged from the disjointed decisions of a great many particular GPs trying to do the best for the particular patients who present with particular complaints.

Market failures will inevitably emerge in these 'quasi-markets' as surely as in genuine ones, leading, for example, to an unduly low revealed demand for public goods such as research and development of new technologies and treatment regimes. Quasi-markets, like real ones, will respond to expressed demand rather than underlying needs, so the long-suffering poor who expect little will get little. Fundholders in quasi-markets will try to cream 'good risks' just as insurance underwriters in real markets do. Quasi-markets will be as sensitive as real ones to the initial distribution of resources, so, for example, fundholders charged with the care of particularly at-risk patients will need to be given an extra 'loading' of some sort. While all of these issues can be addressed, they can only be addressed outside the model of market accountability itself – by central authorities of responsible government.

The personal responsibility crisis

In New Right rhetoric, the unaccountability of traditional state welfare providers was matched by the irresponsibility of welfare recipients. Ensuring everyone a right to welfare led to a 'demoralisation' of society, both discouraging and devaluing personal effort. In place of the old virtues of self-reliance, there arose a 'culture of dependency'. This was said to be nowhere more evident than in the breeding behaviour of much maligned welfare mothers – 'babies having babies' well before they were either emotionally or financially ready to bear the burden (Murray 1984; Himmelfarb 1994).

These dependency critiques are often linked to – both feeding off and feeding into – arguments in terms of affordability and accountability. Welfare dependency is said by some to inhibit economic growth and, in so doing, to undermine what is our best hope for reducing poverty overall and in the long run. In Charles Murray's famous phrase, 'we were winning the war [against poverty] until Lyndon Johnson decided to wage it' (1984, p. 16). Granting anyone an automatic right to welfare, regardless of their own complicity in the chain of events that led to their plight, is said by many to undermine notions of accountability and personal responsibility.

In the end, it is this moral challenge that constitutes the most distinctive aspect of the dependency critique of the welfare state. Women who recklessly or wantonly court pregnancy, knowing that they will have no recourse but to rely upon state assistance to support the ensuing child, are said to be behaving patently immorally; and their immorality is taken to be a template for a whole raft of other reckless or wanton behaviour which leads others to fall onto the welfare rolls as well.

Whether this is an apt characterisation of the predicament or calculations of welfare mothers, whether it is a model for others, whether any moral fault follows from it, or whether any future-oriented policy prescriptions follow from backward-looking calculations of fault are all radically open questions (Fraser and Gordon 1994; Goodin 1997). But this is certainly how the situations are presented, and in ways which apparently resonate on all sides of the present political spectrum, judging from the way in which in 1996, overturning practices of sixty years' standing, a Republican Congress enacted, and a Democratic president Clinton signed, legislation withdrawing Aid to Families with Dependent Children from welfare mothers who had been on the rolls continuously for two years or intermittently for five.

According to received opinion, the solution to welfare dependency is 'workfare'. Education and training programmes designed to make welfare recipients work-ready constitute a 'hand up, not a hand out', thus enhancing self-reliance rather than undermining it. In thus solving the moral problem posed by welfare dependency, workfare programmes also address issues of affordability as well, constituting as they do 'investments in human capital' and an inducement to future economic growth (Bane and Ellwood 1994; King 1995). How successful they can realistically expect to be in either dimension is of course open to question: many (counting the age pension, most) welfare recipients are not objectively in social situations in which we ordinarily expect people to work, being too young, too old, physically or mentally handicapped or burdened with very young children. Furthermore, whatever remedial education and training workfare provides for them, most long-term welfare recipients are never likely to be much more than marginal, low-paid workers. Thus, workfare solutions to welfare dependency are more a matter of ideology and appearances than they are of economics or even genuine morality. Still, there is no overestimating the political importance of ideology and appearances.

The feminist challenge

Feminists are quick to point out the perversity of the 'dependency' critique of the welfare state. The objection is not to dependency as such, but merely to dependence upon the state for needed assistance. The 'self-reliance' being advocated is consistent with, and indeed entails, reliance upon all manner of family and friends and private charities. But that is as illogical as it is sexist.

If there really is some 'defect of character' involved in people relying upon agencies outside themselves for things they need and could easily provide for themselves, it should in principle be the same in both cases (Goodin 1988, ch. 12; 1997; Fraser and Gordon 1994). And shifting the burden of care in that way from the state to the community entails yet greater burdens for typically female caregivers, who are increasingly trying to hold down paid employment at the same time (Ungerson 1987).

Furthermore, feminists point out, some of the most maligned aspects of the welfare state – financial assistance to unwed mothers, most especially – actually contribute to independence of this broader sort. It assists women in setting up a separate household, thus escaping their dependence upon men, be they their fathers or partners, for support (Orloff 1993). The women in question remain incapable of securing a market income sufficient to support themselves, so their dependence is not so much reduced as merely shifted from family to state. But dependence on an impersonal agency like the state, whose agents have minimal discretion in the distribution of those needed resources, entails far less risk of manipulation and exploitation than does reliance upon the inherently discretionary largesse of family and friends and voluntary charities – a point on which feminist critics of patrimony echo earlier advocates of welfare rights (Orloff 1993; Titmuss 1973).

In various other more modest ways, as well, welfare states can be set up so as to promote independence, rather than dependence, for women within the household. One old welfare state tradition was to underwrite a 'family wage', through both labour market and social transfer policies, the effect of which was a 'breadwinner's welfare state' increasing and underwriting the dependence upon a typically male breadwinner. The newer, more female-friendly alternative is to provide welfare on an individualised basis, assisting individuals rather than families and doing so on the basis of their own rather than their household's needs and assets (Fraser 1994). Some countries have done this to some extent for quite some time, others are just beginning. Clearly, however, it is the trend of the future, with considerations of gender justice happily converging with the practicalities of social administration in a world of increasingly complicated domestic couplings and decouplings (Land 1994; Sainsbury 1996; O'Connor *et al.* 1999).

The future

Under the weight of those challenges, the traditional universalistic cradle-to-grave welfare state is probably politically 'dead' for the foreseeable future.

There is an unmistakable trend toward a leaner, more tightly targeted system of social services and income supports (Atkinson, 1995, chs. 12–16).

These reforms are not all of a cloth, however. Some of them seem to amount to sheer capitulation to the critics of the unaffordability of old-style welfare states. That seems clearly the case, for example, where programmes which used to be universally available to everyone regardless of income or assets are increasingly means-tested in respect of availability, charges or benefits. In other cases, though, reforms seem to amount more to reshaping than simply retrenching old-style welfare states. In place of uniform benefits to all clients, tailor-made packages are increasingly being put together by social-service analogues of GP fundholders that are more responsive to the particular needs of particular clients (Rothstein 1998).

Even if talk of 'cradle-to-grave security' is distinctly out of fashion, social programmes still particularly concern themselves with people at each end of the lifecourse. Programmes for income security in old age are being readjusted in the light of looming affordability crises, but nowhere are they under fundamental attack (Korpi 1995); and the same is true, in most countries, with programmes of child support and family allowances. Death benefits remain a central, if seldom discussed, plank even of reformed welfare states. There will be no return any time soon to the ignominy of paupers' graves. Public provision for ante-natal and neo-natal care and at least modest maternity leave and other benefits remain, even where health services and labour law have been radically reformed. Even the leanest of the new welfare states still offer support to children in the womb and the cradle, and state support continues throughout most of the school years.

It is in the middle of the lifecourse where welfare reforms bite hardest. Those who could in principle work for a living are increasingly being expected to do so, rather than relying upon state support. But they are also being increasingly assisted in doing so, through a range of 'workfare' education and training programmes (King 1995; Bane and Ellwood 1994).

With this increasing emphasis upon self-support through the labour market comes, also, renewed reflection upon the classes of people who we think ought legitimately to be excused from service in labour markets. The young, the old and the physically disabled have always been so excused, without much comment (Titmuss 1955). But renewed emphasis upon labour markets as the prime mode of welfare provision should, and inevitably will, bring to the fore of public discussion questions of whether, for example, mothers of very young children might not be performing a greater social service staying home to raise the next generation than they would be labouring in some factory for low wages (Land 1994; cf. Bane and Ellwood 1994, ch. 5). Those caring for elderly relatives or performing other forms of voluntary charitable labour likewise might be performing a greater social service than they would in the paid labour market (Ungerson 1987).

Where the internal logic of such reflections will eventually lead is of course hard to predict. But in the limiting case, such logic might eventually lead us to pay out of the public purse a 'participation wage' to everyone performing any of a range of useful public services outside the paid labour market (Atkinson 1996), and that itself might take us a very long way toward paying a 'basic income' to everyone in society (Van Parijs 1992). Basic income proposals have been around for a long time, in various forms – most famously, previously, as Friedman's (1962, ch. 12; Friedman and Friedman 1980, ch. 4) 'negative income tax'. Such proposals pose familiar questions both of affordability and of accountability, of whether we really want to remove all 'strings' tied to present 'categorical benefits' and of just how much we could pay everyone even by cashing out all categorical benefits (recalling, of course, that basic income payments would be taxable, for those over the tax threshold). Beyond pragmatics, however, are questions of principle – of whether it is right that people get 'something for nothing' in this way (cf. Van Parijs 1992). Many who think it is not are drawn to the idea of a 'participation wage', paid generously to everyone providing any of a wide range of social services (including most especially caring for the young or old at home), in consequence.

Another class of people who would have to be excused from labour market participation are those who are 'structurally unemployed'. If the 'natural rate of unemployment' in our economy is, say, 5 per cent, then logically we simply have to excuse 5 per cent of otherwise eligible workers from earning a living for themselves in the labour market. Identifying who is structurally unemployed and who is voluntarily unemployed is of course administratively difficult. We impose 'availability for work' tests upon recipients of unemployment benefits, and spend substantial sums policing them. As technological change makes increasing numbers of people structurally unemployed, it might eventually prove simpler and more efficient, once again, simply to compensate them through less conditional programmes of income support – eventually leading once again, in the limiting case, to something that might approximate a basic income (Hamminga 1995; Mead 1995).

In an important way, all this amounts to a 'return to Beveridge' – or, rather, a rethinking of the basic Beveridge strategy for income support, in the light of new social circumstances. Beveridge's original plan for flat-rate national insurance benefits linked to employee contributions, per *Social Insurance and Allied Services* (Beveridge 1942), clearly presupposed something like full employment (Beveridge 1945), so everyone will have made (or had made on their behalf) qualifying contributions. Furthermore, Beveridge (1948) also explicitly assumed that the limits of flat-rate income support would be made good by 'voluntary action' of a charitable sort in the non-government sector. With increasing structural unemployment, the first condition is not met; with increasing pressure toward two-income families, would-be caregivers are increasingly otherwise occupied (Ungerson 1987; Land 1994). Basic income, or a 'participation wage' to compensate people for contributions to society outside the labour market, might go some way towards making good both shortcomings in the basic preconditions of the original Beveridge model.

Social insurance is once again becoming increasingly central in new-style welfare states. One aspect of that, already mentioned, is a transfer across the lifecourse – from high-earning middle years to the non-earning years of childhood and old age. What looks from one perspective like a transfer from one group to others (from the middle-aged to the young and old) is, from another perspective, simply a transfer across one's own lifecourse.

Categorical programmes of social assistance have traditionally been earnings-related, aimed explicitly at stabilising the incomes of people whose ordinary earnings have been interrupted by some specific form of catastrophic injury or illness (Goodin 1990). Social assistance more generally is being increasingly conceived similarly as provisional assistance, tiding people over particular crises until they are able to support themselves again.

That reconceptualisation is clearly hard on welfare mothers and others who genuinely need to rely on public support in an on-going way, and who are increasingly under threat of being denied benefits after a relatively brief period. But the genuine seriousness of their plight ought not to obscure the fact that the great majority of recipients of public assistance use it only in this transitional way (Duncan 1984; Duncan *et al.* 1988; Bane and Ellwood 1994; Goodin *et al.* 1999). Furthermore, these precipitating life crises – unemployment, protracted illness or loss (by death, disability or divorce) of a family's breadwinner – might happen to anyone, so insurance of this sort is something virtually everyone might find of benefit (Duncan 1984, p. 119).

The political point of reconceptualising transfers as 'insurance against interrupted earnings' in this way is clear enough. *Ex post*, the lucky end up cross-subsidising the unlucky. But *ex ante* anyone might have turned out to be unlucky, and in that sense everyone benefits from the insurance provided (Goodin and Dryzek 1986; Barr 1987). Substantial redistribution, of a sort, is thus justified without any appeal to old-style and increasingly unfashionable values of equality or altruism. The 'solidarity' of the shared risk pool, and the efficiencies of providing social insurance on a public rather than private basis (Goodin 1988, ch. 6; 1997; Barr, 1989), may be quite enough to motivate support for something rather like the welfare state into the indefinite future.

Part II
Varieties of Marxism

10
The Second International: socialism and social democracy

DICK GEARY

Introduction

In 1889 the Second International Working Men's Association was formed at a congress in Paris of trade unionists and socialists from several countries. In the following decades this organisation became the forum of major debates between different kinds of socialists. The Second International was not simply a talking shop for intellectuals, however; its membership embraced mass organisations, such as the Austrian, German and Russian Social Democratic parties, the Belgian Labour Party, the French socialists, who united in 1905 to form the Section Française de l'Internationale Ouvrière (SFIO), and the Italian Socialist Party (PSI). Between 1889 and 1914 Marxist intellectuals were not detached from practical party politics: socialist theory flourished hand in hand with the growth of the labour movement. Eighteen eighty-nine, for example, was a year of massive strikes, including the great London dock strike and industrial action on the part of thousands of miners in the Ruhr. In the next fifteen years millions of workers joined unions; a third general strike led to the introduction of universal male suffrage in Belgium; in the wake of the Dreyfus affair a socialist (Millerand) actually entered the French government; Russia experienced revolution in 1905; and the PSI gained control of local government in several cities in northern Italy shortly before the outbreak of the First World War. In 1910 the British Labour Party secured forty-two parliamentary seats; and just two years later the German Social Democratic Party (SPD) mobilised four million voters and over one million individual members. The SPD was the largest political party in Germany and the largest socialist party in the world. On account of its size and organisation, as well as the status of its theorists (Kautsky, Bernstein, Luxemburg, Parvus), the SPD became the most powerful force in the International, whose discourse was to a large extent dominated by the 'orthodox Marxism' of Karl Kautsky, the 'Pope' of socialism. Of course non-Marxist variants of socialist thought had far from disappeared. Christian socialists could be found in most countries; and Keir Hardie was much more likely to quote from the Bible than from the classics of Marxism. The British Labour Party had no socialist programme at this point in time; and the Fabians remained largely uninfluenced by Marx. In Spain, Italy and France anarcho-syndicalism could claim a significant following; whilst the SFIO contained a 'possibilist' faction, led by Paul Brousse, which believed in gradual reform through the municipalities. Most socialist parties contained competing ideological strands; yet debate within the Second International was indubitably Marxist. It deployed the language of 'class conflict' and 'capitalism'; and at its congresses the intellectual lead was provided by the SPD.

Orthodox Marxism

It was in the 1880s that Marxism became dominant in German social democracy. This was a period of worldwide economic depression and of political repression in Germany, which seemed to validate Marx's prognosis of capitalist crisis and his analysis of the state. The theory was transmitted by Karl Kautsky and Eduard Bernstein (no 'revisionist' yet), who had met Marx and Engels in London and who remained in contact with the latter until his death. They published newspapers and journals which circulated clandestinely in Germany during the 'anti-socialist law' (1878–90) and which spread the Marxist message. Kautsky was also the founding editor of *Die Neue Zeit*, which became the focus of international theoretical debate and could count Lenin amongst its most avid readers. Together with Bernstein he wrote the SPD's 1891 Erfurt Programme, which subsequently became a model for other parties. This programme and Kautsky's numerous articles in *Die Neue Zeit* defined Marxism for the generation after Marx and constituted the fundament of 'orthodox Marxism'.

Kautsky's Marxism was in most respects derivative but not unsophisticated. He explained and defended the theories of surplus value, immiseration, class polarisation and capitalist crisis. He never imagined that the Marxian concept of exploitation, as expressed in the theory of surplus value, could be reduced to a proposition about low wages. What it said was that as long as the proletariat had nothing to sell but its labour power, appropriated by the capitalist for profit, then workers would never receive the full value of their labour. Thus capitalism inevitably rested upon the exploitation of the working class and could only end when workers themselves owned the product of their labour, i.e. in socialist society. As capitalism developed, workers became increasingly 'impoverished'; but this did not mean that wages fell in absolute terms. Kautsky insisted that immiseration was relative, not absolute. He realised that trade union struggle or state intervention could bring about improvements in wages and working conditions; but these improvements had to be seen in the context of higher productivity, engendered by an intensification of labour and technological modernisation. So the workers ended up receiving a smaller share of the value of their labour than hitherto, even if their wages rose in absolute terms. This was demonstrated by the Reich income-tax statistics; for profits rose much faster than wages and higher incomes much faster than lower incomes in Imperial Germany.

Capitalism not only exploited workers. It made their material existence insecure as a consequence of unavoidable economic crisis. As long as competition and production for profit, i.e. capitalism, existed, crises and unemployment would continue. Cartels and trusts might lessen the impact of depression on capitalists but they intensified the problems confronted by the worker by increasing inflexibility and hence unemployment when crises did take place, and by controlling wage levels through a reduction in competition for labour when business was booming. Cartels were designed to keep prices high and maximise profits; they were not meant to protect the working class from insecurity. In short, organised capitalism meant an increase in exploitation and class conflict, in which the trade unions found it increasingly difficult to defend their members' interests against powerful organisations of industry. The last decade of industrial relations in Germany before the First World War bore out this gloomy prognosis.

The origins of the capitalist crisis Kautsky located in the most fundamental facet of capitalism: production for profit and competition. The precise mechanisms that led to crisis, however, he described variously. Having worked with an under-consumptionist model, Kautsky subsequently identified the disproportionality of the consumer and producer goods sectors as the origins of recession. The specific theory of imperialism, to which he subscribed until 1911, was a response to those who believed that capitalism could regulate itself; for imperialism transferred capitalist competition from the domestic to the international market. As he explained in *The Road to Power* (Kautsky 1909), a pamphlet that left a profound impression on Lenin, imperialism brought economic crises of ever greater dimensions, entangled class conflict with colonial revolt and led to war. (This position, which was shared by August Bebel and Rosa Luxemburg, was ultimately rejected by Kautsky after 1911, when he developed his concept of 'ultra-imperialism', as we will see.)

Kautsky also defended the thesis of capital concentration and class polarisation with vigour. This was a crucial issue, for if the proletariat were not increasing in size and consciousness, then a strategy of working-class self-reliance, the linchpin of SPD politics, would be nonsensical and the chances of revolution thin. Therefore Kautsky sought to demonstrate that the continued existence of small peasants and the emergence of a 'new middle class' of white-collar workers did not prevent or dilute class polarisation. Insisting that industrial capital would become more concentrated and that smaller businesses would be forced to the wall by their larger and more efficient competitors, Kautsky did recognise that developments in agriculture were somewhat different. His *Agrarian Question* (Kautsky 1899a), which Lenin admired, argued that concentration was less marked in agriculture, but at a cost. Some small farms were only able to survive because their peasant proprietors took up ancillary employment in rural factories or became out-workers in domestic industry. Their economic survival involved high levels of self- and family exploitation, as well as their integration into the capitalist market. Hence the number of industrial workers was continuing to grow without the expropriation of the peasantry. The peasant had indeed survived: but at the expense of agricultural progress and the urban consumer. In any case, smallholdings would not be able to produce the surplus necessary for the future socialist society.

Kautsky's arguments about the peasantry were not only about economics, however; and this was because he did not regard the peasantry as a class. Its existence did not alter the reality of increasing conflict between capital and labour because peasants were incapable of independent political action. Hostile to advancing capitalism, they nonetheless clung to the ideal of private property. They were not the bearers of a new social order, unlike the bourgeoisie and the proletariat. The peasantry, like the lower middle class more generally, veered from course to course in its political allegiances; but it was becoming increasingly reactionary and had sold out to protectionism. Under the banner of imperialism, the peasantry and petty bourgeoisie had allied with the anti-socialist elites. (Interestingly Kautsky did not apply the same conclusions to the Russian peasantry. Believing that the 'bourgeois revolution' in Russia would have to be led by the industrial working class, on account of the weakness of the indigenous middle class, he had come to the conclusion as early as 1892 – and in contrast to Plekhanov – that there would also be a role for the peasantry, a point he continued to develop after 1900 and which explains his initial popularity with Lenin and Trotsky.)

In industrial Europe, however, Kautsky not only believed there was no future in alliances with an increasingly reactionary peasantry; he also rejected the idea that the emergence of a 'new middle class' constituted a problem for his model of class polarisation. He was aware of the group's existence, but he did not believe that it constituted an independent class. The upper strata – bank and company managers, for example – would identify with capital in the class struggle, whilst clerks, confronted with increasing competition and automation, would come closer to the proletariat in both their objective situation and their subjective beliefs. As a result it made no sense for socialist parties to abandon their working-class identity. This advocacy of proletarian self-reliance was reinforced by the rightward trajectory of middle-class politics. The bourgeoisie was becoming stronger and better organised, as the rising failure rate of strikes in Germany indicated. Trade union work alone could only bring temporary and partial successes, but was a 'labour of Sisyphus'. The alliance of former liberals with older conservatives, which constituted the hallmark of bourgeois politics in Imperial Germany and was, according to Kautsky, even noticeable in Britain at the time of the Boer War, suggested that workers could expect more hostility and more repression in the future. As he wrote: 'Should parliamentary democracy develop in such a way as to threaten the rule of the bourgeoisie, then the bourgeoisie will prefer to repress democratic forms of government . . . rather than capitulate peacefully before the proletariat' (*Die Neue Zeit* [*NZ*] (1909), 27(1): 45).

This analysis, shared by Bebel and Luxemburg, linked the development of imperialism with new class alliances and the brutalisation of politics. The decline of Manchester and liberal ideals went hand in hand. Any idea that the interests of labour could be furthered by anything more than the most temporary alliances with the bourgeoisie were thus illusory. The necessary social revolution could only be the product of the industrial working class. It required 'the dictatorship of the proletariat'.

In his bitter polemic with Lenin after 1917 it was clear that Kautsky did not associate proletarian 'dictatorship' with violent repression; but this had long been the case. As early as 1893 he had argued that parliamentary democracy could be a tool of working-class rule. What 'the dictatorship of the proletariat' meant to him was a government in which the representatives of the proletariat ruled alone and not together with the representatives of other classes. Thus it was yet another manifestation of proletarian self-reliance rather than a call for violent revolution. From the start Kautsky held that parliamentary democracy and socialism were complementary. Where he differed from Bernstein was in his recognition that Germany before 1914 did not yet enjoy parliamentary government and that a revolution was therefore necessary to create it. Kautsky here reiterated Marx's position of 1872 that a peaceful transition to working-class rule might be possible in states with a large, well-organised labour movement, universal suffrage and parliamentary sovereignty.

Kautsky's belief that democratic institutions constituted the ideal basis for the development of the proletariat and for its exercise of power, a belief shared by most members of the Second International including Lenin before 1914, raised the question, however, of what should be done if such institutions were threatened by an alliance of former liberals and the traditional, reactionary elites, as the German Social Democrat himself had predicted. In abstract his answer was clear: the proletariat must be prepared to use force to defend itself. It might also think of calling a general strike. However, as a mass strike to bring about suffrage reform was put on the agenda by the Belgian general strike of 1902 and even more pressingly by the SPD's radical left after the 1905 Revolution in Russia, so in practice Kautsky shied away from advocating this particular course of action. Indeed his position was described by Anton Pannekoek as one of 'action-less waiting... the theory of passive radicalism' (*NZ* (1912), 30(2): 694), a phrase which applied equally to the Marxism of Plekhanov in Russia, Jules Guesde in France and Enrico Ferri in Italy. Thus Kautsky listed an enormous number of preconditions before a mass strike could be attempted: the existing regime had to be weak, the great majority of workers had to be organised already and they all needed to participate in any mass strike. In any case, such a strike could only be successful where it was spontaneous. Interestingly Parvus and Lenin both agreed that Kautsky's understanding of the German situation was much more realistic than Luxemburg's. However, his advocacy of caution was not restricted to this specific situation but was repeated whenever he discussed the overthrow of reactionary regimes, as in the case of the Bolshevik government, which he saw as a dictatorship over the proletariat, in the 1920s and of Nazi rule in the 1930s. Even his radical masterpiece, *The Road to Power*, of 1909, which talked of impending revolution, world war and colonial revolt, said absolutely nothing about tactics, as was realised by the lawyer hired by a troubled SPD executive to vet the text in the light of possible prosecution. As Kautsky had said as early as 1881, 'it is not our task to organise the revolution, but to organise ourselves for the revolution' (*Der Sozialdemokrat* (1881), 8, p. 1). Later, in 1904, he claimed that the task confronting the SPD was not 'to fight or not', but 'to prepare for the fight or not' (*NZ* (1904), 22(2): 581). Such a position was also revealed by his perpetual insistence that the proletariat had to be 'mature' (*reif*) before revolutionary action could be undertaken.

In Kautsky's case this 'passive radicalism' was to some extent a product of his cautious temperament. However, the popularity of such a position within the SPD points to something else, namely the position of his party in Imperial Germany. Partly repressed but allowed to build a massive organisation and compete in elections, the SPD could never be unambiguously revolutionary or uniformly reformist, especially given the non-parliamentary nature of Wilhelmine government. It was also confronted by a powerful military regime, which mobilised significant support not only from the landowning and bureaucratic elites but also from an increasingly organised and anti-socialist *Mittelstand* and peasantry. Inaction and isolation were products of this situation, which Kautskyite Marxism articulated much more accurately than either the revisionist optimism of Bernstein or the revolutionary optimism of Luxemburg. This was why neither the revisionist intellectual Bernstein nor the Polish revolutionary Luxemburg mobilised much support at SPD conferences.

This is only a partial explanation of the tactical silence of orthodox Marxism, however, not least because Marxists of the same generation in other countries subscribed to a very similar kind of theory. Moreover many German socialists held views of historical development that were even more passive and fatalistic than those of socialism's 'Pope'. Some revisionists subscribed to the belief that the evolutionary laws of society obviated the need for revolution. Some 'Marxists' thought that an inevitable 'collapse' of capitalism would usher in the socialist society, a belief central to Bernstein's critique of Marxism, but one to which neither Marx nor Kautsky subscribed. For Kautsky it was the conquest of political power by the proletariat, not economic collapse, which would bring about socialism. His rejection of an economic reductionism is nowhere clearer than in his stress on the necessity for political organisation and the belief that revolutionary consciousness could never be the product of the economic and sectional struggles of the trade unions alone, but had to be imported into the labour movement from the outside by revolutionary intellectuals and a revolutionary party. (He saw the SPD as just such a party, as did Lenin before 1912.) This theory, which was lifted explicitly by Lenin from Kautsky in *What Is To Be Done?* (Lenin 1960–70, vol. V [1902], pp. 347–529), clearly negates the claim that Kautsky was an economic reductionist.

However, a crucial role in Kautsky's formulation of Marxism was played by a model of social change borrowed from the 'law-governed' natural sciences. Ignorant of Hegel, Kautsky, like so many of his generation, came to Marx through that most positivistic reading of Marx, Engels' *Anti-Dühring*, and through the work of Darwin, which he had experienced as a 'revelation' in his youth. *Die Neue Zeit* was founded expressly to propagate both Marxism and Darwinism; and for most of his life its editor saw social development as 'law-governed'. It is true that Kautsky's Marxism borrowed less from evolutionary models than some other Marxisms. He attacked 'Darwinising' sociologists and insisted that Marxism was not 'fatalistic'. Men did make their own history, economic processes did not operate mechanically and capitalism was not doomed to extinction through purely economic causes. Thus one can make a case from Kautsky's general observations that he was no mere regurgitator of a positivistic, scientistic reductionism.

Yet the charge is not without foundation, especially when his general views of social change are brought together with his analysis of human agency in particular situations. Kautsky's attempts to defend 'the materialist conception of history' against charges of a false 'scientism' and 'economic reductionism' were far less assured and far less successful than his demolition of Bernstein's statistics or his understanding of Wilhelmine society. He was not interested in philosophy and admitted to Plekhanov that it had never been his strong point. He did see socialism as a 'science' – the outcome of a correct analysis of capitalist society and not a question of moral choice. If socialism were a question of individual morality, and not the consequence of the interests of a particular class in capitalist society, then there was no reason either to believe in the inevitability of its victory or to shun alliance with the bourgeoisie. (Here he realised the intimate connection between the Neo-Kantianism of the revisionists and their advocacy of class collaboration.) For Kautsky ethics were predicated by class; and only the working class had an objective interest in socialism. It was this that made revolution and the victory of socialism 'inevitable'. Kautsky's discourse was one of 'natural necessity', 'natural laws' and 'economic necessity', even if he did believe that the laws of society were different from those of nature. When he backed away from advocating action against the German Imperial government before 1914, or against a repressive Bolshevik regime in the 1920s, or against the Nazi state in 1934, his argument was always the same: we must prepare ourselves for the moment when economic forces render the survival of these regimes impossible. His claim that the 'necessities of production' were more powerful than the bloodiest terrorism in the 1920s was structurally identical to his arguments for inaction in Germany before the First World War: a repressive regime was bound to fail against a class with 'economic necessity' on its side. Accurate though Kautskyite Marxism was in its assessment of the difficulties and dangers of attempted insurrection in Imperial Germany, its claim that 'revolutions cannot be made but arise out of conditions' (Kautsky 1964, p. 63) was unlikely to be of any help to socialist movements when confronted with revolutionary opportunities in 1917/18.

This 'deterministic' reading of Marx was also embraced at a general (though not a tactical level) by Engels, most obviously in the *Dialectics of Nature* and *Anti-Dühring*. It was common to many other Marxists: to Jules Guesde and Paul Lafargue in France, to Gyorgy Plekhanov and the first generation of Russian Marxists, to H. N. Hyndman and the English Social Democratic Federation, and to Enrico Ferri in Italy. I would also argue that a belief in 'laws' of historical development informed Luxemburg's theory of imperialism, which proclaimed the inevitability of a great capitalist crisis, and her reliance on the spontaneity of the masses, just as it did Lenin's general views of historical development. The latter saw the materialist conception of history as a 'scientifically demonstrated proposition' (Lenin 1950, vol. I, p. 250) and believed in 'laws' of historical development, even if such beliefs stood in marked contradiction to the voluntarism of his revolutionary tactics.

There were of course exceptions, even in Kautsky's generation of Marxist intellectuals. Antonio Labriola, the prime populariser of Marx in Italy, was one; but he was not a party activist and he had been an academic philosopher long before he became a Marxist. More significantly he came to Marx through Hegel and was open to other theoretical influences, including a historicist anti-positivism and Kant. He did believe that philosophy expressed specific historical circumstances, but he was antipathetical to attempts to schematise history. For him the future was unpredictable and he lacked the certainty of Kautsky or Guesde, even though he joined them in condemning revisionism. The Austro-Marxists too embraced Kant and were suspicious of positivism. They agreed amongst themselves that Marxism was not a self-contained system and were critical of Engels' 'materialism'. However, with the exception of Karl Renner, whose position came close to that of Bernstein, most Austro-Marxists, including Otto Bauer and Viktor Adler, rejected bourgeois alliances and revisionism. They continued to subscribe to the theory of surplus value and class conflict; and class remained central to their politics. Jean Jaurès represented yet another intellectual tradition: for him socialism was a continuation of the French republican and revolutionary tradition. Influenced by Marx, he nonetheless reconciled the most varied intellectual positions and thought that socialism was essentially a moral concept, which was not class-specific (a position befitting a product of the Ecole Normale Supérieure). He believed that reforms in the present could so accumulate as to constitute the socialist future. The thinkers discussed above, however, never engaged in a frontal attack on the major premises of Marxism. From the mid-1890s, these came under sustained and explicit attack, not only from bourgeois politicians and social scientists but also from within the socialist camp.

Revisionism

Most of the socialist parties affiliated to the Second International had reformist politicians as well as Marxist radicals in their camps. However, practical politicians and their trade union allies, primarily concerned to win short-term gains, were usually uninterested in theory, except when it impinged on their behaviour. The 'revisionist' attack on 'orthodox Marxism', mounted by Eduard Bernstein in the mid-1890s, was different, despite his contention that he remained a 'Marxist'. In a series of articles entitled 'Problems of Socialism', published in *Die Neue Zeit* between 1896 and 1898, and subsequently in his major work *Die Voraussetzungen des Sozialismus* (Bernstein 1899), usually translated as *Evolutionary Socialism*, Bernstein refuted the theories of surplus value, impoverishment, capital concentration and crisis. Workers were not becoming poorer; the number of peasants was not declining; a 'new middle class' was growing in size and importance; share ownership refuted the claim of capital concentration; and capitalism was developing mechanisms to reduce competition and remove recurrent economic crisis. (Significantly Bernstein was writing at the end of the 'Great Depression' of 1873–96, which some misguided Social Democrats had regarded as the final crisis of capitalism.) As he summarised: 'peasants do not shrink; middle class does not disappear; crises do not grow ever larger; misery and serfdom do not increase' (Gay 1962, p. 250). Under these circumstances workers would not be revolutionary; and without a global economic crisis, the prospects of revolution became exceedingly thin. Hence it made much more sense for the SPD to abandon its revolutionary rhetoric and its policy of proletarian self-reliance, and to join with progressive elements of the bourgeoisie to bring about gradual change, possibly through the municipalities. There were clear similarities between these views and those of both Paul Brousse in France and the English Fabians, with whom Bernstein had been in fairly continuous contact during his lengthy stay in London in the 1880s and 1890s; but the fact that they came from a former propagator of Marxism, to whom Engels had bequeathed Marx's papers and who was an important figure in the SPD, was bound to cause a furore. Bernstein also came to doubt that 'scientific socialism' was possible and stressed the ethical basis of socialist commitment, which disconnected socialism from class interest and thus raised the prospect of cross-class cooperation. Indeed, this issue of relations with bourgeois politics was the very nub of the 'revisionist controversy', as Franz Mehring noted at the time.

We have already seen Kautsky's response: Bernstein had misunderstood the meaning of 'revolution', which was not to be associated with 'Blanquist' violence – an accusation that Kautsky was also later to lay at Lenin's door; he had misread the social statistics and he was overly sanguine about capitalism's ability to control economic crisis, not least in an age of imperial conflict. Influenced by British circumstances, he had failed to see that Germany was not Britain and that no democratic route to socialism was possible in the semi-autocratic Reich; and he had overlooked the rightward trajectory of the middle classes away from liberalism, especially in the context of colonial expansion and conflict. Bernstein thus provided no grounds for the SPD to change its proletarian strategy. (Given that 90 per cent of the SPD's membership was recruited from manual workers, it is scarcely surprising that Kautsky won the day!)

The criticisms of revisionism articulated by younger radicals, such as Rosa Luxemburg and Parvus, were not substantially different from the above. In *Social Reform or Revolution* (Luxemburg 1902) Luxemburg saw her major task as that of defending the objective necessity of socialism. As she wrote, 'in our opinion the crux of Bernstein's remarks is not to be found in his views about the practical tasks of Social Democracy but lies in what he has to say about the objective development of capitalist society' (Luxemburg 1969, p. 13). She did not demand that the party renounce its parliamentary strategy; and she recognised that the 'daily struggle' was a 'bourgeois' tactic. What linked the day-to-day struggles of the party to the final goal of socialism was not a specific revolutionary tactic but revolutionary theory. The same applies to Parvus (Israel Helphand), who was the first to denounce Bernstein publicly. His famous article 'Opportunism in Practice', which appeared in *Die Neue Zeit* in 1901, was another vindication of a revolutionary goal behind reformist reality. He was concerned to link parliamentary activity to the final goal of socialism, not to devise a new tactic. What none of these social democratic radicals did was to posit an organisational solution to the threat of reformism or revisionism. It was Lenin who did this, when he demanded the expulsion of the ideologically impure from the revolutionary party. To Luxemburg, and also to Trotsky in 1904, such a solution was artificial and dangerous, for it detached the party from the class and threatened bureaucratic sclerosis. In the revisionist controversy neither Parvus nor Luxemburg contradicted the SPD's existing strategy; for them it was theory which constituted the link between practical politics and the future revolution, not a specific revolutionary strategy in the present. It was in the context of another debate, that over the mass strike, that differences between Kautsky and the younger radicals were to become more apparent.

The radical left

Kautsky claimed in the face of later criticism that he had been the first German Social Democrat to propagate the idea of a mass strike; and as early as 1893 he had called for his party to discuss the matter, in case the few democratic rights already enjoyed in the German Empire were threatened by a reactionary coup. The issue became more acute in 1902, after the failure of the second Belgian general strike, and was subsequently fuelled by the gigantic upheavals in Russia three years later. Kautsky was one of those who pressured the SPD's executive to debate the issue, against its wishes and those of the powerful unions; and he wrote a foreword to Henriette Roland-Holst's *General Strike and Social Democracy* (Kautsky 1905). He saw the mass strike as the purest weapon of the class war, a weapon that might replace the barricades of past revolutions. More immediately it was the weapon to be deployed against any threat to democratic institutions.

What soon became clear, however, and what had been true even in 1893, was that Kautsky's defence of the right to discuss the general strike and his contemplation of its use in the abstract, was never matched by the advocacy of its use in any concrete historical situation. When radicals like Rosa Luxemburg (and others, including Bernstein after his return to Germany) urged the SPD to unleash a general strike to bring about suffrage reform in Prussia, he produced an exhaustive and essentially impossible list of preconditions for such action: the working class had to be strong, disciplined and class-conscious, united in a single political organisation. For success the strike required the cooperation of all workers and not just the organised; mass action had to wait upon the education and organisation of the proletariat. Furthermore, the mass strike could only be successful where a regime was already crumbling, which was manifestly not the case in Imperial Germany.

Rosa Luxemburg's position was, of course, different; and not only because she read the German situation differently (and probably wrongly). Impressed by the 1905 Ruhr miners' strike and even more by the revolutionary upheavals in Russia, she believed that social democracy confronted the choice of placing itself at the head of the swelling ranks of revolution or of being pushed aside by them. A revolutionary party could not simply sit back and do nothing. As she declared at the Jena party congress of 1905, 'the time has come which our great masters Marx and Engels foresaw, when a period of evolution gives way to one of revolution' (*Protokoll*, 1905, p. 320). However, Luxemburg not only assessed the probability of defeat differently from Kautsky but she approached the question from an utterly different perspective. Her older colleague believed that an unsuccessful strike would jeopardise the strong organisation that was a prerequisite for successful revolution. For Luxemburg the point of mass strikes was not simply to achieve specific, short-term goals; for her the danger lay not in the threat to the party's organisation but conversely in 'organisational fetishism'. She believed the proletariat developed its capacities through action, not organisation. Indeed organisation, education, consciousness and action were not separate and sequential moments in a revolutionary process; they were different aspects of the same process. For her, organisation and consciousness were the product of the struggle itself. (In this regard her critique could and did apply to Lenin as much as Kautsky. Her essay on the 'Organisational Problems of Russian Social Democracy', which appeared in 1904, made this clear.) Opportunism was to be fought not by erecting a tightly centralised party, which treated the worker in much the same way as the factory supervisor, as a cog in a machine, but by the actions and struggles of the workers themselves.

It should be noted, however, that Luxemburg's stress on the dynamics of proletarian action was not without its contradictions. Luxemburg herself, unlike Lenin, did not address the question of state power and its overthrow any more concretely than Kautsky. Pannekoek's observation that 'the struggle of the proletariat is not simply a struggle against the bourgeoisie for state power, but a struggle against the power of the state' (1910, quoted in Fetscher 1965, vol. III, p. 334) remained a relatively isolated observation outside Russia. Luxemburg did not argue that the mass strike should replace the SPD's parliamentary strategy. She was no revolutionary syndicalist. Nor would such a strike necessarily be violent. Above all the mass strike could not be called at will, any more than it could be prevented by decree when the time was 'ripe' (note the Kautskyan terminology). Unlike the council communists, such as Pannekoek, she never elaborated on the connection between new organisational forms and the 'spontaneity' of the masses.

Excursus: Russia

The immediacy of revolution in a society still largely unindustrialised gave rise to a very specific kind of Marxism in Russia. In its early stages indebted to Kautsky, Marxism was initially adopted by 'Westernisers', intent to argue that Russia could not avoid the same path of historical development that Marx had described in industrial Europe: feudalism was to be followed by capitalism and a direct, peasant route to a new society, as advocated by the Populists, was inconceivable. (The fact that Marx himself was more flexible on this issue appears to have been ignored by or unknown to them.) Gyorgy Plekhanov took up the Marxist cudgel, but for more explicitly political purposes: the development of a revolutionary party of industrial workers. Playing the same populising role as Kautsky in Germany, the 'father' of Russian Marxism catechised Marxian theory and subscribed to a philosophical materialism. He also likened Marx to Darwin; and the Marxist laws of historical development to the Darwinian laws of nature. The Kantianism of the revisionists he saw as an invasion of proletarian socialism by a bourgeois mentality; and though he did discuss philosophical questions and even Hegel, his view was decisively influenced by Engels' materialistic construction of the dialectic. As far as Russia was concerned, economic development was too far advanced for the peasant commune to serve as the basis for a future socialist order, as the Populists mistakenly hoped. (In this Plekhanov and Lenin were of one mind.) The coming revolution would be a 'bourgeois revolution', albeit one that required the participation of the industrial proletariat, given the weakness and cowardly nature of the Russian middle class. Thereafter would come a stage of capitalism, to be followed by a socialist revolution, which would be the work of the working class alone. To arrive at revolutionary consciousness, however, the working class would require intellectual guidance and the leadership of a revolutionary party. Thus Plekhanov's view of the role of the party was at this stage not unlike that of Kautsky or Lenin; and hence he found himself in the Bolshevik camp when Russian social democracy split in 1903. At this stage, however, the plea for a party of professional revolutionaries was not an advocacy of conspiratorial elitism. There are good reasons to believe that in 1902 Lenin saw the SPD as a model. The arguments for secrecy and conspiracy in *What Is To Be Done?* are contingent (upon Tsarist repression), whereas the justification for the role of the professional party is necessary and borrowed expressly from Kautsky and not from the Russian conspiratorial tradition or Blanqui, at least in the text.

However, Plekhanov soon accused Lenin of ultra-centralism and moved to the Menshevik camp. He feared the party was in danger of detaching itself from the working class and had become Blanquist. At the same time disagreement grew between the 'father of Russian Marxism' and his erstwhile disciples over the role of the peasantry in Russia, with Trotsky, Lenin and, as we have seen, even Kautsky holding a much more positive view of the revolutionary potential of rural Russia. In 1902 Kautsky had even suggested that the epicentre of revolution was moving eastwards to Russia; and this perception was subsequently developed by Parvus and Trotsky. Parvus, a Russian Jew who had found his political home in the SPD, had already noted that as a democratic revolution in Russia would have to be led by the proletariat and therefore bring to power the Russian Social Democrats, these would then find themselves obliged to push the revolutionary process yet further towards socialism. After 1905 Trotsky took this argument a stage further: the absence of a strong and independent middle class in Russia, partly the result of economic backwardness and partly of the fact that foreign capital dominated new industry, meant that the democratic revolution would not stop at the 'bourgeois' stage. Supported by the peasantry during the first revolution, the proletariat would find itself isolated inside Russia in a second 'socialist' revolution; but this second revolution would hit international capital at its weakest link and thus trigger a socialist revolution in the capitalist heartlands, in particular in Germany. (Until April 1917 this view was not shared by Lenin.) Thus the opportunity to engage in revolutionary action in Russia led rapidly to a revision of attitudes towards the peasantry and a concern with tactics, which was largely absent in the West. Here they knew that the state had to be 'smashed'. Yet Trotsky and Lenin, though they had few allies for democratic centralism amongst the radical left in France and Germany, were nonetheless in unison with the French socialists Jean Jaurès and Gustav Hervé, and with Parvus, Luxemburg, Pannekoek and even Kautsky before 1911, in believing that there was an intrinsic relationship between imperialism, war and revolution.

Imperialism and war

Initially debates about 'imperialism' within the socialist movement were primarily concerned with colonial expansion and the treatment of subject peoples by the colonial powers, rather than a fundamental restructuring of capitalism. Some within the International believed that advanced societies had a duty to 'civilise' the non-European world. This position was widespread in the United Kingdom and was adopted by the Dutch socialist van Kol, for example, as well as by Eduard Bernstein. There were, on the other hand, socialists, like Wilhelm Liebknecht, who perceived that colonial rule was anything but civilised. Kautsky agreed that colonial expansion invariably involved 'plunder' and the exploitation of the natives. Relatively quickly, however, Kautsky's writings about 'colonialism' went beyond this moral criticism. In 1884 he attempted to explain overseas expansion on the part of the European powers in terms of the laws of capitalist development. For Kautsky, as subsequently for August Bebel and many other European socialists, commodity production produced a surplus of goods, for which there was insufficient domestic demand. Foreign markets within Europe could no longer absorb this surplus because of the tariffs introduced in the Great Depression (thus colonialism was structurally linked to protectionism and the ending of free trade); and thus colonial territories had become essential for the survival of capitalism. However, there was also a limit to the absorptive capacities of the colonies; and in any case (so thought Kautsky even in 1884), independence movements in the colonies threatened the whole system with collapse.

This under-consumptionist model was subsequently joined by others. Kautsky himself, for example, changed his position repeatedly. Between 1898 and 1902, when he began to use the term 'imperialism' to describe Britain's turn away from free trade and its involvement in the Boer War, he argued, like the Italian Turati and as Joseph Schumpeter was to do later, that it was reactionary elites that fuelled imperial politics, as well as financial capital. To protect the higher rates of return on investments overseas, when these were falling in Europe, finance capital, supported by military and bureaucratic interests, demanded the annexation of overseas territories by the state. This turn to the state, which was also a characteristic of domestic politics, had even occurred in Britain, where reaction had been historically weak;

and this was the historical conjuncture in which the bourgeoisie abandoned its former liberalism. Thus around the turn of the century Kautsky linked increasingly reactionary domestic politics with protectionism and imperial expansion. The connections were pursued further in 1907 in *Socialism and Colonialism*, which drew together the processes of capital concentration, monopolisation, over-production, depression and colonial expansion. The armaments race was also incorporated into this syndrome.

Many of these propositions were commonplace in the European socialist movement, as was the general belief that capitalism could not endlessly reproduce itself, as in Luxemburg's *Accumulation of Capital* and Lenin's *Imperialism: The Highest Stage of Capitalism* (Luxemburg 1951 [1910]; Lenin 1950 [1917]). What is more, the association of imperialism with war became central to socialist discourse. In the *Road to Power*, and often elsewhere, Kautsky had claimed that an age of revolution and war was at hand; and that this was related to the translation of economic rivalries into the colonial sphere. The German Social Democrats Konrad Haenisch and Paul Lensch thought war so inevitably rooted in the capitalist mode of production that it was pointless to advocate disarmament: war would only end with the destruction of capitalism. For Lenin this was why imperialism was the last stage of capitalism. Significantly, however, Lenin did not see imperialism simply as an issue of colonialism. Rather the phenomenon was related to the dominance of financial capital and overseas investment, not just formal annexation. In this sense Russia too was a colony: a country tied to the advanced economies by her dependency on foreign capital. This attention to finance capital as the core of imperialism (and not formal colonialism) came at least in part from the Austro-Marxist Hilferding.

In 1910 Rudolf Hilferding's *Finanzkapital* was published. It attempted to analyse the development of capitalism since the death of Marx, and claimed that capitalism had undergone a qualitative change in its nature. The need to mobilise capital on an ever greater scale, as a result of capital concentration and technological modernisation, required the emergence of joint-stock companies and banks. As the banks became increasingly involved, they sought to reduce competition amongst their industrial customers by creating industrial monopolies; and thus industry became increasingly dependent on the banks. There was a fusion of industrial and financial capital. Hilferding did not believe that there was an absolute limit to the possible cartelisation of industry, which theoretically might end in a universal cartel, i.e. to all intents and purposes a planned economy. Until then, however, crises remained inevitable under capitalism; and crises increasingly affected the worldwide economy. In them the concerns with the largest capital survived and the dominance of finance capital became ever more assured. This dominance involved a change in the relationship between the state and the market. Finance capital required a strong state to facilitate the export of capital through both imperialism overseas and protection at home, in order to sustain the rate of profit; and it created an increasingly polarised society by rendering obsolete conflicts between the upper and lower middle class, though it also encouraged an increase in the number of company managers and technicians.

From Hilferding Lenin concluded that the revolution in Russia had a role to play in the global breakdown of capitalism; but Kautsky drew very different conclusions. The prospect of international cartelisation actually reduced the risk of conflict between capitalist nations. Imperialism would continue and would have to be combated by the international socialist movement; but it no longer necessarily meant war. The solution of the Samoan crisis, Franco-German compromises in Morocco, the resolution of the Second Balkan crisis at the London conference, and other diplomatic solutions between 1910 and 1912, seemed to indicate a new atmosphere in international relations, which Kautsky from 1911 specifically related to 'ultra-imperialism'. (He was not alone in noting this transition: Hermann Molkenbuhr, a prominent member of the SPD executive, the enigmatic Parvus, Turati in Italy, the Austrian Karl Renner and even August Bebel in his old age came to believe that the capitalist powers were becoming less bellicose.) The theory of ultra-imperialism stated that capitalist firms from different countries were cooperating to exploit colonies, as in the case of French and German firms in Morocco, and that capitalists were coming to realise that war itself constituted the greatest threat of all to their interests. Now they saw that it was not the 'furtherance but the abolition of militarism' which was the prerequisite for economic growth. Thus capitalists would seek a peaceful resolution of international conflicts through a process of diplomatic agreement and economic cartelisation. In complete contradiction of his position in *The Road to Power*, therefore, Kautsky now thought that war could be prevented through cooperation with those sections of the bourgeoisie with an interest in free trade and international peace (a position not only at odds with Luxemburg and Lenin, but also with Hilferding).

What to do in the event of war or to preserve peace constituted one of the greatest problems for unity in the Second International. Some, like Jules Guesde, believed nothing could be done, as war was inevitable under capitalism. The SPD leadership said they would do all they could to prevent war but refused to commit themselves to any particular strategy (as usual) and thought that a general strike would have disastrous consequences. Others, such as Jean Jaurès, Gustav Hervé and Rosa Luxemburg, did advocate a general strike in the event of war. Karl Liebknecht subscribed both to this position and to an advocacy of international diplomacy for peace and disarmament, revealing considerable theoretical confusion; and Kautsky thought war could be avoided through alliance with pacifistic, free-trading elements of the bourgeoisie and international disarmament. For Lenin, however, as for Anton Pannekoek, Paul Fröhlich and Karl Radek, a general strike was not simply to be a tactic to prevent war, which in any case was not to be avoided. It was to turn war into revolution.

The First World War led to revolutions in Russia, Austria, Germany and Hungary, though only in Russia did the socialist revolution (of a sort) triumph. It also produced a split in the ranks of international socialism between Social Democrats and Communists. Faced with revolutionary success in Russia and failure elsewhere, history, as Trotsky would have it, had condemned the 'passive radicalism' of orthodox Marxism to the rubbish heap. It also revealed the centrality of the nation state and nationalism, even to working-class identity; and this constituted another problem for the popularisers of Marx.

It was the Polish Marxists (without a state before the First World War) and the Austro-Marxists (inhabiting a multi-national empire), as well as the Russians (also living in a multi-national state), who thought most seriously about the national question. For most Polish social democrats the re-creation of a Polish national state was a necessary and desirable step on the road to socialism. To Luxemburg, who found her home in German social democracy, nationalism, like feminism, was a distraction from the realities of international capitalist repression. In fact Polish capitalism could not be separated from Russian capitalism; and it was capitalism that lay at the root of repression. To demand the restoration of Poland, therefore, was utopian. It was also reactionary, as it worked against the solidarity of the proletariat in the Russian, German and Austrian empires. In Russia Lenin reached very different conclusions. Whether for reasons of principle or opportunism, he did advocate the cause of national self-determination, realising that this was a force that could be unleashed against the Tsarist autocracy. Kautsky and others also supported independence movements in the colonies. In Austria-Hungary, however, a more differentiated analysis of the relationship between class, culture and nation appeared. Otto Bauer's *The Nationalities Question and Social Democracy* (1907) began by criticising spiritual and racist theories of the nation as metaphysical and ahistorical. It saw 'national character' as the prime determinant of nationhood; but this changed over time and was itself a product of natural and cultural factors. With socialism national differences would not disappear, but would, on the contrary, grow, as culture was brought to the masses. Increasing differentiation, however, did not mean that national rivalries and hatreds would become intensified, as national oppression was seen by Bauer as the consequence of class oppression, which socialism was to destroy. Socialism was therefore in favour of national self-determination, but not of national rivalries under capitalist conditions. Therefore the different national groups in the Austrian Empire should not fight divisively for separate statehood. The best solution in present society was for national autonomy within a multi-national state.

Conclusion

In August 1914 it became clear that most socialist parties subscribed to the theory of national self-defence, an anathema to Luxemburg and Lenin, who declared that, in an age of imperialism and capitalist war, the proletariat had no homeland. The enemy, capitalism, lay within. Only the Serbian and Russian Social Democratic parties, however, opposed the war from the start. In this sense the Second International had failed in its self-assigned task of uniting the international struggle for socialism. The Russian Revolution, combined with the failure of socialist revolution in western and central Europe, saw the strength and apparent relevance of the Second International eclipsed by that of the Third; whilst Marxism, in the hands of the Bolshevik Party and especially under Stalin, experienced a theoretical closure and dogmatism unknown before 1914. What is more, the generational rejection of 'scienticism' and positivism around the turn of the century, combined with the rediscovery of the Hegel in Marx by Lukács and Korsch, and the discovery of Marx's *Paris Manuscripts*, located orthodox Marxism in a bygone intellectual age.

11
The Russian Revolution: an ideology in power

NEIL HARDING

The Bolshevik Revolution of October 1917 marked the beginning of the global conflict between communism and capitalism that was to dominate the politics of the twentieth century and redraw the map of modern ideologies. On the mainstream left a bitter schism developed between gradualist 'Western' social democracy and revolutionary 'Eastern' communism. On the peripheries a host of splinter groupings emerged whose identities revolved around their conflicting interpretations of the Soviet experience. Socialism was, hereafter, organisationally and ideologically fractured: at war with itself.

The revolution and the Soviet experience also became, of course, the Other for many ideologies of the right and a cautionary tale for their seminal thinkers. The lapse into authoritarian or totalitarian practices was variously attributed to the pretensions of socialist states to eliminate the free market economy (Hayek 1976), their contempt for the civilising restraints of the rule of law (Friedrich 1954; Schapiro 1972) or their reckless pursuit of messianic patterns of thought that lie deep within the Western intellectual tradition (Talmon 1961; Popper 1980; Walicki, 1995).

It is clear that for both left and right the fate of revolutionary Marxism and that of the Russian Revolution were closely entwined. This chapter concerns itself with the manner in which the Bolsheviks redefined revolutionary Marxism in the twentieth century. It examines some of the disputations that surrounded the Bolshevik seizure of power in October 1917 and the theories that were developed to justify the state-building process that then ensued. It is the condensed story of an ideology coming to power, legitimating a unique state formation and, finally, imploding as an explanatory or justificatory system of ideas.

Could a socialist revolution in Russia be justified in Marxist terms?

There were two revolutions in Russia in 1917. The first occurred in February. It was largely spontaneous and supported by virtually all sections of the populace. In brief, the appalling management of the war with Germany and the consequent privations suffered by the people had become intolerable. The dynasty of the Romanovs was abruptly terminated by a largely bloodless popular uprising led by the workers of Petrograd. When the troops called out to suppress the huge street demonstrations went over to the insurgents, the Tsar abdicated. Power in the state was assumed by a group of aristocratic and middle-class politicians hitherto prominent in the Duma (which the Tsar had been obliged to convoke following an earlier revolution in 1905). The Duma had been merely a consultative body with no control of the budget or the ministry. Now regenerated as an executive Provisional Government it set itself the tasks of more effectively organising the war effort, feeding the populace and placating the increasingly radical demands of the urban workers and the land hunger of the peasants, as well as introducing democracy and civic freedoms to Russia for the very first time. It became apparent that to attempt to deal with all these tasks simultaneously was not possible.

The position of the Provisional Government was, from the outset, compromised by the existence of another centre of power and authority – the soviets (Russian for 'councils'). Workers' soviets had emerged in the revolution of 1905 primarily to coordinate the economic and political strikes that came close to overthrowing the Tsar. They were revived in February 1917 as the principal vehicles of worker organisation and expression (Anweiler 1974, pp. 97–143). Soldiers' and sailors' soviets were rapidly formed and, crucially, they merged their activities with the workers' soviets. At the head of this vibrant and often chaotic network of debating and deliberating bodies stood the Petrograd soviet. Most of the principal leaders of the main socialist parties sat on its executive and in the eyes of millions they had a greater legitimacy and authority than the unelected members of the Provisional Government.

It is undeniable that, had they so desired, the soviet leaders in Petrograd could simply have assumed power on the day they (and the Provisional Government) came into existence. As the year progressed, and especially after July, there were insistent calls, from the insurgent populace and from the soldiers, that the soviet leadership should take the power that was offered to them. They constantly refused. Russia, they insisted, was not in Marxist terms ripe for a socialist revolution. The slogan 'All power to the soviets' was, according to the Menshevik Statement of July 1917, 'a dangerous one' threatening to divide the revolutionary forces. There could be no separate peace and no fomenting of anti-capitalist sentiment: 'our immediate aim [is] to help the state in its struggle against the economic chaos' (Ascher 1976, pp. 98–9). The Mensheviks (generally considered to be the orthodox Marxists) and Socialist Revolutionaries (or SRs, a mainly peasant party) supported the war, called for order and discipline and became increasingly identified with the unpopular policies of the Provisional Government.

The Mensheviks argued that Russia had only just overthrown three centuries of Romanov autocracy; she was just at the threshold of a bourgeois democratic revolution. Elections for a Constituent Assembly were in the offing, civic rights and the rule of law were just emerging and the country was immersed in a debilitating war of defence against Germany. The nation would not lightly forgive adventurers who, in this critical situation, threatened its unity by counselling a civil war for socialism. In the Menshevik view, such people would assuredly be adventurers, for the good reason that they flouted the exacting conditions that Marx had specified in the matter of deciding whether conditions were ripe for a socialist revolution.

There were, in the first place, 'objective conditions' having to do with the development of productive forces. Since socialism presumed an end to material scarcity, it could only be securely based upon an extensive and advanced industrial system. This meant, in turn, the refinement of what Marx termed the 'forces of production' – machines and technology and the buildings that housed them and the communications networks that they required to exchange materials, goods and labour. In Marx's account of history, the development and refinement of productive forces are always progressive and so long as social, economic and political conditions allow such development, there could be no prospect of revolution. 'No social order ever perishes before all the productive forces for which there is room in it have developed; and new, higher relations of production never appear before the material conditions of their existence have matured in the womb of the old society itself' (Marx and Engels 1962, vol. I, p. 363). Manifestly, Russia had not reached the point where capitalism had exhausted its progressive potential.

Just as importantly, Marx had specified the maturation of certain 'subjective conditions' having to do with the consciousness and organisation of the class that was destined to accomplish the socialist revolution – the proletariat. The minimal definition of this class was that they shared a common relationship to the ownership of the means of production – they were all non-owners and they were obliged to sell their labour power. This common designation made them a class 'in themselves' but not 'for themselves'. For the class to emerge as historical actor, it had to be capable of articulating its *general* interests (as distinct from local, trade or gender interests). Therefore, it had to be organised as a distinct political party, because 'every class struggle is a political struggle' (Marx and Engels 1962, vol. I, p. 42). A lengthy period of democratic experience would be necessary to prepare the proletariat for power. It was, in the view of the Mensheviks, adherence to the restraints that these conditions enjoined that *defined* a Marxist in Russia. The existence of a power vacuum in a volatile situation was no warrant for a Marxist to attempt a seizure of power. On the contrary, it behoved Marxists to counsel restraint and to invoke a self-denying ordinance until such time as the conditions for a genuine majoritarian and conscious advance to socialism had properly matured. The alternatives, the Mensheviks fervently believed, were likely to issue in authoritarian violence exercised against the whole Russian people.

The soviet movement was both a product of, and an actor in, the extraordinary radicalisation of social and political attitudes that occurred in Russia in 1917. The fall of the Romanov dynasty saw, coincidentally, the collapse of the social power of the nobility and the gentry. Their economic power, too, was rapidly eroded by peasant expropriations of their estates. In the towns the workers were increasingly unprepared to accept the authority of their bosses. There was an escalating 'plebian war on privilege' in which 'the popular term *burzhooi*... was used as a general form of abuse against employers, officers, landowners, priests, merchants, Jews, students, professionals or anyone else well dressed, foreign looking or seemingly well-to-do' (Figes 1997, pp. 522–3). A considerable factor promoting this radicalisation was, of course, the Bolshevik Party, especially Lenin.

Lenin had been a central figure in the Marxist revolutionary movement for more than twenty years prior to 1917, both as an activist and as a theorist. In 1903 he was instrumental in splitting the Russian Social Democratic Labour Party into two sections: Mensheviks (or men of the minority) and Bolsheviks (or men of the majority). He was the undisputed leader of the Bolshevik, or ultra tendency which, in 1918, constituted itself as the Russian Communist Party.

When Lenin returned to Russia in the famous sealed train in April 1917, he announced to his colleagues and to the people of Russia a programme of such extreme radicalness that virtually all his associates, including those who had been closest to him in the past, were scandalised. 'Lenin's voice, heard straight from the train, was a "voice from outside"' (Sukhanov 1955, p. 274). His April Theses denounced the war as 'a predatory imperialistic war' inseparably connected to capitalism. Ending the one could only be achieved by overthrowing the other. Russia, Lenin went on, is passing from the first stage of the revolution, where power had been gifted to the bourgeois, to the second stage, where the proletariat and poor peasants would take power. It followed that there could be no support for the Provisional Government and that the 'soviets of workers' deputies are the *only possible* form of revolutionary government' – all state power should pass into their hands. Police, army and bureaucracy were to be eliminated and replaced by the armed people; all officials were to be elected and their mandates revocable; all land was to be nationalised and a single national bank created; there was to be no retreat to a parliamentary republic but a state form 'modelled on the Paris Commune'; finally, a genuinely revolutionary Socialist International was to be created – these were the tasks of the revolution (Lenin 1960–70, vol. XXIV, pp. 21–6).

Lenin's April Theses constituted a clarion call for the restitution of revolutionary Marxism. As a theory and practice of revolution, Marxism had all but withered away by the beginning of the twentieth century. In practice, and increasingly in theory, the politics of gradual peaceful transformation of capitalism through democratic means was overwhelmingly dominant in the socialist parties of Europe. The creation of mass social democratic parties led, as Michels and Weber had pointed out, to the growth in power of centralising bureaucratic structures and the waning of local activism. The proletarian element of the movement was increasingly discounted. 'The tendency is', Rosa Luxemburg lamented, 'for the directing organs of the socialist party to play a conservative role' (Luxemburg 1951, p. 93). The climax of this reformist politics came on 4 August 1914, when the French and German socialist parties, assembled in parliament, voted war credits for their governments. The Social Democrats came in from the cold into the warm embrace of the national (capitalist) community. The threat of war demanded social peace – a *union sacrée* or *Burgfrieden*, with the social democratic and labour leaders as its most authoritative officers. In Lenin's view, there was no more conclusive evidence of the canker of reformism and the erosion of revolutionary commitment than the activities of so-called Marxists joining national governments and pledging their support to bourgeois states at the very moment of their greatest frailty. His conclusion in 1914 was that all such social traitors had abnegated the right to be called Marxists. They had become recruiting sergeants and policemen of the imperialist state formation and were therefore, unambiguously, part of the enemy camp.

Lenin spent the years from 1914 to 1917 pondering and theorising the sources of what he took to be the apostasy of the theoreticians and leaders he had hitherto revered, especially Karl Kautsky, the erstwhile Pope of European socialism. So fundamental were their derelictions that the source of their errors had to lie deep in their methodologies. His first concern after the outbreak of war was to explore in Marx, Hegel and Feuerbach the true nature of Marx's dialectical method. He then went on to examine how the changing nature of the world economy led to war and to the growth of revisionism. Finally, Lenin embarked (1916–17) on a study of the relationship between the capitalist state formation and the demands of monopoly capitalism. He concluded from these theoretical studies that: (i) the dominant economic realities were global; monopoly capitalism was international capitalism; (ii) monopoly capitalism repressed rather than advanced the development of the productive forces and was therefore historically regressive rather than progressive; (iii) it also produced fierce competition for economic territory (imperialism) leading to militarism and global war; (iv) its capacity to sustain and reproduce itself was undoubtedly tied to a hugely expanded and oppressive state; (v) there could be no peace without the simultaneous overthrow of finance capital and its organisational focus, the imperialist state; (vi) the appropriate administrative form to replace the state was the one outlined in Marx's account of the Paris Commune; (vii) assessment of ripeness for socialist revolutions had to be conducted on a global rather than a narrowly national basis; and (viii) the barbarism and slaughter of imperialist war could be terminated only by international socialist revolution organised and coordinated by a Communist International organisation.

These formulations, the bedrock of Lenin's revolutionary analysis, were far from being mere slogans. They summarise a complex process of theoretical analysis in the period 1914–17. His voluminous *Philosophical Notebooks* (Lenin 1960–70, vol. XXXVIII) were followed by the economic analysis of *Imperialism: The Highest Stage of Capitalism* in 1916 (Lenin 1960–70, vol. XXII) and the extensive (if unfinished) reconstruction of the Marxist theory of the state in *The State and Revolution* (Lenin 1960–70, vol. XXV). He had theorised the nature of modern capitalism, the origins and character of the war, social democracy and the contemporary state, the conditions for global revolution and the imperatives for beginning it, long before arriving in Petrograd.

The theoretical disputes regarding Russia's ripeness for socialist revolution were, very largely, dialogues of the deaf. The Mensheviks and their foreign allies consistently maintained that within Russia neither the objective nor the subjective conditions had been realised. A socialist revolution in Russia, Kautsky warned, could only constitute 'a grandiose attempt to clear by bold leaps or remove by legal enactments the obstacles offered by the successive phases of normal development' (Kautsky 1965, p. 98). For many commentators, then as now, the Bolshevik programme of 1917 was fundamentally a rehash of Lenin's earlier work on party building, *What Is To Be Done*? (Lenin 1960–70, vol. V). There, it is widely maintained, Lenin first despaired of the proletariat as the bearers of socialism and proposed substituting for them the disciplined party of conscious revolutionaries. The elitism and voluntarism of his formative years is conventionally projected forward to account for his advocacy of a premature seizure of power by the Bolshevik Party. The revolution was, in this account, a minority coup not a popular revolution: Jacobin rather than Marxist, Eastern rather than Western. It was fated, because of its prematurity, to impose the will of a party/state upon the recalcitrant realities of the Russian economy and the cultural backwardness of the Russian people. To make both fit for socialism would, it was predicted, entail wholesale restructuring of society and the coercive refashioning of attitudes and dispositions. This analysis of a Jacobin impatience with backwardness fed into, and was complemented by, later Western theories of totalitarianism. The dystopia of arbitrary power, terror and the extinction of civil society, and autonomous selfhood arose, in these interpretations, from the unbridgeable gap between the limitless aspirations of a ruling elite and the finite malleability of people and things.

A great burden of subsequent analysis and interpretation bears down upon the question of revolutionary ripeness, but it is clear that no authoritative answers can be found in Marxism itself. There is, in the first place, the vexed question of which Marx we are to take. According to some, Lenin's revolutionary stance in 1917 fits perfectly comfortably with Marx's in the period 1848–51 (Wolfe 1956). Marx too, it has frequently been observed, was far from punctilious in attempting to measure the maturation of objective and subjective conditions. He had, after all, attempted to provoke international socialist revolution in 1848 in countries that were then no more developed than Russia in 1917. Engels was later forced to admit that 'History has proved us, and all who thought like us wrong. It has made it clear that the state of economic development on the continent at that time was not, by a long way, ripe for the elimination of capitalist production' (Marx and Engels 1962, vol. I, p. 125).

It was part of Lenin's case that the true disciples of Marx were revealed by their consistent application of his method rather than the ritual intoning of his prescriptions. And Marx's method, Lenin rediscovered in 1914, was emphatically dialectical, and therefore revolutionary. This method, Lenin insisted, had nothing to do with the optimistic positivism or vulgar evolutionism of the revisionists. Its principal finding was that the evolutionary development of all phenomena (including, evidently, classes, modes of production and epochs of history) had always a finite limit – the break or rupture – at which point they were abruptly transformed into different phenomena. All things at all times were to be understood as being in a state of constant change: they never were, they were always becoming. They could and did undergo a process of incremental change (the addition of an extra quantum at each particular moment) and this was referred to as quantitative change. However, a point was always reached at which the addition of a further quantum could no longer be accommodated by the form of the given phenomenon and it was abruptly transformed into something qualitatively different. In the social, economic and political realms the dialectic expressed itself, as Marx and Engels reminded their followers, as the history of class struggle. 'Proletariat and wealth', they insisted 'are opposites' (Marx and Engels 1975–86, vol. IV, p. 35). Class war was, therefore, irreducibly present in bourgeois society. It could not be negotiated away or suspended for the duration of the war because it transgressed 'national unity' or was unpopular or dangerous. The real traitors to Marx were those who renounced the implications of Marx's revolutionary method and made common purpose with the bourgeoisie to make war on their brother proletarians. The doctrine of unripeness was, in 1917, a veil to hide the cowardice of the class collaborationists.

The cowardice of the defencist socialists in Russia in 1917 was, according to Lenin, the more wretched because in Russia uniquely the workers were supported by the soldiers, they had their own powerful organisational foci – the soviets – and they had unrestricted freedoms of assembly and publication. They owed to the workers of the belligerent countries the responsibility of beginning the revolution against war, against finance capitalism and its oppressive Leviathan state. Russia being uniquely blessed in these respects had a responsibility to *begin* the global revolution for socialism. All of this, of course, presupposed that the world as a whole was ripe for socialism.

The analysis of imperialism and the imperialist war

The crucial transformations of capitalism that had occurred at the turn of the century, and had accelerated during the preparations for and prosecution of the war, had barely been noticed by the Russian proponents of unripe time. Marxist theorists such as Hilferding (1910), Luxemburg (1951) and the Bolshevik Bukharin (1972) had, from the 1890s onwards, begun to articulate an analysis of a qualitatively new phase in the development of capitalism that had been only half anticipated in Marx's writings. Their conclusions were that the 1890s had witnessed a remarkably rapid concentration of capital under the control of the big banks, which consequently became the directing centres of the accumulation and reproduction of capital. Under their direction there occurred a simultaneous process of amalgamation of productive units into huge corporations or trusts that effectively monopolised whole sectors of industry. Finance (or banking) capital came to prevail over manufacturing or industrial capital and monopoly displaced competition. But as competition was eroded, so capitalism finally forfeited its historical right to exist, for, in the Marxist canon, only competition kept it progressive. Without competition the imperative constantly to revolutionise the forces of production ceases to operate. Capitalism becomes historically retrogressive. This finding was, clearly, fraught with large revolutionary consequences. If the theorists of monopoly capitalism were right, then it followed that capitalism had entered its final degenerate stage. This account of an epochal transition formed a central part of Lenin's mindset (and his popular propaganda in 1917). It was a crucial element in what Lukács called Lenin's sense of the 'actuality of the revolution': the revolution was here, it was now (Lukács 1970).

Among the problems that Marxist theorists had to explain was how capitalism had succeeded (a) in reproducing itself on an extended level; (b) in absorbing its own product; and (c) in avoiding the revolutionary spiral predicted by Marx consequent upon a decline in the rate of profit. The theories of monopoly capitalism that Lenin absorbed provided answers to all these problems.

The problem of the reproduction of capital and absorption of the product had indeed become acute in the leading manufacturing countries in the 1880s and 1890s. They suffered from a glut of goods that could not be absorbed on the home market. This was followed by an over-production of capital that could find no profitable employment. Goods and capital had, therefore, to be exported on a massive scale in order for the cycle of the reproduction of capital to be completed and renewed. There would, naturally, be resistance to the intrusion of cheap goods and superabundant capital that threatened to disrupt and destroy the host economies. Powerful armies and navies would have to be developed to expand the economic territory available to metropolitan capital. Imperialism was, in this account, a function of monopoly capitalism. Monopoly capitalism, in the age of imperialism, had finally succeeded in realising Marx's prediction that capitalism 'must nestle everywhere, settle everywhere' (Marx and Engels 1962, vol. I, p. 37); that it was to be the first world historical mode of production (Marx and Engels 1975–86, vol. V, p. 49). The frantic imperialist expansion of the 1880s and 1890s finally saturated the territory of the whole world with (monopoly) capitalist relations.

The epoch of global capitalism necessarily universalised the contradictions of capitalism and, in the process, gave rise to a new phenomenon – that of exploiter *nations*. The argument, in brief, was that the export of goods and capital to protected (non-competitive) markets, combined with the ruthless extraction of surplus value from colonial workers unprotected by trade unions (or moral scruples) produced super-profits: that is, profits greatly in excess of those on the home markets. The monopoly capitalists were able to use these super-profits to arrest the general tendency for the rate of profit to decline. They were also able to use part of this surplus to buy off industrial militancy by developing a stratum of better-paid, more secure workers – a workers' aristocracy – whose interests became directly tied to imperialism. It was this stratum that had, in Lenin's view, formed the constituency for revisionism and the politics of gradualness that had issued in the shameless defencism of social democratic leaders.

Not only had Lenin found a materialist explanation for social democratic treachery, he had also set capitalism, and therefore the revolution, against it, in a wholly new perspective. Global capitalism could only be defeated by global revolution. It followed that the assessment of revolutionary ripeness had to be conducted on the integrated global mode of production rather than on the specifics of a national market. The analysis also showed that exploitation was most severe (and revisionism least developed) in the periphery of the global system. It was therefore plausible that the global anti-imperialist revolution might begin in the colonies or the semi-colonies (like Russia). The imperialist chain would break at its weakest link, not in its metropolitan fortresses.

The imperialist state formation

The war itself was, according to the Bolshevik analysis, the necessary outcome of the ferocious competition for economic territory that mature capitalism was bound to generate. This was, inevitably, a competition between states and it was, equally inevitably, accompanied by the growth of militarism and the reorientation of the economic system to produce means of destruction rather than means of production or consumption. The barons of finance capitalism had, by the first decade of the twentieth century, already recognised the huge importance of the state as authoritative organiser and guarantor of contemporary capitalism and had, therefore, moved in to take control of it. It was the state, after all, that alone had the authority to levy taxes and impose tariffs to pursue an appropriate foreign policy, commit armies and navies and create colonial administrations. The changing nature of capitalism was bound to impact upon the bourgeois state formation. Nikolai Bukharin was the most outstanding theorist of the Bolshevik Party and he anticipated many of Lenin's ideas in the period 1914 to 1917. In 1916 Lenin fell out with Bukharin over what he took to be the near-anarchism of Bukharin's conclusion that smashing finance capitalism entailed smashing the imperialist state; by early 1917 Lenin came to agree with this conclusion. Bukharin led the way in theorising the degeneration from the minimal non-interventionist liberal state to the massively interventionist and totalising imperialist state (Bukharin 1925).

The wartime imperialist state was, in Bukharin's account, far more threatening in its pretensions than any state known to history. It aspired to, and was in the process of implementing, a system of controls that were total and all-embracing in their scope. It had subordinated to itself the hitherto autonomous groupings of civil society. It had annexed the professional bodies: 'Philosophy and medicine, religion and ethics, chemistry and bacteriology – all were "mobilised" and "militarised" exactly in the same way as industry and finance' (Bukharin 1925, p. 29). Finally, it had extinguished the autonomy of the socialist parties and the labour movement. They too absorbed its mythology of the national interest and even vindicated the étatisation of social and economic life as increments towards 'state socialism'. They had sold the militant, heroic role of the proletariat in history for some crumbs of state-provided welfare and a few words of flattery. They had treacherously connived at the conversion of the movement into the pliant Labour Department of the imperialist state.

What had occurred, in the view of both Bukharin and Lenin, was the comprehensive swallowing of society by the state. Nothing and no-one escaped its iron grasp: 'Thus there arises the finished form of the contemporary imperialist robber state, an iron organisation, which envelops the living body of society with its tenacious, grasping claws. It is – The New Leviathan, beside which the fantasy of Thomas Hobbes seems but a child's plaything' (Bukharin 1925, p. 30). Bukharin and Lenin were clear that the imperialist state was unlike any previously known to history. It promulgated a single compulsory ideology, effectively decreed the end of politics and bent people's minds to its purposes. In its wartime imperialist form, the state had been brought to its ultimate, putrescent, militarist inversion of purpose. Far from assisting the development of productive forces and the market, the state now served to develop the forces of destruction and had embarked upon the most gigantic process of mutual annihilation in the history of humanity. This was the necrosis of a civilisation, a mode of production and epoch of history. It had become a vast graveyard drenched in the mud and carnage of the world's first total war conducted by the world's first total states. At this juncture in the history of mankind socialism was the only alternative to barbarism. To escape war meant smashing capitalism and this entailed smashing the state. The programme of the revolution was now as radical as it was possible to conceive within the framework of Marxism. The big question that now had to be answered was: if the state had to go, what was to replace it?

It is one of the larger paradoxes of twentieth-century history that the regime that was to epitomise totalitarianism in the popular (and scholarly) mind, began its career as a virulent opponent of the nascent totalitarianism of the contemporary bourgeois state. The Russian revolutionary project of 1917 was expressly theorised as the antidote to this nightmare vision of the modern Leviathan – the militarist, limitless and blood-soaked imperialist robber state (Harding 1996).

The Bolshevik theorists of the Russian Revolution shared with Marx the article of faith that state and society were, historically, locked in a zero-sum game in which the presence of the one was the denial of the other. They were, at least in 1917, unique in resurrecting a discourse that many had thought to be hopelessly outmoded and naïve even at the time when Marx had given it voice. They enthusiastically recovered, and integrated into their twentieth-century analysis, Marx's narrative about the growth of the state being accomplished only at the cost of society.

The soviets as contemporary forms of the Commune

For Marx the archetype of untrammelled state power was the regime of Louis Bonaparte. He had profited from the class equilibrium revealed by the revolution of 1848. He had played one class against the other (and the peasants against both) to secure the virtual autonomy of the executive and its swollen bands of bureaucrats and generals. In the process of its growth, and as a condition of it, the state had emasculated and exhausted society. 'Only under the second Bonaparte does the state seem to have made itself completely independent' (Marx and Engels 1962, vol. I, p. 333). It was hardly surprising that when the revolution against Louis Bonaparte's regime broke out, it took the form of a revolution not against this or that particular form of the state but a revolution 'against the state itself, of this supernaturalist abortion of society, a resumption by the people, for the people of its own social life. It was not a revolution to transfer it from one faction of the ruling class to another but a revolution to break down this horrid machinery of class-domination itself' (Marx 1970, p. 166). This was the zero-sum: following all state and no society was to dawn the era of all society and no state. The Commune that displaced Louis Bonaparte moved immediately to abolish the standing army and the police. There were no longer to be any 'separate bodies of armed men'; nor were there to be separate bodies of politicians, bureaucrats, judges, jailers or functionaries of any sort. Definitionally, therefore, the state ceased to exist. It was precisely this extraordinary and radical discourse that Lenin spent much of 1917 recovering and restating as the warrant and guide to Bolshevik strategy and the programme of the Russian Revolution. It was to form the substance not only of his bookish manual *The State and Revolution* but of his programmatic and agitational writings too. He rescued from the oblivion into which they had fallen Marx's writings on the Paris Commune of 1871. He identified the Russian soviets as the contemporary forms of the Commune and invested them with the same virulently anti-statist role. Socialists of all lands had tragically forgotten Marx's lesson that there was an alternative to the state.

The history of the state had, thus far, been the history of the development of the pretensions, powers and exclusive prerogatives of specialised functional and political groups. It was an account of the ideas, institutions and practices in which these prerogatives were located and through which they were justified. The nature of the new time, of the epochal transformation of all these old patterns of domination and subordination, was that the universally armed people, organised in their militias, communes, soviets, factory and regional committees and so on, were to appropriate to themselves all these lost powers. The idea of the revolution had concretised itself as anti-statism or, more properly, socialism – the empowerment of society. It was a revolution against the nation-as-state: the dominant idea of politics since the French Revolution.

This new beginning, Lenin insisted, had become inescapable, not because of theoretical imperatives but because there were no remaining alternatives for the contemporary world. Russia itself, in the six months since the February Revolution of 1917 overthrew the Tsar, had coursed its way through the gamut of available institutions and forms of government. It had been, variously, a monarchy, an aristocratic then a banker's government, a pseudo-constitutional executive of the centre, then of the centre left and, all the while, Russia lurched deeper into crises. The war continued, the dead and maimed piled up, the economy and the communications structures collapsed, and inflation and unemployment spiralled out of control, whilst speculators and profiteers benefited from the general misery and the country fell easy prey to its enemies. All other political forms, Lenin insisted, had been tried and found wanting. None answered, or could answer, to the public needs, because each presumed that leadership and organisation proceeded exclusively from the state. Only the Bolsheviks had the courage to step outside these narrow confines to invoke the raw energy and initiative of the mass. Only in this way, Lenin insisted, was it possible *in practice* to avert the slide to catastrophe. The theoretical imperative had become a practical necessity (Lenin 1960–70, vol. XXV, pp. 323–67).

The political structures of monopoly capitalism were, as we have seen, to be demolished and destroyed. Here the revolution had to be thoroughgoing and radical. As far as the *economic* structures of finance capitalism were concerned, however, Lenin counselled the greatest caution. This part of the inheritance from finance capitalism was not to be 'smashed' or negated. It was, on the contrary, to be allowed to develop all its luxuriant potential. Socialism could, in this way, attach itself unreservedly to the coat tails of modernism. This was the modernist Lenin of the single state bank as the mechanism to bring about a nationwide system of bookkeeping and accountancy, which would 'constitute as much as nine tenths of the socialist apparatus'. This was to be a system of production and distribution that built upon and developed monopoly capitalist institutions like the trusts and cartels. They not only enormously simplified the business of bringing industry under social control, they also provided mechanisms that lay 'ready to hand' that could be set in motion 'at one stroke by a single decree' and made to serve the needs of the majority rather than the profits of the few. Capitalism had, in short, bequeathed a splendidly articulated set of institutions through which socialist society could effect 'the administration of things' (Lenin 1960–70, vol. XXVI, p. 106). Nor was there any great mystique about the enterprise. The capitalists themselves, after all, did not administer anything. They simply recruited hirelings to do their bidding. In any case, they had so simplified the processes of production, distribution and control that these were accessible to any literate person. Literally all must be taught the art of administration and they would learn it only by experience, by taking upon themselves the responsibility for controlling their own lives. This was, as Lenin tirelessly insisted in the early months of the revolution, the sum and substance of the project for socialism in Russia, the quintessence of the Marxist promise of emancipation.

Class analysis and strategy

The basic questions of the revolution were, according to Lenin, what class could most be trusted with power and what form of state power would best facilitate an advance of socialism? In answer to the first term of the question there were, he maintained, only three possible class contenders in Russia – the bourgeoisie, the peasantry, the proletariat. The policy of the Mensheviks and SRs was, effectively, to fight tooth and nail against the radicalisation of the people in order to ensure the continued allegiance of the bourgeoisie to the revolution. But, in Lenin's view, the bourgeoisie would, as soon as the moment was opportune, betray the democratic revolution, turn on the soviets and rely upon sheer coercion to put down the threat of socialism. They would do this because their economic and social position and their future security demanded that they did so. This was, after all, the burden of Marx's reflections on the European revolutions of 1848 and the lesson of the Russian Revolution of 1905. To imagine that the fate of the revolution and of the soviets was safe in bourgeois hands was, therefore, worse than naïve: it actually disarmed the workers, making them easy prey to the coup that was coming.

According to this analysis, the Provisional Government and the soviets could not co-exist because they embodied two opposing class positions. One signalled the leadership of the bourgeoisie and the other of the proletariat. One sought to restrict then crush the revolution, the other to expand and develop it. The way forward in class terms was, for Lenin, crystal clear: an end to dual power – all power to the soviets, with the land-hungry peasants and the radical urban workers taking control of production. Thus all movements that extended and deepened the revolution, i.e. sapped the economic and social power of the bourgeoisie and the gentry, were to be supported.

The period after February was for Lenin a period of temporary class equilibrium. It was the crucial period in which each class would maximise and prepare its forces and occupy the best positions for the final confrontation. For the proletarian party this meant, in the first place, securing a majority in the soviets – the representative organs exclusively representing the working class and the peasantry. In the second place, it meant mobilising and directing a preponderance of armed force at the right time and in the right places. Revolutions, Lenin reminded his colleagues, were, in the final resort, trials of arms. The mobilising and military aspects of seizing power had, therefore, to be taken seriously and treated as an art (Lenin 1960–70, vol. XXVI, pp. 22–7). There could, in the matter of making a revolution, be no fetish about parliamentary forms or formal democracy. The soviets were the contemporary form of the Commune and the Commune was, as Marx had insisted, 'the political form at last discovered under which to work out the economic emancipation of labour' (Marx and Engels 1962, vol. I, p. 522). It was the only administrative form suited to the task of socialist construction, immeasurably superior to the talking shops of formal or bourgeois democracy: superior because it was participatory, because it expressly set out to involve the whole of the population, especially the ill-educated, poor and dispossessed, in making, implementing and policing all the policies that most affected their lives. It was the final word of the socialist project because it made of socialism a relationship between equals and a restless activity. In this strategy the activity of the mass to empower themselves was simultaneously the process through which they tested and expanded their capacities for social self-management and the process by which the powers and authority of the state and the old governing classes were neutralised and usurped.

It was, of course, not Marxist theory that shelled the occupants of the Winter Palace into terrified submission, took the Post and Telegraph Offices, secured the bridges and won over the crucial garrisons in October 1917. All of this was the work of organised activists prepared to fight for the revolutionary cause. Their motives for doing so were diverse, but there is general agreement that, in the months from July to October 1917, there was a massive ebbing of support for the government and the political parties supporting it. After the failure of the Galician offensive, upon which the Kerensky government had, in a sense, gambled everything, the writing was on the wall. Defeat after defeat followed sacrifice after sacrifice; the ordinary Russian people had no more stomach for the war or the government that promoted it. Predictably the officer corps became the focus of a movement on the right to restore order, resurrect patriotism and re-create a disciplined fighting force capable of defending Russia. And all this, they believed, would necessitate a temporary dictatorship exercised by a charismatic leader. It would also, clearly, involve the suppression of all those parties and institutions that threatened their programme – the meddlesome soviets and the parties of the left. As self-appointed saviour of the nation, General Kornilov rallied his Cossack forces in July and set off on his mission to cleanse Petrograd of its anti-national scourges. As an attempted coup it fizzled out ignominiously, but its consequences were to be enormous. There was, in the first place, sufficient ambiguity about the Provisional Government's role in the Kornilov affair for large numbers of people to accuse it of complicity. Worst of all, in order to be seen to be dealing with the Kornilov coup, the Provisional Government had to enlist the help of all forces that would oppose it. It turned to the Petrograd soviet which promptly established a Military Revolutionary Committee. Bolshevik leaders who had been imprisoned after the abortive spontaneous rising in July were released and immediately assumed control of the arming of pro-soviet worker detachments. The Military Revolutionary Committee was from the outset under their effective control (via Trotsky and his colleagues).

With the failure of Kornilov's coup, the Bolsheviks basked in the glory of the true defenders of the revolution. Their predictions had come true. The bourgeoisie *had* gone over to the counter-revolution, supporting a military adventurer and would-be Napoleon: 'The Kornilov crisis was the critical turning point, for it seemed to confirm their (the Bolsheviks') message that neither peace nor radical social change could be obtained through the politics of compromise with the bourgeoisie' (Figes 1997, p. 457). *None* of the basic problems besetting the people had been attended to – the land, the war, employment or popular welfare. The parties comprising the Provisional Government had comprehensively demonstrated that they could not govern, while the people were increasingly declaring that they would not be governed in the old way. The conditions for a successful seizure of power were maturing. The radical alternative proposed by the Bolsheviks was rapidly gaining ground. By September the Bolsheviks commanded a majority in the soviets of Moscow and Petrograd. They were on course for a majority in the Second All-Russia Congress of Soviets due to convene on 25 October. They had won the allegiance of the key towns, industrial areas, garrisons and naval bases. The revolutionary moment, Lenin insisted, had now arrived. The resistance was at its weakest; the revolutionary forces were in the ascendant. To delay would be fatal. The demands of the world revolution made action in Russia imperative. Russia was honoured to be the first to break the imperialist chain. Lenin now assaulted the hesitant and fearful Central Committee of his party with ever more insistent demands that they mobilise their forces and effect a seizure of power before the Congress of Soviets took place (Lenin 1960–70, vol. XXVI, pp. 19–21). With considerable reservations the decision was finally taken to mount an assault on Petrograd during the night preceding the opening of the Second Congress of Soviets. Almost without resistance the insurgents in Petrograd captured all the positions of power and arrested all the personnel (with the exception of Kerensky) of the old regime. The battle for Moscow proved to be more prolonged and bloody.

The impact of the Bolshevik Revolution upon Russian society was proportionate to the extreme radicalism of its initial programme. That programme not only corroded the legitimacy of the state and all power-holders, it arguably made any sort of social order or continuous production and circulation of goods impossible. The Bolshevik slogan of an end to bossing was taken up with such fervid enthusiasm that it made the very possibility of constituting and justifying authority within the administrative, economic and social life of the country highly problematic. The peasants expelled their landlords and seized the land. Since they no longer had to produce cash crops for sale on the market in order to service debt repayments (now annulled by the revolution), their only incentive to trade in the market was to obtain cash in order to purchase consumer goods they could not themselves produce. But if these goods were not available in the market there could be no remaining incentive for the peasant to trade. He would, as a rational actor, retreat into self-sufficient production for immediate consumption rather than production for the market. And so he did. Urban life and industrial production were in real danger of being starved to extinction by the peasants' refusal to trade.

As far as the industrial workers were concerned, they too had agendas that often ran flatly counter to Bolshevik plans and exhortations. They were not inclined to discriminate as fastidiously as Lenin had insisted that they should between ownership and control. A spate of nationalisations from below was accompanied by a rejection of all things bourgeois, including all learning and specialist skills. *Spetsii* and men with glasses, anyone with education, and all authority figures were now perceived to be enemies of the people. The October Revolution, Bukharin lamented in 1920, brought merely dissolution of the old patterns of authority and legitimation within society and the state. It dissolved, at every level and in all spheres of activity, the linkage between the technical intelligentsia, the managerial cadres and the workers. The consequent costs were as extensive as the scale of this dissolution. It led to a catastrophic decline in industrial production: 'it must be *a priori* evident that the *proletarian* revolution is inevitably accompanied by a strong decline of productive powers' (Bukharin 1971, p. 106). The compulsion of the capitalist wage relation (i.e. work or starve) had not yet been replaced by alternative moral or material incentives to ensure discipline and application within the work process. No *positive* principles yet informed the mode of production and civilisation that was striving to replace capitalism. What had thus far occurred was the essentially negative process of dissolving and devaluing the old structures of power and their sustaining attitudes.

The dictatorship of the proletariat – discipline and security

By 1920 it was apparent that a great gulf had opened up between the actual practices and power structures of the regime and its foundational legitimating principles. Russia's only representative body ever elected by manhood suffrage was forcibly terminated as soon as it convened in January 1918. The Constituent Assembly (elected in November 1917) had a majority of SRs and would not accept the Bolshevik demands that it approve all the measures enacted since October and acknowledge the supremacy of the soviets. A civil war that was bitter, brutal and centralising then ensued. The leading figure in the civil war was undoubtedly Leon Trotsky. He first rose to prominence during the revolution of 1905 when his fiery oratory and great energy secured his election as deputy chairman of the Petrograd workers' soviet. Subsequently he tried to preserve an independent conciliatory role in the Bolshevik/Menshevik disputes, but by 1917 he sided firmly with Lenin. As Commissar for War, Trotsky reintroduced the authority of army officers and restored discipline and cohesion to the Red Army.

By late 1920 the civil war was effectively over. In the final resort the peasants disliked the Bolsheviks less than they feared a white revival of the power of landlords. Internal opposition and external intervention had failed to unseat the Bolsheviks. They had, however, as Lenin lamented, grievously impeded the possibilities of building socialism in Russia. Now that the civil war was over, there were powerful voices within the party and outside that called for the retraction of the centralising measures in the military, economic and political spheres that had been justified by the civil war state of emergency. Workers' control of production was the watchword of the Workers' Opposition platform. The Democratic Centralists demanded a restitution of democratic procedures in the party and outside. Prominent soviets demanded a restoration of their powers and freedom for all socialist parties to compete. But Lenin and the Bolsheviks knew that to return to the foundational principles of the revolution would effectively sweep their power away. Free elections would yield majorities to their political opponents. Russia was on its own internationally; internally the Bolsheviks were a diminishing minority, their popular support had ebbed away and pathetically few people – 'a few thousand throughout Russia and no more' (Lenin 1960–70, vol. XXXII, p. 61) – were actually engaged in the business of government and administration: 'the proletariat is declassed, i.e. dislodged from its class groove' (Lenin 1960–70, vol. XXXIII, pp. 23–4). Their proletarian base had, as Lenin reminded the party, withered away.

The old model of socialism as people's power and the legitimating principles of radical commune democracy could no longer serve. The alternative 'positive' model of state development that Marx proposed to his followers was the dictatorship of the proletariat. It is the state form recommended in the Communist Manifesto and expanded upon in the 'Critique of the Gotha Programme' (Marx and Engels 1962, vol. II, pp. 18–37). The dictatorship of the proletariat was everything that the Commune was not. It was tightly centralised rather than devolved, transitional rather than the finished form of popular administration. Whereas the Commune sought to transform power relations, the dictatorship of the proletariat set out to transform property relations. The one was necessarily participatory and democratic, the other was wholly agnostic to structures of power and patterns of accountability. Whereas the Commune defined itself in organisational and procedural forms, Lenin's new relativism declared that: 'The form of government has got absolutely nothing to do with it' (Lenin 1960–70, vol. XXVIII, p. 238). If the Commune was socialism as freedom, as activity, the dictatorship of the proletariat was socialism as efficient production and equitable distribution; it was a condition of being free from material need. Its goal was not the end of alienation but the much more manageable goal of the end of exploitation. It was Marxism in the mode of modernity. Its voice was passive.

By 1920 Lenin, Bukharin and Trotsky insisted that socialism had nothing to do with autonomy, self-activity and freedom. 'We do not promise any freedom, or any democracy' (Lenin 1960–70, vol. XXXII, p. 495). In a chilling phrase that perfectly expressed the new mood, he declared that: 'Industry is indispensable, democracy is not' (Lenin 1960–70, vol. XXXII, p. 27). Bukharin, Trotsky and Lenin were now agreed that the absolute priority was the maximisation of production and this, they insisted, meant maximal discipline and accountability and the imposition of authoritarian control of the process of work. Bukharin was clear that '*revolutionary* state power [as] the mightiest lever of economic revolution . . . turns *inward*, by constituting a factor of the *self-organisation and the compulsory self-discipline of the working people*'. State compulsion and coercion would have to be extended to the ruling class itself, even to its 'proletarian avant-garde which is united in the party of the revolution' (Bukharin 1971, pp. 151–6). Trotsky was more emphatic still. The only model of organisation appropriate to the transition period was the army. Only the army had absolute jurisdiction over the lives of its members, to direct and punish them and to subject them to the unchallengeable authority of one man. The militarisation of labour and of the state was, Trotsky repeatedly insisted in 1920 and 1921, the only way in which a recalcitrant workforce and dislocated economy could be reformed so that the single goal of socialism – the maximisation of production – could be obtained (Trotsky 1961, p. 144). Lenin too was clear that a divided and degraded working class that had become 'dislodged from its class groove' could not create its own dictatorship. Its class power could only be effected by its conscious vanguard concentrated in the party.

The dictatorship of the proletariat was, on the face of it, a much more promising basis than the Commune for establishing the legitimation of state power. The Commune was, from first to last, bitterly anti-statist and its message was emphatic – restore to society all the powers leached by the state. It was a tale about the utmost dispersal of power. Its key words were collegiality, recall, answerability and the absence of mediation or material advantage. It smacked of golden-ageism – a reversion to the face-to-face intimacy of pre-modern society. It implicitly presumed that the volume and complexity of public business was manageable and accessible to the whole population. It was no basis upon which to build an account of modernity or of any permanent structure of power of any sort. The dictatorship of the proletariat, however, was emphatically a form of state, the most authoritarian form of state, the first openly partisan form of state that admitted and valued only workers. It was to be a centralising body charged with concentrating all the forces of production, distribution and exchange into the hands of the state authority. It was unambiguously modern in its embrace of the machine, division of labour and the virtues of large-scale authoritative organisation. It was bound by no law, morality or convention, but ruthlessly pursued the class interest of the proletariat. It openly recognised, and was proud to declare, that its state power rested upon coercion and terror if need be. By 1920 Bukharin, Lenin and Trotsky all agreed that the road to socialism lay through the maximum conceivable amplification of the state's powers. In formal terms the soviet state would, Bukharin insisted, mimic the centralising authoritarianism of the imperialist state, especially in its control and direction of the economy. The promise of socialism in this second moment of the development of soviet power was to repair and remedy the deficiencies, wastage, planlessness and inequities of the capitalist mode of production. But in order to accomplish these productivist and distributivist goals, it imperatively had to control, on a national scale, the productive forces, the investment resources, the labour power and the distribution of goods and services of the entire society. In the perilous situation in which Russia (and therefore socialism) found itself in 1921, this set of ideas and conception of socialism appealed with compelling force. The country had been devastated. War, civil war and industrial dislocation had reduced gross production, in almost all spheres, to approximately 20 per cent of the 1913 figure; 'in the case of iron and steel it was actually below 5 per cent' (Hosking 1985, p. 120). The towns had been depopulated, the proletariat destroyed and the peasantry devastated by famine. The European revolution that was to redeem Russian backwardness had, against all the predictions of theory, failed to materialise. Isolated internally ('we are but a drop in the ocean of people', Lenin frequently lamented) and isolated externally, the Bolsheviks were in a desperate situation. Their support had ebbed away. They had no significant solid social base. At the most elemental level how were they to reproduce their own power? How were they to guarantee the power of the state which had become their own last bastion?

It was in this situation that Bukharin reflected upon the manner in which the besieged forces of the imperialist bourgeoisie had managed to cling on to power and reproduce their mode of extracting surplus value. They had survived, Bukharin argued, by abrogating democracy, forging a single near-compulsory ideology of national unity, and, above all, by utilising the power of the state to intervene massively in the economy so as to guarantee the reproduction of their own capital and the continuation of their complex systems for extracting surplus value from the population at large. In all essentials, Bukharin argued, the proletarian state would be the mirror image of the state of the monopoly capitalists: 'Thus the system of state capitalism transforms itself into its own inversion, into the state form of workers' socialism' (Bukharin 1971, p. 79).

Soviet state ideology – the promise of plenty

The theoretical underpinnings of a socialist Leviathan state had been articulated by Lenin, Trotsky and especially Bukharin between 1920 and 1921. However, they proved impossible to implement at that time. In the spring of 1921 the regime faced an accumulation of crises that all but swept it away. Worker unrest in Petrograd was followed by the revolt of the sailors in the ultra-radical Kronstadt naval base, whilst, simultaneously, peasant revolt swept western and southern Russia. The final fling of the post-war revolutionary movement came to an ignominious end with the crushing of the German communists' action of March 1921. The hopes of an international proletarian rising to redeem Russia's backwardness had, evidently, to be indefinitely postponed. The regime was hanging on by its fingertips, presiding over a ruined, disaffected and isolated country.

It was in this situation that the strategic retreat of the New Economic Policy was introduced. The grandiose schemes for comprehensive state direction and management of the economy were put into reverse. The state withdrew from the ownership and management of small and medium enterprises, retaining only the very large-scale strategically important parts of industry and communications. Freedom for peasants and traders to market their goods was extended as the state withdrew. The experiment in War Communism came to an end. Socialism as a new mode of production was put on hold.

It was evident from the outset that comprehensive national planning required state control of all the factors of production – land, capital, labour, transport and the distribution of the product. In 1928 the Russian Communists were, arguably, further from realising this control than many European regimes. It took the Stalin revolution, unleashed in the two five-year plans that were to follow, to transform this situation and to effect, for the first time in history, what came to be known as a planned economy. Stalin had been consistently promoted by Lenin as a reliable apparatus man in charge of the allocation of key personnel within the party and state machines. After Lenin's death he presented himself as the chosen interpreter of what he termed Leninism and used the power base he built up within the party to attack first the left (associated with Trotsky and his supporters), then the right (grouped around Zinoviev and Kamenev). By 1928 effective control of the party/state machine was in his hands and he proceeded to announce radical plans for the rapid industrialisation of the country and the collectivisation of agriculture. The moderacy of the New Economic Policy was abruptly reversed. We cannot here go into the divergent accounts of the motives behind this abrupt transformation or explore the rival calculations of premature deaths that this holocaust produced, but we can say beyond doubt that this was the most savage and traumatic transformation suffered by any modern society at the hands of its state. An ancestral way of life with all its traditional signifiers, securities and points of identity was smashed forever; and with it whole classes perished. Villages were destroyed, forced labour camps established, crops burnt, livestock slaughtered and the consequent famine killed millions. At unspeakable cost the regime now secured the land under its control. It secured, too, a vast dispossessed workforce to build the cities and industrial complexes, dig the canals and build the hydroelectric stations to fuel the headlong drive for increased production. Stalin presided over this reckless (and largely unplanned) agricultural and industrial transformation (Nove 1992).

It had been a central argument in Stalin's long battle with Trotsky that the Soviet Union could indeed build socialism in one country. It could not, of course, *complete* the building of communism but it could (indeed it had to) proceed to construct a mode of production that would demonstrate its superiority to capitalism (Stalin 1953–5, vol. VI, pp. 110–11). At the most obvious level, socialism as a mode of production had to profess (and ultimately demonstrate) its superiority to capitalism. Chronologically it superseded a mature or degenerating capitalism and its progressive nature rested upon its claim to liberate technological innovation that had been stifled by capitalist monopolies. It promised to end duplication of productive capacity and to eliminate the recurrent gaps between production and consumption that produced successive booms, slumps, wastage of resource and unemployment.

In line with the Saint-Simonian variant of Marxism that thereafter dominated the ideology of the Soviet state, the purpose of society was to assure the individual the continuous satisfaction of material needs. Individuals had elemental needs for food, shelter and clothing that imperatively had to be satisfied. They could, moreover, through imagination, conceive of more extensive and refined needs. Their existential plight was, however, that as lone individuals not even elemental needs could be continuously satisfied. The foundational concept of Soviet-style socialism is that of a creature with extensive material needs (but limited individual productive capacity) entering society in order to secure their satisfaction. The individual entering society is endowed not with a bundle of pre-existing rights but, rather, with a capacity to labour. Individuals enter society as bearers of labour power. As a condition for enjoying the security and needs satisfaction that society alone can provide them with, individuals must now renounce autonomous control over their labour power. Control over it must be ceded to society, or, more properly, to the authoritative, organising institution of society – the state. The state evidently could not negotiate, monitor and reward a labour plan for each individual. It recognised only more or less sizeable aggregates of labour power, which, in turn, were integrated into national structures controlled by central government ministries. One contributed socially useful labour (and therefore qualified for citizenship) only as a worker within an enterprise contributing to the plan. The work collective had the responsibility to ensure that all its members had proper attitudes towards the disciplined and conscientious performance not only of their work but also of their social responsibilities. It disposed moreover of a graduated hierarchy of welfare inducements and welfare sanctions to ensure that each individual did indeed fulfil the labour targets set. In the first place, and crucially, it was the work collective that effectively decided upon the remuneration of each individual worker. Within the work collective it was the party-dominated management that decided upon appropriate candidates for training and skills acquisition and so determined promotional prospects. It determined what sorts of jobs were done by whom.

The work collective had, however, far broader economic social and moral/political concerns. It often disposed of the available housing stock, determining access to flats and deciding who got the most desirable ones. It disposed of scarce and therefore extremely valued durable consumer goods like cars, colour televisions and washing machines. It ran the recreational facilities available to workers and often owned rest homes and holiday facilities. The work collective was the compulsory and unavoidable locale in which every citizen made his or her way, aware at every juncture of its power over them – its power to grant or withhold all of the most scarce and highly valued goods that the society had to offer. It is hardly to be wondered at that from an early age individuals were socialised, by family, friends and neighbours, into patterns of behaviour and external significations that proved effective in gaining access to scarce resources. Diligent and disciplined work was, of course, the single most important signifier but it had to be complemented by appropriate dress codes, signals of accepted civility (turning up for meetings, raising the hand, voting, making supportive comments) and the endorsement of current policies and leadership personnel. The enterprise/collective was, therefore, the locus in which not only the material values but also the moral and political values sustaining the whole society were generated and reproduced and reinforced each other.

According to Soviet precepts of distributive justice, the more one produced the more one was to receive. But the greater the stock of values created by the individual and his/her collective, the greater the volume of values accruing to the central planning agencies; that is, the more the strength of the central state apparatus was augmented. The planning system, articulated through ministries, trusts, enterprises and work collectives, was the uniquely all-embracing vehicle whereby the Soviet state formation extracted the social surplus from the whole of the population. *In abstracto* it was a perfect system for reproducing the power of the power-holders – the central allocators. It was they, after all, who by dictating the price of all commodities, goods and services, by controlling taxes and the wages of labour, could thereby control the volume of the social surplus, the disposition of which was exclusively their preserve. Through astute management of the social surplus, and through carefully graduating the returns and benefits obtained by elite groups, the central allocators could guarantee the expanded reproduction of their own power. Everyone within this system was caught in complex webs of complicitous legitimation in which the more one received the more one had to signify, and signifying was, as we have seen, the condition for access at any level (Konrad and Szeleyni 1979; Feher, Heller and Markus 1983; Harding 1984).

The pathology of the Soviet economic system reads as an indictment of the positivist Marxism from which it was derived. The Soviet experience confirmed the view that, in proportion as the units of the Soviet economic system became modernised, complex and interdependent, so they proved increasingly impossible to plan. Far from being the great panacea that finally freed industry from inefficiency and unleashed technological innovation, the State Plan proved itself to be in almost all respects an insurmountable obstacle to innovation and efficiency. The State Plan increasingly became the problem rather than the answer. The modernist, positivist assumptions that informed the planning project proved to be hopelessly optimistic. Even the best mathematical minds, utilising the most sophisticated computer equipment, proved themselves to be woefully inadequate in their attempts to grasp the volume of variables in their infinite combinations that the central direction of a planned economy had to deal with. It became apparent to more and more people and, finally, to the planners themselves, that planning had failed in its promises. It simply was not assuring to its citizens/producers a greater stock of material benefit than any competitor systems. Nor was it rewarding them according to their productive inputs. But it was these promises that had justified the lack of personal autonomy and control over one's own labour. It was these promises that had been central to the legitimation of the Soviet regime. The sting in the tail of all social contract theories is, of course, that when the state fails to deliver, the citizens are relieved of their obligation. By the late 1980s, it was evident that the modes of legitimation retailed from Marx and practised within the Soviet Union would no longer serve as the anchor of state power.

Conclusion

Each of the variants of the Marxian emancipatory project had been tried and each had ended in failure. The project for socialism as self-activity and commune-based freedom ended in hunger, isolation and devastation. The project for socialism as efficiency and state-guaranteed security had issued in the terrorist austerity of the Stalin period. Finally, the project for socialism as the promise of plenty generated by the planning mechanisms of the all-people's state terminated in elite corruption and chronic shortages of consumer goods. Only at the very end was there any theoretical (or practical) attempt to grapple with the genuine complexities of modern politics.

There is a strong case to be made that Marxism impoverished political discourse throughout the Soviet period and, arguably, still impedes the emergence of a healthy relationship between state and civil society in Russia. In the entire course of the Soviet experiment issues like how we are to control, limit and hold power-holders accountable were simply undiscussable. Politics as contestation, the open canvassing of alternative political or economic strategies, or public appeal to particular constituencies, simply did not exist. Only at the very end, and even then only fitfully, did Soviet social theorists and political leaders begin to think seriously about the complex reciprocal relationships between civil society, the individual and the state. Only at the end was civil society rediscovered as a sphere that could and should have its own degree of autonomous development, and this, in turn, required new attitudes towards law and due process. Only at the very end of the Soviet experiment were the virtues of pluralism hesitatingly canvassed. These very radical innovations were hesitantly suggested in Mikhail Gorbachev's programmes *perestroika* (reconstruction) and *demokratisatsiya* (democratisation). Far from stabilising and renewing the Soviet systems of power they had the exactly opposite effect. Democratisation, especially, proved to be radically corrosive of the Communist monopoly of power. It facilitated the rise of new political and national constituencies that soon dissolved the Soviet Union. It was, finally, only with extreme reluctance that certain groups and individuals were allowed to step outside the constraints of the State Plan and the work collective to create cooperative or individual enterprises. But as soon as this dispensation to control one's own labour was conceded, the party and the state saw their power seep away. The power of the party to control access, to grant or withhold welfare benefit, promotional prospects and so on, was abruptly terminated. The regime could no longer reproduce either the material or the moral values necessary for its own survival. It yielded place to the unfettered operation of a perverse variant of capitalism, the luxuriant growth of plebiscitary democracy, and the darkly seductive charms of nationalism.

12
Asian communism

DAVID McLELLAN

Historical context

Marxism, initially the product of reflection upon the economic, social and political consequences of the industrial revolution, is firmly anchored in Europe. Its application to Asia, therefore, has been problematic – except on the view that 'the more advanced countries simply hold up to the less advanced the mirror of their own future' (Marx 1995, p. 12). In effect, Marxism could only make progress in Asia by adapting to two factors. First, Marxism had to come to terms with indigenous cultural values. Although not every Marxist would agree with U Ba Swe, secretary general of the Burmese Socialist Party, who claimed in 1951 that 'Marxist theory is not antagonistic to Buddhist philosophy. The two are, frankly speaking, not merely similar. In fact they are the same in concept' (Trager 1959, p. 11), at least some adaptation to cultural patterns and beliefs was essential. The words of Mao Zedong, 'for the Chinese communists who are part of the great Chinese nation, flesh of its flesh and blood of its blood, any talk about Marxism in isolation from China's characteristics is merely Marxism in the abstract, Marxism in a vacuum' (Mao 1965–77, vol. I, pp. 209ff.), applied *mutatis mutandis* to all Asian Marxism. Second, Marxism arrived in Asia in support, ostensibly at least, of anti-colonialist and nationalist aspirations. Although in Marx's more simplistic statements, the workers were considered to have no fatherland, Marxist analyses of imperialism and of nationalist movements in the non-European world became more urgent as the twentieth century progressed.

The Bolshevik victory in 1917 meant that Asian Marxism emerged under the tutelage of the emergent Soviet Union (see Carrere d'Encausse and Schram 1969, pp. 69ff.). At the Second Congress of the Communist International in 1920, the leader of the Indian delegation, M. N. Roy, argued strongly that the fate of the revolution in Europe depended on its success in Asia which would deprive European capitalism of its super-profits (on Roy's views, see further Gupta 1980). Lenin, by contrast, adopted a more cautious approach, was more interested in protecting the nascent Soviet state, and advocated the advisability, in some circumstances, of subordinating the communist movement in backward countries to the emergent 'bourgeois-democratic' nationalist movements. While Lenin was sympathetic to peasant-based movements, Roy argued that in Asia the working class was already sufficiently large and class-conscious to lead the revolutionary movement. But the new Communist parties failed to make headway in areas where, on orthodox Marxist principles, they might be expected to. In India, the Communist Party failed to become central to the struggle against British rule. And in Japan, which already had a large industrial working class, the Communist Party only became a force to be reckoned with under post-war US occupation. It was rather in China that a distinctive form of Asian Marxism began to develop – but only after the traumatic decimation of the Communist Party by the very bourgeois-nationalist movements to which Soviet policy subordinated it.

Chinese Marxism

The Chinese Communist Party (CCP) was founded in 1921 with Mao Zedong one of the thirteen members present. From the start, the Chinese Communist Party was confronted with the traditional problems of what policies to adopt in what seemed to be a nationalist, republican, 'bourgeois' revolution (see further here Luk 1990). In early 1920, most revolutionary nationalist forces supported the Kuomintang (KMT) of Dr Sun Yat-sen which had succeeded in establishing itself, with Russian aid, in south China based on Canton. Trotsky considered the KMT to be a bourgeois party, unlike Stalin who thought it a coalition of different classes. The latter view prevailed and, under Russian pressure, the Chinese Communist Party formed a United Front in 1923 with the KMT as its left wing. In early 1926, under the leadership of Chiang Kai-shek who had succeeded Sun, the Kuomintang mounted the successful Northern Expedition to drive out the warlords and the Western imperialists who abetted them. But when the Communists organised a successful uprising in Shanghai (which held China's biggest concentration of industrial workers) Chiang turned ruthlessly against them. Hundreds of their members were killed and the party as a whole was proscribed. Under the leadership of Mao, the Communist soldiery retreated to the wild, mountainous region of the Jingkangshan on the eastern borders of Hunan province where Mao had been born. Pursued by the KMT and eventually encircled, the increasingly Stalinised Central Committee of the party favoured a disastrous policy of meeting the KMT head on. Eventually the only course left was for the Red Army to break out and seek refuge elsewhere. They did so in 1934 and trekked 6,000 miles during twelve months over the most difficult terrain before finding a secure base in Yenan in north-west China. It was during this Long March that Mao became undisputed leader of the party and was able to give Chinese Marxism its distinctive character.

It is obviously difficult to determine how much Mao's version of Marxism owes to Chinese culture. The fact that Chinese thought is basically more empirical and pragmatic than its Western counterpart may well have influenced Mao's Marxism. There were also dialectical elements in Buddhism and Taoism, both of which tended to think in terms of opposites – everything being imbued by the contradiction of yin and yang. On a more immediate level, Mao was undoubtedly influenced by his reading of classical Chinese novels such as *The Water Margin*, with their glorification of peasant revolts and military exploits. What was clearer was that the central role in the revolutionary movement would be played by the peasantry, whom Mao described as 'the vanguard of the revolution' (Mao 1965–77, vol. I, p. 30). What this meant in practice became plainer as the Communists established themselves in Yenan where a moderate agrarian policy was pursued: confiscation; rents were limited to one third of the yield; there were no incentives for land reclamation which helped the Communists to attain virtual self-sufficiency in food; and, to lessen the need for government finance, the army and the party officials took part in farming and other productive activities. But the embattled nature of the Communist enclave meant that more emphasis than ever was put on the army. In this context Mao famously declared that 'every Communist must grasp the truth, "Political power grows out of the barrel of a gun" ', although he continued: 'our principle is that the Party commands the gun, and the gun must never be allowed to command the Party' (Mao 1965–77, vol. II, p. 224). One of the enduring legacies of the historical origins of Chinese communism was the secrecy surrounding the internal debates of the party hierarchy. Whereas the Russian Communists fought their (brief) civil war after they had achieved power, and conserved an atmosphere of relatively open debate in the party well into the 1920s, the Chinese Communist Party was engaged in almost constant warfare, either against the KMT or against the Japanese invaders, for the two decades before its final victory.

The military nature of early Chinese communism meant that one of the most original contributions of Mao to the theory and practice of contemporary Marxism was his conception of guerrilla warfare. Drawing on the classical Chinese tradition in such writers as Sun Tzu, Mao declared that 'our strategy is to "pit one against ten", and our tactics are to "pit ten against one"' (Mao 1965–77, vol. I, p. 237). He considered that guerrilla forces should be so organised that, through rapid concentration, they could mount local offensives with superior forces despite an overall inferiority. As soon as possible, they should operate in conjunction with regular troops working behind the enemy's lines, disturbing communications, etc. Most importantly, the guerrillas should control bases to which they could periodically retire. These should be areas that were geographically difficult of access – mountainous, bordered by swamps or deserts. In these areas, the troops themselves should work land and be active in production. They should help raise the productivity of the local inhabitants and, if possible, organise elementary social services. This would both avoid their being a burden on the locals and counter the boredom of periodic inactivity that sapped the morale of all traditional armies. These tactics were later applied successfully by Tito's partisans in Yugoslavia, by the FLN in Algeria, during the Cuban revolution, and, of course, in Indo-China.

The success of these tactics and the steady expansion of Communist power in north-east China enabled Mao to set out his views on the future of the Chinese revolution. In keeping with the Leninist doctrine which was particularly emphasised by the Stalinist Popular Front policies of the Third International after 1935, he now spoke of revolution by stages – a bourgeois, democratic revolution preceding the Socialist revolution: 'In the course of its history, the Chinese revolution must go through two stages, first, the democratic revolution, and second the socialist revolution, and by their very nature they are two very different revolutionary processes' (Mao 1965–77, vol. II, p. 341). But because of the phenomenon of imperialism, the world revolution, of which China was a part, was a socialist revolution, and therefore the Chinese revolution, although bourgeois, could be conducted under proletarian hegemony: 'The first step in our revolution will result in the establishment of a new democratic society under the joint dictatorship of all the revolutionary classes of China headed by the Chinese proletariat. The revolution will then be carried forward to the second stages, in which a socialist society will be established in China' (Mao 1965–77, vol. II, p. 347). Mao went beyond Lenin in stating that the dictatorship would be one of several revolutionary classes. He wished to emphasise the revolutionary character of the Chinese people as a whole. The emphasis on the bourgeois character of the revolution was satisfying to the peasantry which had no enthusiasm for socialism. And when he mentioned the proletariat what he really meant was the CCP, which was standing in for an 'absent' working class. The rapid transition to socialism and the China-centred nature of the post-1949 development were not yet part of Mao's thinking.

While meditating on the nature of the political revolution to come, Mao also devoted himself to giving the party a philosophical basis and produced two essays entitled *On Practice* and *On Contradiction*. In the first, Mao emphasised that 'above all, Marxists regard man's activity in production as the most fundamental practical activity, the determinant of all his other activities' (Mao 1965–77, vol. I, p. 295). Mao thus continued the Marxian tradition as exemplified in Lukács, Gramsci and the later Lenin. *On Practice* married the *Theses on Feuerbach* with a crude, inductive, natural scientific method, and denied that Marxism had any ontological basis or underlying metaphysic. This chimed well with Mao's own aversion to book-learning and dogmatism, and also his desire to give a theoretical justification for his own policies. The very practical success of the Yenan regime – though unorthodox by Communist standards – was its own justification. For the Marxist philosophy of dialectical materialism 'emphasises the dependence of theory on practice and in turn serves practice. The truth of any knowledge or theory is determined not by subjective feelings but by the objective result in social practice. Only social practice can be the criterion of truth' (Mao 1965–77, vol. I, p. 297).

In his second essay, *On Contradiction*, Mao set aside talk of the 'laws' of the dialectic and put the notion of contradiction into the centre of his view of the world (see Knight 1990). But more than the universality of contradiction, Mao was concerned to emphasise its particularity. Dogmatists 'do not understand that conditions differ in different kinds of revolution and so do not understand that different methods should be used to resolve different contradictions; on the contrary, they invariably adopt what they imagine to be an unalterable formula and arbitrarily apply it everywhere, which only causes setbacks to the revolutions or makes a sorry mess of what was originally well done' (Mao 1965–77, vol. I, p. 331). Different contradictions demanded different methods of resolving them. For example, 'in Russia, there was a fundamental difference between the contradiction resolved by the February Revolution and the contradiction resolved by the October Revolution' (Mao 1965–77, vol. I, p. 322). More specifically, Mao wished to analyse what he termed a principal contradiction and a principal aspect of a contradiction. He wrote: 'there are many contradictions in the process of development of a complex thing, and one of them is necessarily the principal contradiction, whose existence and development determines or influences the existence and development of the other contradictions' (Mao 1965–77, vol. I, p. 331). The implications for current policies was evident: the war against Japan was the principal contradiction and the struggle against the KMT was for the moment secondary. With regard to the general principles of historical materialism, Mao's views involved a substantial reformulation. He wrote:

> The productive forces, practice and the economic base generally play the principal and decisive role; whoever denies this is not a materialist. But it must also be admitted that in certain conditions, such aspects as the relations of production, theory and the superstructure in turn manifest themselves in the principal and decisive role. When the superstructure (politics, culture, etc.) obstructs the development of the economic base, political and cultural changes become principal and decisive (Mao 1965–77, vol. I, p. 336).

This approach implied a possible emphasis on politics and culture that Mao was later to exploit in full.

The victory of the Chinese Communist Party in 1949 enabled Mao to give full rein to this emphasis on superstructural elements, particularly during the Cultural Revolution. After three years spent reconstructing an economy ruined by civil war, the first five-year plan of 1953–7 saw much faster economic progress towards socialism than had been envisaged in 1949. This was partly due to the inevitable clash between planning and the existence of private property, whether in industry or in agriculture, and partly to the Korean War which imposed strains on the Chinese economy and hastened the reduction in economic power of classes who were potentially hostile to the regime. In the agricultural sector, the drive towards cooperatives and collectivisation was originally intended to halt a slide in the opposite direction. Like Bukharin, Mao believed that industry should serve agriculture and he promoted the communes in order to foster peasant accumulation – not in order to extract the surplus for the benefit of heavy industry like Preobrazhensky and Stalin. By the end of 1956, virtually all peasants were in cooperatives and the vast majority in fully socialist ones – ten years ahead of the goal set in 1953. This haste involved a certain clumsiness in implementation and some resistance on the part of the peasantry – but nothing on the scale of the Soviet Union in the early 1930s. Haste was necessary for two reasons. The first was the need to increase agricultural production in order to promote industry. Mao's faith in the revolutionary potential of the Chinese countryside and his preference for men over machines led him eventually to think that a rise in agricultural production would have to precede or at least accompany a rise in industrial production, in opposition to the traditional view that mechanisation would have to precede collectivisation – the view consistently supported by Liu Shaoqi. The second reason was the need to support the increase in population, which began to rise dramatically on economic recovery.

This acceleration of the progress towards socialism was accompanied by revision of the nature of class and contradiction in Chinese society. Whereas in 1945 Mao had declared that 'it would be a sheer illusion to try to build a socialist society . . . without a thorough-going bourgeois-democratic revolution of a new type led by the Communist Party' (Mao 1965–77, vol. III, p. 283), the view was that the transition to socialism had actually begun in 1949. In his essay of 1957 entitled *On the Correct Handling of Contradictions Among the People*, Mao stated that a socialist victory had been achieved in China and that socialism was in the process of being built, but that contradictions would still remain – contradictions with the enemy and those among the people. 'In capitalist society', he wrote, 'contradictions find expression in acute antagonisms and conflicts, in sharp class struggle; they cannot be resolved by the capitalist system itself and can only be resolved by socialist revolution. The case is quite different with contradictions in socialist society; on the contrary, they are not antagonistic and can be ceaselessly resolved by the socialist system itself' (Mao 1965–77, vol. V, p. 393).

The antagonistic contradiction – that with the counter-revolutionary enemies of the people – had been to a large extent eliminated in the violence when the Communists took power. Those that involved the peasantry, the national bourgeoisie and the intellectuals were being dealt with in a more continuous manner. The contradictions that still existed among the people were being handled by an authoritarian party. The defeat of the urban-based Communists in 1927 and the de-industrialisation of the east coast by the Japanese invaders had deprived the Communist Party of any appreciable working-class base to which they might be even notionally responsible. In 1949, Mao nevertheless laid emphasis on the cities, but with the movement away from the Russian model of development in the mid-1950s, the non-proletarian nature of Maoism became plain. The proletariat was still maintained as a reference point, but the real areas of focus were the party and the peasantry. Thus, as Schwartz has written: 'The term "proletarian" had already acquired new connotations. It had already come to refer to a cluster of proletarian moral qualities which could be set before both Party and masses as a norm of true collectivist behaviour. To a considerable extent, it had already been disengaged from its concrete class reference' (Wilson 1977, p. 24). Indeed, Mao often talked vaguely of 'the masses', by which he meant an agglomeration of the lower ranks of the peasantry and the urban petty bourgeoisie. The absent proletariat could not fulfil a hegemonic role against these groups so the party had to act as its substitute. This phenomenon of 'substitutism' – the party playing the role of the proletariat in the face of the peasantry whose initial aspirations were not socialist – goes a long way to explaining the authoritarian nature of the party.

The role ascribed to the people in China's progress towards communism was essentially passive. In a classic passage on what he termed 'the mass line' Mao wrote:

> All correct leadership is necessarily 'from the masses to the masses'. This means: take the ideas of the masses (scattered and unsystematic ideas) and concentrate them (through study turn them into concentrated and systematic ideas), then go to the masses and propagate and explain these ideas until the masses embrace them as their own, hold fast to them, and translate them into action, and test the directness of these ideas in such action. Then once again concentrate ideas from the masses and once again go to the masses so that the ideas are persevered in and carried through. And so on, over and over again in an endless spiral, with the ideas becoming more correct, more vital, and richer each time. Such is the Marxist-Leninist theory of knowledge (Mao 1965–77, vol. III, p. 119).

The question remained as to who was going to write the words and paint the beautiful pictures. The initiatives of the masses tended not to be well received if they were not impregnated with Mao Zedong's thought. Mao himself claimed that he had only fostered the cult of his personality as a counter-weight to the party bureaucracy. But the grotesque lengths to which this was taken only served to caricature the essentially authoritarian and paternalistic nature of the relationship of the charismatic leader to the masses: in accordance with the Confucian tradition, the people were regarded as essentially good, but their ignorance required an enlightened leadership to be responsible for their well-being. According to Isaac Deutscher, 'national history, custom and tradition (including the deep philosophical influences of Confucianism and Taoism) have been reflected in the patriarchal character of the Maoist government, the hieratic style of its work and propaganda among the masses, and the magic aura surrounding the leader' (Blackburn 1977, p. 213).

This characteristic of the party's attitude to the masses in China was clear in the fate of two movements which seemed – temporarily – to negate the essential paternalism of the party: the Cultural Revolution and the preceding One Hundred Flowers campaign of 1956–7, launched under the slogan 'let a hundred flowers bloom and a hundred schools of thought contend'. But the resultant criticisms, unrest and even direct opposition to the party led to the imposition of strict criteria to distinguish 'fragrant flowers' from 'poisonous weeds'. The same process of an attempted shake-up of the bureaucracy through mass participation which was later brought under strict party control was visible in greater detail in the Cultural Revolution, which began in August 1966 in the universities with a mass campaign to eliminate those seen as 'rightists', to re-emphasise the importance of Mao's thought, to lessen specialisation, and substantially to restrict the role of examinations. At the plenum of the Central Committee in August 1966 it became clear that Mao and Lin Biao were advocating a return to the policies of 1958–9, as embodied in the disastrous Great Leap Forward, in the face of opposition from Liu and Deng. The Maoists won and a decision was taken to promote mass mobilisation outside the ordinary party channels. The aim was to attack 'those within the Party who are in authority and are taking the capitalist road'. The vehicle was to be the movement known as the Red Guards. However, when Red Guards attacked the offices of party officials and tried to involve the workers in their demands, the movement began to get out of control and there was widespread dissension on tactics among the Guards themselves. As the party struggled to regain control, the People's Liberation Army (PLA) played an increasing role in setting up the new administration, sometimes in alliance with the Red Rebels and sometimes against them. The shaking up of the old bureaucracy and the mutual hostility and transitory nature of many of the rebel groupings left a power vacuum that could only be filled by the PLA, which was a fairly cohesive and unified body.[1] However, the swift fall of Mao's designated successor Lin Biao in 1971, and the campaign against the Gang of Four in 1976, marked the re-emergence of many of the elements – Deng Xiaoping, for example – previously disgraced in the Cultural Revolution (see Tang Tsou 1986).

The phenomenon of the Cultural Revolution was in keeping with Mao's general philosophy. At the time of the Great Leap Forward, talk of stages

1. For detail on the Cultural Revolution, see MacFarquhar and Fairbank (1991, vol. XV, esp. chs. 2 and 4).

in the revolutionary movement gave way to talk of 'permanent' or 'interrupted' revolution. This perspective was used to justify the introduction of institutions – communes – that were proper to a Communist society. 'After winning one battle', Mao said, 'we must immediately put forward new tasks. In this way, we can maintain the revolutionary enthusiasm of the cadres and the masses and diminish their self-satisfaction, since they have no time to be satisfied with themselves, even if they wanted to' (Wilson 1977, p. 57). And later: 'the advanced and the backward are the two extremities of a contradiction, and 'comparison' is the unity of opposites . . . disequilibrium is a universal objective law. Things for ever proceed from disequilibrium, to equilibrium, and from equilibrium to disequilibrium, in endless cycles . . . but each cycle reaches a higher level. Disequilibrium is constant and absolute; equilibrium is temporary and relative' (Wilson 1977, p. 58). Even communism itself was not exempt from such 'revolutions'. This general attitude of Mao became more pronounced in the 1960s when he summed up his view of philosophy as follows: 'Engels talked about three categories, but as for me, I don't believe in two of those categories . . . there is no such thing as the negation of the negation. Affirmation, negation, affirmation, negation . . . in the development of things, every link in the chain of events is both affirmation and negation . . . Socialism, too, will be eliminated, it wouldn't do if it were not eliminated, for then there would be no Communism' (Schram 1974, p. 226). This idea of 'permanent revolution' may sound akin to that of Trotsky, but is in fact very different. Mao had – perforce – to allot a much more important role to the peasantry in the revolutionary movement than Trotsky, who was even more pessimistic concerning the revolutionary potential of the peasantry than was Lenin. Consequently, Mao refused to adopt the emphasis on heavy industrial development at the expense of the peasantry that Stalin – in accordance with the previously expressed views of Trotsky – had implemented.

In slightly more concrete terms, the Chinese version of Marxism privileges the relations of production over the forces of production and the former are obviously more malleable than the latter. The Sino-Soviet split of 1960 was undoubtedly partly due to international power politics: détente with the USA left China exposed and the USSR had not offered China the expected support in her border dispute with India. Of more long-term significance, however, were different models for the achievement of socialism. Beginning with the 1955 drive towards raising agricultural productivity by means of almost total cooperativisation, China had begun to move from the Soviet model – the only one available to them in 1949. In contrast to the

Soviet Union, there was an emphasis on the peasants and the countryside that was equal to, and sometimes greater than, that on heavy industry. The continued application of the Soviet model would have meant creating an unacceptable gulf between city and country. The peasants were, after all, the makers of the revolution. They could not be relegated simply to a source of surplus to be invested in heavy industrial development. Therefore, in order to avoid the 'natural' alternative of a Bukharinist accumulation through small peasant plots, immense efforts were necessary to push the peasants towards socialism; hence the campaigns for cooperatives and communes, and the Cultural Revolution itself. These campaigns were pervaded by a high moral tone. Confucianism had always linked morality with politics in a unified and intolerant system of thought. It is striking how moral criteria are intermingled in Maoist documents with more strictly Marxist categories. As Schram has said:

> Consider the definition which Mao put forward in the 1950s for the so-called 'five bad elements', still used today. Landlords, rich peasants, counter-revolutionaries, bad elements and rightists. Two of these categories are sociological, two political and one moral. Mao did not appear to see any contradiction or problem in lumping them all together. Did he not perhaps see the revolution as the work of proletarians, peasants and good men? Does not all the available evidence suggest that Mao in fact shared with Liu Shaoqi the very Chinese and indeed Confucian notion that it is impossible to separate the inner moral world of the individual from his outward behaviour and from the political realm as a whole? (Wilson 1977, p. 65).

However much Mao believed that power grew out of the barrel of a gun, he was even more insistent that 'Weapons are an important factor in war, but not the decisive factor; it is people, not things, that are decisive. The contest of strength is not only a contest of military and economic power, but also a contest of human power and morale. Military and economic power is necessarily wielded by people' (Mao 1965–77, vol. II, p. 143).

Thus Maoism has continued the traditional emphasis in China on moral and political attitudes. These views more than any other were held to define a society and give it its particular character. It is in keeping with this tradition that the events of 1966–9 should be described as a cultural revolution. Hence, particularly during the Cultural Revolution, class struggle was said to take place in the individual's consciousness which veered between collective and private interests. Hence, too, the incessant praise of the spirit of self-sacrifice, the fanatical rejection of material incentives, and the general asceticism and puritanism that pervaded Chinese society, and appeals to the common good in a way more reminiscent of Rousseau than of Marx.

Asian Marxism outside China

The success of the Chinese revolution meant that the Chinese Communists had the space to deploy their ideas even before their accession to power. The same is true, to an extent much more limited by war and international power politics, of Vietnam, North Korea and Kampuchea. Elsewhere, Marxists in Asia have devoted themselves to socio-economic analyses of their societies and developing (unsuccessful) strategies to gain political power.

The basic question confronting Marxists in Asia was how to adapt the Marxian doctrine of historical materialism to their societies. This doctrine had seen societies as moving through various stages of modes of production with communism as the final result. Marx himself had talked of an 'Asiatic' mode of production: 'in broad outlines Asiatic, ancient, feudal, and modern bourgeois modes of production can be designated as progressive epochs in the economic formation of society' (Marx 1977, p. 390). What Marx meant by this was that the necessity of providing vast public works to achieve satisfactory irrigation had led to a highly centralised government built on a sub-stratum of self-contained villages and the entire absence of private property in land.[2] But however interesting such a conception may be historically, it had little influence on Asian Marxism, which operated largely with the analytical parameters of historical development laid down by Lenin and Stalin. Thus the question confronting Asian Marxists was whether their societies were analysable as predominantly feudal in the European sense. In Japan, for example, there was an intense debate on whether the Meiji restoration was essentially a bourgeois revolution introducing a capitalist society, as argued by Yamakama, or whether important feudal elements remained – as held by the Japanese Communist Party.

These rather broad considerations had more immediate political implications. Put simply, would one revolution or two be needed to achieve socialism? As noted above, this question was answered very differently by the Chinese Communists in the 1950s from the views they propounded in the 1930s. In Vietnam, the leading party theoretician Truong Chinh held that the feudal landowners and the small indigenous bourgeoisie were dependent on the French colonial power, and that therefore the national liberation struggle could harmonise nationalism and socialism. In Japan the dispute over the nature of the Meiji restoration led to a division between those who considered Japan already capitalist, and therefore in need of a

2. On Marx's subtle and variegated conception of Asian society, see Melotti (1977).

single revolution, and the Japanese Communist Party which held that a bourgeois democratic revolution was first necessary to overcome the feudal elements still powerful in Japanese society.[3] In Indonesia, which contained the biggest Communist Party in the non-Communist world and a relatively substantial proletariat, feudalism and proletarian revolution could be directly combined. As D. N. Aidit, the most prominent post-war leader of the PKI wrote: 'The Indonesian proletariat is exploited by three forms of brutal exploitation, that is, imperialism, capitalism and feudalism' (Aidit 1958, p. 62). Here the successive stages of orthodox Marxism are radically telescoped.

Historical periodisation and revolutionary strategy obviously depended on a class analysis of Asian society. Crucial was the role allotted to the peasantry. One of the reasons for the success in West Bengal and eventually in Kerala of the Communist Party (Marxist), which broke away from the Communist Party of India in 1964, was that it merged the thinking of Lenin and Mao to give equal prominence to the working class and poor peasants in its campaigns; and, in a more academic vein, Indian Marxists have produced an impressive literature debating the nature of the mode of production in agriculture (see, for example, Patnaik 1989). In Vietnam, Ho Chi Minh highlighted the revolutionary potential of the peasantry before Mao did. And in Kampuchea the Communist Party actually emptied its urban areas of workers and set about transforming all its inhabitants into peasants. A corollary of this was a reluctance to describe post-revolutionary governments as dictatorships of the proletariat and a tendency in China pre-1949 and Vietnam to talk more vaguely of 'the people'. Opinions have also differed on the persistence of class struggle in post-revolutionary society. Vietnamese Communists – whose leadership has been remarkably consensual – disapproved of Mao's views on this, rejected the Cultural Revolution, and, on this point if on few others, sided with Deng Xiaoping and the post-1978 rejection in China of class struggle as a principal contradiction. Indeed, in Korea class struggle was claimed to have been completely eliminated.

The role of the party has proved equally problematic. Since Asian Marxism has been of the Marxist-Leninist variety, the party was conceived as a vanguard leading the various interests that it represented. In this respect Vietnam has proved the most orthodox. In Indonesia, the Communist Party in the 1950s adopted a Gramscian stance and promoted itself as an ideological force. In China in the 1960s, by contrast, the Cultural Revolution produced

3. The most interesting work to come out of this controversy is that of Kozo Uno. See his comprehensive restatement of Marxism (1980) and also the work of his disciple Makoto Itoh (1988).

a violent anti-party reaction, whereas in Korea the party was said to be the creation of its individual leader Kim Il Sung.

The espousal of violence as the midwife of revolution has depended on political culture and the degree of economic development. In China, Korea, Vietnam and Kampuchea, careful thinking about guerrilla warfare contributed to the success of revolution. Non-violent approaches failed to yield political power, except in the Indian states of Kerala and West Bengal. The attempt to transfer Maoist guerrilla tactics to India in the Naxalite movement of 1967, under the charismatic leadership of Mazumdar, was a failure.[4] The Naxalites never managed to draw on nationalist sentiments, and capitalism proved to be too firmly entrenched in the Indian countryside to be overturned by guerrilla action. The Communist Party of India itself had embraced the doctrine of peaceful transition to socialism as early as 1958, following their victory in Kerala the previous year. The preamble to the party's new constitution set as a goal the achievement of 'full democracy by peaceful means' and represented 'a deep blow to the non-violent and democratic traditions of India' (S. Gupta 1972, p. 52). Similarly the post-war Japanese Communist Party adopted the parliamentary road to socialism, and Indonesian Marxists in the years before their brutal suppression in 1965 evolved a strategy for infiltrating and transforming the state by peaceful means. With the biggest Communist Party in the non-Communist world, Indonesian Marxism could appear as the ideology of a counter-elite who, as well as being relatively hospitable to the more left-leaning elements in Islam, held that the state had a dual aspect – pro-people as well as anti-people. The struggle for ideological hegemony could emphasise the pro-people element in the state and gradually transform its nature (Aidit 1964, pp. 42ff.).

If there is one striking characteristic of Asian Marxism, it is the emphasis on the superstructure. It is, of course, true that Western Marxism typically re-evaluated the force of ideology and culture as compared with the Marxism of the Second International. But this happened in a context where the leading Marxist theoreticians were increasingly isolated from Marxist political movements (Aidit 1964, pp. 44ff.). In Asia, however, the theoretical re-evaluation of the superstructure was achieved within the Marxist movement itself. In Mao's China it was felt that the socialisation of the economic base of society had progressed faster than the consciousness of the people, which was still imbued with conservative attitudes inherited from pre-revolutionary society. Constant struggle was necessary to keep the

4. See further the comprehensive account of Mohan Ram (1971).

ideological superstructure abreast of the economic base, in contrast to Mao's successors who have returned to the more traditional Marxist view on the development of the productive forces. In Vietnam, one of the major factors making for the success of the revolution was the ability of Ho Chi Minh and his followers to imbue their movement with strong feelings of patriotism. Indigenous landowners and the bourgeoisie had so compromised themselves with the colonial power that the anti-imperialist nationalist revolution and the social land-reforming revolution were identical. In Korea, the emphasis was on the independence, creativity and consciousness of humankind – all factors necessary for the creation of a new society and the individual leadership of, for example, Kim Il Sung to guide this creativity in the right direction. Here the Marxist view of the centrality of material factors for understanding and transforming society has been abandoned. Even more so was this the case in Kampuchea under Pol Pot, where two views combined to form a lethal cocktail.[5] The first, taken from a crude dialectical materialism, was that all things were interrelated; the second was an extreme form of voluntarism which held, given the correct consciousness, that any obstacle could be overcome. Thus no misfortune could ever really be an accident: things being interconnected, there was always a cause and this resided in the individual's refusal to effect the necessary change in his/her consciousness. The added chauvinism and sectarianism which characterised the Communist Party of Kampuchea produced an ideology which, both in its substance and in the importance attributed to it, was very far removed from the mainstream Marxism perhaps best displayed by the gradualist Gramscian approach of the Communist Party in Indonesia.

As Marxism travelled east, it inevitably underwent a profound transformation. Marxism was originally devised as a critical tool for dealing with capitalist societies. In Asia, the societies in which it was successful were far from capitalist. Revisions of the traditional Marxist periodisation of history were essential, as well as a most un-Marxist emphasis on ideology and consciousness. From a Marxist point of view, these revisions and distortions are connected with premature attempts to construct socialism. As a distinguished Chinese scholar has recently claimed: 'According to Marx's theory of the social formation, the history of those so-called socialist countries is nothing but the history of societies from pre-capitalism to capitalism' (Duan 1996, p. 126). Asian Marxism thus appears in a compelling example of Hegel's irony of history, as a modernising precursor of capitalism.

5. See further Ben Kiernan, 'Kampuchea as Stalinism', in Mackerras and Knight (1985, p. 232).

13
Western Marxism

DAVID McLELLAN

Introduction

The character of Marxism in Europe during the middle of the twentieth century was profoundly marked by the collapse of the Second International in 1914 and by the defeat of the working-class movements in Western Europe in the following two decades. This collapse meant that the centre of gravity of Marxist thought initially moved east, where it was soon suppressed by the rise of Stalin. Unlike the previous generation of Marxist theoreticians, most of the thinkers grouped under the rubric of 'Western' Marxism were not important figures in political parties. They tended to be academics rather than activists, writing in a period of declining working-class activity and therefore in comparative isolation from political practice. Thus philosophy, epistemology, methodology and even aesthetics bulk larger in their works than do politics or economics – though all were insistent on the political implications of even their most abstruse writings. In a period when parliamentary democracy became normal throughout the advanced capitalist countries and their economies enjoyed a period of unprecedented growth, an atmosphere of resigned pessimism spread among many Marxist intellectuals – a pessimism that was not alleviated by considering the repressive nature of Soviet bureaucracy. Geographically, Marxist thought was concentrated in Germany, France and Italy, countries with large Communist parties. Whereas Marx started with philosophy and moved to economics, the typical thinkers of Western Marxism have moved in the opposite direction and in some cases sought inspiration in philosophers anterior to Marx – Spinoza, Kant and, above all, Hegel.

Within this context, the term 'Western Marxism' normally excludes orthodox communists of strict Marxist obedience, and even Austro-Marxists such as Otto Bauer or Karl Renner, and is confined to the (still rather loose) collection of thinkers that centred around the work of Lukács and Korsch in central Europe, that of Gramsci in Italy, and, perhaps above all, of the Frankfurt school in Germany. Western Marxism is thus a philosophical meditation on the defeat of Marxism in the West. These meditations have profound implications for politics, but Western Marxism was rarely directly political: a rethinking of the philosophical premises of Marxism was seen as a necessary precondition for a successful politics. And Western Marxism was happy to engage with 'bourgeois' philosophy to achieve this rethinking. Thus the spirit of Hegel was revived by the flux and changes that followed the First World War, with its theoretical counterpart in the writings of the late Lenin and, particularly, of the early Lukács. The impact of Freud's theories was felt in the work of the Frankfurt school, especially in Reich, Marcuse and the early Habermas. The rise of Nazism and its consequences shifted the centre of Marxist theory in the West to France and saw the advent of existentialism and then structuralism as the dominant mode of philosophising. And more recently, in the Anglo-Saxon world, some of the more interesting contributions to discussions of Marxism have used analytical philosophy to reinterpret Marxism through the individualistic ideology of the Reagan–Thatcher years. While some might question whether these modes of thought were really compatible with anything recognisable as Marxism, they undoubtedly extended the horizons of Marxist discussion beyond the rather limited perspectives of the Second International and Leninist orthodoxy. Gramsci's concept of hegemony and its consequences for political culture, the treatment of Freud by Marcuse, the drastic critique of the Enlightenment in Horkheimer and Adorno – all these attempts to remedy weaknesses or gaps in the classical Marxist tradition have produced a compelling, if sometimes rather convoluted, literature on philosophy, politics and society.

The impact of Lukács

A figure who lies somewhat outside the contours of Western Marxism as described above, but who nevertheless helped to shape those contours, is the Hungarian philosopher Georg Lukács. Lukács' early work forms a bridge between the success and prestige of the Russian Revolution and its subsequent degeneration. This work is an idealised picture of the revolutionary movement and Communist parties that had led the risings of 1918–19 in Germany, Austria and Lukács' native Hungary. But the picture remained at some distance from reality as these revolutionary movements proved a failure and Lukács found himself theorising in a socio-political vacuum. His most influential work, entitled *History and Class Consciousness*, was written in exile in Vienna after the suppression of the Hungarian Commune. In its search for philosophical inspiration outside traditional Marxism, its emphasis on consciousness, and its antipathy to seeing Marxism as a science, Lukács' work established themes that were to resonate through the whole of Western Marxism. Although Hungarian by birth, Lukács studied widely in Germany and, in the pre-war years, had assimilated the debates surrounding the demise of the neo-Kantian school, the beginnings of phenomenology, and the growing influence of intuitionist and Romantic tendencies, all of which currents, epitomised in the work of Dilthey, were reacting against the primacy attached to the methodology of the natural sciences. But it was to Hegel that Lukács chiefly looked to conceptualise the problems of his time. With the possible (and rather minor) exception of Labriola, Lukács was the first Marxist thinker seriously to evaluate the role of Hegel in the formation of Marx's thought and recapture the Hegelian dimension of Marxism. In this, Lukács strikingly anticipated the new light cast upon Marx's thought by the publication around 1930 of *The Economic and Philosophical Manuscripts*. Like the young Marx, Lukács had found his way to Marxism through Hegel. This approach involved Lukács in opposing the theoretical presuppositions both of the economism practised by the Socialist Trade Union leaders for the previous two decades and the emphasis on natural necessity so evident in the scientism of so many previous Marxist philosophers. He criticised the idea of a dialectics of nature and the reflection theory of knowledge, and took Engels to task for his deficient understanding of dialectics. For Lukács, the dialectical method, which was the essence of Marxism, meant a particular approach to the world in which thinking about the world also involved changing it: the dialectic was an integral part of a practical commitment to the revolutionary process. In long and detailed analyses, Lukács attempted to show how previous thought had not been able correctly to perceive the world since it radically separated subject from object. Only with Hegel was this separation overcome – albeit in an idealist fashion. The only class which could unite subject and object was the proletariat, which expressed in its subjective thought (at least in so far as it was fully class conscious) what it was objectively doing in history. This historical interaction of subject and object was for Lukács the basic form of the dialectic.

Thus the central thesis of Lukács' main work was that the two terms of its title – history and class consciousness – were in fact one and the same. In his discussion of class consciousness, Lukács went beyond the actual subjective consciousness of the proletariat and talked of 'ascribed' consciousness, i.e. the consciousness a class would have if it were fully aware of its own interests. Until the advent of the proletariat and its unification of the roles of subject and object, understanding the world was blocked by the phenomenon for which Lukács popularised the term 'reification'. Lukács started explicitly from Marx's analysis of the fetishism of commodities in *Capital*, in which the social relations between persons became transformed both subjectively and objectively into relations between commodities. The world of things ruled over human beings through objective laws that appeared to be independent of them. People became objects: passive spectators of a process that structured their lives for them. Starting from the economic division of labour, Lukács traced the progress of this reification in the state and in modern bureaucracy, here borrowing from Max Weber's concept of 'rationality'.

Linked to the notion of reification in Lukács was that of totality. One of the results of reification was 'the destruction of every image of the whole'. The specialisation of labour and the general atomisation of society meant that people and the world surrounding them were viewed as discrete, separate entities with no intrinsic connection. The bourgeoisie had necessarily to view things like this, for it was essential to their way of life. The central impetus of the reification process up till the present had been the all-pervasiveness of objectivity: in a reified world there were no subjects. However, the evolution of capital in society had now reached a point where the proletariat could destroy reification and become the subject of the historical process. The partial and static views of the bourgeoisie could never attain knowledge of society.

Lukács' work was condemned by the Fifth Comintern Congress in 1924. His approach was too labile, too keen on dialectics at the expense of materialism, and too sympathetic to the idea of workers' councils and the legacy of Rosa Luxemburg for it to be acceptable in the increasingly authoritarian and dogmatic world of the emerging Soviet Union. This emphasis on the role of consciousness and its political counterpart in the workers' councils was stressed by Lukács' colleague, the prominent German Communist Karl Korsch. Korsch was also the first writer systematically to apply Marx's own ideas to the history of Marxism. For his pains he was expelled from the German Communist Party in 1926. Lukács, on the other hand, moved to the Soviet Union and to the less controversial fields of literary criticism and, later, social ontology. But his influence remained strong. The spirit of his work was continued in a direct way by his pupil Lucien Goldmann in France and by the efforts of such writers as Agnes Heller and Ferenc

Feher, who formed the core of the Budapest school which flourished in the 1960s. More widely, Lukács' treatment of class consciousness influenced the sociology of knowledge and resonated throughout Western Marxism. He revived interest in the Hegelian element in Marxism and his treatment of the concepts of alienation, reification, totality, etc., were fundamental to later Marxist critiques of bourgeois culture. Utopian and prophetic, his incorporation of the Romantic anti-scientific tradition into Marxism and his passionate resistance to the kind of positivistic calculus that has progressively colonised so many areas of life means that his thought has an abiding interest for critics of the contemporary *Zeitgeist*.

Gramsci

Like that of Lukács, the thought of Antonio Gramsci, perhaps the most influential Marxist political thinker in the West during the twentieth century, forms a bridge between the high point of Marxist success during the first two decades of the century and the more ruminative style of later Western Marxism. Gramsci was an active advocate of workers' councils during the revolutionary years in Italy of 1919–20. He helped to found the Italian Communist Party in 1921 and became its leader for the two years before his arrest and imprisonment in 1926. The *Notebooks* which he compiled in prison helped to mediate many of the themes of Western Marxism to the Communist parties of Western Europe in the post-Stalin years. For while Gramsci could be seen as a Leninist (of sorts), his innovative writings contained approaches, particularly to political culture, that were foreign both to the classical Marxist and the Leninist traditions. Gramsci was a profound historicist in that he considered all human activity only to have meaning in relation to the historical process of which it was a part. Thus Gramsci tended to analyse the base through the superstructure, and was well aware of the very multi-dimensional sense in which historical materialism should be interpreted, He was one of the most dialectical of Marxist thinkers, and his analysis, particularly in the *Prison Notebooks*, of the relationship of necessity and liberty, of the superstructure, of the connection of intellectuals to the working class, etc., was constantly informed by a dialectical approach.

Fundamental to political culture for Gramsci was the role and function of intellectuals in society. Much of his research was devoted to a series of historical studies out of which he drew a distinction between traditional and organic intellectuals. Traditional intellectuals were intellectuals who mistakenly considered themselves to be autonomous of social classes, and who appeared to embody a historical continuity above and beyond socio-political change. Examples would be writers, artists, philosophers, and, especially, ecclesiastics. Traditional intellectuals were those who survived the demise of the mode of production that gave them birth. The fact that they were linked to historically moribund classes and yet pretended to a certain independence involved the production of an ideology, usually of an idealist bent, to mask their real obsolescence. While the notion of a traditional intellectual was primarily a historical one, that of an organic intellectual was much more sociological. The extent to which an intellectual was organic was measured by the closeness of the connection of the organisation of which he or she was a member to the class which that organisation represented. Organic intellectuals articulated the collective consciousness of their class in the political, social and economic sphere.

Drawing on his experience of workers' councils in Turin in the immediately post-war years, Gramsci held that the task of these organic intellectuals was to draw out and make coherent the latent aspirations and potentialities already inherent in working-class activity. The relationship of organic intellectuals and their class was thus a dialectical one: they drew their material from working-class experience at the same time as imparting to it a theoretical consciousness. The formation of organic intellectuals was much more difficult for the proletariat than for the bourgeoisie, which had enjoyed its own life and culture in the interstices of feudal society. Occasionally Gramsci even went as far as to say that the proletariat could only really produce its *own* intellectuals *after* the seizure of state power.

The most important role of intellectuals was to organise and articulate the skein of beliefs and of institutional and social relations that Gramsci called hegemony and whose analysis was perhaps Gramsci's most important contribution to political thought. As with the concept of intellectuals, so with that of hegemony, he modified and enriched the Marxist tradition by extending a concept that had previously had rather a narrow application – in this case in the work of Plekhanov and Lenin. Drawing, again, on his experience in Turin, Gramsci broadened the concept of hegemony to include in it an analysis of the means by which ruling classes obtained the consent of the subordinate group to their own domination. The world view of the ruling class, in other words, was so thoroughly diffused by its intellectuals as to become the 'common sense' of the whole of society. The bureaucratic and technological rationalism analysed by Weber was part of the capitalist ideological hegemony which functioned to repress any creative or innovatory initiatives of the working class. Gramsci considered this realisation that for the most part the ruling class did not have to resort to force to maintain its dominance to be the core of his theory.

In Gramsci's view, the hegemony of the bourgeoisie lay in its dominance of civil society rather than its control of the repressive force of state power, and it was to the analysis of civil society that he devoted most of his energy. Although both Gramsci and Marx claimed to be getting their concept of civil society from Hegel, their use of the term was, in fact, very different. Whereas Marx used the expression civil society to mean the totality of economic relationships, Gramsci used 'civil society' to refer mainly to the superstructure. Sometimes Gramsci did talk of civil society as fulfilling a mediation function between economics and politics. Usually, however, civil society denoted for Gramsci all the organisations and technical means which diffused the ideological justification of the ruling class in all domains of culture. And Gramsci's conception of ideology was both extremely wide, including even most aspects of natural science, and extremely varied, extending its appeal from philosophy to folklore. Thus civil society had above all a cultural function and, through the hegemony of the ruling class, presented the 'ethical content of the State'.

One result of this approach was to draw a distinction between different revolutionary strategies in the East and the West. In less-developed societies, such as Russia, the state had rightly been the object of frontal attack; in more-developed societies, it was civil society that first needed to be infiltrated. Borrowing terms from recent studies of military science, Gramsci termed the first sort of attack 'a war of movement or manoeuvre' in which artillery could open up sudden gaps in defences and troops could be rapidly switched from one point to another to storm through and capture fortresses, and the second a 'war of position' in which enemies were well balanced and had to settle down to a long period of trench warfare. The French bourgeoisie, for example, preceded its success in its 1789 Revolution by a war of position in the shape of a lengthy cultural assault on the ideological supports of aristocratic power. And Gramsci considered that the war of position became more important as capitalism developed.

Given his contrast between East and West, Gramsci was opposed to what he saw as the blunt internationalism of Trotsky. Although he agreed with Trotsky in seeing fascism as a movement of the petty bourgeoisie reacting to their loss of power, he came down in favour of Stalin in the argument over socialism in one country. Gramsci supported the idea of different national roads towards the achievement of communism and thus could be read as a mentor for the Euro-communist tendencies which emerged in the 1960s.

As the intense debate over his legacy demonstrates, Gramsci was, with the exception of the Russian revolutionaries, the most original Marxist political thinker in Europe over the last fifty years. His contribution spanned the entire spectrum of Marxist politics in the decade following the October Revolution. He talked the same language as the council communists such as Pannekoek and Gorter and yet was active in the Third International. His work on the system of hegemony, and on the intellectuals as an organic link between base and superstructure, builds directly on the work of Marx and, to a lesser extent, that of Lenin. Yet it contained, at the same time, a rationale for the more reflective, academic analyses of capitalist society and culture that were characteristic of much of Western Marxism.

The Frankfurt school

Central to what is ordinarily meant by 'Western Marxism' is the work of the Frankfurt school, which took its name from the Institute of Social Research founded in Frankfurt in 1923. Originally concentrating on a more orthodox form of Marxism, the Institute changed its orientation with the appointment of Max Horkheimer as director in 1930. He was soon joined by Theodor Adorno and Herbert Marcuse whose work, together with the later contributions of Habermas, formed the core of the Frankfurt school. Driven into exile in the United States by Nazism, the Institute was re-established in Germany in the early 1950s. The writings of the Frankfurt school thus have as their background, and are a reflection upon, the events which had so forcefully shaped the lives of its members: the collapse of working-class movements in Western Europe and the rise of fascism, the degeneration of the Russian Revolution as the grip of Stalinism stifled intellectual debate, and the lengthy capitalist boom in post-war Europe. They considered that the traditional Marxist approach of historical materialism needed to be supplemented by the work of thinkers outside the Marxist tradition such as Weber or Freud. The original Marxian concern with political economy needed to be allied with other disciplines which were necessary to account for crucial phenomena such as the expansion of state activity, the industrialisation of culture, and the increase of authoritarianism. They broadened the notion of the political by reference to problems created by the growth of bureaucracy, by family structures, and by the impact of mass culture. Thus psychoanalysis, sociology, even extended discussions of the role of art in society, all became part of their repertoire. They used these perceptions to contest overly deterministic interpretations of historical materialism and concentrated more on the forces currently shaping the identity and attitudes of those who, however much they might now be subject to historical laws, were, at least potentially, also their agents.

The term which leading members of the Frankfurt school used to describe their enterprise was 'critical theory'. The criticism contained in this theory was directed above all against a positivism and empiricism which, however progressive they may have been during the rise of capitalism, had become a source of reification and an endorsement of the status quo. Horkheimer's seminal article of 1937 entitled 'Traditional and Critical Theory' opposed what he saw as positivism's simplistic approach to objectivity. In this 'traditional' theory, he wrote, 'the genesis of particular objective facts, the practical application of the conceptual systems by which it grasps the facts, and the role of such systems in action, are all taken to be external to the theoretical thinking itself' (Horkheimer 1972, p. 208). Critical theory, on the other hand, refused these dichotomies. They were an 'alienation' which involved a separation of value and research, of knowledge and action. The thinker was always a part of the object of his or her studies and it would be a mistake either to see the intellectual as 'free-floating' above society (as in Mannheim) or as completely embedded in society (as in vulgar Marxism). As opposed to the traditional view,

> in the materialist conception, the basic activity involved is work in society, and the class-related form of this work puts its mark on all human patterns of reaction, including theory. The intervention of reason in the processes whereby knowledge and its object are constituted, or the subordination of these processes to conscious control does not take place therefore in a purely intellectual world, but coincides with the struggle for certain real ways of life (Horkheimer 1972, p. 248).

In their attempt to transcend the difference between empirical and evaluative judgements, the Frankfurt school follow the line of Lukács – though without his reference to the proletariat. In a wider sense they saw themselves as inheritors of the whole Western philosophical tradition.

Thus, in their approach to society, thinkers such as Horkheimer tried always to adopt a critical perspective which was above all concerned with a critique of ideology, by which they meant all systematically distorted accounts of society which tried to conceal and legitimate the distribution of power. They attempted to show how the conflicts over this social power were expressed in thought and how intellectual activity served to justify various forms of domination. By exposing the nature and causes of this domination, they hoped to encourage action and change.

Historically, the target of much of this critical theory was the Enlightenment. In their influential book *Dialectic of Enlightenment*, Horkheimer and Adorno set out to investigate why the Enlightenment and the progress of Western reason and science in general had so signally failed, as they saw it, to deliver what it had promised. The book was written against the background of the authors' experience of Nazism which they viewed as an exceptionally dramatic illustration of the universal barbarism towards which the world as a whole was headed. The 'dialectic' of the title refers to the fact that, whereas science and reason were supposed to liberate humanity from the oppression of myth and superstition, they had produced the very opposite of liberation: a new all-embracing utilitarian pragmatic ideology which reduced everything to its quantitative aspect and thus drained it of all meaning. Indeed, by converting individual things and human beings into abstractions, this approach created the preconditions for twentieth-century totalitarianism.

Horkheimer and Adorno defined their subject as 'the self-destruction of the Enlightenment' and set out to investigate the paradox that 'the enlightenment has always aimed at liberating men from fear and establishing their sovereignty. Yet the fully enlightened earth radiates disaster triumphant' (Horkheimer and Adorno 1972, p. 3). Central to their book was the contrast between two types of reason. The first was concerned to discover means for the liberation of human beings from external constraints and compulsions. The second was an instrumental reason whose function was to exercise a technical control over nature and which received its main impetus from the eighteenth-century Enlightenment. In its more recent manifestations, this type of reason had degenerated into totalitarianism:

> For the Enlightenment, whatever does not conform to the rule of computation and utility is suspect. So long as it can develop undisturbed by any outward repression there is no holding it. In the process, it treats its own ideas of human rights exactly as it does the older universals. Every spiritual resistance it encounters serves merely to increase its strength. Which means enlightenment still recognises itself even in myths. Whatever myths the resistance may appeal to, by virtue of the very fact that they become arguments in the process of opposition, they acknowledge the principle of dissolvent rationality for which they reproach the Enlightenment. Enlightenment is totalitarian (Horkheimer and Adorno 1972, p. 6).

By implication, Marx's thought, too, contained elements of instrumental reason: Marx's emphasis on labour (which had been viewed positively in 'Traditional and Critical Theory') and on nature as an object for human exploitation put him in the Enlightenment tradition. Thus class struggle and political economy took second place in the Frankfurt school to a broader account of the way in which the relationship between man and nature had become vitiated.

Even further away from man was Adorno's major work *Negative Dialectics*, an intentionally unfocused and tangential book whose main theme was to combat the 'identity principle' with a dialectical approach. The identity principle treated each thing as it was and analysed it by means of abstract general concepts. Dialectic, by contrast, identified each object by its own individual reality and not by general categories. It considered what the object should be according to its own individual concept but had not yet managed to become. The result was a provocative critique of first principles, but one which represented the Frankfurt school's furthest remove from the Marxist tradition.

Two important areas where the school attempted to supplement the Marxist tradition were psychology and art. Both these obviously reflect Western Marxism's interest in the superstructural elements of society. Lukács devoted much effort to study of the nineteenth-century bourgeois novel and his pupil Lucien Goldmann, in his study of Pascal and Racine (Goldmann 1964), produced what is perhaps the most impressive contribution by Western Marxism to literary criticism. The Frankfurt school cast its net wider and held that great works of art, while inevitably rooted in their own society, afforded a perspective on that society which was to some degree autonomous, non-conventional and potentially subversive. In its negative aspect, art was a protest against prevailing conditions and transcended society in so far as it hinted at more humane values. Adorno, for example, who was particularly interested in music, contrasted Schoenberg, whose atonal music expressed the disharmonies of contemporary society, favourably with Stravinsky who merely adapted pre-bourgeois music to the tastes of contemporary society. Hence, also, the Frankfurt school's critique of mass culture which had become a commodity and an industry. As such it simply served as a distraction from everyday life, which effectively duplicated and reinforced the social structures from which it temporarily diverted people.

While a concern with aesthetics had, from Marx onwards, always been a part of the Marxist tradition, the attempt to come to terms with psychology was a new departure. Strongly influenced by psychoanalysis, and particularly Freud, the Frankfurt school tried to assimilate this material into what remained of their Marxism. The only professional psychologist among them, Erich Fromm, produced detailed work on Freud and evolved an approach which combined Freudian insights with a strong historical perspective based on ideas of alienation and humanism taken from Marx's early writings. Fromm eventually drifted away from the school; but those who remained within its orbit directed their attention to the relationship between psychoanalysis and contemporary politics. Their general view, as expressed for example by Marcuse, saw Nazism as the culmination of the trend towards irrational domination inherent in the growing emphasis on instrumental reason and technological efficiency that was the legacy of the liberal Enlightenment traditional in the West. From a psychological perspective, however, they investigated the ways in which, as they saw it, the decline of paternal authority in the traditional family enhanced the power of role models coming from fascism in that the child looked for a father figure to replace weakening and arbitrary paternal control. In their classic post-war survey *The Authoritarian Personality*, Adorno and his collaborators tried to show the connections between the eponymous personality, which relied on superstition, stereotypical thinking and automatic submission to authority, and political opinions which tended towards fascism. The most determined (and optimistic) effort to marry Freud with Marxism, Marcuse's *Eros and Civilization*, claimed that, with the advance of technology, the repressive subordination of the instincts analysed by Freud would no longer be necessary: Marcuse here anticipated a society in which labour would be replaced by a kind of aesthetic play which would finally destroy the power of the death instinct.

While some members of the Frankfurt school, such as Adorno, developed a strong pessimism about contemporary society and others such as Horkheimer abandoned Marxism altogether, Marcuse continued to be more directly involved in political and social struggle. As the most prominent theorist of the New Left, it was Marcuse who, in the 1960s, popularised, particularly in North America, the ideas of the Frankfurt school of which he was the clearest and most systematic exponent. Prior to the radical utopia outlined in *Eros and Civilization*, Marcuse had devoted himself to Heidegger and pioneering studies of the relationship of Hegel to Marx which, like the work of Lukács, involved sustained attacks on positivism. While his *Soviet Marxism* contained a severe critique of state socialism, it was his all-embracing attack on advanced industrial society entitled *One-Dimensional Man* that proved his most popular book. Building on the work of Horkheimer and Adorno's *Dialectic of Enlightenment*, Marcuse aimed to show how late capitalist society totally controlled the consciousness of its members. Echoing a theme central to the Frankfurt school, he wrote that what distinguished current society was 'a flattening out of the antagonism between culture and social reality through the obliteration of the oppositional, alien, and transcendent elements in the higher culture by virtue of which it constituted *another dimension* of reality' (Marcuse 1964, p. 58). Such a regime could only be overturned by those who existed outside orthodox politics: 'the substratum of the outcasts and outsiders, the exploited and persecuted of other races and other colours, the unemployed and the unemployable' (Marcuse 1964, p. 201). In spite of this rather pessimistic conclusion, Marcuse remained committed to a radical politics that most of his colleagues had abandoned.

Western Marxism has been characterised by attempts to recover aspects of human experience neglected in the main Marxist tradition. While art and psychoanalysis, for example, proved difficult to recover, it might be thought, given the negative attitude of Marx and his immediate followers, that religion would be impossible. But some bold souls at least made the attempt. Lukács' pupil Lucien Goldmann produced brilliant analyses of Jansenism in seventeenth-century France. And Gramsci's subtle meditations on the lessons to be learnt from a historical comparison between Marxism and Christianity remain, at least in a historical perspective, the foremost Marxist contribution to the study of religion. Others, however, had a more evaluative and positive approach. Horkheimer, for example, had an abiding, if peripheral, interest in religion and pointed to the iconoclastic potential of Christianity, in that the idea of a radically transcendent divinity implied a relativisation and even criticism of all political and social arrangements: the legacy of religion was the idea of a perfect justice which, while it might be impossible to realise in this world, yet served as a constant basis of opposition to the powers that were. Adorno's younger friend Walter Benjamin called himself a historical materialist. But the images and language of his essays on philosophy and literary criticism were heavily imbued with theological themes such as redemption and messianism, producing a peculiar theology of revolution in which religious motifs were juxtaposed with, rather than subordinated to, materialist analyses. But it was Ernst Bloch who published the most extended, if rather allusive and uncoordinated, meditations on religion and Marxism. Although a friend both of Benjamin and of Lukács, Bloch had no direct connection to the Frankfurt school and professed allegiance to more or less orthodox communism throughout the most productive period of his life. From *The Spirit of Utopia* published in 1918 to his *magnum opus*, the three-volume *The Principle of Hope* of the 1950s, Bloch endeavoured to retrieve the Romantic and utopian elements of Marxism – what he called its 'warm current'. Bloch returned to the early Marx's comments on religion as 'the sign of the oppressed creature' and 'the heart of a heartless world' and took them further: religion, for Bloch, was no mere illusion, and the taking seriously of some of Marx's statements might 'open the way to conversations between believers purged of ideology and unbelievers purged of taboo'. Religious belief of some sort was a normal part of the human condition while there was still something for which to hope. Even under socialism there would be room for a socialist church to express the utopian aspirations of humankind. There was a strong continuity between Marxism and some forms of Christianity: Marxism was to make real the content of Christianity. In order to achieve this, Marxist atheism could not be simply negation. It had to be an active humanism that would bring to reality the 'hope treasures' of religion. These treasures were to be found in a secular messianism in which redemption is always possible in this world.

Habermas

The work of the Frankfurt school reflected in the main the world of the 1930s and 1940s. Although Marcuse continued to carry forward these ideas into the 1970s, the most influential figure in the 'second generation' of the school is Jürgen Habermas. In adapting the ideas of the school to the late twentieth century, Habermas has examined the philosophical presuppositions which had allowed the transformation of reason from an instrument of liberation to one of domination. Whereas in his later writings Habermas has been increasingly concerned with the discursive foundations of ethics, in his early work he attempted a basic reformulation of historical materialism. He did not wish, like Horkheimer and Adorno, to reject labour as a fundamental category of human activity; but he considered that implicit in Marx was a distinction between labour and interaction. The first was purposive rational action on an external world; the second involved communication between subjects. These two spheres (which corresponded to some extent with the classical Marxist division between forces of production and relations of production) were separate though related dimensions of social evolution. Each dimension had its own mode of knowledge and its own criteria of rationality: in the sphere of instrumental action, this involved extending technical control; in that of cultural development it involved the extension of forms of communication free from distortion and domination. Habermas then attempted to provide a theoretical framework for ideal communication, declaring that 'today the problem of language has replaced the traditional problem of consciousness'. Habermas claimed that technological society could only be rational if its policies were subject to public control. But discussion and opinion had to be free from manipulation and domination. The very act of speech involved the supposition of the possibility of an ideal speech situation in which the force of the better argument alone would decide the issue. This was only possible if all members of society had an equal chance to participate in the discussion; and this involved the notion of the transformation of society in a direction that would enable such a communicative competence to characterise all members of society. The ultimate goal of social emancipation was therefore inherent in any and every speech act.

It was to this 'linguistic turn' that Habermas devoted himself through most of the 1970s and 1980s. He developed a 'theory of communicative competence' which he saw as a self-reflexive social theory concerned to validate its own critical standards. Rather like Rousseau's General Will, the results of emancipated communication would be justified not by their contents corresponding to some external norm, but by the method through which they were attained. Taking a more optimistic view of the Enlightenment than Horkheimer and Adorno, Habermas saw it as an unfinished project. He replaced the former subject-centred conception of rationality by a communicative conception grounded in interactions *between* human subjects where the norms to govern society had yet to be constructed. This has enabled Habermas to preserve, at least counterfactually, concepts of truth, morality and political legitimacy. In this he has found himself at odds with the proponents of postmodernity such as Foucault, Derrida or Rorty who are sceptical of any universal values. Habermas, by contrast, has retained his confidence in 'modernity' and its implicitly universally justifiable norms, and devoted his encyclopaedic analyses to explaining the trends in contemporary society which frustrate their realisation.

Conclusion

Western Marxism can thus be seen as an attempt fundamentally to revise the Marxist tradition by going backwards to its Hegelian roots and forwards to the incorporation of later sociological approaches mainly of a Weberian inspiration. As such, it has its own distinctive tradition which finds itself at variance with other West European attempts to come to terms with Marx's legacy. In France, for example, Sartre trying to reconcile his existentialism with Marxist principles or Althusserian Marxism and its anarchic successors inhabits a different intellectual world which obviously owes a lot to Descartes. In the United States and Britain, the development of what has become known as 'analytical' or 'rational choice' Marxism is equally alien. It is a product of the *Zeitgeist* and particularly the rampant individualism of the Thatcher/Reagan years. Marxist social scientists applied methods employed in neo-classical economics such as game theory and general equilibrium theory. The work of Elster and Roemer in particular reinterpreted man through the framework of a strict methodological individualism and held that to explain social phenomena it was necessary to show that rational individuals would freely choose to behave in ways that would result in the phenomena to be explained. For the Western Marxism of Lukács, Gramsci and the Frankfurt school such approaches are too influenced by contemporary economics and neglect the critical, philosophical, reflective legacy of Hegel. Deeply imbued with German idealism, these Western Marxists have rejected the traditional Marxist approach of interpreting and changing society through its economic base, and even more the view of Marxism as a universal science of nature and history. They thus had no time for dialectical materialism – the doctrine that physical and chemical matter was in some way dialectical. Western Marxists were concerned rather to produce a theory of society. In their view this involved primarily a theory of culture and of consciousness.

As well as the influence of classical German philosophy, world events shaped the approach of Western Marxists and encouraged them to resurrect the more superstructural side of their inheritance. The Stalinisation of the working class and the rise of fascism drove many of them into exile and removed the opportunity for practical politics. Faced with these twin catastrophes, many Western Marxists, particularly in the Frankfurt school, failed to appreciate the complexity of politics. Faced with the starkness of contemporary events they overestimated the capacity of existing powers to stabilise society and absorb all opposition. They thus tended to neglect the various crises afflicting capitalist societies and the political struggles that stemmed therefrom. It is an attention to these that distinguishes the work of, for example, Habermas from the previous generation of Horkheimer and Adorno. Their milieu was undoubtedly burdened by a pessimism about the trajectory of politics which could only encourage their interest in such subjects as epistemology or aesthetics. As the prospects for revolution ebbed in the West, many Marxists turned their attention to philosophy almost as an end in itself, and to subjects – such as aesthetics – apparently far removed from politics. Indeed, it is a measure of how far Marxist thought has travelled over the last century that the two areas in which much of the most interesting theoretical work is currently being done are development studies, with special reference to the third world, and aesthetics. In thus expanding its analyses into areas neglected by its predecessors, Western Marxism has produced a powerful literature. Its authors have investigated the impact of technological advance, its accompanying rationalising ideologies, and the various forms of domination that it produces and reproduces. In so doing they have not only enriched the Marxist tradition but also evolved a critical theory of society that continues to have considerable influence.

14
French Marxism – existentialism to structuralism

SUNIL KHILNANI

Introduction

In its nineteenth-century heyday, Marxism was an avowedly internationalist doctrine promising universal human emancipation; its twentieth-century fate, though, was to splinter under the pressure of more local concerns, and to be forced into restrictive national boundaries. In the East, Marxism became an ideology of the state; in the West, it remained outside the portals of state power, in some countries relegated to the margins of public life, in others achieving a certain cultural centrality. In France, the latter was emphatically the case.

Of all these national forms taken by Marxism in the West, the French species developed comparatively late. It came to prominence after 1945 – almost three decades after the wave of revolutionary upheaval had swept other parts of Europe. Yet after the end of the Second World War, France – or more precisely, Paris – almost overnight established itself as the most important forging house for Western ideas of revolution. The theories and ideas that emanated from the French capital gained a spectacular eminence in Marxist thought across the globe, and provoked developments that took Marxism into areas quite remote from its founding preoccupations. The history of this intellectual episode is, therefore, a vital and vivid fragment of the history of twentieth-century radical thought.

The history of Marxism in France lends itself to bold narrative-shaping. It has a definite beginning – signalled by its meteoric post-war entry into French debate – and an equally decisive terminus, marked by its swift collapse in the mid-1970s. To the articulate and intense minds that participated in it, it is a story told often in tragic or confessional mode. The bright hopes of the early years, when revolution seemed possible, yield to a history of defeated ambitions – to disappointment and ultimately to rejection of the very idea of revolution itself, which came to be seen as intrinsically twinned to political terror. Indeed, the exit from Marxism was, for the French themselves, as important a part of French Marxism's history as its actual content.

During the almost three decades that Marxism dominated the French intellectual landscape, it provided, in Jean-Paul Sartre's phrase, the 'unsurpassable horizon' of all French thought. How it came to enjoy this ascendancy is a story of some intricacy and one quite specific to the inflections of French history and politics. Despite the presence of a Communist Party more orthodox than any of its Western counterparts, French Marxism was vigorously plural – even promiscuous, both in its prior filiations and in its wide-ranging contemporary connections, which criss-crossed the entire field of the social sciences and the humanities. The broad diversity of Marxisms that flourished in France is striking. Almost every extant strain of Marxism has at some time or other found expression and adepts in France: Leninism, Trotskyism and Maoism, as well as French innovations such as existential Marxism, Althusserianism and '*gauchisme*'. What united them all, and imprinted them as distinctively French, was a shared political history and a set of shaping predicaments and preoccupations which were defined by longer rhythms and punctuated by more proximate events.

Those long-term patterns included the presence, since the French Revolution of 1789, of a sharp cleavage between left and right, and a vigorous revolutionary tradition that encompassed social groups, political organisations and a rich array of symbols. More immediately, the experience of war and defeat, of collaboration with and resistance to fascism, of the wars in colonial Indo-China and Algeria, and of the establishment of Charles de Gaulle's Fifth Republic and the events of 1968, all framed the political context of French Marxism. These traditions and experiences defined a set of recurring thematic concerns – a preoccupation with the idea of revolution, with the status of the Communist Party and its relation to the working class, with the role of theory and the place of intellectuals, and with France's own historical role as a vanguard nation. But French Marxism showed virtually no interest in the central concern of classical Marxism: economics. Marxism was transplanted into a French cultural context in which literature and philosophy held a privileged status, and in keeping with an emphasis common to Western Marxism as a whole, French Marxism was more attentive to matters of culture and ideology: the origins of both existential and structural Marxism lay squarely in literary and philosophical concerns.

The claims of French Marxism were grand – to generate, variously, a universal philosophy of freedom, or an objective science of society. The conceptual content, theoretical inventiveness and ambitious scope of French Marxism are all important in explaining its remarkable influence and impact on radical thought across the world. But, equally, its firmly contextual character is neglected at peril. Erratic, regularly subject to local rhythms, the French contribution figures centrally in the elaboration of Marxism in the second half of the twentieth century; and the effects of its collapse were severe for the broader fate of Marxist theory.

There are difficulties in trying to delineate the identity of French Marxism very precisely: its intellectual boundaries were permeable, and there was always regular traffic with non- or pre-Marxist thought. Additionally, after 1945, French radical intellectuals, unlike others in Western Europe (with the exception of their Italian counterparts) were not operating in a political vacuum. What made Marxism unavoidable for them was the presence in France of the largest working-class movement in Western Europe, led by a Communist Party with close links to the Soviet Union. French Marxism was thus always split between the 'official' doctrines of the party and the philosophical theories of intellectuals, who chose to work either within or outside the party. A great deal of French Marxist theoretical reflection and argument centred on the nature of this divide between intellectuals and the party. It followed also that the cognitive status of Marxism was constantly debated, since on this turned the issue of who could legitimately claim authority to interpret it. Should Marxism be viewed as the direct expression of working-class consciousness, which merely required articulation by the Communist Party? Or were the truths of Marxism embedded in texts that required theoretical interpretation? And if the latter, whose interpretations were to count as authoritative?

The intellectual elaboration of Marxism in France was further complicated by the shadow cast over French intellectual life by the Soviet experience. While other strands of Western Marxism managed earlier – and more decisively – to disconnect themselves from the Soviet Union, this was not the case in France. The enduring entanglement had to do with the initial French response to the 1917 Bolshevik Revolution, which assimilated that event to France's own revolutionary tradition, and which generated an entire lexicon of historical-political symbols that linked together the French and Soviet revolutions, portraying the latter as the genealogical inheritor of the former. French Marxism's great and finally self-destructive failure was never to develop an adequate, plausible critique of the Soviet experience – especially Stalinism – nor to address the implications of this experience for Marxism as a whole.

The context of Marxism before 1945

Marx's own thinking was shaped by his understanding of French history, but in the nineteenth century Marxism itself had relatively little direct impact in France. A strong native working-class movement, proud of its own revolutionary traditions – divided between syndicalism, Guesdism and Jaurèsian socialism, but all contained within a broad socialist church – monopolised the politics of the left. The Bolshevik Revolution of 1917, however, changed that. The 1917 Revolution, with its claim to be the vehicle of universal revolutionary ambitions, usurped the privileged position of the French Revolution, and it provoked divergent responses within the French left. In 1920, the French socialist movement split as a result of its inability to agree on the domestic implications of the events in the Soviet Union: the French Communist Party (PCF) was formed, explicitly committed to Marxist-Leninist doctrine – which it believed could be grafted directly onto the indigenous Jacobin revolutionary tradition. The Communists acknowledged a shift in the theoretical and practical epicentre of revolution away from Paris and eastwards, towards the Soviet Union. The Socialists, under Léon Blum, on the other hand, clung to the hope that a distinctive French path to socialism remained available.

The Communists, initially a small sect of pacifists and revolutionaries, began from the mid-1930s to establish themselves as a mass movement, winning popular support by their committed anti-fascism. Their subsequent role in the resistance to Nazi occupation (and conversely the failure of the Socialists to organise themselves for this task) meant that by the 1940s the Communists had emerged as the largest party of the left. For French Communists, Marxism in its Leninist formulation was the crucial link between the French and Soviet revolutions. Leninism was of course the monopoly of the Communist Party of the Soviet Union (CPSU), and the PCF duly subordinated itself to the ideological *diktats* of its Soviet counterpart. It was able to attract intellectuals – especially writers and artists (for example, the Surrealists), philosophers and historians. During the 1930s, Communist philosophers like Paul Nizan (1971 [1932]), Georges Politzer, Georges Friedmann and Henri Lefebvre launched critiques of the predominant styles of French philosophy – targeting in particular what they called 'bourgeois' positivism, as well as the influential ideas of Henri Bergson. But this work left little lasting trace – many of its authors did not survive the Second World War, and only Lefebvre went on to become a theorist of importance (Lefebvre 1968 [1940]).

The more enduring consequence of these early ventures in Marxist philosophy under the party umbrella was the publication in 1933 of Lefebvre's edition of Marx's 1844 *Economic and Philosophical Manuscripts* (Lefebvre and Guterman 1934). This made available in France the most significant of Marx's early writings, and introduced French intellectuals to concepts like alienation and praxis – which had been absent from the debates in Communist Party journals like *La Pensée*, heavily influenced as they were by Soviet doctrinal tastes. Perhaps even more important than the young Marx's writings was the French discovery of Hegel. Hegel was to become the central reference point for all French thought for nearly half a century, from the 1930s to the 1980s, and the character of French Marxism was determined by the changing fortunes accorded to Hegel's reputation in France (Descombes 1980 [1979]; Roth 1988).

The single most important interpreter of Hegel to the French was Alexandre Kojève, a Russian émigré who settled in Paris. In 1933 he began a course of lectures at the Ecole des Hautes Etudes devoted to Hegel's *Phenomenology of Spirit* (Kojève 1969 [1947]). Kojève portrayed Hegel in conflictual, non-liberal terms, and took the master–slave dialectic to be the clue to understanding the dynamic of modern history. Developing Hegel's idea of 'the end of history', Kojève argued that the truth or falsity of an idea was determined by its success or failure in the arena of historical action. His interpretation imprinted itself upon the imagination of a whole generation (his auditors included Jean-Paul Sartre, Maurice Merleau-Ponty, Simone de Beauvoir, Georges Bataille and Raymond Aron), and it gained a monopoly over French understandings of Hegel (a French translation of the *Phenomenology of Spirit* did not appear until 1947). To the restless intellectuals of Paris in the 1930s and 1940s, the attraction of Hegelian styles of thought lay in the promise of a holistic, totalising philosophy with a radical edge. The effects of Kojève's dialectical conception, with its fascination for terror and the historical uses of violence, would become apparent in subsequent French debate – Merleau-Ponty's *Humanism and Terror* (1969 [1947]), Sartre, and the New Philosophers of the 1970s all owed a debt to Kojève.

The years between 1939 and 1945, years of war and of defeat, of collaboration with and resistance to the Nazi occupation, set the conditions for Marxism's flourishing in post-war France. France's military defeat was experienced also as a cultural collapse: it brought down the entire edifice of Third Republican political and intellectual life. The purges of collaborators after the liberation of France in 1944 shattered settled conceptions of a French national political community, and the nation could no longer see itself as the advance guard of historical progress (an image it had cultivated ever since 1789, in such forms as the Jacobin myth of 'la grande nation'). The war had accentuated divisions between left and right, and left the right fatally tainted by collaboration with the Nazis; conversely, the Communist Party, by claiming a large role in resisting the Nazis, enjoyed great popular support. The war also lent new urgency to the perennially French issue of the intellectual's role: of political commitment and responsibility.

Existential Marxism

In the years immediately after 1945, Marxism in France meant to all intents the Leninist doctrines of the PCF, propagated by party theorists in journals like *La Pensée* and *La Nouvelle Critique* (Garaudy 1945). But a wider intellectual ferment was astir, driven by an injured sense of French backwardness and the need to modernise. This prompted an openness to broader currents in European – and especially German – thought, and in these circumstances Marxism held up the promise of being a revolutionary politics as well as a modern method for understanding history and society.

The most eloquent and influential responses to the post-war predicament came from two men central to the formulation of existential Marxism: Jean-Paul Sartre and Maurice Merleau-Ponty. They, along with Simone de Beauvoir and a cohort of colleagues, defined the intellectual landscape for at least a decade after the end of the war. They did so through their individual works, and also collectively through the pages of *Les Temps Modernes*, a monthly journal designed to be encyclopaedic in its worldly concerns, engaged in its stance, and dedicated to the creation of a radical 'concrete philosophy'.

Sartre, already by the war's end an established novelist, had in 1942 published a work of philosophy, *Being and Nothingness* (1966 [1942]). In an analysis stimulated by his study of Heidegger and Husserl, Sartre rendered here an existentialist concept of freedom, understood as the very ground of being: 'Man does not exist *first* in order to be free *subsequently*; there is no difference between the being of man and his *being-free*' (Sartre 1966, p. 30). This radical freedom – a conception which saw man as the creator of all values, all of which were thus in some sense arbitrary – was a source of daily anxiety, but also a somewhat abstract conception. The experience of war and Resistance had, however, thrown people into situations of radical choice and forced them to act (and so to define their freedom) – thus, Sartre came to argue, giving practical force to the ideas of existentialism. It had made real the possibility of a 'situated' freedom. Furthermore, politics in the form of a strong Communist movement – in the late 1940s, the PCF could claim the support of around 30 per cent of the electorate – made an encounter with Marxism unavoidable.

Sartre was drawn to Marxism from these existentialist premises, and his concerns with freedom, praxis and a non-determinist view of history attracted him to Marx's early writings. But now the Communist Party stood between Marxism and the independent intellectual, and claimed for itself a monopoly over the interpretation of Marxist doctrine. The party itself claimed to represent the most vibrant social energies – it stood for the French working class, as well as the Soviet Union, the historically chosen vehicle of world revolution. Sartre and his fellow intellectuals had, therefore, to take a position towards the proletariat and the PCF as its self-proclaimed representative. The choice between affiliation to – or independence from – the PCF was to divide the entire subsequent history of French Marxism. What came to be called 'existential Marxism' was itself as much a political manoeuvre designed to wrest revolutionary politics away from the orthodoxy of the Communist Party as it was a philosophical project.

Existential Marxism was an attempt to enrich the philosophical and conceptual vocabulary of French Marxist thought, and to shift it away from the positivist and determinist presuppositions which characterised Communist doctrine. Its history divides into two phases, the first from 1945 to the mid-1950s, the second from the mid-1950s till the early 1960s. What differentiated each period was the attitude of existential Marxists towards the question confronting all radical intellectuals: was it the case, as the Communist Party insisted, that Marxism-Leninism was the unique philosophy or ideology of revolution (supplanting other forms of emancipatory politics)? If answered in the affirmative, then the Bolshevik Revolution had to be accorded a universal and prior status – a status that could be used to justify all acts committed in its name. The positions of Sartre and his colleagues wavered, from initial endorsement of the Soviet Union and the Communist Party to increasing distance.

The term 'existential Marxism' covers a broad range of approaches: it is important, for instance, to distinguish Sartre's work from that of Merleau-Ponty (which aimed to develop an existentialist phenomenology), and also from that of younger thinkers who began under Sartre's spell, like André Gorz, but moved towards ecological themes (Gorz 1982). However, it is possible to identify four areas of common interest within existential Marxism: the nature of individual freedom, and its relationship to social collectivity; the direction and meaning (*sens*) of history, which revealed it to possess a rational, progressive order, but without predetermined outcomes; the role of the party, as representative of the proletariat and as 'collective intellectual'; and the status of Marxism as a universal method and philosophy.

Sartre himself never joined the Communist Party (although for a time he enjoyed close relations with it), and though not in any obvious sense a Marxist, his recasting of Marxist ideas helped to frame the terms of radical debate among the first post-war generation. In the pages of *Les Temps Modernes* Sartre, Merleau-Ponty and others developed a polemical critique with a distinctive voice: anti-bourgeois, anti-capitalist, anti-American and anti-liberal, populist in its political instincts (if resolutely elitist in its aesthetic and literary sensibilities), aligned with the Communist movement and defensive of the Soviet Union. Initially Sartre's radicalism owed more to the Romantic tradition of French literary prophetism (stretching from Hugo via Michelet to Malraux) than it did to Marxism. In *Qu'est-ce que la littérature?* (*What is Literature?*) (in Sartre 1947–76), he disputed implicitly the claims of the party to be the unique spokesman of the working class, and argued that it was the individual great writer alone who was in contact with and able to express the aspirations of 'the people'. Unsurprisingly, Communist Party ideologues came down heavily against this, attacking Sartre and his colleagues as 'bourgeois stooges' (Kanapa 1947).

By the early 1950s Merleau-Ponty, increasingly troubled by events in the Soviet Union, was drifting away from politics and Marxism towards a deeper engagement with philosophy. Sartre's response to Communist Party criticism, however, was to announce his commitment to the party. In *The Communists and Peace* (a series of articles written between 1952 and 1954: Sartre 1969a), he tried to theorise the practice of the party, and show why it was the sole legitimate representative of the working class. Sartre drew a picture of an emaciated working class, without capacity for self-organisation, subject to systematic attrition by the bourgeoisie. It was not the lone intellectual, but the party, Sartre now agreed, which could represent and act for the proletariat: without it, the latter was nothing but 'dust', an atomised mass of individuals. And the close alliance between the party and the Soviet Union was historically correct, since it embodied the progressive direction of historical movement.

Ironically, Sartre had drifted closest to the Communist Party during the very years when, after Stalin's death in 1953, Soviet communism was for the first time showing flickers of self-doubt. Khrushchev's 1954 report on the 'cult of personality', and the Soviet suppression of the uprising in Budapest in 1956, fed criticism of the Communist project. In fact, the previous year, two important critiques of Marxism were published by former associates of Sartre, one from the left, the other from a liberal position: Merleau-Ponty's *Adventures of the Dialectic* (1955) and Raymond Aron's *The Opium of the Intellectuals* (1955).

Adventures of the Dialectic was arguably the most subtle and ultimately damaging of French critiques of Marxism, in both its orthodox and Sartrean renditions. Merleau-Ponty, himself steeped in German philosophy and social science and familiar with the central European debates of the 1920s (in which Georg Lukács and others had participated), developed an argument whose sophistication was far in advance of any other Marxist reflection in France. Merleau-Ponty now rejected his earlier convoluted attempt to justify the Moscow Trials of the 1930s (Merleau-Ponty 1969 [1947]), and expressed a sweeping scepticism about the entire Marxist project. In essays on Western Marxism, on the dialectic, and on what he dubbed Sartre's 'ultrabolshevism', Merleau-Ponty repeatedly exposed the weakness of Marxism as a philosophy of history. Rejecting the Hegelian idea of 'the end of history', he concluded that 'if one completely eliminates the concept of the end of history, the concept of revolution is relativized' – and therefore the consequences of any particular revolution had to be assessed empirically, rather than by reference to some teleological schema. Merleau-Ponty went on to affirm the importance of bourgeois institutions of representative democracy, declared his disillusion with the Soviet Union, and called for 'the birth of a non-communist Left' capable of developing a 'new liberalism' (Merleau-Ponty 1973 [1955], pp. 203–30).

The call to a 'new liberalism' would remain unheeded for at least another three decades: only in the late 1980s and 1990s would French intellectuals – most notably François Furet – begin to respond to the call. But the echoes of Merleau-Ponty's arguments carried far, and provided sustenance for younger intellectuals who yearned for an arena of radical debate beyond the shadow of the Communist Party – itself increasingly compromised, not only by the actions of its Soviet counterpart, but by its support for defence of French colonialism in Algeria. In particular, Merleau-Ponty's arguments were taken up and advanced by younger thinkers like Claude Lefort and Cornelius Castoriadis, who in the late 1940s had together founded a Trotskyite journal,

Socialisme ou Barbarie. Both Lefort and Castoriadis attacked the Marxist faith in the historical mission and agency of the proletariat; Castoriadis went on to show – through empirical analysis – the bureaucratic and exploitative nature of the Soviet state, while Lefort analysed Marxism as a totalitarian ideology. Though marginalised in the 1950s, the arguments developed by Lefort and Castoriadis were to resurface in the late 1960s and 1970s, their power augmented by their belated rediscovery in a changed political context.

These critiques – both internal and external to Marxism – when joined by others, constituted the moment of 'revisionism' in France. The founding of journals like *Arguments* (1956), which brought together younger intellectuals like Edgar Morin, Roland Barthes, Colette Audry and Kostas Axelos, the publication of Lucien Goldmann's 'Marxist humanist' cultural criticism (Goldmann 1956; 1959), and the re-launch in 1957 of the journal of the Catholic left, *Esprit*, dedicated to a more reformist politics, were all testimony to the effort to spark an intellectual debate that drew on Marxist themes and concepts but was not beholden to Communist Party strictures. The intellectuals of the *Arguments* group were more open than were many other French intellectuals to developments in transatlantic sociological thought (Raymond Aron was an important conduit for these into France), and they shifted attention away from the revolution against capitalism and the proletariat's role in bringing this about, towards a more general critique of industrial society.

Revisionism engendered two major responses: from Sartre and from Althusser. The single most ambitious work to emerge from the revisionist interlude was Sartre's gigantic fragment, the *Critique of Dialectical Reason* (1960), preceded by a companion essay, *Search for a Method*. The *Critique* was the grandest of all French efforts to produce a philosophy of revolutionary politics that escaped the Marxist-Leninist orthodoxies of the Communist Party. The latter Sartre dismissed as ideological; like the bourgeois thought it opposed, this 'lazy Marxism' was unable to grasp reality. In its place Sartre proposed 'dialectical reason': this method of totalising knowledge would reveal that 'there is one human history, with one truth and one intelligibility' (Sartre 1991 [1960], p. 69). It would, that is, recoup the universalist dimension of Marxism. Breaking with positivist readings of Marx that spoke of an 'objective dialectic' located in nature, Sartre argued the need for a distinctive epistemology and method in order to understand the humanly created world.

If there was one human history with a fundamental truth to it, this presupposed a stable historical subject of (and for) whom there could be such a truth. Much of the *Critique* was given over to identifying, by means of an abstract typology of social groups, an authentic form of human sociality. In the *Critique*, Sartre hoped to show how a genuine political society, what he called a 'fused totality' could come into existence and maintain its identity over time. This would be a post-bourgeois, post-revolutionary society, without need of a state and the division of labour, and one where the claims of individual and collectivity would receive equal respect. More specifically, he wished to show how a revolutionary class, the proletariat, could unite and accede to power, could absorb the functions of the state, without having to use as its instrument the distorting institutions either of the Communist Party or of bourgeois politics (with its paraphernalia of democratic elections, parliaments and political parties). Sartre defined the proletariat not by its structural position within an economic mode of production, but as the product of antagonism with the bourgeoisie: the very identities of bourgeois and proletariat, like those of master and slave, were given by their opposition to one another, and by their desire to annihilate each other. The proletariat was for Sartre a philosophical concept, a 'totalisation' of the historical process.

The second volume of the *Critique* (1985), never published in Sartre's lifetime, signalled the failure of Sartre's effort to reconstruct Marxism. In the course of a lengthy account of the fate of the Bolshevik Revolution, Sartre tried to explain why the revolutionary 'group-in-fusion' had collapsed into a more conventional human society under the dictatorship of a 'sovereign': Stalin. The promise and then collapse of the Bolshevik Revolution had, Sartre now concluded, sabotaged hopes for a universal revolutionary theory. Marxism, 'a universalist ideology and practice, born in the most industrialised European country', had been deformed into the 'historical monstrosity' of 'socialism in one country': its reduction to the national dogma and realpolitik of a single state had swept away its universal scope and left it broken and 'particularised'.

Sartre's prognosis for Marxism was bleak. The success of the Bolshevik Revolution paradoxically shattered Marxism's universal character, by opening it to the contingencies of history. The destruction of Marxism's unity and dialectical universality left two 'particular universalities': on the one hand, it produced the revolutionary movements of the West, instances of 'abstract universality' and umbilically tied to the Soviet Union. On the other hand, it engendered Soviet Marxism, a pure particularity unable to explain or account for its own history. Sartre wrote with disdain of how the 'backward Russians' had assimilated Marxism. Hitherto the privileged revolutionary theory of the intellectual, Marxism was now freely available to 'these crude workers, so hastily created, so close to the peasants; men and women who 'transformed Marxism as they absorbed it... it was vulgarised even as it refined them'. Adopted by these 'mystified peasants', Marxism's universalist purity was corrupted. The subversion of its universalist scope led Sartre to cancel his project of a 'totalising' historical narrative, which he had hoped might have explained Stalinism as a 'deviation', a temporary setback in a larger progressive development.

Structuralism: the moment of Althusser

Sartre's efforts to rebuild Marxism as a philosophy – a theory distinguished by its ability to explain its own history (including the era of Stalin) – failed for internal reasons. It was also displaced by other developments. Sartre's attempt at a 'total history' fell victim to a sweeping reaction against historicist approaches, and against Hegelian thought in particular – a reaction that amounted to the sternest rebuff to the Hegelian impulse in Western Marxism. This anti-historicist current represented a convergence between two schools of thought: the traditions of French positivism and rationalism, as upheld by philosophers of science like Georges Canguilhem and Gaston Bachelard, and structuralist linguistics. Drawing on these ideas, thinkers like Claude Lévi-Strauss, Michel Foucault and Jacques Derrida dismissed the desire for a 'total history' – and indeed, the very idea of history itself – as no more than a Eurocentric myth, an ideology of the bourgeois age. In place of historicism, they proposed instead the method of structuralism, which could reveal universal and transhistorical structures of thought and society.

Structuralism had an electrifying effect on French thought of the 1950s and 1960s, and quickly established itself as the main challenger to Marxism's claim to comprehend human society. Derived originally from the theories of the Swiss linguist, Fernand Saussure, in France it was taken up in particular by literary critics such as Roland Barthes. But it was rapidly extended to new realms: into anthropology by Lévi-Strauss, into psychoanalysis by Jacques Lacan, into philosophy by Derrida, and into history by Foucault. Primarily a method designed to show meaning as the product of relations internal to a text, object or activity (indeed, to any system that could be treated as analogous to a text), the structuralist method promised knowledge that claimed the certainty of scientific truths. Its rise coincided with the consolidation of Charles de Gaulle's Fifth Republic, itself committed to a technocratic vision that stood 'beyond ideology'. Structuralism refused to accord any privilege to the authenticity of individual experience – which had been so important to existential Marxism. From a structuralist viewpoint, lived experience, whether it be that of worker or capitalist, was the realm of ideology and of false knowledge.

At this vulnerable moment for Marxism, Louis Althusser emerged on the scene, promising to show how Marxism could claim for itself the status of a science and so repudiate its ideological past. Althusser drastically shifted the focus of Marxist theoretical interests – away from the philosophy of praxis, away from economic analysis, away from Hegelian philosophy of history, away from any precise political analysis, and towards the cold frontier of epistemology.

Unlike Sartre, Althusser was throughout his working life a Communist Party member (he called himself a 'Communist Philosopher'), and a professor at the elite Ecole Normale Supérieure. Although Althusser should not be mistaken for a 'Party Philosopher' – he could be critical of the party, particularly in his call for greater independence for intellectuals – nevertheless his basic intention was to provide a defence of Leninist principles in a context where French radical intellectuals were drifting away from them. He saw a dual function to his own work: it was designed to establish 'the principles of science and philosophy founded on Marx', but his arguments were also 'interventions in a definite conjuncture'.

As Althusser described it, this conjuncture was defined by two events: Khrushchev's speech to the Twentieth Congress of the Communist Party of the Soviet Union which had criticised the 'cult of personality' surrounding Stalin, and the Sino-Soviet split, which had blown apart the putative internationalism of the Communist movement. In fact, in addition to this global context the conjuncture was defined by more local concerns, identifiable from Althusser's introduction to *For Marx* (1977 [1965]). Here he pointed to the overbearing presence of the French Communist Party, whose combination of 'dogmatism' and 'pragmatism' had squeezed out any real Marxist theory. He bemoaned the etiolated quality of French theory and philosophy, a legacy French Marxism had inherited. As a consequence, the party had been 'born into a theoretical vacuum' (1977 [1965], p. 26), which had come to be filled by the exigencies of politics.

For Althusser, the way to salvage Marxism in this situation was to establish its philosophical credentials. But the problem as he saw it was that Marx's philosophy was not explicitly present in his writings: rather, it had to be painstakingly elicited from the internal structure and logic of his work. Rejecting the bias Western Marxism had shown towards Marx's early writings, Althusser insisted that the core of Marx's philosophy was to be found in his later works, especially *Capital*. The true significance of *Capital*, Althusser claimed, lay not in its economic theories and analysis, but rather in the implicit epistemology secreted within it, an epistemology that bore few evident traces of the baneful Hegelian dialectic.

Although the essays in *For Marx* had all been published on earlier occasions, their collected appearance in 1965 immediately captured attention and propelled Althusser to the position of leading Marxist philosopher in France. *For Marx* outlined a rigorously logical approach, and it caught the imagination of young leftists (in fact, Althusser's influence on young intellectuals was out of all proportion to the regard in which he was held by his peer generation). By the mid-1960s he had already assembled a formidable array of young philosophers in his seminar at the Ecole Normale – among them Etienne Balibar, Jacques Rancière, Dominique Lecourt, Pierre Macheray – all of whom were to play roles in the subsequent fortunes of French Marxism. Out of the seminar came Althusser's second major work, *Reading Capital* (Althusser and Balibar 1970 [1968]).

In these works, Althusser wished to move away from the economic determinism of orthodox communism; but, equally, he wished to resist the pulls of historicist readings of Marx associated with Western Marxism. If one of his targets was Stalinist dogmatism, another was what he saw as a 'humanist' drift within the French left. By this he meant the attempts in the late 1950s and early 1960s to cement alliances between Communists, Socialists and Catholics, on the basis of a philosophical reading of Marx that emphasised the importance of early Marxian concepts like alienation over those such as exploitation and the analysis of surplus value. By ridding French Marxism of its imprecision and compromises, Althusser hoped to demonstrate that Marxism was an encompassing knowledge system 'indispensable not only to the development of the science of society and of the various "human sciences", but also to that of the natural sciences and philosophy' (Althusser and Balibar 1970 [1968], p. 26). To secure this ambitious claim, Althusser stressed the autonomy of theory, vis-à-vis both the party and the traditions of bourgeois scholarship cultivated in the university. Theory was also granted autonomy and priority over the realm of experience: proletarian consciousness, for instance, imprinted by the experience of exploitation, could claim no privileged understanding of reality. That belonged uniquely to rigorous theory, as developed by specialised theoreticians.

Althusser's resort to epistemology may be seen as an attempt to immunise Marxism against its actual historical record. By switching from a common political vocabulary of 'success and failure' to one of 'truth and error', the issue of Stalinism could be contained – it need not affect Marxism's basic 'scientific validity', which rested on epistemological grounds.

The defining orientations of Althusser's reformulation of Marxism lay in four directions, and yielded him a new conceptual lexicon. From psychoanalysis he imported concepts developed by Sigmund Freud and Jacques Lacan. The most important of these was 'overdetermination', a Freudian term used to signify the condensation of multiple contradictions in what Freud termed the 'dream-work'. Althusser found here a concept which could explain uneven historical change without recourse to the Hegelian idea of contradiction. The great puzzle for Marxist thought was how to explain the occurrence of revolution in Russia. Gramsci had called the 1917 revolution the 'revolution against *Capital*', since – according to the classical Marxist schema, based on Hegelian premises – revolution should have occurred in the most advanced capitalist country, not in a backward country like Russia. Drawing on Lenin's notion of the 'weakest link', as well as Mao's essay 'On Contradiction', Althusser argued that to explain the Russian Revolution, Marxist theory had to break with the 'simplicity of Hegelian contradiction'. Hegel could 'represent universal theory from the Ancient Orient to the present day as "dialectical"; that is, moved by the simple play of a principle of *simple* contradiction'. But the Russian Revolution was the result of multiple contradictions, present at different levels internal to the society (economic, political, ideological) as well as internationally, which had fused together into a particular revolutionary configuration. The concept of over-determination, Althusser argued, enabled an analysis that could reveal the real political potentialities of a society. It would help also to drive Hegel's 'phantom back into the night' (Althusser 1977 [1965], p. 117) and exorcise Hegel from the Marxist tradition.

From structural linguistics and from Lévi-Strauss's anthropological studies, Althusser borrowed the notions of 'decentring' and of 'structural causality' (as distinct from linear or expressive causality). This allowed him to portray society as a 'structure in dominance', constituted by ideological, political and economic 'instances' or 'levels', no one of which was reducible to any of the others. The economic base of the classical Marxist model retained its causally determining role; but, in Althusser's reformulation, this now need apply only in the 'last instance'. By this, Althusser wished to avoid the presumption that the economic base could in a direct and unmediated way determine the shape of a society; rather, the economic base determined which 'instance' – the political, the ideological, or, as it may happen, the economic – was in fact actually dominant and determining in any particular case. By thus extending and loosening the causal chain, he intended to give a more flexible form to the base-superstructure model of classical Marxism. If structuralist ideas allowed Althusser to modify the classical Marxist models of causality, their other significant effect was to extinguish individual agency from his theory: the individual was transformed into a 'support' or bearer of systemic, structural effects, and as such was no more than an ideological construct.

Althusser also turned to French philosophy of science, in particular the studies of Gaston Bachelard and Georges Canguilhem. From them, he adopted the notions of 'epistemological break' and 'problematic'. The former Althusser used to designate what he claimed was the crucial shift in Marx's work – which he saw as occurring with Marx's 'Theses on Feuerbach' (1845) (Marx and Engels 1962). This marked Marx's move from philosophy to science. The concept of the 'problematic' suggested an anti-intentionalist interpretative methodology, which was 'centred on absence of problems and concepts within the problematic as much as their presence'. Such a methodology proceeded through a 'symptomatic reading' of the silences within a text in order to elicit the true theoretical claims it contained. Lurking behind this heavily rationalist French philosophy of science was the presence of a fourth shaping influence: that of Baruch Spinoza, from whom Althusser borrowed an emphasis on totality or holism, as well as a concern for the ideas of truth and error.

It was out of this, by Marxist standards wildly eclectic, *mélange* that Althusser fashioned his Marxism. Perhaps Althusser's most significant departure from the shared elements of Western Marxism was his categorical break with Hegelian aspects and themes. Marxism proper began, Althusser argued, at the point where Marx left behind the idealist philosophy and historicism he had imbibed from Hegel and set forth to chart the 'new continent' of theory and science. 'There is', Althusser declared, 'an unequivocal "epistemological break" in Marx's work' which 'divides Marx's thought into two long essential periods: the "ideological" period before, and the scientific period after, the break in 1845.' By repudiating the centrality accorded by Western Marxists to the work of the young Marx, by describing it as humanist, historicist, mired in philosophical anthropology and hence ideological, Althusser hoped to undermine the efforts of both Sartre and of the revisionists to establish a humanist Marxism. Most importantly, he hoped thereby to resolve – or rather bypass – the problem of Stalinism. The concept of structural causality allowed Althusser to argue that Stalinism did not signal in any way that socialism was failing in the Soviet Union – it was merely a symptom of mistakes at the level of the political superstructure, and it in no way affected the socialist economic base. Stalinism was a case of political repression, not very different from the dictatorships of Latin America and elsewhere; it did not signify any fundamental exploitation of the citizenry.

This narrow, brittle conception of power was to implode in the years after 1968. The 'events' of May 1968, when a students' revolt combined with a general strike to paralyse France for a few weeks and threatened to bring down the regime, seemed briefly to throw Paris back to the age of the revolutionary *grandes journées* of the nineteenth century. Althusser, following the Communist Party line, held back from endorsing the attempted revolt. He broke his silence only later, with his last major essay, on 'Ideology and Ideological State Apparatuses (ISAs)' (Althusser 1971 [1969]). This gloomily suggested that a modern capitalist society such as France was incapable of any substantial change – the self-reproducing powers of ideology precluded that. Althusser's reformulation of Marxism was, on the face of it, the most sweeping and innovative in Western Marxism. But the political intention behind it remained constant: a defence of Leninist principles.

The collapse of French Marxism

The dominance of Marxism in France, and of French Marxism across the globe, seemed to be most complete in 1968. In that year, students and workers across the world took to the streets, inspired in large part by ideas drawn from France: from Berkeley to Tokyo, from Prague to Calcutta, politics was in upheaval. In France itself, Marxism appeared to offer a common and convergent frame for the radical protests that swept across the country: yet, although it provided many of the participants with a common terminology, Marxism had actually ceased altogether to be the subject of any shared understanding. The events of 1968 revealed how fragmented and internally contested French Marxism had become. 'Gauchisme' – the general term used to describe those leftist currents outside the Communist Party – in fact encompassed a broad array of radical positions: Althusserians, Maoists, Trotskyites, situationists, ecologists and feminists. What they did all share was deep antipathy to hierarchical organisations and structures of authority: an anti-authoritarianism that expressed itself in vehement criticism and rejection both of the French state in its Gaullist Fifth Republican incarnation and of the French Communist Party, based on the Soviet model of 'democratic centralism'.

Gauchistes of all hues remained committed to the idea of revolution, but the temper of their politics marked a drift away from the Marxist conception of this idea. Influenced by the news of the 'Cultural Revolution' in Mao's China, they rejected the view that the party, or a vanguard of revolutionary intellectuals, would lead the proletariat towards revolution, in favour of a 'spontaneist', populist conception which involved 'going to the people' and allowing them to speak directly rather than claiming to speak on their behalf – emphases that tapped strong anti-intellectualist currents in French thought (see Sorel 1919; Foucault 1977). But, paralleling these intellectual shifts, the political parties of the left were making electoral gains in the early mid-1970s, leading to a growing possibility that they might soon enter government. Far from welcoming this, *gauchistes* now began to train their sights on the Communist Party, and on the Soviet state which loomed behind it.

What finally triggered this attack to devastating effect was the publication in 1974 of a French translation of Alexander Solzhenitsyn's epic of the Stalinist period, *The Gulag Archipelago*, which recounted the story of Stalin's terror and the prison camps. In the first year of its French publication, 600,000 copies of the book were sold, and its appearance provoked a huge and belated media debate about the significance of the Soviet experience for Marxism and for revolutionary politics. The most significant intervention, at least in terms of its effects, was the writing of the self-labelled 'New Philosophers': consisting mostly of renegade *gauchistes*, the group included André Glucksmann (1975) and Bernard Henri-Lévy. Where their predecessors had found ways to ignore or explain away Stalinism and Soviet terror by appealing to local factors, the New Philosophers insisted on a vaguer but more sweeping explanation – one that saw twentieth-century totalitarianism as the product of Enlightenment rationalism, of which Marxism was one particularly dangerous example.

The most decisive blow to Marxism in France came, however, not from the florid jeremiads that the New Philosophers directed against their previous selves and beliefs, but from within the discipline of history, and in particular from within French revolutionary historiography – which had for longed served as the terrain on which the French did their political thinking and arguing. It took the shape of François Furet's critique of the idea of revolution (1981 [1978]). Furet's interpretation of the French Revolution dissented from the prevailing historiographical conventions, which had been established by a long line of distinguished left-wing and Marxist historians, all with socialist or communist affiliations – a line that stretched from Jean Jaurès to Albert Soboul. Furet attacked what he called the 'revolutionary catechism' upheld by these historians, which claimed that the French Revolution of 1789 was the progenitor of a still to be completed revolutionary project of universal scope – and whose contemporary representative was the Soviet Revolution and the state to which it had given birth.

Furet in part endorsed this claim; but he reversed its value. He refused to see the French Revolution as a monolithic event, as forming an indivisible 'bloc' – as all on the French left had seen it since the late nineteenth century. Instead, he separated what he saw as the positive, liberal aspects of the revolution from the period of the Jacobin Terror. The latter, he agreed, did have filiations with the Soviet project; but now he turned the tables against this claim: 'In 1920, Mathiez justified Bolshevik violence by the French precedent, in the name of comparable circumstances. Today the Gulag is leading to a rethinking of the Terror precisely because the two undertakings are seen as identical.' The Russian example, like a lethal boomerang, had now returned to strike at its French origin; and this in turn struck at Marxism itself. 'Marx, today', Furet wrote in a review of Solzhenitsyn's book, 'can no longer escape his legacy, and the boomerang effect is all the more powerful for having been delayed for so long.'

Furet's critique of revolutionary politics, coming at the moment it did, had wide effects, and helped to undermine the credibility of Marxism in France. This happened, ironically, at the very moment when the French Socialists entered government in 1981. During the final decades of the twentieth century, Marxism virtually disappeared from French intellectual life – perhaps the sole significant figure to use Marxist ideas was the sociologist Pierre Bourdieu, although arguably even he owed more to the French tradition of positivist sociology than to Marxism itself. Interest shifted towards the recovery of a distinctively French liberalism – a political liberalism that could be used to revive and reinvent the model of the French Republic, and one that the French were careful to distinguish from the economic liberalism of the free market which they associated with the Anglo-Saxon countries. In this effort, Alexis de Tocqueville rather than Marx was the favoured intellectual touchstone. The Communist Party, meanwhile, was politically sidelined by François Mitterrand's Socialists, and with the break-up of the communist world in the years after 1989 the party split, leaving an electorally insignificant hardcore rump. The broad political circumstances that had infused life into French Marxism, making it a subject of fervent and fertile debate, had now passed. With the collapse of French Marxism, one of the most powerful utopian critiques and visions of modern times, which had received ingenious interpretation in French hands, passed from the political and intellectual horizon.

Part III
Science, modernism and politics

15
Positivism: reactions and developments

MELISSA LANE

Born of the aspiration of Saint-Simon and Comte to cleanse science of metaphysics, 'positivism' came to signify the nineteenth-century desire to make natural science the sole model of knowledge, even for inquiries into human history and culture. Many thinkers, while not hostile to science or intellect as such, began to chafe at this restriction (Collingwood 1946, p. 134). In contesting the hegemony of natural science, anti-positivists typically appealed to two important forms of human experience which fell outside its domain. Some pointed to the consciousness and self-consciousness which soared above the phenomenal domain of natural science, while others unearthed the unconscious or pre-conscious aspects of mental life which lay below it.

Consciousness was celebrated by idealist philosophers as the indispensable basis of both knowledge and freedom, practically a substitute for God. Pragmatists, on the other hand, saw experience not in conscious concepts but in the 'blooming buzzing confusion' of the pre-conscious mind experiencing the world. Even more subversive of the consciously rational agent presupposed by idealists and positivists alike were the inquiries of writers like Nietzsche, Bergson and Freud, who evoked the many and subtle ways in which unconscious motives influence behaviour. Whether appealing to consciousness or unconsciousness, then, reactions to positivism stressed aspects of the human mind which mechanistic pictures of natural science were unable to grasp.

This chapter considers the following instances of reactions to, and developments of, positivism: neo-Kantianism and hermeneutics; idealism and liberalism; sociology and positivist social science; vitalism and pragmatism; and, finally, logical positivism, behaviourism and the 'demise' of political philosophy. Though Marxists were influenced by such debates, the relations between Marxism and positivism are addressed in chapter 13.

Neo-Kantianism and hermeneutics

The problem of the distinction between the natural sciences and what J. S. Mill had called the 'moral sciences' (translated into German as *Geisteswissenschaften*) preoccupied the neo-Kantian movement which arose on the ruins of Hegelianism, and in particular the south-west German school led by Wilhelm Windelband. Kant's analysis of knowledge in the natural sciences rested on the universality of laws and concepts, which left the status of individual objects obscure. How could there be knowledge of particulars if genuine knowledge required conceptual generality? Although in practice German schools of historical law and historical economics flourished in opposition to the purported abstractions of political economy, the philosophical framework for the moral sciences, particularly history, had not been resolved.

Windelband attacked this problem in his inaugural lecture as rector of the University of Strasbourg in 1894, described by an auditor as 'a declaration of war on positivism' (Hughes 1979 [1958], p. 47). He distinguished between two 'incommensurable' scientific methods for dealing with experience. The 'nomothetic' or law-postulating method seeks general laws and treats particular individuals only as types or instances of such laws. This is the method used by the physical sciences of nature. The 'idiographic' method, by contrast, understands individual objects by picturing or grasping their distinct features, such as the style of handwriting of a particular historical record (Windelband 1919). Windelband retained the idea that mental or cultural facts can be dealt with by science, but rejected the aspiration to form positive laws for these sciences, which deal in unique entities rather than in laws.

While this vein of neo-Kantian epistemology was an important source of education for such thinkers as Benedetto Croce and Max Weber, more immediately productive was the new science of hermeneutics elaborated by Wilhelm Dilthey. A decade before Windelband's address, Dilthey had already argued that Kant's critique of reason must be stripped of its pretensions to timeless universality and made a 'critique of historical reason'. Dilthey was particularly concerned with the status and nature of history, and the anti-positivist current which he initiated was labelled 'historicism'. Unlike Windelband, he did not distinguish history and the human sciences on the basis of the concepts used to study them, but rather in terms of their object of study: the products of human action (Bellamy 1987, pp. 78–9).

Human action for Dilthey inescapably involved will and bodily self-awareness. Dilthey proposed that this acknowledgement of the body could resolve the ancient quarrel between realism and idealism, stripping the latter of its false coating of Kantian nominalism. 'From the perspective of mere representation, the external world always remains only a phenomenon... [but] for the whole human being who wills, feels, and represents, external reality is given simultaneously and with as much certitude as his own self' (Dilthey 1989 [1883], p. 51). For one person to understand the action of another was not to infer concepts about it but to re-experience it (*nacherleben*) and so gain an intuitive and direct understanding (*Erlebnis*) of it. As we will see, Max Weber, a student of Windelband's school, developed this notion of understanding the meaning of an action (*Verstehen*) in his account of social science. Dilthey himself used it in elaborating a science of hermeneutics which could interpret social facts and cultural artefacts by grasping their specific meanings, a science which was wholly distinct from the purported positivist model of natural science.

Idealism and liberalism

T. H. Green in England and Benedetto Croce in Italy exemplify another use made of Kant (as well as Hegel and, for Green, Plato): building an idealism linked to liberal politics. Green's liberalism was integral to his philosophy, which sought to construct an alternative to mechanistic utilitarianism by depicting an idealism aligned with the Christian God. Croce reoriented his philosophy of culture toward liberal politics only later in life, when after 1924 he became perhaps the most powerful exemplar of the intellectual resistance to fascism. Idealism for both represented the claims of moral value in relationship to freedom, which rival philosophies – whether utilitarian, fascist or socialist – threatened to destroy.

Green indicted British empiricism as logically circular.[1] Neither Locke nor Hume could explain the mental origin of ideas of relations except by appealing to comparison and contrast, themselves relations. For Green, the only viable alternative was to hold with Kant that knowledge presupposes formal conceptions, such as relations, which are the products of mind. Rejecting the Kantian thing-in-itself as intrinsically unknowable, however, he advocated a holistic view of experience as involving 'concrete universals',

1. This paragraph draws on the clear analysis provided in Hylton (1990, pp. 21–43).

and located these in a single, eternal self-consciousness (which both underwrote and was underwritten by his religious commitments).

The fact that self-realisation of each tends toward the unity of all in the eternal consciousness constitutes a moral good and a legitimate end for the community as a whole. This interplay of self-realisation shaped Green's ethics. He was hostile to what he saw as the utilitarian ideal of freedom as pursuing one's desires without unnecessary restraint. For Green, following Plato, desire was unstable and its true end, the necessary and ultimate aim of all action, was rather the good. Correspondingly, freedom could not be adequately understood or valuably maintained as the freedom from constraint presupposed by classical ideas of freedom of contract. 'Freedom in the positive sense' involved rather 'the liberation of the powers of all men equally for contributing to a common good' (Green 1888a [1881], vol. III, p. 372). The positive freedom of each individual was therefore a legitimate concern for the community and so for the state.

Departing from John Stuart Mill's classical liberal horror of paternalism, Green defended temperance legislation partly on the grounds that drunkards harmed themselves by destroying their own ability to act autonomously and pursue the good (Richter 1983 [1964], p. 366). But Green's ideal state, while concerning itself with the conditions necessary for individuals' self-realisation, did so mainly by protecting their respective rights and duties. The state was never elevated to a status separate from or higher than the people it served. In his lectures on the principles of political obligation in 1879–80, he distinguished between the perfect political obligation owed to the ideal state and its problematic implications for those flawed states which violate their citizens' rights and fail in their duties.

Green inspired a generation of young men to engage in local educational and charity work, making the Evangelical tradition of philanthropy intellectually respectable. His influence, perhaps even more in this practical than philosophical vein, helped inspire British 'New Liberalism' to depart from the previous dogmas of free trade and negative freedom in countenancing state intervention to foster morality and welfare (Clarke 1981 [1978]; Freeden 1978). The same aspects of Green's thought also influenced the American pragmatist John Dewey. Such civic activism presupposed a certain level of comfort with existing political institutions, however imperfect these might be. Croce, in contrast, had to contend first with the corrupt political cronyism of turn-of-the-century Italy, torn between Catholics and socialists, north and south, and then with the moral catastrophe of fascism. His own defence of liberalism reflected these pressures.

Croce's first philosophical essay attacked Italian positivism, which was influential in state social policy, by seeking to mediate the debate between Windelband and Dilthey outlined above. The young Croce viewed history (the human science which most concerned him as a practising antiquarian) as a sub-set of art. Like art, historical study involves intuiting and empathising with the blend of intellect, will and bodily expression which characterises all human action (as for Dilthey), studied as particular events and not for the sake of eliciting general laws of human behaviour (here accepting Windelband's conceptual distinction). While art portrays possible human actions, history studies only that sub-set of possible actions which have 'actually occurred' (Bellamy 1987, p. 74).

This neo-Kantian position remained central to Croce despite his grappling with Marx, Hegel and Vico. However, he modified it significantly in the 1909 revision of his *Logic* by arguing that history, like all thought, does require concepts, and in particular involves judging universals to be incarnate in particulars. The universal is a mere abstraction, whereas the individual or particular really exists. Croce, like Green, used this Hegelian idea of the concrete universal to defy positivism. Whereas the positivist programme of Hippolyte Taine had used facts to search for general laws, Croce declared that a fact itself incorporated all that one could ever know of its cause (Croce 1917). All reality then is history and all knowledge is historical knowledge. Philosophy formulates abstractions from the reality grasped by history, while natural science deals not with reality or truth but only with abstract pseudo-concepts reified for the sake of utility.

This distinction between the useful and the true, which Croce compounded into a fourfold distinction between the fundamental values of the useful, the true, the beautiful and the good, became key to his criticism of Hegel (who confounded these 'distincts' into false opposites) and to his rejection of socialism. Socialism threatened to collapse all values into judgements of economic utility, and so like utilitarianism failed to offer any genuine moral theory at all. The Marxist philosophy of history, meanwhile, fell into the naturalistic fallacy of ignoring the forms of spirit which constitute human action. Croce was thus able to befriend the syndicalist Georges Sorel, who celebrated the general strike as morally rejuvenating myth-making, while remaining hostile to the Italian communist parties.

Until the 1920s Croce concentrated on his research and the publication of his journal *La Critica*, sharply distinguishing the realm of economics and politics where force and utility belonged, from his own chosen realm of history and aesthetics. But he had turned against Mussolini by 1924, and when his erstwhile collaborator Giovanni Gentile began to defend fascism by drawing on Croce's own prior endorsement of political Machiavellianism, Croce was impelled to articulate a new ethico-political liberalism which stressed that politics was a moral domain after all. But this meta-political liberalism, based on Croce's account of history as the story of liberty, was not connected to any specific institutional structures and proved practically feeble after the war (Bellamy 1992, pp. 144–55). Even after his anti-fascist turn, Croce continued to oppose 'mathematical and mechanical' conceptions of equality which he thought democracy idolised. He was a liberal rather than a democrat, insisting that the two doctrines belonged together only in certain historical circumstances (Croce 1945 [1924], p. 116).

Green and Croce are exceptions to the general claim that the anti-positivists tended to be partisans of science, though on their own terms. Unlike his idealist colleague F. H. Bradley, Green was not much interested in the status of history or of any social science, while Croce's elevation of history left scant intellectual space for any conception of social science. They rejected not only positivism but also the sociology (or aspiration to social science) which was its offspring. We turn now to several attempts to rescue or refashion sociology from its positivist birth, attempts which also bear the marks of engagement with the neo-Kantian and idealist philosophies we have encountered.

The evolution of positivism and the emergence of sociology

We begin with Vilfredo Pareto, a Swiss-Italian correspondent of Croce's who carved out a roughly inverse political trajectory. While the instinctively conservative Croce was galvanised by fascism into a renewed commitment to liberalism, Pareto began as a committed liberal whose progressive political embitterment led him ultimately to embrace fascism. Pareto studied engineering and worked for the Italian railways for almost twenty years, during which time he campaigned for a liberal and democratic free-market society on terms heavily influenced by Mill and Spencer. On taking the Lausanne chair in political economy in 1893, he still defended free competition and a differentiated social order on positivist terms in his *Cours d'économie politique* (1896), although he was sympathetic to the suffering of the proletariat and admired the moral energy of the socialists.

But in 1900, jaundiced by the new liberal ministry in Italy which he thought was bowing to the selfish pressure of a wave of strikes, Pareto started to warn of the dangers of socialism as simply another ruse for class spoliation.

The socialists, he argued, would simply use political power to defraud others and enrich themselves just as the liberals and conservatives had done in their turn. This was the germ of the 'elite' theory of politics developed from various angles by Pareto, Gaetano Mosca and Roberto Michels (see chapter 3). Power circulated from one elite to the next on the basis of their success in using force or ideological fraud, so that any claim to empower the common people was always an excuse for a new elite to gain power.

As the machinations of self-interest began to seem to him ubiquitous, Pareto shifted his interests from economics[2] to sociology. Perhaps this new science could explain why people typically sought to aggrandise or avenge themselves instead of peacefully maximising their utility as instrumental rationality would dictate. His *Trattato di sociologia generale* (1916) offered an extensive classification of 'irrational' instincts, interests and rationalisations, the most striking of which were modelled on Machiavelli's foxes who use cunning against the brute strength and persistence of the lions. By the time that Mussolini took power, Pareto saw authoritarian fascist politics as the only way to free the market (a continuity with his earliest beliefs) from the corruption of democratically circulating elites and the threat of socialism (Bellamy 1992, p. 138).

If Pareto's early positivism mutated into a narrow view of instrumental reason and a cynicism about political morality, that of Emile Durkheim remained resolutely committed to a broad conception of reason and the renewal of public morals. Durkheim's intellectual career has often been interpreted as a movement from positivist beginnings, in his doctoral dissertation which became *De la division du travail social* (1984 [1893/1902]), to an idealistic conclusion in his last major work *Formes élémentaires de la vie religieuse* (1912). Yet Durkheim can be consistently construed in his own terms as a rationalist, and in this light as the renovator of one particular strand of positivist ideas. He was steeped in the Saint-Simonian tradition which had proclaimed the sacred mission of sociology to discover a new basis for moral and social order. But, unlike Saint-Simon, Durkheim was a confirmed democrat and republican, and he emphasised conscious mental facts rather than physiological ones. As a Jew, the non-observant son of a rabbi, he was initiated into the French elite at the Ecole Normale Supérieure, and later attempted to articulate a moral basis for the secular industrial society of the Third Republic (see chapter 17).

2. Among Pareto's landmark contributions to economic theory was the principle of social choice which still bears his name. The 'Pareto principle' identifies Pareto-optimal distributions as those distributions departure from which could make no-one better off without making someone else worse off.

Durkheim began by distinguishing the irrational instinctual will from the cognitive 'representations' that constituted the proper focus of social study. In Durkheim's view, these representations were fundamentally social and constituted the *conscience collective* or collective consciousness of society. As with T. H. Green, such an emphasis on consciousness marks a departure from positivist materialism, although Durkheim insisted that 'social facts' nonetheless manifest external regularities for the sociologist to study (a method he applied most famously in his study of suicide).[3]

Durkheim was firmly opposed to utilitarian and Kantian moral approaches in the study of society. Both put unwarranted faith in deductive methods, whereas he (despite his rationalist view of the nature of human cognition) wished to promote the inductive and empirical study of social phenomena. And the most striking fact about modern social phenomena, to which he devoted his career, was the shift in the social division of labour from what he would call 'mechanical' to 'organic' solidarity. Whereas in societies displaying mechanical solidarity there was little division of labour and most people were united by the similarities of their habits, tasks and ideas, in industrialised societies individuals were integrated instead by their reciprocally differentiated functions.

The arch-positivist Herbert Spencer had likewise emphasised the growing differentiation in social life as an exemplar of his general law of development from homogeneity to heterogeneity. But Durkheim thought that Spencer's view put the cart before the horse by making individual orientations drive social change. He argued that far from being a natural attribute, true individualism was a cognitive achievement, a representation, which had to be educated and cultivated to restrain the selfish egoism of the will. Spencer's analysis was therefore callow. And it was morally obtuse. For Durkheim, organic solidarity, welcome as it was, nevertheless bore the risk of moral disintegration. In *Le suicide* (1976 [1930]) he pointed to a new phenomenon in modern organic societies: to the familiar types of 'egoistic' and 'altruistic' suicides were now added 'anomic' suicides reflecting the failure of social integration. Anomie threatened social coherence and so the health of the more vulnerable members of society who simultaneously lost their sense of individuality and of social meaning.

For this reason Durkheim worked unceasingly for the renewal of French education and for associations to integrate migrants to the new urban centres.

3. It is interesting that the positivist historian Henry Buckle had already used the regularity of various national and regional statistics about suicide as an example of what he took to be the determinism of social facts (Buckle 1882, vol. I, pp. 20, 26–9).

And, like the French positivists Saint-Simon and Comte, he treated the state as the brain of the social organism, leading the people intellectually and administratively. Because democratic society was uniquely 'conscious of itself' it could grow and shape the state in response. So the reigning political programme of 'solidarism', to which Durkheim subscribed, was shown to be precisely the *conscience collective* needed to sustain organic French solidarity. (American political scientists would some decades later similarly assume that the existing values of their society were uniquely functional.)

Durkheim's influential role as a social scientist in French politics is often compared to that of Max Weber in Germany. But whereas Durkheim was never reticent in prescribing morals, Weber scrupulously distinguished his studies as a scientist from the advice he could offer as a political man (see chapter 17). Where Durkheim blended positivism and idealism into a heady brew of prescriptive sociology, Weber clung to the neo-Kantian critical standpoint he had learned as a student in Heidelberg and Strasbourg, seeking to keep fact and value clearly distinct.

If consciousness was the *leitmotif* of Durkheim's sociology, Weber's was the related set of notions of reason, rationality and rationalisation. He distinguished between instrumental rationality (*Zweckrationalität*) which assesses the most efficient means to reach a postulated end, and value rationality (*Wertrationalität*), which counts actions as rational insofar as they display and exemplify commitment to a given value such as religious asceticism. Not all action is rational, and Weber recognised the existence of other motives for action, such as following traditional rituals. However, insofar as the sociologist must seek to understand the meaning of the actions studied for the agents themselves (here Weber developed Dilthey's account of *Verstehen*), the most intelligible forms of action would be those which were instrumentally rational. The sociologist could easily assess how adequate a choice of means was to attain the given end. Just as importantly, the other actors in the society being studied could also rely on the transparent rationality of the instrumentally adequate action.

The transparency of instrumental rationality created an internal dynamic which affected both individual attitudes and public institutions. The paradigmatic rationalised institution was bureaucracy, which Weber saw as increasingly indispensable in capitalist firms as well as in the civil service and the law. Consumers like citizens demanded reliable, repeatable, equitable impersonal treatment and this generated the need for ever-increasing layers of bureaucracy, which then fostered the demand for such treatment, and so on. Though he never adhered to a deterministic picture of social change,

Weber feared that the trend toward bureaucratic domination would eventually drive capitalism to the wall and culminate in a socialism which would control all aspects of life through bureaucratic procedures. Lecturing on socialism at the height of the world war and German revolution, he attacked the fond socialist fantasy that bureaucracy could simply disappear from the modern world, or that the experience of mass organisation would change significantly once virtuous socialists were in charge (here influencing the elitist theory of his student Robert Michels – see chapter 3).

Two questions arise for this view. First, what is the origin of the 'ends' which *Zweckrationalität* pursues, and what gives them individual or social validity? Second, what is the role of politics in a society where both public administration and economic firms have become bureaucratised? As we will now see, the answers to these questions for Weber are intertwined.

His answer to the first question drew profoundly on the thought of Friedrich Nietzsche. Believing Christianity's sway over the Western mind to be ending, and so famously proclaiming the 'death of God', Nietzsche had ruptured the religious unity between truth and moral value. Values could no longer be accepted as the purportedly impartial and universal dictates of right reason. Their real role was as chosen ends which articulated an individual's drive toward healthy and vital flourishing. But only a few individuals, the free spirits or philosophers, were strong and self-aware enough to shape such potent values for themselves or for others. Figures like Moses, Jesus and Socrates had to act as moral legislators for the rest of humanity.

Weber followed Nietzsche in seeing the source of moral value in the self-legislation of a few rare individuals (his own exemplar was Luther, in his lecture on the vocation of politics to students in January 1919: Weber 1978 [1919]). Like Nietzsche, he stripped the Kantian image of self-legislation of its claim to rational universality. But, more explicitly than Nietzsche, he acknowledged a 'polytheistic' universe of competing and rationally irreconcilable values. Individual character was formed (here articulating the German tradition of *Bildung* or education) by committing oneself to an overriding value and expressing it in one's conduct and personality. For Weber such commitment merged elements of instrumental rationality with those of value rationality. In the case of the politician, it demanded responsibility for the consequences of one's decisions as well as the burning passion for a cause.

The concern with the nature of the politician marks another important difference between Nietzsche and Weber. Whereas Nietzsche had simply loathed the levelling tendencies of modern egalitarianism, Weber took seriously the task of articulating how such commitments to value on the part of politicians could fit into the modern world of secular, liberal, capitalist democracies. The First World War marked a watershed in his view of democracy, as he came to accept as inevitable and important that the masses of people who had risked their lives as soldiers must have some share in political life. Modern mass society required a democracy in which party competition tested and toughened political leaders, while a bureaucratic civil service maintained the impartial rule of law in its procedural integrity. Such a constitution, which Weber helped to devise for the Weimar Republic that emerged from the ashes of German defeat in the First World War, could also ward off the dangerous blandishments of the socialists who had so unrealistic a view of the bureaucratic and legal requirements of modern politics (Weber 1984 [1918]).

The danger was that party competition would degenerate into cronyism, leaving the polity to the mercy of politicians seeing their posts as paths to self-enrichment rather than expressions of a vocation. As the newborn Weimar Republic struggled to assert its authority in the face of recalcitrant elements in the press, judiciary and army, Weber called for a strengthening of the role of the president – a plebiscitary president – in order to sustain this role of political leadership. It has been much debated whether Weber's demands for a strengthened president helped open the door to Hitler's rise to power. His austere view of political life and the irrationality of all value choices at least left open the door to nihilism for those of weaker moral and intellectual character than Weber himself.

Vitalism and pragmatism: the claims of 'life'

Pareto, Durkheim and Weber all sought to develop sociology within the space bounded by their positivist predecessors, even while proposing major changes in the ways the social sciences were to be understood. The next two reactions to and developments of positivism to be examined were more extreme, seeking to serve not science but 'life'. Those we may call vitalists (Nietzsche, Bergson and Sorel) developed a sense of the recalcitrance of experience to science, while the pragmatists (Peirce, James, Dewey) developed a subtly different account of science as continuous with the human response to manifold experience.

The little that was said about Nietzsche above will have to suffice to indicate in what ways his 'vitalism' was manifest. Especially in his early writings, he invoked the health of 'life' as the real aim and sole standard of all choices, although sick and perverted people such as priests would hide this in purported supernatural sanctions; in his later writings the claims of life were wrapped up in the difficult idea of the 'will to power'. Nietzsche's celebration of the demands of life and individuality explain his decided hostility to positivism, which he attacked as a shallow and hedonistic determinism. Julien Benda classed him with Bergson and Sorel as a pragmatist traitor to the intellectual life (Benda 1927). But Nietzsche is not best understood as a pragmatist; his rupturing of the Christian harmony between truth, morality and salvation implies that truth may well be antipathetic to the claims of life or morality.

The question of the relation between vitalism, pragmatism and positivism is complicated further in the case of Henri Bergson. Like Durkheim an assimilated Jew, he dominated the French intellectual scene more briefly but even more powerfully than did Croce the Italian (Grogin 1988). His political and intellectual allegiances were murkier than those of the committed republican Durkheim. Ensconced at the Collège de France, where his lectures drew such crowds in the years before the First World War that it was proposed to move them to the Opéra, Bergson attracted admirers from across the political spectrum – his disciples including Charles Péguy and Georges Sorel.

Like Dilthey, Bergson saw himself as dissolving metaphysical pseudo-problems, seeking a new conception of mental life to supersede what he saw as the pseudo-conflict between free will and determinism. And, like the positivists, he rejected the metaphysical delusion that 'we can find behind the word a thing'. But instead of trying to unify the sciences, Bergson articulated new dimensions of experience – the flow of consciousness or duration and the importance of the unconscious – which preceded and exceeded all scientific concepts. He insisted that he was an empiricist in attending to reality, but his was a world deeper and stranger than any imagined by positivism.

From Schopenhauer, Bergson developed the notion of an unconscious which underlies, infuses and often contradicts our conscious waking world. The idea of an unconscious dimension of the mind threw the traditional ethical and explanatory schemata into question: how could one understand human action or social order if not as the product of transparent rational connections? Bergson responded with the idea of intuition, which could generate actions and create knowledge in a holistic way. Intuition, furthermore, could be used to show that time was experienced in consciousness as duration, as a lived flow, rather than as the mathematised time of physics.

This resolved the problem of free will. Freedom need not, and cannot, be reified in the manner of space, into a point of pure free willing. It is indefinable and unanalysable, for 'if we persist in analysing it, we unconsciously transform the process [of willing] into a thing and duration into extensity [*sic*]' (Bergson 1910 [1889], p. 219).

The flow of consciousness was central to Bergson's appeal to the life force (*élan vital*) as an ever-renewing expression of creativity in action. The claims of 'life' explain Bergson's reciprocated admiration of the pragmatist William James. Yet with Croce, against the American pragmatists, he saw science not as serving life but as abstracting from it, making pallid abstractions of the colourful concrete flow of reality. Like Croce again, Bergson came to think that this picture of 'creative evolution' demanded a broadly liberal form of society. In his last major work, *The Two Sources of Morality and Religion* (1935 [1932]), he favourably contrasted an 'open society' which would unite all humanity in a dynamic and intuitive religion, with the natural human tendency to form 'closed societies' which fight each other in the name of their private myths. But he saw the effort to establish the open society as a constant struggle which, though enriched by the effort of each rare individual who promoted it, would inevitably collapse. And the mysticism which clung to the notion of the *élan vital* meant that despite Bergson's personal liberalism, leaders of the extreme French right and others opposed to freedom and reason drew succour from his ideas.

In this connection it is worth saying something more about the impassioned career of Bergson's disciple Georges Sorel. Sorel was, like Pareto, a trained engineer who worked for many years in that field before retiring to devote himself to writing. But, whereas Pareto was committed to the market, Sorel always despised the utilitarian calculations of the capitalists. He was attracted to syndicalism for reasons he had derived from Bergson's philosophy of action. According to Bergson, at least on Sorel's reading, science could only rationalise false abstractions. It was myth that propelled and invigorated the life force.[4]

In his best-known work, *Réflexions sur la violence* (1969 [1908] published initially as articles in 1905–6), Sorel urged that the violence used by the proletariat in a general strike could purify and inspire, unlike the calculating uses of force under the capitalist status quo. Rather like Pareto again, he became disillusioned by the experience of socialist politics and in the years before

4. The negative reflections on myth in *Deux sources* appeared some thirty years after the time when Bergson directly influenced Sorel.

the outbreak of the First World War flirted instead with the budding fascist right. But he was sickened by the right's celebration of the outbreak of war in 1914, seeing the war not as national glory but as bureaucratic carnage, and returned to socialism in time to enthuse about the Bolshevik Revolution. To the end he combined rejection of positivism with the demand for a science and a form of revolution which could resist the sordid sullying of selfish calculation.

We turn now to the question of pragmatism proper as a movement both influenced by and hostile to positivism. Pragmatism was pre-eminently an American movement. Its main epistemological tenet was sketched by the philosopher Charles Sanders Peirce, who argued that the meaning of beliefs could only be assessed in terms of their consequences as rules for action. As Peirce wrote in his seminal paper of 1878, 'How to Make Our Ideas Clear', 'there is no distinction of meaning so fine as to consist in anything but a possible difference of practice' (Peirce 1986 [1878], vol. III, p. 265). It was left to the Harvard psychologist William James to develop this view into a full-fledged philosophical standpoint, and for John Dewey to articulate it into a new vision of science and democracy as mutually sustaining and interdependent.

Peirce's insistence that beliefs must be manifestable in order to be meaningful has some similarities to Comte's call for observable correlations as the hallmark of positivist science. William James brought pragmatism even closer to positivism; he identified himself as positivist in a gesture unusual after 1890 (James 1891, vol. I, p. vi). James conceived of knowing as an active process rather than a passive mirror of reality. So far, so Kantian. But whereas Kant had located spontaneity specifically in the constitutive features of the mind, James rooted it more broadly in the effortful action of humans as embodied creatures. The human drive to know could not be divorced from the other projects and drives of a human being.

James turned against Kant further in rejecting the idea, central to idealists such as Green, that the mental production of relational concepts structures all our access to reality. And he likewise rejected the Hegelian view of relations as requiring something higher to hold them together. Instead, his 'radical empiricism' consisted of the view that (against Kant) the world itself, not the human cogniser, contains all the relations which give it structure, and that (against Kant and Hegel) human experience is not at bottom a matter of concepts and relations but of a preconceptual immediate given. Concepts and relations, like 'truth', enter only at a later stage, and are valid insofar as they are functional for the purposes of knowers.

Developing his pragmatist picture of the social world, James famously spoke of moral truths as constituted by a 'credit system' of reputable assertions exchanged by individual agents with their own purposes and aims (James 1976 [1907], p. 207). This image helps to explain why pragmatism attracted the hostility of Durkheim. For James, moral truths, indeed all truths, could easily come and go according to the vagaries of everyday individual interactions. For Durkheim, the formation of moral bonds was a matter of the exceptional crystallisation of certain paradigmatically religious concepts and experiences. Collective effervescence was far from the bickering of a credit system. Pragmatism was for Durkheim an impious attack on the holies of the collective mind (Durkheim 1983 [1913]).

Despite Durkheim's attack, William James was as committed to accounting for the social and cognitive value of religion as the Frenchman, and as anxious as the arch-positivists Comte and Spencer to prevent science from squeezing out religious faith. While Durkheim's strategy was to redescribe faith as society worshipping itself, James adopted a version of the older positivist strategy of leaving room for faith by emphasising that there is no way to know the nature of things as opposed to the laws of their interaction. Because reality always outstrips human concepts, relics as they are of the attempt to freeze and abstract some small piece of reality, concepts and so science can never grasp the whole. Room therefore remains for religion. Moreover, if truth is constituted by what it is best for us as active beings to believe, then a pragmatist justification will save (or, if you will, sacrifice) religious truths alongside others. The purpose of James's important work *The Varieties of Religious Experience* (1902) was not to expose religion as a fake, but on the contrary to show it serving and expressing a diverse range of human purposes. James did not intend to cater for self-deception or moral enervation by allowing people to make something true simply by believing it. He himself clung like Nietzsche to an ideal of dispassionate, even heroic, objectivity (James 1891, vol. II, p. 579), though it is not clear that his own theory can fully underwrite this stance.

It was for John Dewey to politicise and more profoundly socialise the pragmatist position. At the height of his career at the University of Chicago where he founded the famous Laboratory school, and then at Columbia, Dewey served as the ubiquitous sage of democracy and philosophy in American public life. He was influenced early by Hegelian idealism and by the synthesis of political principles achieved by T. H. Green. While he knew James's writing from early in his career, and James saluted the Chicago *Studies in Logical Theory* (Dewey 1903) which Dewey organised as a parallel effort to that of pragmatism, Dewey remained sufficiently idealistic to resist calling himself an empiricist. Instead he socialised the idealist emphasis on consciousness, acknowledged the total context of physical, mental and emotional experience, and insisted on 'experimentalism' as a naturalistic method for solving problems (Ryan 1995, pp. 85, 20).

Social communication was the key to Dewey's vision of science and democracy alike. Both apply 'intelligent action' to solving the problems which arise in the embodied experiential world of everyday life; both exclude snobbery and hierarchy, depending as both do on the widest possible context for articulating, challenging and refining beliefs. Indeed democracy will eventually assimilate not only the pervasive practice of science but also the aspirations of organised religion into a single, pulsing and interconnected civic life. Except in the case of educational reform, where his ideas were widely influential, Dewey offered few specifics about political change or public policy. He was the philosopher of a meta-political democracy, the high priest and preacher of democratic principles, insulated like Croce's meta-political liberalism from the world of parties, power and conflict.

Neo-positivism, behaviourism and the 'demise' of political philosophy

More even than the pragmatists, the logical positivists in philosophy and the behaviourists in the social sciences can be viewed as legitimate heirs of the positivist creed. 'Logical positivism' was baptised in 1931 by two young members of the 'Vienna circle' formed around the logician and philosopher Moritz Schlick (Smith 1986, p. 28). The logical positivists sought to advance the positivist aim of demarcating meaningful science from metaphysical nonsense by denying (contra Kant) that there could be any synthetic a priori truths. Instead, all truths were classed as either analytic and a priori (such as the axioms of logic and mathematics) or else as empirical and a posteriori (such as the theorems of the natural sciences).

Having postulated this distinction, it was the structure and nature of the analytic truths of logic which most preoccupied the thinkers of the circle. While they admired the empiricism of Mill and Comte, they baptised themselves 'logical' positivists to distinguish their concerns from the psychologistic inductivism of Mill (Feigl 1969, p. 652). And although Schlick and Otto Neurath would enthusiastically found an international 'Unity of Science' movement, their view of how to unify science was more abstract than that of the positivists Comte or Spencer, both of whom had insisted on the distinctiveness of each branch of science.

The Viennese instead focused on articulating a single meta-scientific criterion for the meaningfulness of statements. This criterion was their verifiability. Carl Hempel, a student of the allied circle in Berlin, summed up the fundamental doctrine:

> The defining characteristic of an empirical statement is its capability of being tested by a confrontation with experiential findings, *i.e.* with the results of suitable experiments or focused observations. This feature distinguishes statements which have empirical content both from the statements of the formal sciences, logic and mathematics, which require no experiential test for their validity, and from the statements of transempirical metaphysics, which admit of none (Hempel 1965, p. 3).

This insistence on empirical verifiability of concepts and theories took the field of analytical philosophy by storm in the 1920s and 1930s. While there is much more to say about logical positivism, our concern is with the consequences of their strict demarcation of meaning for morality and politics. For whereas the classical positivists and pragmatists sought to defend or reconstitute moral values, moral truths seemed to fall foul of the Viennese distinction. Suddenly the old fact/value distinction seemed to stand on new and irreproachable ground, now marking not just a categorical difference but the difference between sense and nonsense.

English logical positivists, however, found two ways to mitigate the meaninglessness of value discourse, which had a bracing (or chilling) effect on anglophone political philosophy in the 1950s and 1960s. On the one hand, the view of meaning as the method of possible verification became, in the hands of A. J. Ayer and others, the more supple doctrine that 'meaning is use'. This allowed T. D. Weldon in *The Vocabulary of Politics* (1953), complete with foreword by Ayer, to argue that the normative claims made by political philosophers are not simply meaningless. They are rather used in a specific way, that is, as rule-like statements. Values can be discussed in the way that the rules of cricket can be discussed, but truth and falsity do not apply, and facts and values remain absolutely separated by an abyss. Other followers of Ayer declared that traditional political philosophy chestnuts like 'Why should I obey any law?' were strictly meaningless, while genuine questions like 'Why should I obey this Conscription Act?' did not need philosophers to answer them (MacDonald 1951).

The alternative approach was inspired by meta-ethicists such as R. M. Hare, who began to suggest that value statements have expressive and prescriptive rather than cognitive meaning. Felix Oppenheim in *Moral Principles in Political Philosophy* (1968) took this tack. But the view that morality could consist only in social convention or in psychological emoting cut the ground out from under the traditional concerns of political philosophy, in which morality and politics were always intertwined. The dominance of these positivist approaches in English philosophy led Peter Laslett to opine that 'for the moment, anyway, political philosophy is dead' (Laslett 1956, p. vii).

As Laslett predicted (Laslett 1956, p. xi), much of the constructive theoretical work of relevance to politics done within the positivist framework came from legal philosophers concerned with the nature of law, its authority and our obligation to obey it, rather than their political counterparts. The classic legal positivism of Jeremy Bentham and John Austin in the late eighteenth and early nineteenth centuries had followed Hobbes in reducing law to the commands of the sovereign. Law had no moral source or authority – we obey it solely because we fear a sanction from the law's sovereign commander and enforcer. Yet this position ignores the fact that courts use the existence of a legal obligation as a reason for deciding a case in a given way, thereby justifying applying a sanction. Later positivists, therefore, sought to analyse the law in ways that preserved its normative character whilst not equating its prescriptive qualities with moral judgements. By far the most influential of these attempts was that of the Austrian legal theorist Hans Kelsen. By contrast to the logical positivists, he returned to Kant to seek the transcendental presuppositions of law's prescriptive force. He argued that any legal order presupposed that the founding act of constitution-making was valid and regulated how force ought to be employed within it. This 'basic norm' or *Grundnorm* was what transformed the commands of a sovereign legislator into binding standards of conduct. Historically, law comes to regulate its own creation with constitutional law validating the drafting of primary legislation, which validates in its turn secondary legislation and so on. Through this process, general norms come to take on a more concrete and less ambiguous form. The state is essentially the personification of this complex legal order and gives it unity (Kelsen 1945).

Though worked out in great detail, Kelsen's argument nonetheless remains ambiguous – caught midway between classical logical positivism and natural law, it posits real or fictitious acts of human will as the origin of law, while ascribing to law a form of justified but non-moral normativity deriving from acceptance of the objective validity of the basic norm. Two of the most interesting developers of Kelsen's argument, the Italian jurist Norberto Bobbio and the British legal philosopher H. L. A. Hart, attempted to overcome this dilemma. Although there were many differences in their approaches, both had also been influenced by linguistic analytical philosophy and focused on elucidating the concept of law as it emerged from legal practice. Bobbio's main contribution was in two books deriving from his lectures as professor of legal philosophy at Turin University – *A Theory of Judicial Norms* (1993 [1958], part 1) and *A Theory of the Legal Order* (1993 [1960], part 2). In these books he sought, on the one hand, to outline the formal characteristics of legal rules, and, on the other, to identify the character of law more intimately than Kelsen had done, with its forming part of an institutional system of rules (Bobbio 1993, pp. vii–x). Unlike Kelsen, however, Bobbio did not believe law was necessarily a unitary system. On the contrary, he argued that any complex legal code would contain a number of conflicting norms. Bobbio was also less concerned than Kelsen with the justificatory as opposed to the systemic normativity of laws. Law, he argued, was a language, which derived its prescriptive quality through the use people made of it to communicate certain norms to each other. Finally, he departed from Kelsen in seeing the state as a political as well as a legal entity, with law intimately related to politics. A student of both the Italian tradition of positivist social science associated with Pareto and Mosca and the classic British tradition of legal positivism from Hobbes onwards, his later writings explored the relationship between the institutional context of law-making and the exercise of power. He argued that the rule of law and rights were historical products of the distribution of power produced by liberal democracy (Bobbio 1995 [1990]), though he followed Kelsen in seeing democracy in its turn as a set of procedural 'rules of the game' (Bobbio 1987 [1984]).

In his important book *The Concept of Law* (1961), Hart also sought to understand law as a practice. He argued that the authority of legal rules and their makers and interpreters rested on widely accepted 'rules of recognition' or rules about which rules should be followed or be legitimately enacted, and by whom. However, against theorists such as Lon Fuller (1969), he insisted that such rules need not be moral, though normative values were usually embedded within them. The task of the jurist became that of simply explicating the 'internal point of view' of the officials of the legal system and the ways they deployed this 'secondary' rule, rather than personal morality of community values, in order to identify and apply the primary rules or laws of the system. Thus jurisprudence was a combination of sociological analysis of the activities of legal practitioners and the logical analysis of the concept of legal rules. Law is not only divorced from morality but also from politics. The role of the legal class lies not in making but in applying the law by reference to rules and procedures that are legally valid within the system. Hart's theory is a powerful account of how the law operates.

Unsurprisingly, however, the revival of political philosophy was to come in part from American sources that objected to the formalities of 'legalism' and regarded the US Supreme Court's overtly political and principled role during the Warren era not as an aberration but as a model (Dworkin 1977).

The importance of the law schools in the revival of American political philosophy was also the result of the dominance of a self-consciously positivist political science. As Bernard Crick observed in the mid-1950s, American political scientists in the first half of the twentieth century were greatly influenced by the peculiarities of that country's democratic experience, as well as by the emerging disciplines of sociology and psychology.[5] Nevertheless, the more alert among them did not hesitate to seek philosophical legitimacy for their nascent discipline by invoking the foreign-made mantle of positivism.

The American dream of useful democratic knowledge and morals led to recurrent calls for a political science, and widespread interest in the works of Comte, Spencer and the British political sociologist Lord Bryce. But the birth of a qualitatively new view of science came in the aftermath of the First World War, when Progressive-era ideals of political reform had been tarnished. Charles Merriam at the University of Chicago initiated a new call for a political science which would be capable of rectifying politics where the unscientific reformers had failed. Merriam announced that America must entrust its fate to 'laboratory science' if it were to avoid a recurrence of the antithetical 'jungle politics' of the war (Merriam 1970 [1925], p. 247, quoted in Crick 1959, p. 139). What was new in Merriam's programme for the discipline was the aspiration to a political science specifically modelled on the natural sciences. This was in part due to the programme of behaviourism in psychological research which the American John B. Watson had initiated. 'Behaviour' correspondingly took centre stage in studies of political behaviour by Merriam's Chicago associates Herbert Tingsten, Harold Lasswell and others, and it was to the measuring, generalising, quantifying and predicting of behaviour that the political scientists devoted themselves.

The political implications of this new 'science of politics' were, as Crick has argued, not pellucid to its proponents. While political scientists insisted on the sharp positivist distinction between fact and value, they nevertheless uncritically oriented their studies toward the accepted foundational American values of equality and democracy. And they tended in Comtean fashion to propose that the power of the state could be used, guided by

5. This and the following paragraph are indebted to Crick (1959). See further chapter 20.

the scientific elite, to promote such equality. Critics attached to the older traditions of political philosophy lost no time in exposing this slide between fact and value, and the unexamined postulate of democratic values, in the works of the new political scientists (e.g. Strauss 1962). An extreme version of this suspicion was manifest in the 1946 Senate debate as to whether the social sciences should fall within the remit of the new National Science Foundation, when several senators insisted that the 'socialist sciences' had no place in an American foundation.

The hegemony and even the coherence of these new aspirations to positivist social science were soon challenged. Philosophers like Peter Winch and Charles Taylor questioned the adequacy of behaviourism as an account of human action. They disputed the view that human behaviour could be adequately described without reference to the intentions, motives and reasons of the actors involved. Drawing on both the earlier hermeneutic critics of positivism and the later work of Ludwig Wittgenstein, they argued further that social practices embodied a 'form of life' involving certain rule-like norms and forms of rationality. A practice such as voting, therefore, could not be understood solely in terms of individual physical movements or even subjective desires, but rather made sense only against the backdrop of a complex set of social norms, values, concepts and practices (Taylor 1985, p. 35). Meanwhile, in a different vein, the American Talcott Parsons sought to reconstruct sociology by discarding what he named its positivist-utilitarian foundations in favour of functionalism (Taylor 1964; Parsons 1947 [1937]). In retrospect Parsons' project appears as the first of many waves of what Quentin Skinner would later call 'the return of grand theory in the social sciences', almost all of which took themselves to be reacting *inter alia* against some sort of positivist tendencies (Skinner 1990).

One example of the return of grand theory in contested form came with a notorious debate in German social science in the 1960s. A major challenge to Vienna-era logical positivism had been made by Karl Popper, who observed that no verification could in principle ever be final since a counter-example might always be found. Popper substituted falsification for verification and argued that social science could contribute to 'piecemeal social engineering' on the basis of its unfalsified findings, though he argued strenuously against socialist aspirations to remould society as a whole which he traced to the malign influence of Plato and Hegel (Popper 1945). But Popperianism itself was soon attacked as excessively positivistic for picturing the growth of science as steadily cumulative, a picture which neglected both the value-ladenness of the formulation of problems and the sudden shifts in perceptual 'paradigms' which Thomas Kuhn (1963) and other critics would highlight.

Popper's presentation on the logic of the social sciences at a conference of the German Sociological Association in Tübingen in 1961 received a reply by Theodor Adorno, which launched a reconsideration of the whole issue of positivism and critical standards in science dubbed the *Positivismusstreit* (Adorno *et al.* 1969). Adorno spoke as a member of the Frankfurt school which was committed to the possibility of critically distinguishing knowledge claims from ideological delusion in oppressive societies. A younger Frankfurt school member, Jürgen Habermas, insisted in his contributions that scientific rationality and knowledge cannot be treated as exhaustive in the manner of positivist thinking (Habermas 1969a; 1969b). Habermas has gone on to construct an important theory of communicative rationality which draws on pragmatism and neo-Kantian sociology as well as many other currents of philosophical thought (e.g. Habermas 1982; see also chapters 13 and 16).

After Laslett's premature announcement of its death, anglophone political philosophy was nursed back to strength in the 1960s (see chapter 22).[6] Rawls offered a constructive method which he claimed could discriminate between various principles of justice on rational grounds, although he sidestepped the problem of value relativism by simply stipulating certain fundamental moral intuitions as starting points. In Rawls' wake, political philosophers have plunged back into the vortex of analysing values, sometimes taken as given, sometimes constructed or defended on other grounds. The related discipline of the history of political thought, for its part, has devoted itself to the elucidation of the meaning of action and of texts in a programme very much indebted to the hermeneutic response to positivism. So far as these disciplines are concerned, the battle against positivism has been won. Meanwhile, however, national political science associations harbour political philosophy as one isolated corner of a field which remains broadly proud of its positivist ancestry. As for the positivist aspirations to social control and reformation, they may be thought to be reviving in eugenicist fantasies reawakened by the dizzying progress in human genetics research. The anti-positivist language of vitalism and the will is less evident today than in the previous *fin-de-siècle* era which has been recounted in this chapter, but the battles between positivism and anti-positivism may not yet be played out.

6. Among those in England who continued to defend political philosophy as a valid discipline were Berlin (1962) and Barry (1965); and in America, Shklar (1957) and Wolin (1960). It was declared alive and fully fit on the publication of John Rawls' *A Theory of Justice* (1971).

16

Postmodernism: pathologies of modernity from Nietzsche to the post-structuralists

PETER DEWS

Defining postmodernism

In the last quarter of the twentieth century the concept of postmodernism, and the associated notion of postmodernity, became a principal focus of discussion in philosophy, cultural analysis, and social and political theory. The notion of 'postmodernism' had originally emerged in an aesthetic context, at least as long ago as the 1930s, but the term was only used sporadically until the boom in its scope and currency from the mid-1970s onwards.[1] This popularisation began in the domain of architecture, where the adjective 'postmodern' was employed to characterise the rebellion against the technocratic functionalism of the 'international style' which was then under way (Jencks 1991 [1978]). But from here its use spread rapidly, first to describe new developments in literature, painting and other artistic media, and then to characterise a whole range of social and cultural developments which were assumed to represent a break with the defining practices and styles of thought of the modern era. Indeed, for some of its more enthusiastic proponents, the emergence of postmodernism signalled nothing less than the transition to a new historical epoch, beyond modernity.

This epochal significance of the postmodern was given an influential pioneering formulation by the French philosopher Jean-François Lyotard in his book, *La condition postmoderne* (*The Postmodern Condition*), first published in 1979. Part of the success of this work, which presented a series of provocative and fertile ideas rather than a carefully constructed argument, was due to the compactness with which Lyotard defined his key term. For Lyotard, the postmodern condition was characterised by the delegitimation

1. Perry Anderson traces the origins of the term back to 1934, when the Spanish critic Federico de Onís coined the word 'postmodernismo' to describe a decorative involution of the modernist movement in the arts, a retreat from its originally subversive dynamic (Anderson 1998, pp. 3–14).

of 'grand narratives', or 'incredulity toward meta-narratives' (Lyotard 1984, pp. 37–41, xxiv). On his account, the grand schemata of historical progress and social development stemming from the Enlightenment, whether liberal or Marxist in inspiration, had finally lost all credibility. The political horrors and moral catastrophes of the twentieth century, combined with the self-avowedly provisional and instrumental character of modern scientific knowledge, had produced a fundamental distrust of such universal stories of human advancement. In some respects, Lyotard's claims were reminiscent of those made during the later 1950s and early 1960s by liberal proponents of the 'end of ideology' thesis. But whereas figures such as Daniel Bell, Seymour Martin Lipset and Ralf Dahrendorf tolled only the death-knell of totalitarian ideologies, of fascism and communism (Waxman 1968), Lyotard also dismissed the notion of the progressive triumph of liberal democracy as another 'grand narrative', another delusive version of the modernist project. Lyotard does not deny that the narrative impulse is central to social existence. Indeed, he insists that story-telling is the fundamental way in which individuals and communities contextualise and make sense of their lives. But he argues that in the future human beings will have to make do with modest local narratives, provisional 'language games' (a Wittgensteinian borrowing), abandoning any comprehensive perspective on social evolution, and the prospect of convergence on a generally shared consensus.

Whatever the strengths or weaknesses of its philosophical argument, *The Postmodern Condition* was an astute encapsulation of the emerging intellectual ambience in the advanced Western democracies. The 1980s witnessed a burgeoning of new forms of cultural, social and political diagnosis marked by a deeply sceptical attitude towards theoretical synthesis, global perspectives and notions of historical progress. These were replaced by an advocacy of epistemological pluralism, an insistence on irreducible socio-cultural diversity, and sometimes even a celebration of subjective fragmentation. If two or three pervasive themes could be selected to summarise these developments, then the following would probably be the most plausible candidates:

(1) *Anti-foundationalism*: a conviction that moral norms and political principles cannot be given an ultimate metaphysical grounding, and that all knowledge claims are relative to linguistic, social and historical contexts.
(2) *The critique of the 'subject'*: a rejection of the notion that human beings can be essentially defined as rational, reflective subjects of experience and as consciously self-determining agents or initiators of action, a notion assumed to be central to the modern philosophical tradition. According

to postmodern theorists, due attention paid to issues of culture, gender and race, and to the vulnerable corporeality of human beings, will lead us to view subjectivity as divided, internally conflictual, and shaped by the opaque workings of unconscious desire.

(3) *Acknowledgement of difference, and the claims of the 'Other'*: a conviction that universalistic moral and political discourse inevitably rides roughshod over cultural, ethnic, gender and other differences between human beings, excluding or marginalising subordinate groups and dissident voices. From this perspective, Enlightenment rationalism and universalism appear as a metaphysically disguised Eurocentrism. Indeed, according to many postmodern thinkers, the exclusion of 'alterity' may be built into the basic structures of the Western conception of reason as such.

Postmodernist thought, as it evolved in the advanced Western world, was decisively influenced by a constellation of French thinkers who came to prominence during the 1960s, and who are usually referred to as 'post-structuralists' (since they respond in various ways to the formalist and anti-subjectivist 'structuralism' briefly fashionable in France in the early to mid-1960s). This group includes Jacques Derrida, Michel Foucault, Gilles Deleuze and Jacques Lacan. (Lyotard did not become influential until the later 1970s; during the 1960s, as a member of the far-left group Socialisme ou Barbarie, he still espoused a version of 'Western Marxism'.) A concern with semantic instability, epistemological rupture and the decentring of subjectivity, combined with a suspicion of developmental and teleological schemata, feature prominently in the work of all these writers. Undeniably, native impulses deriving from Surrealism, and from allied thinkers who emerged in the 1930s such as Maurice Blanchot and Georges Bataille, are evident in post-structuralism (Bürger 2000). But the work of this generation of French thinkers, a generation of incontestable, often dazzling inventiveness and originality, was fundamentally shaped by two of the most important European philosophers of the late nineteenth and twentieth centuries: Friedrich Nietzsche (1844–1900) and Martin Heidegger (1889–1976). In different ways, and in varying combinations, all the post-structuralist thinkers incorporate, develop and respond to Nietzschean and Heideggerian concerns.

The precursors of postmodernism: Nietzsche and Heidegger

The relation between these two key figures is itself a highly fraught issue. But most commentators would agree that Nietzsche and Heidegger share a philosophical diagnosis of modernity as the culmination, and turning point, of the history of the West. Both have been retrospectively characterised as 'postmodern', and this description seems justified in at least one fundamental sense: they share the conviction that modern consciousness, and modern forms of social life, cannot ultimately legitimate, and hence stabilise, themselves. They regard modernity as a period of irresolvable crisis, and they anticipate a new historical dawning, a transition to a new mode of experiencing, a transformed relation between human beings and the world, 'beyond' modernity. It is this basic radicalism which most profoundly influenced the post-structuralist generation. Of course, in another sense it would be an anachronism to describe Nietzsche or Heidegger as 'postmodernist' thinkers – and their French followers, too, have for the most part repudiated the label. Nonetheless, the patterns of feeling which were articulated by French avant-garde thought from the 1960s onwards, and which circulated thence into a global postmodernism, cannot be understood without a sense of their origins in Nietzsche and Heidegger.

Nietzsche's work revolves around a diagnosis of Western culture and civilisation as crippled from the beginning by their orientation towards a transcendent reality, an otherworldly, timeless truth. This conception of truth, he suggests, was first formulated by Plato, and later joined in a fatal alliance with the world-denying asceticism of the Christian religion. For Nietzsche this conception of truth relies on a basic misapprehension: that there is a pure knowing subject, which can – in principle – gain access to reality without any bias or partiality, and that – at the other pole of the epistemic relation – there is an objective reality to be known. Nietzsche rejects both these assumptions. He regards the notion of a 'subject' of cognition and agency as fiction which masks the conflicting multiplicity of emotions, interests and drives (often unconscious) which motivate human beings. And just as the notion of the knowing subject is an abstraction – one which suppresses the complex intertwining of the mental and the corporeal in human existence – so is the idea of an ultimately 'true' world behind the flux and diversity of appearances:

> From now on, my dear philosophers, let us beware of the dangerous old conceptual fable which posited a 'pure, will-less, painless, timeless knowing subject'... Perspectival seeing is the *only* kind of seeing there is, perspectival 'knowing' the *only* kind of knowing; and the *more* feelings about a matter which we allow to come to expression, the *more* eyes, different eyes through which we are able to view this same matter, the more complete our 'conception' of it, our 'objectivity', will be (Nietzsche 1996 [1887], p. 98).

Much of the power of Nietzsche's thought derives from the fact that he does not simply *oppose* his own naturalistic, anti-dualistic vision of the world to the predominant strains within Western thought and culture. Rather, his 'genealogical' method, centred on the underlying power struggles which shape subjectivity, exposes the self-destructive dynamic built into the 'ascetic ideals' espoused by the Platonic – Christian tradition. It is the notion of a world-transcending truth, to be pursued regardless of any human interest or consideration of consequences, which has ultimately led to the collapse of the assumptions which set up the ideal of truth in the first place. As Nietzsche writes in an early unpublished text, 'Truth kills; indeed kills itself (insofar as it recognises that it is grounded in illusion)' (Nietzsche 1979, p. 92). For Nietzsche even the modern notion of objective scientific knowledge is simply one more manifestation of the West's self-denying 'will-to-truth'. Indeed, he regards modern secularism in general as the result of the ascetic ideal: 'Absolute, honest atheism... is an awe-inspiring *catastrophe*, the outcome of a two-thousand-year training in truthfulness, which finally forbids itself the *lie of belief in God*' (Nietzsche 1996 [1887], p. 134).

Nietzsche's response to atheism as an existential disaster suggests the profound seriousness with which he confronts the historical crisis he has diagnosed. He believes human beings have reached a turning point: they must begin to create meaning and value for themselves, through the exercise of the creative, self-transcending capacity he terms 'will-to-power'. However, the majority of moderns are incapable of doing this, and hence they languish in a state of 'nihilism'. Conformists without conviction, they no longer truly believe in inherited values, but lack the strength to generate new ones. For Nietzsche, the tenets of what is now usually described as 'liberal democracy', tenets which – in the late nineteenth century – were still more a political programme than a reality, are simply another expression of the herd mentality, of life-denying Christian–Platonic values:

> Take a look at the periods in the history of a people in which the scholar comes to the fore: they are times of exhaustion, often of twilight, of decline... The predominance of mandarins is never a good sign: just as little as the advent of democracy, of international courts of peace instead of wars, of equal rights for women, of the religion of compassion, and whatever other symptoms there are of life in decline (Nietzsche 1996 [1887], p. 129).

But what would it mean to create values sovereignly, in opposition to the impotent rationalism and conformist mediocrity of the modern world? And what picture of reality would such creation presuppose? These are issues Nietzsche strives repeatedly to elucidate, without ever reaching a conclusive answer. He comes closest in his evocations of a world of perpetual, cyclical becoming, a vision which only those without remorse and regret can confront and affirm. But while Nietzsche's positive vision remains elusive, his targeting of modern shibboleths has been profoundly influential. His attack on metaphysical notions of truth has encouraged a widespread relativism and perspectivism, while his bold probing beneath the surface of consciousness has provided a model for postmodernism's suspicion of the self-available subject. Furthermore, the key doctrine of the 'eternal return of the same' has offered a challenging antidote to teleological conceptions of history. And, finally, his restless, experimental writing, the sometimes playful, sometimes apocalyptic language in which he conveys his sense of epochal crisis, have been crucial influences on postmodernism's intellectual style.

Martin Heidegger shared Nietzsche's sense of the exhaustion of the Western metaphysical tradition, and a belief that the crisis of modern culture can only be resolved through a drastic new beginning. As a charismatic young lecturer at the University of Freiburg in the early 1920s, he left his students in no doubt that philosophy must be a response to the urgency of the present moment, of '*being-now*' (*Jetztsein*); its task is 'communicating *Dasein* [Heidegger's term of art for self-concerned existence] to itself... hunting down the alienation from itself with which it is smitten' (Heidegger 1999a, pp. 14, 11). But, significantly, Heidegger denied that this new notion of philosophy involved being 'as modern as possible' (Heidegger 1999a, p. 15). Rather, what was required was a profound engagement with, and 'deconstruction' (*Abbau*) of, the philosophical tradition: 'What is needed is to get beyond the position we started from and arrive at a grasp of the subject matter which is free of covering up. For this it is necessary to disclose the history of the covering up of the subject matter... The tradition must be dismantled... Such is possible today only through fundamental *historical critique*' (Heidegger 1999a, p. 59). This conception of method, announced so early in Heidegger's career, remained central, despite all the twists and turns, throughout his intellectual development.

Heidegger's determination to deconstruct the tradition was guided by the conviction that the apparatus of modern thought, and in particular the centrality of the knowing 'subject' within that apparatus, had led to a disastrous objectification of the world. In his view, this tendency does not begin with Descartes, but is in fact latent in the entire history of Western thought, from the Greeks onwards. In his 1927 masterpiece, *Sein und Zeit*

(*Being and Time*), Heidegger sought to counter the entrenched modern construal of experience in terms of a subject–object polarity through a phenomenology of our way of 'Being-in-the-world'. He tried to show that, primordially, we do not encounter a world of 'objects' from the standpoint of an observing and theorising subject, but are practically engaged in the world in ways which imply a 'pre-understanding' of 'Being', of what it *means* for *Dasein*, and for the surrounding web of 'ready-to-hand' things with which *Dasein* engages, to be. This 'pre-understanding' is typically covered over by the theoretical stance of philosophy and the sciences. But it can be recovered from experiences in which *Dasein* is forced beyond the limits of explanation, and confronts the groundlessness of its own existence. The most fundamental of these experiences is the anxiety in which *Dasein* comes to realise that death is its 'own most "non-relational" possibility, since it is that which includes and cancels all other possibilities' (Heidegger 1962 [1927], p. 294). However, *Dasein* tends to flee this anxiety into the neutral, depersonalised mode of existing which he calls '*das Man*' (the 'They'). For the early Heidegger authenticity (*Eigentlichkeit*) involves resolutely facing our always imminent end, and seizing the possibilities of existing which this 'Being-towards-death' throws into relief. These possibilities are not created by *Dasein*, but are taken over from the historical and cultural world to which we belong, in a process which Heidegger calls 'repetition' (*Wiederholung*).

In retrospect it is clear that the rhetoric of Heidegger's early philosophy, his distaste for the utilitarianism, shallowness and 'idle curiosity' of modern society, and his longing for 'a *moment of vision* in which *Dasein* brings itself before itself as that which is properly binding' (Heidegger 1995, p. 165) has close affinities with the language of the 'radical right', which was prevalent in Germany and elsewhere in Europe in the 1920s and 1930s (Bourdieu 1991, pp. 7–39). Nonetheless, his enthusiasm for the Nazi seizure of power, and his joining of the NSDAP in 1933, shortly after becoming rector of Freiburg University, came as a shock to many of his students and colleagues. For a period of about ten months Heidegger made enthusiastic speeches in favour of the regime, pushed forward the *Gleichschaltung* of the university, and even organised a 'study camp' (*Wissenschaftslager*) in the Black Forest for pro-Nazi faculty members and students. However, Heidegger was no crude Nazi ideologue, and he seems to have been free of personal anti-Semitism, despite some deplorable accommodations to the racism of the regime. His vision of a radical renewal of the German spirit was idiosyncratic, and never wholly congenial to the authorities. He resigned the rectorship after less than a year, apparently disillusioned with the increasingly pragmatic attitude of his political superiors.[2]

Inevitably, this episode has cast its shadow over Heidegger's entire philosophical career, and its meaning and implications are still hotly disputed. For commentators unsympathetic to Heidegger, the lesson is clear: attempting to think 'beyond' a modernity diagnosed one-sidedly in terms of social atomisation and loss of meaning is disastrous. It can lead only towards the destruction of those distinctive modern achievements, political democracy and individual freedom (Ferry and Renault 1990, pp. 50–80). It must be admitted that Heidegger never acknowledged anything positive in liberal democratic values – throughout his life, his view of the modern world remained unremittingly bleak. Nonetheless, during the 1930s, Heidegger's thinking did undergo a major 'turn' or *Kehre*, in which the unresolved problems of his earlier thought, and the chastening effects of his abortive political engagement, undoubtedly both played a role. He moved away from his central focus on *Dasein* towards what he began to call the 'history of Being' (*Seinsgeschichte*). This is an meditation on the ways in which Being has both disclosed and concealed itself in the history of the West, through a sequence of fundamental modes of response to the world: styles of experience which find their most explicit articulation in metaphysics.

Briefly put, for Heidegger the defining trait of European thought, after the pre-Socratics at least, has been its misapprehension, its 'forgetfulness' of Being. This forgetfulness was no accident, since Being is essentially a play of disclosure and self-concealment, or what Heidegger later comes to call an 'event' (*Ereignis*). Nonetheless, its consequences have been fateful. This is because Being (the sheer untheorisable *fact that* anything exists, we might say, as opposed to *what* it is) comes to be viewed within metaphysics as a kind of primordial 'super-entity', one which is the ground and cause of all others. Furthermore, what it means to be is defined in general in terms of enduring 'presence'. According to Heidegger, this privileging of presence, which begins with Plato's vision of transient, finite items as imperfect instantiations of eternal ideas, leads to the progressive obnubilation of Being. The encompassing site of human dwelling is transformed into 'nature', and then into a mere 'standing-reserve', a source of raw material for industrial exploitation (Heidegger 1993 [1954]). Technology, then, is far from being a 'neutral' means for achieving human aims. The practical outcome of the long history of Western metaphysical thinking, its obscure dynamic,

2. For the details of Heidegger's political engagement during the 1930s and its aftermath, see Ott (1993).

pervades our experience – and yet its 'essence' eludes us. The remorseless quest for power and efficiency which characterises modern life blots out the resonances of time, place and language, leaving us homeless in a world drained of meaning. From such a perspective the Nazism which Heidegger had once actively espoused comes to appear as one of the ills of modern society, another manifestation of the same manipulative rage, rather than as the beginning of its overcoming.

While Heidegger's diagnosis of modernity has affinities with that of Nietzsche, temperamentally they are far removed. Whereas Nietzsche's thought turns on the notion of the will-to-power, of the sovereign individual who legislates his own values, Heidegger recommends attentiveness, a submissive harkening to the 'voice' of Being. He anticipates that the nihilism of the technological age will lead to a reversal in which the very depth of the 'forgetfulness of Being' will reawaken the question of Being. Human beings will only be 'saved' if they can rediscover a new sense of reverence and receptiveness to the world, and this may require the emergence of a new divinity (cf. the obscure meditations on 'the last god' (*der letzte Gott*) in Heidegger (1999b, pp. 288–93), and the posthumous interview, published in *Der Spiegel* in 1976, where Heidegger makes the famous claim, 'Only a God can save us' (Heidegger 1976)). From this perspective, Nietzsche's demolition of metaphysics, since it recognises nothing higher then the power of willing, is in fact the culminating expression of metaphysical thought. In a cycle of lectures delivered between 1936 and 1940 Heidegger explores the thought that, while Nietzsche reveals the nihilism of the modern age, he is unable to transcend it. Nietzsche simply *inverts* Platonism – endless becoming, in the form of the 'eternal return of the same', instead of static being: the plastic subjectivity of the will rather than the immutability of presence. Nietzsche therefore leaves no room for the 'truth of Being' (*Wahrheit des Seins*) and for a new 'remembrance of Being' (*Andenken des Seins*), informed by respect for the 'ontological difference', the distinction between all which is (*das Seiende*) and Being itself (*das Sein*), which the long history of metaphysics had occluded (Heidegger 1979–87 [1961]).

Whatever the aptness of Heidegger's assessment of Nietzsche – and there is much dispute about this – the two thinkers clearly represent contrasting ways of envisaging a passage beyond modernity into 'postmodernity'. Both are convinced that the modern project of a rational self-grounding of moral and political norms is superficial and doomed to failure, but they draw opposite conclusions from this. Nietzsche often seems to push the modern experience of uprootedness and dislocation even further, denying that human beings are beholden to any higher power, and portraying himself, in one of his favourite images, as setting forth on uncharted open seas. He exacerbates the modern notion of autonomy, as it were arguing that value and meaning can only be posited by human beings themselves, or at least by sovereign individuals. Heidegger, on the contrary, often describes the desolate condition of the modern world in terms of 'homelessness', and implies that the instrumental frenzy of modern science and technology will not subside until human beings are able once more to acknowledge a source of significance which lies beyond themselves. To the unsympathetic, this has looked like a ingenuous, even kitsch attempt to conjure up piety in an essentially post-religious world.

French post-structuralism and postmodernism

As we have noted, Nietzsche and Heidegger are crucial points of reference for the French post-structuralists, who provided the theoretical armoury of postmodernism. But the position of individual thinkers within the force field set up by these exemplars varies from case to case. Thus, Michel Foucault, whose diverse body of work reflects almost all of the fundamental impulses of postmodernism, stressed on several occasions that his formative intellectual experience was the encounter, during the 1950s, with the thought of Nietzsche (e.g. Foucault 1991 [1978], pp. 29–32, 44–6). In the early 1950s Foucault was briefly a member of the French Communist Party, influenced by the existentialist, Hegelian and Marxist currents which prevailed in France in the immediate post-war period. Reading Nietzsche, he later claimed, taught him two essential lessons: first, to distrust the immediate evidence of experience on which phenomenology relied, and to look for the background structures and forces which determine what appear to be intuitively obvious meanings; second, to distrust all notions of development, direction and purpose in the analysis of social and historical processes. More broadly, Nietzsche encouraged Foucault in his suspicion of the heritage of the Enlightenment and his sense of the damage wrought by the rationalisation and instrumentalisation of the modern social world. But damage to what? Nietzsche has an encompassing answer to this question: 'life'. Metaphors of health and sickness, of vitality and decadence, are central to his diagnosis of modern culture and the pathologies of the modern world. For Foucault, however, the answer is far more elusive. Indeed, the various phases of his work could almost be defined in terms of his different approaches to answering this question.

Foucault's first major achievement was *Madness and Civilization*, a book influenced by the 'historical epistemology' pioneered in France by Gaston Bachelard and Georges Canguilhem. Here Foucault begins from the idea that the deep assumptions governing the way in which what we now call 'madness' has been experienced, interpreted and treated have shifted several times in the course of European history since the Renaissance. The book is a close description and analysis of these different modes of experience and frameworks of interpretation, combining detailed historical investigation with philosophical reflection and vividly poetic evocation. It is a many-layered and ambiguous work, but – ultimately – the story which Foucault tells is one of decline.

During the Renaissance, Foucault suggests, there was still a sense of interdependence between reason, on the one hand, and what was then termed 'folly' or 'unreason' on the other. Reason did not regard itself as all-powerful and exclusive; it acknowledged in unreason the possibility of a different kind of wisdom. With the rise of the modern rationalism inaugurated by Descartes, however, this dialogue was cut off: 'Beginning with the seventeenth century, unreason in the most general sense no longer had much instructive value. That perilous reversibility of reason which was still so close for the Renaissance was to be forgotten, and its scandals were to disappear' (Foucault 1967 [1961], p. 78). Foucault correlates this intellectual shift with the 'Great Confinement' – the process whereby, in the mid-seventeenth century, the insane, along with other kinds of socially disruptive and errant individuals, were interned in workhouses in France and other countries across Europe. Gradually, such indiscriminate forms of incarceration were refined, and the insane were isolated. But Foucault suggests that madness still retained something of its transcendent aura into the eighteenth century: 'madness did not disclose a mechanism, but revealed a liberty raging in the monstrous forms of animality' (Foucault 1967 [1961], p. 83). It was only with the introduction of the first insane asylums, towards the end of the eighteenth century, that the disenchantment of madness became complete. The notion of mental 'illness' began to emerge, bringing with it the objectifying knowledge and quasi-medical classification and treatment of the insane which are familiar to us today.

As Foucault emphasises, the inventors of the asylum regarded themselves as humanitarian reformers. Yet *Madness and Civilization* is pervaded by a deep sense of loss. It is clear that the reduction of madness to an object of scientific investigation is felt by Foucault as an impoverishment, a severing of contact with some untamable source of power and illumination. Furthermore, the model of rational and responsible subjectivity to which the insane are to be restored is more oppressive, Foucault strongly implies, than physical incarceration. But right from the beginning this sense of loss and decline vied in Foucault's thought with a deeply relativistic bent – a tendency to regard different cognitive and interpretative frameworks as sheerly incommensurable. Thus in his next book, *The Birth of the Clinic*, which deals with the emergence of modern clinical medicine, different historical classifications of maladies and their symptoms and different conceptual maps of the diseased body are regarded as effectively constituting different realities: there is no underlying 'truth' of disease. Foucault's later works of the 1960s went even further in this direction, adopting an ostensibly 'structuralist' mode of analysis, in which epochal cognitive grids called '*epistemes*' (*The Order of Things*), or more multiple and fluid 'discursive formations' (*The Archaeology of Knowledge*), are described as determining both subject and object positions, and therefore the very possibilities of experience and knowledge. *The Archaeology of Knowledge* explicitly targets the notion of a domain of 'pre-discursive experience' which the patterns of discourse exclude or repress.

At the start of the 1970s, however, Foucault's position began to shift again. In his 1970 inaugural lecture at the Collège de France, he suggested that the rules of discourse function as principles of social regulation and exclusion, determining who may speak about what, and in which context. Adopting an explicitly Nietzschean tone, Foucault proclaimed that his intention, henceforth, was to investigate the metamorphoses of the Western 'will-to-truth'. There duly followed ambitious historical studies of the emergence of the modern prison system (in *Discipline and Punish*), and of our modern ways of theorising and regulating sexuality (*The History of Sexuality*, vol. I: *An Introduction*). *Discipline and Punish*, in particular, seems to loop back to the themes of *Madness and Civilization*: the historical connection between new post-Enlightenment institutions of confinement, mechanisms and procedures of observation and control, and the emergence of the human sciences. In both books Foucault, directly inspired by Nietzschean genealogy, portrays the formation of rational, responsible subjects as a process of the internalisation of constraint.

The major difference between the early book on the asylum and the book on prisons lies in the introduction of an explicit concept of 'power', which is further developed in *The History of Sexuality*. In a move which was to have an immense influence on postmodernist thought in general, Foucault describes power as a mobile, pervasive feature of all social relations, reinforced by, and in turn reinforcing, the forms of knowledge it makes possible. Power, on this view, is not primarily exclusionary or negative, but rather constitutive or 'productive'. But perhaps even more influential than Foucault's conception of power was his general attitude to intellectual work, his Nietzschean experimentalism, in which questions of historical or philosophical truth, as conventionally understood, were no longer the overriding concern. In an interview given in 1978, Foucault confessed: 'I consider myself more an experimenter than a theorist; I don't develop deductive systems to apply uniformly in different fields of research. When I write, I do it above all to change myself and not to think the same thing as before' (Foucault 1991 [1978], p. 27). An equally influential concomitant of this outlook was Foucault's deep reluctance to propose social prescriptions or political solutions.

In Foucault's work, the influence of Nietzsche, and the role of concepts directly derived from Nietzsche, such as 'will-to-truth', 'genealogy' and 'power', are patent. Heidegger's influence is more difficult to pin down, but may perhaps be descried in Foucault's concern with historically shifting frames of world disclosure, an echo of Heidegger's *Seinsgeschichte*. In the case of Jacques Derrida, however, the balance of influence, and the sensibility at work, are quite different. Derrida derives his basic orientation from Heidegger. 'What I have attempted to do would not have been possible', he has stated, 'without the opening of Heidegger's questions' (Derrida 1981a [1972], p. 18). More specifically, the notion of the 'deconstruction' of metaphysics, which was central to Derrida's early writings, relies heavily on Heideggerian precedents, including the crucial claim that Western philosophy has been dominated by the equation of Being with presence. Like Heidegger, Derrida seeks for ways of thinking beyond the 'closure' produced by this equation, a closure which he also understands as a comprehensive exclusion of '*différance*' – his term for the transcendent productivity of differences. But at the same time he is resistant to what he perceives as the nostalgic tonalities of Heidegger's thought: the emphasis on responsiveness and belonging. The resistance is often Nietzschean in inspiration.

In Derrida's early work, this ambiguous relation to Heidegger is played out through his portrayal of the history of Western philosophy as a battle for status between speech and writing. Derrida traces the way in which – from Plato to Husserl, and beyond – the apparently living immediacy of the voice, the speaker's experience of the direct coincidence of an intended meaning and its verbal expression, is contrasted with the 'artificial', supposedly derivative medium of writing. Script, Derrida claims, has traditionally been regarded as no more than an imperfect representation of the spoken word, one severed from the source of meaning, and from the thoughts or intentions of the writer. But since writing can function in the total absence of its author (for example, after his or her death), it opens the possibility that meaning may go astray, that words, placed in new contexts, may start to signify something other than what was 'originally' intended. Indeed, the very notion of an 'original' meaning starts to look problematic. For Derrida argues that semantic instability and uncertainty are in fact intrinsic to language. He suggests that all language can be viewed as a kind of 'text' or 'writing', in which meaning emerges from the play of the differential relation between elements, rather than primarily expressing a thought or intention present in the mind of the language user.

This provocative account of the relation between speech and writing formed the original template for the philosophical strategy which Derrida has made famous as 'deconstruction'. Deconstruction begins with a moment of reversal, in which the subordinate term – such as writing, the material, the corporeal or indeed the feminine – is freed from its inferior status. But this phase of reversal must be accompanied by a second phase, in which the very opposition is put in question, just as conventional opposition of speech and writing is ultimately engulfed, in Derrida's work of the 1960s, by a more encompassing notion of language as 'arche-writing' (Derrida 1974 [1967], p. 56). Without this second phase, deconstruction would be indistinguishable from those forms of philosophical critique which seek to recover some original truth or reality from occlusion or alienation. But Derrida is even more sceptical about such retrievals than Foucault. On his view, any attempt to rescue a repressed truth, or disclose an ultimate underlying reality, will simply repeat the structures of the 'metaphysics of presence'. It will overlook the fact that what is construed as truth and reality is always relative to the play of the text; that – in a formulation which became notorious – 'il n'y pas de hors-texte [there is no outside-text]' (Derrida 1974 [1967], p. 158). In Derrida's view, Nietzsche's reflections on language may be more radical than those of Heidegger because they are no longer oriented towards the notion of truth at all, not even a truth of Being more primordial than all metaphysical truth:

> Radicalising the concepts of *interpretation*, *perspective*, *evaluation*, *difference*, and all the 'empiricist' or nonphilosophical motifs that have constantly tormented philosophy throughout the history of the West . . . Nietzsche . . . contributed a great deal to the

> liberation of signifier from its dependence or derivation with respect to the logos and the related concept of truth or the primary signified, in whatever sense that is understood (Derrida 1974 [1967], p. 19).

Although Derrida would reject the characterisation of his thought as 'postmodern', the Nietzschean revamping of Heideggerian themes which typified his early work provided the jumping-off point for many developments in postmodernist thought. On the one hand, the language of deconstruction provided a lingua franca for a wide range of protests against forms of exclusion and oppression. Derrida's reversal of the relation of speech versus writing, of the philosophical *logos* and its excluded, derivative others has proved a tempting model to apply to a wide variety of political and social hierarchies. Theoretically inclined adherents of many social and political protest movements have been able to discern in Derrida's gesture towards the marginalised 'Other' a reflection of their own concerns. At the same time, however, Derrida's sense of the power of 'logocentric metaphysics' is so pervasive that it becomes extremely difficult to specify what the result of an emancipation of the 'Other' from its constraints would be. He often comes very close to implying that there *are* no other ways to reason than those prescribed by metaphysics, so that alternatives become literally unthinkable. The consequence is a curious oscillation, characteristic of much postmodernist thinking, between an almost apocalyptic mode of discourse, which invokes the radical 'beyond' of modernity, and a kind of political evasiveness, even defeatism.

Postmodernist thought in the English-speaking world

Foucault and Derrida have probably been the most influential of French post-structuralist thinkers. But a number of other writers who came to prominence during the 1960s and 1970s – the psychoanalyst Jacques Lacan, the philosopher Gilles Deleuze and the social theorist Jean Baudrillard – also contributed to the articulation of the postmodernist outlook. These Parisian thinkers provided the concepts powering the postmodernist trend, which touched every discipline in the humanities and social sciences, not least in the anglophone world. However, this wider domain of postmodernist thought is so complex and varied that it may be useful to differentiate between three broad socio-political currents within it. The first of these incorporates the critique of metaphysical foundationalism, but does not see this critique as posing any particular problem for liberal democratic values, or as implying any deep challenge to contemporary society; the second current does regard postmodernism as a basis for questioning existing political and social institutions, but not as implying a need for their total overhaul (this current often finds the value of postmodernism in its heightened sensitivity to the claims of the Other, but regards this as requiring a more *flexible* version of modern notions of justice (see Young (1990) for one of the most thoughtful examples of this approach); finally, there is a current of postmodernism which reaches more dramatic conclusions concerning the remoulding of subjectivity and the transformation of social relations which would be desirable, or is supposed to be currently in train.

The North American philosopher Richard Rorty provides probably the best-known example of the first outlook. In 1980 Rorty published *Philosophy and the Mirror of Nature*, a book which carried to its ultimate conclusion the shift away from foundationalism in analytical philosophy after Quine. According to Rorty, the efforts of modern philosophers, from Descartes onwards, to establish definitive criteria for the true representation of reality have finally run aground. In a move which strikingly echoed the contemporaneous claims of Lyotard's *The Postmodern Condition*, Rorty argued that anticipation of finding ultimate truth should be abandoned in favour of an open-ended conversation between divergent points of view. In a spate of subsequent publications, Rorty, marrying postmodernism with his version of American pragmatism, extended this argument into the moral and political domain. On his account, the discovery that our beliefs, including our moral and political beliefs, lack metaphysical foundations does not leave us staring into the abyss. Since reason, truth and justice simply *are* what a given community defines them as being, since there is no more ultimate court of appeal, we have no reason to abandon the beliefs of the community to which we already belong. Denizens of the modern West, therefore, have no reason to abandon the principles of liberal democracy, or even to doubt the superiority of their principles over those of other traditions. Hence what Rorty dubs 'postmodernist bourgeois liberalism' turns out, on inspection, to be just bourgeois liberalism dispensing with philosophical justification (Rorty 1993).

Other thinkers influenced by postmodernism, such as the political theorist William Connolly, take a rather different view. Following Nietzsche and Foucault, Connolly stresses the exclusionary features of political and social identities, indeed the 'cruelty' which may be required to forge a unified self. Capturing an elemental postmodernist thought, Connolly writes:

'Identity requires difference in order to be, and it converts difference into otherness in order to secure its own self-certainty' (Connolly 1991, p. 65). The paradox which this conception generates, of course, is that the politically marginalised and excluded can only find an equal place within the polity by achieving recognition for their distinct identity. But since identity is regarded as marked by intrinsically constraining or repressive features, any such achievement of recognition or inclusion appears as a pyrrhic victory. Yet having stated this 'paradox of difference', as he calls it, Connolly does not draw the conclusion that the liberal project of acknowledging difference and individuality should be abandoned. Rather, he calls for an 'alternative, militant liberalism' based on a 'multifarious politicization of difference' (Connolly 1991, pp. 93, 87).

But politicisation for what? Here we reach the third strand of postmodernism. For once one accepts that there are 'pressures in the human condition to naturalise conventional identities' (Connolly 1991, p. 80), then the disruption of identity, the fracturing of subjectivity, the fostering of plurality tend to become an end in themselves. The anarchic celebrations of unleashed desire in works such as Deleuze and Guattari's *Anti-Oedipus* and Lyotard's *Economie libidinale* are obvious examples of this trend in France. In the English-speaking world such an extreme position is less common, but Judith Butler's *Gender Trouble* may come close to it. Butler argues that 'there is no ontology of gender on which we might construct a politics, for gender ontologies always operate within established political contexts as normative injunctions' (Butler 1990, p. 148). But since, on this account, *any* definition and practice of gender is a construction, it is hard to find a reason to oppose any specific construction, other than the purely negative 'aim' of disrupting gender identity as such. For obvious reasons, such stances can scarcely be taken as expressing a political perspective at all, and this suggest a pervasive problem in postmodernist thinking. For to the extent that exclusion is taken to be anchored in the very structures of Western reason, or the ineluctability of power-defined identities, then the 'Other' in whose name a protest is raised – the 'feminine', for example, in the influential early work of the French feminist Luce Irigaray (1985a; 1985b) – seems condemned either to the ineffectual limbo of the unthinkable, or to irrationalist celebration. The reverse side of this dilemma is the starting point of the thought of the social theorist Jean Baudrillard. For, beginning from a similar premise, namely that in contemporary society there is no outside to the 'hyperreal' universe of endlessly shifting signs, Baudrillard concludes that the very notion of emancipation has become chimerical. The 'Other' of the system is itself another product of the system: 'when everything is repressed, nothing is anymore' (Baudrillard 1994 [1981], p. 147).

Habermas's critique of postmodernism and the 'ethical turn'

It is precisely this central theoretical and political dilemma of postmodernist thought which was highlighted by its most eminent critic, Jürgen Habermas. As the doyen of the 'second generation' of the Frankfurt school, a tradition of social theory rooted in Western Marxism, Habermas sympathised with many of the critical impulses of postmodernism. But he was also convinced that a foreshortened understanding of modernity had led the postmodernists to misdirect their fire. In a lecture delivered in 1980, 'Modernity – An Incomplete Project' (Habermas 1993 [1981]), and in a full-scale book published a few years later, *The Philosophical Discourse of Modernity* (Habermas 1987a), Habermas laid out his alternative diagnosis. Essentially, Habermas contests the view that modernity can be adequately defined in terms of the rise of a domineering principle of subjectivity, and the consequent restructuring of social reality in line with the dictates of functional efficiency. This was, of course, the basic conception of the modern world which postmodernism had inherited from Nietzsche and Heidegger. In Habermas's view, the basic error of this negative response to modernity lay in the equation of reason *as such* with a restricted, 'instrumental' conception of reason. Once this equation is made, then protest can only be expressed through an appeal to irrational powers. Madness, eroticism, the dionysian, are invoked to disrupt a subjectivity which is entirely equated with the capacity for reflective self-objectification and self-regulation.

In opposition to the developments that culminate in the paradoxes of what he terms a 'totalising critique of reason', Habermas proposes his conception of 'communicative reason'. Rationality, he claims, is not exhausted by the drive for instrumental calculation and control. It is also exemplified in our ability to raise, respond to and assess the validity claims (for example, claims to truth) which are raised in linguistic communication. This ability, in turn, would not be possible without a capacity to identify with or put ourselves in the place of the interlocutor, the Other. And, indeed, on Habermas's account, it is precisely through the development of this ability that reflective subjectivity emerges in the first place. Since, on Habermas's account, communication is guided by the aim of reaching general agreement concerning validity claims, there is no *intrinsic* opposition between universalism and the claims of the Other. The notion of communicative reason allows us to move beyond the assumption that reason itself is inevitably dominating and exclusionary, since, on Habermas's account, the rational goal of achieving consensus depends precisely on the *recognition* of the claims of the Other as potentially more valid than my own (Habermas 1987a, pp. 309–16). Furthermore, whereas postmodernists have typically construed the collapse of metaphysical foundations as a licence for relativism, Habermas's conception of agreement as the intrinsic, albeit idealised, aim of communication provides, so he claims, a 'post-metaphysical' account of our orientation to a context-transcending truth. On Habermas's account, modernity, in both its capitalist and bureaucratic socialist versions, is characterised by a 'colonisation' of the human life-world by instrumental reason. But since this represents a *one-sided* realisation of the potential of modern reason, which prioritises functional imperatives over the rationality inherent in life-world communication, it is a historical distortion which could *in principle* be corrected, and hence provides no grounds for bidding farewell to modernity as such (cf. Habermas 1987b, pp. 303–31).

Arguably, reservations similar to those expressed by Habermas, but arising from the internal dynamic of postmodernism, began to have an impact from the 1980s onwards. In the final years of his life, for example, Foucault made a surprising turn towards the concept of freedom, which he acknowledges as the necessary contrastive notion to that of power (Foucault 1982, pp. 221–2). Foucault's working out of his conception of freedom in terms of an 'aesthetics of existence' – the idea that individuals should fashion their own lives in conformity with an individual project of self-shaping – is still resolutely anti-universalist, but it nonetheless ushers a notion of self-conscious and purposeful subjectivity back onto the stage.

Later developments in Derrida's thought have been, if anything, even more striking. We have already considered Derrida's notorious early dictum, 'il n'y pas de hors-texte'. The implications of this aphorism have been much disputed, but, at a minimum, it surely implies that there is nothing which cannot be relativised; that linguistic meaning and existential orientation do not flow from any experience or reality prior to language and difference. By the 1980s, however, Derrida's position had changed quite drastically, since he began to elaborate the notion of a call, a messianic appeal, an 'experience of the impossible', which appears to be the unconditioned precondition of deconstruction itself. Thus, to take one example, Derrida argues that the possibility of deconstructing any determinate conception of justice depends on 'the sense of a responsibility without limits, and so necessarily excessive, incalculable, before memory' (Derrida 1992, p. 19). He suggests that: 'deconstruction takes place in the interval that separates the undeconstructibility of justice from the deconstructibility of *droit* (authority, legitimacy, and so on). It is possible as an experience of the impossible, there where, even if it does not exist (or does not yet exist, or never does exist) *there is* justice' (Derrida 1992, p. 15). Deconstruction, then, arises from and is oriented by an anticipation of justice. In a similar vein, in his book *Specters of Marx*, Derrida affirms that 'what remains irreducible to all deconstruction, what remains undeconstructible as the very possibility of deconstruction, is perhaps a certain experience of the emancipatory promise' (Derrida 1994, p. 59).

This shift in Derrida's work, and in postmodernist thought more generally, is inseparable from the increasing influence of Emmanuel Levinas, a thinker of Jewish–Lithuanian origin who was active in Paris for over sixty years. Like many of the twentieth century's leading philosophers, Levinas began as a follower of Heidegger, studying with him in Freiburg during the 1920s. From Heidegger he inherited the notion that Western metaphysics as a whole has been an immense apparatus of forgetting. But whereas, for Heidegger, what has been forgotten is the *Seinsfrage*, the 'question of Being', for Levinas it is the primordiality of our ethical relation to the Other, a sense of boundless responsibility which constitutes us as subjects, but which philosophy cannot grasp in its objectifying categories. Like Derrida, but for rather different reasons, Levinas argues that the notion of 'ontological difference' is not – as Heidegger assumes – the escape route from objectifying metaphysics. 'Being', for Levinas, is not sufficiently transcendent, since it offers itself to comprehension in what Heidegger calls 'the clearing of Being' (*die Lichtung des Seins*). Indeed, for Levinas, Being is far from representing the last repository of wonder. On his account, we experience naked being in the form of what he terms the '*il y a*' (the 'there is'): as anonymous, neutral, oppressive, horrifying. Our only window onto transcendence, and escape from the claustrophic pressure of being, Levinas suggests, is to be found in the face of the human Other. In the face-to-face relation we experience an irrecusable ethical obligation, encapsulated in the primordial commandment 'Thou shalt not kill', which drives us beyond the egotistical involution of the self. Indeed, we can only make sense of the absolute character of this obligation if we assume that it is through the face-to-face relation – and in fact *only* here – that we catch a glimpse of the divine (Levinas 1969 [1961]).

Although Levinas's work has been widely regarded as pioneering a 'postmodern' ethics, its relation to the typical features of postmodern thought is profoundly ambiguous. Clearly, there are affinities with postmodernism in the radicality of his attack on the tradition of Western philosophy, and his claim that this tradition as a whole has been complicit in the violent suppression and reduction of otherness. But, at the same time, his thinking is not located in the field of polarities established by Nietzsche and Heidegger, the terrain of so many other postmodern thinkers. Heidegger regards Nietzsche's announcement of the 'death of God' with the utmost seriousness: the inherited value schemas of the West have indeed devalued themselves, and the only appropriate response is a new beginning, the transition to a post-philosophical 'remembrance of Being' (*Andenken des Seins*). By contrast, Levinas scarcely registers the Nietzschean proclamation, except to brush it aside as a kind of childishness – for the 'onto-theological' notion of God as supreme being and ultimate source of value was never more than an idolatrous hypostatisation anyway, one which bears little relation to that elusive trace of the divine which is disclosed through our ethical response to the human Other.

Perhaps the primary respect in which Levinas might be regarded as 'postmodern' is in his refusal to base his ethical stance on metaphysical foundations or principles. His work seeks to evoke phenomenologically the asymmetrical structure of obligation disclosed in the face-to-face relation as such. But since this structure is universal, Levinas had no sympathy for the contextualism and relativism typical of the postmodern outlook. Indeed, in an essay dating from 1964, which explicitly reflects on the logic of post-war decolonisation, Levinas states: 'The saraband of innumerable and equivalent cultures, each justifying itself in its own context, creates a world which is, to be sure, de-occidentalized, but also disoriented . . . the norms of morality are not embarked in history and culture' (Levinas 1996 [1964], pp. 58–9). Elsewhere Levinas vigorously attacks what he regards as Heidegger's 'paganism' of Being and the homeland. The Heideggerian emphasis on dwelling and place he dismisses as a recipe for hostile division. It conceals the essential dislocation of human beings, which allows the ethical claim – what Levinas calls the 'nudity of the face' – to shine through. Furthermore, far from embodying the final occlusion of Being, as Heidegger suggests, technology makes possible an emancipation from the mythical power of place. Technology, like Judaism, 'has demystified the universe. It has freed Nature from a spell' (Levinas 1990 [1961], p. 234).

Although some posmodernist writers have sought to use Levinas's work to develop a pluralist and multiculturalist ethics, it seems clear that all such efforts are doomed (Badiou 2000, pp. 18–23). Indeed, the growing influence of Levinas, in particular on the thought of Derrida, raises questions about the very possibility of an ethical turn *within* postmodernism. For, as the philosopher Martin Seel has argued, both Nietzsche and Heidegger elaborate what could be termed an 'ethics of play'. In other words, in their thinking, all criteria of normative rightness are subordinated to an openness to the 'world-play of Being' (Heidegger), or the sovereignty of a will which is itself caught up in the endless play of the will-to-power (Seel 1989). Hence both thinkers fail to articulate that universalism which is an essential feature of modern moral consciousness. If this is the price of 'postmodernism', then it is a price which increasingly came to appear unacceptable. Significantly, Derrida's work of the 1990s contains a new recognition of the legitimate claims of the universal. Indeed, in his book *Specters of Marx*, Derrida numbers himself amongst those who have 'ceaselessly proceeded in a hyper-critical fashion, I will dare to say in a deconstructive fashion, in the name of a new Enlightenment for the century to come. And without renouncing an ideal of democracy and emancipation, but rather by trying to think it and put it to work otherwise' (Derrida, 1994, p. 90). Derrida even calls for the formation of an 'new international' to combat the depredations of multi-national capitalism (cf. Derrida 1994, pp. 83–6).

Conclusion

These developments highlight one of the central paradoxes of postmodern social and political theory. As we have seen, there is a tendency for postmodernist thought to magnify its sense of the crisis of the modern world into adumbrations of an epochal transition. But, at the same time, the perspectivism, and even relativism, which are central to the epistemology of postmodernism, prohibit such comprehensive historical claims. To take the most obvious example, Lyotard's *The Postmodern Condition* seems to founder on a basic contradiction, since it tells the 'grand narrative' of the end of grand narratives. Indeed, one could argue that, in its eagerness to supersede modernism and modernity, postmodern thought often displays precisely that hyperbolic rejection of the past, that dynamic of future-oriented transcendence, which is central to modernity as such. In view of these basic inconsistencies, it is perhaps not surprising that the thinkers who have proved best able to appreciate the *symptomatic* status of postmodernist theory, as an expression of postmodern culture, have explained the rise of this culture in terms uncongenial to postmodernism, namely from within a broadly Marxist orientation.

The most prominent of such thinkers is the American critic Fredric Jameson. In a celebrated essay, first published in 1984, Jameson outlined a phenomenology of postmodern culture, characterised in terms of 'depthlessness', 'waning of affect', the displacement of any authentic sense of historical continuity by recycled images of an indeterminate, mythified past, and an accompanying sense of subjective dissociation akin to schizophrenia. These transformations in the quality of experience, Jameson suggested, were not indications of a transition to a postmodern *era*, but rather the correlates of the unprecedented commodification of social life achieved by contemporary global capitalism. In a society where no uncommercialised residue of nature or the psyche seems to remain, the fundamental contrasts between surface and interior, the authentic and the inauthentic, signifier and signified become eroded. Members of the advanced Western societies now live in an image-saturated world, governed by the vast circuits of multinational capital, which apparently lie beyond all control, and even beyond our powers of imagination and representation (Jameson 1991, pp. 1–54). In support of his analysis, Jameson invoked the work of the Marxist economist Ernest Mandel. But, as critics were swift to point out, the primary aim of Mandel's major treatise, *Late Capitalism* (Mandel 1975), was to theorise the long boom following the Second World War, and it could therefore not be used to substantiate Jameson's argument for a cultural rupture which first made itself felt during the 1970s.

A few years later, a more plausible economic periodisation was proposed by the geographer David Harvey, in his book *The Condition of Postmodernity*. Drawing on the French 'Regulation school' of political economy, Harvey correlated the rise of postmodernism with shift from a 'Fordist' to a 'post-Fordist' regime of accumulation. The Fordism which powered the prosperity of the immediate post-war decades had been based on high levels of employment for the white, male working class in mass-production industries, and on the corresponding spread of consumerist lifestyles. But in the 1970s, partly in response to the shock of the 1973–4 oil crisis, and to pressure from groups excluded from the benefits of these arrangements, a new 'post-Fordist' regime of accumulation began to emerge. Post-Fordism is characterised by the breakdown of larger economic units, the rise of flexible and part-time employment, complex outsourcing and sub-contracting arrangements, rampant international financial speculation, and an enhanced ability of multi-national firms to initiate global shifts of investment. Under such a regime, Harvey argued, the 'capacity for instantaneous response to changes in exchange rates, fashions and tastes, and moves by competitors is more essential to corporate survival than it ever was under Fordism' (Harvey 1989, p. 159). On his account, 'High modernist art, architecture, literature, etc. became establishment arts and practices in a society where a corporate capitalist version of the Enlightenment project of development for progress and human emancipation held sway as a political-economic dominant' (Harvey 1989, p. 35). By contrast, 'Flexible accumulation has been accompanied... by a much greater attention to quick-changing fashions and the mobilisation of all the artifices of need inducement and cultural transformation that this implies' (Harvey 1989, p. 156). These developments, summarised by Harvey in terms of a further intensifying round of the repeated 'time-space compression' which has defined the history of capitalism, have led to a world of increasing instability, disorientation and insecurity. It is these phenomena, he claims, which postmodernism as a cultural movement reflects.

Other Marxist commentators have contested both the accuracy of this socio-economic account and its explanatory value, presenting postmodernist theory rather as an expression of the political disillusionment of the post-'68 generation (Callinicos 1989). Yet it seems ungenerous to deny that postmodernism, as an intellectual movement, has functioned as a powerful and sensitive seismograph of social, cultural and political trends. At the same time, postmodernism's relativist bent has undoubtedly hampered its ability to contextualise and comprehend the historical developments with which it is entwined. Significantly, from the 1990s onwards, the star of postmodernism began to wane, and a new term rose to prominence in the domains of social and political theory, namely 'globalisation'. And it is striking that, in many cases, the very phenomena which were once cited as indicating our entry into 'postmodernity' (the compression and dislocation of time and space, a sense of the opacity of economic and social processes too vast and complex to be brought under control) began to be addressed under this new rubric. From the perspective of globalisation theory, the hybrid, disparate, commercialised character of postmodern *culture* can be seen as a direct effect of a historical process – the continuing expansion and consolidation of the capitalist world market – which, far from indicating an epochal transition, is still essentially modern. Of course, the new rhetoric of globalisation has brought its own style of hyperbole and simplification (Rosenberg 2000). But it does suggest what may turn out to be one enduring verdict on postmodernism. As a term employed to describe the exhaustion of the self-purifying – but also self-etiolating – dynamic of modernism in the arts, to evoke the rise of pastiche and parody, the mixing of disparate historical styles, and the increasing crossover of high and mass culture, the notion of postmodernism has an undoubted legitimacy. But, in its extension to social and political phenomena, the postmodernist outlook paid for its sensitivity to the local and the particular with a narrowing of scope, an almost wilfully self-induced cognitive constriction. The challenge for social, political and cultural thought in the twenty-first century will be to produce new modes of analysis which are both sufficiently flexible and wide-ranging, and sufficiently attuned to the dangers of a Eurocentric teleological bias, to make sense of what is now – undeniably, and sometimes traumatically – one single interconnected world.

17

Weber, Durkheim and the sociology of the modern state

ANTONINO PALUMBO AND ALAN SCOTT

Modern social theory offers three main models of the state: an instrumentalist, a realist and a pluralist. These models can be respectively represented by the names Karl Marx, Max Weber and Emile Durkheim. Of those three theorists, perhaps only Marx can claim to be a key originator of 'his' model of the state. In Weber's political sociology the influence of political realism stretching back at least as far as Machiavelli and Hobbes is quite transparent. Furthermore, while rejecting any form of socialism and what he took to be the economic reductionism of Marxist theory, Weber nevertheless sought to retain elements of a materialist methodology denuded of its original political aim. Finally, Weber's conception of power as an expression of will, and his view of both politics and society as increasingly rationalised (and 'disenchanted') and as sites of eternal struggle owe a great deal to his reading of Nietzsche. His achievement might be described as one of synthesising elements of realism, materialism and nihilism, and of translating these into the language of the modern social sciences. In Durkheim's political sociology the influence of both French and German political theory is no less evident. His view of the state as the deliberative organ of political societies and as the guardian of their *conscience collective* echoes Rousseau's general will, French socialist thought (in particular Saint-Simon's) and Comte's positivist approach to the study of society. Moreover, his emphasis upon the normative role of secondary associations (as both a source of identity and as a counter-balance to the growing power of the state) has precedence not only in Montesquieu and Tocqueville, but also in those German political theorists who tried to rescue elements of the '*Standestaat*' (polity of estates) for a modern pluralist society. Durkheim's objective was to use scientific method to show how the individual and the social, the value of freedom and the requirement of solidarity, might be reconciled.

Whereas Weber's influence is ubiquitous almost to the point of invisibility – it could be said that most political scientists speak Weber's language – Durkheim's contribution appears to be much more marginal and represents something of a dissenting tradition within twentieth-century political thought.[1] The initial impression is that the search for a specifically *sociological* approach to the state was the only common factor.[2] Furthermore, their political ideas are closely related to the two national political and intellectual contexts in which they worked, and the general methodology of social science and conception of society that they espoused (see Bellamy 1992 and Levine 1995). It is the general concept of the society–state relation and social-scientific method that will provide us with our entry point into the comparison. Our central contention is that Weber and Durkheim are both liberals, but not conventionally so. Neither accepts the core argument of economic liberalism that markets are self-generating and self-reproducing. At the same time, they rejected both the anti-modernism of backward-looking conservatives and the anti-capitalism of forward-looking revolutionary socialists. Both thinkers were engaged in giving active but critical support to the political regimes under which they lived and sought to ground their political prescriptions in sociological analysis. While this is the source of points of contact and agreement between them, their views concerning democracy, the state and the nation diverge significantly.

The state, capitalism and modernity

In one vital respect, Durkheim and Weber share a common account of modernity and one which makes their contributions distinctly sociological: they offer an account of the process that caused the emergence of modern market society which resists both the naturalism of classical political economists and Marx's historical materialism. Both theorists seek to identify a set of non-economic institutional and cultural preconditions for the emergence of money economies and market societies. Also, they highlight the importance of non-contractual elements in preventing the market from developing self-destructive dynamics and reducing the dehumanising side-effects of modernity itself.

1. See Lukes (1973), Gane (1984) and the editor's introduction to Giddens (1986) for attempts to point out the significance of Durkheim's political sociology. Cladis (1992) offers a detailed discussion, drawing parallels between Durkheim and contemporary liberal communitarianism.
2. This lack of apparent intellectual contact is also reflected in the fact that they worked in apparent ignorance of each other's contribution (see Tiryakian 1965). Tiryakian suspects that there must have been mutual knowledge despite the complete lack of reference in either to the work of the other.

For Durkheim and Weber, the emergence of capitalism in the West required an extraordinary combination of contingent factors: economic, cultural and political. Capitalism is not merely a mode of production, it is also a set of perceptions, beliefs and motivations: a 'form of life' quite distinct from any other in human history. Far from being in unison with human nature, as economists since Adam Smith have insisted, the forms of activity associated with capitalism have an almost 'unnatural' quality. Durkheim explicitly argues against utilitarian naturalist accounts in his first major work, *The Division of Labour in Society*, first published in 1893. For him, 'by nature we are not inclined to curb ourselves and exercise restraint' (Durkheim 1984, p. xxxiv). He claims that:

> if the division of labour produces solidarity, it is not only because it makes each individual an agent of exchange, to use the language of the economists. It is because it creates between men a whole system of rights and duties joining them in a lasting way to one another... If economists have believed that it would produce enough solidarity, however it came about, and in consequence have maintained that human societies could and should resolve themselves into purely economic associations, it is because they believed that only individual and temporary interests were at stake (Durkheim 1984, pp. 337–8).

Against the economic reductionism of classical political economy, Durkheim argues that the division of labour has a moral dimension that is more important than its technical one and that it is a *social fact*. He takes the division of labour out of Smith's pin factory and defines it more broadly as a constitutive element of modernity. What distinguishes modern from pre-modern societies is the distinct source of social solidarity which underpins them. Pre-modern societies are sustained by a strong '*conscience collective*' (sense of common belonging) grounded in similarity and in collective ritual ('every consciousness beats as one') (Durkheim 1984, p. 106). By contrast, modern societies are inherently pluralistic, with a corresponding weakening of the *conscience collective* and a correspondingly stronger sense of personal identity and social differences. Such societies are sustained by the interdependence of the persons and groups who constitute them and by a common respect for the rights of the person. Reversing Tönnies's categories, Durkheim labels the former 'mechanical solidarity' and the latter 'organic'. Using a biological metaphor, the division of functions and institutional specialisation in modern societies are likened to bodies with specialised but interdependent organs. The state is the brain: 'the social brain [the state], like a human brain, has grown in the course of evolution' (Durkheim 1957, p. 53). For

Durkheim the state is also the main historical agent that initiates the process of modernisation:

> We might say that in the State we have the prime mover. It is the State that has rescued the child from patriarchal domination and from family tyranny; it is the State that has freed the citizen from feudal groups and later from communal groups; it is the State that has liberated the craftsman and his master from guild tyranny (Durkheim 1957, p. 64).

Against the economic reductionism of Marx's historical materialism, Durkheim argues that 'just as it appears to us to be true that the causes of social phenomena must be sought outside the representations of the individual, so it seems false to us that they can in the last resort be ascribed to the state of industrial technology or that the economic factor is the mainspring of progress' (Durkheim 1897, p. 134). Thus he stresses the influence of religion as well as the state in initiating and directing social and economic phenomena: 'it is from religion that have emerged, through successive transformations, all the other manifestations of collective activity – law, morality, art, science, political forms, etc. In the beginning everything was religious' (Durkheim 1897, p. 135).

Weber's account of the process that brought about modernity and a capitalist market society is strikingly similar to Durkheim's. Like Durkheim, Weber views the working of the market economy as quite 'unnatural':

> The old economic order asks: How can I give, on this piece of land, work and sustenance to the greatest possible number of men? Capitalism asks: From this given piece of land how can I produce as many crops as possible for the market with as few men as possible? (Weber 1948, p. 367).

Also, unlike in the 'old economy', we do not stop working when we have satisfied our basic needs or even when we have acquired sufficient wealth to live in luxury. Work has ceased to be a means to an end and has become an end in itself. Weber's explanation for this remarkable change is his famous Protestant ethic thesis. Early Protestantism, and especially Calvinism with its doctrine of salvation via election, induced anxieties which led to the search for 'outward signs of inward grace' through the adoption of a 'this-worldly asceticism' which, in contrast to the 'other-worldly asceticism' of the monasteries, allowed, indeed encouraged, the acquisition but not the garish display of personal wealth. The central concept in Weber's search for an 'elective affinity' (a term he uses to avoid implying a straightforward causal connection) between the Protestant ethic and the 'spirit of capitalism' is that of a 'calling' or 'vocation' (*Beruf*) which, as we shall see later, is also key to understanding his view of modern politics: 'What God demands is not labour in itself, but rational labour in a calling' (Weber 1930 [1904–5], pp. 161–2). *Beruf* becomes detached from its religious origins and connotations and becomes attached to worldly economic activities such as the accumulation of wealth through entrepreneurial activity or the pursuit of a career. The kinds of external 'rational discipline' (Weber 1948, ch. X, p. 1) previously associated with near-total institutions such as religious orders or armies (with the 'cloister communism' of bachelor households, i.e. monasteries and barracks) become internalised as part of the personality of the modern subject. The failure of modern rational forms of capitalist activity to emerge in, for example, Russia or particularly China (where the technical conditions appeared even more favourable than in Europe), illustrates for Weber the path-dependent nature of tradition where it is not disrupted by contingent cultural transformations.

This emphasis upon the cultural revolution necessary for the emergence of modern capitalism is not as far removed from Weber's theory of the formation of the modern state as it may appear to be. Both capitalism and modern 'legal-rational' authority rest upon instrumental rationality ('*Zweckrationalität*'), calculability and, for the state above all, proceduralism. 'The modern state "speaks the law" in almost all aspects of its functioning' and rational (unlike cadi) law is mechanical and predictable in it workings (Poggi 1990, p. 29). 'Traditional legitimisation' is too rigid, whereas 'charismatic legitimation' is too arbitrary, to be compatible with rational capitalism, which requires stability and predictability of outcome. Only 'legal-rational' authority meets this requirement:

> The main inner foundation of the modern capitalist business is *calculation*. In order to exist, it requires a system of justice and administration which, in principle at any rate, function in a *rationally calculable* manner according to stable general norms, just as one calculates the predictable performance of a *machine* (Weber 1918a, pp. 147–8).

Like Durkheim, Weber insists, against Marx and liberal economists alike, that the state cannot be reduced to the requirements of capitalism (see Poggi 1990, pp. 95–7). Its institutional autonomy rests upon its monopoly of the means of legitimate coercion within its territory (Weber 1922, part I, ch. I, sec. 17). Economic and political activities are thus described as two distinct spheres of human activities that have followed a parallel and complementary course:

> The development of the modern state is set in motion everywhere by a decision of the prince to dispossess the independent 'private' bearers of administrative power who existed alongside him... The whole process is a complete parallel to the development of the capitalist enterprise [*Betrieb*] through the gradual expropriation of independent producers (Weber 1919a, p. 315).

In sum, in their closely interdependent cultural and political sociologies Durkheim and Weber seek to show, against individualists or utilitarians such as Bentham, Mill and Spencer, that capitalist modernity is not a spontaneous by-product of rationally self-interested individuals pursuing their own interests in their own ways. First, these rational individuals are themselves the product of a historically contingent cultural revolution. Second, there are supplementary institutional (political and administrative) structures that have to be in place in order for modern rational capitalism to work.

The state and civil society

Weber and Durkheim not only represent two versions of a possible sociological critique of economic explanations, whether utilitarian or Marxist, of the rise of the modern state and market, they also display remarkably similar attitudes towards the critique of modernity and the market economy put forward by socialists and conservatives.

According to Durkheim, modernity is not simply the emancipation of the individual from the constraints of the *ancien régime*, but a destructive force that could expose the individual to the loss of identity and lead society into anarchy. Thus he breaks with the celebratory attitude of nineteenth-century economic liberalism and assumes a more pessimistic perspective: 'unless one relies a great deal upon Providence, as Bastiat [and, we can add, Smith] did, it seems difficult to him [Fouillée] for there miraculously to emerge a harmony of interests from the spontaneous interplay of individual egoisms' (Durkheim 1885, p. 92). In this sense Durkheim acknowledges the arguments put forward by Marxists and traditionalists who pointed out, on the one hand, the negative effects of the market economy in terms of commodification of social relations and, on the other hand, the perverse influence of an individualist and secularist culture on society. Modernity's chief pathology is labelled 'anomie', a term employed to indicate 'a form of deprivation, of a loss of membership in those social institutions and modes in which norms, including the norms of tradition-constituted rationality, are embodied' (MacIntyre 1988, p. 368).

Echoing Marx, Durkheim notes that the worker is 'no more than a lifeless cog, which an external force sets in motion and impels always in the same direction and in the same fashion' (Durkheim 1984, pp. 306–7). Like the traditionalists, he recognises the anarchic tendencies implicit in modernity: 'Over a very short space of time very profound changes have occurred in the structure of our societies . . . Thus the morality corresponding to [the segmentary] type of society has lost influence, but without its successor developing quickly enough to occupy the space left vacant in our consciousness' (Durkheim 1984, p. 339). However, Durkheim rejects both diagnoses and prescriptions of revolutionary socialists and reactionary Catholics alike and continuously stresses the practical and theoretical faults of those two opposing perspectives. Thus, against the traditionalists, he argues that: 'The remedy for the ill is nevertheless not to seek to revive traditions and practices that no longer correspond to present-day social conditions, and that could only subsist in a life that would be artificial, one only of appearance' (Durkheim 1984, p. 340). Similarly, he rejects the revolutionary solutions advocated by Marxists and syndicalists. First, revolutionary action would not lead to the emancipation of mankind because it rests on false essentialist notions of human nature: 'Man is the product of history and hence a "becoming"; there is nothing in him that is either given or defined in advance. History begins nowhere and it ends nowhere' (Durkheim 1960, p. 429). Second, the history of France demonstrates that revolutions cause counter-reactions and social instability and can even strengthen reactionary forces. Finally, in a Weberian fashion, the socialist goal to abolish private property merely turns society 'into an army of civil servants on more or less fixed salary' (Durkheim 1885, p. 88).

However, unlike Weber who displays distaste for socialism in any form, the intention behind Durkheim's critique was to rescue what was valuable in socialism from Marxism. Given that class conflict (the 'forced division of labour') was for Durkheim one of the key pathologies of modernity, he was not prepared to endorse a political ideology that called for its intensification. Instead he wanted to retain elements of socialism in its reformist and more pluralist mode. As he explains in his sympathetic review of Merlino's *Formes et essence du socialisme*:

> It would be a considerable step forward . . . if socialism finally abandoned confusing the social question with that of the workers. The first includes the other, but extends beyond it . . . It is not a question of merely reducing the share of one group so as to increase that of another, but one of refashioning the moral constitution of

society . . . Here also we should doubtless praise his [Merlino's] justifiable mistrust of unilateral solutions. It is absolutely certain that in the future societies, of whatever kind they may be, will not be based upon one single principle . . . however future society is organised, it will include, in a state of coexistence, the most varied types of economic management. There will be room for all kinds (Durkheim 1897, pp. 141–3).

Weber's account of modernity as a combined process of rationalisation and the decline of magical beliefs (*Entzauberung*) shares many of Durkheim's worries and goals. Several scholars have pointed out the influence Nietzsche had on Weber's interpretation of modernity (see Hennis 2000 and Owen 1994). Indeed, Weber's characterisation of modernity as a process of progressive rationalisation is inherently dualistic and circular. On the one hand, rationalisation and bureaucratisation represent the means by which modern princes emancipated themselves from the barons by transferring to the state the monopoly of legitimate physical force. On the other hand, the same process fostered the separation of the state from the church, severing the chains linking the individual to local communities and estates. In the process the 'ethic of conviction' and the 'ethic of responsibility' became separated and 'legality' became the prevalent form of legitimation.

Here the similarities with Durkheim are substantial and not coincidental, as each was influenced by both Simmel's sociology of social forms and Nietzsche's philosophical obituary for God.[3] Weber shares Durkheim's rejection of revolutionary socialism. While Durkheim argued that the abolition of private property would not alter the 'problems around us' (Durkheim 1957, p. 30), Weber went further to argue that it would merely exacerbate those problems by restoring a key feature of pre-capitalist societies, namely the coincidence of economic and political power where 'the master was not a simple employer, but rather a political autocrat who personally dominated the labourer' (Weber 1989, p. 165). In a lecture on socialism, Weber (1918b) argues, based on a close observation of Russian politics from the attempted revolution of 1905 onwards, that where the state is both employer and political 'master' the worker is no better, indeed worse, off than under capitalism, and that the state will merely displace the employer as the focus of class conflict. However, Weber and Durkheim drew quite different lessons from their common rejection of Marxism. Weber extends his critique of Marxism to include all 'socialist' measures, however moderate. All such measures will

3. Nietzsche's influence on Durkheim was as pervasive as it was on Weber. Durkheim discusses Nietzsche's philosophy at length in his lectures on pragmatism (Durkheim 1960).

merely reinforce modern society's tendency towards bureaucratisation – towards a new enslavement. His version of the modernity story is one of the cunning of reason. The Protestant Reformation in the name of God brought about increasing secularisation and in the name of individualism created new relations of domination and obedience based upon the exact rational calculation of means and ends which left Weber asking 'how is it at all possible to salvage any remnant of "individual" freedom of movement in any sense, given this all-powerful trend towards bureaucratisation?' (Weber 1918a, p. 159). Accordingly, he viewed all forms of state regulation with deep suspicion and developed a critique of Bismarck's welfare measures which appears similar to what we would now call 'neo-liberal'. Unlike the latter, however, he perceived political action as crucial in countervailing both the monopolistic drives of global capitalism and the bureaucratisation of modern society.

If the recognition of the self-destructive and dehumanising nature of modernity did not lead Weber to accept the arguments of the socialists, neither did it lead him to embrace the anti-modernist arguments of reactionaries. Weber is highly critical of those conservative *littérateurs* who argued for the retention of pre-modern economic and political forms (the communal economy and the polity of estates, respectively). He came to view this form of German conservative nationalism as merely 'the *parasitic ideals* of a stratum of prebendaries and *rentiers*' (Weber 1917, p. 84), which displayed a 'profound ignorance of the nature of capitalism' (Weber 1917, p. 89). In modern capitalism the pursuit of gain through rationally disciplined labour is grounded in an ethic of responsible professionalism and as such receives Weber's full support. Underlying this analysis lies a different interpretation of capitalism from that offered by Durkheim, for whom markets are essentially 'amoral' and thus in need of normative supplement if they are not to disrupt social reactions and undermine the basis of trust upon which they themselves ultimately rest. For Weber, by contrast, modern economic activity has its own internal ethic which leads him to reject in the strongest terms anything which looks like a proposal to return to pre-capitalist community-based economic relations grounded in solidarity and reciprocity: 'anyone still unaware of the difference between these things [e.g. guilds, clans, etc. and modern single-purpose associations] should learn his sociological ABC before troubling the book-market with the products of his vanity' (Weber 1917, p. 91). As Scott notes, 'this crass dismissal was not, but might well have been, aimed directly at Durkheim' (Scott 2000,

p. 37), were it not for the fact that Durkheim too characterises just such Romantic traditionalism as a mere 'mystic solution' to the problems created by rational capitalism (Durkheim 1957, p. 54). However, Durkheim's rejection of such mysticism leads him to endorse a constructivist ethical project for promoting organic solidarity, rather than the radically modernising constitutional prescriptions that can be found in Weber's later political writings.

The multi-faceted analyses of modernity supplied by Durkheim and Weber contrast with the simplistic understanding of the relation between the state and civil society found in liberalism; that is, a relation resting on an inherent trade-off. For Durkheim the state remains the main actor that preserves individual freedom by regulating the potential conflict between the individual and the group and the various secondary associations composing political society. Weber is sceptical about the regulative power of the state and its neutral role in assessing the conflicting claims of the individual vis-à-vis the group and the group vis-à-vis the state itself. However, his picture of modern society as the locus of an on-going struggle for power (both economic and political) between individuals, classes and states is incompatible with the liberal portrait of civil society as a self-sustaining moral order. Civil society in Weber's view is not coincident with Hayek's catallaxy (i.e. a system of exchanges capable of transforming an 'enemy' into a 'friend' and thus a state of nature into a market *order*), but retains a problematic Hobbesian character where a pre-emptive strike assures personal and national success. From this perspective, both Durkheim and Weber renounce the anti-political claims of classical and neo-liberals and subscribe to a pluralist vision of the economic, social and moral spheres and of the relations between them.

The state and democracy

In discussing how to avoid the negative predicament of modernity, however, Durkheim's and Weber's positions diverge significantly. Like Weber, Durkheim's political theory is closely linked to a cultural sociology. In both cases markets, unsupplemented, do not have self-generating capacities. But in Durkheim's case, much more than in Weber's, informal norms are thought to play as vital a role as political regulation. Thus Weber defines the state in terms of the *material basis* of its power (its increasing monopoly over legitimate violence), while Durkheim defines it in terms of its *regulative function*.[4]

According to Durkheim, as society becomes more complex and differentiated, so the need for coordination of the whole by a higher organ becomes more intense. The word 'state' here is short for the set of institutions regulating a political society: 'We apply the term "state" more especially to the agents of the sovereign authority, and "political society" to the complex group of which the state is the highest organ' (Durkheim 1957, p. 48). A political society is such when it is composed of many groups: 'political societies are of necessity polycellular or polysegmental' (Durkheim 1957, p. 47). The state is autonomous from society because the latter is polycellular, but it is not in opposition to the associations (or secondary groups) composing political society. In brief, Durkheim's is a pluralistic theory of the state. The state's task is to address the central dangers implicit in modern society: failure to replace pre-modern with modern norms ('anomie') and class conflict (the 'forced division of labour'): 'there exists today a whole range of collective activity [i.e. economic activity] outside the sphere of morals and which is almost entirely removed from the moderating effect of obligations' (Durkheim 1957, p. 10). Under these conditions destructive forms of normless egotism are encouraged. It is the state which calls the individual 'to a moral way of life' (Durkheim 1957, p. 69). The state, Durkheim writes, is 'a special organ whose responsibility it is to work out certain representations which hold good for the collectivity' (Durkheim 1957, p. 50), and he adds: 'the whole life of the State, in its true meaning, consists not in exterior action, in making changes, but in deliberation, that is in representations' (Durkheim 1957, p. 51).

Those remarks have often been taken as an indication of the inherent totalitarian character of Durkheim's political thought: a totalitarianism which reaches back to Rousseau's essentialist conception of the general will and Hegel's organic view of the state as an ethical entity. In our view, nothing could be more mistaken. In fact, he labels those conceptions 'mystic solutions' that 'try to revive the cult of the City State in a new guise' (Durkheim 1957, p. 54). Durkheim's main goal is to strike a balance between those rights-based liberal positions that make the state a residue of society and those Romantic theories that collapse society into the state.

4. It is the centrality of norms in Durkheim's thought which has led David Lockwood (1992), rightly, to characterise him as a 'normative functionalist' in contrast to later systems-theory functionalists such as Parsons and Luhmann who provide a sociological variant of the spontaneous order argument rather than a critique of it.

Against the former, he argues that 'the state was not created to prevent the individual from being disturbed in the exercise of his natural right . . . rather, it is the state that creates and organises and makes a reality of these rights' (Durkheim 1957, p. 60). Concerning the latter, Durkheim explains:

> The State, in our large-scale societies, is so removed from individual interests that it cannot take into account the special or local and other conditions in which they exist. Therefore when it does attempt to regulate them, it succeeds only at the cost of doing violence to them and distorting them . . . The inference to be drawn from this comment, however, is simply that if that collective force, the State, is to be the liberator of the individual, it has itself need of some counter-balance; it must be restrained by other collective forces, that is . . . secondary groups . . . Their usefulness is not merely to regulate and govern the interests they are meant to serve. They have a wider purpose; they form one of the conditions essential to the emancipation of the individual (Durkheim 1957, p. 63).

What Durkheim is espousing here is a pluralist theory of the state that advocates a division of powers by means of *social* checks and balances on the authority of the state.

For Weber, by contrast, modern societies are essentially large-scale mass societies and the state form necessarily reflects that fact. In mass societies political rule (*Herrschaft*) 'necessarily and inevitably lies in the hands of *officialdom*' (Weber 1918a, p. 145) and is exercised via the routine management of everyday administration. Put bluntly (and Weber was no stranger to bluntness) political society for Weber consists essentially of rulers and ruled. He thus addresses questions of political representation and democracy as though they were technical questions of institutional design: how to design institutions which enable political leaders to counter-balance the ever-increasing power of technical administration while tying the masses into those decision-making processes without submitting to the essentially irrational and negative nature of mass politics. This leads Weber to think about the nature of modern democracy in narrower terms of (I) the proper personality and orientation of political leaders and (II) the design of institutions that facilitate both effective leadership and political legitimation. In his view:

> The demos, in the sense of an undifferentiated mass, never 'governs' larger associations. Rather it is governed and changes only the manner of the selection of executive leaders and the extent to which the demos, or better social circles within its midst, is able, via so-called 'public opinion', to influence the content and direction of administrative activity (Weber 1922, p. 568).

This position was modified somewhat towards the end of the First World War and in its aftermath when Weber argued with increasing forcefulness that modern representative democracy is the only potentially effective technical instrument for assuring political leadership and mass legitimation. Thus his most famous political essay, 'The Profession and Vocation of Politics' (Weber 1919a), focuses on the ethical stance and personality structure appropriate to those who 'live for' rather than 'live off' politics. The appropriate ethic is one of responsibility, but one moderated by conviction. The true politician should possess '*Leidenschaft mit Augenmaß*' (passion with a sense of perspective). Many of his other late political writings address questions of institutional design, including the technical constitutional questions which occupied Weber at the time due to his ambition to influence the new constitution of post-First World War Germany (see, especially, Weber 1918a). In these writings it is apparent that Weber believes that pure legal-rational authority and legitimation are insufficient either to counter the power of bureaucracy or to ensure mass support for the political system. The trick is to design institutions which institutionalise the negative politics of the masses and an element of charismatic authority, without giving way to irrationality in either case. Mass democracies, particularly of a plebiscitary nature (Weber 1919b), can both give political leadership the mass support it requires in order to counter the power of administration and offer the masses the opportunity to acclaim or reject that leadership at regular intervals. The rational and the irrational can be held in balance.

The technical nature of Weber's proposals, their concentration on leadership and the essentially elitist nature of the model of political society that underlies them would be anathema to Durkheim. In the first place, Durkheim thinks of charismatic legitimation as a mode of the past, doomed to aggravate social instability by piling sectarian divides (e.g. cults of personality) on top of class conflict. Second, he maintains that external solutions need to be supplemented by institutional devices that promote internalisation within the individual conscience, i.e. to educate individuals such that they are able to grasp the significance of interests beyond the narrow horizons of their own selfish concerns. The moral education advocated by Durkheim is by no means the Foucauldian regimented discipline of the market or the factory:

> We must never lose sight of what is the goal of public education. It is not a matter of training workers for the factory or clerks for the warehouse, but citizens for society. The teaching must therefore consist essentially of moral instruction . . . But

it is neither by the rule of three nor by Archimedes' principle that one will ever inculcate morality to the masses. Only aesthetic culture can act in so profound a fashion upon the human spirit... However, this purely literary education plainly cannot suffice. In addition the future citizen must be equipped with exact notions of politics and economics (Durkheim 1885, pp. 90–1).

This is in marked contrast to Weber's view that technical rather than humanist education was the chief function of the modern university (see Weber 1919a and Ringer forthcoming, ch. 1).

Even more distant from Weber's solution is the second of Durkheim's proposals: the creation of secondary associations, seen as a source of potential moral solidarity ('a moral environment' for their members) (Durkheim 1984, p. xli) *and* as key intermediaries between the individual and the state. Weber views secondary associations largely as self-seeking '*Zweckverbände*' (purposive associations) which pursue monopolistic strategies in order in improve their members' 'market situation', distorting the market in the process. Weber, following Simmel, also argues that modernity means a further differentiation of identities with individuals enjoying a growing multiplicity of affiliations of which occupational standing is only one. For these reasons he does not share Durkheim's optimistic vision of modernised guilds replacing family loyalty and local identity as these decline. Durkheim is at great pains, however, to stress that the guilds can only perform this function if they themselves modernise and develop an internally democratic structure. Behind this vision lies a notion akin to subsidiarity (originally a term in natural law): decisions should be made at the lowest possible level so as to maximise participation and decentralisation, but at a sufficiently high level to prevent self-interest from dictating outcomes. A balance is to be struck such that decisions are left neither to group egoism nor to aloof mandarins.

Weber's and Durkheim's contrasting attitudes towards the protective function of the state against the effects of markets represent a final point of disagreement. Whereas Durkheim argues for a proactive state role in the protection of workers, Weber's rejection of modern welfare policies, which he views essentially as a modern form of patrimony, is as unambiguous as it is dramatic:

This housing, so praised by our naïve littérateurs, will be augmented by the shackles chaining each individual to his firm (the beginnings of this are to be found in so-called 'welfare arrangements'), to his class (by an increasingly rigid structure of ownership) and perhaps at some time in the future to his occupation (by state provision of needs on a 'liturgical' principle, whereby associations structured along occupational lines carry a burden of state responsibilities) (Weber 1918a, p. 159).

In sum, whereas Weber sought a solution in institutional design changes that could promote charismatic leadership as the only means to bridle the masses, reverse bureaucratic sclerosis and rejuvenate the German state, Durkheim stressed the need to educate the masses through their active involvement in secondary institutions, to foster deliberative forms of democracy that recognise and protect the rights of the person and to deploy the powers of the state to ameliorate the damage wrought by unrestrained market capitalism. The differences between Weber and Durkheim are here at their sharpest.

The state and the nation

Those two distinct perspectives are reflected in the role and aim the two authors attribute to the nation. A standard reading of the political thought of Weber and Durkheim presents the latter as a human-rights theorist who justified the French Third Republic on objective moral grounds and the former as a *Machtstaat* theorist committed to German world power. In this section we argue that such a standard reading is too simplistic and we employ the categories of 'inwardness' and 'outwardness' to arrive at a better account of Weber's and Durkheim's views of the nation and patriotism.

Weber distinguishes between ethical activity guided by 'two fundamentally different, irreconcilably opposed maxims. It can follow the "ethic of conviction" or the "ethic of responsibility"' (Weber 1919a, p. 359). This distinction seems to advocate a Machiavellian separation between means and ends, between the feasible and the desirable. According to this reading, statesmen ought to follow standards which are incompatible with those arrived at by moral philosophers:

> Anyone wishing to establish absolute justice on earth by *force* needs a following in order to do so, a human 'apparatus.' He must promise these people the necessary inner and outward prizes . . . because the apparatus will not function otherwise . . . The outward rewards are adventure, victory, booty, power and prebends. The success of the leader is entirely dependent on the functioning of his apparatus. He is therefore dependent on *its* motives, not his own (Weber 1919a, pp. 364–5).

This call to the reality of power struggle is not, however, a licence to seek power by any means. Weber maintains that only those who perceive politics as a calling have the quality to become great leaders. The question is, what sort of principles ought those with a vocation for politics follow? Weber advances two seemingly inconsistent answers: first he maintains that there are no absolute values which can be objectively justified and that the choice between ends is merely subjective; second, he justifies nationalism as the paramount value and advocates a strong *Machtstaat* politics for Germany. David Beetham explains this seeming inconsistency as follows: 'for Weber it was the choice between an inward- and an outward-looking society, between a narrow preoccupation with the nation's internal affairs and the development of a wider consciousness through the pursuit of "world-political tasks"' (Beetham 1974, p. 143). This distinction between inwardness and outwardness gives us a clue to the differences between Weber's and Durkheim's nationalism.

Weber's nationalist beliefs are spelled out in his Freiburg inaugural lecture (Weber 1895). Here he offers two main reasons to support the absolute priority ascribed to the national interest vis-à-vis other competing values. The first and most general pertains to the Hobbesian logic underlying international relations: 'the economic struggle [*Kampf*] between the nationalities runs its course even under the semblance of "peace" ... In the economic struggle for life ... there is no peace to be had. Only if one takes the semblance of peace for its reality can one believe that the future holds peace and a happy life for our descendants' (Weber 1895, p. 14). As in Hobbes, in this context the only rational strategy is pre-emptive action and any internal strife that prevents the unity and readiness of the body politic for either self-interested concerns or spurious appeals to ultimate moral values must be put to an end. The second reason is more idealistic and controversial. Weber saw *fin-de-siècle* Germany threatened by the invasion of 'starving Slavs' and as the last champion of Western civilisation against Russia. Hence, he maintains that 'the German race should be protected in the east of the country, and that the state's economic policies ought to rise to the challenge of defending it' (Weber 1895, p. 13). Moreover, he claims that only an unqualified commitment to Germany in the struggle for economic markets and political hegemony could engender 'those characteristics which we think of as constituting the human greatness and nobility of our nature' (Weber 1895, p. 15). Weber makes clear that the national interest is the overriding value to which personal and class interests must surrender: 'From the standpoint of the nation, large-scale enterprises which can only be preserved at the expense of the German race deserve to go down to destruction' (Weber 1895, p. 12).

For Beetham, 'Weber's commitment to the nation [is] based on a more universal premise than simply allegiance to the specific value of *German* culture'. In his view, 'it was as a vehicle for, and embodiment of, "*Kultur*" ... that the nation had supreme value for Weber' (Beetham 1974, p. 127). In addition, he notes that for Weber the nation was a 'community of sentiments', the 'source of solidarity' rooted in objective facts and 'the only form of status superiority available to the masses at large' (Beetham 1974, p. 122). Similarly, other authors have pointed out that Weber's case for Germany's world power is related to the maintenance of an open and pluralist international system to promote interstate competition and its attendant beneficial effects (Bellamy 1992, pp. 178–9). Indeed, Weber's distinction between nation and state stresses the cultural element of the nation in opposition to sheer power politics. The nation represents a community (*Gemeinschaft*) of feelings and solidarity and it is to the preservation of this community that the state (as a *Gesellschaft*) owes its existence and *raison d'être*. Furthermore, throughout his work Weber shows a strong faith in the creative power of Nietzschean struggles for existence and affirmation of the self. Thus, for Weber patriotism is at one and the same time a way of preserving valuable cultural elements, of creating a cultural identity, of feeding into the masses a sense of embeddedness and of maintaining a pluralist and dynamic international setting.

This position is modified in light of the First World War (see Ringer forthcoming, ch. 2). From having been a pan-Germanist, during the war he actively opposes the expansionist plans of the military establishment. Moreover, in light of Germany's defeat, Weber argues against conservative nationalists and for the Westernisation of German politics, economy and culture. This emerging political position is reflected at the theoretical level by Weber's increasingly constructivist analysis of the nation and of national identity, and by his growing opposition to racism and pseudo-scientific racial theories (see Weber's response to A. Ploetz 1910, discussed in Peukert 1989). Nevertheless, the greatness of the nation remains the ultimate value. Even in the late political essays we do not find Weber taking the kind of cosmopolitan turn recommended by Durkheim. Instead he substitutes economic for political means as a way of creating a nation that is vigorous (*tüchtig*), happy (*glücklich*) and valuable (*wertvoll*) (Weber 1918a, p. 134). Likewise, modern constitutions with their guarantees of human rights, freedom of speech and so on remain largely a means to the modernising end rather than values in themselves.

On this point the contrast with Durkheim is instructive. Durkheim claims patriotism needs to be justified on moral grounds. The moral theory subscribed to by Durkheim is what we would now identify as 'constructivist': an approach that, while denying the existence of ultimate and absolute values, asserts the need to establish common moral principles. For Durkheim, modern capitalist nations with an extended division of labour ought to develop elements of organic solidarity that recognise the 'cult of the person' as the main suitable substitute for religion in secular society. In the 1898 essay 'Individualism and the Intellectuals' written as a response to the Dreyfus affair and in support of the Dreyfusards, Durkheim identifies moral individualism as the suitable substitute for religion as the source of solidarity within a modern secular society. While he recognised that elements of mechanical solidarity are still displayed by modern nations in collective national rituals ('civic religion'), patriotism finds its ultimate legitimation not in national chauvinism but in the degree to which universal rights celebrating the cult of the person are embedded in the nation and in its constitution. The heritage of the French Revolution means, for Durkheim, that the moral unity of modern France is rooted in the principles upheld by the revolution and enshrined in the Declaration of the Rights of Man and the Citizen. Thus he advocates a 'constitutional patriotism' that views individual autonomy as an overriding moral goal on the grounds that such a value is rooted in shared collective representations underpinning the moral constitution of the nation. This justification departs from traditional natural rights arguments for reasons very like those employed by Weber himself: 'those who believe in [the] theory of natural rights think they can make a final distinction between what is and what is not a right. However, a closer study will show that in reality the dividing line they think they can draw is certainly not definite and depends entirely on the state of public opinion' (Durkheim 1957, p. 67). However, Durkheim does not share Weber's radical subjectivism or his elitism. Only a democratic, inward-looking constitutional patriotism could supply the moral basis for the development of organic solidarity in modern society compatible with the preservation of the *conscience collective* of the French nation.

Durkheim's notion of inwardness first appears in his lectures on professional ethics and civic morals:

> there is an inward activity that is neither economic nor commercial and this is moral activity. Those forces that turn from the outward to the inward are not simply used to produce as much as possible and add to creature comfort, but to organise and raise the moral level of society, to uphold this moral structure and to see that it goes on developing (Durkheim 1957, p. 71).

Inwardness has nothing to do with the materialistic concerns that worried traditional nationalists and the Weber of the Freiburg lecture. On the contrary, it is a concern with the inner morality of a nation and with the latter's ability to arouse the support of its citizens and promote a healthy social milieu. Against Weber's realist arguments (which also inspired French nationalists), Durkheim points out that chauvinism is neither the only nor the best way to build national identities. First, he claims that: 'as long as there are States, so there will be national pride, and nothing can be more warranted. But societies can have their pride, not in being the greatest or the wealthiest, but in being the most just, the best organised and in possessing the best moral constitution' (Durkheim 1957, p. 75). Second, he maintains that those allegedly realist arguments actually rest on highly controversial psychological assumptions concerning the ability of outward-looking policies to develop a sense of embeddedness into the masses. For Durkheim, without secondary associations that can mediate between the state and the individual and turn the masses into responsible citizens, outward-looking patriotic policies will simply reinforce the anomic tendencies existing in large-scale nation states and exacerbate the distributive conflicts between classes and interest groups.

The opposition between outward-looking and inward-looking patriotism is further elaborated in the wartime pamphlets (e.g. Durkheim 1915). Here Durkheim discusses the unintended effects of German aggressive nationalism in perpetuating the Hobbesian condition of international relations and in promoting the First World War. According to Durkheim the war is a reflection of the German mentality: a mentality expressed in the work of the pan-German writer and teacher of Weber, Heinrich von Treitschke. Durkheim reduces this mentality to a set of propositions that establish the basic principle that state sovereignty is absolute: (I) the state is above international law; (II) the state is above morality (its ends justify any means); (III) the state as the realm of unity is above and opposed to civil society (the realm of plurality and difference). Durkheim is careful not to imply that all Germans privately believed this; rather it is a public ideology the original aim of which was to foster the process of unification pursued by Bismarck. He notes that it is this public ideology which has generated a permanent policy of confrontation ever since, and caused the response in kind from the other European nations that led to the outbreak of the war. From this perspective, Weber's post-war disillusion with the German industrialists, the military establishment and the Kaiser for the way in which they handled German diplomacy and the war justifies Durkheim's analysis of the self-defeating logic of outward-looking nationalism and of its inability to be a vehicle for, and embodiment of, '*Kultur*'. Moreover, Weber's increasing scepticism about the creative power of economic and political struggle endorses Durkheim's critical views on the ability of unbounded competition (either at the national or at the international level) to stimulate beneficial processes of change.

In sum, Weber considers outward-looking policies as the best way to preserve Germany's national culture and strengthen the national character of the German people. Durkheim espouses an inward-looking perspective which views true nationalism as based upon the values and principles underpinning the moral constitution of the nation and supporting the Rights of Man. While the former continues and extends the realist approach to nation-building, state affairs and international relations, the latter anticipates current deliberative models of citizenship, democracy and constitutional patriotism (cf. Habermas 1996).

The sociology of the modern state after Weber and Durkheim

As we indicated at the outset, Weber's influence on subsequent debate has been considerably greater than that of Durkheim. Modern political science and political sociology have both been shaped, almost subliminally, by the ambiguous heritage of Weber's texts and problems. But in this process that heritage has been interpreted and adapted in ways that do not always represent an improvement on the original. First, prominence has often been given to Weber's economic analysis (so as to make it akin to that of classical political economy) rather than to his historical and multi-causal account of modernity. This has encouraged a tendency to explain political phenomena in terms of economic decision-making, thereby ignoring Weber's own more subtle analysis of the nature of social action. Second, later thinkers, particularly those sociologists who have appropriated Weber via Talcott Parsons, have tended to focus more on his formal apparatus than on his historical and comparative methodology.

Weber's influence on political science has strengthened both the realist approach to politics, with its emphasis upon struggle and its analogy between political and economic competition, and the concern with institutions and institutional design that informed Weber's later political writings in particular. The key link between Weber and modern political science is the competitive elite theory of Joseph Schumpeter, whose view of modern democracy as 'that institutional arrangement for arriving at political decisions in which individuals acquire the power to decide by means of competitive struggle for the people's vote' (Schumpeter 1943, p. 269) extends Weber's arguments in the direction of an economic decision-making model. This economistic view of politics was later formalised by Anthony Downs (1957) and is now the core of rational and public choice theories. However, this development stands in a no less problematic relationship to Weber's perspective than does, say, Carl Schmitt's decisionism (Schmitt 1928), which has also occasionally been interpreted as a natural development of Weber's political analysis (e.g. Habermas 1971). While the latter overlooks the seriousness with which Weber took the institutions of formal democracy, the former overlooks Weber's insistence that economic action is merely a special form of *social* action. The economism and formalism which have recently influenced political science are, from a Weberian perspective, one-sided. However, the fact that his analysis of modernity as a process of rationalisation and political inclusion *can* be developed in the direction of a formal decision-making model perhaps suggests that Weber did not break sharply enough with an economic perspective.

In the work of those political sociologists who have been sensitive to the comparative and historical nature of Weber's work, his influence has led to the study of long-term processes of state formation understood as the concentration of the means of coercion on the one hand, and the increasingly procedural ('legal-rational') nature of the legitimation of political power on the other. This research programme has involved sociologists who, like Reinhard Bendix (1977), Ernest Gellner (1983), Anthony Giddens (1985), Michael Mann (1993) and Gianfranco Poggi (1990), share Weber's general outlook, as well as authors more influenced by Marx – e.g. Perry Anderson (1974), Barrington Moore Jr. (1969), Charles Tilly (1992) and Theda Skocpol (1979). For both groups, formal political inclusion (as opposed to Durkheim's moral integration) has come to represent the hallmark of the modern state and the criterion for assessing its future development. The ubiquitous nature of Weber's influence is especially evident in the way in which his analysis of modernity has been applied to the study of totalitarianism, and the Holocaust in particular, often by his own critics. Here the view – shared by the first generation of critical theorists (e.g. Horkheimer, Adorno and Marcuse), natural rights theorists (e.g. Strauss and Voegelin), Hannah Arendt (1951) and more recently Zygmunt Bauman (1989) – is that the increased concentration of power in a single body (the nation state) that is itself under-regulated from above, plus the pacification of the population that is the other side of the monopoly of coercion, plus bureaucratic domination, are among the central preconditions for forms of barbarism which are essentially *modern*.

However diverse and all-pervasive Weber's influence, changing conditions make his version of political modernism increasingly problematic, while highlighting the resourcefulness of Durkheim's cosmopolitan alternative. The basic unit of Weber's political analysis is the sovereign nation state – i.e. that body which enjoys a monopoly of legitimate violence within a bounded territory. The developments which the catch-all term 'globalisation' seeks to encapsulate have cast doubt on the proposition that the sovereign state is the only, or even the most, appropriate starting point for an analysis of political phenomena and for the definition of modern collective identities. Increasing interdependence *between* states, greater cultural diversity *within* states, and the growth of what Durkheim would call social – as opposed to territorial – differentiation, have exposed the limits of both the sovereign state and formal political inclusion. On the one hand, the effectiveness of political action has been systematically undermined by market forces operating at the global (or at least international) level, and thus beyond the reach of the sovereign state. On the other hand, in order to govern effectively, in national and transnational political communities 'power and decision-making have been handed along to points ever further away from citizens: from local to provincial, from provincial to national, from national to international institutions, that lack all transparency or accountability' (Klein 2001, pp. 86–7); hence the widespread perception that democratic governance has been hollowed out and a growing disenchantment towards liberal democracy and especially the minimal institutionalised negative politics of the ballot box advocated by Weber.

The intellectual response to these perceived democratic deficits has been the revival of forms of communitarianism, civic republicanism and deliberative models of democracy, but concern about the more violent aspects of these processes at the international or global level has also revived an interest in institutional design where Weber's suggestions still exercise a strong and pervasive influence. According to the latter project, the instability caused by unregulated global market forces can be counteracted by creating supranational political institutions that in essence replicate the process of vertical integration followed by the nation state (see Held 1993). The European Union represents a clear attempt to establish such a political counter-weight to market expansion, and to retain competitive pluralism in a post-Cold War world dominated by a single superpower (see Habermas 1996). While we must be careful not to exaggerate the extent or impact of globalisation on the hegemony of the nation state (for a corrective, see Hirst and Thompson 1999), it seems clear that the Weberian solution does not address the underlying problems adequately and needs to be at least supplemented by Durkheim's cosmopolitan alternative. As we argued in the last section, Weber's outward-looking nationalism and competitive model of democracy overrate the ability of the nation state to foster stable collective identity and effective forms of governance without at the same time establishing intermediate political bodies that can mediate between the state and the individual. Thus an expansion of the Weberian model at European level (let alone beyond it) would not in itself address the growing distance between the state and the individual and might merely magnify the weaknesses affecting traditional nation states.

By contrast, Durkheim's inward-looking cosmopolitanism articulates an alternative political solution where forms of subsidiarity, functional representation and local participation combine to produce a decentralised system of governance capable of fostering stable collective identities.

> Durkheim's analysis suggests that while inclusion remains an important variable in the construction of democratic stability, the most decisive factor may be the ability of the political system . . . to transform particularistic concerns to some common universalistic commitments and where the protection of the democratic individual is at the heart of the political process (Prager 1981, p. 946).

Where growing interdependence and pluralisation have been institutionalised peacefully, as in the case of the European Union, and where there has been a degree of decoupling of legal authority and political power and a partial loosening of what Gellner (1983) has called the 'monopoly of legitimate culture', we occasionally find more optimistic arguments to the effect that a space for new forms of democratic multi-level governance may be opening up in which no single level can claim a monopoly, be it of sovereign power or legitimate culture (see, for example, MacCormick 1995). Such arguments have distinctly Durkheimian overtones in their emphasis upon the dispersal of power throughout a system (subsidiarity), the role of intermediate institutions, forms of liberal nationalism or constitutional patriotism, and in the necessity for levels of governance both above and below the nation state. Here interesting affinities emerge between Durkheim's notion of moral integration and new forms of civil republicanism and deliberative democracy developed in response to the difficulties faced by liberalism in dealing with phenomena like complexity, multiculturalism and globalisation. Each position emphasises, though with varying weight, the centrality of citizenship, civic education and civic virtue, and the necessity for forms of democratic participation beyond mere representation.[5]

The fate of the dominant Weberian model in part depends on the continued hegemony of those political forms it so brilliantly analyses. Where the hegemonic model confronts its own limits, we shall continue to see the search for alternatives. It is to this project that Durkheim's political sociology retains its relevance today and warrants a more considered assessment of his contribution to the discipline vis-à-vis Weber's.

5. Although Durkheim is by no means the only source of such arguments (see Hirst 1997, p. 32), French corporatist thinking (including that of Léon Duguit as well as Durkheim) has clear affinities with much contemporary debate. For a detailed account of the historical connections between French political thought and its English counterpart in the works of G. D. H. Cole, John Neville Figgis and Harold Laski, see Laborde (2000). These affinities can also be seen in the recent work of Paul Hirst (especially 1994 and 1997), who grounds his version of a pluralist 'associative' democracy on the British writers, but whose own views and proposals bear a strong resemblance to those of Durkheim, at least as we have presented them here.

18

Freud and his followers

PAUL ROAZEN

In the late 1890s Sigmund Freud (1856–1939), who had been trained as a Viennese neurologist, created a new field, psychoanalysis, which was designed to understand and treat neurotic afflictions. Although not a political thinker per se, Freud contributed indirectly, and some of his followers directly, to modern political theory. Politically, Freud was something of a conservative liberal, sceptical in outlook and suspicious of utopian schemes. His followers did not always follow him faithfully down the trail he had blazed in the new discipline of psychoanalysis; nor did all agree with his political views. Some were conservative to the point of reaction, others radical Marxists and utopians. Some revised Freudian theory almost beyond recognition. All were alike, however, in finding in Freud the outline and essentials of a new and fruitful way of thinking about man and society.

Freud's thought

An essential key to Freud's thinking about psychopathology lies in the character of the last days of the Hapsburg Empire. A yawning gulf between reality and official ideology stimulated a general intellectual revolt and a search for the actualities beneath the pious formulae of public truth. This uprising was led by those ideally placed to see the discrepancy because they had nothing to gain from accepting the official view: the educated Jews. Mordant irony was their weapon for piercing the veil of the structure of formal beliefs. The cultural conflict between East and West that had its vortex in Vienna's cosmopolitan intellectual life, and the sense that liberal culture was on the verge of being undermined, would be reflected throughout Freud's mature thought (Zweig 1953; Roazen 1968; Johnston 1972; Schorske 1979).

Freud's starting point as a therapist was the existence of inner conflicts that interfered with the lives of suffering patients. He proposed that symptoms be looked upon as substitute satisfactions, the result of failure adequately to deal with early childhood patterns. Freud highlighted persistent infantilism as the ultimate source of adult neurotic problems. He held that neuroses are psychologically meaningful, and he interpreted them as compromise formations between repressed impulses and censoring parts of the mind. One portion of every symptom was understood as the expression of wish fulfilment, and another side represented the mental structure that reacted against the primal drive.

Initially Freud thought that neurotic anxiety arose from sexual sources; specifically, he indicted dammed-up sexuality as the physical basis for neurosis (Freud 1900; Roazen 1975; Roazen 2001a). Freud conceived sexuality so broadly as to include virtually all aspects of childish pleasure-seeking. Fantasies of sexual gratification stemming from early childhood were allegedly the source of adult neurotic dilemmas. Freud proposed that a person's emotional attitude toward parents encapsulated the core problems of neurosis, and he coined the term 'Oedipus complex' to describe a boy's first childish desires for his mother and a girl's earliest affection for her father. Freud understood that someone's emotional attitude towards a family consisted of conflicting emotions involving rivalry and guilt, not just desire. And he believed that the most troublesome feelings stemmed from emotional problems about which the individual remains unconscious (Jones 1953–7).

Freud was proposing that people have motives that can be operative without their knowing anything about them. His special viewpoint was that of a psychologist, and he sought to pierce the mysteries of memory and false recollections. Freud thought that the compromise formations in constructing our image of the past were just like those in dreaming, as well as the ones underlying neurotic symptomatology and everyday slips of the tongue or pen (Freud 1901). He thought that the past lives on in the present, and psychoanalytic treatment consisted in the exploration of each patient's early history.

Freud was ambitious as a theorist, and his notion of neurosis became part of a full-fledged system of thought. A central implication of his approach amounted to an assault on confidence in our ability to think rationally. For Freud was insisting that people are fundamentally self-deceptive. Neurosis was a form of ignorance, and Freud saw it as his task to utilise the power that came from enlightenment. Yet, much as Freud's work can be understood as a critique of the capacity for self-understanding, he was superlatively rationalistic about psychoanalysis itself. He thought he had discovered a science of the mind, and that he had uncovered a realm of meaning that could be objectively verified. The technique of free associations, which he relied on during treatment, was one that others could be trained to use. Once patients submitted to the analytic situation, involving daily meetings each lasting fifty minutes, such commitment could be used by the analyst to promote personal autonomy. Freud was relying on a structured situation to make people free (Roazen 1990).

One of the chief defects in Freud's approach was his unwillingness to concede the full philosophical underpinnings of it. He was convinced that psychoanalysis was capable of transforming thought and undermining previous moral positions, yet he fancied that he had been able to do so without importing any ethical baggage of his own into his teachings. Nonetheless, Freud was clearly expressing a morality of his own; he once explained to a patient that the moral self was the conscious, the evil self being the unconscious. Freud qualified this distinction by maintaining that his approach emphasised not only evil wishes but also the moral censorship that makes them unrecognisable. He was insistent that morality was self-evident, but that at the same time he himself held to a higher standard of ethics than, supposedly, humanity as a whole (Rieff 1959; 1966).

Freud's Enlightenment heritage led him boldly to denounce religious belief. Indeed, religion was the one social coercion Freud felt to be humanly unnecessary. In each of the last three decades of his life he wrote a book centring on different aspects of the psychology of religion. He made the analogy between religion and obsessional neurosis, and pointed out how often outer forms have obliterated the inner religious intention, as with any other self-defeating neurotic structure. Yet despite his critique's affinities with the liberal rationalism of the eighteenth century, Freud departed from liberalism in stressing, in *The Future of an Illusion*, the inner instinctual core that strains beyond culture's reach and which is one of the sources of religion's psychological appeal (Freud 1927).

After 1927, Freud insisted that human helplessness was at the origin of religious conviction; people need religion because of the failure to outgrow the dependency of childhood. Religion is an illusion in the sense that it is the product of wish-fulfilment. Freud sceptically saw religion as a pack of lies, fairy-tales that were a product of emotional insecurities. Because religion is based on irrational fears, its unreality may undermine the civilisation it currently supports. Illusions are dangerous, no matter how comfortable. Freud ignored his earlier comments on religion, relating it to fears of death and guilt, as he now concluded that superstition is intolerable. He was so intolerant of the infantile and the regressive that he had difficulty understanding their constructive functions.

Freud saw the family as the prototype for authority relationships. As he had argued that God the father was needed to allay the deepest fears, so he thought that the Oedipus complex also illuminated the social cohesion of political groups. He elaborated these ideas in his *Group Psychology and the Analysis of the Ego*. Freud was suspicious of the masses and disdainful of the lower classes; his elitism lay behind a good deal of his social thinking. Religion always seemed to Freud a more intolerable irrationality than political authority (Freud 1921). Politically he was impressed by the extent of human inner instability and the craving for authority. Although Freud's whole form of therapy aimed at liberation and independence, politically he was a pessimist.

In *Civilization and its Discontents* Freud eloquently expressed his full sense of the conflictedness of life. He stressed the inevitable pervasiveness of suffering in civilised society. Although he could, as in *The Future of an Illusion*, write like an eighteenth-century libertarian, here his sense of the inevitable cruelties of life was uppermost in the argument. For civilisation to be powerful enough to protect people from each other and against nature, it must, according to Freud, have at its disposal an equally intense energy. Throughout Freud's thought there is a sense of the limits of life, the truth behind the maxim that one cannot have one's cake and eat it too. Social unity can only be achieved on the ruins of human desires. People need the security of civilised life so deeply that they renounce the gratification of instincts in exchange for society (Freud 1930). Freud concluded that the frustration of sexual and aggressive drives is entailed by their very character. Only if society can successfully internalise human instinctuality can civilisation be maintained.

As has already been suggested, Freud's own views can best be aligned with a conservative reading of aspects of Enlightenment liberalism. However, Freudians have been found in most of the main ideological camps – from socialism and Marxism, to conservatism and fascism. Each will be examined in turn, returning at the end to a discussion of the ambiguous concept that provides the starting point for the political use of Freud's ideas – the notion of normality implied by his theories. We start, however, with Freud's own approach to liberalism.

Liberalism

In his respect for the dignity of his patients that made his innovations possible, and by means of his conviction that despite appearances all people are psychologically the same, Freud ranks as a great heir of the Enlightenment. He was also a liberal in being among those who are ever demanding more freedom. At the same time, however, in the development of psychoanalysis the open-ended quality of liberalism led to a revision of some of its most cherished premises. For Freud represents an aspect of liberalism's self-examination.

It was an Enlightenment ideal to relate political impulses with the aim of achieving the best in us. The trouble with the liberal tradition was its narrow understanding of these impulses. It is frequently maintained, for instance, that *The Federalist* exhibits a realism about human motives, as well as a lack of utopianism about history, that might well benefit contemporary political thinking (Hamilton, Madison and Jay 2003 [1787–8]). Yet, in comparison to Freud, *The Federalist* seems as shallow on human nature as much of the rest of liberalism. For while Madison, Jay and Hamilton had a shrewd eye for human motivation, they lacked a sense of the limitlessness of human lusts and ambitions. Madison tells us that ambition can be made to counteract ambition; human drives can supposedly be rearranged and engineered until a clock-like mechanism of checks and balances emerges to ensure constitutionalism. This smacks more of a utilitarian gimmick than of modern psychological depth. In Freud's quest for an understanding of human feelings he transcended liberalism and joined hands with thinkers usually associated with traditions alien to it. Along with Burke, he recognised the intensity of destructive urges and the sense in which societal coercions can be psychologically necessary. With Marx he extended our appreciation of the extent of self-deception, self-alienation and bad faith.

Although Freud worked on behalf of autonomy, the implications of his ideas may have helped undermine central features of the liberal ideals of individualism and privacy. Liberalism in the spirit of John Stuart Mill has long sought for an elaboration of what a fully developed person would be like, and psychoanalytic conceptions of normality, including notions like individuation and the life cycle, are at least one such model of humanity (Mill 1974 [1859]). Indeed, Freud's whole therapeutic approach encouraged a kind of self-expression that was congenial to the aims of thinkers like Mill. Like most liberals, Freud distinguished between liberty and licence. Whatever the excesses to which psychoanalytic ideas were sometimes put, the historical

Freud did not advocate self-indulgence; he might romantically posture in defiance of Western traditions but he stood for order and civility (Clark 1980; Roazen 2001a). Yet Freud also challenged traditional liberal democratic theory. He demonstrated the degree to which the child lives on within the adult, the way psychological uncertainties prevent people from ruling themselves.

Likewise, Freud might be appalled how the public now craves personal knowledge about historical figures and all public people, so that privacy today is used in a manipulative way, and this state of intimacy is a political and social reality of contemporary life. However, Freud himself used his disguised autobiography, in his *The Interpretation of Dreams* and *The Psychopathology of Everyday Life*, to establish his principles. By daring to treat dreams and symptoms as meaningful, therefore, Freud had marked the end of an era that considered such material legitimately personal and outside the bounds of historical inquiry.

Socialism

Many left-wing thinkers have long dismissed psychoanalysis as a decadent form of soul-searching. At least starting with Lenin, Marxists have been unsure about what to do with Freud. Yet within socialism there has been a history of theorists eager to unite Marxist concepts with those of Freud. Trotsky, for example, was open-mindedly receptive to the significance of Freud's teachings, and he was in personal contact in Vienna with Alfred Adler (1870–1937), one of the earliest members of Freud's circle, which was first founded in 1902. Adler, although one of Freud's first students, was also a socialist who went on to found a school of 'individual psychology' apart from Freud's own (Ansbacher and Ansbacher 1956; Hoffman 1994). Adler had a special concern with the social and environmental factors in disease, and highlighted the role of compensations for early defects in his study of organ inferiority; he was proposing that under the best circumstances defects in a child could create a disposition toward better performance. Adler was not as exclusively concerned with infantile sexuality as Freud, but was instead preoccupied with ego mechanisms and aggressive drives. In contrast to Freud's own lack of interest in politics, Adler sought to improve the world through education and psychotherapy.

In 1911 Freud decided to bring his differences with Adler to a head, and the result was Adler's resignation, along with half the membership of the Vienna Psychoanalytic Society. Adler was stressing the extent to which emotional problems stemmed from current conflicts and cultural disharmonies rather than from the patient's childhood past. Adler interpreted symptoms as a weapon of self-assertion, often arising from deep-seated feelings of inferiority. But he looked on the patient's wholeness as the key to neurosis; Adler was concerned with what are now known as character problems.

Adler proposed to help patients with their feelings of inferiority by leading them out of their self-preoccupied isolation into participation in the community. Through the cultivation of social feeling and by means of service to society one could subdue egotism. Adler was a pioneer with his interest in the ego as an agency of the mind, and thought he could thereby help to bridge the gap between the pathological and the normal. By 1920 Adler had directed his efforts to setting up consultations with schoolteachers: he had been intrigued all along with the psychology of the family group. He was especially compassionate toward victims of social injustice, and thought it of primary importance to help promote human dignity (Sperber 1974). Women in particular were suffering from socially patterned oppression. Adler understood how people, out of their own inadequacies and lack of self-esteem, could bolster themselves by degrading others. Once a group or class has been treated as inferior, these feelings can be self-sustaining and lead to compensatory manoeuvres to make up for self-doubts. Chronic neurotic suffering stems from psychological over-sensitivity, and feelings of inferiority are often compensated for through protest and fantasies of greatness. Adler understood some of the key social bases for destructiveness, and those concerned with race as a psychological force in the modern world – including Frantz Fanon and Kenneth Clark – have acknowledged themselves in Adler's debt (Roazen 1975).

Wilhelm Reich (1897–1957) was a Viennese psychiatrist who was also one of Freud's most talented pupils. Freud had conceived of neurosis primarily as a memory problem, while Reich tried to show that the real issue to be studied was not symptomatology but the whole personality. In his work on character analysis in the 1920s, Reich broadened the earlier conception of what was suitable for analytic concern.

While Reich helped to shift the focus of attention to non-verbal means of expression, he failed to convince analysts of the diagnostic significance of orgastic sexual satisfaction. Reich thought that mental health depended on orgastic potency, and he was in favour of full and free sexual expression. (Freud sharply disagreed with these ideas.) As a practical reformer Reich held that many adult problems would never develop if sexual expression were not prematurely stifled. What orthodox analysts called sublimation, the transmutation of instinctual drives into cultural expression, was deemed by Reich to be the rationalised product of bourgeois sexual inhibitions. He started to argue in the late 1920s that Freud was betraying, out of conformist pressures, his original revolutionary stand on behalf of the rights of libido. Freud in turn objected that Reich was trying to limit the concept of sexuality to what it had been before psychoanalysis (King 1972; Sharaf 1983; Roazen 1990).

Reich was not only a Marxist but also a communist, and he became one of the few analysts to start building bridges between psychoanalysis and social thought. He proposed to prevent the rise of Oedipal problems rather than simply study and cure them after the fact. The key, he thought, was to ameliorate human suffering through changes in the traditional Western family structure. He believed that only the dissolution of the middle-class family would lead to the disappearance of the Oedipus complex. Freud viewed neurosis as an outgrowth of the biological necessity of the family, and composed his *Civilization and its Discontents* as an answer to Reich's position (Freud 1930; Reich 1970 [1935]).

Reich's *The Mass Psychology of Fascism* first appeared in Germany in 1935, and was written at the high point of Reich's involvement with Freudian and Marxist concepts. The central interpretive thesis was that modern man is torn by contradictory impulses toward conservatism and revolution. He craves authority, fears freedom, but is simultaneously rebellious. The authoritarian patriarchal family, Reich held, distorted some of man's most generous and cooperative instincts. Fascism represents not so much any one political party as the organised expression of the average man's enslaved character. Reich's main sociological point was that society is capable of transforming man's inner nature, producing a character structure that then reproduces society in the form of ideologies. In Reich's time, the distressed German middle class became members of the Nazi radical right, and he chose to explain modern nationalism as an outgrowth of suppressed genital sexuality.

Erich Fromm (1900–80), another Marxist psychoanalyst, published *Escape from Freedom* in 1941, and it immediately became a notable event in intellectual history. He won the enmity of the orthodox analysts of his day for daring to discuss factors such as the role of the environment in personality development, and the creation of 'social character'. Societies do tend to produce and reproduce the character types they need to survive and perpetuate themselves; 'social character' is shaped by the economic structure of society through processes of psychological internalisation. In turn, the dominant personality traits become forces in their own right in moulding the social process itself. As external necessity becomes part of the psyche, human energy is harnessed for a given economic or social system. In this way, we become what we are expected to be (Fromm 1941; Fromm 1947; Fromm 1956; Birnbach 1961; Schaar 1961; Burston 1991).

Fromm was concerned with the pathology of normality and considered it legitimate to speak of an 'insane' society and what happens to people in it. Fromm's earliest papers in the 1930s had focused on the alleged defects of the middle-class liberalism implicit in Freud. As Fromm turned away from the pessimism of Freud's instinct theory, Fromm insisted on the potential significance of changes in the social environment as a means of altering the human condition. (Fromm acknowledged the impact of Reich's general influence on him.) Freud had not been much interested, aside from criticising sexual mores, in the social sources of suffering and exploitation. Fromm, by contrast, was intrigued with the way our culture fosters conformist tendencies by suppressing spontaneous feelings and thereby crippling the development of genuine individuality.

Instead of seeing the unconscious as something frightening, Fromm held that truth is repressed by an unconscious that is basically socially determined. He also thought that too often we fear our superior potentialities and, in particular, the ability to develop as autonomous and free individuals. He traced destructiveness to unlived life rather than to Freud's mythical death instinct. If cruelty is one of the ways of making sense of existence, it only illustrates Fromm's theory that character-rooted passions should be considered psycho-social phenomena.

For Fromm selfishness was not, as in Freud, the same as self-love. Fromm thought these traits were diametrically opposite, and therefore the possibility of altruism as an aspect of self-expression becomes a real one. Whereas Freud liked to debunk the legitimacy of altruism, Fromm – like Adler – tried to combat egocentricity. Too often we hold our ego as a possession, the basis for identity, a thing.

In addition to assailing egotism, Fromm set out to combat greed and human passivity, bewailing the prevalence in the modern world of competition, antagonism and fear. He distinguished between subjectively felt needs and objectively valid ones. He had in mind the aim of self-realisation; for him self-affirmation was a process of exercising human reason in a productive activity. Fromm believed that reason properly exercised will lead to an ethic of love. Love for Fromm was a process of self-renewing and self-increasing. Society has aimed not, as Freud thought, to repress sex, but to vilify sex for the sake of breaking the human will. Social conformism succeeds to the extent that it breaks independence without our even being aware of it.

In 1955 Herbert Marcuse (1898–1979) published *Eros and Civilization*, an important critique of so-called revisionist Freudian psychology like that promoted by Fromm. With great polemical skill, Marcuse punctured the inspirationalist pretensions of writers who had tried to update psychoanalytic thought in a culturalist direction. Marcuse had first turned to a serious examination of Freud during the late 1930s, when he felt forced to reformulate Marxist premises. Bourgeois society had survived economic crises, the proletariat was susceptible to fascist appeals, and the Soviet Union, both domestically and internationally, had not fulfilled revolutionary hopes. Marcuse disclaimed an interest in the clinical side of psychoanalysis, but selectively picked those concepts from within orthodox Freudian writing that might support his purposes. Relying on what he called a 'hidden trend' in psychoanalysis, Marcuse tried to demonstrate the feasibility of a non-repressive society. He maintained that Freud was the true revolutionary and that his cause had been betrayed by those who had diluted his message for purposes that turned out on inspection to be socially conservative (Marcuse 1955; Robinson 1969; Jay 1973; Jacoby 1975).

Marcuse had launched a fundamentalist Freudian attack on revisionists like Fromm. By drawing on the reasoning in *The Future of an Illusion*, and through building on the Marxist concern with alienation, Marcuse was able to make use of classical psychoanalytic theory for socially utopian purposes. It seemed to Marcuse that to abandon, or minimise, the instinctivistic side of Freud's theories was to give up those concepts that underlined the opposition between man and contemporary society. Marcuse relied on Freud's instinct theory in order to ensure an energy and drive basis within individuals in the hope of challenging the status quo.

It had been Fromm's intention to alter psychoanalytic thinking in the direction of socialism. Fromm and Marcuse, former colleagues in the Frankfurt school of critical sociology, represent (adapting a distinction of William James's) the tender-minded and the tough-minded union of Freud and Marx. But although Marcuse was accurate in pointing out the somewhat Pollyannaish-sounding flavour to much of the psychoanalytic writing since Freud's death, Marcuse did not sufficiently appreciate the pragmatic and moral grounds on which these writers set out to alter their earlier commitments to certain doctrines. They had, for instance, abandoned Freud's instinct theory for the sake of avoiding what they saw as his unnecessary pessimism that could seem to border on therapeutic nihilism.

Marcuse relentlessly pursued what he considered the banalities of the revisionists. In addition to attacking Fromm, Marcuse went after the ideas of Karen Horney and Harry Stack Sullivan (Horney 1937; Sullivan 1953); he indicted their emphases on the relevance of the need people have for growth, and how cultural biases blinded Freud to his biologistic prejudices (Thompson 1950). Despite the injustices of Marcuse's attacks, it is hard not to admire the conceptual power of his mind as he criticised the way analysts can belabour the obvious. A kind of potential social conformism can be seen as implicit in the sort of mental massage advocated by such revisionist theorists. For Marcuse there was no possibility of free personality development in the context of a fundamentally unfree society, in which basic human impulses have been made aggressive and destructive.

Conservatism

If psychoanalysis has been used by Marcuse and others for radical social purposes, Freud has proved no less useful for conservative aims. Carl Gustav Jung (1875–1961) led the most painful of the 'secessions' from psychoanalysis; of all the pupils in Freud's life, Jung played the most substantial intellectual role. His contact in the 1930s with the Nazis only put the final seal of disapproval on a man Freud's pupils had already learned to detest.

There were long-standing sources of difference between Freud and Jung, even during their period of cooperation from 1906 until 1913; but Freud had come to depend on Jung as his 'crown prince', destined to lead the psychoanalytic movement in the future, especially in the world of psychiatry which in central Europe was then distinct from neurology. Nevertheless, Jung had hesitated to extend the concept of sexuality as broadly as Freud wished, and Jung came to interpret many so-called infantile clinical phenomena as of secondary rather than primary causal importance; current difficulties, he held, could reactivate past conflicts. Jung insisted that the past can be used defensively to evade the present, a clinical point which would command widespread later agreement; but at the time they split apart Freud saw Jung as merely retreating from the boldness of psychoanalysis's so-called findings (Jung 1966; Ellenberger 1970).

Less rationalistic and suspicious of the unconscious than Freud, Jung began to formulate his own views on the compensatory functions of symptoms. No better critique of Freud's excessive rationalism can be found than in

Jung's collected works. He proposed that symptoms are always justified and serve a purpose. Also, he was interested in stages of the life cycle other than the Oedipal one. It is still not widely known how early Jung emphasised the central importance of the personal rapport between patient and analyst if therapy is to be successful, as he warned against the dangers of authoritarianism implicit in neutral-seeming analytic technique. And Jung also, as the son of a pastor, took religion as a far more deep-rooted and legitimate set of human aspirations than Freud would acknowledge.

At the time of their falling out before the First World War, Freud publicly accused Jung of anti-Semitism. After Hitler came to power, Jung accepted the leadership of a German psychiatric association, in what he described as an attempt to protect psychotherapy there. Continuing to live in Switzerland during this time, he helped numerous Jewish therapists to escape to England and elsewhere. But Jung had described some of the characteristics of Freud's psychoanalysis as Jewish, and Jung allowed his comments on the differences between Jewish and 'Aryan' psychology to appear in a 1934 article published in Nazi Germany. The closeness of Jung's distinction to the Nazi one between 'Jewish science' and 'German science' has to be chilling. Despite the opportunistic collaboration with the Nazis, which has damaged Jung's historical standing, his genuine psychological contributions deserve to be acknowledged.

Freud's seeing creativity as the result of the denial of other human capacities was to Jung, and Reich too, an expression of Freud's sexual inhibitions. While Freud was consistently suspicious of the human capacity for regression, Jung saw the non-rational as a profound component of human vision. Jung had appreciation for the creative potentials of the unconscious, and saw in the unknown as much of the life forces as of death drives. Jung held that the therapist must be prepared to meet the patient at all levels, including the moral. He tried to deal with the philosophical dimensions of depth psychology, and was willing to discuss the implications of these ideas for a modern conception of individualism. Further, Jung used his notion of the collective unconscious to stress that an individual always exists in the context of a social environment.

The issue of the rise of Hitler serves as a reminder of how easily psychology can be misused for the worst kinds of conformist purposes. Dr Matthias Göring, a distant cousin of Hitler's deputy, headed an institute that claimed to be housing psychotherapists (Cocks 1985). To a remarkable extent in Nazi Germany, so-called psychotherapists were able to achieve the support of professional institutionalisation. The success of the Göring Institute, its links to the notorious SS and its part in helping the Luftwaffe promote the war effort, has to besmirch the whole tradition of German 'psychotherapy'. We should be wary of the implications of any ideas that aim to harmonise the individual and the social order, a point that stands out when the society is Hitlerian. Since the practice of psychoanalysis could only be preserved in Germany by means of the departure of Jewish analysts and the cover of the Göring name, a fatal flaw had to mar the existence of the psychotherapeutic profession in Hitler's Germany.

Matthias Göring's organisation had solid links to pre-Hitlerian practitioners, as well as to those in post-Second World War Germany. Göring had joined the Nazi Party as a matter of conviction and national loyalty, and he also condemned the Jewish influence in his occupation. As early as 1933–4 Göring made *Mein Kampf* required reading for all his therapists. Göring was sufficiently partisan that his relationship with his deputy ruptured in early 1945, over Göring's insistence that those in charge of the institute serve as advisers to the last German units defending Berlin against the Russians. Göring insisted, in the face of the argument that such actions were futile, that it would be defeatist to do otherwise.

For reasons that are worrisome in terms of intellectual history, earlier philosophical ideas, and in particular a Romantic tradition in German psychology, could be made use of by the Nazis. A special irony can be found in the Nazi conviction that in principle mental disorder within the 'master race' could not be considered essentially an organic or biological matter, which was why Göring's applied depth psychology had its special role to play under the Third Reich. It might almost go without saying that therapists at the Göring Institute were not permitted to treat Jews. To protest against the Nazi regime would have risked not only personal destruction but also damage to the whole profession of 'psychotherapy' itself, which amounts to a damning indictment of what Göring's institute accomplished. No-one has ever been able to understand how patient confidentiality could be maintained under totalitarian political circumstances. So the Nazi regime had succeeded in destroying psychotherapy, as it should be known. The German practitioners of their craft betrayed an obligation they owed to patients, humanity at large, and the people in countries that the Nazis assaulted.

Although I hesitate to bring it up after discussing Hitler's Germany, and without exploring the abuses of psychiatry in Soviet Russia and the People's Republic of China, the full-scale development of ego psychology, one of the main currents in psychoanalytic theory since the late 1930s, had its own special conservative implications. And it was Freud himself who set this theoretical change in motion. In the 1920s he maintained that the ego functions as a protective barrier against stimulation, whether coming from the drives in the psyche or from external reality. The ego's main task is to keep an individual on an even keel of psychological excitation. Anxiety is a danger signal against the threat of helplessness in the face of overwhelming stimulation. The ego was increasingly discussed as a coherent organisation of psychic forces (Coles 1970; Friedman 1999).

One does not have to look far within early psychoanalytic theory to find how Freud's negativism had been reflected in his earlier work, and why ego psychology later proved so attractive. His whole system was designed to explain motivation when a person is in conflict, and the ego has relatively failed at its integrative task. As a therapist Freud was preoccupied with pulling problems apart and tearing fixations asunder, on the assumption that the patient's ego would be able to put the pieces back together again. For Freud analysis was automatically synthesis; constructive processes had originally been taken for granted by him, an issue which Jung had challenged him on.

Freud was a master at understanding the means of self-deception, but he ignored many processes of self-healing. Therefore, a main trend after his death was to correct this imbalance, and to focus on the ego as an agency integrating inner needs and outer realities (Roazen 1976). The ego has a unifying function, ensuring coherent behaviour and conduct. The job of the ego is not just the negative one of avoiding anxiety, but also the positive one of maintaining effective performance. The ego's defences may be adaptive as well as maladaptive. Adaptation is itself bedevilled by anxieties and guilts; but the ego's strength is not measured by the earlier psychoanalytic standard of what in a personality is denied or cut off, but rather by all the extremes that an individual's ego is able to unify.

A defective ego identity can be responsible for pathology that once would have been traced to instinctual drives. Rage, for example, can result from an individual's blocked sense of mastery. Aggression can stem from an inability to tolerate passivity. Because of ego psychology's explicit attention to the interaction of internal and external realities, it opened up possibilities for interdisciplinary cooperation in the social sciences.

At the same time that ego psychology shifted from the more traditional concern with the defensive ego to the problems of growth and adaptation, it looked for the collective sources of ego development. For instance, there can be a need for a sense of identity to be confirmed by social institutions, as Erik H. Erikson (1902–94) pointed out; and here organised religion and ritual can play a positive role (Erikson 1950; Erikson 1968). But there are those who have wondered whether the upshot of ego psychology must not be inherently conservative. Society can either stimulate or cripple the development of the individual self, and also offer a pseudo-identity in place of the authentic self.

It is possible for ego psychology to give an undue weight to conformist values. Erikson was correct, in that the role of work was often neglected in earlier Freudian thinking. Yet it would be misleading to look at work just individualistically and not also socially; the spirit in which work gets done may matter little if its social purpose is questionable. It may even turn out to be an advantage not to have a secure sense of self. A peripheral standing can be a source of creativity, and alienation may be meritorious. Ego psychology can fail to distinguish between genuine and artificial continuities, in keeping with its tolerance for myth and legend.

It is striking how Erikson could take one-sided views of his biographical subjects (Erikson 1958; Erikson 1969). In studying Martin Luther, Erikson concentrated on the young man, isolating the ethical preacher from his career as an active political leader with mixed results for human betterment. And Erikson saw Mahatma Gandhi as only a reconciler of religious and political propensities. In each case Erikson sanctified a hero, leaving the impression of advocating bold change while ignoring the reactionary implications of the life under scrutiny.

Erikson's concepts always specified respect for the inner dimension of experience. But the 'sense' of identity can be different from genuine identity, and illusory feelings do not equal social reality. Ego psychology can communicate too much of what we want to hear, and hopefulness should not be only linked to social conservatism. Ego psychology needs to confront the possibility that there may be few social groups worth being 'integrated' with. On the other hand, Freud's own kind of hostility to illusions does not guarantee that psychology will not be used complacently to justify the status quo. His own politics in the 1930s led him to justify a reactionary Austrian regime, and he wrote more warmly about Mussolini than one might have liked; Freud's International Psychoanalytic Association cooperated with the Nazi regime, agreeing that the Jewish members in Germany should resign 'voluntarily' in order to 'save' psychoanalysis there (Roazen 2001b).

Walter Lippmann (1889–1974), the foremost American political pundit of the twentieth century, was one of the first in the English-speaking world before the First World War to recognise the significance of Freud's contribution to moral thought. When the British Fabian socialist Graham

Wallas was teaching at Harvard while Lippmann was still an undergraduate, Lippmann became his course assistant; and Wallas, already the author of a famous text on *Human Nature in Politics*, had a lasting influence on Lippmann's orientation (Wallas 1948 [1908]). Lippmann seems to have first picked up on the significance of Freud through a friend who was translating Freud's *The Interpretation of Dreams* (Freud 1900). The First World War had a central impact on Lippmann's political thought; and starting with his *Public Opinion* (1922) he grew increasingly critical of liberalism's naïve hopes for public participation in decision-making. The book was centrally concerned with the role of the irrational. Lippmann introduced an unforgettable contrast between the complexities of the outside world and the distortions inherent in our need for simplifications in our heads. This antithesis between the immense social environment in which we live and our ability to perceive it only indirectly has continued to haunt democratic thinkers. Not only do our leaders acquire fictitious personalities, but symbols can govern political behaviour (Lippmann 1922).

Between each of us and the environment there arises what Lippmann considered a 'pseudo-environment'. He thought that political behaviour is a response not to the real world but to those pseudo-realities that we construct about phenomena that are beyond our direct knowledge. The implications Lippmann drew went beyond the importance of propaganda. Along with other critics of utilitarian psychology, Lippmann held that social life cannot be explained in terms of pleasure–pain calculus. Despite all the criticisms of Benthamism that many writers (from Dickens to Dostoevsky) have advanced, self-interest still dominates the motives social science is apt to attribute to people; yet advantage, Lippmann believed, is itself not an irreducible concept.

In the light of the psychological insights he was emphasising, it is no wonder that Lippmann questioned idyllic conceptions of democracy. It is still hard for many people to accept the degree to which democracy, designed for harmony and tranquillity, rests on symbols of unity, the manufacture of consent, and the manipulation of the masses. Yet Lippmann offered reasons enough for permanent scepticism about dogmas of popular sovereignty.

Perhaps the peak of Lippmann's conservatism came during the Eisenhower years, when the place of businessmen in high public office helped to evoke his most elitist proclivities. His *The Public Philosophy* was a natural law critique of democratic government, and yet his writing continued to belie his own most reactionary principles; in seeking to be a public educator, he never lost the rationalist faith that clear-headedness on public matters can be communicated to the people effectively (Lippmann 1955). He did not relinquish the democratic ideal that the voters can be rallied in defence of the public interest. Although Lippmann became doubtful about the capacity of democracy to survive under the complicated conditions of modern life, he devoted his journalistic talents to the democratic ideal of purifying the news for the public's consumption (Steel 1980). He remained troubled by the inability of the democratic electorate to secure the needed information on which to act rationally.

Feminism

In thinking about ourselves few concepts cut deeper than that of gender, of male and female, as feminist theorists reminded us in the early days of the women's movement in the late 1960s and 1970s. It was then de rigueur to criticise Freud for his 'patriarchal' and condescending view of women, the 'phallocentrism' inherent in his concept of 'penis envy', and the generally masculine orientation of his thought (Daly 1978; Butler 1990, ch. 2). Freud was of course a man of his age and culture, which was not without its misogynist aspects. But he was also in some respects a man ahead of his time. To take one notable example, Freud may be said to have given a significant stimulus to modern feminist theory. At the outset of his career many of his most prominent patients were women, and although, as we saw, he rejected Adler's pre-First World War invitation to change psychoanalytic thought to acknowledge the social sources of the plight of women, Freud's movement proved attractive to women who became leading analysts. As early as 1910 the issue of equality arose connected with a proposal for admitting women as full members of the Vienna Psychoanalytic Society. Freud personally insisted that it would be a 'gross inconsistency' to 'exclude women on principle' (Nunberg and Federn 1962–75, vol. II). Although the members were a generation younger than Freud, a vocal minority was opposed to Freud's open-mindedness, and he claimed at the time that it would therefore require him to proceed with great caution on this point. In fact Freud almost immediately did as he pleased and went on to welcome women analysts to an unusual extent, and in the context of the history of twentieth-century professions his field became outstandingly receptive to the contributions of women.

As a matter of fact the novel ideas of two of his followers, Helene Deutsch (1884–1982) and Karen Horney (1885–1952), helped push Freud in the 1920s to composing essays specifically on femininity. Freud was characteristically sensitive on the issue of priorities, and he suspected that these women disciples were in danger of stealing a march on the topic of female psychology. Although it is these particular articles that Freud wrote in response to the innovations of Deutsch and Horney that created the body of Freud's work that in the 1960s and 1970s would be subjected to so much later feminist criticism (Brownmiller 1975), it has still gone relatively unnoticed how Deutsch in particular was able to succeed in departing from Freud while at the same time remaining loyal to his basic conceptualisation. Deutsch's *Psychoanalysis of the Sexual Functions of Women* first appeared in 1925, a work where she was proud to have brought 'the first ray of light on the unappreciated female libido' (Deutsch 1991). It was to be the first book by a psychoanalyst on the subject of femininity (Roazen 1985). (According to Freud's thinking, libido had to be necessarily masculine.) In later books Deutsch went further in the direction of developing her own views on women that substantially differed from Freud's theories (Deutsch 1944–5, Roazen 1985). Horney, though, had publicly disagreed with both Deutsch and Freud, and it was Horney's views on the role of culture (Horney 1967), in line with those of Fromm, that were subsequently heralded as a pioneer of modern feminism.

The issue of normality

Much of the political use and abuse of Freud centres on seeking social conditions that will remove certain supposedly pathological psychological states. However, it is clear that Freud did not envisage a utopian version of personal happiness; anxiety and despair were to him inevitable parts of the human condition. Freud sought not to eradicate human conflicts, but to teach how to come to terms with such anguish.

Since Freud wrote so much about abnormality, it might seem that he would have been obliged to discuss his picture of mental health. But whatever Freud had in mind has to be teased out of his system of thought, since he remained loath to deal frontally with a concept like normality. Normality is one of those ideas that can be discussed endlessly, not because it is an unreal question but precisely on the grounds that psychological health remains such a challenging idea. When one thinks what it might mean to treat patients in the context of a social environment of varying degrees of cruelty or social injustice, the significance of having some broad view of normality – as opposed to proposing a conformist adaptation to whatever the status quo might be – should be apparent.

The humanistically oriented revisionists of Freud's views, like Fromm or Erikson, were trying to inject genuine humanitarianism into a psychoanalytic world view that appeared to end in therapeutic despair and ethical nihilism. In Fromm's neglected retort to Marcuse's famous dissection of neo-Freudianism, Fromm accused Marcuse of ultimately advocating a nihilistic position (Fromm 1955). There may be less danger in psychoanalysis being a devastating threat to Western culture than its lending undercover support to objectionable conformist practices. As an aspect of the success of Freudian ideas, psychodynamic notions of normality have become part of the prevailing social structure around us. One need only think about how Anna Freud (1895–1982) and her collaborators at Yale Law School came up with defending the idea of 'psychological parenthood' and used it to support the notion that continuity in child custody cases should prevail over what these 'experts' considered mere biological parenthood (Goldstein, Solnit, Goldstein and Freud 1996). The value of continuity can be as unthinkingly enshrined as a part of middle-class morality as the alleged dangers of traumas were once used to frighten people into conformity.

In correspondence and conversation Freud acknowledged that health was only one value among others, and that it could not exhaust morality as a whole. If he was wary about this whole subject of normality it was because he realised what kind of potential quagmire he was in danger of entering. He touched on the subject of normality only on the rarest occasions. Once, in an essay designed to refute Jung's views on psychological types, Freud said that an ideally normal person would have hysterical, obsessional and narcissistic layers in harmony; his idea communicated one of his characteristic demands about how high a standard he expected of people, for to be able to bear that much conflict and still function effectively presupposes a considerable degree of self-control and capacity to endure stress. Freud typically took for granted that the people he liked best to work with were creative and self-disciplined.

Freud feared that the more original and disturbing aspects of his ideas would be destroyed by the widespread acceptance of his work in the New World. But I wonder whether he did enough to prevent precisely this outcome. By not providing more hints about normality, and not owning up publicly to the wide variety of psychological solutions he found both therapeutically tolerable and humanly desirable, Freud contributed to what he most sought to prevent. He had set out, in the spirit of Nietzsche, to transform Western values; he was eager to go beyond accepted good and evil.

When he assaulted 'love thy neighbour as thyself' as both unrealistic and undesirable, he was explicitly trying to overturn Christian ethics.

It is logically impossible to talk about neurosis without at the same time implying a standard of maturity, and yet despite how powerful psychology can be in outlining human defects and weaknesses, it has not been nearly as successful in coming to terms with the positive side of human strength and coherence. In the end, the issue of the significance of normality and its relationship to nihilism has to be left an open question. Freud's psychology did contribute to our understanding of what it can mean to be human, and in that sense his ideas will be permanently interesting to political theorists. But it is impossible to attempt to spell out in a definitive way the ideological implications of psychoanalysis. For the writers who have been influenced by Freud constitute a wide enough range of people to satisfy his fundamental aim of using his concept of the unconscious to transform how we think about ourselves.

It was Helene Deutsch, an old analyst and loyal disciple of Freud, whose ideas we explored above, who had the most appropriately philosophic attitude toward the perplexing issue of normality. In her earlier years, when she had been one of the most prominent teachers in the history of psychoanalysis, she used to make it a practice to ask prospective analysts in the course of interviewing them for acceptance into training what they thought a normal person would be like. It is of course an ultimately unanswerable conundrum, and yet one that as civilised people we too are obliged to raise repeatedly. Like all genuine questions in political philosophy, the problem of what is 'normal' or 'natural' can never be solved; it remains a real issue, nonetheless, to the extent that we choose to find it intolerable to contemplate a universe lacking in moral values.

19
Modernism in art, literature and political theory

WALTER L. ADAMSON

In politics these people [who uphold the 'materialist creed'] are democrats and republicans... In economics these people are socialists... In science these men are positivists... In art they are naturalists (Kandinsky 1977 [1911], pp. 10–11).

Modernism is a term of Anglo-American provenance with both literary-critical and art-historical variants.[1] It arose in the 1920s (Sultan 1987, p. 97), but did not become popular until the two decades after 1945 when formalist criticism held sway. Such 'new critics' thought of modernism as an approach to literature and the arts, emerging just before the First World War and dominant in the inter-war period, that emphasised aesthetic autonomy and formalism, detachment and irony, mythic themes, and self-reflective attention to acts of creation and composition. The novels of Joyce and Woolf, the plays of Pirandello and Yeats, the music of Schoenberg and Stravinsky, and the abstract art of Kandinsky and Mondrian were paradigmatic. The term was then appropriated by Western Marxists debating the properly revolutionary approach to aesthetics and cultural critique.[2] More recent usage has greatly expanded and somewhat altered the concept, but it remains historiographical in the sense that the artists, writers and movements considered modernist by the critics rarely used the term to refer to themselves. It also remains essentially contested; there is no single, widely accepted usage. I will therefore begin by indicating how it is being used here.

Most current writers on modernism use it as an umbrella term for a group of intellectuals and cultural movements that dominated the European and American scene between 1890 and 1930. Beyond the individuals mentioned

1. There is a related but distinct usage in Hispanic criticism; see Davison (1966).
2. The usual terms deployed in this debate, however, are 'Avantgardismus' and 'die Moderne', not 'Modernismus'. Lukács (1964 [1955]), for example, uses the word 'Avantgardismus', which the English translator renders as 'modernism'. In his reply to Lukács, Adorno (1984 [1970]) favours 'die Moderne' but occasionally writes of 'Modernismus'.

above, now considered 'high modernists' in their relative isolation, movements like German expressionism, French cubism, and English vorticism and imagism are generally included.[3] I follow this usage but also include movements such as Italian and Russian futurism, Zurich dada and its successors and French surrealism, which are sometimes separated out as 'avant-garde' in contrast to 'modernism'. Although this division can be defended by claiming that avant-gardes sought to 'aestheticise life' while modernists sought 'autonomy' in both the aesthetic and social senses of the term, the present argument is that, on close inspection, these two goals turn out to be two sides of the same coin. Both avant-gardism and modernism responded to the increasing commodification of Western culture, the one by somehow decorrupting or extracting the otherness out of the commodified object to produce art, the other by fleeing the commodified object altogether in quest of art as 'pure form'.

In comparison with its original usage, then, the concept of modernism has been broadened by extending it beyond individuals to cultural movements, and beyond stylistics to the social, economic, cultural and political contexts modernists were responding to and seeking to reshape. Increasingly, it is understood in relation to the rise of the modern metropolis, the *fin-de-siècle* cultural crisis with its explosive mixture of utopian hopes for cultural renewal and fears of descent into 'mass-cultural' barbarism, and the 'space-time compression' associated with newly developed technologies of communication and transportation. Despite this contextual enrichment, however, the word continues to be used primarily in a narrow aesthetic sense, with either that adjective or 'artistic' or 'literary' frequently preceding it. Modernism is, from this perspective, an aesthetic or, at most, a cultural outlook to which a political theory might be attached. Such a conception is tempting since modernists could adopt quite a variety of political positions. Yet the fact that modernists cannot be conveniently located at one or even at two or three stable points on the ideological spectrum should not lead us to conclude that politics for them was merely a private matter separate from their main concerns. Modernists were, on the contrary, intensely political in their 'aesthetic' activities; they wanted to renew modern life and they organised themselves in movements to this end. To understand the politics of modernism one must therefore immanently reconstruct the political logic of their aesthetic activities. To do so is to see that modernism was bound

3. Kandinsky and Stravinsky are exceptions to the high-modernist label. Interestingly, the late Stravinsky promoted a high-modernist self-image but, as a young man, he had been deeply immersed in Russian avant-gardism and its exploration of folk culture; see Taruskin (1982).

up with a political theory of its own, and that it should be understood as a political ideology comparable to socialism, anarchism, liberalism and conservatism, rather than as an aesthetics attached to one or another of these ideologies.

By modernism I mean the collection of intellectuals and cultural movements which, with greatest intensity between 1905 and 1925, sought to foment a 'cultural renewal' of Europe. Modernists were forward-looking, yet they were highly critical of the actually existing modernisation process and aimed to disrupt the hegemony of bourgeois political institutions and cultural taste and to reinvigorate the public sphere through an insistence on the primacy of aesthetic issues and concerns.[4] Modernists differed in how they proposed to do this. Some, probably most, sought to develop a new cultural sphere based on the 'pure' qualities of each 'autonomous' art, or on a synthesis of the pure qualities of various arts. Such autonomy meant rejecting the idea of art as a 'representation' of the external world in favour of art as a 'presentation' of itself. Others preferred to mock commodified, bourgeois art in the belief that this might somehow release new, non-commodified cultural forms that could then provide the basis for a new hegemony of the aesthetic. Still others accepted commodified mass culture but sought to wrest control of it for themselves and to rebuild it in terms of avant-garde values. But all modernists believed that bourgeois society had subordinated cultural life in general, and the arts in particular, to economic-utilitarian values, bureaucratic-political modes, and standardised, industrially produced styles. In contrast to existing anti-bourgeois ideologies, which they sometimes supported but also criticised as being too beholden to processes of commodification and reification, modernists sought to make the aesthetic into an ideology that functioned against these processes and, in that sense, against all existing politics. Theirs was an effort to reconceive the political in an aesthetic key, to put values of cultural creation at the centre of society. To develop an oppositional political ideology in the usual way was, in their view, to become complicitous with now deeply entrenched bourgeois or 'materialist' modes of life, as the epigraph from Kandinsky suggests. Yet, unlike many of their Romantic forebears, they rejected all notions of a return to the pre-industrial past and believed that 'modernity' should be affirmed by reconnecting it with the myth-making and

4. 'Public sphere', used here in the sense of Habermas (1992 [1962]), refers to those institutions and venues between the governmental and private realms where citizens can present and discuss their ideas about matters of collective concern. Modernists aimed to reinvigorate this sphere by giving primacy to aesthetic over both rational-scientific and commercial values.

metaphor-creating capacities of humankind as revealed above all in 'primitive' religion and art.

In the sense that they sought to reinvigorate the public sphere by insisting on the primacy of the aesthetic, modernists aestheticised politics. Notoriously, the modernist aestheticisation of politics did prepare the ground for would-be totalitarian movements like Italian fascism and genuinely totalitarian ones like Nazism, as Walter Benjamin pointed out long ago (Benjamin 1978b [1936], pp. 241–2; on the Italian case, see Adamson, 1993). Yet this does not mean that modernism has uniformly disastrous political consequences, as some advocates of postmodernism have implied.[5] Modernists were united in their desire to aestheticise the public sphere, but the political values and aesthetic forms they associated with this sphere were quite various. Thus, modernism could and did function as a prelude to fascism and tyranny, but it could also exhibit a disruptiveness and playfulness much closer to anarchism or libertarian individualism. It was sometimes associated with political irrationalism, but sometimes also with efforts to deepen rationalism by reconnecting analytical rationality with intuition, involuntary memory, dreams and Dionysian dimensions of experience. It could imply myth, violence, sensuousness, intoxication and will, but also discipline, hardness, rigour, self-control and focus. It did sometimes imply closure but also, in other instances, a carnivalesque resistance to closure.

The claim that modernism is always and everywhere an aesthetic ideology with totalitarian potential is perhaps best viewed as an overreaction to the new-critical founders of modernist discourse who denied it any political valence at all. Another such overreaction to the new-critical version of modernism, which has gained increasing currency in recent years, is the claim that modernism is best understood as an elite-oriented market segment of an emerging mass culture industry rather than, as its champions have always argued, as a 'pure' alternative to mass culture.[6] Yet while it has been shown that modernist artists were quite capable of positioning themselves to benefit financially from the new markets for 'high' art (Jensen 1992 and 1994; FitzGerald 1995), the claim that they cynically exploited the myth of themselves as social outcasts and that their aims can be reduced to status-seeking

5. For one such argument, which traces modernist avant-gardism back to the Jena Romantics, see Lacoue-Labarthe and Nancy (1988 [1978]). For a critique of such postmodern arguments, see Jay (1992). For a postmodern conception of 'aesthetic politics' that bears many resemblances to that of the modernists, see Ankersmit (1996).

6. The notion that modernism and mass culture should be understood as alternatives is deeply ingrained in the critical literature. For two canonical statements, see Greenberg (1992 [1961]) and Adorno (1991).

and financial gain is too crude.[7] Modernists held various attitudes towards participation in mass culture, but they uniformly refused to accept the notion of the economic market or of a mass audience as the final arbiter of value and taste. Rather they retained the illusion that they remained firmly in control not only of the content and nature of their art but also of the criteria by which its value would be determined. And many modernists, even some of those most interested in pursuing a 'pure' art free of commercial contamination, actively pursued mass-cultural forms like cinema and vaudeville precisely as modes of accessing the mythic and 'primitive' in a modern context.

Baudelaire and the culture of modernity

Since modernism is often loosely deployed to denote all of early twentieth-century European culture, it is not surprising that some sceptical writers have denigrated it as the effusions of a few intellectuals who 'wrote primarily for each other, and only rarely if ever reached wider audiences in or near the seats of power' (Mayer 1981, p. 281). Undeniably, intellectual modernists included a number of extraordinary writers and artists. A list limited to those born between 1880 and 1885 would include Guillaume Apollinaire, Béla Bartók, Alban Berg, Andrei Biely, Alexander Blok, Umberto Boccioni, Georges Braque, Max Brod, Carlo Carrà, Robert Delaunay, André Derain, Walter Gropius, Jaroslav Hasek, T. E. Hulme, James Joyce, Franz Kafka, Ernst Ludwig Kirchner, D. H. Lawrence, Fernand Léger, Wyndham Lewis, Georg Lukács, Franz Marc, Ludwig Meidner, Robert Musil, Giovanni Papini, Pablo Picasso, Ezra Pound, Gino Severini, Igor Stravinsky, Anton von Webern, Virginia Woolf and Stefan Zweig. Yet what makes modernism important is less the number or quality of intellectuals who can be counted under its banner than the window it opens on a process of cultural disintegration and recomposition associated with the watershed known as 'modernity'.

Between 1880 and the First World War, the pace of technological, economic and urban development in Europe so accelerated that it appeared to create almost a new human condition (Kern 1983; Asendorf 1993; Harvey 1989, pp. 3–38 and 240–83). Features of this new and now familiar 'culture

7. Nicholls (1995, pp. 98–102) makes a similar case specifically for Italian futurism. For a reply, see Adamson (1997).

of modernity' included the enormous expansion of capitalism, commercialism and urbanisation (Schivelbusch 1995 [1983]; Zola 1992 [1883]; Handlin 1963); new industries of mass entertainment often based on new technologies like cinema (Charney and Schwartz 1995); an explosion in literacy and a greatly expanded market for newspapers (Berlin, in 1914, had about 100 dailies to complement its approximately 200 cinemas); a railway network that shrank the continent and 'industrialised' the perception of space and time (Schivelbusch 1986 [1977]); inventions such as the personal Kodak camera, bicycle, automobile, aeroplane, trolley bus, wireless telegraph and telephone that not only further shrank the globe but allowed humankind to celebrate some of its oldest fantasies (Wohl 1994); and new sciences and medical technologies designed to help humanity cope with the new speed of life (Rabinbach 1992), but which also supplied new diversions such as the opening of morgues to tourism (Charney and Schwartz 1995, pp. 297–319).

The poet Charles Baudelaire died in 1867, just as these processes of disintegration and recomposition were beginning to emerge. Yet, sensitive and prescient observer that he was, Baudelaire not only intuited the experiential nature of the modern city and of what Walter Benjamin (Benjamin 1978b [1936], pp. 221–3) has made famous as the 'loss of aura' in modern mass culture, but he also began exploring the disruptive and remedial possibilities of a new aesthetic politics.

What distinguishes Baudelaire from previous poets of the city, such as Blake and Wordsworth, is that he emphasises how modern cities, with their open and fluid patterns of circulation, bring every conceivable human type into a random and intense, if fleeting, commingling. These patterns, he fully understands, are the result of the new boulevards and new economic relations of production that separate home and work. Where not long before we had hardly ventured from our own small *quartier* and knew the faces of nearly everyone we encountered, now, in crossing the city to reach work or the new department store, we encounter the old, the blind, the poor, the dirty, the deviant, the mad, and countless others who are simply unfamiliar to us. Such people shock us and threaten our self-identities merely by presenting themselves. The ever-moving mass of deracinated individuals, anonymous but varied, make the city a spectacle which 'envelops and saturates us like the atmosphere' but which we mostly 'fail to see' (Baudelaire 1992 [1846], p. 107). Only the poet is sensitive enough to appreciate how 'marvellous' the new spectacle is: 'it's not everyone who can take a bath in a crowd; to enjoy crowds is an art' (Baudelaire 1991 [1861–9], p. 355).

Yet the poet pays a huge psychic price for his receptivity to this experience. Entering the crowd as a *flâneur*, he attempts to use the power of his gaze to control the spectacle before him and yet finds deeply threatening both the unexpectedness of what he discovers in this urban phantasmagoria and, perhaps even more, the return of its gaze upon him. Part of this latter threat is its visuality: the undeflected gaze, like the evil eye, can stop the poet in his tracks and plunge him into self-doubt; it may even threaten him with madness and will certainly deprive him of any sense of control. But part of the threat also lies in the momentariness of human encounters, which reduce the poet to the status of a contingent observation, a reproducible instance, a mere *passant*. 'What are the perils of the forest or the prairie compared with the daily shocks and conflicts of civilisation?' he asks (Baudelaire 1975 [1887], p. 663). Nonetheless, threatening as the experience is, he finds it exhilarating. As Benjamin (1983 [1938], p. 45) remarks about Baudelaire's *passante*, 'the delight of the city-dweller is not so much love at first sight as love at last sight'. If she could be held onto her appeal would be lost, and the fact that her gaze is fleeting means that his power to record his experience in language can be preserved. The 'aura' of the prolonged returned gaze 'disintegrates', as Benjamin argued (1978c [1939], pp. 188–91), in the modern 'experience of shock', but that shock is the basis of a new kind of culture which, for Baudelaire, makes possible 'the heroism of modern life' (Baudelaire 1992 [1846], p. 104).

Already in Baudelaire, then, we find a connection between the changed nature of modern urban experience and the character of modern culture, which will depend more and more upon what is reproducible rather than original: that is, as his famous definition of modernity has it, upon 'the ephemeral, the fugitive, the contingent, the half of art whose other half is the eternal and the immutable' (Baudelaire 1964 [1863], p. 13). Yet a single question haunts both realms. Can the poet retain his autonomy in the midst of modern crowds? Can his work remain genuinely autonomous, or does it, in the new world of reproducible commodities, become just another sign within the endless flow of signs? In the many encounters Baudelaire's poetry stages with the 'Other' (fallen women, beggars, the blind), it continually raises the possibility of empathy only to assume ironic distance. This seems to be because, were the poet to identify with others, he would greatly risk his autonomy, his integral self. How do I know that my desires, choices and perceptions are mine and not just acquired through identification with others? The problem is usually seen as central to the nineteenth-century novel (Girard 1980 [1961]), but it is equally pressing for Baudelaire, and it is what leads him to a stance of ironic detachment and anti-social self-privileging.

In making this move, Baudelaire implicitly makes a second one as well: he refuses to situate himself in terms of class. He is like the poor in terms of the way the bourgeois regards him; he is like the bourgeois in terms of outward appearance; he is like the aristocrat in terms of inner character and values; he is like all of these, but he is none of them. Baudelaire seeks to adopt a stance that is outside the social order, and to do so without falling back into some pre-modern utopia or primal human nature but by embracing modernity and contingency. He refuses to cede modernity to those currently in power, but he also refuses to attempt to remake it through any alliance with an existing social class. Hence his third move: to preserve his autonomy and to eschew existing class politics, while also and simultaneously reaching out to modernity, he becomes a champion of the aesthetic as a central public value. In this way he creates the basis for a political ideology that, like Marxism, is favourable to modernity but, unlike Marxism, finds nothing redemptive in bourgeois society and refuses to side with any present social group against it. Rather, insofar as Baudelaire has hope, he pins it on a relentless critique of every bourgeois value – of time as measurable, continuous evolution; of art as an arbiter of moral truth; of pity as an ethic; of mimesis as an artistic goal; of the natural as an aesthetic ideal; and of the naturalised individual, cleansed of any trace of the demonic, as a social norm. Only through such a cultural critique can modern public life be redeemed.

But can such an aesthetic politics succeed? There is little in Baudelaire to suggest a positive answer, which, possibly, is why, though he prepared the ground for the formulation of such a programme, he does not actually formulate it himself. His charm is that, even as he knows his efforts will fail (except as poetry), he never loses his enthusiasm for pressing forward into the urban crowd. In this regard he is bolder than the other writers of his era, like Flaubert, Dostoyevsky and Nietzsche, who shared his anti-bourgeois individualism, his refusal of class politics, and his new anti-historical sense of time as a kind of perpetual emergency, and whose work similarly suggested the need for a strategic shift from political confrontation to aesthetic outflanking. Together they represented a formidable aesthetic opposition both to bourgeois society and to existing forms of anti-bourgeois politics like socialism and aesthetic naturalism, even if they were unable to see beyond a politics of tragic impasse. Only Nietzsche, with his idea of decadence as a seedbed for cultural rebirth, seriously contemplated the way forward. But, as he knew all too well, his readers were as yet unborn.

Aesthetic politics and the emergence of modernism

Baudelaire's generation were the modernist pioneers of aesthetic opposition to what they saw as an emerging world of commercial degradation, spiritual decadence and cultural pastiche aimed at concealing the disruptive effects of the new. Yet, given their ineffectiveness in launching the transvaluation of values they sought, those in the next generation who inherited their commitment to cultural renewal faced the challenge of better articulating how it might be forged. For the French symbolists, especially their leading poet Stéphane Mallarmé, the answer lay in a more aggressive deployment of the non-social, 'literary' or 'world-disclosing' dimensions of language.

First formulated in a manifesto by Jean Moréas (1992 [1886], p. 224), symbolism was to be built on 'an archetypal and complex style: unpolluted words, firm periods to act as buttresses and alternate with others of undulating faintness, the significant pleonasm, the mysterious ellipsis, the suspended anacolutha, every trope daring and multiform'; in short, a writing that would 'hurl the sharp terms of language like Thracian archers their sinuous arrows'. Yet, in Mallarmé's hands, these poetics operate much more timidly than such metaphors suggest, a fact not lost upon Moréas who broke publicly with symbolism in 1891 in favour of the more potent, nationalistic medicine of the *école romane* he then co-founded with the young Charles Maurras.[8] Mallarmé believed that the way to a purified language was to 'still' the poet's own voice (Mallarmé 1956a [1886–95], p. 40) and to let 'that part of speech which is not spoken' (Mallarmé 1956b [1894], p. 33) take the initiative – speech being 'no more than a commercial approach to reality' (Mallarmé 1956a [1886–95], p. 40). Drawing in part on Baudelaire's notion (Baudelaire 1991 [1861–9], pp. 28–31) of 'correspondences', the result is a hermetic poetry of cool hyper-refinement that owes much to Platonism but also something to the typographical innovations of modern consumer advertisements, which intrigued Mallarmé despite his aversion to commercialism (Drucker 1994, p. 51). By the 1890s, however, symbolism had become mired in aestheticism and decadence, standpoints also given to solitude and withdrawal to advance hopes of cultural renewal. In the hands of a writer like Gabriele D'Annunzio, for example, the decadent transformation of symbolism led to macabre, sado-masochistic fantasies of misogyny, suicide and murder, but, however shocking, such images merely reinforced

8. Modern nationalist politics was rooted in a break with the symbolist or aestheticist movement not only in France but also in Italy, where the key nationalist figure, Enrico Corradini, began as an aestheticist. On the Italian case, see Drake (1981) and Adamson (1993).

cultural pessimism, cynicism and privatism rather than leading to any public assertion of aesthetic values.[9]

Only after 1900 would Baudelaire's aesthetic and Nietzsche's notion of decadence as a seedbed for cultural renewal be seized upon as the basis for a new political initiative by literary and artistic intellectuals, who now commonly organised themselves as self-conscious avant-gardes dedicated to public displays of vitality and dynamism.[10] The first major movement was German expressionism which, though named as such only in 1911, had already begun to develop by 1905 among the Dresden artists known as die Brücke. Their art was marked by an interest in primitivism (a parallel inquiry into which was begun almost simultaneously by Picasso), through which they hoped to reignite a cultural imagination grown dim by civilisation, and which led them to explore the aggressive effects of colour, distortion and a radical simplification of form. In 1911 another group of artists, led by Kandinsky and Franz Marc, organised Blaue Reiter in Munich, and soon published an 'almanac' exhibiting their sense of cultural emergency and the aesthetic means through which they hoped to foment 'spiritual revolution'. At about the same time, groups of writers calling themselves expressionist, and actively pursuing such a spiritual revolution, began to take shape in many German cities, above all Berlin.

Compared with the Baudelairean tradition in France, expressionism was more ambivalent about modernity, especially modern technologies, machines and urbanism. The fact that capitalism in Germany meant the reinforcement of the military might of the state as much as it did private consumerism, and that the state was seen as allied with a feudal past of conservative and military values, surely contributed to this ambivalence. Expressionist art and literature are strongly marked by the critique of patriarchal authority, one frequently dramatised through an atmosphere of violent emotion and Oedipal crisis. Ideals of libertarianism and pacificism are also more prevalent here than in other modernist movements, as is the sharp juxtaposition of dark images of the city – of tenements, factories, sexual depravity, crime and disease – with apocalyptic images of utopian hope. Yet if a rediscovery of the primitive was a major source of this hope, this 'primitive' was to be found not only in ethnographic museums but also in

9. D'Annunzio's pre-war literary opus stands in contrast to his capacity, demonstrated in and after the war, to wield poetic imagery in a public performance that greatly influenced the subsequent symbolic politics of Italian fascism.

10. Bourdieu has plausibly argued (1992, p. 174) that French symbolism is already an 'avant-garde'. But it weakened in the 1890s, and was unable to spawn comparable movements elsewhere.

the new urban life itself. 'We have forms that absolutely enthral everyone in exactly the same way as the fire dance enthrals the African or the mysterious drumming of the fakirs enthrals the Indian', wrote August Macke (1974 [1912], pp. 87–8), a young Blaue Reiter painter killed in the first weeks of the First World War. 'At the movies the professor marvels alongside the servant girl; in the vaudeville theatre the butterfly-coloured dancer enchants the most amorous couples as intensely as the solemn sound of the organ in a Gothic cathedral seizes both believer and unbeliever.'

Berlin's foremost journal of expressionism was *Der Sturm*, edited by Herwarth Walden. Despite its expressionist ambivalence towards modern technology, *Der Sturm* was enthusiastic in its reception of Italian futurism, organising two major exhibitions in 1912 and 1913, publishing many of its manifestos, and helping futurism's impresario, F. T. Marinetti, make his month-long tour of Russia in February 1914. Yet this relationship was at least as much the triumph of Marinetti who, despite his nationalism, was unbounded and unparalleled in his enthusiasm for bringing avant-garde modernism onto an international stage.

Tireless promoter and self-promoter, Marinetti launched futurism in February 1909 with a manifesto in *Le Figaro*, thus establishing from the outset its international character and his talent for utilising the power of the press and advertising. Within a year he had brought many poets and artists into his movement, and by the onset of the war, having spent much of the past five years shuttling by rail between European capitals, he was in command of an Italy-centred but genuinely trans-European movement. In essence, Marinetti conceived futurism as a direct translation of modern space-time compression into an aesthetic of *velocità*, an aesthetic that would inform every aspect of modern public life, from architecture and education to politics and sexual relationships, to food, clothing and entertainment. Moreover, his mode of publicity, which depended heavily on achieving notoriety through public performances known as *serate*, was no less linked to the modern condition than his aesthetic and the politics it implied. 'I believe that the most fertile and reinvigorating ideas cannot [any longer] be propagated by the book', he wrote to an admirer (Adamson 1997, p. 100).

> Ideas in books are hopelessly bewildering to people, given the flood of industrial and commercial forces, and the sickness and tiredness of the human brain, shaken by the incessant racket of economic interests in a life that has become, for almost everyone, more cinematographic and anxious than ever. We must therefore adapt the movement of ideas to the frenetic movement of our acts.

More than any other modernist, Marinetti understood that modern life was based on a dominance of vision, that visual images would not only increasingly displace written forms but also reorient print media by heightening the visual dimensions of their typography. He understood that such images were commodified, implying the need to reconstruct one's public persona as a set of masks and poses. Though he himself began as a symbolist poet, he was contemptuous of intellectual movements that pursued *recherché* language because he understood that modern public life was also inherently democratic.[11] In his own poetry, he insisted on a radical suppression of psychic interiors and an accessible presentation in typographical designs that drew upon and, in turn, influenced modern advertising. Moreover, the innovations he and other futurists produced in literature, painting, film and theatre were frequently linked to the newer mass entertainment venues, such as variety theatre and cabaret, and his *serate* are best understood as a wholly new sort of mass-cultural performance in which the audience is teased into becoming the source of their turbulent, raucous and sometimes violent drama. Like Baudelaire's *flâneur* in the Parisian crowd, the futurist poets wandering onto the stage depend upon the audience to provide spontaneity and constant shocks; the result is a performance that breaks free of mimesis, acting out the modernist imperative to have art 'present' rather than 'represent'. Indeed, for Marinetti and the futurists, not only were modernism and mass culture compatible, but only through a reconstructed mass-cultural performance was it possible to realise a pure, non-mimetic art.

That Marinetti launched futurism from Paris and did much of his early writing in French testified to the mythic status of that city within the international modernist avant-garde. Long celebrated for a *vie de bohème* that offered cheap living amidst intellectual freedom and cosmopolitan tolerance, Paris by the late nineteenth century was attracting many of Europe's foremost writers and artists, who arrived by rail to live for months or years in the city and then, sometimes, moved on or returned home to reinvigorate their cultural roots. In addition to Marinetti, prominent avant-gardists meeting this description included Apollinaire, Picasso, Severini, Mécislas Golberg, Blaise Cendrars, Serge Jastrebzoff, Giorgio de Chirico, Ardengo Soffici, Arthur Cravan and the art dealer Daniel-Henry Kahnweiler. They

11. Though Marinetti rejected parliamentarism, he always insisted on the concept of democracy when discussing futurism's cultural politics, which was relentlessly anti-monarchical, anti-clerical and anti-classical. See Marinetti (1983b [1919]).

contributed significantly to avant-garde institutions such as the Salon des Indépendants and the Salon d'Automne, as well as to reviews such as *Gil Blas, La Plume* and, in the two years before the First World War, *Les Soirées de Paris*, co-edited by Apollinaire and Jastrebzoff.

Though intertwined with every other modernist avant-garde and quite varied and dispersed in its own right, the Parisian movement coalesced from 1908 to 1912 primarily around cubism – both the Montmartre cubism led by Picasso and Braque, which also included Apollinaire, Kahnweiler, André Salmon, Maurice Raynal and Max Jacob, and the group at suburban Créteil (later Puteaux) that included Albert Gleizes, Jean Metzinger, Alexander Mercereau, Roger Allard (who would contribute to the *Blaue Reiter Almanac*), and the pre-futurist Marinetti. By 1913, Apollinaire was supporting the 'orphism' of Robert Delaunay, first exhibited that spring, over cubism's relative austerity, and he and Cendrars also briefly participated in futurism, which took off in Paris after its first major exhibition there in February 1912. Cendrars (1922 [1917], p. 265) was especially excited by futurist insights into the way commodification was linked with space-time compression such that 'produce, from five parts of the globe, is united on the same plate, in the same dress'.

Like the German expressionists, the cubists immersed themselves in 'primitive' art in order to upset naturalised bourgeois versions of the modern, release repressed libidinal energies, and test the boundaries of the mimetic. Indeed, their juxtapositions of modern and primitive were often more violent (as in Apollinaire's poem *Zone*) than those of the expressionists, who seem to have found greater human continuity between the primitive and themselves. Like the futurists, the cubists were interested in the modern for what they perceived as its dynamism, but they conceived it not as movement or speed but as 'simultaneity', which they explored by freezing time, emphasising the plasticity of forms, and rejecting unitary perspective in favour of connections among multiple, spatially defined perspectives. This effort led them, partly under the philosophical influence of Henri Bergson (Antliff 1993), to dissociate language (pictorial or verbal) from practices of discursive analysis, and to reconceive it as an intuitive synthesis of memory and experience. In this conception, the active role of the viewer or reader was much increased. As Gleizes and Metzinger (1964 [1912], p. 12) put it: 'in order that the spectator, ready to establish unity himself, may apprehend all the elements in the order assigned to them by creative intuition, the properties of each portion must be left independent, and the plastic continuity must be broken into a thousand surprises of light and shade'.

For Apollinaire too, the forms on Picasso's canvas or in his own poetry were material for an active search for the object. Thus, while representation had not entirely escaped, the idea of art as a window on the world was rejected, and emphasis was placed on the audience's active perception, remembering and creative constitution. Yet the problem he found in cubism (especially Braque's) was its excessive intellectualism. His excitement about Delaunay lay in the latter's theorisation of simultaneity in terms of colour and 'simultaneous contrasts' which ensured 'the dynamism of colours'.[12] Apollinaire's brief flirtation with futurism also arose from its heightened emotional pitch, though he soon realised that, for him, futurism was not intellectualist enough. He always insisted on a concept of language as a human activity confronting experience and resisting the transcendence of the subject–object dichotomy that the futurists, like the symbolists before them, believed a properly performative language could provide.[13] But he did accept their interest in mass culture and recognised the importance for avant-garde art of signs, posters and advertisements (Apollinaire 1972b [1913], p. 269).

The transformation of modernist politics during and after the First World War

In addition to German expressionism, Italian futurism and French cubism, modernist movements existed in many other European cities, often as spin-offs like British vorticism or Russian futurism, both of which were heavily influenced by Marinetti. In the atmosphere of 1913–14, most of these movements saw the coming war as an opening to the bolder modernity of their dreams, and they actively campaigned for it, but when it proved neither heroic nor short, the atmosphere became dispirited and cynical, and new avant-gardisms reflecting it, like dada, were born. At the same time, the pre-war movements lost momentum, were put on the defensive by their interventionism, and, by 1918, commonly submerged themselves within more politically organised movements of both right and left. The pre-war project of modernist cultural renewal based on a reinvigoration of the aesthetic in the public sphere now appeared naïve and futile, and it was never again put forward in quite the same way.

12. Apollinaire (1972a [1912], p. 263). The citation is from Delaunay, 'On the Construction of Reality in Pure Painting', a declaration embedded within Apollinaire's article, which appeared originally in the December 1912 issue of *Der Sturm*.
13. On futurist *parole in libertà* (words set free), see Marinetti (1983a [1913]). Though aimed at the same goal, this programme for a language that breaks down the subject–object dichotomy is much more activist and irrationalist than the symbolist notion of 'stilling the poet's voice'.

Dada arose in February 1916 in Zurich, where German expressionists like Hans Arp, Hugo Ball, Emmy Hennings and Richard Huelsenbeck gathered with other modernists opposed to the war at the Cabaret Voltaire, run by Ball. The most notorious among them was the Romanian Tristan Tzara who best personified the movement's black humour, sense of outrage and fantasies of destruction, and who took it to Paris in 1920. Unlike earlier modernisms, Tzara's dada had no positive programme. As André Breton declared (1981 [1924], p. 203), 'cubism was a school of painting, futurism a political movement: dada is a state of mind' – elements, however artificially separated, that he would later seek to recombine in surrealism. Yet Tzara got much mileage out of mocking earlier avant-gardes while adopting futurism's performance style. He wrote 'manifestos' proclaiming that 'in principle I am against manifestos, as I am also against principles' (Tzara 1981a [1918], p. 76), and he composed and performed 'simultaneous poems', in which multiple voices recited the parts at the same time in different languages. Like Marinetti, one of his aims was notoriety but, unlike Marinetti, he had no hope for a constructive transformation of modern culture. In that sense, his avant-gardism, and that of dada generally, were self-contradictory.

Another contradiction in dada is best illustrated by the artist Marcel Duchamp, a friend of many of the dadaists and editor of *New York Dada* (1921), who nonetheless declined to join them in Zurich. In and out of the early cubist circle around Gleizes and Metzinger, Duchamp withdrew in 1912 when they declined to exhibit his painting because it failed to fit their programme, and during the next years when his notorious ready-mades appeared (the last and most famous, the urinal by 'R. Mutt', is from 1917) he lived as a loner on the edge of avant-gardism, illustrating what Tzara may have meant when he declared that 'the true dadas are against dada' (Tzara 1981b [1920], p. 92).

Despite these contradictions, however, many modernists after the war still saw dada as the best hope for realising their pre-war project in a world in which, as Gleizes put it (1981 [1920], p. 298), 'the hierarchy of bourgeois capitalism is crumbling . . . and men are being tossed this way and that, with very little idea of what is happening', while 'political parties from the extreme right to the extreme left continue to accuse one another of every crime'. Certainly the more organised and programmatic surrealism that Breton developed in 1922 owed much to dadaist experiments with objective chance, automatic writing and group writing, as well as its interest in the 'uncanny' (Nicholls 1995, p. 279; Foster 1993, pp. xi–xii), which was then also being explored by Sigmund Freud. Surrealism also inherited dada's intense anti-nationalism and anti-militarism. Yet, unlike dada, it accepted the need for new structures, even if the way to them lay through the unconscious mind, which surrealism closely connected with the Freudian death instinct. Surrealism hoped to locate such structures by unearthing from objects the 'veiled-erotic' and 'fixed-explosive' elements of human desire (Foster 1993, pp. 21–8). Once our sense of how reality has been shaped by human desires was reawakened, they assumed, we would be able to break through the commodity fetishism of modern life, 'win the energies of intoxication for the revolution' (Benjamin 1978a [1929], p. 189), and re-enchant modern public life by recovering the 'marvellous' buried within it. In this sense, they returned to the political project of pre-war modernism, supplementing pre-war Bergson with post-war Freud. Yet, just as pre-war modernism collapsed on the shoals of the First World War, surrealism gave way under the pressure of the Great Depression and Stalin's 'left turn', as Breton's bitter second manifesto of 1929 sadly testifies.

Though they zealously guarded their independence as movements, both dada and surrealism were clearly on the left. Dada's leftism is best illustrated by the German dadaists, who returned to Berlin in 1918 to fight side by side (though not always harmoniously) with many expressionists in favour of a socialist revolution. Likewise surrealism's flirtation with French communism is well known, even if its ambivalences and their internal disagreements are sometimes underestimated. Other modernisms, like Italian futurism, allied themselves with fascism, though again there were many tensions and complexities in such associations. By the end of the war, pressures on modernists to associate with a political party of the clearly defined left or right were intense. Experiences of 'conversion' in 1918, such as Lukács' sudden embrace of communism, were only the most dramatic instances of this politicisation of modernism.

In pre-war modernism, by contrast, distinctions of left and right tended to blur, as those who argue, for example, that the German expressionists were 'left-wing Nietzscheans' ultimately discover.[14] Partly, this blurring was a function of issues chosen: whether to accept or reject consumer-oriented mass culture, or how to overcome a naturalising, bourgeois aesthetic, were not questions that lent themselves to left–right thinking, rooted as such

14. This argument is made in Taylor (1990). Yet, he is forced to confess that one important component of German expressionism, Der Neue Club, 'did have a right-wing tendency and their cultural critique shared many of the characteristics of the critique of Wilhelminian Germany made by revolutionary conservatives. It would be wrong, though, to conclude that this is true of all or even a majority of expressionists' (p. 54).

thinking is in political debates about 'liberty, equality, and fraternity' rather than in aesthetic or cultural ones. Partly, too, it was a function of what one student of expressionism has called the 'fragile balance between national identity and international aspirations' (Lloyd 1991, p. 59) that characterised that movement and most modernist movements elsewhere. As previously noted, modernists often crossed national boundaries to come together in cosmopolitan centres, having left behind some provincial, popular culture to which ambivalent, emotional attachments remained. Though estrangement from moribund localisms frequently provided the motivation to leave them, they could equally well become a source of inspiration for modernists labouring to counter the degraded commercialism of the urban cultures they had joined. Amidst rising international tensions and approaching war, the creative stimulus they found in local cultures often pushed them towards nationalist sentiment, even as their common cosmopolitan life, and the avant-garde linkages among cities they built, made them internationalist as well.

One of the best-known theoretical texts of pre-war German expressionism was Wilhelm Worringer's *Abstraction and Empathy*, which sought to contrast the psychological underpinnings of the aesthetic of 'abstraction' dominant in 'primitive' art with the realist aesthetic of 'empathy' more dominant recently, an investigation mostly conducted on a universalist level. Nonetheless, Worringer could not resist aligning primitivism and abstraction with 'Northern peoples', in contrast to the greater realism of 'Romance peoples' (Worringer 1953 [1908], pp. 31–3). Similarly, the main thrust of French cubism was universalist but, especially in the group around Gleizes and Metzinger, a species of 'Celtic nationalism' prevailed that led some of them to join the Celtic League, founded in 1911 amidst an intensifying French debate on cultural identity (Antliff 1993, pp. 106–34). With such an affiliation, they believed, their politics could appear as an attractive, progressive alternative to Action Française and other forces of the new right.

For the German and French avant-gardes, as well as for the Italian futurists, nationalist commitments were useful in lending political concreteness to the explorations of the mythic dimensions of culture in which they were all engaged. And, with a distinct nationalism of their own, they not only countered the conservative rhetoric of new-right movements but also distinguished themselves from socialism and symbolism (which had largely repressed its creative kinship to folk art). The difficulty was that, with their contradictory amalgam of nationalist and internationalist elements, their refusal to take sides in the established political confrontation, and their inability to specify what an anti-bourgeois cultural politics would finally amount to, modernists were never able to translate their utopian aspirations for modernity into a vision transcending the merely negative politics suggested by Kandinsky's enemies' list of 1911.

In hindsight, of course, modernism as a political theory may appear to have been doomed more by the overwhelming power of the forces over which it sought control – the emerging international industries of commodified, mass culture – than by its own shortcomings. By the 1920s mass culture in Germany had reached the level of 'cartelisation' (Gay 1968, p. 133), and a new generation of modernist critics associated with the Frankfurt school like Theodor Adorno and Max Horkheimer, as well as others closely allied with them like Benjamin and Siegfried Kracauer, would turn their theoretical imagination and energy to the political implications of mass culture. Yet even if one accepts the direst Frankfurt school verdict on modern culture as articulated in Horkheimer and Adorno's *Dialectic of Enlightenment*, it can still be argued that, like Marx's idea of proletarian revolution (similarly vanquished in this century by international capitalism, or so it now appears), avant-garde modernism immeasurably enriched the mass cultures that ultimately engulfed it.[15]

The era between the late nineteenth-century onset of the culture of modernity and the Second World War appears in retrospect as a first, transitional phase of mass society in which the relation between the aristocratic standards of a 'persistent old regime' and the market forces and mass-audience appeals associated with a rising mass politics and culture was being renegotiated. Modernists were pivotal participants in this renegotiation. Though they generally detested the old elites who sought to preserve their privileges through the institutions of state, army and university, they shared many elite values. And though they were generally sympathetic with popular cultures and mass aspirations, they feared the vulgarisation and their own disempowerment that a mass culture portended. Thus their political choices and 'conversions' in the inter-war period, however wide-ranging, reflected their common desire to create a public life of mass inclusion without surrendering to exchange value as the arbiter of cultural value. Ultimately, none of their efforts to do this succeeded, and, as Jürgen Habermas argued after the war (Habermas 1992 [1962], pp. 159–95), the modern public sphere has

15. For a parallel argument regarding twentieth-century Marxist revolution, specifically the Soviet case, see Hobsbawm (1994, pp. 7–8).

largely been transformed from a 'culture-debating' to a 'culture-consuming' sphere, a mere 'platform for advertising'.[16]

More important than modernism's success or failure, however, is the neglected truth about early twentieth-century political ideology in Europe to which its political ideas call attention. While many of the central antagonisms of those tumultuous years involved the political and economic dimensions of modernity, and are thus appropriately understood in the left–right terms ultimately rooted in class and class conflict, these years were also about what constitutes the public life and culture most appropriate to modernity. Appreciating modernism as a contributor to this latter struggle helps to clarify otherwise intractable problems connected with left-versus-right understandings of early twentieth-century politics. Did Benjamin, for example, let his passion for a culturally redeemed modernity lead him into an implicit collaboration with the fascist aestheticisation of politics he himself exposed, as one critic has charged (Bersani 1990, p. 60)? It is true that Benjamin remained a believer in the modernist project of revitalising the modern public sphere through its aesthetic dimension but, however nostalgic he may sometimes have been in his portrayal of the auratic cultural world we have lost, he would never have sought to recapture it with anything approximating fascist public rituals. Benjamin's concept of modernism, like Adorno's, is at the polar opposite of the Schillerian model of a reconciled wholeness that postmodernists fear. The two differed in their concept of a modernist politics: Benjamin hoped that the end of art as a 'beautiful illusion' distanced from everyday life might provide the opportunity for its democratisation, while Adorno feared that any strategy other than a high-modernist withdrawal from the public sphere would only hasten the fall into propagandistic mass art or commercialised mass culture. But they shared a modernist belief in art as a last refuge of modernity's utopian aspirations, as well as a modernist hesitancy to theorise the institutional basis for renewing modern life. Their modernist visions, in their utopian passion and practical open-endedness, illustrated again what had always been the great strength of modernism as political theory: its uncompromising tenacity in thinking through the needs of the historical present. Unfortunately, they also replicated its fatal weakness: an inability to generate a political vision sufficiently hardheaded to command serious attention in the push and pull of actually existing politics.

16. My difference with Habermas (1992 [1962]) is that he pushes the starting date for this deterioration back to 1850, while I would date it from 1945 and treat the intervening period as a complex negotiation over the institutions and values of an emerging mass culture.

20
The new science of politics

JAMES FARR

The political scientist must be something of a utopian in his prophetic view and something both of a statesman and a scientist in his practical methods (Charles E. Merriam 1925).

New ways to comprehend and control politics have been prophesied for the last half-millennium. Machiavelli blazed a 'new route' to traverse Renaissance statecraft. Hobbes constructed a new 'civil science' to pacify the revolutionary 1640s. Hume anticipated the novelty of the Enlightenment enterprise 'to reduce politics to a science'. Adams conjured a 'divine science of politics' to consecrate a constitutional order without precedent. Hamilton heralded the 'vast improvements' and 'wholly new discoveries' in 'the science of politics' for post-revolutionary republics. Tocqueville foresaw 'a new political science . . . for a world itself quite new'. The pattern continues into the third millennium, marking more than a century since the academic discipline of political science emerged in the 1880s. A 'new science of politics' was anticipated in the 1920s and 1930s, and was followed by a 'behavioural revolution' in the 1950s and 1960s. The conceptions of science backing these anticipatory 'new' schemes varied considerably, as did the political contexts within which they developed and the political projects to which they contributed.

The twentieth-century chapter in the venerable new science of politics is best understood, in its political dimensions, as a species of democratic theory, marked by increasingly technical methods and a healthy dose of realism about power, propaganda and public opinion. It is less famous than those grand 'isms' that have dominated twentieth-century political thought. But it intersects them, especially modernism, positivism, liberalism, socialism and fascism. It has been implicated by historians in more complex 'isms', including consensus liberalism, American exceptionalism, disenchanted realism, even scientism (see, variously, Crick 1959; Somit and Tanenhaus 1967; Seidelman and Harpham 1985; and Ross 1991). When the accent falls on *science* – as opposed to political theory generally – the twentieth century's chapter has been most vocally an American affair. In the 1920s and 1930s, the dominant figures were Charles Merriam and Harold Lasswell. This is not to deny worldwide contributions and consequences (see Farr 2004), nor the fact that Merriam and Lasswell followed Graham Wallas and allied with George E. G. Catlin, two crucial English political scientists, among others. Their shared emphases on psychology, control and the problems of democracy – including those confronting propaganda – were reactions to nineteenth-century statism, formalism and the rise of a mass public. Their followers in the 1950s and 1960s carried on as self-styled behaviouralists who were making revolution. This chapter is a short history of their contribution to twentieth-century *political* thought, with as close attention to their words, texts and contexts as space allows.

The psychological science of control

The 1920s witnessed new zeal to make the study of politics a genuine science. The first National Conference on the Science of Politics was held in 1923. Behind the conference lay the earlier efforts of the American Political Science Association's (APSA) Committee on Political Research; and behind this a forward-looking inventory of 'The Present State of the Study of Politics' that aimed at 'the reconstruction of methods' (Merriam 1921, p. 174). Two more national conferences followed in 1924 and 1925, as did a manifesto hailing *New Aspects of Politics* (1925). These conferences, committees and writings resulted from the labours of Charles Edward Merriam. A public figure and presidential adviser, Merriam also founded the Social Science Research Council (SSRC) in 1923 and forged the influential 'Chicago school' of political scientists (see Karl 1974). Before the Second World War, a number of Merriam's colleagues and students – especially the imaginative and prolific Harold D. Lasswell – would join him in constructing and publicising a new science of politics that was enthusiastic about methods and realistic about democracy in the wake of the First World War. Their efforts would be continued well into the 1950s and 60s by their behavioural descendants.

Merriam and company struck a pose against the reigning styles of political study. Traditional political theory was stigmatised as formalistic, and its history a memorial of dead dogmas. Although his early career fitted this mould, Merriam came to dismiss the 'airy hypotheses' of most political theorists from Plato onwards. George E. G. Catlin disparaged 'the unguarded field of political theory' as 'the rubbish of uncritical speculation' (Catlin 1927, p. 143). Political theory and its historiography needed overhauling. Thus, in *New Aspects of Politics*, Merriam opined that 'a history of the process of political thinking, as distinguished from the history of political theory, would be very valuable' (Merriam 1970 [1925], pp. 79, 132, 300n). By political thinking he meant 'the methods of political reasoning' and by history a compressed sketch of four stages:

1. the a priori and deductive method, down to 1850;
2. the historical and comparative method, 1850–1900;
3. the present tendency toward observation, survey, measurement, 1900–;
4. the beginnings of the psychological treatment of politics.

Merriam's influential sketch was noteworthy, quite apart from its decidedly Whiggish bent. In the name of new thinking, it pronounced dead all deductive methods of a non-empirical kind, as well as the nominally empirical method of historical comparison. The latter was associated with such earlier German, English and American figures as Johann Bluntschli, Francis Lieber, Henry Sumner Maine, John Seeley, John W. Burgess, Woodrow Wilson and James Bryce (see Collini, Winch and Burrow 1983; Gunnell 1993). Their collection of comparative 'facts' about ancient and modern states served as the methodological foundation for their own 'new science' (Macy 1917, p. 4), namely, 'the science of the state'. Reports of its death were premature, but dating an end was rhetorically useful for rejecting statism, historicism and empiricist simplicities like Bryce's: 'it is the Facts that are needed; Facts, Facts, Facts'. In their place, the twentieth-century's new science advanced *psychology* and *control*. These words convey much about the self-understanding of the new scientists, and recall Graham Wallas's influence.

Wallas was famous for his own scientific 'manifesto' (Lippmann 1913, p. 78), *Human Nature and Politics*. Published originally in 1908, it was in its third edition by 1921 on the eve of Merriam's efforts to organise his national conferences on the science of politics. 'The study of politics is just now in a curiously unsatisfactory position', it began. The traditions of rationalism and intellectualism that had dominated political study had failed to analyse 'man' underneath formal institutions, including representative democracies. In particular, the dark realities of psychological emotion, behaviour and opinion had been virtually neglected, save for a few pioneering studies by Gabriel Tarde and Gustave Le Bon concerning mass hysteria and crowd psychosis. Rationalism and intellectualism failed, furthermore, to explain how those elites most experienced in representative democracies were the most 'disappointed and apprehensive' about it. A proper science of politics, therefore, needed to be placed upon a psychological foundation with considerable investment in statistics and quantitative methods of the sort for which Karl Pearson was noteworthy. Only this would allow the understanding and 'control' of the 'empirical art of politics', namely 'the creation of opinion by the deliberate exploitation of sub-conscious non-rational inferences' (Merriam 1921, pp. 18, 25, 75).

Praised by Merriam as 'brilliant, stimulating and suggestive, rather than systematic' (Merriam 1970 [1925], pp. 130f.), Wallas's manifesto illuminated an agenda for the new science. His particular allegiances to associationism proved more incidental to his American followers. Lasswell, for example, gravitated toward Freudianism, and Merriam toward behaviourism (loosely conceived). Indeed, Merriam hailed a 'science of political behaviour' that named the movement of the next generation (Merriam 1970 [1925], p. 348). But Wallas's manifesto broke ground for crucial studies like *Public Opinion and Representative Government* (1913 and 1921) by A. Lawrence Lowell, professor of government and president of Harvard. In *Public Opinion* (1922) and *The Phantom Public* (1925) Wallas's most famous student, Walter Lippmann, underscored both the incompetence of the masses to govern themselves and the need for scientific expertise in government. William B. Munro proposed 'the law of the pendulum' as one of the few 'inexorable laws' of politics that explained how mass opinion swung from one ideological extreme to the other (Munro 1927, p. 35). Reflecting this rather pessimistic mood, Merriam imagined writing the 'history of political unreason, folly and prejudice' (Merriam 1970 [1925], p. 338). Lasswell nearly realised this ambition in *Psychopathology and Politics* (1930) and *World Politics and Personal Insecurity* (1935). The titles capture Lasswell's assessment of the psychic extremities of politics in the inter-war era, and the texts advocated science as an instrument for controlling them.

Two senses of control were embraced. The first concerned scientific practice itself, as Merriam's chronology and Catlin's groundwork, *Science and Methods of Politics* (1927), made clear. Observation, survey and measurement were techniques of scientific control that constituted practices internal to science. To them were added experimentation, quantification, operationalisation and many specific methods, notably sample surveys and depth interviews. These techniques, allegedly, were normatively neutral (or value-free) respecting the phenomena being studied. They also systematically ordered data collection and the testing of generalisations or laws (ideally 'inexorable' ones, as Munro thought). These generalisations or laws, not mere facts, constituted scientific theories capable of explanation and prediction. Natural science was the cognitive ideal. To judge by citations to Pearson and P. T. Bridgman – as well as gestures to European positivism and American pragmatism – that ideal was an instrumentalist one.

The second sense of control idealised the social function of science when it solved or prevented problems in politics external to itself. Political science was thus 'the science of political control' (Merriam 1970 [1925], p. 312), and political scientists were 'technicians . . . of the political' (Merriam 1934, p. 39). Lasswell called them 'skill specialists' and the next generation 'policy scientists'. Most agreed that political scientists were to use their new science to remedy problems associated with governmental inaction, administrative inefficiency and uninformed or discontented citizens. The last of these problems cried out for citizen education, now thematised by the technical interest in control. Merriam thought that citizen education could be another science of control: 'the science of civic training' (Merriam 1931, p. 348).

The science of civic training was to be a proper science. That is, it sought to develop generalisations, at best laws, about the processes of civic education, based on comparative research and the psychological insight of expert professionals. It also sought to develop techniques for the actual control and training of citizens. ('It is possible to build the citizen from the ground up' (Merriam 1931, p. 331).) The techniques varied according to the primary agencies of training, including language, literature, the press, the military, political parties and (especially) schools. Behind these arose the spectre of modern propaganda, especially as practised in Germany, Italy, Great Britain, the Soviet Union and the United States during the First World War. These countries formed the core of Merriam's nine-nation 'Civic Training Series' which he summarised as *The Making of Citizens* (1931).

Political science's confrontation with propaganda was unavoidable and perhaps over-determined in an era of mass democracy and international hostility. This confrontation reveals so much about the political thought, intentions and context of the new political scientists that it deserves closer attention, even in so short a history as this.

The political science of propaganda

Propaganda was firmly impressed upon the modern psyche by the 1920s. There was the older history associated with religious (especially Catholic) dogma. Other dogmas, like Soviet Marxism, consciously produced their own 'propaganda' for agitation and motivation. By the turn of the twentieth century, commercial publicity had proved so successful that Lowell called it 'the Age of Advertisement' (Lowell 1921, p. 58). But the First World War proved to be particularly important. German propaganda was made infamous – and bested – by Allied propaganda. British fabrications of German war crimes were revealed after the 1915 report of the Committee on Alleged German Outrages headed by James Bryce. In the United States, the wartime success of the Committee of Public Information (CPI), created by Woodrow Wilson and placed under George Creel, did not ensure its survival past 1919 because of disillusionment with war propaganda on all sides. For many, the term 'propaganda' was permanently tarnished; for others, including the new political scientists, its aura of manipulation and power held enormous fascination for research and control amidst red scares, Nazi threats, and public relations.

Political scientists extensively analysed the theory and practice of propaganda during and between the two world wars. This is intellectually and sociologically crucial. Merriam served on the CPI, as did Lippmann and Edward Bernays, the founder of modern public relations and author of *Crystallizing Public Opinion* (1923) and *Propaganda* (1928). As commissioner in Rome, Merriam recounted his experiences in 'American Publicity in Italy' (1919). When a larger project failed to interest the University of Chicago Press, Merriam complained that 'the technique of propaganda . . . remains largely unexplored' (Merriam 1970 [1925], p. 304). However, he advised his star student, Lasswell, to pursue it for a dissertation. When *Propaganda Technique in the World War* was published, Lasswell clarified his frank intent 'to evolve an explicit theory of how international war propaganda may be conducted with success' (Lasswell 1927a, p. 12). Theoretical intentions aside, it was also a work of surpassing rhetorical power and bracing political judgement.

> Propaganda is a reflex to the immensity, the rationality and wilfulness of the modern world. It is the new dynamic of society, for power is subdivided and diffused, and more can be won by illusion than by coercion. It has all the prestige of the new and provokes all the animosity of the baffled. To illuminate the mechanisms of propaganda is to reveal the secret springs of social action, and to expose to the most searching criticism our prevailing dogmas of sovereignty, of democracy, of honesty, and of the sanctity of individual opinion (Lasswell 1927a, p. 222).

A decade-long series of works established Lasswell as 'the world's foremost specialist . . . in the scientific analysis of propaganda' (Smith 1969, pp. 56f.). This made him Merriam's choice to head the SSRC's new Committee on Pressure Groups and Propaganda in 1931. On the committee, Lasswell was joined by many scientifically minded colleagues, including Harold F. Gosnell, E. Pendleton Herring and Peter Odegaard. With Ralph Casey and Bruce Lannes Smith, Lasswell completed *Propaganda and Promotional Activities: An Annotated Bibliography* of 4,500 titles related to 'the practice of scientific propaganda' (Lasswell, Casey and Smith 1935, p. ix). Casey subsequently served on the board of the Institute for Propaganda Analysis, as did other social and political scientists such as Robert Lynd, Leonard Doob and Charles Beard (see Sproule 1997). Domestic communism became the subject of Lasswell and Dorothy Blumenstock's *World Revolutionary Propaganda: A Chicago Study* (1939). When war broke out, Lasswell became director of the Experimental Division for the Study of War-Time Communications at the Library of Congress where he constructed and supervised the World Attention Survey to gather basic intelligence about nations' views of each other. The collected papers of the Experimental Division were later published as the *Language of Politics* (Lasswell and Leites 1949). In his and related organisations – including the Office of War Information, the Foreign Broadcast Information Service, and the Morale Division of the United States Strategic Bombing Survey – Lasswell found or influenced scholars who were or would become famous for new-scientific thinking, including Paul Lazarsfeld, Bernard Berelson, Edward Shils, Morris Janowitz, Gabriel Almond, David Truman, Heinz Eulau, Daniel Lerner, Nathan Leites, Alexander George and Ithiel de Sola Pool, among others. These scientists were discharging their patriotic duties as they honed their skills in analysing 'behaviour'.

Dominating the scene, Lasswell provided numerous influential definitions. His first made propaganda 'the management of collective attitudes by the manipulation of significant symbols' (Lasswell 1927b, p. 627). Subsequent definitions (in Lasswell 1928, p. 259; 1934, p. 13; 1935a, p. 126; 1935b, pp. 188–9; 1941, p. 41; and Lasswell and Blumenstock 1939, p. 10) substituted 'control' for 'management' and noted that the attitudes to be manipulated were 'controversial' ones. Moreover, manipulation, management and control were 'deliberate'. This precluded 'unintentional' propaganda, contrary to Doob (1935, p. 71). Propaganda was also itself 'rational' despite playing upon the 'irrational' or 'unconscious components of human action', especially 'emotions' (Catlin 1936, p. 128). Attitudes affecting 'the promotion of loyalty' needed special control. Symbols of loyalty were 'representations' that assumed various forms – spoken, written, pictorial or musical. Swastikas, hammers-and-sickles, and the Star Spangled Banner struck the popular imagination. But words were symbolic representations, too, especially those 'master symbols' like nation, class and democracy.

Thus defined, the term 'propaganda' was ready for scientific use. It did not cross the threshold from fact to value, the new scientists proclaimed. It was 'a mere tool no more moral or immoral than a pump handle' (Lasswell 1928, p. 264; 1934, p. 521). It needed analysis, not moralistic condemnation. Propaganda *analysis* followed a simple formula: 'who says what in what channel to whom with what effect?' (Lasswell, Casey and Smith 1935, p. xx). The propagandist ('who') could be analysed for emphasis, repetition and intent. Radio, film, press and speeches were media 'channels' whose differential impact could be measured. The psychological attentiveness or concentration of the audience 'to whom' propaganda was directed could be measured on the Attention Index and Concentration Index (Lasswell and Blumenstock 1939, pp. 237ff.). However, the analysis of content ('what') dominated the exercise. *Content analysis* was a research technique for the systematic and quantitative description of propagandistic symbols. It was the successor of humanistic and hermeneutic analyses of literary and sacred texts. It represented a methodological advance in the inter-war years, complementing sample surveys and depth interviews. Individuals could use the method on a select group of texts to discover their political leanings, as Lasswell did on Prussian schoolbooks in 1925. On the scale of the World Attention Survey in the early 1940s, it required an army of readers and listeners who would identify, tabulate and enumerate items in newspapers or radio to discover both 'manifest' and 'latent' content in the symbols employed by friends, enemies or alleged neutrals.

In due course, propaganda furthered the development and gave particular shape to psychological theories of politics, especially public opinion. It helped refashion citizen education as civic training, and democratic theory as a species of political realism. As more nations entered the Second World War, the matter became clearer and more urgent. In *Democracy through Public Opinion*, Lasswell acknowledged 'the propaganda aspect of civic education' when concluding an ominous counterfactual: 'If democracy is to endure, democracy must make propaganda in favour of itself and against propaganda hostile to itself' (Lasswell 1941, p. 98). The explicit connections echoed the broader debate about democracy and democratic theory into which Wallas and the new scientists had earlier been drawn.

The realistic science of democracy

Advocating the cause of democracy was unremarkable by the 1920s and 1930s. However, taking the longer view that the new scientists themselves took, this made for its own revolution in political science. Most political scientists of the nineteenth and early twentieth centuries were not democrats, even in the United States; or, like Burgess, they conflated democracy with the existing nation state without demanding popular participation or an expanded suffrage (Dietz and Farr 1998). Such democratic theorists as existed in the nineteenth and early twentieth centuries were regarded by the new scientists as unscientific and unrealistic. Echoing Wallas, Lasswell decried 'romantic democrats', blinded by the 'formal etiquette of government' and 'eulogistic' views about the people (Lasswell 1928, pp. 258, 262, 264). Twentieth-century democracy needed 'political realism', Merriam noted. This meant adopting 'the scientific attitude in handling social and political problems', as well as acknowledging the realities of money, pressure groups, and national planning in a 'mass governed world' (Merriam 1934, pp. 43, 50, ch. 10). Propaganda itself cultivated 'an attitude of social realism' which helped the 'liquidation of the sentimental basis of democratic government' (Lasswell 1928, p. 262; 1935b, p. 188). Democrats needed to confront the psychic limitations of the citizenry and the hostile challenges posed by anti-democratic propaganda. The new scientists constructed a complex and realistic structure of argument: how propaganda was not inherently undemocratic; why democracy needed its own propaganda; and what form democracy might take in the era of propaganda and mass public opinion. They also had to deal with a problem of their own design (see Ricci 1984), namely, how to reconcile the values of democracy with the facts of science.

The new political scientists recognised that their views regarding technical expertise and normative neutrality precluded scientific justification of any value system, including democracy. 'As an expert, a political scientist... might show how to build successfully an aristocracy, a democracy, a monarchy, a technocracy, a plutocracy, a centralized or a decentralized government; how to organize methods of propaganda and counter-propaganda' or serve as a 'technical adviser to a fascist state, or an oriental or an occidental system, or a capitalist or a communist or an anarchistic regime'. Political scientists could well be democrats, but only by 'assuming an agreement upon the democratic ideal' (Merriam 1934, pp. 39, 40f., 43). They were democrats, then, not by science, but by choice, faith, even propaganda. Ordinary citizens were on no firmer ground; and they were the more likely targets of democratic propaganda. In one of his blunter assessments, Lasswell announced: 'democracy has proclaimed the dictatorship of palaver, and the technique of dictating to the dictator is named propaganda' (Lasswell 1927b, p. 631).

Realism and science rendered the active, participatory side of democracy mainly an affair of elites and experts who could manage public opinion in the service of democracy. While Merriam invoked popular decision-making 'in the last analysis' and was concerned with non-voters, his research gravitated towards elites in the inter-war years. Alongside Lippmann and Bernays, as well as the Italian theorists Gaetano Mosca and Vilfredo Pareto, Lasswell was frankly elitist in welcoming as inevitable 'the few who would rule the many under democratic conditions'. It was for this reason that propagandists needed 'an ethical rehabilitation in democratic society' (Lasswell 1928, pp. 259, 261). Bernays hailed 'a leadership democracy administered by the intelligent minority who know how to regiment and guide the masses' (Bernays 1928, p. 114). He went on to ask, and answer: 'Is this government by propaganda? Call it, if you prefer, government by education.' This was a purportedly realistic assessment; and realistic democracy was still superior to the leadership cults and indoctrination practices of fascist, Nazi and communist dictatorships.

None of the events of the 1930s, much less the Second World War or the electoral realities of the 1940s and 50s, forced much reconsideration of this democratic realism. 'The members of the great society', Lasswell noted with the phrase made famous by Wallas, 'cannot live up to democratic morals.' So the new scientists could and must help by providing 'an arsenal of implements for the achievement of democratic ideals' – which Lasswell in an essay honouring Merriam called 'the developing science of democracy'. That arsenal included 'new methods', 'new instruments' and 'new procedures of observation' in search of 'scientific laws' by a 'staff of skilful observers' (Lasswell 1942, pp. 25, 33, 46, 48).

The enlightened elitism of democratic realism survived the war within the empirical and policy framework of the new science of politics. The survival was both mitigated and complex because of Allied victory, the onset of the Cold War, the duty to democratise (or perhaps Americanise) the post-war world (especially the emergent nations of the third world) and the 'revolution' in the study of mass and elite behaviour. Leonard D. White of the Chicago school proclaimed that 'we have a practical task of world education in the American way of life and in the spirit of American government, made in its image' (White 1950, p. 18). In *The American People and*

Foreign Policy, Gabriel Almond – Merriam's student, Lasswell's co-author and erstwhile propaganda analyst – acknowledged that world leadership was 'thrust' upon the United States facing an 'opponent which tends to subordinate all values to power'. He worried about the mass public's psychological abilities to comprehend foreign policy. Thankfully, however, a smaller 'attentive public' existed which formed the proper audience for a realistic, democratic social science.

> The institutions of higher learning – and the social sciences in particular – have a potential function which cannot be sufficiently emphasized. The attentive public . . . is largely a college-educated public, and the political, interest and communication elites are also largely college-trained. It is in the social sciences in the universities that a democratic ideological consensus can be fostered and a democratic elite discipline encouraged (Almond 1950, pp. 3, 234f.).

The legacy of symbol analysis, opinion manipulation and elite communication – in short, propaganda – was still in evidence.

The value of propaganda analysis as 'a tool of intelligence and research for policy making purposes' was subject to debate in this context (George 1959, p. viii). The debate was fuelled by continuing concerns for the psychological stability of mass publics, as well as the fight for a democratic future for new nations. Whether (or with what success) political scientists should be involved turned partly on an assessment of previous performance. The work of Lasswell and others was criticised for not being 'very satisfactory when tried under operational conditions', that is, held up to its own professed standards by propaganda analysts such as Alexander George (1959, p. 29), writing under the auspices of the RAND Corporation. Out of this debate, new methods of analysis and psychological warfare emerged with contributions from many wartime experts or their students (see Simpson 1994). More importantly, if diffusely, propaganda and propaganda analysis left decisive marks on post-war political science and democratic theory. Content analysis had a bright future in political communications, especially when given more quantified treatment (Berelson 1952). So did public opinion research on candidate platforms, consumer products and communist parties (in, for example, *A Study of Bolshevism* (Leites 1953) and *The Appeals of Communism* (Almond 1954)). The power of symbols or a 'symbolic, charismatic leader' – not to mention the legacy of Merriam's civic training series – animated the most important work of political culture and socialisation in the 1950s and 1960s, *The Civic Culture* by Almond and Sidney Verba (1963, p. 503).

Labels like 'empirical democratic theory' and 'the theory of democratic elitism' – with nods to Mosca, Pareto and Joseph Schumpeter – were used to describe behavioural theorising about domestic politics, especially public opinion and voting behaviour in a representative democracy with a robust civil society of secondary associations. 'Realistic research on contemporary politics' placed voting at the centre of a systemic model of democracy, according to two of the most famous new scientists and propaganda analysts, Berelson and Lazarsfeld. That research downplayed individual citizens' virtues and highlighted electoral competition between elites: '*Individual voters* today seem unable to satisfy the requirements for a democratic system of government outlined by political theorists. But the *system of democracy* does' (Berelson, Lazarsfeld and McPhee 1954, pp. 306, 312). Furthermore, the system was 'pluralistic', composed of individuals acting in groups pursuing their interests in a competitive environment. In different arenas, different groups would negotiate, bargain and otherwise vie for influence over policy and governance. (The most influential democratic pluralist and behaviouralist, Robert A. Dahl, called the overall system of distributive influence 'minorities rule': Dahl 1956, p. 132.) The system was stabilised by overlapping and competing interest groups, as well as a basic consensus on liberal democratic values (which during the inter-war years needed propagandising), like liberty, individualism, free speech and free trade. Consensus on values was articulated most consistently by elites, but steadily enough by ordinary citizens who were otherwise apathetic about actual participation. Neither elites nor most ordinary citizens were ideological, either, at least in the sense of holding political ideas so passionately as to border on the fanaticism associated with fascism, communism or extremist movements. In this way, the American case in particular held out signs of an 'end-of-ideology' among post-war liberal democracies (see Waxman 1968). In factual contrast to twentieth-century instability in Europe and elsewhere, American-style liberal democracy was – as a theorist of the end-of-ideology, Seymour Martin Lipset, famously remarked – 'the good society itself in operation' (Lipset 1959, p. 439).

The empirical science of democracy – variously described as realism, pluralism and elitism – was among the new science of politics' most significant contributions to twentieth-century political thought. It continued to assume various methodological guises as the new scientists came increasingly to call themselves 'behaviouralists' and to think of their methodological rout of traditional political theory as a 'revolution'.

The revolutionary science of behaviour

Behaviouralism was the direct descendant of Merriam's 'science of political behaviour'. It was broadly identified with methods, behaviour and (as noted above) American-style pluralist democracy viewed realistically. 'Method' meant any quantitative or operationalised instrument with which to experiment or analyse data. 'Behaviour' referred not only to actions, but to psychological states, as well as the properties of larger systems. But however broad the referral, the sense was clear: 'behaviour comes first: ruling before government, obeying before authority, voting before decision, demanding before value, fearing before sanction, coercing before power, persuading before influence, fighting before conflict, believing before ideology' (Eulau 1963, p. 5). Behaviouralism thus proved to be not so much a specific or unifying theory, but more a methodological orientation or, as Eulau (1963) dubbed it, a 'persuasion'. Behaviouralism was expressed in a distinctive idiom of empirical research (see Somit and Tanenhaus 1967, pp. 190f.). It also acknowledged its applicability to public policy, and hence its political relevance, without violating the fact/value distinction. 'Policy science' – a phrase popularised by Lasswell himself – was thus the applied form of behaviouralism, useful to policy-makers of varied allegiances and normative commitments. Continuities with the Chicago school were direct, since many leading behaviouralists were educated under (or acknowledged alliance with) Merriam, Lasswell and their associates, although the behaviouralists' technical sophistication was far superior. Wallas, too, was frequently remembered for originary inspiration.

Behaviouralism's crucial decade fell between 1951 and 1961, with 1953 its most symbolic date. Most importantly, David Easton published *The Political System: An Inquiry into the State of Political Science* (1953) soon after his arrival at the University of Chicago and his lauding of Lasswell as the 'policy scientist for a democratic society'. Here was behaviouralism's manifesto, doing for Easton's generation what Merriam's *New Aspects of Politics* and Wallas's *Human Nature in Politics* had done for their respective generations. Sounding much as they had, Easton criticised 'traditional' inquiry into the state, the 'historicism' of political theory and the 'hyperfactualism' of Brycean empiricism. The 'political system' should orient political research, and 'the authoritative allocation of values' should replace 'power' at the conceptual core of politics (Easton 1953, chs. 4–5, 10). In the spirit of Easton's manifesto, behaviouralists produced a prodigious quantity of research and reinvigorated the time-honoured appeal to scientific method. The appeal to science carried considerable cultural authority; but it also brought down upon the behaviouralists condemnation from certain critics. In Eric Voegelin's *The New Science of Politics* (1952) and other works, classical political theory and traditional normative values were pitted against science. Here was a harbinger of things to come.

The later 1950s and 1960s witnessed a series of striking proclamations and strident debates over behaviouralism. The stakes had been raised by the boast, first articulated by David Truman (1955) of the Chicago school, that a 'revolution' in the behavioural sciences as a whole was transforming political science as well. Soon enough, Dahl frankly acknowledged that 'the revolutionary sectarians have found themselves . . . members of the Establishment' (Dahl 1961, p. 765). Leading behaviouralists like Almond and Truman, as APSA presidents, hailed the accomplishments of behaviouralism (somewhat ironically) in terms of Thomas Kuhn's new philosophy of science. Despite Kuhn's own anti-positivism and hesitations about social science, behaviouralism was made to appear as a 'paradigm' in the wake of its revolutionary successes. In this environment, behaviouralism was seriously challenged by scholars of a more 'traditional' or 'normative' sort. The émigré political theorist Hannah Arendt thought 'the unfortunate truth about behaviourism and the validity of its "laws" is that the more people there are, the more likely they are to behave and the less likely to tolerate non-behaviour . . . The rise of the "behavioural sciences" indicates clearly the final stage . . . when mass society has devoured all strata of the nation' (Arendt 1958, pp. 443, 445). A volume of *Essays on the Scientific Study of Politics* by followers of the conservative political philosopher and émigré Leo Strauss took direct aim at behaviouralists as the latest 'manifestations of the new science of politics', including the 'scientific propaganda' of Lasswell. Strauss concluded the volume by praising 'classical political science' and excoriating 'the new political science' for scientism, relativism and blindness to 'the most dangerous proclivities of democracy'. A facetious twist concluded his fiery denunciation of behaviouralism: 'One may say of it that it fiddles while Rome burns. It is excused by two facts: it does not know that it fiddles, and it does not know that Rome burns' (Strauss 1962, pp. 311, 327). There followed books of more left-leaning tilt, such as *Apolitical Politics* (1967), *The Bias of Pluralism* (1969) and *The End of Liberalism* (1969). These and books like them captured the anti-establishment mood made possible by the established success of behaviouralism. More constructively, they also hailed the power of ideas, the resilience of ideology and a more participatory democratic theory than had been imagined or allowed by behaviouralism and its political realism.

Civil rights protests, urban riots, the Vietnam War, and the emergence of feminism, among other social forces, provided a context and exacerbated debates over behaviouralism. The ferocity of debate suggested the limits of liberal pluralism and democratic realism, not to mention the behaviouralists' failure to predict actual behaviour or sustain a brief for the end-of-ideology. But the debates and forces also brought out the imaginative power of things yet new. A left-leaning Caucus for a New Political Science was formed in 1967, critical of behaviouralism for having 'failed to study, in a radically critical spirit, either the great crises of the day or the inherent weakness of the American political system' (in Seidelman and Harpham 1985, p. 198). A (or, rather, another) 'new' political science must reverse these misfortunes; if not, the caucus anticipated *An End to Political Science* (1970). Even erstwhile behaviouralists recognised the import of the times. It was a defining moment for behaviouralism – arguably, the symbolic finale of the twentieth-century new science of politics – when David Easton delivered his APSA presidential address. 'A new revolution is underway in American political science', he began. It was a 'post-behavioural revolution' now that 'the last revolution – behaviouralism – has . . . been overtaken by the increasing social and political crises of our time'. These crises suggested the scientific 'failure of the current pluralist interpretations of democracy' and the political failure of a discipline to appear 'more as apologists' than 'objective analysts' of American policy (Easton 1969, pp. 1051, 1057, 1061). Easton called for post-positivist methods and a credo of relevance to revitalise scientific reform (if not control) of politics.

The new revolution of post-behaviouralism, as it turned out, was short-lived, if it lived at all. The same proved true of a new political science of academic radicals. But those very aspirations, articulated in the idiom of a 'new' science, reaffirmed the venerability of novelty expressed so powerfully by Merriam, Lasswell and their revolutionary descendants. The time-honoured ritual of prophesying the new would soon enough, and to this day, be heard in yet other quarters. A 'genuinely scientific enterprise' is underway, we hear, amidst a 'rational choice revolution' (Shepsle 1989, p. 146) that draws its inspiration from economics and game theory, making possible a 'new institutionalism' and, more generally, a new political science. Whether the prophets of *this* new revolution surpass the statesmanship or practicality in the methods of the last prophets remains to be seen.

21
Utilitarianism and beyond: contemporary analytical political theory

DAVID MILLER AND RICHARD DAGGER

General features

In this chapter we sketch a body of political thought that became predominant in the second half of the twentieth century among academic political philosophers, primarily in the English-speaking world, but increasingly elsewhere, too. To call this type of political thought 'analytical' may not be particularly revealing, but no other term better describes the movement in question. Sometimes 'liberal political theory' is used, and there is indeed a close connection between analytical theory and liberalism. But that label is in one way too broad and in another too narrow for this kind of political thinking: too broad because liberalism has assumed many different philosophical guises in the course of a history much longer than that of our subject; and too narrow because those who engage in this kind of political theory use methods of analysis and techniques of argument that are not confined to liberals.

Indeed, the political theorists and philosophers of the analytical school often disagree sharply over questions of practical politics, and some have embraced positions, such as Marxism, that have been historically hostile to liberalism. They form a school not because of a common ideological stance, then, but because of certain shared assumptions about the aims and methods of political thought. These assumptions fall under the following five headings.

First, political theory can be detached from deep metaphysical questions about the meaning of human life and the place of human beings in the cosmos. There is no need to settle such questions in order to discover how people should live in societies and order their common affairs. Although political theorists must know something about how human beings behave and what they value, they need not preface their theories with a general account of 'the human condition', if that means asking such questions as 'What can we know?', 'What is the ultimate good?', 'Does God exist?', 'Is there life after death?' In particular this means that political theory must begin from secular premises, whatever the personal beliefs of the person who engages in it. This feature distinguishes analytical theory from many other schools of political philosophy, past and present, and leads some critics to describe it as comparatively shallow (Parekh 1996). Analytical theorists would say in reply that since we cannot expect to find agreement on the deep metaphysical questions, yet have to live together in political communities as best we can, we must find principles to live by that can be justified in less ambitious ways.

The second feature of analytical theory, as its name perhaps suggests, is its commitment to conceptual clarity and argumentative rigour. Analytical theorists begin with the observation that many of the ideas politicians and the public invoke in political debate are ill-defined and often confused. Concepts like democracy, freedom and equality are used rhetorically without the speaker or writer having any clear idea of their meaning. So a first task of political theory is clarification, which may involve giving an exact definition of a term like 'democracy' or perhaps more often distinguishing between two or more ways in which such a term can be used, as Isaiah Berlin did in his celebrated lecture on 'Two Concepts of Liberty' (Berlin 1969). This feature derived originally from the influence of analytical philosophy, the mid-century movement which held that the task of philosophy was to dissolve philosophical problems by carefully tracing the ways in which concepts were used in ordinary language. Initially this had a somewhat stultifying effect on political theory, because it implied that political theory could not go beyond the analysis and clarification of the terms of political discourse (e.g. Macdonald 1951 and Weldon 1953; for a critical appraisal, Miller 1983). But conceptual clarification soon came to be seen as a preliminary to the justification of principles and the defence of political positions: it is necessary to state clearly what democracy and related concepts mean, for example, if one is to explain why democracy is valuable (see Benn and Peters 1959; Barry 1965; Pitkin 1967; and the essays collected in Quinton 1967; De Crespigny and Wertheimer 1970; and Flathman 1973).

According to analytical theorists, the arguments used to justify principles should be set out explicitly in as rigorous a way as possible. The ideal is to present a series of deductive steps from premises to conclusion. Although the arguments given are rarely so logically tight as this, analytical theorists attempt to display the structure of reasoning that leads to a particular conclusion. Equally, they strive to avoid forms of argument that are prevalent in other, less reputable, forms of political thought: appeals to tradition or to the authority of Great Books, use of rhetorical devices or loose analogies, and obscurantist jargon. In this respect they follow the example of John Locke when he complained that 'vague and insignificant Forms of Speech' and 'hard or misapply'd words' are frequently mistaken for 'deep Learning and heighth of Speculation' (Locke 1975 [1690], p. 10).

The third feature of analytical theory is that its aim is a normative one, namely to establish political principles that can govern the constitution of states and the making of public policy. It attempts to answer the questions that face citizens and their representatives when they vote, or pass legislation, or allocate resources to one project rather than another. Ought the constitution to include a bill of rights? Should financial support be given to those who cannot find work? Ought hate speech to be outlawed? These are the kinds of questions that political theory should answer by establishing general principles – of liberty or justice, for instance – from which specific recommendations can be derived. It is political theory written from the perspective of the responsible citizen, one might say, and its aim is to encourage such citizens to think more clearly and consistently about the issues they face in the politics of the day. In this respect it diverges radically from forms of political theory whose avowed aim is to promote the cause of a social class or other sectional group, or whose purpose is the unmasking of power relations in contemporary society.

Fourth, analytical theorists all confront, in various ways, the phenomenon of value-pluralism. That is, they acknowledge that deciding political questions such as those listed above requires us to consider a number of apparently conflicting ideals – liberty, justice, democracy, economic prosperity and so forth – each of which may suggest a different answer to the question at stake. Some thinkers in this camp hold that political philosophy has simply to cope with the irreducible plurality of political principles: a view eloquently expressed in Berlin's lecture 'Does Political Theory Still Exist?', in which he argues that the human condition does not allow us to achieve all of our ideals simultaneously, but forces us to make choices that involve the sacrifice of one value for another (Berlin 1962). Other thinkers believe that we have good reason to give precedence to one value: John Rawls, whose theory will be discussed later in the chapter, has argued in this way for the priority of *justice*[1], while both Robert Nozick and Ronald Dworkin insist that

1. 'Justice is the first virtue of social institutions, as truth is of systems of thought . . . [L]aws and institutions no matter how efficient and well-arranged must be reformed or abolished if they are unjust' (Rawls 1971, p. 3).

individual *rights* should take precedence over other political values (Nozick 1974, esp. ch. 3; Dworkin 1977, ch. 7). Perhaps the most ambitious attempt to come to terms with value-pluralism has been utilitarianism (discussed in the next section), which appeals to the principle of greatest happiness as a supreme arbiter to resolve conflicts between liberty, justice and all other goods.

Fifth, in a broad sense, analytical political theory must be described as liberal. It aims to serve as the public philosophy of a society of free and equal citizens who have choices to make about how their society will be organised; it assumes that such citizens will often disagree, but that clear thinking and careful argument can lessen the disagreement and uncover principles that can win widespread support. Within this broad agreement, analytical theorists have taken a wide variety of political stances, from free-market libertarianism at one extreme to egalitarian socialism at the other. (They include, for example, analytical Marxists, who have attempted to reconstruct Marxian political theory by abandoning dialectics and using analytical methods borrowed from non-Marxian economics and philosophy: see Elster 1985; Roemer 1986.) Analytical theory is liberal, then, but not in the narrow sense that entails a particular view about the rights of individuals or how extensive the role of the state should be.

The legacy of utilitarianism

In its origins, analytical theory both grew out of and reacted against the utilitarian outlook which had achieved a kind of dominance-by-default in the English-speaking liberal democracies in the twentieth century. Jeremy Bentham, John Stuart Mill and other 'philosophic radicals' had gained prominence in the first half of the nineteenth century with the argument that questions of government and policy should be answered by choosing the available option that appeared likely to contribute most to the aggregate happiness of those affected. In Britain, especially, this was a great reforming philosophy, underpinning major changes in economic policy, legal practice and the machinery of government. But in the later years of the century it came under attack from various quarters, and was displaced in the universities by the idealism of F. H. Bradley, T. H. Green and their disciples. In the first half of the twentieth century no utilitarian political philosopher mounted a systematic defence of utilitarianism to rival Henry Sidgwick's *The Methods of Ethics*, first published in 1874.

Yet utilitarianism remained a powerful current among economists, especially those 'welfare economists' who sought ways to measure and achieve 'maximum aggregate utility' (Rescher 1966 provides a succinct summary). It also enjoyed a quiet revival among moral philosophers after the Second World War. These philosophers were more concerned to elucidate moral concepts and to explain the meaning of moral propositions than to put forward substantive criteria by which actions and practices might be assessed, but when they did turn to matters of substance it was often a form of utilitarianism that emerged. Richard Hare, for example, gave an account of moral judgements as universalisable prescriptions – that is, action-guiding judgements that everyone must be able to endorse, no matter what their place in the world. Arriving at a universalisable prescription required the moral agent to give equal weight to the preferences of everyone who would be affected by the judgement's implementation and to follow the course of action that would achieve the greatest possible satisfaction of preferences. Hare's substantive criterion for testing moral principles was thus utilitarian, with 'preference-satisfaction' replacing the traditional 'happiness' in the utilitarian formula (Hare 1963; 1981). In the USA, Richard Brandt's work followed a parallel path, from his analysis of moral language to a defence of a sophisticated form of rule-utilitarianism (Brandt, 1959; 1992). Even John Rawls, who was soon to become a leading anti-utilitarian, wrote an early paper defending a form of rule-utilitarianism that he thought would overcome familiar criticisms, such as that utilitarianism might justify punishing the innocent (Rawls 1955).

Utilitarian thinking also seemed to come naturally to politicians and civil servants in democratic governments charged with making policy decisions that affected the welfare of very large numbers of citizens. Over the first half of the twentieth century, New Liberalism in Britain and the New Deal in the USA brought a steady expansion of the powers of government, with new social programmes in education and health, and, under the influence of J. M. Keynes, a more interventionist style of economic policy. Economic planning in wartime, and the post-war preoccupation with national defence, amplified these powers still further. Responsible public servants had somehow to justify such policies to a democratic electorate: but how was this to be done when these policies typically produced both winners and losers? Most obviously, by counting the interests of each citizen equally, and then showing that on balance the gains of the winners outweighed the losses of the losers. In this way, utilitarianism became the unconscious public philosophy of a generation of administrators and their advisers; after all, as one of them later wrote, 'the welfare state was itself an essay in utilitarianism' (Annan 1991, p. 413).

The perception that democratic governments were following the utilitarian principle provoked a reaction from several political philosophers, who argued that unconstrained utilitarianism might justify abhorrent policies. They criticised utilitarianism primarily from two directions. First, because policies were assessed simply by weighing total gains and losses, it was possible on utilitarian grounds to justify policies that violated the basic rights of certain individuals or groups, or harmed them in some other way, so long as these costs were outweighed by greater gains elsewhere. Thus draconian forms of punishment might be justified if these acted as an effective deterrent to potential criminals, or economic policies that imposed severe costs on a few people could be defended on the grounds that they enhanced economic efficiency overall. Utilitarianism appeared to have no place for the idea that each person has a claim to just treatment that could not be overridden even if doing so produced great benefits for others. This failure to recognise that a gain to A does not automatically compensate for a loss to B led to the complaint that utilitarianism 'does not take seriously the distinction between persons' (Rawls 1971, p. 27). So it was necessary to look elsewhere – to a non-utilitarian theory of justice, a theory of human rights, a theory of freedom, or some other source – to find acceptable principles for a free society.

The second attack on utilitarianism took a slightly different form. Critics in this camp pointed out that the injunction to do whatever will produce the best overall consequences places no fixed limits on what people might do. Absolute restrictions of the form 'It is always wrong to perform actions of type X', where X might stand for 'taking innocent life' or 'betraying one's friends', are simply not allowed. At the personal level, this meant that utilitarianism must collide with the belief that it is always dishonourable – a violation of personal integrity – to act in certain ways (Williams 1973). At the public level, the charge was that utilitarianism encouraged a kind of cynicism in which nothing the state did could be described simply as morally intolerable, since it was always possible to find consequentialist reasons to justify what had been done. In the century of Stalin, Hitler and the Holocaust, this was no merely abstract consideration. Later, the Vietnam War was thought to show what may happen when governments make their decisions on the basis of a kind of cost-benefit analysis, admitting no absolute moral limits on what they can do (Hampshire 1978).

During the 1960s and 1970s, then, political theorists began to search for alternatives to utilitarianism that could remedy these defects while still providing firm foundations for the liberal state. Utilitarianism became, and has since remained, a minority view, even though it has continued to find vigorous defenders (see Smart 1973; Singer 1979; Hardin 1988; Goodin 1995). The strongest argument that can be made on its behalf is perhaps that it can provide coherent guidance to legislators and policy-makers, who must consider the general long-term consequences of the decisions they make and the overall welfare of the people affected by those decisions. Yet even in this role – as a public political philosophy rather than a personal ethic – it faces difficulties. There are formidable problems associated with the utilitarian calculus itself – the problem of discovering how much welfare or happiness each person would derive from the implementation of different policies, and the problem of aggregating these individual utilities into an overall measure of social utility. Even if these problems could somehow be overcome, most political theorists would continue to argue that non-utilitarian principles – principles of liberty, equality, individual rights and others – set limits to what governments may legitimately do in pursuit of the general happiness. Utilitarianism, therefore, cannot serve as a complete public philosophy.

Political obligation, authority and civil disobedience

Utilitarianism's incompleteness is especially evident with regard to political obligation and civil disobedience. For the utilitarian, whether one ought or ought not to obey the law is a matter of deciding which course of action will produce the better consequences. But this response simply bypasses the question of whether citizens – especially the citizens of a democratic state – have a moral *obligation* to comply with properly enacted laws.

In the political climate of the 1960s and 1970s, this old question of political obligation took on a new urgency. People involved in the civil rights and anti-war movements in the USA, and in campaigns against nuclear weapons in Britain and elsewhere in Europe, had to decide whether their protests should remain within the bounds of law or whether the gravity of the issues at stake could justify flag-burning, draft-dodging, illegal occupation of military sites, and other acts of civil disobedience. Analytical political philosophers in the 1950s had argued that the problem of political obligation could be dissolved by observing that acknowledging an obligation to obey the law was simply part of what it meant to belong to a political society (Macdonald 1951; Weldon 1953; McPherson 1967). Such views were hard to sustain, however, when democratic governments were following policies that significant numbers of their citizens regarded as immoral.

Utilitarians aside, most liberals had accepted Locke's argument that citizens were bound to obey because they had consented, either expressly or tacitly, to the state's authority over them (Locke 1963 [1689–90]). But showing that citizens had generally behaved in a way that implied consent proved an embarrassing problem. Despite Plamenatz's attempt to revive consent theory in something like its traditional form, this embarrassment led analytical theorists to search for an alternative (Plamenatz 1938). Some turned to *hypothetical* consent as the grounds of political obligation. What counts, on this view, is not whether one *has* consented to obey the laws of one's country but whether one *would* consent, freely and rationally, to obey them. What counts, in other words, is whether the state in question is legitimate, or the kind of state to which one ought to consent (Pitkin 1965–6; Kavka 1986, pp. 398–407). But this proves to be a consent theory in which the idea of consent does no work at all. If the legitimacy or worthiness of the government or state is what matters, then one may as well dispense with the idea of consent (Schmidtz 1990). Or one could take consent quite seriously and insist that it must be actual rather than hypothetical or implied, which entails that states must undertake reforms that give people suitable opportunities to express their consent and reasonable alternatives should they withhold it (Beran 1987). Such a theory of 'reformist consent' cannot ground an obligation to obey the laws of existing states, however, for none of them, no matter how worthy, provide the requisite opportunities and alternatives; nor is it likely that these can be provided (Klosko 1991).

Reflection on the difficulties of consent theory has led some thinkers in the analytical tradition to espouse 'philosophical anarchism'. These 'anarchists' deny not only that most people have a general obligation to obey the law but also that states or their officials even have the authority to enact and enforce laws. The anarchists' arguments take a stronger and a weaker form. The stronger claim is that it is impossible to provide a satisfactory account of a general obligation to obey the law. Any such obligation must rest on the belief that political authority is 'the right to command, and correlatively, the right to be obeyed', and this belief is at odds with our 'primary obligation' of autonomy, which requires us to decide for ourselves, not merely to follow orders (Wolff 1970, pp. 4 and 18). The weaker form of philosophical anarchism holds that none of the many attempts to ground political obligation have succeeded, which suggests that none will. The conclusion, then, is that only those relatively few people who have explicitly committed themselves to obedience have anything like a general obligation to obey the laws under which they live (Simmons 1979). Philosophical anarchists of both kinds admit that we probably have good reasons, moral as well as prudential, to obey the laws, but an obligation to obey those in authority is not one of them.

Other philosophers have stopped short of philosophical anarchism by accepting the first conclusion – that there is no general obligation to obey the law – but not the anarchists' denial of political authority. They do this on the grounds that political authority does not entail an obligation to be obeyed by those subject to the authority (Green 1988; and the essays by Smith, Sartorius, Raz and Greenawalt in Edmundson 1999). In this dispute, much depends upon what counts as the proper analysis of 'authority'.

Most recent attempts to justify political obligation have appealed either to *fair play* or *membership*. As formulated by H. L. A. Hart (1955) and Rawls (1964; but cf. Rawls 1971, §§18, 19, 51, 52), the principle of fair play (or fairness) holds that everyone who participates in a just, mutually beneficial, cooperative practice or endeavour has an obligation to bear a fair share of the burdens of the practice. This obligation is owed to the others who cooperate in the practice, for cooperation is what makes it possible for the practice to produce benefits. Anyone who enjoys the benefits without contributing to their production is liable to blame and punishment as one who takes unfair advantage of others, even if his or her shirking does not directly threaten the survival of the practice.

The principle of fairness applies to a political society only if that society can reasonably be regarded as a cooperative enterprise. If so, the members of the polity have an obligation of fair play to do their part in maintaining the enterprise. Because the rule of law is necessary to this end, the principal form of cooperation is obeying the law. Fair play allows that overriding considerations may warrant civil disobedience, but in their absence the members of the polity qua cooperative practice must honour their obligation to each other to obey the laws.

The principal objection to the fairness theory is that political societies, even the best of them, are not cooperative practices that generate political obligations. As developed forcefully by Nozick (1974, pp. 90–5) and Simmons (1979, ch. V), the criticism is that fair play requires the voluntary acceptance of benefits – otherwise, people could foist obligations on us by giving us unsolicited benefits – and this kind of voluntary acceptance is too rare to provide the basis for political obligation. The principle's advocates have responded by arguing that voluntary acceptance is not as rare as the critics charge (Dagger 1997, ch. 5; Kavka 1986, pp. 409–13), and that obligations of fairness may obtain even when people cannot avoid the receipt of such benefits as national defence and the rule of law (Arneson 1982; Klosko 1992).

The belief that obligations need not derive from voluntary commitments is also central to the membership (or associative) theory of political obligation. Here the key idea is that the political community, like the family, generates obligations even among those who have not chosen to be members. Like 'family and friendship and other forms of association more local and intimate', political association 'is in itself pregnant of obligation' (Dworkin 1986, p. 206). There is thus no need to justify political obligation by appealing to voluntary commitment or some fundamental moral principle, for political obligations, like other associative obligations, grow out of 'deep-rooted connections with our sense of who we are and our place in the world, [and] have a particularly fundamental role in our moral being' (Horton 1992, p. 157).

Critics of the membership theory charge that it depends upon an implausible analogy between small and intimate associations, such as the family, and the large and impersonal state (Simmons 1996; Wellman 1997). As with fair play, the complaint is that membership may generate obligations, but not *political* obligations. We are left with contending theories of political obligation, then, and no consensus as to which of them is best – or (as the essays in Edmundson 1999 attest) whether any of them is even satisfactory.

There are, however, two points on which there is wide agreement among analytical theorists. The first is that the obligation to obey the law, if it exists at all, must be defeasible rather than absolute, for it is always possible that other moral considerations may override this obligation. The second point of agreement, following from the first, is that civil disobedience is sometimes just and proper. No matter how free, open and democratic a state may be, there is always a chance that some injustice will be done to some of its members, or perhaps to foreigners, that warrants civil disobedience. What counts as *civil* disobedience remains a matter of dispute – must it be direct disobedience of the law(s) in question, for instance, or may it allow disobeying one law, such as trespass, as an indirect protest against another? – but the possibility of justifying civil disobedience does not.

The contractarian alternative to utilitarianism

The attempt to answer questions about political obligation leads quickly, as we have seen, into other issues, such as authority, justice, rights and the common good, thereby pressing political thinkers toward more comprehensive and systematic theories. The most important systematic political philosophy developed as an alternative to utilitarianism in the analytical tradition has been social contract theory, especially in the form advanced by John Rawls. Its attraction lay mainly in two features. First, it embraced the individualism at the heart of utilitarianism, but promised to rid it of the possibility that the interests of the few might be sacrificed to the greater welfare of the many. According to contractarianism, a political order is legitimate when it is based on principles that everyone in the society in question can accept. Everyone enjoys a veto, so to speak, on the principles that will govern the society, thereby ruling out principles whose operation might prove detrimental to particular persons or groups of people. Second, contractarians such as Rawls believed that this test would select a clear and consistent set of principles of justice, so that public policy might be guided with more precision than utilitarian criteria provided. Rawls' aim, then, was to lay out certain principles of justice, and then to show that every citizen who thought rationally about how his or her society ought to be governed would agree to these principles.

In the earliest version of his theory, Rawls envisioned a social contract that people, taken just as they were, would agree to sign when they reflected on the long-term gains and losses they would incur under alternative sets of principles (Rawls 1958). But by the time the theory took definitive form in *A Theory of Justice*, Rawls had modified his argument so that the contract was now to be made behind 'a veil of ignorance' (Rawls 1971, §24). This required his readers to imagine that the people choosing principles of justice would know the general facts of social life but not their personal tastes, abilities or social positions. Rawls claimed that the choosers would select two principles. The first specified that each person should enjoy the greatest degree of personal liberty consistent with everyone else enjoying an equal liberty, which in practice meant that they should enjoy rights to speak and act freely, to associate with others and to vote in elections – in other words, the civil and political rights well established in liberal democracies. The second governed the distribution of social and economic resources: income, wealth and opportunity. Rawls argued that his choosers would start by assuming that these should be distributed equally. They would soon see, however, that there were circumstances in which an unequal distribution might be to everyone's advantage – if, for instance, economic inequalities served as incentives to those who produced goods and services, thus leading to a greater overall volume of production – and they would accept such inequalities if they were fairly gained. So Rawls' second principle stated that material inequalities were fair when they could be expected to work to the greatest benefit of the least advantaged members of society, and so long as they were attached to social positions that everyone had an equal opportunity to fill. This principle required equality of opportunity in the education system and the job market, and redistribution of resources from the better-off to the worse-off up to the point at which further attempts to redistribute would backfire by undermining incentives. The outcome of Rawls' hypothetical social contract, therefore, was a social democratic state which preserved and privileged liberal freedoms, but constrained the workings of the market in the interests, primarily, of the least fortunate.

Is Rawls' theory formally valid? That is, would rational people placed behind a veil of ignorance actually choose the two principles he lays down? This is one of two main questions prompted by Rawls' theory. The second is how much weight, if any, we should give to a hypothetical contract – a thought experiment in which people are deprived of personal information that they do, of course, have in their daily lives. Rawls' aim was to propose a public conception of justice – a conception that would allow people in actual societies to justify their shares of material and immaterial benefits to one another even when the size of those shares is fully known. If my income is much larger than yours, can I justify this inequality to you by arguing that you would have chosen a principle that permits inequalities of this kind behind a veil of ignorance?

Rawls has been widely criticised on both counts. Few critics were persuaded that choosers behind a veil of ignorance would give liberty the absolute priority over material resources that Rawls requires, or that they would assess alternative material distributions exclusively in terms of the share of resources going to the worst-off group (e.g. Hart 1973; Barry 1973). Indeed, some critics argued that the natural outcome of Rawls' social contract would be a modified form of the principle of utility – an ironic consequence, given that Rawls' whole endeavour had been directed at finding a contractarian alternative to utilitarianism (Harsanyi 1982; Arrow 1973). Others argued that appealing to a hypothetical contract was the wrong way to generate a public conception of justice. In stripping his choosers of all knowledge of their beliefs, tastes and capacities, Rawls had also stripped away elements essential to the personal identity of some members of existing political societies (Sandel 1982). One could not, for instance, justify freedom of conscience to a religious believer by asking him to consider what principles he would choose if he did not know whether he was a believer or an atheist. If he took his religious convictions to be an inescapable part of his identity, he might well regard that question as ethically irrelevant.

In the years following publication of *A Theory of Justice*, Rawls responded to these criticisms by softening the contractarian element in his thinking. Although he continues to stand by his two principles of justice, he relied less on the hypothetical contract to justify them and more on two other claims: that they can form the basis of an 'overlapping consensus' between people of diverse moral, philosophical and religious outlooks, and that they are potentially stable, in the sense that people will find them acceptable in practice and become increasingly attached to them over time. People in contemporary democratic societies are irreversibly divided over questions of ultimate value, but nonetheless they must live together on the basis of principles that each person (or at least each 'reasonable' person) can accept – principles, Rawls argued, that his theory is uniquely qualified to provide (Rawls 1993).

Although Rawls' version of the social contract remained the most influential by far in the second half of the twentieth century, other philosophers have devised other forms of contractarianism. These fall roughly into two categories. In one are theories that attempt to provide a more 'realistic' alternative to Rawls by scrapping the veil of ignorance and analysing contracts that would be made under conditions of full information. How would people choose to arrange their social institutions if they all know how they are likely to fare under the various institutional arrangements that may be proposed? The key idea here is that everyone must gain relative to a baseline where common institutions are absent – a state of nature, so to speak, where individuals are free to act as they please and no principles of justice are in place. If institutions are to win universal consent, they must ensure that each person at least does better than he or she would do in what Hobbes called 'the condition of meer Nature' (Hobbes 1968 [1651], p. 196). Two questions then immediately arise: how are we to identify the relevant baseline, and how should we choose between different ways of distributing the gains of social cooperation? Contractarians of this type tend to assume that only a state with quite limited powers would emerge from this process; they assume, in other words, that the state of nature resembles an economic free-for-all, and those who fared well in it would not agree to redistribution on the scale envisaged by Rawls, say. They are happy to accept Rawls' idea that society is a 'cooperative venture for mutual advantage', but they go on to insist that 'mutual advantage' must be interpreted literally and under conditions of full knowledge (see especially Buchanan 1975; Gauthier 1986; and for discussion Barry 1995, ch. 2).

A contrasting interpretation of the social contract has been offered by moral and political philosophers who claim that the contract should be understood as an agreement between morally motivated individuals. Principles, especially principles of justice, are acceptable if and only if they could not reasonably be rejected as a basis for 'informed, unforced general agreement' by people seeking to find principles that others with a similar motivation could also accept (Scanlon 1982, p. 110; elaborated in Scanlon 1998). The most important contractarian theory of this type has been put forward by Brian Barry, who claims that a number of relatively concrete principles of justice will be selected by the reasonable rejection test – for instance that 'all inequalities of rights, opportunities and resources have to be justifiable in ways that cannot reasonably be rejected by those who get least' (Barry 1998, p. 147).[2] In theories of this kind, a great deal turns on the notion of reasonableness, which leads critics to object that this form of contractarianism can be made to work only by smuggling the desired practical conclusions into the motivations of the parties to the contract.

Rights theories

As we have seen, one of the most powerful objections to utilitarianism was that the principle might in certain circumstances license policy-makers to override the basic rights of some individuals in the name of the greater good of the many. The idea that individuals have rights which must on no account be violated has a long and distinguished pedigree in liberal societies, so it is hardly surprising that rights-based theories have proved a popular alternative to utilitarianism among political theorists in the analytical tradition. What may be more surprising is the sharp opposition within the tradition about the nature and justification of the rights they seek to defend. There has been an on-going debate about what it means to have a right – about the conditions under which we can correctly say that some person P has a right to some advantage A. Alongside this there has been a more overtly political disagreement between libertarians, who believe that rights are negative,

2. For the full statement of Barry's view, see Barry (1995).

protective devices that secure individuals and their property against invasion by other individuals and the state, and their various opponents, who believe that individuals also have positive rights to a range of opportunities and resources, often requiring state provision for their protection.

We cannot do justice here to the intricacies of the first debate. The most important contenders have been the *choice* theory of rights, according to which having a right is to have control over other people's duties – to be able to require them to fulfil a duty, or to waive that requirement – and the *benefit* theory, according to which having a right is to stand to benefit in an appropriate way from the performance of the duty. Both theories have been refined and developed in a variety of ways, with significant implications for questions of political obligation, the relationship between law and morality, and other issues in legal and political philosophy. (See Hart 1955 and Raz 1986, ch. 7, for important statements of the choice and benefit theories, respectively; and Jones 1994; Martin 1993; Waldron 1984 for surveys of the debate and general discussion of the concept of rights.)

Robert Nozick's *Anarchy, State, and Utopia* (Nozick 1974) touched off the debate between libertarians and their opponents over the substance of rights. Nozick's book begins with the claim that in order to recognise the inviolability of persons – that it is never morally justified to sacrifice one person for the greater good of others – we must attribute to everyone a set of rights that tightly constrains how others may treat him or her. This set includes rights to use and control our own bodies and full ownership of external resources that we have justly acquired. So powerful are these rights that they put in question the very legitimacy of the state. Nozick asks us to imagine people living in a state of nature with no political authority, and entrusting the defence of their rights to private protective agencies that would punish rights-violators and compensate their victims. In these circumstances, Nozick argues, an institution that we would recognise as a state could emerge spontaneously from interaction between such agencies, but it could only be a 'minimal state', restricted in its functioning to the protection of personal and property rights. Individuals may band together to pursue other goals or goods, but the state is prohibited from using its powers of compulsion for any purpose other than rights protection: thus taxation is only legitimate to cover the costs of external defence and administering a legal system.

Nozick goes on to show how a rights theory of this kind excludes not only utilitarian principles, but Rawlsian principles of justice that require the state to redistribute resources to the worst-off, principles of equality, and any principle that requires more than a 'minimal state'. Because individuals have strong rights over their possessions, any political project that infringes these rights will be illegitimate unless it can command the unanimous support of those whose rights are in question.

Two issues have dominated the critical reaction to Nozick's claims. The first concerns Nozick's move from the anti-utilitarian premise that individuals must in some sense be treated as inviolable and not be used for the benefit of others to the conclusion that they have rights of the sort that he endows them with. In particular critics have argued that self-ownership rights – rights to bodily integrity and control – and external property rights have very different implications (see especially Cohen 1995). If I am awarded rights over some physical thing – a tract of land, say – this immediately prevents you from using that thing without my permission. My freedom may be enhanced, but yours is restricted. So to justify property rights merely from the perspective of the right-holder is myopic. Connected to this is the second issue, namely, how individuals originally acquire the rights that are later to be treated as sacrosanct. Nozick follows John Locke in maintaining that people may legitimately acquire property by mixing their labour with unowned things, and may exchange or transfer the property so acquired in any way they wish, provided that their acquisition does not worsen the position of anyone else. But critics have argued that for property rights of this kind to be justified, people must at least have had an equal opportunity to acquire property in the first place. Even within the libertarian camp, some, such as Steiner (1994), have insisted that each person must initially be credited with an equal share of the earth's natural resources before property exchange and transfer is allowed to proceed.

This more egalitarian form of libertarian rights theory still conceives of rights negatively as requirements that others should not interfere with my person or property. For critics, this negative construal misses the essential point about rights, which is that they should safeguard the conditions under which human beings can lead worthwhile lives. These conditions include protection of person and property, but they may also include the provision of vital resources – food, medicine, education and so forth. The idea of human rights, which has assumed increasing importance in international affairs in the second half of the twentieth century, is usually taken to include positive rights of this kind. Within the analytical tradition such rights have been justified by appeals to *moral agency* or to *needs*. On the moral agency view, no one can choose and act morally unless he or she enjoys a certain minimum level of freedom and well-being. It follows that, regardless of the particular form of morality one embraces, one must recognise fundamental rights to freedom and well-being as a precondition of *any* morality (see Gewirth 1978; 1982; 1996; Plant *et al.* 1980). A more naturalistic approach grounds rights in needs – such as needs for health and adequate nutrition – that are common to all human beings regardless of the particular lives that they choose to lead (see Shue 1980; Donnelly 1985). Both views claim that the distinction between negative and positive rights is morally arbitrary: it is as damaging to a person to be deprived of food by famine as it is by theft, so if individuals have rights not to be deprived of the food they have grown, they also have a right to be supplied with food if their crops fail through no fault of their own.

Social justice after Rawls

As noted above, libertarian rights theorists such as Nozick argued for a minimal state and ruled out any compulsory redistribution from rich to poor in the name of social justice. Critics argued that states were morally obliged to protect the (positive) rights of every citizen by guaranteeing the provision of minimum levels of welfare. Rawls had gone further still in arguing that justice required not merely the provision of a social minimum but that inequalities in society must always work to the greatest benefit of the least advantaged members. Rawls, though, did not object to economic inequalities as such: if they served as incentives encouraging the talented to be more productive, then his difference principle would justify them. Subsequent theories of social justice in the analytical tradition have argued for a stronger form of equality. A common theme has been that justice requires the elimination of all morally arbitrary inequalities, where 'morally arbitrary' means that the individuals in question cannot be held personally responsible.

Ronald Dworkin's theory of equality of resources has been particularly influential in this field (Dworkin 1981). The theory rests upon a basic distinction between a person's circumstances and her choices – between features of someone's situation for which she cannot be held responsible and those for which she can. Dworkin believes, in particular, that it would be wrong to try to give people equal levels of well-being, because a person's well-being depends on her tastes and preferences, and in normal circumstances people can properly be held responsible for their tastes and preferences. Equally, people can be held responsible for the choices they make about how to use the resources available to them. The level of resources available to someone forms part of her circumstances, however, so everyone must initially enjoy an equal share of such resources. For Dworkin, these resources include not only wealth, commodities and other external resources, but personal talents and handicaps. Justice requires, therefore, that every citizen have access to an equal bundle of resources, taking both internal and external resources into account; but justice permits subsequent inequalities that result from choices or preferences.

Since people will value resources differently depending on their preferences, Dworkin's theory requires some way of deciding whether resource bundles are equal or not. For external resources he proposes the device of a hypothetical auction, where resources are divided into lots and each citizen is given an equal number of tokens with which to bid. The auction continues until each person is satisfied that he has made the best bids he can given the number of tokens he has and the rival bids of others. The resulting distribution of resources will be 'envy-free' in the sense that no-one prefers anyone else's bundle to his own. An equal distribution of external resources, therefore, is defined as one that could have emerged from such a procedure.

Dworkin faces greater difficulties when dealing with personal resources – personal talents and handicaps. His theory of justice requires that people with handicaps should be compensated by being given additional external resources, and that people with greater talents should be penalised by having fewer such resources: the principle is that, overall, everyone's bundle should be equally valuable to avoid morally arbitrary inequalities. But this requires that personal resources should be valued in some way, and the auction device is not appropriate here. Instead, Dworkin resorts to the idea of insurance. He asks how much people would be prepared, on average, to pay to insure against a particular form of disability, or to insure against having low levels of talent, if they did not know what talents or handicaps they actually had. He argues that the state should use its powers of tax and transfer to simulate such an insurance scheme – taking resources from the talented in the form of income taxation to track the insurance premiums they would have paid, and giving resources to the untalented and the handicapped to track the payouts they would have received, if such a scheme had existed.

Despite its technical difficulties, Dworkin's theory of justice ranks alongside Rawls' as a remarkable attempt to give a principled basis for the distributive practices of modern liberal democracies. Yet critics sympathetic to the egalitarian thrust of the theory have argued that it focuses too narrowly on *resources*. Even if people enjoy equal access to resources in the way that Dworkin's theory requires, they may still be relatively advantaged or disadvantaged for reasons that are not traceable to their choices or preferences – in particular, they may be more or less able to convert resources into personal well-being. A handicapped person, for instance, may not only have fewer opportunities but may also suffer personal distress as a result of the handicap, and the distress would not count as a resource deficiency. So theorists have looked for a new 'currency' that avoids the difficulties of welfare and of resources in which to measure egalitarian justice. Amartya Sen has proposed 'basic capability equality' – the principle that people should as far as possible be made equal in their capacity to perform a range of functionings such as being adequately nourished, being able to move about freely, and avoiding premature death (Sen 1982; 1992). G. A. Cohen has proposed 'equal access to advantage', where 'advantage' is taken to mean some combination of resources and welfare (Cohen 1989).

A noteworthy feature of all these theories, and one they share with Rawls', is that they reject *desert*, as that idea is commonly understood. Social justice does not, for instance, mean that people who make a larger economic contribution deserve to receive a higher income. According to egalitarian theorists, since the size of someone's contribution depends in part at least on natural talents, and since natural talents are regarded as morally arbitrary features, no one can deserve income or other benefits simply for contributing more; at best someone might deserve something for making an effort or a choice. This feature sets egalitarian theories significantly apart from public opinion in the societies to which they are meant to apply, where desert retains a central place in popular conceptions of social justice. Some analytical theorists have attempted to rescue the idea of desert from egalitarian criticism and to argue that a complete theory of social justice must find room for desert alongside equality and other distributive principles (see Lucas 1980; Sher 1987; Miller 1999).

A quite different way of understanding the meaning and value of equality has been proposed by Michael Walzer (1983). Walzer rejects the idea that justice can be understood as the equal distribution of any single currency. Instead, justice is irreducibly plural, in the sense that different social goods – money, political power, education, recognition and so forth – compose separate spheres in each of which a different principle of distribution applies. Yet so long as the separation of spheres is maintained – so long as people are prevented from converting the advantages they gain in one sphere into advantages in another, in defiance of the distributive principle that rightfully applies in the second – a certain kind of equality may be achieved. Walzer calls this 'complex equality'. A society of complex equality is one in which some people are (justly) ahead in the sphere of money, others are ahead in the sphere of political power, and so on, but no one wins out in all the spheres, and so everyone enjoys an equal standing overall. This also means that Walzer is able to find a limited place for desert within a theory of equality. So long as specific forms of desert are confined to particular spheres, and no overall scale of desert is established, recognising desert need not threaten social equality.

The challenge of communitarianism

Another problem with contemporary theories of justice, according to Walzer, is that they are too abstract and universalistic. Against them he opposes his 'radically particularist' approach, which attends to 'history, culture, and membership' by asking not what 'rational individuals . . . under universalising conditions of such-and-such a sort' would choose, but what would 'individuals like us choose, who are situated as we are, who share a culture and are determined to go on sharing it?' (Walzer 1983, pp. xiv and 5). Walzer thus calls attention to the importance of community, which he and others writing in the early 1980s took to be suffering from both philosophical and political neglect.

Nor do these *communitarians* believe that theoretical indifference has merely coincided with the erosion of community that they see in the world around them. In various ways Walzer, Alisdair MacIntyre (1981), Michael Sandel (1982) and Charles Taylor (1985), among others, have all charged that the philosophical emphasis on distributive justice and individual rights works to divide the citizens of the modern state against each other, thereby fostering isolation, alienation and apathy rather than commitment to a common civic enterprise. This concern with the pernicious effects of individualism is hardly new – Hegel, de Tocqueville, Durkheim and the British idealists sounded similar themes in the nineteenth century, as did Rousseau and others even earlier – but it was given a new life and a new opponent as part of what became known, for better or worse, as the liberal-communitarian debate.

Those enlisted on the communitarian side of the debate have pressed four major objections against their 'liberal' or 'individualist' opponents. The first is the complaint, already noted in Walzer, that abstract reason will not bear the weight philosophers have placed on it in their attempts to ground justice and morality. This 'Enlightenment project' (MacIntyre 1981) is doomed by its failure to recognise that reasoning about these matters cannot proceed apart from shared traditions and practices, each with its own set of roles, responsibilities and virtues. Second, the liberal emphasis on individual rights and justice comes at the expense of civic duty and the common good. In Sandel's words, 'justice finds its limits in those forms of community that engage the identity as well as the interests of the participants'; 'to some I owe more than justice requires or even permits . . . in virtue of those more or less enduring attachments and commitments which taken together partly define the person I am' (Sandel 1982, pp. 182 and 179). Contemporary liberals are blind to these enduring attachments and commitments, according to the third charge, because they too often rely on an atomistic conception of the self – an 'unencumbered self', in Sandel's terms – that is supposedly prior to its ends and attachments. Such a conception is both false and pernicious, for individual selves are largely constituted by the communities that nurture and sustain them. When Rawls and other 'deontological liberals' teach individuals to think of themselves as somehow prior to and apart from these communities, they are engaged quite literally in a *self*-defeating enterprise. The fourth objection, then, is that these abstract and universalistic theories of justice and rights have contributed to the withdrawal into private life and the intransigent insistence on one's rights against others that threaten modern societies. There is little sense of a common good or even a common ground on which citizens can meet. As MacIntyre sees it, the conflict between the advocates of incommensurable moral positions has so riven modern societies that politics now 'is civil war carried on by other means' (MacIntyre 1981, p. 253). The best that we can do in these circumstances is to agree to disagree while we try to fashion 'local forms of community within which civility and the intellectual and moral life can be sustained through the new dark ages which are already upon us' (MacIntyre 1981, p. 263).

Before turning to the 'liberal' rebuttal, we must note that the communitarian critics of liberalism neither form a well-defined school nor pose a distinctly extramural challenge to liberalism. Some theorists with communitarian leanings persist in calling themselves liberals (Galston 1991; Spragens 1995). Indeed, it sometimes seems that the communitarians' fundamental worry is that *other* liberals are so preoccupied with the rights and liberties of the abstract individual that they put the survival of liberal societies at risk. Whether this worry is well founded is a question that the 'liberal' side has raised in response to the 'communitarians'.

Here we may distinguish three interlocking responses. The first is that the communitarians have misunderstood the abstractness of the theories they criticise. Thus Rawls maintains (1993, lecture I) that his 'political' conception of the self as prior to its ends is not a metaphysical claim about the nature of the self, as Sandel believes, but simply a way of representing the parties who are choosing principles of justice from behind the 'veil of ignorance'. Nor does this conception of the individual as a self capable of choosing its ends require liberals to deny that individual identity is in many ways the product of unchosen attachments and social circumstances. 'What is central to the liberal view', according to Will Kymlicka, 'is not that we can *perceive* a self prior to its ends, but that we understand ourselves to be prior to our ends, *in the sense that no end or goal is exempt from possible re-examination*' (Kymlicka 1989, p. 52, emphasis in original). With this understood, a second response is to grant, as Kymlicka, Dworkin (1986; 1992) and Gewirth (1996) do, that liberals should pay more attention to belonging, identity and community, but to insist that they can do this perfectly well within their existing theories. The third response, finally, is to point to the dangers of the critics' appeal to community norms. Communities have their virtues, but they have their vices, too – smugness, intolerance and various forms of oppression and exploitation among them. The fact that the communitarians do not embrace these vices simply reveals the perversity of their criticism: they 'want us to live in Salem, but not to believe in witches' (Gutmann 1992, p. 133; see also Friedman 1992). If liberals rely on abstractions and universal considerations in their theories of justice and rights, that is because they must do so to rise above – and critically assess – local prejudices that communitarians must simply accept.

Communitarian rejoinders have indicated their sensitivity to this last point. Some, such as Sandel (1996), have adopted 'republicanism' as the proper name for their position. By allying themselves with the classical or civic republican tradition of political thought, they have shown that they are not willing to accept community in all its forms; they have also reduced the distance between themselves and those who have embraced 'civic republicanism in the liberal mode' (Dworkin 1992, p. 220; also Burtt 1993; Pettit 1997). Others have preferred to retain the communitarian label, but their rejoinders to 'liberal' criticisms stress their desire to strike a balance between individual rights and civic responsibilities (Etzioni 1997) and to 'move closer to the *ideal* of community life' – a life in which 'we learn the value of integrating what we seek individually with the needs and aspirations of other people' (Tam 1998, p. 220, emphasis added).

Mistaken or not as a critique of liberalism, communitarianism certainly has touched a political nerve. There is a communitarian journal, *The Responsive Community*, a Communitarian Platform and a Communitarian Network that extends throughout Europe and North America. If there is no Communitarian Party competing for office, communitarian ideas and rhetoric have certainly been evident in a number of other parties and places – notably the Clinton administration in the United States and Tony Blair's Labour government in Britain. Among practising politicians, in fact, communitarians may have achieved more influence than those whose abstract and individualistic theories they have sought to counteract.

Conclusion

Any attempt to assess the accomplishments of twentieth-century analytical political philosophy must confront two difficulties. The first is that our subject clearly continues to be a going enterprise – a growth industry, one might say, in which practitioners of the analytical approach take up new topics and spread around the globe. Indeed, space limitations prevent us from surveying the breadth of analytical political theory in this chapter. In addition to the topics we have discussed, a full treatment would explore the analysis of authority, freedom, power and other political concepts; survey contributions to the understanding of voting schemes, systems of representation and other topics in democratic theory; attend to the use of prisoners' dilemmas, free riders and other concepts of social choice theory to clarify various problems of politics; and take account of significant work on law and legal systems in analytical jurisprudence.

The second difficulty lies in determining what counts as success and failure for an enterprise of this kind. If the goal is to achieve fixed and uncontestable understandings of key concepts or to arrive at nearly unanimous agreement on basic principles, then analytical theorists have thus far failed. Even when a particular analysis of a concept seems definitive – as may be the case with Hanna Pitkin's work on representation (Pitkin 1967) – this conceptual agreement does not lead to agreement on the political or institutional form that representation should take. By this standard, however, it is doubtful that any political theory could ever succeed. Nor is it a standard that most analytical theorists have aspired to reach. According to Berlin and other value-pluralists, in fact, the conflict among incommensurable goods forecloses the possibility of nearly unanimous agreement on substantive principles. Moreover, conceptual analysis has taught most analytical theorists that political concepts are such constitutive parts of political contests – perhaps even 'essentially contestable' parts (Gallie 1966; MacIntyre 1973; but cf. Ball 1988, ch. 1) – that they do not lend themselves to precise definition. As a form of activity that proceeds through argument, debate and deliberation, that is, politics necessarily relies on concepts. Insofar as conceptual analysis changes the way people define and employ such concepts as freedom, justice, democracy and the public interest, it must therefore change the way they think and act politically (Ball, Farr and Hanson 1989). However much they may desire to be dispassionate scholars, analytical theorists thus find themselves engaged in an enterprise that is inescapably political. In these circumstances, they will almost certainly fail to reach agreement on fixed and uncontestable understandings of key concepts.

But if the goal of the analytical school is the more modest one of bringing conceptual clarity and argumentative rigour to political thinking, thereby encouraging citizens to think more clearly and consistently about the politics of the day, then analytical political philosophy has surely achieved some success. The continuing importance in political debates of such concepts as positive and negative liberty, equality of opportunity, human rights and the public interest is one form of evidence. Another is the way in which analytical theorists have been able to bring their skills to bear upon new concerns as the politics of the day shifts and changes direction. This has been particularly evident in recent years as many of these theorists have looked to issues such as education, multiculturalism, nationalism, threats to the environment, and global and intergenerational justice. Analytical theorists may be academics, but they are academics who believe that their theory can and should inform political practice. In this respect, analytical political theory continues to be political theory written from the perspective of the responsible citizen.

Part IV
New social movements and the politics of difference

22
Pacifism and *pacificism*

MARTIN CEADEL

Since the start of the modern political era, if not longer, most people in almost all countries have believed that the incidence of international war is most likely to be reduced if countries repudiate aggression yet maintain armed forces, and if necessary also military alliances, strong enough to stop others being tempted into expansionism by the prospect of easy pickings – a deterrent stance whose credibility requires a perceived willingness to fight.

This majority viewpoint is here labelled 'defencism' because it regards national defence efforts as the best prophylactics against war and believes that self-defence is a sufficient justification for fighting (Ceadel 1987, ch. 5). Its rejection of aggression distinguishes it both from militarism, which glorifies fighting and believes that the conquest of weak states by strong ones advances civilisation, and from crusading, which believes that aggressive force is justified where by promoting justice it ultimately contributes to peace (Ceadel 1987, chs. 3 and 4). Frequently summed up by the Latin tag *si vis pacem, para bellum* ('if you want peace, prepare for war'), defencism was generally treated by its supporters as a self-evident truth until early in the Cold War when a 'realist' school of academic students of international relations began to articulate its intellectual assumptions in order to justify them. However, it has long been associated with an ethical tradition which has attempted to delimit the circumstances in which a 'just war' can be declared (*jus ad bellum*) and the methods of fighting which can be used in its name (*jus in bello*) (Johnson 1975; 1981).

This chapter is concerned neither with defencism and its associated just-war tradition, nor with militarism and crusading. Instead, it analyses the ideas of the minority which, in addition to rejecting aggression, has regarded defencism as too negative because it aspires to no more than a stable truce between armed and watchful states and an amelioration of warfare once it eventually breaks out. This minority, which has become known as the 'peace movement' – a term which entered English usage as early as the 1840s, eventually supplanting the late eighteenth-century label 'friends of peace' – has insisted that war can be abolished by moral or political reform and a true and lasting peace created.

Ever since its emergence in the late eighteenth century, the peace movement has consisted of both absolutists and reformists (Ceadel 1996; 2000). Absolutists have argued that military force can be dispensed with immediately and completely if citizens develop a conscientious objection to the defence effort. They have insisted that all war is always wrong, a stance which originated in religious fundamentalism, though its nearest equivalent in domestic politics is anarchism of the non-violent kind (as noted, for example, by R. Sampson, in Wright and Augarde 1990, p. 51). Reformists have argued that war can be abolished through change at the level of political structures rather than individual consciences. They have accepted that, until the causes of aggression are eradicated, military force will be needed, though it must be not only defensive (as defencists also insist) but compatible with the progressive cause which will eventually abolish war: for example, some reformists believe that fighting to retain a colonial possession, though undoubtedly a defensive act, is none the less unjustified because colonialism is an obstacle to a peaceful world order. Products of the Enlightenment, reformist ideas about international relations are the counterparts of progressive ideas about domestic politics.

Though the distinction between the absolutist and the reformist approaches was understood from the outset by most peace activists, it was little recognised by the general public, in part because of a lack of agreed terminology. Prior to the twentieth century there was no generally accepted label for either an absolutist (though 'non-resister' was sometimes used) or a reformist (though 'peace advocate of defensive war', used in 1846 by the American absolutist Elihu Burritt (Ceadel 1996, p. 28), was one of the more succinct of the many circumlocutions resorted to). The appearance of the word 'pacifism' initially increased rather than dispelled the etymological uncertainty. It was coined in French in 1901,[1] and caught on within a decade in most languages, although for a while purists tried to insist on 'pacificism' as its correct English form. Intended to show that the peace movement had

1. By the French peace activist Emile Arnaud, who did so originally in August, 1901, in an article in *L'Indépendance Belge:* see Cooper (1991, p. 60). He reprinted this article in the same month's *Les Etats-Unis d'Europe*, p. 1 – a source I owe to Irwin Abrams. After Arnaud spoke at the following month's peace congress in Glasgow, the official report translated 'les pacifistes' as 'friends of peace' – a term dating back to the eighteenth century: see *Proceedings of the 10th Universal Peace Congress* (1901, pp. 74, 79).

a positive programme, and moreover one that was broader than the international federalism to which one faction wished to confine it, the neologism began as an umbrella term. Therefore, because reformists were more numerous than absolutists, it implied little more than opposition to defencism (and to militarism and crusading). In continental Europe, where absolutism has been much weaker than in the English-speaking world, pacifism has never lost this rather general meaning; and on the comparatively rare occasions when the absolutist position needs to be specified it has been distinguished by the addition of an adjective such as 'absolute' or 'integral'.

However, in Britain and the United States, where the absolutist strand has been somewhat more influential, the more rigorous meaning of pacifism gradually gained primacy. This semantic shift began during the First World War, as a result of the publicity attracted by conscientious objectors to whom in particular the label 'pacifist' was applied. It was completed in the second half of the 1930s, when, as will be noted, reformists generally accepted that military force would have to be used defensively to resist German, Italian and Japanese expansionism. They therefore tacitly surrendered the label 'pacifist' to that minority which insisted that even a defensive war against totalitarian aggression could not be justified.

This left the English language without a word for the reformist majority of the peace movement, a lack which led the Oxford historian A. J. P. Taylor to suggest that 'pacificism' be adopted (Taylor 1957, p. 51). He seemed unaware that this had once been a purist variant of 'pacifism' rather than a separate word. But his suggestion had the merit of identifying those who, without being fundamentalist opponents of military force in all circumstances, were 'pacific' in their approach to international relations; and, in the absence of a better alternative, it is used in this chapter.

Pacifism (absolutism) and *pacificism* (reformism) are sufficiently distinct to require separate discussion here. The latter is taken first, both because it was the more popular viewpoint and because its progress or otherwise was contextually significant for pacifism but not vice versa.

Pacificism

Pacificism had first appeared during the eighteenth century,[2] when beliefs in the harmony of international interests and in the capacity of public pressure

2. For what distinguishes *pacificism* from earlier blueprints for the improvement of international relations which had been produced intermittently since the early fourteenth century, see Ceadel (1996, pp. 6–7, 63–6).

to alter government policy both began to develop. It was strongest in Britain, on which this chapter will therefore mainly focus, followed by the rest of the English-speaking world and then by the Low Countries and Scandinavia. It fragmented into as many strands as there were reforming ideologies, beginning with radical and liberal variants: from the 1790s onwards radical *pacificism* blamed war on the incompetence and selfishness of elites and vested interests, and saw popular control as the remedy; and, especially after the 1830s, liberal *pacificism* blamed war on an irrational obsession with state prestige and proposed international remedies – economic interdependence, improvements in international law, and (albeit finding little support before the First World War) international organisation. By the mid-nineteenth century both radicals and liberals propounded the view, most famously identified with the English free-trade publicist Richard Cobden, that as the aristocracy lost power to the commercial classes a more peaceful foreign policy would result.

In the latter part of the nineteenth century, however, *pacificism* was thrown onto the defensive by Social Darwinism, by Germany's unification and industrialisation, and by growing imperial competition, all of which were widely seen to support the defencist or even the militarist world view. *Pacificism*'s counter-attack towards the end of the century was led by two intellectuals with Russian connections, Jacques Novicow and Ivan Bloch. Novicow, the cosmopolitan son of a Russian manufacturer, argued in 1893 that the real implications of Darwin's thinking were anti-war. Although human existence was indeed a series of struggles, intelligence rather than belligerence would ultimately prevail. The laws of science would eventually eliminate 'the state of perpetual war among civilized nations'; and peace activists could further this process by appealing to man's self-interest rather than to his emotions and by campaigning for a practical goal such as European federation rather than for a utopian one such as perpetual peace (Novicow 1893, pp. 424, 691–5; for 'peace biology' generally, see Crook 1994). In a later popularisation of his views for the peace movement, Novicow emphasised that 'war is a selection for the worse, which destroys the more cultivated and leaves the more barbarous', and claimed: 'The Darwinian law in no wise prevents the whole of humanity from joining in a federation in which peace will reign' (Novikow 1912, pp. 67, 164). Bloch, a banker and railway constructor of Polish-Jewish origins often credited with influencing the Tsar to summon the 1899 Hague Conference, drew on recent technological developments to argue in 1898 that 'war has become impossible, except at the price of suicide': the magazine rifle meant that in a major future conflict there would 'be increased slaughter... on so terrible a scale as to render it impossible to get troops to push the battle to a decisive issue'; and a war of attrition would develop, resulting in famine, national bankruptcy, social collapse, and socialist revolution (Bloch 1899, pp. xvi–xvii, xxxi).

At the start of the twentieth century two British writers, J. A. Hobson and Norman Angell, produced influential adaptations of radical and liberal *pacificism* to changed circumstances. Faced with popular enthusiasm in Britain for the Boer War, the radical Hobson conceded that the 'lay multitude' had succumbed to jingoism, in part because of the deleterious effects on their nervous systems of the 'bad conditions of town life in our great industrial centres' as well as the influence of a 'biassed, enslaved, and poisoned press' (Hobson 1901, pp. 1, 7, 125). But in his classic work *Imperialism: A Study* he rejected 'the merely sentimental diagnosis which explains wars or other national errors by outbursts of patriotic animosity or errors of statecraft' and insisted that war, though irrational 'from the standpoint of the whole nation', was 'rational enough from the standpoint of certain classes in the nation' – namely those financiers who, unable to find profitable investment at home because of the insufficient mass purchasing power of an unequal society, invested abroad and expected the state to use force to protect or even promote their interests. Though Hobson's economic analysis was new, his policy prescription was that of traditional radicalism: 'Secure popular government, in substance and in form, and you secure internationalism: retain class government, and you retain military Imperialism and international conflict' (Hobson 1902, pp. 52, 171).

As a liberal, Norman Angell (whose full name was Ralph Norman Angell Lane) disagreed with the proposition 'that if financial influence is kept well in hand by democratic control, nothing is to be feared'. Instead, influenced by a study of crowd psychology (Le Bon 1895) as well as by his personal observation of popular xenophobia in Britain, the United States and France, he stressed the role of 'non-economic factors' such as the emotionalism of the 'mass mind' in frustrating Cobden's hopes (Lane 1903, p. 30). As the Anglo-German naval race intensified he became increasingly convinced of the validity of the Cobdenite belief that financial considerations pointed in an anti-war direction. In a pamphlet published in 1909, which the following year he expanded into the bestseller *The Great Illusion*, he insisted that, because of 'the complex financial interdependence of the capitalists of the world' (Angell 1909a, p. 44) even a successful war of conquest would be counter-productive: if Germany seized Britain's wealth or colonies it would trigger systemic financial difficulties which in the end would make it a net economic loser. However, apart from distancing his overtly materialistic 'new pacifism' from the moralism of the 'old' peace movement – as Novicow had urged – and directing it more towards political elites than towards the masses, Angell offered no remedy other than education.

Socialists responded to these radical and liberal critiques by blaming capitalism for war. Though intermittently voiced as early as the mid-nineteenth century, this strand of *pacificism* could not establish itself within the peace-or-war debate until socialism became a force to be reckoned with in domestic politics. It was thus early in the twentieth century that assertions such as that by the Scottish politician Keir Hardie in 1907 became commonplace: 'I see no hope for the triumph of peace principles until society has been reorganized on the communistic non-competitive basis. It is for this, amongst other reasons, that I am a Socialist.'

To *pacificists* of all kinds the First World War came as a shock, but also as a stimulus. The English journalist H. N. Brailsford's prediction only months previously that 'there will be no more wars among the six Great Powers' (Brailsford 1914, p. 35) articulated a complacency which had managed to co-exist with concern about the arms race. Prior to 1914 the vast majority of Anglo-American liberals had either expected arbitration to work merely through bilateral arrangements (assisted by the panel of arbiters provided by the 1899 Hague Conference) or talked expansively but cloudily of federation. Now they rapidly united in support of a 'league of nations', a permanent international organisation which would require its member countries to submit all international disputes to a third party (though not in all cases to abide by the latter's verdict), to offer each other assistance against aggression, but not otherwise to surrender national sovereignty.

The main instigator of this remarkable pro-league consensus was the Cambridge political scientist Goldsworthy Lowes Dickinson, who argued that the German militarism which occasioned the war was itself caused by an international 'anarchy' for which all countries were responsible. (See Dickinson 1915; 1916; 1917. The best-known statement of his ideas did not appear until a decade later: see Dickinson 1926.) The league idea found most favour in Britain and the United States, a Dutch peace activist noting in 1917 that 'on the Continent one generally speaks of the further building up of the work of the Hague Peace-Conferences' instead (de Jong van Beek en Donk 1917, p. 10). The triumph of the League of Nations was assured when an American convert, President Woodrow Wilson, brought his country into the war. As a result, radical *pacificists* and defencists offered their own blueprints for a league, the former ambitiously wanting it to be a supranational body tackling economic causes of war as well as political ones, and the latter more conservatively wanting it to be merely an institutionalised and globalised Concert of Europe. (For analysis of the various schemes see Ceadel 1991.) Only socialists regarded the league idea as irredeemable because capitalist. Their own strand of *pacificism* found its fullest and most famous expression in Lenin's *Imperialism*, published in 1916, which adopted much of Hobson's economic analysis but insisted that the overthrow of capitalism itself, rather than democratic control, was the only solution.

The League of Nations that was agreed in 1919 and came into existence the following year was hated by socialists, who continued to insist that capitalism not international anarchy caused war (for the debate between socialists and League supporters see Brinton 1935), and disliked by radicals, who criticised it as in practice a league of governments not peoples. None the less it was such an innovation that for a decade and a half it was the focus of most *pacificist* hopes, especially in Britain. Even the academic discipline of international relations, created in the aftermath of the First World War, had so strong a normative commitment to it that the Oxford classics professor Gilbert Murray, a leading campaigner for the League, could describe his country's university chairs in the subject as 'the special League of Nations Professorships'.

However, the League was progressively discredited by the Japanese seizure of Manchuria in 1931, the collapse of the World Disarmament Conference in 1933 and – most decisively – Mussolini's conquest of Ethiopia, completed in 1936. This last event, along with Hitler's remilitarisation of the Rhineland and Franco's rebellion in Spain in the same year, polarised opinion in democratic countries as to whether to contain or to accommodate the aggressors. Albeit reluctantly, some *pacificists* supported containment: some liberals did so under the label of 'collective security', to indicate that the threat of force was validated by its internationalist character; and some socialists talked of a 'peace front' of European democracies plus the Soviet Union, to show that it was the progressive character of the states attempting containment which legitimised the policy. But they accepted that, even when given a progressive ideological gloss, containment in practice bore an embarrassing resemblance to the defencist policy of rearmament and alliances, justified with reference to national interests, to which *pacificism* had always aspired to provide an alternative. For that reason a rather greater number of *pacificists* initially favoured accommodation, abandoning the League and advocating appeasement under the name of 'peaceful change'. This term was also taken up by academics (Angus 1937; Cruttwell 1937; Manning 1937) and many previously pro-League professors moved towards what became known as a realist position, E. H. Carr leading the way (Carr 1936; 1939).

However, idealistic internationalism did not disappear. A few liberal *pacificists* argued that the League's failure showed that a more ambitious experiment in supranationalism should be tried. In particular, inspired by the fact that federation had succeeded in the United States after confederation had failed, a *New York Times* journalist, Clarence K. Streit, called for a comparable federation of the leading democracies of the world. His book, *Union Now: A Proposal for a Federal Union of the Democracies of the North Atlantic*, made a considerable impact, partly because its publication was almost immediately followed by Hitler's seizure of Prague in March 1939, which, by demonstrating that Hitler was not a mere pan-German but an expansionist seeking control over non-Germans too, discredited appeasement. With war inevitable and other outlets for international idealism lacking, federalism attracted considerable attention. Although later fragmenting into separate strands – Atlanticist, Europeanist, globalist and functionalist – it came, as a left-wing intellectual noted in 1940, 'to hold the same place in the public mind as had been held by the concept of the League of Nations during the latter half of the war of 1914–1918' (Strachey 1940, p. 7).

Yet despite the formation of the United Nations and some progress towards the integration of a European bloc, idealist hopes faded soon after Germany and Japan were defeated in 1945. Indeed, the first decade of the Cold War reduced *pacificism* to a very low ebb. The bipolarisation of the international system largely frustrated the expectation of its liberal strand that the Second World War would bring about what American Vice-President Wendell Wilkie called 'one world' (Wilkie 1943), though a nucleus of federalists kept the idea alive: as late as the early 1960s Amitai Etzioni was to observe that 'world government has been advocated as an immediate cure-all for international violence at the rate of one book per three years for the last generation', and to venture the judgement that the possibility of the United Nations developing into a supranational body could not be wholly dismissed (Etzioni 1962, pp. 173–5; 1964 pp. 226–35). The Soviet Union did a major disservice to socialist *pacificism* in the West by appropriating its rhetoric for blatantly communist 'peace' campaigns. Realism not only became the dominant 'paradigm' of the rapidly expanding international relations profession, its message being disseminated most effectively in a much reprinted textbook by political scientist Hans Morgenthau (1949), but also supplied an intellectual justification for NATO's policy of containing the Soviet bloc.

None the less, during two subsequent phases of the Cold War nuclear weapons provoked considerable public disquiet in Europe and the United States: during the late 1950s and early 1960s the radioactive fall-out generated by atmospheric nuclear tests caused widespread anxiety; and during the early 1980s the installation of a new generation of nuclear weapons, mounted on Cruise and Pershing missiles, raised fears that these might be intended for war-fighting rather than deterrence. Although many who called for unilateral nuclear disarmament did so in an ideological vacuum, others integrated nuclear weapons into either a modified version of traditional radicalism, which enjoyed something of a revival after several decades of playing second fiddle to the socialist perspective, or two new *pacificisms* arising out of the women's liberation and green movements which appeared in advanced countries.

The radical critique had been boosted by the appearance of the military-industrial complex, a phenomenon against which even President Eisenhower had warned in his farewell address. In the United States in particular it was further stimulated by the Vietnam War, which caused many Americans to see their own domestic political and social structures as a primary cause of international conflict. Radicalism could fit nuclear weapons into its analysis by noting that the secrecy and hair-trigger response which they required militated against democratic accountability, and that the popular control which their abandonment would make possible would produce a peaceful foreign policy. Indeed, as the threat which nuclear war posed to humanity as a whole came to be recognised as invalidating a purely class-centred analysis of international relations, radicalism recovered a little from its eclipse during the previous half century. In the 1980s E. P. Thompson, a distinguished historian of English radicalism as well as a former Communist who had subsequently helped to create the independent Marxist 'New Left', began to blame the senseless nuclear arms race on the Soviet defence lobby as well as on its Western counterparts. Unlike traditional radicals, he saw these lobbies not as simple pressure groups – though he admitted their relative autonomy – but as integral parts of a new state structure called 'exterminism', his argument being that 'the USA and the USSR do not *have* military-industrial complexes: they *are* such complexes. The "leading sector" (weapons systems and their supports) does not occupy a vast societal space, and official secrecy encourages low visibility; but it stamps its priorities on the society as a whole' (Thompson 1980, p. 23). However, at times Thompson sounded just like an orthodox radical, as when he claimed: 'What is needed is less "arms control" than control of the political and military leaders who control these arms' (Thompson 1982, p. ix; for further instances of radical rhetoric in the movement against nuclear weapons, see Ceadel 1987, pp. 119–21).

Women's peace activism already possessed a long history, but had previously concentrated on mobilising women in support of pacifism or of liberal, radical or socialist *pacificism* rather than formulating a distinctive analysis of its own. The women's liberation movement of the 1970s produced an explicitly feminist *pacificism* which indicted patriarchy as the cause of war, and was able to apply this gender-based critique to the nuclear issue at the beginning of the next decade. For example, in 1980 the British organisation Women Oppose the Nuclear Threat identified 'nuclear weapons as a specifically feminist issue', one of its activists, Lucy Whitman, arguing: 'Like a lot of feminists, I am convinced that nuclear weapons and nuclear power are in fact the most brutal manifestation of the murderous patriarchal system which has brought about so much misery throughout recorded history' (*Spare Rib*, Nov. 1980).

The green movement had also appeared in time to interpret nuclear weapons as a particularly clear illustration of its own warnings about the dangers of upsetting the ecological balance. It thus insisted that 'nuclear weapons are not just a nasty mistake in an otherwise healthy world. They are the logical outcome of the kind of society we have created for ourselves, the epitome of an exploitative, uncaring, unthinking worldview', to quote a British campaigner, Jonathon Porritt. Refusing to go as far as pacifism, Porritt preached eco-*pacificism*: 'Lasting peace can be based only on a genuine understanding of the relationship between people and planet... Ecologists insist therefore that one cannot talk about peace in a vacuum; it must be related to one's way of life... Of necessity, industrialism begets belligerency' (Porritt 1984, pp. 60–1, 156, 160–1).

Within the discipline of international relations, moreover, the realist emphasis on power relations among states came under criticism. The development by Scandinavian exponents of the new sub-discipline of peace studies of such notions as 'structural violence' (Galtung 1969), the emphasis by influential American political scientists on 'transnational' relations among civil societies and their positive contribution to 'interdependence' (Keohane and Nye 1971; 1977), and the exploration of the theory that democracies do not fight each other (Doyle 1983) – which, though often attributed to Kant's *On Perpetual Peace* (Kant 1903 [1795]), can be found in slightly earlier works by Paine and Godwin (Ceadel 1996, pp. 38–9) – were all symptoms of a renewed academic interest in an essentially *pacificist* agenda.

Moreover, statesmen rediscovered an interest in reforming the international system after the Cold War ended. American President George Bush and United Nations Secretary-General Boutros Boutros-Ghali expressed hopes for a new world order which had echoes of Wilsonianism. And Bill Clinton's administration was initially enthusiastic about the theory that democracy leads to peace.

However, these expectations proved illusory as conflicts which had previously been held in check by Cold War disciplines began to erupt. In consequence, *pacificism* left the twentieth century less confidently than it entered it. Admittedly, the just-war tradition, which had been almost moribund despite the fact that the 'area bombing' of the Second World War had infringed long-accepted *jus in bello* restrictions, had enjoyed a revival (e.g. Walzer 1977; Johnson, 1984), thanks in considerable part to Roman Catholic ethicists (e.g. Ramsey 1961; Finnis, Boyle and Grisez 1987), but, as already noted, it has never held out hope for the abolition of war. And the last vestiges of militarism have died away, despite a brief cult of guerrilla fighting in the 1960s and early 1970s. But crusading revived in the 1990s, particularly in the form of support for military action to punish Serbia for its treatment of Muslims in Bosnia and Albanians in Kosovo. And defencism remains the dominant perspective on international relations. Even among progressives, the tradition of claiming that war can be abolished altogether by political change has fallen on hard times.

Pacifism

Pacifism also passed its peak of popular support earlier in the twentieth century. As an ideology (as distinct from as an expression of sectarian peculiarity) it is no older than *pacificism*, having found its way from Christian sects, such as the Quakers and Mennonites, into mainstream Protestantism – albeit only as a tiny minority even within its evangelical wing – in both Britain and the United States by the end of the eighteenth century. This transition presented it with two problems which had become more acute by the second half of the nineteenth century: how to apply an absolutist idea to worldly politics; and how to sustain a religious idea at a time of increasing secularisation.

In respect of the political sphere, pacifism in effect faced a choice of three orientations. At one extreme was the optimistic view that a nation could be converted to pacifism fairly quickly and thereafter use it as an effective national policy: a disarmed country would escape aggression, either because God would protect those who showed true faith (as some evangelical pacifists argued early in the nineteenth century) or because aggressors would feel moral or psychological shame at attacking the non-violent (as Gandhians were to imply a hundred years later). At the other extreme was the pessimistic view that conversion would be slow and that until all nations had undergone it pacifism had nothing to offer the world of politics: pacifists could merely bear witness to their faith as a long-term ideal. As a widely favoured half-way house between these optimistic and pessimistic extremes, a collaborative orientation accepted that pacifism itself was not in the foreseeable future a practical policy, but insisted that its adherents could participate in politics by supporting *pacificist* proposals which had a realistic chance of being implemented and offered a real chance of reducing the incidence of war.

Each of these orientations had a drawback, however. The optimistic one, though inspirational in favourable circumstances, took a more sanguine view of the workings of God or the international system than experience usually warranted. The pessimistic one, though proving robust in situations of real adversity, was too quietist to encourage those of an activist temperament to take up the cause. And the collaborative one, though a seemingly sensible compromise, posed a particularly difficult question: how, if pacifists accepted that reformism offered the best practical hope of abolishing war, could they sustain and justify their own personal absolutism? The world's first pacifist association of any substance and durability, the Peace Society (established in London in 1816), found it increasingly hard to sustain its original faith: it devoted so much of its effort from the 1840s onwards to collaborating with promising new *pacificist* schemes for arbitration and general disarmament rather than expounding its own doctrine of non-resistance that it gradually forgot its absolutist character. Some Quakers, who felt obliged by their religious affiliation to remain pacifists but accepted that in terms of worldly politics only *pacificism* made sense, ceased to justify pacifism as a universal creed: they stopped urging non-Quakers to adopt their absolutist view, on the grounds that it was not in the best interests of society to have a pacifist majority.[3] However, this version of collaborative pacifism was hard to distinguish from mere 'exemptionism' (Ceadel 1987, 139–41) – the belief of the elect or the elite that war is wrong only for them and not for the majority

3. See, for example, J. W. Graham's letter challenging the proposition 'that for any Christian government to make war is a sin', while insisting that he personally remained loyal to the Quaker peace testimony: *Friend*, Dec. 1882, p. 304. The issue is discussed further in my forthcoming study of the British peace movement from the Crimean War to the Second World War.

whose willingness to use military force is indeed essential. Though for obvious reasons rarely articulated, exemptionism was to be encapsulated during the First World War in the reply of a member of London's 'Bloomsbury Group' to a woman who asked him why he was not fighting for civilisation like most other men of his age: 'Madam, *I* am the civilisation they are fighting for' (Holroyd 1967, vol. I, p. 416).

The need to adapt to a society in which religious belief was slowly losing ground was another cause of uncertainty among late nineteenth-century pacifists. Increasingly, even those who remained devout Christians were reluctant not only to argue that God would rescue a disarmed country but also to ground their pacifism on theological considerations alone. They therefore emphasised the inhumanity, disutility and impolicy of war, whilst claiming these to be secondary to its incompatibility with Christian teaching. Yet even though free thought had by mid-century given rise to at least one instance of avowedly agnostic pacifism (the Chartist Thomas Cooper), it had not progressed sufficiently for humanitarian, utilitarian and political versions of pacifism to establish themselves as acceptable alternatives to Christian pacifism.

The difficulties which mainstream pacifism was experiencing by the late nineteenth century explain the appeal of the uncompromising no-force pacifism based on the 'Christian life conception' which was propounded from the 1880s onwards by the aristocratic novelist and former soldier, Leo Tolstoy – a further instance of the creative contribution of Russian intellectuals to peace thinking at the end of the nineteenth century (Tolstoy 1885; 1894). Though mainly reacting against his own, particularly repressive, political system, Tolstoy had also been influenced by the Christian anarcho-pacifism preached nearly half a century previously in New England by William Lloyd Garrison and others who had been similarly alienated from their political system by its toleration of slavery; but most Garrisonians – like the American peace movement in general – had later supported military force against the slave-holding states, thereby compromising their pacifist tradition. Tolstoy's perfectionism, his injunction always to return good for evil, and his criticism of *pacificist* palliatives such as the Hague Conferences, contrasted excitingly with the messages being received from many members of the Peace Society and the Society of Friends. And, though derived from Christianity, his 'law of love' had universalistic and socially revolutionary qualities that appealed to humanists, socialists and anarchists. The extent of his international influence can be inferred from the claim made in 1915 by a British opponent of the peace movement that pacifism had 'long found its strongest expression among the Society of

Friends – or "Quakers". But, during recent years, it has been based largely upon the teachings of Tolstoi' (Ballard 1915, p. 16).

The First World War led most pacifists to accept Tolstoy's view that a personal rejection of war entailed a personal commitment to create the conditions under which human beings could live without violence. Even the largely quietist Christian pacifists who formed the Fellowship of Reconciliation recognised that they were 'called to a task of a more radical character than that of stopping the war', namely 'a struggle to destroy the spirit and the way of life which bear the fruits of war' (Roberts 1915, p. 33). In addition, the introduction in the English-speaking world of conscription enabled pacifists to distinguish themselves from *pacificists*; and the limited (though none the less path-breaking) provision for conscientious objection enabled the most courageous of them to make a public stand on behalf of their beliefs. Prominent among those suffering most were the handful of socialists, such as the young ILP activist Clifford Allen, who interpreted their political philosophy as forbidding the taking of human life. Admittedly, wartime circumstances limited their opportunities to articulate their socialist-pacifist creed and sometimes led them expediently to leaven it with socially more acceptable Christian arguments. Moreover, the Russian Revolutions of 1917 caused a number of them, including Allen, to reinterpret their socialism as allowing military force to be used in defence of a workers' state – in other words, to conclude that on reflection they were really *pacificists* not pacifists (Ceadel 1980, pp. 52–6). None the less, an explicitly political pacifism had made its first appearance.

In the aftermath of the First World War the influence of the League of Nations was so great that many pacifists supported it in the hope that it would have sufficient moral authority not to need the coercive sanctions for which, troublingly to their consciences, its Covenant made provision. However, not all pacifists adopted this collaborative orientation: some criticised the League and optimistically claimed to have a more effective policy to offer. Most notably, in a book published in 1925, the Labour politician Arthur Ponsonby criticised not only defencists ('No so-called adequate armaments... will give security against war') but liberal *pacificists* ('A League of Nations war will not just be a tidy little police affair'), and claimed that by contrast pacifists were 'intensely practical'. Ponsonby's confidence on this score rested on two questionable assumptions. The first was that, because 'in the world as we find it to-day, aggression, except perhaps on the part of the great powers against backward and weaker tribes on other continents, may be ruled out as a motive for war', wars were caused by mistakes alone. The second was that no pacifist movement which reached 'proportions which really count, could be confined to one nation alone', so that disarmament would never in practice be unilateral.

Ponsonby was more persuasive in his claim to have discovered a 'neglected' inspiration for pacifism – 'the scales of the balance of reason applied to war', as distinct from 'religious', 'humanitarian' and 'socialist' principles (Ponsonby 1925, pp. 85–9, 101–3, 109, 137, 139, 153). This self-consciously consequentialist pacifism was a response to the growing awareness of the harmful effects of the First World War and to the expectation that, because 'the bomber will always get through' (as Conservative leader Stanley Baldwin was to tell parliament on 10 November 1932 in arguably the most repeated saying of the inter-war years), any future war would be even more damaging.

The ingenuous Ponsonby had assumed an international system without real quarrels or illiberal regimes; but to be credible as a policy pacifism had to recognise the possibility of aggression and authoritarianism and offer a strategy for dealing with them. There was thus a widespread hope among pacifists in the early 1930s that the techniques of non-violent resistance pioneered by Mohandas K. Gandhi against British rule in India could also be applied to international conflict. For example, an American labour lawyer, Richard B. Gregg, published a book in 1934 which insisted that Gandhian techniques constituted a 'moral jiu jitsu' which would 'operate in different ways in different nations, but... operate effectively against them all, as sure as violent war has operated against them all' (Gregg 1936 [1934], p. 90).

Such ideas attracted most attention after the League of Nations was fully discredited in 1936. It was during May of that year that the Peace Pledge Union (PPU) was founded in London, establishing itself as the world's largest pacifist association (with 136,000 members at its peak in April 1940). Though its founder was a prominent Anglican clergyman, Canon H. R. L. ('Dick') Sheppard, the PPU left explicitly Christian pacifism – which was in any event facing a theological assault on its immanentist and liberal assumptions from Karl Barth, the distinguished German scholar, and the American lapsed pacifist Reinhold Niebuhr – to the Fellowship of Reconciliation. It concentrated instead on humanitarian and utilitarian arguments which were refined by the most distinguished 'sponsors' ever to support a pacifist association. For example, the novelist Aldous Huxley, enthused by Gregg and yearning to devote himself to a moral cause,[4] put forward the humanitarian case:

> Mankind is one, and there is an underlying spiritual reality. Men are free to deny or affirm their unity in the spirit. Acts and thoughts which tend to affirm unity are right; those which deny it are wrong. War is the large-scale and systematic denial of human unity, and is therefore wrong. Pacifism is also good policy – the only sensible policy that anyone has suggested in the circumstances of modern life (*Nash's Pall Mall Magazine*, July 1936, p. 77. See also Huxley 1936).

And the philosopher Bertrand Russell, a *pacificist* of long standing, embraced pacifism in 1936 mainly because he had convinced himself that air power made any future war too destructive to justify any conceivable benefits. In a book which he sent in draft to Ponsonby, who had put forward similar utilitarian arguments a decade before, Russell accepted the justice of military force used by a legitimate world government ('The evil of war is quantitative, and a small war for a great end may do more good than harm'), and concluded: 'What is right and what is wrong depends, as I believe, on the consequences of actions, in so far as they can be foreseen; I cannot say simply "War is Wicked," but only "Modern war is practically certain to have worse consequences than even the most unjust peace"' (Russell 1936, pp. 151, 211–12).

At first the PPU believed that it might be able to prevent war and, following Gregg, sought to train its followers in non-violent resistance. But once it realised that it would never reach 'proportions which really count', as Ponsonby had put it, many of its members abandoned the optimistic orientation for the collaborative one of backing those *pacificists*, such as Clifford Allen (now Lord Allen of Hurtwood), who were now campaigning for peaceful change.

However, the PPU's most thoughtful members moved instead towards the pessimistic orientation, long adopted by most members of the Fellowship of Reconciliation, which saw pacifism as more a faith than a policy. Even Huxley, after withdrawing to the United States in 1937, wrote a book which, without retracting support for the 'short-term policy . . . of war-resistance', insisted that 'there must be more than a mere deflection of evil; there must be a suppression at the source, in the individual will', and concentrated on the 'long-term' policy of pursuing, through meditation, the oriental goal of 'non-attachment', as the sole means by which the necessary awareness

4. The best source on Huxley pending the publication of David Bradshaw's biography is Bradshaw (1996).

of 'oneness with ultimate reality' could be achieved (Huxley 1937, pp. 24, 151, 298).

Another PPU sponsor, the literary critic John Middleton Murry, went through an even more extreme version of this transition. Initially he asserted that it was 'probably as near to a certainty as human reckoning can attain that, against a Pacifist England, Fascist Germany would be completely incapable of making war' (Murry 1937, pp. 26, 114). However, he then switched to the view: 'The pacifist cause will be won, if it is won, only by those who have come to see that winning is a secondary affair. What matters is that men and women should bear their witness – and bear it, if need be, to the end.' As Murry's pacifism thus moved from an optimistic to a pessimistic orientation, it also changed from a political to a Christian inspiration, noting approvingly that in Huxley's case too a 'previous scepticism has completed changed, under the urgency of Pacifism, to a religious mysticism' (Murry 1938, pp. 9, 12).

Although the intellectually volatile Murry later swung back briefly to a belief in practical pacifism, many PPU intellectuals began thinking about creating communities in which they could nurture pacifism as a long-term ideal within a political world which they knew to be far from ready for it.

The Second World War inflicted lasting damage on pacifism as a policy, while helping to legitimise it as a religious and ethical faith that was too exigent to have mass appeal. In particular, Germany's military successes of 1940 caused a number of PPU members, including Russell, to recant. Those who did not, and availed themselves of the improved provisions for conscientious objection (available only in the liberal and Protestant countries of the English-speaking world, Scandinavia and the Netherlands), often felt uneasy about their pacifism, and strove to offer their fellow citizens social, in lieu of military, service. When Hitler's extermination camps were discovered in 1945, they were almost universally interpreted not as evils generated by the conflict itself but as definitive demonstrations that greater evils than war existed. Some pacifists continued to claim that their policy could have avoided the Second World War. For example, A. J. Muste, who was later described as ' "Mr Pacifist" to a cold war generation' in the United States (Chatfield 1971, p. 370), asserted: 'If we had been willing to spend one-tenth or one-twentieth of the money, energy and brains we put into the war on the economic rehabilitation of Germany and other countries, there would have been no war – could have been no war' (Muste 1947, pp. 11–12).

Understood to be the viewpoint of a tiny minority, pacifism gained increasing acceptance in liberal-democratic countries during the post-war era, as reflected in the decision by Roman Catholic countries, such as France in 1963 and Italy in 1971, to recognise conscientious objection. However, many refusals of military service – for example, those of the Greens in West Germany and white radicals in South Africa during apartheid – were protests against the political system requiring it rather than against bearing arms as such. Pacifist books and pamphlets appeared in a steady trickle, particularly from Christian authors helped by the turning of the tide of theological fashion back from Barthian and Niebuhrian preoccupations towards liberalism. Some, notably those of John Yoder, an American Mennonite ethicist, were of a high quality (Yoder 1976) but none had a major impact on either intellectual or general opinion.

The interest which non-violence aroused for a time in progressive circles might have been expected to boost pacifism. However, it was favoured as a means of pursuing a political struggle rather than as an expression of a principled commitment to social or international reconciliation: in the 1970s John Hyatt, an activist in the much diminished PPU, noted 'a strong swing within the non-violent movement away from principled non-violence and pacifism towards trying to propagate non-violence as a technique which can be used by anyone without any philosophical or ethical basis for that non-violence' (Hyatt 1972, unpaginated); and Gene Sharp, the American theorist of non-violence, acknowledged that his subject embraced 'non-violent coercion' (Sharp 1973, pp. 741–4). (Similarly, Carter, Hoggett and Roberts 1970 was 'primarily about a technique of action, not a dogma'; and two of its compilers made the transition from activists to prominent academic students of non-violence: see Carter 1973 and Roberts 1967). Moreover, it was understandably applied more easily to domestic issues, such as race relations in the United States, than to international relations: significantly, when Gregg's *The Power of Nonviolence* was re-issued in 1960, the foreword was by the leading campaigner for African-American rights, Martin Luther King.

Nuclear weapons might also have been expected to boost pacifism of a utilitarian or humanitarian kind in the same way that 'the bomber' had in the inter-war period. Indeed, some people did decide that 'they were not going to support the idea of armed conflict for whatever purpose . . . because the potential end-product of any armed conflict was the use of nuclear weapons', in the words of one such, Pat Arrowsmith, a prominent activist in Britain's Campaign for Nuclear Disarmament (Mackay and Fernbach 1983, p. 65). However, the vast majority did not, as was shown by the use of the phrase 'nuclear pacifist' to describe someone who had repudiated nuclear but not conventional weapons, rather than someone like Arrowsmith who had been converted to pacifism proper by the risk of nuclear escalation in any war. To avoid confusion, therefore, the latter is best labelled a 'nuclear-era pacifist' (Ceadel 1987, pp. 144–5).

Other intellectual approaches benefited from the nuclear revolution more than pacifism. *Pacificism* did so to some extent, as already noted. A bigger beneficiary was the just-war tradition. However, despite the unprecedented stringency of their interpretation of the *jus in bello*, the leading exponents of this tradition distanced themselves from pacifism: Ramsey did so explicitly (Ramsey 1988); and Finnis, Boyle and Grisez, though admitting that their moral theory 'is more restrictive than traditional versions, even that of Thomas Aquinas', also insisted that it 'by no means entails pacifism' (Finnis, Boyle and Grisez 1987, p. 315).

Although neither non-violence nor nuclear weapons stimulated pacifism as significantly as might have been expected, America's unsuccessful military involvement in Vietnam from 1965 to 1973 led to the formulation of a 'contingent' version of it founded on near absolute distrust of politicians and the military. The influential political philosopher John Rawls argued that

> the conduct and aims of states in waging war, especially large and powerful ones, are in some circumstances so likely to be unjust that one is forced to conclude that in the foreseeable future one must abjure military service altogether. So understood a form of contingent pacifism may be a perfectly reasonable position: the possibility of a just war is conceded but not under present circumstances (Rawls 1971, pp. 381–2).

Paradoxically, however, this same distrust led many of America's existing pacifists to support the use of military force against what they regarded as imperialism. For example, Dave Dellinger, chairman of the National Mobilization to End the War in Vietnam, asserted in 1967: 'I practice non-violence, but I do not repudiate or oppose what I sometimes call the violence of the victims' (Lewy 1988, p. 102). Admittedly, pacifists have always drawn the line in different places: indeed, we have already noted that Tolstoy rejected all force, whereas Russell and Arrowsmith accepted that some international wars had been justifiable prior to the invention of, respectively, the bomber and nuclear weapons. Provided that they can explain why they draw the line where they do, therefore, pacifists can coherently reject all international war but support just civil wars and just revolutions: indeed, Ponsonby had explicitly taken this position (Ponsonby 1925, p. 16). Yet during the Cold War American pacifists failed to produce a considered justification of their line-drawing: their desire to be politically relevant caused them to condemn their own political system out of hand, yet endorse violent movements for national liberation uncritically.

The end of the Cold War has thrown pacifists onto the defensive: by removing certain obstacles to nationalist aggression while diminishing the risk of nuclear escalation, it has strengthened the case for limited uses of military force, for example to defend vulnerable minorities in the former Yugoslavia. As a member of the executive committee of the War Resisters International, Christine Schweitzer, admitted at a meeting in Zagreb in 1996 with the recent Bosnian conflict in mind: 'Pacifists have not been able to come up with very good answers to questions like: How do you defend the enclaves? How do you stop the shelling of civilians? How do you put an end to the detention camps?' None the less, noting that the Spanish Civil war, the Second World War, the Vietnam War, wars of national liberation and the Gulf War had posed similar problems, she insisted: 'There is certainly a crisis of pacifism, but it is not historically unique, nor is it as definitive as those who declare "the end of pacifism" seem to believe' (*Peace News*, Feb. 1997, pp. 12–14).

At the end of the twentieth century pacifism was widely respected as the moral conviction of a small minority but possessed little credibility as a practical policy. For absolutists even more than for reformists, the abolition of war seems almost as remote as ever.

23
Feminisms

SUSAN JAMES

Throughout the twentieth century, the feminist movement has been made up of shifting and more or less closely connected groups, united by the conviction that women are unfairly disadvantaged by comparison with men. While this minimal consensus contributes to an understanding of feminism as an enduring position, it exists alongside great internal diversity. The normative conception of disadvantage around which consensus revolves stands in need of analysis and has in fact been interpreted in strikingly divergent ways, giving rise to a variety of feminisms, some of them with conflicting goals and theoretical commitments. Feminism is therefore internally complex, but the divisions within it can be traced to enduring disputes and differences.

One of these sources of conflict concerns the relation between theory and practice. During the first quarter of the century, feminism gained much of its identity from a series of political campaigns aimed at improving the lives of at least some women, and in many quarters it has continued to represent itself as a practical programme striving for social and political reform. Like any movement which challenges the status quo, it depends on a critical kind of theorising – on an ability to expose the limitations or inconsistencies of established principles in order to undermine the practices that flow from them. Within feminism, however, critical theorising of this sort has sometimes developed a degree of autonomy that has separated it from practical politics, and this in turn has led to divisions between feminists concerned with immediate political change, and those with more abstract philosophical interests (Barrett 1980, pp. 201–19; hooks 1984, pp. 17–31; Yeatman 1994, pp. 42–53). But although the balance between these two preoccupations varies, they are rarely completely disjoined. During the campaigns for female suffrage, for example, assessments of what was politically achievable were offset by arguments about the justice of enfranchising all women, only some women, different groups of men and women, or all men; and in the 1970s debates about wages for housework, and theoretical discussion about how such a policy might be justified, went along with a more practical interest in how it might be organised.

The problematic relation between theory and practice is complemented by a further tension surrounding the roles of critical and constructive theorising. For the reason just given, critical analysis is often seen as an essential aspect of feminist politics. Furthermore, for feminists who understand themselves as confronting political systems and philosophies which serve to legitimate and uphold male power, criticism is an entirely appropriate stance. At some point in the process of theorising, however, the exposure of flaws gives way to the vulnerable task of articulating new categories, arguments and possibilities. Such constructive theorising often moves away from immediate engagements with practical questions, but insofar as it borrows concepts or methods from political theories which implicitly uphold male power, it runs the further risk of assimilating the very norms that critical theorising aims to expose, and of losing its distinctiveness (Whitford 1991a, p. 97). So within the history of feminism there is often an uneasy accommodation between two stances: that of a theorist who uses her marginality as a source of critical insight, and that of a theorist who, in the course of constructing a view of her own, appropriates the language of the powerful. Once again, there have been times and places at which one approach has predominated over the other.

A third divisive issue relates to the scope of theorising and action. Some feminists have attributed the disadvantages suffered by women to relatively local and specific arrangements (for instance, to the lack of legislation outlawing sweated labour), while others have identified much more extensive forms of subordination, rooted in a far-reaching and long-lasting patriarchal system. Each theoretical framework yields different interpretations of the phenomena on which it focuses, and suggests a different conception of the relation between feminism and other political movements. For example, where the first may be optimistic about the amount that can be achieved through legal reform, the second, persuaded of the range and adaptability of patriarchal power, is likely to take a more sceptical view.

As these areas of pervasive disagreement indicate, feminism is, and always has been, highly sensitive to its own theoretical and political setting, and has engaged with the resources of surrounding social and political theories, whether by criticising, rejecting, incorporating, inverting or adapting them. Because many varieties of feminism are deeply indebted to non-feminist political theories as well as to each other, and because feminisms have in turn had an effect on some of the non-feminist theories with which they have come into contact, the development of feminism as a whole is best seen in the context of this extended network of relationships (ecofeminism is briefly discussed in chapter 25). These relationships are not always easy-going. Some break down completely and others are poisoned by the fear of betrayal. Nevertheless, it is in this highly charged and politicised environment that feminism has grown to a point where it is arguably the most original and challenging contributor to contemporary political philosophy.

During the last few years, it has become common to distinguish a first wave of modern feminism, dating from the mid-nineteenth century to 1930, a second wave lasting through the 1970s and a third wave rising in the latter half of the 1980s. This chronology highlights the absence of specifically feminist campaigns between the 1940s and 1970s and awards special importance to a shift in the character of anglophone feminism during the late 1980s; but it needs to be used cautiously, since it is liable to obscure the diversity of feminist movements within a single wave, and to overemphasise the discontinuity between one wave and the next. Both these points are worth noting. The first applies especially to the first wave, a long period in which diverse women's movements contributed to many kinds of social reform. The second is relevant to the relations between all three waves: although the second was separated in time from the first, it took up many of its central themes and preoccupations; and although there is a significant transition from the second to the third, there is also a great deal of continuity between them.

The first wave

First-wave feminism provides a compelling illustration of the general point that feminism is internally diverse; it encompasses, for instance, campaigns for women's rights in Europe and America, Alexandra Kollontai's efforts to transform women's labour in revolutionary Russia, and, again in America and Europe, Emma Goldman's defence of the importance of sexual freedom. It also exemplifies the claim that feminisms have both criticised and drawn on a wide range of theoretical perspectives; while campaigns for women's rights were often conducted within a broadly liberal framework, Kollontai based her reforms on the work of Marx and Engels, and Goldman was inspired by anarchism. Finally, it contains within itself differences of opinion about the sites of women's disadvantage and thus about the sorts of changes needed in order to overcome it. Where many feminists set store by the reform of existing political and economic institutions, Kollontai saw the emancipation of women as an aspect of a revolutionary movement, and Goldman argued that the only way to escape oppression is to live outside the institutions of the state, including marriage.

Although allegiances such as these are extremely significant in relation to the history of feminism, it is important not to exaggerate the disparities in the theoretical approaches associated with them. For example, defenders of equal rights for women, who can be broadly classified as liberal, were nevertheless sensitive to women's difference. While they argued that what were regularly described as natural differences between men and women were in many cases nothing more than instances of discrimination concealing the need for equal treatment, they also appealed to sexual difference to portray women's distinctive contribution to public life, and to allay widespread fears about the social upheaval that might follow from female emancipation (Banks 1981, p. 84; Lewis 1984, pp. 88–9; Kent 1990, pp. 206–7). At the same time, they were alive to the connections between the public and private spheres. By demanding a range of civil and economic reforms, liberal feminists challenged both the deeply embedded assumption that (whatever the realities of working-class life) women were not capable of conforming to the norms governing the political realm and the workplace, and the assumption that it was their duty to be an angel in the house, safely protected by men (Evans 1977; Banks 1981; Lewis 1984; Rendall 1985; Kent 1990).

For the members of the first women's movements, female emancipation was often an element in a programme of more wide-ranging social reforms, and their success in gaining rights for women could be helped or hindered by their other political aspirations. For example, in America, Australia, Denmark and New Zealand, temperance and suffrage movements were interlinked, and the female franchise was seen as a step towards the moral improvement of the polity (Evans 1977, pp. 53, 60–3, 78). In much of Western Europe and Scandinavia, an interest in women's welfare derived in part from anxiety about population decline (Evans 1977, pp. 26–8). Because alliances between feminism and other causes depended on local circumstances, it is extremely difficult to generalise about its development or achievements. In each country, the women's movement followed its own course.

There is, however, a certain amount of uniformity in the problems feminists addressed. By the beginning of the twentieth century, many of the types of disadvantage from which women suffered had been identified and aired, and the question of how they might be alleviated had begun to be tackled. In some countries, preliminary reforms had been made. In others, however, progress was slower, and legislation guaranteeing basic rights for women belongs to the twentieth century. Several of the early women's movements were relatively successful in gaining access to more than minimal education. In America, 40,000 women were enrolled in colleges of higher education by 1880, and in New Zealand more than half of all university students were women by 1893 (Evans 1977, p. 50). Swedish education for women expanded rapidly from the 1860s, and the first institutions offering higher education to British women date from the 1840s (Evans 1977, p. 70; Millett 1977, p. 75). During the same period, moreover, women began to gain entry to the professions. By 1890, American women had been admitted to the federal bar, and there were 4,500 physicians and 250,000 teachers (Evans 1977, p. 51). Legislation passed in the 1850s and 1860s allowed Scandinavian women to become teachers, and in Britain women were first admitted to medical school in the 1870s (Porter 1997, p. 356). These changes came more slowly, however, in France and Germany. Women were not allowed to attend lectures at the Sorbonne until 1880 and only gained admission to German universities as full-time students after 1902 (Evans 1977, p. 128).

The gradual recognition of women as legal persons capable of exercising their own rights also began comparatively early. Women started to acquire the rights they needed in order to engage in economic activity. In Sweden, for example, laws enabling women to inherit property were passed during the 1840s and a law restricting women's access to certain occupations was repealed in 1864, while French women gained the right to hold post office accounts in 1884 (Evans 1977, pp. 70, 128). At the same time, the legal status of married women began to change. The passage of Married Women's Property Acts (in America during the 1840s, in Britain during the 1850s, and in New Zealand in 1870) was one of a large number of factors which focused attention on the asymmetrical positions of women and men as regards marriage, divorce and custody, and helped to initiate a lengthy process of reform. Divorce laws, albeit restrictive ones, were in place in Britain, France, Sweden and America by 1900 (Millett 1977, p. 67; Bolt 1993, pp. 95–104). Disparity in the basic economic and social rights of men and women was thus one of the first areas addressed by feminist movements, and it has remained a pressing concern up to the present day.

During the first wave, campaigns to improve women's legal status were closely connected to campaigns for sexual rights, a topic which was important in a number of feminist movements from an early stage. In the 1880s, state regulation of prostitution was a contested issue in Denmark (Evans 1977, pp. 77–8), as well as in England where Josephine Butler led a successful campaign for the repeal of the Contagious Diseases Act, a law which punished female prostitutes suspected of carrying venereal disease but not their male sexual partners. Butler's campaign drew attention to the sexual double standard underlying the law, and also encouraged the recognition that this affected all sexually active women – married and unmarried, prostitutes and respectable ladies. As long as men were sexually promiscuous, so she and her Danish counterparts argued, the health and well-being of women would be endangered, and women should therefore fight for a society in which men controlled their bestial sexual urges (Kent 1990, pp. 60–79; Caine 1997, pp. 102–15; Jordan 2001). Although not all feminists regarded the regulation of prostitution as an urgent issue, campaigns such as Butler's marked the beginning of a series of demands for greater sexual equality (demands, for instance, for an end to a husband's untrammelled right to sex with his wife, for abortion or for contraception) some of which only became central during the twentieth century (Kent 1990, pp. 157–83).

Alongside these sexual issues went a broader concern for the welfare of women, both as workers and as mothers. Efforts to improve working conditions and rates of pay varied widely from country to country, as did the proportion of paid female workers. (For example, 48 per cent of French women were employed in 1901 and 54 per cent in 1921, as compared with 36 per cent of British women in 1901 and 35 per cent in 1921.) In England, factory inspection was extended to women's work during the 1880s, and attempts were made to protect women from the worst excesses of sweated labour. From 1909, women were able to sit on some of the Trade Boards where wages were negotiated, but differential wages for men and women remained common at least until the 1970s (Mappen 1986, pp. 235–60; Caine 1997, pp. 147–58). In France, the first laws protecting women from exceptionally heavy work, and limiting the working day, were introduced in 1874, and further bills restricting working hours were passed in 1900 and 1905. Here, though, as elsewhere in Europe, the struggle for equal wages proceeded slowly, and although the kinds of work done by women expanded during the First World War, this change was not in general sustained (Kent 1993, pp. 3–11; Harrison 1987, pp. 322–3; Alberti 1989, pp. 135, 219; Bolt 1993, pp. 236–76). Meanwhile, American legislation followed a somewhat different course. A minimum wage was guaranteed for women earlier than men on the grounds that women were unable to protect themselves from exploitation; but it did not always work to their advantage and sometimes functioned to keep them in the most poorly paid jobs.

Women's work was of course profoundly affected by the demands and expectations placed on mothers, and during the opening decades of the twentieth century women's movements throughout Europe played a part in the reform of laws relating to maternity. For example, short spells of funded maternity leave became the norm between 1910 and 1920, followed in the inter-war period by the introduction of child allowances (Bock and Thane 1991).

It is difficult to generalise about the relation between economic and social reforms, and political ones. Campaigns for the vote were an early feature of all nineteenth-century women's movements (for example, Elizabeth Cady Stanton and Susan B. Anthony initiated one such campaign in New York in 1868, and another was launched in England in 1866 when John Stuart Mill and Henry Fawcett presented the first of many petitions to Parliament) (Bolt 1993, pp. 119–25; Kent 1990, pp. 184–219). Since the fortunes of suffrage movements were largely determined by local circumstances, they met with varying degrees of success. In some countries the franchise was won relatively quickly; for example, women gained the parliamentary vote in New Zealand in 1893, in Finland in 1906, and in Australia in 1908, and won the right to vote in state elections in nine American states by 1900 (Evans 1977, pp. 58–63, 214–15). In these parts of the world, the struggle for further rights was therefore conducted by women who were in one sense full citizens. Elsewhere, where progress was much slower, the vote tended to become, as Christabel Pankhurst put it, a symbol of freedom and equality for women, and in America, as well as in many parts of Europe, it was the object of protracted, and sometimes violent, campaigns (Sarah 1983, p. 269). To take another example, the right to vote in national elections was granted to American women in 1920, to Swedish women in 1921, to English women in 1928, and to French women in 1945 (Evans 1977, *passim*).

By using the resources of the liberal state to reform the law relating to the family, and to increase women's access to the public sphere, the tradition of broadly liberal feminism altered the lives and prospects of women living in certain parts of the world. Nevertheless, it was subjected to internal and external criticism. On the inside, many activists were disappointed by the fact that, once the vote was won, women did not on the whole use their new-found power to press for further political reforms. On the outside, feminists remained dissatisfied by the extent to which the reforms that had been achieved benefited middle-class more than working-class women, and were strengthened in their conviction that the source of women's oppression did not after all lie in their lack of political rights.

The aspiration to improve the condition of women in the ways so far sketched was by no means confined to liberal theorists and activists (Evans 1987; Stites 1978). One of the most theoretically sophisticated and practically effective opponents of what she referred to as bourgeois feminism was Alexandra Kollontai, Commissar of Social Welfare in the Russian revolutionary government of 1917 (Kollontai 1977; Stites 1981). Influenced by Engels (1985 [1884]), Kollontai believed that women were principally disadvantaged by the labour demanded of them within the family, and she oversaw the drafting of far-reaching though short-lived legal reforms designed to relieve them of the 'triple load' of wage worker, housekeeper and mother. These reforms were organised around the distinction between productive and non-productive labour and aimed to free women from the burden of non-productive domestic tasks (cleaning, cooking, washing, caring for clothes and many aspects of child-rearing) so that they could engage in productive labour alongside men. At the same time, women's work was to take account of their capacity to bear children which Kollontai regarded as productive labour of a distinctively female kind. They were not to do heavy jobs which might damage their health, or to work long hours or night shifts; and they were to have paid maternity leave and health care during pregnancy. Once their children had passed beyond infancy, they would be cared for in crèches, kindergartens and schools, which would also provide meals and clothing (Kollontai 1984a). According to Kollontai, the dictatorship of the proletariat would abolish the family, and with it bourgeois sexual morality. For although the state has a legitimate interest in the children who will make up the next generation of revolutionaries, it need not concern itself with the relations between men and women, who should be free to experience many forms of love, unimpeded by the restrictive institution of marriage (Kollontai 1984b). In pursuit of this ideal, Kollontai gave women full civil rights, introduced civil marriage and divorce laws, guaranteed the same rights to legitimate and illegitimate children, and legalised abortion (Stites 1981; Williams 1986, pp. 60–80; Farnsworth 1980; Clements 1979; Porter 1980).

Kollontai shared with her liberal contemporaries the view that women are disadvantaged by being excluded from certain activities undertaken by men, and by the fact that the value of their distinctive contribution goes unrecognised. Her belief that women should be able to engage in productive labour thus parallels the liberal feminist conviction that women are disadvantaged by being excluded from paid work and civil life. Furthermore, the advocates of the two approaches are alike in conjoining the notions of equality and difference. For Kollontai, both men and women need to engage in productive labour in order to be free and in this respect should be treated equally; but because there is a distinctively female form of productive labour, they are able to realise their freedom by making different contributions. There remains, however, an important divergence between Kollontai and her liberal counterparts: whereas many liberal feminists viewed conventional notions of marriage and the family as compatible with female emancipation, Kollontai did not.

Kollontai's view that women's subordination is rooted in the traditional family, and her belief in the importance of sexual freedom for both men and women, were shared by a variety of feminist authors, but were developed by Emma Goldman to ground a set of far-reaching political conclusions (Goldman 1972; 1987; Haaland 1993; Wexler 1989). Writing in the first decade of the twentieth century, Goldman argued that access to education and work, for which the emancipationists had fought so hard, only succeeds in producing 'professional automatons', and that when women enter the public sphere they are co-opted into an impure state which prevents the development of a kind of freedom springing from sexual intimacy. Moreover, while all citizens are distorted by this experience, women are particularly badly affected, since love is even more important to them than it is to men. Because Goldman believes that freedom is the fruit of erotic self-expression, she is adamant that women can only achieve it once they cease to be the sexual possessions of their husbands. She therefore holds that, as well as keeping out of the public sphere, women must reject an institution of marriage in which, driven by economic need, they purchase financial security at the price of their independence, and must instead learn to recognise and follow what Goldman calls their instinct – the sexual intimacy and love which will make them free. Here, liberty is conceived as a process of individual exploration which needs to be pursued outside the state, has little to do with work, and is only contingently related to motherhood.

Of these three currents, only liberal feminism gave rise to any lasting reforms; but contributions such as those of Goldman and Kollontai were nevertheless influential and important. This was partly because – along with some strands of liberal feminist thought – they located women's subordination primarily in the multi-faceted institutions of marriage and the family, and in doing so helped to highlight the issue of sexuality, but it was also because they regarded women's oppression as systematic, and consequently believed that only extremely radical measures would get rid of it. These two lines of thought were taken up during the 1970s and 1980s by Australian, European and North American feminists, who to some extent replicated the theoretical divisions within the movements mentioned so far.

The second wave

After 1930, some of the gains made during the first wave were consolidated. For the most part, however, this consolidation did not occur in the name of feminism, and during this period political activists tended to direct their energies to other causes. Women did not fail to notice that first-wave feminism had been only a limited success, and that in many areas such as wages, pension rights or access to certain sorts of jobs, formal equality did not exist. Nor were they unaware that the division of labour within the family remained largely unchanged, and that even in areas where women possessed the same rights as men, they continued to lag far behind in exercising them, so that the equality of the sexes remained more formal than real. But it was only in the 1970s that women again began to organise around feminist campaigns. In America, this change was partly prompted by the civil rights movement, which gave the mainly white and middle-class women who went on to identify themselves as feminists experience of consciousness-raising (Cardy 1974; Evans 1979; Eisenstein 1981, pp. 177–200). And in both the United States and Europe an awareness of diverse forms of disadvantage and exploitation was fostered by the radical student movements of the late 1960s (Mitchell 1971, pp. 1–39; Meehan 1990, pp. 189–204; Rowbotham 1992, pp. 257–83). Although the condition of women as such was not central to student radicalism, sexual mores were, so that issues such as the double standard, contraception and childcare came to be re-examined, and consciousness-raising groups provided women with an opportunity to explore these 'personal' themes. At the same time, many women interpreted their experience of sexism in the light of theoretical and political approaches to which they were already committed, so that a series of distinct if mutually defining positions developed, of which the most important were liberal feminism, Marxist-socialist feminism and radical feminism (Strathern 1987, p. 276).

While advocates of each of these approaches were keen to differentiate their own position from the others, each listened carefully to what was being said elsewhere and all three shared a range of theoretical resources. At least some women of each persuasion were sympathetic to consciousness-raising as a means of refining their understanding of their own circumstances and of the systematic disadvantages to which they were subject, and took as authoritative their individual or collective experience. At least some women of each persuasion were in search of a systematic account of the cause of women's oppression and thus shared the urge to construct a grand theory which was so characteristic of social and political philosophy during this period. Finally, all three positions were to some degree influenced by Simone de Beauvoir's *Le deuxième sexe* (*The Second Sex*), first published in 1949, first translated into English in 1953, and republished in English in 1972.

Beauvoir sets out to explain the unparalleled efficaciousness of men's power over women. While domination is usually a fragile and temporary achievement, women have been subject to men for many millennia and in many cultures. The question therefore arises, 'Whence comes this submissiveness?' In answering it, Beauvoir draws on and extends Hegel's discussion of the relation between master and slave. At the heart of his account, she argues, lies the deep insight that there is 'in consciousness itself a fundamental hostility to every other consciousness; the subject can be posed only in being opposed – he sets himself up as the essential, as opposed to the inessential, the object' (Beauvoir 1972, p. 17). In order to become a subject, each consciousness needs recognition, a recognition it can only acquire by dominating the Other and turning it into an object. In the public realm, men strive to become subjects by fighting, and out of their battles are born uneasy masters and unwilling slaves. There is, however, a further dimension to this struggle which enables all men to become subjects. Women are conscious beings capable of recognising male subjects; but rather than fighting for subjecthood by trying to objectify men in their turn, they allow themselves to be dominated, and even cooperate in their own subordination. By possessing them, men acquire an Other who is supportive rather than threatening, and against whom they have no need to struggle. But they purchase subjecthood at the expense of woman, who has no Other, and is unable to escape from her position as man's object (Beauvoir 1972, p. 483; Chanter 1995, p. 65; Mackenzie 1998, pp. 123–4; Butler 1989).

Although Beauvoir locates her work in a Hegelian framework, she is concerned throughout most of *The Second Sex* to chart the cultural images of masculinity and femininity in the light of which men and women understand themselves, together with the possibilities and obstacles that their self-understandings contain. Her interpretations of the multitude of social practices that conspire to keep women in a subordinate position and prevent them from seeking their own transcendence inspired many second-wave analyses of the diverse ways in which women are disadvantaged. At the same time, her depiction of woman as man's Other fed into a broader theoretical account of the gendered associations which shape our understanding of sexual difference. The claim that the hierarchical relationship between man and woman is symbolically represented in a sequence of further pairs, such as mind and body, public and private, or reason and emotion, offered second-wave feminism a valuable interpretative tool, which informed its contribution to political philosophy (Lloyd 1984; Ortner 1974; Elshtain 1981; Bordo 1987; Flax 1983; Landes 1998). Finally, Beauvoir's celebrated pronouncement that one is not born, but becomes, a woman, placed the issue of social construction at the centre of the stage, where it has remained ever since.

Many second-wave feminists, alive to the failures of the emancipationist movements of the first half of the century and influenced by the radical politics of the late 1960s and 1970s, tended to view liberal feminism as timid and lacking in vision. Attempts to commandeer the liberal apparatus of rights would, they believed, fail to overcome some of the most profound aspects of women's subordination, among them the forms of material oppression on which Marxist feminism focused, and the conceptions of sexual subordination central to radical feminism.

Since so many of the disadvantages to which women are exposed can be traced to their economic circumstances (low wages, exclusion from better-paid kinds of work, economic dependence on men), it is hardly surprising that many feminists were attracted by Marxism, which offered both a model of an overarching explanatory theory, and of a theory of oppression (Hartsock 1979; O'Brien 1979, pp. 99–116; MacKinnon 1989, pp. 1–80). Marx had pointed out that women in capitalist societies undertake the domestic labour of washing, cooking, cleaning and so forth which keeps male workers in a position to go on producing surplus value. Kollontai had pointed out that women were also responsible for the reproduction of the workforce, and had classified this contribution as productive labour. Engels had argued that women's subordination to men arises with the institution of private property and is a feature of all class societies. In short, there already existed within the Marxist tradition an account of women's oppression which was ripe for elaboration. In fact, however, many of the most interesting contributions of the 1970s engaged critically not just with the place awarded to women within Marxist theory, but also with some of Marxism's key concepts and distinctions (O'Brien 1979; Hartman 1981a, pp. 109–34; Barrett 1980; Mitchell 1971; Brennan 1993). An example in point is the 1970s debate about whether women should be paid wages for doing housework (Hartman 1981b, pp. 109–34; Delphy 1977; Delphy and Leonard 1992, pp. 75–104; Bubeck 1995, pp. 17–126; Nicholson 1987). Advocates of this view argued that, since housework contributes to surplus value, it should be classed as productive labour and should be rewarded. Their proposal raised a number of questions. Does housework in fact contribute to surplus value? Should women be paid for all the work they do in the home? Who should pay them? Should a man be paid for emptying the rubbish bin? Should women be paid for bearing children? These in turn prompted revisions of Marx's conceptions of productivity, labour and value. The view that value arises from labour, which in turn consists in transforming one form of matter into another, fits certain activities which we normally think of as productive quite neatly, but does not seem to describe aspects of the reproductive work for which women are primarily responsible. For instance, is pregnancy to be understood as labour, or cleaning the kitchen to be understood as the transformation of matter? By failing to address such questions, Marxism implicitly assumes that women are excluded from productive work, except insofar as they share the tasks undertaken by men.

A comparable discussion asked whether women's oppression could be assimilated to class oppression, or whether, in treating women as members of the classes to which their menfolk belonged, Marxism had once again ignored the peculiarities of their position. Women who do not work for wages or own the means of production, and who are therefore not workers or capitalists by virtue of their position in the mode of production but by virtue of their relationship to a man, possess only provisional class membership. Their vulnerability, it was suggested, lies not so much in their class position as in their dependence on the man from whom their class position derives, as one can see in societies where divorce causes a woman of any class to lose her status (Delphy and Leonard 1992, pp. 105–62; Wittig 1988a).

These arguments were often allied to the claim that Marxism underestimates or ignores the extent to which women are oppressed not only by capitalism but by men. While the position of women in bourgeois society does benefit capital, it is also to the advantage of male capitalists and workers, who therefore have a shared interest in maintaining this aspect of the status quo. To put it in Beauvoir's terms, even the lowliest worker may have a woman to be his Other, and to see to his sexual and material needs (Beauvoir 1972, p. 483; Delphy 1977; Barrett 1980).

In the course of the second wave, many feminists came to believe that Marxism suffered from grave limitations. While some continued to argue that it could be satisfactorily modified to produce a unified Marxist–feminist account, others favoured a position known as dual systems theory (Eisenstein 1979, pp. 41–55; Mitchell 1974; Hartman 1981a, pp. 1–41; Young 1981, pp. 43–69). This was the view that Marxism could be supplemented by a theory of patriarchy – a theory of those material and social relations between men which create solidarity between them and enable them to dominate women. At the same time, radical feminists developed theories of patriarchy intended to stand by themselves and to provide comprehensive analyses of the sources of gender oppression.

Radical feminists who identified themselves in opposition to Marxist feminism nevertheless shared its aspiration to arrive at a comprehensive analysis of the structural factors oppressing women. Where Marx had traced oppression to the economic relations between classes, radical feminists focused on the ways in which women are disadvantaged by their sexual relations with men, and by the clusters of institutions and practices in which sexual power is manifested (Frye 1983; Wittig 1988a, pp. 431–9; Rich 1987, pp. 23–75; MacKinnon 1989, pp. 155–236; Dworkin 1981). The fundamentally heterosexual forms of life through which women are dominated include marriage, and extend to prostitution, rape, battery, pornography and harassment. These latter practices, radical feminists claimed, are much more widespread than is generally acknowledged and they are usually not understood as acts of sexual violence. This is because they are interpreted, in male-dominated societies, in terms which conceal their coercive character. For example, rape is often described as voluntary sex, or sexual harassment as paying a woman a compliment. Such descriptions, and the practices to which they contribute, both construct male and female sexuality and legitimise the use of sexual violence against women. So although women are disadvantaged in various ways, including economic ones, the root of their oppression lies in an interpretation of female sexuality which represents them as submissive and serves to maintain their subordination to men (Firestone 1970, pp. 11–22; Millett 1977; Brownmiller 1976, pp. 309–22; Rich 1987; Frye 1983, pp. 17–51; MacKinnon 1989, pp. 157–70).

The oppressive character of sexual relations could be traced to biological differences between the sexes (Firestone 1970, pp. 11–22) or attributed to a masculinist state (MacKinnon 1989, pp. 157–70). Like their Marxist counterparts, however, some radical feminists drew back from the aspiration to construct a grand theory organised around a unified, primary cause of oppression, and instead began to develop accounts of a patriarchal system made up of interconnected institutions and practices. Patriarchy may be maintained, for example, by the system of production, the state, the legitimation of male violence and institutionalised heterosexuality, but none of these need have causal priority or ultimate causal responsibility, and their respective roles may vary with time and place (Walby 1990, pp. 19–22, 23–4). Furthermore, the subordination of women may be kept in place by a variety of mechanisms or processes, some enduring and some more historically specific.

If people encounter and internalise norms of masculinity and femininity from an early age and in many areas of their lives, some of the mechanisms by which they do so must be psychological. With this thought in mind, second-wave feminism pursued what has proved to be an exceptionally fruitful set of interconnections between psychology and politics. Initially, when feminists looked to psychology and psychoanalysis, they were struck by its sexism and, again following Beauvoir, responded with a series of robust criticisms (Gilligan 1982; Mitchell 1974). Yet out of this critical phase there grew a range of profoundly influential and creative efforts to use psychological theories, above all the resources of the psychoanalytic tradition, to cast light on the workings of patriarchy. In this field, more than any other, anglophone feminists learned from work being done in France; for example, many of them took up Luce Irigaray's claim that women are altogether excluded from the symbolic, and must create an *écriture féminine* in order to be able to express themselves as women (Brennan 1989; Burke, Schor and Whitford 1994; Whitford 1991b; Grosz 1989; Moi 1987; Gallop 1982). In parallel, however, the anglophone community developed positions of its own, some of them grounded on Anglo-American interpretations of Freud (Brennan 1989; Benjamin 1990; Richmond 2000). Winnicott's object relations theory, for instance, provided the theoretical framework for the suggestion that the internalisation of masculine traits by boys, and feminine ones by girls, stems from the way young children are cared for, specifically from the fact that both boys and girls are mainly looked after by women (Chodorow 1978). But as well as generating particular explanatory hypotheses, the conviction that the subordination of women is partly maintained by unconscious processes which give both women and men an investment in existing political and social arrangements added an enormously important dimension to feminist work.

These moves towards a multi-faceted conception of patriarchy turned out to be extremely significant, partly because they embodied the recognition that a grand theory of women's oppression was not likely to be forthcoming, and partly because the new approach opened up fruitful avenues of enquiry. Second-wave feminism generated an awareness of the sheer variety of ways in which the hierarchical relations between men and women are sustained and reinforced, and at the same time revealed the gendered quality of divisions between the political and the apolitical. Issues such as domestic labour or sexual violence against women were classified as apolitical by states which took little or no responsibility for them, and were regarded as marginal within the tradition of political philosophy. But insofar as these issues played a part in the subordination and oppression of women, they were seen to be the very stuff of feminist politics.

A more inclusive conception of politics, epitomised in the slogan 'The personal is political', is one of the most incisive and powerful contributions of second-wave feminism. Besides using it to initiate new lines of research, feminists took it as a vantage point from which to criticise the liberal tradition. While radical and Marxist opponents of liberalism tended to claim that it lacked the theoretical or practical resources to counter women's oppression, they sometimes grounded this judgement on the mistaken belief that liberals could only countenance rights which belonged equally to all citizens, and could not consistently impose rights and obligations on areas of life classified as private. Since neither of these assumptions applied to welfare liberalism, liberalism as a whole was always more malleable than these critics allowed, and in a number of states liberal tools were in fact employed to introduce some of the reforms advocated by Marxist and radical feminists (Pateman 1989, pp. 210–25; James 1992). In addition, however, the insights of these groups into the disadvantages suffered by women gave rise to a series of telling criticisms of liberal political philosophy.

A first line of objection focused on the disparity between the theoretical claim that the citizens of liberal polities are equal by virtue of possessing the same rights, and the comparative absence of women from public life (Pateman 1989; Elshtain 1981; Phillips 1987, pp. 1–23; Voet 1998). The civil and political rights generally awarded to citizens, it was pointed out, were initially articulated in societies where women were barred from citizenship and were largely under the control of men. The rights of citizens were therefore adapted to a situation in which men controlled the domestic labour and sexual services performed by women. Moreover, because women were not citizens, their relations with men were not a subject of political negotiation; and because these relations were not a subject of political negotiation, the areas of life in which women were most heavily involved were understood as lying outside politics (Canovan 1987; Pateman and Grosz 1986, pp. 63–124; Gatens 1991, pp. 9–47). As women gained citizenship, they were awarded rights which had for generations belonged to men and had been interpreted in the light of men's circumstances and capabilities. Women therefore won these rights on terms other than their own, and their formal equality with men consequently only became real in circumstances where they could simulate masculinity. A middle-class woman might be in as good a position to get to the polls as her husband, but might be less well placed than him to run for office if, for example, she had young children and no independent income. More generally, the assumption that sexual and family relations are not central to the business of the liberal state, and that legislation in these areas is liable to infringe what are regarded as important aspects of individual liberty, disadvantages women in two major ways: it leaves their subordination within the sexual division of labour unchallenged and perpetuates the assumption that in these areas women are under the control and protection of men; and it fails to alter conditions which undermine the worth of their rights as citizens (Dietz 1998; Young 1990a).

The conclusion that the figure of the liberal citizen is implicitly masculine also led feminists to question an aspect of recent North American liberal philosophy – the claim that the purpose of the state is above all to guarantee justice. Is it true, they wanted to know, that the method of arriving at principles of justice proposed by Rawls really succeeds in dealing fairly and impartially with the interests of both men and women? (Baier 1994, pp. 18–32; Okin 1989; Code 1987; Benhabib 1982; Jaggar 1983). Furthermore, is the view that justice is the primary political value a gender-neutral one, or does it embody a masculine bias so that states which give priority to justice disadvantage women? This latter query gained an added urgency when it was considered in the light of psychological studies which claimed to show that girls and boys tend to adopt different approaches to solving moral problems. While boys readily accept a broadly Kantian conception of justice as an adequate ethical norm, girls are said to employ an ethic which gives priority to the value of care, and is designed to devise ways to meet the needs of particular individuals (Gilligan 1982). Whether or not men and women do in fact differ in the way this research suggests, it gave rise to a wide-ranging debate. Some theorists argued for a feminine polity which would privilege care, the value around which mothering and women's work revolves, over justice, and would order its institutions and practices accordingly (Ruddick 1989; Noddings 1984). Others rejected this approach on the grounds that it encouraged women to conform to the very stereotypes from which they were trying to free themselves (Dietz 1985). A third group of writers dwelt on the relations between a public sphere committed to justice and inhabited largely by men, and a private realm in which the work of caring is mainly done by women. The former, they pointed out, is materially dependent on the latter. Furthermore, by failing to acknowledge the fact that political communities depend on care, liberal theory once again depoliticises a contribution which is mainly made by women, and which, even where this is not the case, remains symbolically feminine (Bubeck 1995; Sevenhuijsen 1998).

The question of how far liberals can meet or accommodate these criticisms continues to be discussed, the more so since liberalism has in effect become a hegemonic ideology with which feminism is bound to engage, whether it likes it or not. In the course of the 1990s, and perhaps in part because it has come to occupy such a dominant position, liberal theorists have been comparatively anxious to absorb insights offered by such competing outlooks as multiculturalism and feminism, for example by developing the idea of special group rights, or modifying its own conception of the political role of the family. But it is not clear how long this openness will last and, particularly in the United States, there are already signs of a backlash against what are felt to be excessive feminist gains.

Within feminism itself, discussion about the potential and limits of liberalism continues to involve the notion of rights, and doubts about the efficacy of appealing to them have arisen from several sources. In the first place, experience has proved just how difficult it is to devise group rights for women which do not indirectly make them worse off. For instance, a right to maternity leave may increase the costs of hiring women, thus making it harder for them to get jobs (Rhode 1992). Second, it is hard to see how changes in the division of domestic labour or in sexual relations between men and women can be made the subject of effective rights and obligations. Third, it has been argued that the machinery of rights is tainted by the individualistic outlook associated with the ethic of justice, and that, by awarding entitlements and obligations to individuals, theories of rights work against the particularised and flexible responsiveness to other people's needs that is central to the ethic of care (Kiss 1997).

Interestingly, attitudes to this issue have always cut across divisions between liberal and radical feminists. While some radicals have argued that liberal polities are beyond reform, others have used the legal apparatus of the liberal state in the very areas where it has sometimes been thought to be least useful, to challenge the sexual subordination of women.

Rights-based campaigns to ban pornography, protect women against marital rape and domestic violence, outlaw sexual harassment and recognise the claims of gays and lesbians, have succeeded, in some cases, in altering the legal landscape. As the first wave of feminism revealed, legal change does not amount to social change. Nevertheless, legal change can alter the terms of the debate, and feminists must now consider whether the introduction of women's rights is positively harmful to their cause, or whether it is just insufficient, by itself, to counter the disadvantages against which women struggle (Eisenstein 1988, pp. 42–78; Lacey 1998; Cornell 1992, pp. 280–96; Minow 1990, pp. 173–224; Irigaray 1993).

The third wave

In the course of the second wave, feminists increasingly looked beyond the political and economic institutions around which established social theories were organised. They turned first to domestic life and sexual relations, and then to the many ways in which femininity, understood as a condition of weakness and dependence, is expressed, for example in dress codes, in the way women move, or in the ideals of beauty to which they are encouraged to conform (Brownmiller 1984; Bartky 1990; Young 1990b; Bordo 1993). This interest has remained absolutely central to third-wave feminism, and marks one of its main points of continuity with the second wave. At the same time, however, the third wave has produced its own interpretations of gendered cultural practices, and has offered new assessments of their significance so that, as so often in the history of feminism, continuity and discontinuity are intermingled.

The rise of third-wave feminism is associated with two striking theoretical shifts, one relating to the scope of feminist theories, the other questioning the terms in which such theories have been couched. The first of these transitions stemmed from the critical observation that both first- and second-wave feminism were largely white middle-class movements which, although they claimed to speak for all women, were oblivious to differences of race. In general, feminist theorists had simply ignored the fact that the rights won by feminist movements had benefited a minority of whites, often at the expense of non-white women who had continued to provide the domestic and sexual services from which the minority had been liberated. As one writer memorably put it, feminism's Other was not so much patriarchy as the non-Western woman (Ong 1988). This criticism was elaborated in work which revealed strands of racism embedded in the feminist tradition, and exposed the parochial basis of much of its theorising (hooks 1984; Spelman 1988; DuCille 1994; Bhavnani 2001, pp. 1–11). Many generalisations about women's status and condition proved to be overhasty by virtue of the fact that they were not applicable to non-white women, and once this point had been made in a racial context it was rapidly applied more widely, with the result that variations in women's circumstances and experiences, whether rooted in nationality, class, religion, sexual orientation or ethnicity, came to the fore. The obtuseness of second-wave feminists who had failed to take account of the diversity of women's lives was, their critics argued, born of an unjustified confidence in their own authority. Their theoretical claims were flawed because they had believed themselves capable of speaking for women in general, and had not known how to hear and acknowledge other female voices.

This powerful appeal to difference put an end to attempts to provide an overarching theoretical account of the nature of women's disadvantage. If the family can be oppressive to some women while functioning as a place of solidarity and resistance for others, what can be said about the family in general (Amos and Parmar 1984; Spelman 1988)? If pornography oppresses some women while empowering others, how can it be roundly condemned (Cornell 2000)? And who can speak authoritatively about social practices and institutions? At the same time, some of the black feminists who opened up the debate about difference took a sceptical view of second-wave talk about women's oppression. Since oppression consists in not having any choices, they pointed out, some women are more oppressed than others and some women are not oppressed at all, so that it is an oversimplification to describe the situation of women in such blanket terms (hooks 1984; Maynard 1994). An emphasis on difference therefore brought with it a renewed sensitivity to the various kinds of relations which obtain between women and men, and a more nuanced use of such terms as oppression, discrimination and subordination. By encouraging theorists to take account of the experiences from which their interpretations spring, third-wave writers have generated a new level of critical consciousness and brought it to bear on earlier debates. Addressing those who doubt the value of rights, for example, some black feminists have suggested that a willingness to do without such guarantees is a mark of social privilege. Relatively powerful and secure women may regard rights as an unduly rigid formality, but women whose notional rights have never been respected may not view the matter in this light, and are likely to demand the protection they have never had (Williams 1991; hooks 1984). Here, as in many comparable cases, the recognition of difference has implications for the way that established political practices are assessed, and the greater the array of differences acknowledged, the more complex the picture becomes (Phillips 2002).

Alongside their interest in the differences between women, third-wave theorists have also brought about a second major theoretical shift by questioning the difference between men and women around which feminism has always revolved. If there are many ways of being a woman, each constructed by a particular social and historical context, why should we not press this line of thought a little further and, following Beauvoir's lead, interpret sexual difference itself as a social construct? Rather than attempting to draw a line between physically determined sexual traits and socially determined gendered ones, much recent feminist work has diminished or collapsed the sex/gender distinction, so that, within this field, gender has become ubiquitous (Scott 1996; Gatens 1996, pp. 3–20; Butler 1990).

Not surprisingly, neither of these two innovations has developed in isolation, and each is indebted to other theoretical currents in political philosophy. A concern with differences between women is reflected in a parallel concern within multiculturalism which, like much of third-wave feminism, regards the identities of individuals as culturally and historically situated and holds that the voices of culturally diverse groups should be audible in the polity (Young 1990a, 2000; Phillips 1995; Squires 2000). Moreover, both approaches are sensitive to the fact that the identities of individuals are not always coherent, and may consist of overlapping and shifting allegiances. For example, one can be a lesbian, feminist, Latina academic (Lugones 1996), and an adequate politics should try not to flatten out such an identity, or ignore the conflicts that it involves.

This same theme is also central to postmodernism which, often in alliance with elements of psychoanalytic theory, has been a second major influence on 1990s feminism (Nicholson 1990; Flax 1990; Braidotti 1991). For reasons of its own, postmodernism has criticised conceptions of the agent as an enduring locus of thought and action, and has instead stressed discontinuity and fragmentation within the self. This approach has in turn offered feminists a philosophical legitimation of claims to the effect that there need be no stable traits by virtue of which a person is enduringly masculine or feminine. Rather, masculinity and femininity consist in the more or less intentional performance of certain culturally recognisable and gendered acts which, because they can be subverted, modified and juxtaposed, do not have fixed meanings. Thus a homophobic insult, for example, can be appropriated by a gay community and turned into a proud acknowledgement of sexual identity (Butler 1990; Benhabib *et al.* 1995). This performative view, as it has come to be known, owes a great deal to the work of Foucault and is, amongst other things, an attempt to counter theories that construe women as the victims of intractable, institutionalised disadvantage. The ability to subvert the gendered codes that constitute us as men and women is offered as a form of empowerment, and as a creative force for social change. Viewed as a political theory, such an approach points towards a politics conducted by small groups who are able to devise their own challenges to entrenched cultural practices, and to communicate new meanings to one another. This slant is reflected in current debate, where performativity is often presented as a vehicle of individual expression – for example as a means of subverting the gendered meanings of dress codes, body-building or hairstyles in ways that are initially only appreciated by insiders but may later come to make sense to a wider audience. The intimacy of these processes of cultural change has provoked a critical reaction from some feminists, who argue that they have little to do with real politics; to opt for an arena of playful subversion is, in their view, to abandon any serious attempt to right the wrongs suffered by women, and amounts to little more than a narcissistic retreat (Jones 1993; Nussbaum 1999). This disagreement reopens old fissures within feminism between those who aspire to create a distinctive kind of politics, attentive to what they see as the most fundamental difficulties facing women, and those who aim to adapt existing political resources in order to achieve feminist ends. For many advocates of a performative politics, the constraints confronting women flow from the stranglehold of a hierarchical, binary conception of sexual difference and the compulsory heterosexuality that accompanies it. Since women can only cease to be subordinate to men once this is overcome, and since traditional political practices are just one manifestation of society's investment in a system which privileges men, this state of affairs can only be changed, insofar as it can be changed at all, by an unconventional kind of politics.

Alongside this disagreement about the nature of feminist politics, there exist a number of attempts to mediate or bypass it by devising modes of political theorising and intervention which will allow issues that affect women most deeply to be addressed within relatively traditional institutional settings. Together with multiculturalists and advocates of deliberative democracy, feminist theorists have outlined approaches designed to give women a more prominent place in decision-making processes and to increase their power to determine what issues are discussed. One strand of argument concentrates on representation and on the question of whether, and why, women should represent themselves (Sapiro 1981; Phillips 1995). Another considers how groups of marginalised women who are not in a position to articulate their interests, and who lack political experience, can acquire the confidence and know-how to engage effectively with the political fray (Young 2000; Benhabib 1996; Voet 1998, pp. 136–47). Another asks how women's diverse experiences can be given more weight, while a closely related strand of research explores and criticises the possibility of a mode of political dialogue in which the participants are sensitive to the interests and priorities of diverse groups, and at the same time able to assess them (Benhabib 1982; Mansbridge 1993). These models deal with various aspects of political decision-making. The more abstract ones are concerned with dialogue between social groups and have relatively little to say about the broader institutional setting in which it would take place (Young 1990b), while others acknowledge the role of the state in promoting and controlling political discussion (Squires 2000). With a few notable exceptions, however, feminist exponents of dialogue have relatively little to say about the relation between culturally defined groups and political parties, so that any political arrangements they envisage remain comparatively remote from existing democratic institutions. Furthermore, and perhaps partly as a result of its distance from the politics of the state, this strand of theorising has been criticised for aspiring to absorb rather than recognise difference, and for failing to face up to the existence of intractable conflicts between women (Brown 1995; Honig 1993). Since dialogue must occur within some sort of normative framework, it has been argued, there remains a danger that the terms of debate will continue to be set by the feminisms of Western, white women, and that the voices of 'other' women will not be heard (Spelman 1988; Ang 1995).

Despite its difficulties, the exploration of dialogue offers a means to link explicitly feminist political concerns to some of the central themes of contemporary political philosophy. It seeks both to maintain the integrity of feminism, and to enter what are agreed to be political debates. At the same time, a set of more historical connections is also being developed. Because so much mainstream political philosophy excluded or marginalised women, first- and second-wave writers generally addressed the tradition in order to criticise it, though in doing so they breathed new life into old debates about contractarianism (Pateman 1989, pp. 33–57; Pateman 1988; Hampton 1993), republicanism (Dietz 1998) and a number of other topics. Recently, feminists have turned again to the tradition, either to reassess the work of women philosophers such as Beauvoir (Evans 1998; Card 2002) or Arendt

(Canovan 1977; Honig 1995), or to draw on the ideas of canonical male authors in order to develop modes of theorising capable of counteracting the many mechanisms used to exclude women from politics. In contemporary work on Spinoza, for example, the concern with the gendering of the body so central to the performative strand of feminism reappears as the basis of a politics in which difference is fundamentally embodied (Gatens and Lloyd 1999).

By the end of the twentieth century, the recognition of women's difference was having an impact on feminist politics. What had begun as a first-world movement had become a global phenomenon, and in many regions groups of women were developing their own accounts of the conditions in which they found themselves and of ways in which these might be improved. Because some of these accounts diverged radically from the terms in which the largely secular, rights-based campaigns of the first half of the century had conceived women's subordination, they were sometimes hard for first-world feminists to recognise and accept, just as the assumptions of first-world feminists could be alien to women from other communities. For feminism, therefore, as for multiculturalism, the problems associated with difference loomed large, and posed intellectual as well as political challenges. At the same time, however, many familiar projects remained in place, and these continue to shape the political philosophy of the new century: women struggle more or less successfully for political and economic rights, governments grant or fail to grant their demands, aspects of daily life are redescribed in ways that make explicit the gendered assumptions contained in them, and novelists, journalists and film-makers comment revealingly on gender stereotypes and relations. When feminist writers worry that an increasingly intellectual approach to gender may destroy feminism by subverting the category of woman, it is arguable that they underestimate the pluralism that has developed within feminism itself. While there is not at present one feminism or one feminist politics, there is a multiplicity of both.

24
Identity politics

JAMES TULLY

Three characteristics of identity politics

'Identity politics' came into vogue in the late twentieth century to describe a wide range of political struggles which occur with increasing frequency and constitute one of the most pressing political problems of the present. The range of political activities 'identity politics' refers to comprises struggles over the appropriate forms of legal, political and constitutional recognition and accommodation of the identities of individuals, immigrants and refugees, women, gays, lesbians, linguistic, ethnic, cultural, regional and religious minorities, nations within existing nation states, indigenous peoples, and, often, non-European cultures and religions against Western cultural imperialism.

The forms of recognition and accommodation sought are as various as the struggles. Feminists, gays and lesbians demand formal and substantive equality and equal respect for their identity-related differences, in opposition to dominant patriarchal and heterosexist norms of private and public conduct. Minorities seek different forms of public recognition, representation and protection of their languages, cultures, ethnicities and religions. Immigrants and refugees struggle not only for the rights of citizenship but also for freedom from assimilation to a dominant culture and language; for culturally sensitive modes of integration. Various models of regional, federal and confederal forms of self-government are advanced by suppressed nations and indigenous peoples within existing constitutional states. Nation states in the Arab and third worlds aim to overcome the continuing Western cultural imperialism of the international system of nation states and of the processes of globalisation. Many of these demands are not only for legal, political and constitutional recognition within existing nation states, but also in supranational associations such as the European Union, international law, the United Nations and by the creation of novel 'subnational' and 'transnational' institutions.[1]

As these examples illustrate, the types of struggle are very different and they are not exclusively concerned with identity, but often involve struggles against exploitation, domination and inequality (Young 1990a). It is difficult to generalise across them. Moreover, many of these types of struggle for recognition have histories which predate the emergence of the concept of 'identity politics' by centuries (Parekh 2000). Nevertheless, roughly since 1961, when Frantz Fanon interpreted decolonisation as a struggle against both an identity imposed by European imperialism and an identity imposed by a dominant national elite after independence, these struggles have been referred to as 'identity politics' because they often exhibit three identity-related characteristics in the present which render them significantly similar to each other and significantly different from their past forms (Fanon 1963; Said 1993, pp. 210, 267–78).

First, what makes these struggles so volatile and intractable is their heterogeneity or 'diversity'. Identity politics is not a politics of many separate, bounded and internally uniform minorities, cultures and nations, each seeking separate and compatible forms of political recognition, as in the national struggles and theories of recognition over the last two centuries. Rather, demands are articulated around criss-crossing and overlapping allegiances: indigenousness, nationality, culture, region, religion, ethnicity, language, sexual orientation, gender, immigration and individual expression. A minority nation or language group demanding recognition from the larger political association often finds minorities, indigenous peoples, multicultural citizens or immigrants within who also demand recognition and protection. Feminists find that their identity-related demands are crossed by national, linguistic, cultural, religious, immigrant and sexual-orientation differences among women, and nationalist and culturalist movements find in turn that women do not always agree with men. Members of a minority seeking recognition against an intransigent majority along one identity-related difference will have cross-cutting allegiances due to other aspects of their identity that they share with members of the other side (Bhabha 1994).

1. For an introduction to the vast literature on identity politics see Benhabib (1996), Deveaux (2000), Gutmann (1994), Gagnon and Tully (2001), Honneth (1995), Ivison, Patton and Sanders (2000), Kymlicka and Norman (2000), Laden (2001), O'Neill and Austin (2000), Parekh (2000), and the journal *Ethnicities*.

It does not follow from the absence of separate, bounded and internally uniform identities (associated with the formation of nations and cultures in the nineteenth century) that identity politics is dissolving through its own fragmentation or that, as a result, humans can now relegate identity to the 'sub-political' realm and agree on universal principles, rights and institutions, unmediated by identity-related differences. Quite the contrary. The increasing diversity and insecurity of identity-related differences fuel the demands for their political recognition and protection. What follows is the more modest observation that, in Jacques Derrida's famous phrase, any identity is never quite identical to itself: it always contains an irreducible element of alterity (Derrida 1992, p. 9). Identity is multiplex or aspectival. Otherness and sameness are both internal *and* external to any identity (individual or collective). Accordingly, 'diversity' or the multiplicity of overlapping identities and their corresponding allegiances is one characteristic of identity politics (Connolly 1991; 1995).

Nevertheless, this 'hybridisation', as Homi Bhabha calls it, should not be treated as if it were *the* fundamental characteristic, even though it is the fundamental experience for some people, especially those living in exile or in multicultural cities. It is certainly possible to bring a group of people to agree together in defence and promotion of one aspect of their identity, such as language or nationality, across their other identity-related differences, and this identification can be sustained for generations (as, for example, ranking one's Scottish or Catalonian identity first). What the multiplicity of overlapping identities entails is the second characteristic of identity politics: the priority granted to one identity, the way it is articulated, the spokespeople who claim to represent the identity-related group, and the form of recognition and accommodation demanded must always be open to question, reinterpretation, and renegotiation by the bearers of that identity over time. An identity negotiated in these human, all too human, circumstances will not be fixed or authentic, but it can still be well supported rather than imposed, reasonable rather than unreasonable, empowering rather than disabling, liberating rather than oppressive. That is, it will be a construct of practical and intersubjective dialogue, not of theoretical reason on one side or unmediated ascription on the other. Consequently, identity politics consists of three processes of on-going negotiation (for legal or political recognition) which interact in complex ways: (1) among the members of a group struggling for recognition, (2) between them and the group(s) to whom their demand for recognition is made, and (3) among the members of the latter group(s), whose identity comes into question as a result of the struggle, whether they like it or not (Gagnon and Tully 2001, pp. 1–34).

The third and most elusive feature of identity politics is the concept of 'identity' itself. It is not one's theoretical identity – what one is as a matter of scientific fact or theoretical reason, as, for example, autonomy is in the Kantian tradition. It is one's practical identity, a mode of conduct, of being-in-the-world with others. A practical identity is a form of both self-awareness and of self-formation in relation to and with others. It is a structure of strong evaluations in accord with which humans value themselves, find their lives worth living and their actions worth undertaking, and the description under which they require, as a condition of self-worth, that others (both those who share the identity and those who do not) recognise and respect them. A practical identity is always relational and intersubjective in a double sense. It is acquired, sustained and renegotiated in dialogical relations with those who share it and those who do not. Any practical identity projects onto those who do not share it another identity, the non-X, who, in reciprocity, seek mutual recognition and respect for their identity, which is seldom the one others project on them. This is why 'negotiation' or 'dialogue' – the exchange of reasons in dialogue over forms of recognition – is so fundamental to identity politics (Taylor 1994, p. 67; Laden 2001, pp. 73–130).

As we have seen from the first characteristic, for most people there will be several overlapping practical identities. They will be a member of the human race, a man or a woman or a transsexual, a member of a religion and an ethnic group, a member of one or more language and cultural groups, a national of one or more nations, and so on. Insofar as these identities are valued, they are not a matter of third-person ascription or projection, but of first-person normative practices of self-consciousness and ethical formation (such as consciousness-raising in feminist movements, the acquisition, use and care for a language, culture, religion, community or nationality with others), and of third-person recognition, respect and, at its best, affirmation and celebration by others with whom one interacts in practices of cooperation.

When identity-diverse citizens coordinate their activities and cooperate in a multitude of ways they always already do so under some forms of mutual recognition and action coordination. That is, they establish and interact in accordance with a relational norm of 'mutual recognition'. The norm involves a form of awareness of oneself and the other, normal modes of covert and overt interaction (of speech, agenda setting, behaviour and the like), and relations of power in accordance with which the relation is established and maintained. A relation of mutual recognition of any political or social practice is often habitual and taken for granted by the participants. Then, the participants compete, dispute and coordinate their activities in accordance with the norms of recognition, modes of conduct and relations of power definitive of the identities of the practice in question (say, over an economic policy). The difficulty is that almost any political interaction can upset the normal relations of mutual recognition and spill over into a struggle for recognition: that is, a renegotiation of the identities under which the participants carry on their interaction (say, if an economic policy, while appearing to treat all as equals, is partial towards men, English speakers, and so on). Identity politics irrupts when a norm of mutual recognition (the identities to which the bearers of the norm are subject) is itself called into question and becomes the focus of struggle and negotiation over its justice and freedom (Foucault 1982; Habermas 1994, p. 106).

The injustice and unfreedom distinctive of identity politics occur therefore when subjects (individuals or groups) are thwarted in their attempts to negotiate and gain reciprocal recognition and accommodation of their respectworthy identities in the norms of mutual recognition in which they interact with others. Their identities are mis-recognised or not recognised at all in the prevailing relations of mutual recognition. Instead, an alien identity is imposed upon them through processes of subjection, either assimilating them to the dominant identity or constructing them as marginal and expendable others – 'lower', 'less developed', 'inferior race', and so on. The extermination of 80 per cent of the indigenous peoples of the Americas over 400 years, the Holocaust, and other instances of ethnic cleansing and genocide are the most extreme and horrendous cases (Stannard 1992). It is now widely acknowledged that participation in the negotiation of imposed identities, the security of these processes of identity formation and their achievements, and the recognition and respect of these by others are the threshold prerequisites to the sense of self-worth of individuals and groups which enable them to become free, equal and autonomous agents in both the private and public life of modern societies. As a result, the demeaning and disrespect of their identities through sexism, racism, nationalist, linguistic and culturalist chauvinism, the psuedo-scientific ranking of cultures and languages in stages of development, and the imposition of dominant cultures through processes which destroy identities and assimilate or marginalise individuals and groups are not only unjust; they also undermine the self-respect and so the very abilities of the people concerned not only to resist these injustices but also to act effectively even if they opt to assimilate. This causes the well-known pathologies of oppression, marginalisation, fragmentation and assimilation: lack of self-respect and self-esteem, alienation, transgenerational poverty, substance abuse, unemployment, the destruction of communities, high levels of suicide and the like (Honneth 1995; Kymlicka 1995; 1999).

Three types of demand for the recognition of identity-related differences

Struggles to overcome an imposed identity and to gain recognition of a non-imposed identity through the three processes of negotiation mentioned above were not normally direct challenges to the principles of twentieth-century democratic politics: freedom, equality, due process, the rule of law, federalism, mutual respect, consent, self-determination and political, civic, social and minority rights. If they were they would be rejected out of hand. One or more of these principles is appealed to by both sides in identity politics: to condemn the imposed identity and to justify the recognition of an identity-related difference on one side and to defend the established relations of mutual recognition on the other. Of course, these principles are interpreted and applied in different ways but it is seldom the principles themselves that are in dispute. For example, gay and lesbian couples demand to be treated equally to heterosexual couples, women to men, indigenous peoples to other peoples of the world who enjoy rights of self-determination, a suppressed nation to other nations, a suppressed language group to dominant language groups, immigrants to other citizens, Muslims to Christians and secularists.

The usual objection to an established norm of mutual recognition is that these shared principles are not interpreted, applied and acted on either in a difference-blind manner, as liberals often claim, or in accordance with a national identity which all citizens share equally, as nationalists often claim, but in a manner that is partial to the identity-related differences of the well-to-do, the able, heterosexuals, males, members of the dominant linguistic, cultural, ethnic, national and religious groups, and so on, and biased against others. Accordingly, when the multicultural and multi-national citizens of contemporary societies participate in the institutions and practices based on these principles they have two choices. They can either assimilate to the prevailing unjust relations of mis-recognition imposed on them or they can call them into question and attempt to initiate their renegotiation with those who support them. The resulting clash is the politics of identity or 'struggles over recognition'.

The solution is not to insist on applying the principles in an alleged impartial manner or in accordance with a common national identity in every case, as difference-blind liberals and uniform nationalists reply (Barry 2000; Miller 1995), for in many cases this is not possible. Politics and public life have to be conducted in some language or other, in accord with some mode of conduct or other, statutory holidays, elections and the like will fall on some religious holidays, some versions of history will be taught in the educational systems and embodied in the public narratives and iconography, and so on. The suggestion of identity politics is rather to interpret and apply these principles in a difference-aware manner: one which is not partial to any particular identity at the expense of others but is based on mutual respect for the plurality of identities of the sovereign citizens of the association (Tully 1995; Kelly and Held 2002).

This suggestion has been controversial because it introduces a second aspect of equality. One standard aspect of equality is that all citizens should be treated equally in the sense of 'impartial' or 'indifferent' to any and all identity-related differences. Members of a political association may cultivate their practical identities in private and voluntary associations but the government remains impartial with respect to them (Waldron 1992). While accepting this aspect of equality as legitimate, defenders of identity politics have challenged its applicability in many cases. In many cases it is impossible to be impartial in this sense. When this is the case, it is necessary to take into account another aspect of equality: that is, to treat the reasonable identity-related differences involved with equal respect. To take a simple example, one person has one vote, yet the campaign and ballot are in different languages where numbers warrant. It is now fairly widely accepted that there are two aspects of the concept of equality that need to be taken into account and that they often conflict (Taylor 1994; Deveaux 2000).

Many liberals have agreed and reconceived liberalism along these lines (Kymlicka 1995; Laden 2001). Several nationalists and communitarians have responded in a similar fashion (Poole 1999). Communitarians and nationalists always held that citizens need to share a common political identity in addition to allegiance to the principles mentioned above, but they took this to be a uniform national or community identity shared in the same way by each. The force of the arguments of identity politics has caused many of them to reconceive national identity along the lines of diversity and public negotiation. This does not mean that each and every identity-related difference gains equal recognition and accommodation. This would be impossible. It means that demands for recognition should be accorded equal consideration in order to determine if they are worthy of recognition and those that are should be given due recognition and accommodation (Carens 2000). Before examining this principle in the following section, it is necessary to survey the types of demand to which it is designed to apply.

The struggles to contest and renegotiate the prevailing relations of mutual recognition can be classified into three main types. The first type of demand is for *cultural diversity*: the mutual recognition and respect of identity-related differences in the cultural sphere. All types of identity politics involve demands to negotiate the ways some members of a political association are currently disrespected and mis-recognised in the broad sphere of cultures and values where they first learn and internalise their attitudes towards others. The aim is first to expose and overcome racism, sexism, ableism, ethnocentrism and Eurocentrism, sexual harassment, linguistic, cultural and national stereotypes and other forms of overt and covert diversity-blind and diversity-partial speech and behaviour. Second, the objective is to foster awareness of and respect for diversity in all areas of society so all members can participate on the basis of mutual respect. This type of demand standardly calls for equity policies in hiring in the private and public sectors, the introduction of cultural diversity in the curricula of schools and universities, and education of attitudes towards culturally dissimilar others in the public life of modern societies (Benhabib 1996).

The second type of demand is for *multicultural and multi-ethnic citizenship*. These are demands to participate in the public, private and voluntary institutions and practices of contemporary societies in ways that recognise and affirm, rather than mis-recognise and exclude, the diverse identities of citizens. Women's movements, gays and lesbians, and linguistic, cultural, ethnic and religious minorities wish to participate in the same institutions as the dominant groups but in ways that protect and respect their identity-related differences: to have schooling in their minority languages and cultures, access to media, to be able to use their languages and cultural ways in legal and political institutions and at work, to reform representative institutions so they fairly represent the identity-related diversity and gender of the population, to have day-care facilities so women and single parents can participate on a par with heterosexual males, to speak, deliberate and act in public in a different voice, to have same-sex benefits, to observe a religious or cultural practice in public and public service without disadvantage, for constitutional charters of rights to be interpreted and applied in a diversity-sensitive manner, to establish minority and group rights where necessary, and so on, so all citizens and minorities can participate equally, but not identically, with others. These struggles also include attempts to modify the immigration and refugee policies of nation states in order to overcome forms of racism and exclusion at the global level. Multicultural policies in Canada, the accommodation of Muslim and other minorities in the USA, the UK, France and Germany, the recognition of three official languages in Brussels and of eleven working languages and several 'lesser-used' languages in the European Union are well-known examples (Kymlicka and Norman 2000; Kraus 2000).

The third type of demand is for *multi-national or multi-people constitutional associations*. These are demands to establish relatively autonomous political and legal institutions separate in varying degrees from the larger political association. Here, suppressed nations within multi-national societies and indigenous peoples argue that the proper recognition of their identity *as* nations and *as* peoples with the right of internal self-determination under international law entails that they have a right to their own political and legal institutions in some spheres. It is only by these means of self-government and autonomy, they argue, that they are able to protect and live in accordance with their identity as peoples and nations. If they are constrained to participate in the institutions of the dominant society, then they are misrecognised (as minorities or individuals within the dominant society rather than as nations and peoples) and their identity-related differences will be overwhelmed and assimilated by the majority.

These *multi-national* demands became increasingly familiar in the latter part of the twentieth century. The most common response has been either the suppression of the demand or a conflict which ends in secession and the establishment of a new nation state. However, the struggles have also given rise to experiments in the federalisation of multi-national political associations: that is, regional autonomy, subsidiarity, dispersed and shared sovereignty, and flexible federal and confederal arrangements. Spain, Belgium, the United Kingdom, Canada, Israel–Palestine and the European Union itself are all examples of this kind of identity politics (Gagnon and Tully 2001). And, in countries that have been established on the displacement and marginalisation of indigenous peoples, such as Norway, Canada, the United States, Australia, New Zealand and South American countries, the struggles of indigenous peoples to overcome internal colonisation and gain recognition as self-determining peoples are giving rise to experiments in new forms of indigenous self-government and treaty federalism with the larger, surrounding non-indigenous governments (Havemann 1999; Ivison, Patton and Sanders 2000).

The third type of struggle is the most complex because it brings into play the full diversity of overlapping identities and the three processes of negotiation characteristic of identity politics (see pp. 519–20 above). Those making the demand must persuade their own people through public dialogue that they are not a province, region or minority of some kind, as the current form of recognition has it, but a distinct nation or people. They must also persuade the majority society, with all its internal diversity, and then persuade them to enter into negotiations to change the current constitutional relation to some form of greater autonomy and lesser association. As these negotiations take place, they almost always provoke the two types of demand for cultural diversity and multicultural citizenship within and often across the nation or people demanding recognition. The diverse citizens within, such as linguistic minorities and multicultural immigrants, wish to ensure that their identity-related differences will not be effaced in the new federal institutions of self-government. Yet cultural diversity and multicultural citizenship have to be recognised and accommodated in a form which does not infringe too deeply, or undermine, the identity of the nation or people, for this is the reason self-governing institutions of nationhood are demanded in the first place. Of course, these multiple struggles of identity politics cannot be avoided either by suppressing the demand for nationhood or by secession. They simply reappear in different and usually more violent forms.

Who decides and by what procedures?

The central questions of identity politics are, first, who decides which, if any, identities of the members of a political association are unjustly imposed and which are worthy of recognition and some form of accommodation? And, second, by what procedures do they decide and review their decisions? The response to the first question marks a democratic revolution in political thought and practice in the twentieth century. It is no longer assumed that the identities worthy of recognition, and so constitutive of citizen identity, are identical and can be determined outside of the political process itself, by theoretical reason discovering some transcultural and universal citizen identity. It is now widely assumed that the identities worthy of recognition must be worked out by the members of the association themselves, through the exercise of practical reason in negotiations and agreements. In John Rawls' famous phrase, the question is 'political not metaphysical' (Rawls 1998, pp. 388–415).

There are several reasons for this. The first is that there is a significant emphasis on democracy (or popular sovereignty) and inclusion in both theory and practice in the latter half of the twentieth century. In theory, *quod omnes tangit* (what touches all must be agreed to by all), one of the oldest principles of Western constitutionalism, has been revived and given dialogical reformulation as the principle of democratic legitimacy: 'only those norms can claim to be valid that meet (or could meet) with the approval of all affected in their capacity as participants in a practical discourse' (Habermas 1994, p. 66; 1996). The sovereignty of the people to reach agreement among themselves on the basic norms of mutual recognition of their political association through deliberation is said to be a principle equal in status to the rule of law (Habermas 1995; Rawls 1995). In practice, there has been a proliferation of practices of democratic negotiation of the conditions of membership of a vast and increasing range of associations, from private- and public-sector bargaining to democratic constitutional change, international agreements and evolving institutions of cosmopolitan democracy. In virtually every organisation of human interaction and coordination, disputes over the prevailing relations of mutual recognition are referred to democratic practices of polling, listening, consultation, negotiation, mediation, ratification, referenda and dispute resolution. Moreover, new disciplines of negotiation, mediation and dispute resolution have developed in universities to train experts in 'getting to yes' and to reflect critically on the burgeoning practices of democratic negotiation of prevailing relations of mutual recognition in many sectors of society (Dryzek 2000).

The second reason stems from the negotiated character of identity politics. It is the people themselves who must experience an identity as imposed and unjust; they must come to support a demand for the recognition of another identity from a first-person perspective; and they must gain the mutual recognition, respect and support of others who do not share the identity. All this requires discussion and negotiation by the people involved in the three processes of negotiation mentioned in the first section; not of elites and representatives alone. On this account, a proposed identity only counts as an identity if it has come to be embraced in this democratic and dialogical manner, and it is recognised only if it has come to be affirmed by others in the same fashion. If an identity is advanced by a political elite without popular deliberation and support, and if it is recognised by another elite or an unelected court without passing through democratic will formation in the broader society, then it is not likely to be supported on either side. That is, it is not likely to be seen as an identity on one side or as worthy of respect in practice on the other. It will tend to be experienced as imposed and the struggle for recognition will be intensified rather than resolved.

The third reason follows from the diversity of overlapping identities in any political association. When a demand for the recognition of an identity-related difference is advanced it is necessary to ensure that this demand has the support of those for whom it is presented and, second, that it does not silence or suppress another identity-related difference equally worthy of recognition. The only way this can be ensured is that the people affected have a voice in the proceedings. People must be able to advance alternative formulations of the demand, which take into account the diversity of the people demanding recognition; others must be able to raise their objections to it and defend the status quo or respond with counter-proposals; and others must be able to advance demands of their own that would otherwise be overridden. It is implausible to assume that all these perspectives could be voiced and taken into account without engaging in the dialogues and negotiations of those involved. Consequently, another classic principle of political negotiations has been reintroduced into late twentieth-century politics: *audi alteram partem* (always listen to the other side) (Skinner 1998, pp. 15–16). The democratic negotiations of identity politics today are not the dyadic dialogues of traditional theories of recognition from Hegel to Sartre, but complex 'multilogues' (Bellamy 1999, pp. 190–209).

The fourth reason is that such popular-based negotiations provide stability for the right reasons. A struggle for recognition signals that a relation of mutual recognition in accordance with which citizens coordinate their interaction has been disrupted. If the dispute is not resolved, it can lead to anything from disaffection to secession. Successful democratic negotiations provide a new or renewed relation of mutual recognition that is stable because the people who must bear it have had a say in its formulation, have come to agree that it is well supported, and know that it is open to revision if necessary. They identify with it.

There is one important limitation to the maxim that struggles for recognition must be worked out through negotiations among the people affected. In many cases of identity politics those demanding the recognition of their identity-related differences are minorities. If their demands are put not only to the discussion of all but also to the decision-making of all, their fate is placed in the hands of the majority. Yet this is precisely the injustice they are trying to overcome. Democratic discussion and negotiation are necessary for the four reasons given above. However, it is not necessary for the final *decision* to be made by a majority or by a consensus of all affected. The former is unfair to the minority and the latter is utopian.

Democratic discussions need to be placed in the broader reflective equilibrium of the institutions of the rule of law: representative governments, courts and the legal, constitutional and international law protection of human rights. The appropriate equilibrium varies with the context. In general, however, if a demand for recognition is fully and openly discussed, supported and agreed to by the majority of the minority making the demand (applying *audi alteram partem* within); if it is well discussed and well supported by the other people affected and to whom it is addressed; if it accords with or can be shown plausibly to be an improvement on existing legislation, minority rights and international covenants; if it finds support in representative institutions and their committees of inquiry; or if the courts rule in its favour, then any of these institutions of the rule of law, depending on the particular case, can and should make the decision, even if there is an organised and vocal opposition to it by a powerful interest group within the majority affected. However, they should make the decision only on the condition that it is open to review and reconsideration in the future. In the real time of politics the force of argument needs to be supplemented by the force of law in cases where the majority has a political or economic interest in upholding a deeply sedimented and biased form of unequal recognition (Tully 2000).

The second question is, what are the procedures by which the people, in conjunction with their legal and political institutions, negotiate and reach agreements over disputed identities? The widely proposed answer is through the exchange of reasons *pro* and *contra*. The basic idea is that an identity will be worthy of recognition and respect just insofar as it can be made good to, or find widespread support among, those affected through the fair exchange of reasons. A fair exchange of reasons will determine which identities are reasonable, and so worthy of recognition, and which are unreasonable, and so either prohibited or at least not publicly supportable. The necessary and sufficient conditions for the fair exchange of reasons are themselves contested by theorists and negotiators, but the following are commonly included. A member (individual or group) of a political association has the right to present demands to modify the forms of recognition of the association, and the others have a duty to listen to and enter into negotiations if the demand is well supported by those for whom it is presented and if the reasons for it seem plausible; the interlocutors in the negotiations treat each other as free and equal and accept that they are bearers of a diversity of other practical identities which deserve to be treated with due respect; they are able to speak and listen to each other in their identity-related terms and ways; and any resolution should rest as much as possible on the agreement of those affected and should be open to periodic review. If the dominant members refuse to enter into negotiations, or drag their feet endlessly in the negotiations and implementation, then those making the demand have the right to engage in dissent to bring them to negotiate in good faith.

These are roughly the minimum conditions of mutual recognition and reciprocity which ensure that a discussion is not biased towards any particular cultural identity from the outset. Muslim, atheist, indigenous, male and female interlocutors will interpret 'free and equal' in dissimilar yet reasonable ways (ways which the others will see initially as unfreedom and inequality) but, since this sort of disagreement is precisely what identity politics is about, it is not possible to filter out these differences at the outset without prejudging which identities are worthy of recognition. Attempts to define these rough conditions more stringently or to add further conditions have so far failed to achieve the generality or universality they claim. In the actual context of particular cases, further conditions are usually accepted by the interlocutors, at least provisionally (Young 2000, pp. 52–120).

The exchange of reasons over the recognition of identities can be classified in two types: those which aim at mutual understanding of, and those which aim at mutual agreement over, the identities in dispute. In the first type of exchange the interlocutors aim to understand the identities in question from the point of view of those who bear them and seek recognition. To gain mutual understanding it is necessary to listen to the reasons why a particular identity is important to the group advancing it, even if these are not reasons for others. An ethnic, religious, cultural or linguistic minority or nation will have reasons for embracing their identity that derive from that identity. These internal reasons will not be reasons for supporting their demand as far as the other members of society are concerned. However, they will be important to the other members in understanding why the identity is so important to them; why the members of the minority can agree to pledge allegiance to the political association only if this identity is secure. Citizens need to gain some understanding of different cultural identities, the narratives in terms of which they have meaning and worth for their bearers, and so on. Through these exchanges citizens are able to move around and see to some extent their shared political association from the identity of other cultures, nations, sexual orientations and so on. In the course of this movement they become aware on reflection of their own identities as partial and limited like the others. Moreover, the interplay of internal reasons unsettles the prejudices and stereotypes internal to their own practical identities. That is, these practical conversations foster a new, shared identity among the interlocutors: an identity that consists in the awareness of and respect for the diversity of respectworthy identities of their fellow citizens and of the place of one's own identity among the diversity of overlapping identities.

The second type of exchange of reasons aims at reaching agreement on which identities are worthy of recognition and how they are to be accommodated, as well as which should be prohibited. These public reasons cannot appeal to particular identities for they need to convince other interlocutors who do not share that identity and its internal reasons, even if they understand and respect it. Exchanges aimed at reaching agreement, therefore, search for reasons that identity-diverse citizens can share. These 'shared' reasons are the various principles of modern politics (mentioned above) to which those struggling for and against recognition appeal. The basic conditions of mutual recognition and reciprocity necessary for stability in modern societies rule out certain identities: those that are incompatible with respect for others. Reaching agreement, then, is a process that involves searching for these sorts of shared reasons, interpreting and applying them *pro* and *con* the identities in dispute, and working towards an agreeable form of recognition and institutional accommodation of the identities that are shown to be justifiable and supportable. The form of recognition and accommodation of identities they agree on will constitute their shared multicultural and multinational identity as members of the same association; an identity they will all have reasons for supporting, not despite their identity-related differences, but rather because it gives due recognition to their diverse identities. It is this complex, shared citizen identity that binds them together as an association and gives them a sense of belonging (McKinnon and Hampsher-Monk 2000, pp. 1–9).

The provisional character of negotiated agreements

It is possible in conclusion to present a few generalisations about the agreements reached in negotiations over identity politics. The agreements are 'overlapping' rather than transcendent (Rawls 1993, pp. 133–73). The interlocutors do not transcend their practical identities and reach agreement on an identity-blind norm. They exchange internal and shared reasons from within their practical identities, moving around to some extent to the perspectives of others, and reach agreements on an identity-sensitive norm of mutual recognition. One of the most important discoveries of identity politics is that people with very different cultural, religious, gender and linguistic identities can nevertheless reach overlapping agreements on norms of mutual recognition, such as charters of individual and group rights and obligations, as long as these are formulated, interpreted and applied in an identity-sensitive manner.

Second, overlapping agreements do not conform to the ideal of a consensus. They are negotiated, provisional and contextual settlements which involve compromise and an element of non-consensus, and require review and often revision. The reasons for this derive from the three characteristics of identity politics. Recall that in a struggle for recognition there are three simultaneous processes of negotiation and they influence one another. As the interlocutors proceed, the rule of *audi alteram partem* is applied again and again by diverse individuals and groups whose identities are affected by the proposed form of recognition, demanding that their identities in turn are given due recognition and accommodation in the agreement. An agreement thus will be an attempt to give each legitimate claim its due recognition and this will always involve compromise (Bellamy 1999, pp. 91–140).

Moreover, negotiations take place in real time and under real constraints. Not all voices will be heard and not all compromises will be acceptable to all. The identities of the participants in the discussions will be shaped by the unjust relations of power that are held in place and legitimated by the contested, prevailing relation of mutual recognition. These relations of power cannot be suspended *in* the negotiations (only the implementation of a new form of recognition *after* successful negotiations can do that). Therefore, they will exchange reasons in unequal and asymmetrical ways in the negotiations (Young 2000, pp. 16–36, 81–120). In some cases a court or other body will not unreasonably bring the negotiations to a close. The dissenters they override may turn out on reconsideration to have been right after all. Any agreement can be interpreted in different ways, and this gives rise to disagreements over the institutions that are supposed to implement the agreement and over the way those institutions operate. As they experiment with the implementation of the agreement over time, conflicts will develop in practice that they did not foresee in the negotiations. For example, a group right established to protect a minority from domination and assimilation by the larger society may turn out to give the minority too much authority over the identity-related differences of their members. For these and other reasons, a legal or constitutional agreement on recognition should be seen as provisional and flexible, open to on-going review and revision in the light of experience with its institutionalisation, in the same way as constitutionalism as a whole is being reconceived in the European Union (Shaw 1999).

Finally, the practical identities of the people engaged in struggles for recognition change in the course of the three processes of negotiation themselves. Nothing has changed more over thirty years of identity politics than the identities of men and women, immigrants and old-timers, Muslims and Christians, Arabs and Westerners, Europeans and non-Europeans, cultural minorities and majorities, heterosexuals and homosexuals, and so on. Part of this identity modification is the acquisition, through the interaction with others, of a shared identity based on the reflective awareness of the diversity of identities of others and of the partiality of one's own. This shared identity does nothing to lessen their attachment to their practical identities and to the great struggles for their recognition. But it puts these in a different light. Their practical identities are now seen as partial, somewhat mutable and overlapping with the similarly partial and somewhat mutable identities of others with whom they contend for forms of mutual recognition and accommodation.

As a consequence, identity politics are unlike traditional struggles for recognition in yet another sense. They are not struggles for the definitive recognition of an authentic, autonomous or self-realising identity, for, as this survey of identity politics has shown, no such fixed identity exists. Therefore, just as the negotiations should not be studied under the regulative ideal of a consensus, so too the forms of mutual recognition should not be viewed under the ideal of a definitive recognition. Such an identity is just as much a chimera as the former impartial liberal identity and the uniform national identity. Rather, because the identities in contention are modified in the course of the contests, the aim of identity politics is to ensure that any relation of mutual recognition is not a fixed and unchangeable structure of domination, but is open to democratic question, contestation and change over time, as the identities of the participants change. Accordingly, identity politics is about the democratic *freedom* of diverse people and peoples to modify the norms of public recognition of their political associations as they modify themselves.

25
Green political theory

TERENCE BALL

There is a widely shared albeit arguably mistaken view that 'ecological' or 'green' political thought is of relatively recent vintage, being a product of the political turbulence of the 1960s and 1970s which saw the emergence of die Grünen in Germany and green parties in Britain and France, the publication of important environmental exposés and warnings,[1] and symbolised by the first Earth Day in 1970. But modern green thought is older still, representing a confluence of several different streams of thought and sensibility. Some have detected the first stirrings of environmental concerns as early as the sixteenth century (Thomas 1984). Others trace the first glimmerings of a green sensibility to Jean-Jacques Rousseau and the Romantic movement, with their acute appreciation of mountains, dark forests and wild nature. Others find the first stirrings of an 'ecological' perspective in the writings of the young Marx, with his vision of the symbiotic interdependence of man and nature (Parsons 1977). Or, more broadly, one might take note of the ecological emphases of German thinkers since the time of Goethe who, with his holistic, anti-reductionist view of nature, so greatly influenced not only German Romanticism but the biological sciences, as well as later German greens such as Rudolf Bahro and Petra Kelly. British environmental thinking was spurred by reactions to the industrial revolution, with its 'dark satanic mills' threatening to overtake the green countryside, and has also been greatly influenced by such Romantic nature-poets as William Wordsworth and by the naturalist Charles Darwin, amongst others whose thinking has influenced modern British greens. Americans are apt to award the laurel to such nineteenth and early twentieth-century conservationists as Henry David Thoreau, John Muir, the Scots-born founder of the Sierra Club, the

1. See especially Carson (1962), Goldsmith *et al.* (1972), Caldwell (1972), Ehrlich (1969), Commoner (1971), Catton (1980); these were followed shortly by political manifestos from die Grünen (1983) and green parties in Britain and elsewhere.

author and adventurer John Burroughs, the forest ecologist and author Aldo Leopold and the biologist Rachel Carson (Nash 1989; Oelschlaeger 1991, chs. 5–7). Amongst Scandinavians, the Norwegian mountaineer and 'ecosopher' (eco-philosopher) Arne Naess (1989) has been especially influential. In India, the ideas of Mahatma Gandhi have greatly influenced Vandana Shiva and other third world environmentalists and ecofeminists. Although none of these were systematic political theorists, all have greatly influenced modern 'green' political thought.

Whatever its origins, green political thought became, in the latter half of the twentieth century, a well-established sub-species of political theory (Dobson 1995; Goodin 1992; O'Neill 1993). My aim here is to trace the origins and development of key concepts and ideas in green political thought. I shall begin with an abbreviated history of the concept of ecology. This is then followed by a brief characterisation of the main features of green political philosophy; these I shall then treat in more detail under the headings of green ends, green economic thought, and the political, institutional and strategic means for achieving green goals.

The concept of ecology

If there is a concept – and a word – that is central to green political thought, it is surely the concept designated by the word 'ecology'. The term *Oecologie* was coined in 1866 by the German biologist Ernst Haeckel (Worster 1994, p. 192). The neologism comes from the Greek *oikos*, or household, and refers to the systematic study of nature's household (*Naturhaushalt*) by biology and the other life sciences. It passed into more popular currency after the International Botanical Congress of 1893 recognised the term and changed the spelling to 'ecology' – the same spelling subsequently used by Haeckel's English translator in his popular *The Wonders of Life* (Haeckel 1904), where the term is defined as 'the science of the relations of living organisms to the external world, their habitat, customs, energies, parasites, etc.' (p. 80). Haeckel's conception of ecology combined two important and influential ideas – vitalism (the view that living entities are animated by a life force that Henri Bergson later called the *élan vital*) and holism (the view that living entities are interconnected parts of some greater and irreducible whole).

The modern science of ecology and its various sub-divisions (animal ecology, plant ecology, etc.) study the flow of energy and information (genetic and otherwise) within and between the interdependent entities that constitute the larger wholes called 'ecosystems'. But when green political thinkers use the term 'ecology', it is rarely this specialised and highly technical branch of the life sciences to which they refer. They refer, rather, to an outlook or an orientation that stresses the interdependence of various species – including human beings. Humans not only depend on each other, but on nature – on the biosphere, the atmosphere and the ecosystems that sustain human and other organisms and life forms. Thus understood, 'ecology' is a kind of outlook or sensibility that stresses interconnectedness – of creatures with each other, and all the habitats that sustain them. As Barrington Moore, editor of the journal *Ecology*, put it in 1920, ecology is 'a point of view', an orientation that stresses the interconnectedness of the parts within some greater whole (quoted by Worster 1994, p. 203).

It is impossible in a brief chapter to do justice to the diversity of views within this wider 'ecological' orientation or sensibility.[2] But it may be possible to identify some of the characteristics common to various green thinkers, moderate 'light green' conservationists and militant 'dark green' radicals alike. Let us begin by considering the green critique of conventional political thought and environmental practices.

Green political theory: key features

Twentieth-century green political theorists agreed about several key points, and more particularly about the shortcomings of conventional political thought, right, left and centre. The first characteristic common to most green thinkers is the widely shared perception that there is a crisis or rather a series of interconnected crises afflicting the natural world and its myriad inhabitants. A second claim is that these crises have been brought about, by and large, by human beings. A third feature is that these humans are the heedless inheritors and practitioners of a perspective variously called 'humanism' or 'anthropocentrism', a hierarchical orientation that stresses the happiness, health, wealth and well-being of humans, with little or no regard for, and at the expense of, other creatures and the natural environment. Fourth, if we are to avert the crises brought on by this way of thinking we must criticise and expose the weaknesses of this outlook. And fifth, we must devise an alternative 'ecological' or 'ecocentric' perspective from which we can recognise and appreciate the complexity, interdependence, and diversity of

2. For a substantial sampling of the diversity of twentieth-century 'environmental discourses' see Dryzek and Schlosberg (1998); see also Sessions (1995).

the natural world and our species' place in it. Let us consider each of these characteristics a little more closely.

First, there was amongst twentieth-century green political thinkers a widely shared sense of crisis, or rather of multiple and interrelated crises, that are coming or are already upon us (e.g. Catton 1980). These interconnected crises include a veritable explosion in the human population, the pollution of air and water, the over-fishing of the oceans, the destruction of tropical and temperate rain forests, the extinction of entire species, the depletion of the ozone layer, the build-up of greenhouse gases, global warming, desertification, erosion of precious topsoil, and the disappearance of valuable farmland and wilderness for housing estates, shopping malls, motorways and other forms of 'development'.

The second point to note is that most if not all of these interconnected crises are the result of human actions and activities – procreation, recreation, and the pursuit of wealth, comfort and convenience. Wild rivers are dammed so that more and cheaper hydroelectric power can be generated. Entire mountainsides are stripped of trees and other vegetation to mine coal or to make way for skiers and ski-lifts and lodges. Whole forests are clear-cut to supply timber and other building materials. Tropical rain forests are razed and burned and wetlands drained to grow crops for hungry and ever more numerous humans. As a result, rivers and streams silt up and animal habitat is greatly diminished, degraded or destroyed. Entire species of plant, animal and insect life become extinct before they can be discovered, classified and studied. In these and many other ways, human beings begin chains of destruction whose end they can in principle foresee; but too often they do not bother to look. Humans have only themselves to blame for the predicament that they – and myriad other species – must face now or in the indefinite future.

Third, the notion that humans are somehow entitled to pursue these ends with scant regard for their effects on ecosystems and the creatures that depend upon them is due to a perverse and misguided way of thinking called humanism or anthropocentrism. This is the view that humans are the apex of creation. And this is (variously) because God gave human beings 'dominion' over the earth that they might 'subdue' it (Genesis 1: 28), because humans belong (as Kant famously put it) to the 'kingdom of ends' and animals and ecosystems are merely means to our own species' health, happiness and survival, and that the successful pursuit of these ends requires the 'taming' or 'mastery' of nature and its creatures for human purposes. Most, if not all, environmental ills can be traced directly or indirectly to 'the arrogance of humanism' (Ehrenfeld 1978). We humans view ourselves as occupying the top of the pyramid of creation, superior to and supported by the lesser creatures below us.

There are deep disagreements amongst greens about which humans and/or philosophical perspectives are most to blame for these benighted views and the environmental destruction that results from acting upon them. Some greens say that 'Western' thought – Christian, liberal-individualist, capitalist or otherwise – is at fault. The Judaeo-Christian perspective places God above and outside nature, and views humans as having a rightful dominion over nature (White 1968; criticised by Berry 1981, pp. 267–81). Social ecologists such as Murray Bookchin argue that it is not human beings as such who are responsible for the systematic and continuing pillage of the planet; the fault lies, rather, with the most powerful and privileged class of human beings – industrialists and large international corporations – who in subjugating human beings dominate the natural environment as well (Bookchin 1990, pp. 19–39). Similarly, albeit from a gender-centred perspective, ecofeminism, which originated in France in the early 1970s with the formation of Ecologie-Féminisme by Françoise d'Eaubonne, contends that the fault lies not with human beings in the aggregate, but primarily with modern Western males who subscribe to a masculine or 'androcentric' or 'patriarchal' belief system which views nature as 'feminine' ('Mother Nature') and therefore rightfully subordinate to the interests and desires of men (d'Eaubonne 1974; 1978). These androcentric beliefs, when acted upon, result in the rampant destruction of wilderness and the creatures it sustains (Plumwood 1993; Kelly 1994). Western androcentrism is said by such ecofeminists as Vandana Shiva (1988) and Ariel Salleh (1997) to wreak particular havoc in the lives and livelihoods of women in the third world.

A fourth characteristic of green political thought consists of a critique of humanism or anthropocentrism. Its flaws and weaknesses are said to be both notorious and legion. It is 'reductionist' in that it recognises only parts, not wholes; it therefore fails to recognise interconnections and interdependencies – including human beings' interdependent relations with other species and the ecosystems that sustain them. In its focus on individuals, humanism neglects the value of community and, more specifically, the 'biotic community' in which humans are 'plain members and citizens', along with other species (Leopold 1949, p. 240). In place of the anthropocentrists' master metaphor – the pyramid of creation, with humans at its apex – ecocentrists propose that we think in terms of the non-hierarchical metaphor of the web of life in which all living creatures are implicated. But there are disagreements about, and variations on, this view. In general, 'dark green' or radical environmentalists hold that there must be a thoroughgoing repudiation of Western political thought – and of liberal individualism in particular – and an almost Nietzschean 'transvaluation of all values' in favour of a radically new (or very old and traditional) non-Western ethic. 'Light green' thinkers, by contrast, contend that Western liberal thought – with its emphasis on individual liberties and human rights (including property rights) – possesses the moral and intellectual resources out of which a robust green ethic might yet be constructed (Ball 2001).

Fifth, whilst still primarily a critical theory, green political theory also has a positive or constructive side – although the differences within the green movement are more pronounced here. All greens are pretty well agreed about what they are against, but they are less than unanimous about what they are in favour of. They are against anthropocentrism of an unthinking or un-self-critical sort; they oppose the heedless destruction of the natural environment and the creatures whose lives and well-being depend upon it; and so on, through a rather long list. But what are greens *for*? To answer that question requires that we turn to a green theory of value – roughly, a view of the ends to which they subscribe.

Green ends: an ecocentric theory of value

In so far as one might speak of a green or ecosystem-centred 'ecocentric'[3] theory of value, that theory holds that the worth of some things does not derive from human appraisals of their utility or beauty, or from their price or market value. Some things have *intrinsic* value, in that they are valuable in and of themselves, quite apart from any human estimate of their worth or any value they might have as means to some other end. This is particularly true of certain natural objects or entities (Goodin 1992, pp. 30–41). For example, since wilderness per se has neither instrumental value nor market value, it is conventionally called 'wasteland'. As Locke put it, 'land that is left wholly to nature, that hath no improvement or pasturage, tillage, or planting, is called, as indeed it is, waste; and we shall find the benefit of it amount to little more than nothing' (Locke 1992 [1690], para. 42). By 'benefit' Locke of course meant *human* benefit; he thereby articulated the

3. Some green thinkers – e.g. Taylor (1986) – speak of a 'biocentric' (or life-centred or biosphere-centred) perspective, whilst others refer to an 'ecocentric' view. The terminological difference seems not to matter much, if at all.

pervasive anthropocentric conception and standard of value that continues to characterise so much of Western political and philosophical thought.

Against Locke and other anthropocentrists, ecocentrists maintain that wilderness has value in itself and for the non-human creatures that inhabit it. 'Wasteland' has enormous benefit for the wild creatures whose habitat it is. Moreover, many (probably most) wild species, such as the endangered California Condor, have no instrumental or market value; they are neither a means to any human end nor are they traded or sold in any market. And yet these and other wild creatures are valuable and worth protecting, for all have intrinsic value and a place and function in the complexly interdependent ecosystems to which they belong.

Greens resolutely reject the anthropocentric view that human needs and wants supply the only measure of value. They accept instead one or another version of the ecocentric view that the health and well-being of the 'biotic community' – for example, an ecosystem and the myriad species it sustains – takes precedence over any of its individual members. This ecocentric conception of value is both naturalistic and holistic. That is, it takes all of nature – and not one of its many species, namely *Homo sapiens* – as the source and measure of value. And it views all creatures as interdependent parts of a larger, life-sustaining whole. As Aldo Leopold put it, an ecocentric 'land ethic changes the role of *Homo sapiens* from conqueror of the land-community to plain member and citizen of it. It implies respect for his fellow-members, and also respect for the community as such' (Leopold 1949, p. 240). From this there follows a standard for judging the rightness of an action or condition: 'A thing is right when it tends to preserve the integrity, stability, and beauty of the biotic community. It is wrong when it tends otherwise.'[4] Greens disagree amongst themselves, however, over what this ecocentric theory of value implies and requires. So-called 'light green' conservationists disagree with 'dark green' or 'deep ecologists'. The latter assert that ecocentrism requires a radical shift in perspectives – roughly, from a hierarchical 'pyramid' with humans at the apex, to an interdependent 'web' in which humans are but one species amongst many (Devall and Sessions 1985). The former, by contrast, are highly critical and wary of any attempt to view *Homo sapiens* merely as one species amongst many. They claim that such a view would diminish the value of human beings more than it would re-value nature. And such a view would fail to recognise the important

4. Leopold (1949, p. 262). Whether this is to commit the so-called 'naturalistic fallacy' of deriving 'ought' from 'is' is discussed by Callicott (1989, ch. 7).

and undeniable fact that, because of their knowledge and technology, human beings have great power over nature and its creatures, and therefore a correspondingly great responsibility for the health and well-being of both (Bookchin 1990; Katz, Light and Rothenberg 2000). To see the human species as co-equal with other species is to be blind to this unique and all-important aspect of human existence: humans are not the only tool-making and tool-using creatures; but our species' tools and technologies have the capacity to transform – even to destroy – the earth and most of its creatures. This in turn introduces another recurring 'green' theme: the use and abuse of scientific knowledge and technology.

Much of Western thought since the scientific revolution of the seventeenth century has celebrated the human species' increasing power over nature. Sir Francis Bacon and other seventeenth-century philosophers saw the natural sciences and technology as means of human 'mastery' or 'domination' of nature (Leiss 1972). Other expressions of this view can be found in later thinkers, including Karl Marx, who praised the prospective pacification or 'humanisation' of nature. The development of the 'productive forces' – roughly, natural resources and the technology used to turn them into humanly useful objects – under capitalism has transformed nature beyond all recognition; and this Marx saw as a commendably progressive process.[5] Arguably, this particular Marxian legacy can be seen today in the massive environmental destruction wrought by communist regimes in the former Soviet Union, Eastern Europe, and China (Shapiro 2001). But, whether communist, capitalist, conservative or liberal, Western political philosophy has by and large envisaged and celebrated the conquest of nature for achieving human ends.

By contrast, green political thinkers are highly critical of any philosophy that views nature only or mainly as a means to human ends and that is correspondingly inattentive to the conditions required to sustain the health and well-being of nature's myriad species. Green political thinkers generally subscribe to one or another version of an ecocentric theory of value. This theory holds that things either have intrinsic value as ends in themselves or have value by virtue of the contribution they make to some larger whole. In the latter, the value of something is determined by its place in, and contribution to, some larger functional entity – an ecosystem or (in Leopold's phrase) a biotic community. Thus, for example, predator species such as

5. The idea that Marx was a proto-environmentalist is defended by Parsons (1977) and disputed by Grundmann (1991). See further Hughes (2000).

wolves have value not only in themselves but because of their function for the ecosystem of which they are an integral part. Wolves cull deer that are ill or lame; by preventing the weaker members of the deer population from reproducing, wolves actually benefit that species qua species. Moreover, by controlling the deer population wolves protect the larger ecosystem which both share with other species. In a reversal of long-standing policy, this ecocentric view of the value of predator species was, at the end of the twentieth century, put into (limited and selective) practice in the western United States, where wolf populations have been reintroduced in several national parks and forest lands over the strenuous objections of cattlemen and sheep ranchers. Wolves and other predators have also been reintroduced in eastern Germany.

To speak of predators and prey, and about anthropocentric versus ecocentric conceptions of value, is 'political' in two senses. The first is that laws, rules, regulations and governmental policies on environmental matters are made on the basis of our beliefs about and attitudes towards nature and its creatures. These include laws and public policies having to do with agriculture, land use and property rights, motorway construction, mining and forestry, tourism and economic development, parks and recreation, reforestation, the preservation of wilderness, the protection of endangered species, and many other controversial issues. Some of the most heated political battles of the past century (and already of the new century as well) have been fought over these and other broadly environmental questions. But there is also a second, and much older, sense in which these controversial matters are recognisably political. For politics, as Aristotle noted, is concerned with the good life and the kind of community in which it might be lived. But unlike Aristotle, who was concerned with the good life as lived by (some) human beings, modern greens have a much broader view of community and a vastly more variegated conception of the good life. Greens include human and non-human creatures as co-members of biotic communities. They also hold that what constitutes or counts as the good life differs from one species to another. What will count as the good life for fish differs from what counts as the good life for monkeys. But what all creatures share is an interest in a healthy habitat. Fish and frogs have an interest in unpolluted water, monkeys in intact tree canopies, whales in plankton, koala bears in eucalyptus trees, etc. These interests are, moreover, morally considerable, that is, deserving of consideration and respect by human beings (Taylor 1986; Johnson 1991).

A great many political debates over environmental issues turn on differences over value (anthropocentric vs. ecocentric; instrumental vs. intrinsic), what counts as the good life, the proper place and role of human beings in the natural order, obligations to non-human creatures and to future humans, and the political means or institutions for implementing decisions about these matters (Dryzek and Schlosberg 1998). Green political thinkers are attempting to articulate and justify an ecocentric view of the good life for human beings and for other creatures with whom they share the earth.

The fact that humans are in a position to know, as non-human animals cannot, what is required to sustain non-human species confers upon us the 'epistemic responsibility' to maintain the conditions conducive to their survival. Our knowledge of these matters also confers upon our species an added measure of moral responsibility (Passmore 1980; Taylor 1986; Johnson 1991). Our ever-expanding knowledge of the natural world brings with it an expanded responsibility to recognise the interests (some greens go further, and say 'rights') of other creatures. And whilst we may not always be able to promote these interests, we must, as moral and political agents, at least accord them serious consideration in making political decisions and public policies that affect their well-being or, indeed, their very existence. The same considerations also apply to generations of human beings who are as yet unborn.

One of the hallmarks of green political thought is its concern for the health and well-being of the near and distant descendants of humans and animals now living. Questions about the interests (and perhaps even the rights) of future people and the responsibilities of those presently living are central to environmental theory and practice, and are often asked and analysed under the rubric of 'intergenerational justice', 'obligations to posterity', or 'responsibilities to future generations' (Partridge 1981; Barry and Sikora 1978; de-Shalit 1995). Theories of justice have heretofore focused mainly on relations between contemporaries: what distribution of scarce goods is fairest or optimally just? Should such goods be distributed on the basis of merit or need? These and other questions have been asked by thinkers from Aristotle to John Rawls.[6] Green political theorists have expanded the circle of moral considerability by asking about just distributions of goods or benefits – and harms – over vast stretches of time and across generations.

6. Rawls was among the first twentieth-century philosophers to explicitly address questions concerning 'the problem of justice between generations' (1971, sec. 44, pp. 251–8).

In the light of the foregoing discussion of green antipathies and criticisms – and most especially a green theory of value – we next need to ask what sort of economic thinking is congruent with green political thought, and in what kind of economic system green aims might best be achieved.

Ecology and economics

Greens tend to be critical of conventional economic thinking, and most especially the claim that market allocations and relations are always or necessarily just. This does not mean, however, that all twentieth-century greens can be classified as socialists of one or another sort (although some certainly are). Indeed it is probably fair to say that the twentieth century produced no sweeping and systematic green economic theory. The closest they have come is perhaps to be found in E. F. Schumacher's conception of 'Buddhist economics' which emphasises spiritual over material satisfactions and maximum individual well-being with minimal environmental impact (Schumacher 1973). More typically, green thinkers have criticised and challenged specific features of conventional market-based economic thought, in as much as such thinking forms the basis and justification for policies regarding resource extraction, energy production and use, and other issues affecting the natural environment.

Four features of green economic thought merit special mention. The first is its scepticism about the infinite 'substitutability' of resources. The second is its critique of the idea and practice of 'social discounting'. The third is the green critique of cost-benefit analysis. And the fourth is its hostility to the idea and the practice of assigning 'shadow prices' to goods not traded in markets.

Some economists argue that people now living need not restrict their consumption of scarce or non-renewable resources in order to save some portion for future generations. And this is because substitutes for these resources will be discovered or devised through technological innovations and new inventions (Simon and Kahn 1984). For example, as fossil fuels become ever scarcer and more expensive, new fuels – grain-based 'gasohol' or fusion-derived nuclear fuel – will replace them. Thus we need never worry about 'running out' of any particular resource, because every resource can be replaced by some sort of substitute that is as cheap, clean and accessible as the resource it replaces. Nor need we worry about generating nuclear wastes that we do not yet know how to store safely, since some solution is bound to be devised sometime in the future by those who have a greater interest than we do in their health and well-being, that is, future people themselves.

This 'cornucopian' or 'promethean' outlook is open to numerous objections (Dryzek 1997, ch. 3). One is that it amounts to little more than wishful thinking in the manner of Dickens' Mr Micawber, who always hoped against hope that 'something would turn up'. Whilst it is possible and perhaps even probable that human ingenuity and innovation will prevail, that is a gamble and not a guarantee. To wager with the health and well-being of future people is surely immoral and unjust. And to leave to them the unpleasant and perhaps unhealthy task of cleaning up our mess is rude and inconsiderate, if not unjust.

A second questionable practice is the 'discounting' of the well-being of future generations by means of a 'social rate of discount'. Roughly, the idea is this: just as individuals discount their own future, so too does an entire society at any given time, t_1, discount its future members' welfare at all later times, t_{1+x}. And, just as it is rational for individuals to discount their own future well-being – I would, for example, prefer to have £100 now to having £101 a year from now – so it is rational for one generation to discount the welfare of future generations.

Greens reply that it is one thing to discount one's own future well-being; it is quite another, and morally much more questionable, matter to discount other people's well-being. I am not entitled, rationally or morally, to discount your future well-being at my personal rate of discount. And yet that is precisely what defenders of social discounting attempt to do for future persons. Green critics contend that one's worth or moral considerability does not vary according to one's place in the temporal order of succession. I am not entitled to discount your well-being, whether you are my contemporary or my very distant descendant. The practice of social discounting, its critics claim, works to the distinct disadvantage of future generations and is clearly unjust (Goodin 1992, pp. 66–73; O'Neill 1993, ch. 4).

A third feature of green economic thought concerns its critique of, and reservations regarding, the practice of 'cost-benefit' analysis (O'Neill 1993, chs. 4, 5). Very roughly, cost-benefit analysis is a technique for comparing and assessing alternative policies or practices. The most desirable alternative would be the one that produces the greatest benefit at the lowest cost. This seemingly simple and common-sense idea becomes quite complicated when one asks what is to count as a cost or a benefit, for whom it is costly or beneficial, and over what time span costs and benefits are to be calculated. Consider, by way of example, the claim that nuclear power is preferable to other alternatives because it has a higher benefit-to-cost ratio than such alternatives as fossil fuel or hydroelectric generation. In practice, the benefits – including access to cheap and plentiful electricity – accrue to those now living, whilst the costs will be borne by future people, in the form of increased risk of radiation exposure and of safely storing and guarding nuclear wastes for tens of thousands of years. To measure the benefits and costs over the short term and to ignore or discount further costs over the longer term is to systematically disadvantage future humans and other morally considerable creatures.

Greens do not necessarily object to cost-benefit analysis per se or in principle, but they do object to taking a too-constricted time-horizon over which to measure costs and benefits. If the well-being of future people is not discounted, and the benefits not enjoyed exclusively by one generation and the costs borne by another, then cost-benefit analysis can be a useful tool of analysis, even for environmentally minded policy analysts, legislators and concerned citizens.

A fourth feature of conventional economic thought that greens criticise is the idea and practice of 'shadow pricing'. Green critics contend that too many economists fit the old description of the blinkered man who knows the price of everything and the value of nothing. Or rather, perhaps more precisely, they are remiss in assuming that everything has a price, even if some things – such as clean air and water or scenic beauty or the continued existence of entire species – are not actually traded in markets. Some economists have devised a way to deal with this inconvenient fact. They reframe the question, 'What is the value of x?' as another – and, green critics contend, very different – question: 'What is the price of x?' That is, what price would x fetch if it were to be traded in a market? This can be determined by assigning 'shadow prices' to scenic beauty, clean air, the preservation of animal species and other environmental goods. The hypothetical price is determined by asking people what they would be 'willing to pay' to (for example) preserve the Northern Spotted Owl or the Grand Canyon or the Black Forest or the English Lake District or the Great Barrier Reef.

Critics of shadow pricing argue that such a practice would cheapen things that are in fact priceless (Sagoff 1988, ch. 4; O'Neill 1993, ch. 7). Some things actually lose value (and quite possibly all meaning or moral import) when they are offered for sale (think, analogously, of the buying and selling of love or respect). This is what would happen if a price, however hypothetical, were to be assigned to the preservation (or extinction) of species and ecosystems.

Entities that have intrinsic value cannot or ought not to be assigned prices as if they were exchangeable in markets, because they are not and their value is therefore not restatable as price, the conceits of some economists notwithstanding.

In sum, it is probably fair to say that green economic thought at the end of the twentieth century was more critical than constructive – more articulate about what is wrong with modern market thinking than about what alternative might be devised.

Green means: agents, institutions, strategies and tactics

A further question remains: how – by what political means – might the world be made a 'greener' place for all creatures, human and non-human, present and future? If it is to be practically effective, green political thought must provide an account of the means required for achieving the ends specified by its theory of value. Following Goodin (1992, ch. 4), we might call this the green theory of agency. This theory operates at both an individual and a collective level. Individual agency is concerned with the characters and characteristics of individual agents; collective agency is concerned with the design and operation of the organisations and institutions within which individual agents act in concert. Thus a theory of agency provides an account of the kinds of actors and institutions that would be required to achieve the ends posited by a green theory of value. Two questions arise in this connection. First, what kinds of agents (political actors or citizens, consumers, etc.) are best able to attain green ends? Second, what form of government, what kinds of political organisations or institutions, and what strategies and tactics are most likely to achieve green goals?

The answer generally given to the first question is that green agents or political actors must have an ecocentric outlook, viewing themselves and their species as a small but important part of a much larger and more inclusive biotic community; they must be motivated by a love of and respect for the natural world and its myriad creatures; their satisfactions and pleasures will not, in the main, be materialistic; their wants will be few and satisfiable in sustainable ways; they will whenever possible act non-violently; and their time-horizon will typically extend further than their own and one or two succeeding generations.

It is worth noting that there is nothing unique or utterly unprecedented in this picture of green political agency. It is a picture painted, with many minor variations, by philosophers from Plato onwards, of the good man (*sic*) and the good citizen motivated by a vision of the good life (O'Neill 1993, ch. 1). The good life for humans is not, or need not be, a life of luxury and material abundance. On the contrary, it involves an appreciation of the superiority of spiritual and intellectual satisfactions over material ones, and of caring about something larger and longer-lived than our own mortal selves. And one way of doing this, greens say, is to recognise our place in the natural world and our responsibility to care for the distant descendants who will one day inhabit it (Passmore 1980). This outlook and way of life not only benefits the soul (as Plato would put it) but the planet as well.

A second question is, what kinds of political organisations, institutions and strategies might best achieve green goals? Here again, twentieth-century green thinkers differed remarkably and even radically amongst themselves. Some are socialists, others anarchists, bioregionalists, ecofeminists, deep ecologists, social ecologists, or self-described survivalists who eschew political solutions altogether (see Dryzek 1997 for a sampling of this variety). But, at a minimum, greens generally agree that the most desirable and effective institutions will be broadly democratic, decentralised to some degree, and as open and participatory as is practicable (e.g. Porritt 1984; Dobson 1995). But even here differences appear. Some greens contend that environmental problems are so complex that their solution requires the kind of coordination that can only come about through the modern state, its allied agencies, and cooperation between states (Ostrom 1991; Goodin 1992). When it comes to protecting the natural environment from human predation there may be no substitute for 'mutual coercion, mutually agreed upon by the majority of the people affected' (Hardin 1968). Other greens go further still, arguing that environmental crises are apt to be so numerous, so pervasive and so severe as to require the harsh interventions of an authoritarian, hierarchical and not necessarily democratic state (Heilbroner 1980; Ophuls 1977; Catton 1980). Such dire predictions and prescriptions have led some critics to suggest that there is both a historical and a logical link between green political thought and fascist or Nazi-like political practice (Bramwell 1989; Pois 1986; Ferry 1995, ch. 5). Although overstated, this serves as a salutary reminder and a warning to greens to beware of fanatics and authoritarians within their ranks.

A third set of questions concerns the shape and structure of green political institutions. Are the interest-group politics of Western-style liberal democracies best able to achieve environmental ends? Should greens organise themselves into political parties and pressure groups? Should they nominate candidates for election to public office and lobby on behalf of their green agenda? Should they be willing to compromise in the hopes of gaining piecemeal political victories? Or should greens remain a broad-based movement, aloof from partisan wrangling and pressure-group politics, and immune from temptations to tailor their message to appeal to a broad band of the electorate?[7]

The answers to these and other questions continue to be debated by greens of differing political persuasions. In two-party systems such as the United States, third parties have little hope of success, and the most effective strategy might be to influence the platforms and policies of either (or, better, both) major political parties. Other political systems hold out other possibilities. In multi-party parliamentary systems, for example, it might be wise to organise green political parties – as has been done in Britain and Germany, for example. Best of all, perhaps, would be a system of proportional representation in which congressional or parliamentary seats are allotted according to the proportion of votes cast for various candidates or parties.

Many militant greens insist that conventional party politics are both ineffective and corrupting to the movement, and that compromise is anathema. Indeed the motto of one such group, Earth First!, is 'No compromise in defence of Mother Earth'; and since compromise is central to politics and legislation, many radical environmentalists look askance at conventional party politics. 'Dark green' radicals tend to favour direct action in the form of civil disobedience, protest marches and demonstrations, and even 'ecotage' or 'monkey-wrenching'. Such action is politically and morally justifiable, they say, if it is non-violent and directed at property and never against persons. Thus, for example, the destruction of wildlife habitat for motorway construction or other kinds of 'development' may be slowed and sometimes even stopped by non-violent civil disobedience. By drawing public attention to such issues, protesters hope to educate or 'raise the consciousness' of their fellow citizens, so as to put pressure on their political representatives, planners and policy-makers. Even more militant green activists advocate and practise 'ecotage' or 'monkey-wrenching' – the disabling of machinery, the destruction of surveyors' stakes, the 'spiking'

7. Some of the most protracted and bitter disputes within green parties arose in connection with these questions. In die Grünen, for example, *fundis* pitted their purist or 'fundamentalist' views against *realos* who counselled political 'realism', compromise and coalitions with other parties. The ascendancy of the latter over the former led several prominent German Green *fundis* (most notably Rudolf Bahro) to resign from the party. See Bahro (1986, pp. 210–11).

of old-growth trees to prevent their being cut, and other tactics. The arguments for and against such measures have been, and will doubtless continue to be, a lively topic of political and philosophical debate amongst environmentalists (Foreman 1991; Goodin 1992, pp. 133–5; List 1993).

Conclusion

Green political thought in the twentieth century was not a single, internally consistent or logically coherent body of theory. It was instead a diverse and disparate collection of themes and concerns, conjectures and questions, arguments and counter-arguments which, taken together, constituted a powerful critique of the dark side of modern industrial (and now perhaps post-industrial) society. At the dawn of the new century green political thought is beginning to assume a more definite, although as yet far from definitive, shape. Among remaining and unresolved questions, several stand out. Does a 'greener' world require a Nietzschean 'transvaluation of all values' or can we create such a world with theoretical resources already available to us (Ball 2001)? Must greens abandon humanism or anthropocentrism entirely? If so, is there not a danger that the rights and interests of human beings might be violated in the name of an ecocentric ethic (Ferry 1995)? How might one reconcile environmental concerns with social justice (Dobson 1998)? Do other mainstream political philosophies – utilitarianism and rights-based liberalism foremost among them – contain the conceptual and theoretical resources out of which a viable green political theory might be constructed?[8] What is the proper relationship between the natural environment and the 'built environment' of cities and other human settlements (Light 2001; Dagger 2003)? These and other controversial questions remain to be answered.

8. Answered negatively by O'Neill (1993) and affirmatively by utilitarians such as Goodin (1992) and rights-based liberals such as Barry (1989).

Part V
Beyond Western political thought

26
Non-Western political thought

BHIKHU PAREKH

Four points of clarification are needed about the theme of this chapter and the title itself. First, from a non-Western perspective the twentieth century could be said to begin in 1905 when Japan defeated Russia, an event that destroyed the widespread myth of European invincibility and was celebrated by millions from China to Peru,[1] or in 1918 when the savagery of the First World War, or what non-Europeans call a European civil war, shook their lingering belief in the cultural superiority of Europe. From a non-Western perspective, the twentieth century has not yet ended and would only do so when their agenda of cultural and economic decolonisation is completed and full equality with the West is attained. Since the beginning and the end of the twentieth century are matters of historical judgement and hence contestable, I have taken the safer route of defining it in strictly chronological terms.

Second, the lives of non-Western political thinkers do not all fall neatly within the twentieth century. Some of them continued to live well into the twentieth century but published nothing or little of substance after 1900. I ignore such writers and concentrate on those who published most or at least some of their major works in the twentieth century and participated in its intellectual life.

Third, the term 'non-Western' is much disputed and its use needs explanation. The limitations of the term are obvious. It is not always clear what parts of the world it refers to. The term 'West' is used in several senses: geographical, politico-economic (when it refers to capitalist democracies), hegemonic (when it refers to countries that once exercised and in some cases still continue to exercise political domination over others), racial (when it

1. This was the first time in modern history that a non-European country had defeated a European power. Its impact on the non-Western imagination was immense.

refers to countries whose population is predominantly white), and so on. And each of these senses classifies different countries as Western and non-Western. Furthermore, the term 'non-Western' is Westocentric and negative, treating some parts of the world as the other of the West, as a kind of global remainder, and denying them a positive and autonomous identity of their own. It also homogenises both the West and the non-West, suppresses their internal differences, and obscures their centuries of interaction and shared heritage. Non-West, especially in the shape of the so-called East, has long been a significant presence in the West. It gave the West its two major religions as well as many of its scientific and philosophical ideas such as Arab astronomy, Indian philosophy and mathematics, and the Chinese printing press and gun powder, and has long been a polemical vehicle of its hopes and nightmares. The West's presence in the non-West is even more extensive especially in the aftermath of European colonisation: so much so that large parts of its ways of life and thought are wholly unintelligible without reference to the West.

Although the term 'non-Western' has these and other disadvantages, it is a useful and economical way of referring to those countries in Asia, Africa, Latin America and elsewhere that were either colonised by European powers or subjected to powerful political and military pressures. Although these countries have different histories, traditions and cultures, they all share this profoundly significant historical experience and have to cope with the problems thrown up by it. They were humiliated by metropolitan powers and exposed to a common set of exogenous ideas and forces, and their intellectual life was for long and in many cases still continues to be dominated by the question of how to respond to Western modernity. In spite of its obvious limitations, the term 'non-Western' has therefore considerable analytical and explanatory value, and I use it in this chapter to refer to countries in Asia, Africa and elsewhere that shared this common historical predicament.

The fourth point of clarification has to do with the term 'political thought'. The term is conventionally taken to refer to ideas concerning the nature of the state, the basis of its authority, ways of constituting and the manner of conducting its affairs. Some non-Western societies do not have or rather are not states in the Western sense. And even in those that are, many writers are highly critical of the state. They see it as an abstract and impersonal institution hovering over and dominating society, and wish to re-embed or even dissolve it in the wider society. Their 'political' thought has, in the Western sense, a non-political or even anti-political thrust. I shall therefore use the term 'political thought' to refer not to the state, nor to politics understood as an autonomous and specialised activity, but to ideas concerning how the collective affairs of a society should be organised and conducted.

Although political theory in the West occurs in the writings of theologians, poets, novelists and so on, it has increasingly become a relatively autonomous and specialised form of inquiry undertaken by those whom we have come to call political theorists or philosophers. And although it has an inescapable normative dimension, it is primarily analytical and explanatory in nature. This is not the case in most non-Western societies. Since the state there was not until recently, and is not fully even now, dissociated from society, it is not an independent and self-contained object of investigation. Academic institutions are not based on the kind of disciplinary specialisation characteristic of Western universities. And theoretical reflection is closely tied to practice, and expected to yield practical wisdom. For these and other reasons much of non-Western political thought is the work not of political theorists but political leaders, activists, creative writers, concerned citizens and public intellectuals, and has a strong practical and normative thrust. It is not articulated in conceptually tidy, abstract and politically detached theoretical systems meant for fellow political theorists, but in politically engaged semi-popular writings addressed to fellow citizens. This does not mean that it is inferior to its Western counterpart for, although it often lacks theoretical rigour, it contains penetrating insights, is seized of real issues, and is enriched by practical experience; rather it is different in its nature and orientation and needs to be read in its own terms. Furthermore a good deal of it is written in local languages. And since many of these writings are not translated into European languages and our knowledge of it is necessarily limited to only a small part of it, no discussion of non-Western political thought including this one can claim to be comprehensive.

Context

By the beginning of the twentieth century most countries in Asia, Africa, Latin America and elsewhere had been exposed to extensive Western influence. Many of them were still under colonial rule; some had just come out of it; and those that had never been colonised, such as China, Japan and Iran, felt culturally, economically and militarily threatened by Western powers. In their own different ways, they were all struck by the enormous power of the West and their own lack of power. The West represented not only power but also a vision of life involving such values as individual liberty and rights, equality, democracy, scientific curiosity and mastery of nature – in short, modernity. Non-Western writers wondered about the sources of Western power, the nature of modernity, and the relationship between the two. They asked how they could stand up to the West, whether they should embrace modernity, and what they should do about their traditional ways of life. In some countries, such as India, which had been exposed to Western influences much longer, the debate had begun in the early years of the nineteenth century. In Latin America, Japan, China and the Middle East, it did not begin until a few decades later, and it did not take off in many parts of Africa until the closing decades of the nineteenth century. By the beginning of the twentieth century, however, it had reached the masses in all countries, had begun to dominate the public agenda, and had acquired a reasonably clear shape.

The question as to how to respond to modernity, acquire the capacity to stand up to the West, and reorganise traditional societies received a wide variety of answers which fell into four broad categories. For analytical convenience I shall call them modernism, syncretism, critical traditionalism and, for want of a better word, religious fundamentalism. The fourfold classification pertains to structures of thought or bodies of ideas, and not to individual thinkers, who often sympathised with more than one of them and do not neatly fit into a single category. These bodies of ideas sometimes overlap in their assumptions and recommendations and are not mutually exclusive. However, each has a different thrust, springs from a different world view, reflects different moral and cultural sensibilities, expresses different fears and hopes, and forms a reasonably distinct world of thought. They did not all emerge at the same time; religious fundamentalism, for example, was the last to appear on the scene and often after the countries concerned had become independent. The four bodies of ideas, again, are not all equally dominant in all non-Western countries, for which of them becomes influential at what time depends on such factors as the historical circumstances of the country, the nature and strength of its cultural traditions, its degree of exposure to modernity, and the extent and urgency of the external threat.

Modernism

Modernist writers are enthusiastic advocates of Western modernity. They argue that traditional ways of life such as theirs are static, oppressive, poor, ridden with superstition and mindless conformity to established customs and practices, and incapable of concerted action. Their societies had paid a heavy price in the form of economic underdevelopment, mental and moral stagnation and colonial humiliation. It was about time they 'woke up from their long historical slumber' and caught up with the West by embracing modern science, technology, rationalism, liberalism, the state and so on. As the influential Indonesian thinker Soetan Sjahrir put it, 'What the West has taught us is a higher form of living... The East must become westernised' (Worseley 1967, p. 20).

Modernists need to convince their countrymen, many of them highly sceptical, that the modern way of life is higher. By and large they rely on three interrelated arguments. First, modernity represents freedom in the sense of freeing the individual from the tyranny of nature, customs, poverty, irresponsible power and so on, and creates a way of life worthy of human beings. Second, it releases individual energy and creativity, creates a resourceful and lively society and contributes to human flourishing and progress. And, third, it generates the kind of economic, technological and political power enjoyed by the West, which every society needs to stand up to the West and interact with it as an equal in the modern world. Since the first two arguments are not easy to defend and do not always convince their countrymen, many a modernist writer relies on the third argument and presents modernisation as an inescapable historical predicament and the only way to acquire power and respectability.

In India modernist ideas were advocated by a large number of liberal thinkers such as Dadabhai Naoroji, Pherozeshah Mehta, M. N. Roy, Motilal Nehru and his son Jawaharlal Nehru, and the communist thinkers such as Dange, Ranadive and Namboodiripad. In their view, mysticism, otherworldliness, the caste system, the 'spirit of localism', and the octopus-like grip of society that prevented the emergence of an independent state and civil associations had kept India degenerate for centuries and stifled all creativity and initiative. India's only hope lay in making a radical break with its past and embarking on a programme of comprehensive economic, political and cultural modernisation.[2] In China, Cai Yuanpei (1868–1940), the modernist chancellor of Peking University from 1916 to 1926, attracted independent-minded Westernised scholars and created a milieu that led to the New Culture and May Fourth Movements, both of which advocated comprehensive modernisation.[3] Chan Duxiu (1879–1942), Li Dazhao (1879–1927), Lian Qicho (1873–1929), Wang Guowei (1877–1927),

2. For a fuller discussion, see Parekh (1999, ch. 2). In Turkey Kamal Atatürk and his followers expressed similar sentiments.
3. For a detailed analysis, see Fairbank (1992, chs. 12–15) and Gernet (1996, chs. 28 and 31).

Ken Wu Yu (1872–1941) and others argued in their own different ways for 'democracy and science' and popularised the slogan of 'Down with Confucianism' (Roucek 1946, pp. 576f.). In their view Confucius, Mencius and even Buddhism had encouraged mindless conformity to traditions, despotism, social inequality, a group-differentiated system of rights and duties, and so on, and had been a source of the country's intellectual and social degeneration and political powerlessness. As Lu Hsun (1881–1936), the 'Gorki of China', puts it: 'It is not so much the question of whether we should preserve the tradition as the question of whether the tradition can preserve us' (Tan 1971, p. 54).

Science and progress were the modernist watchwords. Progress was defined and measured in terms of Western modernity, and involved transforming traditional societies along Western secular, liberal and democratic lines. Science was defined in positivist terms and used as a neutral authority with which to attack traditions, religion and so on, and uncover the laws governing the progress from barbarism to civilisation. Many, though by no means all, early modernists were deeply impressed with the writings of Comte, Spencer, Montesquieu, J. S. Mill and Darwin. These were all widely read and quoted in India. In China, Yen-Fu (1853–1921) translated some of them with extensive commentaries, and his writings were highly influential. In Latin America, positivism was the official philosophy of the newly created Brazilian republic, which even built a positivist church from whose membership it drew many of its leaders. In many non-Western countries, modernists read liberalism and Marxism in positivist and historicist terms, and saw them as scientifically based bodies of thought revealing the secrets not only of history but of moral and political life in general (for a fuller discussion, see the article by Harold Davis in Roucek 1946).

Modernist political thinkers, then, demand a radical break with the past. Some of them appreciate that not all their traditional beliefs and practices deserve to be rejected. However, they are convinced that these are few in number and cannot be retained without encouraging the dangerous spirit of 'revivalism', and that the best course of action is to begin with a clean slate. Many of them also wonder if alien ideas and institutions can take root without being embedded in, or at least somehow linked to, existing beliefs and practices, but are persuaded that this is not necessarily so. After all, post-Renaissance Europe had managed to break completely with the medieval ways of life and thought, and even in their own societies wholly alien Western educational institutions had gained widespread popularity.

Modernists are just as enthusiastic about the modern state as about science and technology. In their view, the state stands for modernity, society for tradition; the state is a realm of rationality, society of irrational beliefs and 'obscurantist' forces; the state represents the will to change, society depends on blind conformity to customs. The state must stand above society in order to undertake the massive task of moral and cultural regeneration. And it can do so only if it is led by a modernist political elite supported by an enlightened bureaucracy. Although modernists favour democracy as a way of educating the people and holding the elite accountable, they are worried about the danger of giving power to the allegedly degenerate masses and the likely influence of reactionary forces. Some of them trust their ability to mobilise the masses around the modernist project, whereas others advocate 'guided' or 'regulated' democracy.

Whether they are liberals or Marxists, modernists are agreed that the state's primary task is twofold: economic development and cultural regeneration. Although they think that the two tasks are closely related, they appreciate that they might also sometimes conflict, and privilege one or the other. Mao Zedong initially thought that the two tasks reinforced each other. When he later realised that they did not, he announced the Great Leap Forward from 1958 to 1960, and later the Cultural Revolution which began in 1965 and lasted in one form or another until his death in 1976. The former introduced collectivist communes which abolished the family and private property and sought to fight 'the Four Olds': namely, old ideas, old culture, old customs and old habits (for a good discussion, see Fairbank 1992, ch. 20). The Cultural Revolution sought, among other things, to purge the state of 'careerists' and 'bourgeois reformists', and to place it in the charge of men and women possessing both the right cultural attitudes and the ruthless determination to transform society accordingly. The fact that all this hampered economic development and caused administrative chaos was a small price to pay for China's cultural regeneration.

Modernists argue that the state should be organised as a nation state and should cultivate and mobilise the spirit of nationalism. This is the only way to unite society, generate the kind of political power it needs to stand up to the West and act as a self-determining agent in a hostile world, and to enable the state to undertake the massive task of social regeneration. Modernists face a difficulty in determining the basis of nationalism. Since they reject the past, an appeal to it is not available to them. And since they find religion reactionary and politically dangerous, it too cannot serve that function. Language does not help because there are many languages, or because it is sometimes shared with outsiders, or because it is by itself too weak to mobilise the masses. Ethnicity is open to similar objections. And a body of shared civic and political values as advocated by civic nationalists in the West is not much help either, for the values are not yet part of the society's way of life and are limited to the political realm.

Modernists turn to two things to generate the sense of nationhood: the fear of Western domination and the kind of colonial humiliation their countries had endured until recently and, second, the widely shared substantive goals or 'collective project' of economic development, cultural regeneration and political power. In their view, the nation is not given, and has to be created by the state by mobilising both the fear of the West and the hope of catching up with it. In its psychological orientation and politico-cultural content, modernist nationalism is heavily dependent on the West, its object of fear and envy. It wants the respect of and equality with the West, and that requires conformity to the latter's standards and norms. In the deepest sense, it signifies heteronymous autonomy: a free decision by the countries concerned to model themselves after the West. The kind of nationalism advocated by modernist writers is neither ethnic nor civic in nature, being too state-centred and volitionalist to be the former and too substantive in content to be the latter. It is a collective project propelled by the powerful motives of fear and hope and mobilising the entire society in the pursuit of comprehensive modernisation.

Syncretism

Syncretists advocate a synthesis of the best in their own and Western cultures. They are highly critical of modernists for their uncritical admiration of the West and equally uncritical condemnation of their own society. For syncretists Western culture has many admirable elements, such as its scientific spirit, intellectual curiosity, determined effort to understand and master the external world, respect for the individual and capacity for organisation and collective action. However, it is also flawed in important respects. It is narrowly individualist, materialist, consumerist, militarist, exploitative of weaker groups at home and abroad, driven by greed and desire for domination and devoid of moral and spiritual depth. The pre-modern West was free of many of these vices, but the modern West rejected its valuable heritage in its eagerness to break with its past. Non-Western societies should avoid that mistake. They are strong where the West is weak, and should aim to evolve a higher civilisation based on the noblest ideals of both. For the syncretists, the West is wrong to claim universal validity for its values, for these are partial and one-sided. True universality can only emerge from a critical dialogue between Western and non-Western societies and the resulting synthesis of the best in both. Like the modernists, syncretists welcome modernity but, unlike them, they refuse to equate it with Westernisation and urge non-Western societies to develop their own alternative forms of modernity.

The idea of creating a new civilisation excites the imagination of many a non-Western writer. It enables them to reap the benefits of Western modernity without jettisoning much of their traditional way of life and thought. It gives them the confidence to learn from the West because they also have something to teach it. Indeed it presents them with the unique historical opportunity to create a civilisation superior to that of the West, and take over from it the task of piloting history to its next stage. In India Bankim Chatterjee, Dayanand Saraswati, Gokhale, Ranade and other leading thinkers see themselves 'sitting at the confluence of two mighty rivers' and engaging in the great moral task of combining 'ancient wisdom and modern enterprise', 'European industries and science with Indian *dharma*', 'ancient faith and modern science', and creating a 'New Dispensation' that is at once 'thoroughly scientific' and 'transcendentally spiritual' (Parekh 1999, pp. 68ff.). Japanese thinkers such as Shazon Sakuma Nishi Amana and Kisaro Nishida want to combine 'eastern morality and western technique', 'western and eastern thinking', 'western rationality and traditional Japanese values', and create a 'new form of modernity' and 'universality'. The two cultures in their view 'complement each other' and together form the basis of a 'complete humanity' and a genuine 'world culture' (Samson 1984 offers a good analysis). In China, too, several eminent thinkers argue for a 'true synthesis' of Chinese culture and Western science, and insist that a regenerated China should have 'Chinese knowledge for foundation, and western knowledge for practice' (Gernet 1996, p. 595).[4] Zhang Junmai (1867–1969) challenges the May Fourth Movement's endorsement of Western modernity, and turns to ancient Confucian, Taoist and Buddhist traditions to provide the basis of the new culture with which carefully selected features of modernity are to be integrated. Xu Fuguan (1903–82) argues that the Confucian conceptions of the self and virtue are the only true basis of society, and that the structure of modernity should to be built on it. In Muslim countries such writers as Taha Abdalbāquí Surur argue for a synthesis of Islamic culture

4. For a useful discussion, see Levenson (1958, pp. 78f.).

with Western science, technology and modes of political organisation; they are 'two friends in agreement, not in conflict' as Muhammed Rashid Rida (1865–1935) reassures his critics (Kerr 1966, p. 191).

At the political level, the syncretist project of a grand cultural synthesis involves combining valuable Western and indigenous ideas and institutions. The Western conception of individuality is to be combined with the non-Western emphasis on community, for when detached from each other individuality degenerates into self-centred individualism and community into collectivism. Individual rights are important, but so are social duties and obligations. Individual liberty is a great Western value, but so is the non-Western emphasis on social discipline and harmony. The Western idea of equality is valuable, but it is too atomistic and needs to be supplemented by the traditional idea of fraternity or community. The modern state is a valuable and vitally necessary institution but should not be detached from, given greater importance than, or allowed to lord over society. The state should rise above sectional pressures and retain a measure of impersonality, but equally it should be organised as a family, sustained by filial loyalty, and run by men of character and virtue who give it a human face and provide political role models. Political parties are vital tools of political integration and education, but they should not be partisan, class-based and divisive. Democracy is a commendable form of government, but the role of the virtuous elite and men of wisdom should not be ignored either.

Although the syncretist project is not inherently flawed, it raises more problems than its advocates realise. It presupposes transcultural criteria to determine what is valuable in each culture, and no such criteria are being offered. It also presupposes rather naïvely that the writers involved are themselves culturally unconditioned and able to rise above and freely choose the 'good points' of both cultures. Again, the syncretist thinkers wrongly assume that the best in each can be harmoniously integrated in thought and especially in practice. They fail to appreciate that liberal democracy which many of them favour sits ill at ease with the authority of the moral elite, that the state cannot both rise above and be embedded in society, and that the culture of individual rights cannot be easily combined with status-based social obligations. Although syncretist political thinkers in India, China, Japan and elsewhere offer penetrating criticisms of Western modernity, liberalism, state and democracy, and throw up many constructive ideas, the grand philosophical synthesis of their dream eludes them, and many of them end up either with suggestive but shallow syncretism or with a form of crypto-modernism that is no less modernist for dressing up Western ideas in an indigenous garb.

Critical traditionalism

Critical traditionalists are highly critical of both modernists and syncretists. They reject the modernist contrast between science and tradition. Science is itself a tradition like any other, and its authority is not neutral and self-evident but derived from the consensus among its adherents on the validity of its values and methods. It is true that science relies on trial and error, experimentation and so on, and that its conclusions are open to criticism and hence corrigible. However, this is also true of traditions. They are never 'blind' and 'irrational' but products of a long process of trial and error in which misguided practices and beliefs often get weeded out and only the useful ones generally survive. Since human beings are not mindless automata but rational beings who wish to lead satisfying lives, no social practice can become part of a tradition and last long unless it has a rationale. Some critical traditionalists go further and challenge modern science itself.[5] In their view, it suffers from rationalist hubris, is obsessed with the ideas of dominating nature and mastering human affairs, has an elitist thrust, and is the source of much violence against nature and human beings. It marginalises other forms of knowledge, including folk knowledge and traditional wisdom, privileges reason and ignores other human faculties, and has little to say about the meaning of life and the best way to live.

For critical traditionalists, modernists are naïve to imagine that human beings are like clean slates upon which one can write what one likes. Human beings are deeply shaped by their society and culture, and have certain characters, temperaments, dispositions and forms of self-understanding. A way of life that is good for one group of people might spell disaster for another. It must suit people, be within their psychological and moral reach, and be capable of connecting with and activating their deepest hopes and aspirations. Rather than ask the incoherent and contextless question as to which way of life is the best or most rational, we should ask which way of life is the best or most desirable for people who are constituted in a certain way, are heirs to certain traditions, and live under particular geographical and historical circumstances.

5. These views are developed in Nandy (1988) and Escobar (1995).

Although critical traditionalists are more sympathetic to some of the syncretist concerns and sometimes advocate similar ideas and institutions, they find the syncretist approach deeply flawed. In their view, syncretists naïvely assume that they can rise above both their own and modern ways of life, and evaluate them from a non-existent Archimedean standpoint by means of equally illusory transcultural criteria. Syncretists also make the further mistake of assuming that values can be detached from the wider ways of life and eclectically combined. Their claim that such a new way of life represents the 'true universal' and is alone worthy of universal allegiance perpetuates the modernist fallacy that one way of life is objectively the best and suits all societies equally. Unlike the modern way of life, which is at least a lived reality in the West and whose strengths and weaknesses are evident to all, the syncretist synthesis is a wholly artificial intellectual construct, theoretically seductive but untested in practice, a dangerous moral gamble which no responsible society should take. Unlike the modernists, who embrace the Western model of modernity, and unlike the syncretists, who advocate an indigenous model of it, critical traditionalists are highly critical of modernity itself.

For critical traditionalists, a society must start with what it is. It is a particular kind of society with particular traditions and history which make its members the kind of persons they are. No society is perfect, and it is bound to throw up beliefs and practices some of which are obsolete or have forfeited their rationale. People's ideas of right and wrong also change, and they might consider wrong today what they once thought right. Furthermore the wider world never remains static, and every society must change with it if it is to survive and flourish. Critical traditionalists have a strong sense of historical flux and emphasise the need to adjust to changing times. Since every society must for these and other reasons accept change as a fact of life, the question before it is not whether but how to change without losing its sense of identity and causing widespread moral and cultural disorientation.

For critical traditionalists, no society is so degenerate as to be devoid of all reformist resources, for then it would not have lasted long. It is, of course, possible that its resources might be limited or inadequate to new challenges, and then it should learn what it can from societies that are better equipped in the relevant respect or have successfully met these challenges. It should treat these societies neither as models to emulate, nor even as sources of ready-made ideas, but rather as aids to critical self-reflection. A society should do its thinking itself, both as a matter of pride and because there is no real alternative to it. It should critically examine its own constitutive principles, psychological and moral resources, needs and so on, stay loyal to traditions and practices it considers right, and borrow from others what in its view will improve and can be integrated into its way of life. Such judicious adherence to the past and borrowing from others are both part of self-regeneration. The borrowing does not signify inferiority but self-confidence and courage, and need not be accompanied by a sense of guilt and shame. And its purpose is not to catch up with the West, nor to create a superior civilisation and become the West's teacher, both of which spring from a sense of inferiority, but rather to reform and regenerate oneself in a manner that best realises one's distinct potential and meets the challenges of the age.

Critical traditionalism commands the allegiance of some of the finest thinkers in non-Western societies. In India Mahatma Gandhi, Tagore, Tilak, Aurobindo and others were its eloquent spokesmen, stressing both the richness of the Indian civilisation and the need to revitalise it in harmony with its spirit (Parekh 1999, pp. 72f.). In the West Indies and parts of Africa many writers, deeply disturbed by the modernist assault on traditional African values, advocated 'cultural resistance', 'return to the source' and the consequent 'reconversion of minds'. Amilcar Cabral wanted African society to 'recapture the commanding heights of its own culture', purge itself of the 'harmful influences of foreign rule', and evolve a suitably regenerated 'national culture' (Miller 1990, p. 46).[6] Aimé Césaire, who explored the psychology of colonialism more deeply than most, urged Africans to piece together their ruptured past, systematically squeeze out the colonial legacy from their language, social practices and modes of thought, and constitute national cultures on suitably revised traditional foundations. Kwasi Wiredu, a distinguished Nigerian philosopher, advocates 'conceptual decolonisation', the 'unmasking of the spurious universals' of Western culture, doing African philosophy in African languages, and the creation of an authentic national philosophy based on indigenous African foundations.[7] Such writers as Renato Constantinu in the Philippines and Chang Chitung in China advance similar views (Constantino 1985, pp. 48f.). For all of them, both national dignity and political realism require that political institutions should be based on national culture, that the latter is not given but needs to be carefully constructed, that this can only be done by building on sensitively regenerated

6. Fanon (1967) devotes a whole chapter to national culture.

7. Wiredu (1966, pp. 3f. and also chs. 10 and 14). See also the articles by Marlene Van Niekerk, Steve Biko and Erasmus Prinsloo in P. H. Coetzee and A. J. P. Roux (1998).

traditional values and ways of thought, and that this calls for close cooperation between the ordinary people and their organic intellectuals. Most of these writers are deeply suspicious of the state and assign it little if any role in the creation of national culture.

Since different societies have different traditions and histories, different critical traditionalists offer different accounts of political life and advocate different institutions and practices. Indeed, the very idea of a universally valid political theory or institutional structure favoured by modernists and syncretists alike is wholly alien to their ways of thinking. Certain general ideas, however, recur in many of their writings.

For critical traditionalists, neither the individual nor the state but society, the complex and rich network of social relations and institutions in which both the individual and the state are embedded, is the starting point of political thought. Individuals are part of the family, the clan, the tribe, the village, the religious community and so on, and are tied to them by the bonds of social and moral obligations. These social institutions shape them, engage their deepest emotions, and cultivate moral and social virtues. Unlike the state, which relies on coercion, society relies on moral and social pressure. And unlike civil society, which is much favoured by modernists and is largely made up of voluntary and functional associations, society is largely involuntary, shapes the moral identity and character of its members, and gives them a sense of rootedness. Critical traditionalists seek to strengthen social institutions and see them as the building blocks of the political community. They want them to take over many of the functions normally assigned to the state, such as resolving conflicts, maintaining order and civility, and providing welfare services. The state is then no longer separated from and hovering over society, but is integrated into it and becomes one of its institutions performing a specialised function. It ceases to be the centre, the linchpin, of society and becomes a largely facilitating and coordinating agency whose coercive sanctions are used only in the last resort. Citizenship does not represent the highest status; rather it is one of several ways in which socially conscious individuals express their concern for each other.

Critical traditionalists are highly critical of both capitalism and communism. The former is based on greed, nurtures narrow individualism, involves domestic and global exploitation, and is inimical to stable communities; the latter is statist, coercive, hostile to the spirit of self-help and narrowly economistic in its goals. For critical traditionalists, each society should evolve an economic system suited to its history and culture. Fanon, Nyerere, Cabral and others want 'African socialism' based on *ujamma* villages organised as agro-industrial cooperatives. Gandhi, the older J. P. Narain, Tagore and others in India advocate self-governing villages, cooperative agriculture, socially responsible industries run along participatory lines, production based on need rather than profit and, whenever possible, decentralised, and a partly regulative and partly indicative national plan to coordinate production (for Senghor's similar views, see Senghor 1965). Their counterparts in Islamic countries additionally plead for an Islamic financial system in which interest on savings is disallowed and individuals voluntarily give away a fixed part of their income to charities.

Critical traditionalists are highly critical of liberal democracy and seek to replace it with 'organic' or 'communitarian' democracy.[8] As they understand it, liberal democracy is based on asocial and atomised individuals pursuing their interests within the limits of the law. They are related to each other not directly but through the state, and their morality is based on the fear of each other and the state. Politics here is largely concerned with the promotion of individual and group self-interest. Elections, in which citizens are expected to express their well-considered opinions on issues which they hardly understand, are inevitably reduced to political auctions and dominated by false promises, demagoguery and the power of money. Political parties, the only way to link atomised individuals to each other and to the state, are broadly divided along class lines, and organised into bureaucratic and highly centralised machines demanding total conformity and prizing leaders for their demagogic and manipulative skills rather than their spirit of self-sacrifice, public service, moral courage and personal morality. As Nyerere put it, 'The politics of a country governed by the two-party system are not and cannot be national politics; they are the politics of groups' (Nyerere 1967, p. 167).

By contrast to liberal democracy, organic or communitarian democracy is built from the bottom upwards. The political community is constituted along federal lines, starting with self-governing local communities and leading increasingly to similarly self-governing wider communities, culminating in the national government. Since people are intimately familiar with local issues and leadership, local bodies are to be directly elected by them, and those above by the elected representatives at the level immediately below. Elections, then, do not involve mass mobilisation, and that is supposed to reduce and even eliminate the power of money and demagogues. Some critical

8. For Gandhi, see Parekh (1989). See also Wiredu's chapter in Coetzee and Roux (1998).

traditionalists advocate 'partyless democracy', with elected representatives making their own judgements on the issues of the day and forming ad hoc alliances; others favour 'one-party democracy' in which a single party, committed to the pursuit of national interest and including within it all major interests and views, governs the country. In either case, such an organic or communitarian democracy is said to be superior to liberal democracy because it socialises the state and limits its power and prestige, eliminates ideological polarisation and rigidification of differences, makes integrated communities rather than isolated individuals its basic units, and ensures that those in power are rooted in the community and possess character and integrity. It is said to be superior, also, because it extends democracy right down to the lowest level of government, and respects the autonomy of, and ensures cultural democracy to, its diverse communities.

Critical traditionalists are deeply divided about the nature and value of nationalism. Some, such as Gandhi and Tagore in India, were hostile to it. In their view it turned the state, an administrative and legal institution, into a moral community and reinforced its power and prestige. It stressed unity at the expense of differences, moulded the entire society in the image of a particular conception of the nation, 'homogenised thoughts and feelings', and corrupted the very way of life it claimed to protect. Nationalism, further, was believed to be basically concerned with collective power not individual freedom, to harbour illiberal and repressive tendencies, and to represent nothing more elevated than collective selfishness. For Tagore, it aroused and mobilised powerful and largely irrational emotions and acted as a political anaesthetic that 'drugs' moral feelings and stifles critical reason (see Tagore 1917 and Nandy 1994). It made a fetish of territory, every inch of which was supposed to be sacred and expected to be defended irrespective of the cost in human lives, and sanctioned militarism and brutal wars. As Tagore put it, nationalism represents a pagan worship of *bhowgolic apdevatā* (the evil gods of geography) with its 'blasphemous prayers' and totems in the shape of flags, and is a moral and spiritual monstrosity.

Tagore, Gandhi and other critical traditionalists sharply distinguish nationalism and even its cousin patriotism from what they call *deshprem* or *swadeshchintā*, an affectionate and critical concern for one's way of life and those who share it. The latter is based on love of one's civilisation and people and not of a particular place or territory. Since love involves promoting the well-being of its object, love of one's civilisation is alert to its defects lest they should lead to its decay and degeneration. It is both critical and committed, cherishes freedom and diversity, respects other societies' similar attachments to their ways of life, and is believed to be inherently tolerant, peaceful and non-homogenising.

Other critical traditionalists take a different view of nationalism. For them, their societies succumbed to internal decay, foreign rule or both because of the lack of a strong sense of nationhood and the unity and power it generates. They must now develop a strong sense of nationalism in order to generate a much-needed spirit of resistance to Western values and to protect and reform their traditional ways of life at their own pace. These writers, however, are confronted with a problem. For a variety of historical reasons, including the arbitrary territorial boundaries imposed by colonial rulers, the state and the nation, the political and the cultural community, often do not coincide in many non-Western countries. No Arab country except Egypt, for example, can claim historical continuity. Their classical periods did not occur within their current territorial boundaries and involved different groups of people. And this was also broadly the case in Africa and many other parts of the world. Nations, defined in terms of language, ethnicity, race, religion or all of them together, cut across states, and members of different states sometimes belong to a single nation. As many Arab writers put it, although Arabs belong to different countries or *watan*, they are all part of a single nation or *quam*. In Latin America some political thinkers argue that although the eighteen Spanish-speaking countries form so many different states, they are all really 'one people' or 'nation' by virtue of their shared *hispanidad*. Their counterparts in Africa argue that despite their membership of different states, black Africans constitute a single nation or community by virtue of sharing common ways of life and thought, attitudes to nature, love of music, sense of rhythm, and so on, all summed up in the popular notion of 'African personality' or 'négritude'.[9]

Political thinkers in these societies have to decide how to respond to this asymmetry between the state and the nation. Modernists and syncretists privilege the state and expect it to foster territorially based nationalism, partly because the territorial boundary of the state is clearly marked and provides the basis for a reasonably cohesive political community, and partly because they do not wish to base the nation on such 'atavistic' and 'reactionary' elements as ethnicity, race and religion. Critical traditionalists are divided in their views and fall into three broad groups. Some privilege the nation, arguing that, unlike the territorially bounded states which are administrative and often historically accidental units and are devoid of moral

9. For discussions of these ideas, see Senghor (1967). The title itself is suggestive.

and cultural significance, nations are sources of identity and values and represent moral and spiritual communities. In their view, when states belong to a common nation, as Arab and black African states are supposed to do, they should over time merge into a single nation state.[10]

Other critical traditionalists give more or less equal importance to the state and the nation.[11] In spite of their often arbitrary boundaries, states have developed reasonably distinct ways of life, created united communities around common national projects, and are genuinely moral units. For obvious reasons nations too are moral communities. The important thing, therefore, is to reconcile their claims. States should retain their independence and foster political nationalism. They should also, however, respect the claims of cultural nationalism and build up strong ties and evolve cooperative political structures with others belonging to the common nation.

Finally, some critical traditionalists question either the reality or the significance of shared nationhood.[12] This is particularly the case in Africa. Many African writers reject the idea of *négritude* or African personality. In their view, it emerged among the francophone Africans as a reaction against the strong assimilationist pressure from the French colonial rulers, and means little to anglophone Africans, whose black identity was never subjected to such pressure. And even among the former, it is largely confined to the blacks in the West Indies, who were cut off from their homeland and needed to make a conscious ideology out of their blackness, and has little appeal in Africa where blackness is taken for granted and does not need to be flaunted against a hostile other. For these writers the idea of *négritude* is yet another tool of colonisation, used this time by deracinated and Westernised francophone blacks to impose a particular form of self-understanding on all Africans. As René Menil put it, the negro as imagined by the proponents of *négritude* is 'really a Sartre that has been darkened... very much in anguish, very existentialist, picturesque and petit bourgeois' (LaGuerre 1982, p. 189). Fanon contended that even if one accepted the fact of shared *négritude*, he could not see how it implied shared values or way of life, for not all blacks

10. For Muhammad Abduh, Muslims have no other nationality save religion, and state nationalism (*asshiyya*) should be subordinated to the *umma*. For this see Kerr (1966). Hasan al-Banna (1906–49), the founder of the Egyptian Muslim Brotherhood, also takes this view.

11. For Nyerere, neither state nationalism nor its subordination to African unity is desirable. 'Both would lead Africa to disaster': Nyerere (1968, p. 216).

12. See Fanon (1967). See also Mphale (1962). For discussions that analyse the contradictions of *négritude*, see Worsley (1967, chs. 2 and 4) and LaGuerre (1982). Among Muslim writers, advocates of state nationalism include Mawdodi, Sayyid Qutb, Allal al-fasi of Morocco and Ali Shariati of Iran.

thought let alone ought to think alike. 'My black skin is not the wrapping of specific values', he wryly commented (Fanon 1970, p. 172). Africa to him represented a land not a people. The only thing common to many, though by no means all, Africans was the experience of slavery. To insist that they all constituted and should behave like a single nation was to be a 'slave to slavery'. For this group of writers, African states should both foster territorial nationalism and evolve cooperative international structures, not because they belong to a common nation or race, but because they have common interests and risk being played off against each other.

Religious fundamentalism

Religious fundamentalism differs from the three bodies of thought discussed earlier in several significant respects. Unlike them it is religiously grounded. Although this is also true of some forms of critical traditionalism and to a lesser extent of syncretism, it differs from both in taking a scripturalist view of religion and a literalist view of scriptures. Unlike them, it sees little of value in and declares a war on the modernist vision of the world. In this respect it is far more radical than them, and exhibits a style of thinking that has no parallel in modern Western history. Religious fundamentalism is to be found in one form or another in most non-Western societies, and takes different forms depending on the nature of the religion involved. Hinduism has no definitive scriptures like the Bible or the Qur'an, no organised clergy and no doctrinal orthodoxy. Although it is not amenable to fundamentalism in the strict sense of the term, that has not deterred Hindu militants from developing a highly politicised and homogenised view of their religion and insisting on a return to traditional social practices. Buddhist fundamentalism in South-East Asia and Sri Lanka faces a similar difficulty, and largely consists of insisting on a body of state-imposed moral values and practices. Unlike its Hindu and Buddhist counterparts, Jewish fundamentalism in Israel has a strong political content, involving the retention or conquest of territories associated with ancient Jewish history and giving the state of Israel a distinct religious identity. Unlike these and other religious movements, which are relatively weak and lack a clearly worked-out political theory, Islamic fundamentalism has in recent years proved to be the most powerful doctrinal and political force, and accordingly I shall concentrate on it.

Islamic fundamentalism is of relatively recent origin and is common to both Shi'as and Sunnis. Its most articulate statement is provided in Sayyid Qutb (1898–1966). The Indian thinker Abu al-Hasan 'Ali al-Nadawi's *What*

Has the World Lost by the Decline of the Muslims?, printed in Egypt with an introduction by Qutb and an instant best-seller in Arabic-speaking countries, adds several new ideas. Ayatollahs Khomeini (1900–89), Talequani (1911–79) and Mutahhri (1920–79) give Islamic fundamentalism a further Shi'ite twist in their highly influential writings.

For the Islamic fundamentalist, man's highest duty is to obey Allah and live according to His will as revealed in the Qur'an, the infallible source of all moral knowledge.[13] The body of ideas associated with modernity denies this fundamental truth and represents *jahiliyya* or era of ignorance. Secularism either denies the very existence of God or His relevance to moral and political life. Rationalism, for which reason is not just a source of secular knowledge, a view many religious fundamentalists accept, but the very measure of what is worth knowing and what constitutes knowledge, denies the importance of faith and God's role in history. Science is only equipped to deal with the empirical world, has nothing to say about the meaning and purpose of life and moral values, and lacks wisdom (*hickman*). The modern state usurps the sovereignty of God, and nationalism is blasphemous because it sets up an alternative religion with its own god (nation), rituals and forms of worship, detracts from the majesty of Allah, and places the nation's or state's interests above the cause of God. Modern liberalism is false because it is largely secular, glorifies individual reason, places supreme value on the individual, makes morality a matter of choice, homogenises and asserts the equality of the sexes when in fact the two are radically different and hence neither equal nor unequal, places no restraints on desires, and so on.

Islamic fundamentalism cannot make much sense of many of the beliefs and practices of democracy either (for a valuable discussion, see Esposito 1998). The latter attributes sovereignty to the people when in fact it belongs to Allah, and gives them a right to make such laws as they consider proper when in fact their supreme obligation is to follow the injunctions of the Qur'an and Shari'a. Elections cannot transmit people's authority to the elected government, for people do not have such an authority in the first instance. And since the masses are fickle and theologically illiterate, they cannot be trusted to elect men of character and wisdom. For similar reasons public opinion cannot be trusted either. For the Islamic fundamentalist, a free press has some value as a means of exposing the misdeeds of the government and articulating popular dissatisfaction with it. However, it

13. For excellent discussions, see Choueiri (1990) and Esposito (1983). See also Algar (1985) and Parekh (1994).

needs to be controlled lest it should become a means of spreading ignorance and disbelief and popularising the ideas and practices of secular Western culture. Political parties have no theological justification, for the true goals of political life are all revealed in the Qur'an and Shari'a and there can be no serious disagreement about them. Rulers do need advice, a practice for which there is ample theological justification, but it is most effective and sincere when given in private and with due humility. Rulers can, of course, misuse their power, something which the Qur'an strongly disapproves of, but the best way to guard against this is to place the wise and the learned in charge of government. Islamic fundamentalists, therefore, advocate the rule of the *ulema*, the 'paramount guardians' of the moral and spiritual well-being of the community. For some, the *ulema* should directly participate in the government; for others, this corrupts both religion and politics, and hence the *ulema* should confine themselves to keeping a keen eye on and indirectly regulating the activities of the popularly elected or selected representatives.[14] The latter, called theo-democracy, is supposed to accommodate the relative autonomy of politics within an overarching religious framework, and to be infinitely superior to the liberal and organic democracy favoured by modernists, syncretists and critical traditionalists.

Since all the central beliefs and practices of modernity are believed to be misguided and blasphemous, it cannot in the fundamentalist view be a worthy object of emulation. Instead, it has to be fought and defeated by a determined struggle (*jihad*) at all levels. The syncretist attempt to combine modernity with traditions and religion is just as flawed because its modernist component is unacceptable and cannot be reconciled with religion. In the fundamentalist view, some of modern technology can and should be borrowed, but nothing else. Fundamentalists are also dismissive of critical traditionalism. It privileges tradition over the revealed text and is guilty of blasphemy; it views tradition as the repository of accumulated wisdom when in fact it is often a collection of error and ignorance; and its concern to borrow judiciously from modernity betrays its continuing thraldom to the latter. Rejection of tradition is a favourite theme among modernists and religious reformers as well. However, while the latter's purpose is to make room for reason and a historically sensitive reading of the Qur'an, the fundamentalist's purpose is to make room for faith and close the doors of *ijtihad* or interpretation.

14. For a good discussion of why traditionalist theologians rule out the clergy's involvement in politics, see Abdo (1998).

In the fundamentalist view, Islamic states are legitimate only to the extent that they are religiously based and run. Since all believers constitute a single *umma*, the existing Muslim states should either be replaced by a single Islamic state, or brought under the hegemony of one that has succeeded in establishing a truly Islamic rule, or should subordinate their narrow national interests to those of the *umma* and work closely together in a spirit of solidarity. In any case, religious identity is infinitely more important than the political. For Ayatollah Khomeini, Bakhtiar's greatest sin consisted in thinking that 'he was an Iranian first and a Muslim afterwards'. For Islamic fundamentalism, the preservation of the community's religious identity is the collective responsibility of all its citizens. They owe it to Allah, and it is also in their own interest, to ensure that none of them backslides and corrupts the rest. Each of them, therefore, has a religious and a political duty to prevent such lapses, to report them to the relevant authority, and in exceptional cases to administer instant justice themselves.

For the Islamic fundamentalist, non-Muslims are a protected minority or *dhimmis* in a Muslim society. They are entitled to all the civil rights including the right to practise their religion, lead their traditional ways of life and even to vote, but not to participate actively in the conduct of public affairs, occupy important official positions, and to do anything that militates against or is likely to corrupt the prevailing Islamic way of life. Since the ethos of the state is wholly religious, non-Muslims cannot be granted full equality of status. Since this is how the Qur'an defines their status, even those who wish to grant them full equality face considerable difficulty giving their ideas a coherent theological basis.

In the fundamentalist view modernity has struck such deep roots in popular consciousness and enjoys such political and economic power that a *jihad* against it is fully justified. The masses must be educated and mobilised, their every action minutely analysed, and their smallest lapses severely dealt with. Foreigners, and foreign countries too, have to be diligently watched, and their often subtle attempts to dilute or corrupt the religious zeal of the community exposed and countered. All this calls for a vast army of true believers enjoying the requisite power. They may need to use 'holy violence' or 'Islamic terror', and this is fully justified. As Khomeini calmly assured those in doubt, 'The glorious Imam [the first Shi'ite Imam] killed in one day six thousand of his enemies to protect the faith.' The violence could be punitive as when it is used against the enemies of Allah, or redemptive as when it is suffered or self-inflicted in acts of martyrdom. Such martyrs who 'rise above ordinary mankind' and set an example of heroic dedication to the cause of God are the 'heart of history', rewarded both in this world and more importantly in the next.

General reflections

I have outlined above four major currents of thought in non-Western societies in the twentieth century. Although all four are present in one form or another in all of them, their influence varies greatly. Modernist thought, for example, is far more dominant in India, China and large parts of Latin America than in Pakistan and parts of Africa and the Middle East. Religious fundamentalism is more influential in Iran, Afghanistan, Sri Lanka and the Sudan than in China, Indonesia, Israel and India. And even in the latter, it is more widespread among some groups such as the orthodox and ultra-orthodox in Israel, the Buddhists in Sri Lanka, the Muslims in Nigeria and the Arabs in the Sudan than among others. Even within the same society, different bodies of ideas acquire dominance during different periods. Critical traditionalism was influential in India and large parts of Africa during most of the first half of the twentieth century, but dramatically declined thereafter, only to undergo a mild revival in recent years. Once these countries embarked on a path of modernist development, old traditions either declined or lost their appeal, rendering increasingly irrelevant the very project of reforming them and making them the basis of the new state or its national culture. This does not mean that critical traditionalism is dead or without its eloquent spokesmen; rather it now largely consists in reviving those isolated fragments of the past which still survive and have widespread appeal. Since the past is dissociated from and does not carry the authority of the tradition, critical traditionalism is forced to defend these fragments on rationalist grounds and is only marginally different from moderate modernism.

Although non-Western political thinkers are familiar with a wide variety of Western thinkers, it is striking that they draw upon only some of them and often interpret them very differently. Broadly speaking they are exercised by such questions as the nature and sources of social change and conflict, how to build states, the basis and limits of the reformist role of the state, the nature of political power, the role of ideology in justifying the rule of dominant groups, the relation between morality and politics, and more recently the nature and basis of human rights and how best to accommodate ethnic and cultural diversity. They are therefore attracted to those Western thinkers who discuss these questions from historical and sociological points of view.

This explains the early non-Western interest in Montesquieu, Comte and Marx, and the tendency to accentuate the positivist and historicist aspects of their thought. J. S. Mill was and is widely read, but more for his philosophy of history and utilitarianism than for his theory of liberty, which even now receives little attention. There is only limited interest in Hobbes, and even Locke has attracted serious attention only in recent decades. Bentham's political thought was and to a lesser extent still is read and admired, but his moral and social thought is largely rejected as an expression of the West's amoral individualism and hedonism. Machiavelli arouses little interest, largely because his amoral view of politics is believed to lie at the basis of the Western treatment of non-Western societies and is to be scrupulously avoided by those keen to build politics on moral and spiritual foundations. Burke and his brand of conservatism are too hierarchical and hostile to change to arouse much interest in non-Western societies.

Among contemporary Western writers, Oakeshott, Nozick, Leo Strauss and even Hannah Arendt enjoy little popularity, whereas Gramsci, Foucault, Derrida and to a somewhat lesser extent Habermas are widely read and written about. While Rawls has received some attention in Latin America, he has received almost none in the Middle East, Africa and until recently even in India. The fact that he is too Western and even American in his philosophical assumptions and cultural sensibilities may explain why he has little to say to non-Western societies. His individualist and voluntarist account of society, his failure to engage critically with or even to take a serious account of non-liberal beliefs, and his concern to detach political thought and practice from comprehensive doctrines also limit his appeal.

Twentieth-century non-Western political thought encompasses a wider range of ideas than its Western counterpart. In the West, political institutions and discourse surrounding them have evolved steadily over a fairly long period of time. As a result there is a broad consensus on a number of core beliefs, such as the nature and importance of the state, individual rights, the relative autonomy of the economy, secularism, constitutionalism, and the nature and conduct of international relations. By contrast, political structures in non-Western societies are still relatively fluid. Some of the inherited institutions of the past continue to be a part of lived reality, historical memories of pre-modern ways of life and thought are still fresh and arouse nostalgia, and political thinkers have available to them not only the intellectual resources of the West but also those of their own traditions.

Although modernist ideas have gained considerable ascendancy, they have not succeeded in silencing their critics and foreclosing the possibility of alternative ways of thought and life. Political imagination in non-Western societies is therefore less 'disciplined' in the Foucaldian sense, is both bolder and more reckless, and is prepared to experiment with a greater range of possibilities than in the West. Disagreements between different bodies of ideas are wide and deep, and extend to such basic issues as the nature of the state, the basis and limits of its authority, the importance of individual rights and constitutional restraints on the exercise of power, and the role of religion in public life. Although there is an increasing cross-cutting consensus among different thinkers on different matters, it is difficult to think of any significant political belief on which they are all agreed.

Given these deep differences, the non-Western political theorist faces a problem. He cannot take his beliefs and assumptions for granted or rest content with their superficial defence, for he is acutely aware that others in his society hold opposite views just as strongly and sincerely. John Rawls can afford to base his political philosophy on the central beliefs of Western liberal democracies without feeling the need to defend them against the possible objections of their critics. His non-Western counterpart is denied such theoretical luxury and has only two alternatives available to him. He must either defend his basic principles and assumptions in a manner that his critics can find persuasive or at least respect, or he can take them for granted, offer a superficial and circular defence of them, and construct a political theory on that basis. In the latter case, his theory has a strong ideological core and carries little conviction with his critics. The former is his only theoretically satisfactory option, but it is most demanding. It is not easy for a non-Western liberal political theorist, for example, to refute the basic premises of the religious fundamentalist or even those of the critical traditionalist. And, unlike Rawls and other Western thinkers, he cannot bracket out comprehensive doctrines and aim at a free-standing political theory, for some of these doctrines have profound political implications and their spokesmen reject the autonomy of political life. The non-Western political theorist, therefore, needs to engage with comprehensive doctrines, undertake a systematic critique of them, expose their logical inadequacies and unacceptable moral and political implications, and base his political theory on a reasonably convincing view of man and the world. Such a philosophical task is not impossible, as the works of Hobbes, Kant and Hegel show. However, it requires sustained and rigorous philosophical analysis, a wide range of intellectual and moral sympathy, an acute sense of history, and so on, and this is beyond the reach of most political theorists. Since it has defeated some of the ablest Western political theorists, it is hardly surprising that no non-Western society has so far thrown up a major political philosopher or even a major work of political philosophy.

There are also other reasons why non-Western societies have failed to throw up major works of political philosophy (Parekh 1992, pp. 549ff.). Some of those who write works of political theory are also men of action, and lack the talent, the leisure and the inclination to undertake a sustained theoretical inquiry. As for the academics from whom major works can be expected, other factors are at work. The degree of intellectual freedom that political theory requires is absent in countries dominated by communism and religious orthodoxy. And even in such free societies as India, there is a strong inhibition against asking searching questions lest they should subvert the prevailing ideological consensus and encourage religious and other forms of extremism. Furthermore, when their countries are facing acute practical problems and fear for their very survival and integrity, political theorists find it much more rewarding to address these questions than to engage in abstract political theory. There is no real demand for works in political theory either, and hence no incentive to write them. Again, in societies in which academics are poorly paid and valued and academic jobs are scarce, many of the most talented students enter the faculties of technology, medicine and management, and politics departments generally recruit those who have nowhere else to go. In the absence of a well-established tradition of political theory, the kind of intellectual training that students of political theory receive is relatively shallow, and the standards by which their works are judged are largely undemanding. Since the problems facing non-Western societies are new and do not admit of easy and borrowed answers, theorising them involves breaking out of conventional modes of thought, and that calls for courage and intellectual self-confidence not easily to be found among those subject to decades and even centuries of colonial rule.

27
Islamic political thought

SALWA ISMAIL

Two interrelated issues are central to Islamic political thought in the twentieth century: the relationship between religion and politics and the role of the Islamic heritage in modern society. The treatment of these issues began in the nineteenth century, in the context of Muslim societies' encounter with the West. Commencing with the Napoleonic invasion of Egypt (1789–1803), and extending through a period of Western Christian missionary activities in Muslim countries, Muslim educational missions to Western countries and, finally, to colonial rule, Muslim societies came into contact with modern Western ideas and ways of life. Through this encounter, the view of Western material progress was impressed on these societies. It was expressed in orientalist constructions of the East and in the apologetic and defensive discourses of the indigenous intellectuals. In Arab and Islamic thought, the problem of *nahda* (renaissance) crystallised. In Istanbul, the seat of Ottoman power, ideas of reform were developed and debated.[1] Muslim reformist views also took shape in India.[2] In Iran, the era in which modernising ideas and concepts were introduced became known as the *asre bidari* (period of awakening) (Mirsepassi 2000, p. 56; Gheissari 1998, pp. 14–15). By the end of the nineteenth century, modernist thought integrated nationalist principles and ideas.

At the turn of the twentieth century, Muslims were chiefly concerned with the problem of civilisational stagnation. The main *problématique* was formulated in terms of a renaissance project for Muslim societies. The articulation of this *problématique* was shaped by the encounter with the West in the modern period. Various intellectual positions were formed during this period of encounter, ranging from Islamic modernism to secularism.[3]

1. For the reform movement in Ottoman Turkey see Mardin (1962).
2. On the reformist ideas of thinkers in the Indian subcontinent see Brown (1999).
3. For more details, see Hourani (1983). See also Muhammad Abid al-Jabiri (1982).

The key questions dealt with the causes of deterioration and backwardness and the conditions for achieving progress. Integral to these questions were issues of government. Reformist thinkers discoursed on the types of political rule and on the role of government in society. Their views involved the reinterpretation of Islamic traditions and attempts to reconcile 'Islam' and 'modernity'.

The questions and issues that engaged Islamic thinkers at the turn of the twentieth century appear to have re-emerged, albeit in new formulations, by the latter part of the century. Thus, Arab Islamic thinkers have re-posed the questions of *nahda*, while Iranian Islamic thinkers have confronted anew the issues of modernity and authenticity. This should not be taken to mean that contemporary thinkers are rehashing old ideas or that Islamic thought is frozen in time. Instead, as will be shown, old questions are re-evaluated from a critical standpoint and new answers are proposed. What of the intervening period between the first turn-of-the-century *nahda* or modernist discourse and the critical writings of the later period? Islamic thought during this period is shaped by the historical context of interaction between the West and non-Western countries, in particular the experience of decolonisation and the rise of the nation state. During this time, the discourse of *nahda* receded into the background, while the ideologies of revolution and nationalism took centre stage. The nation state, it so appeared, had captured the project of modernity. Whether secular republican Turkey, or Arab socialist Egypt, catching up with the West, development and progress were claimed by the nation state. Nationalism was the framework for identity politics that reconciled the people with the project of modernity. Modernisation, as the articulating principle of the nationalist project, attained near hegemonic status, backed up, as it was, by the coercive apparatus of the state. This hegemonic principle was articulated within official and oppositional discourses beginning in the 1940s. The rise of Islamist movements and ideologies in the 1960s challenged this hegemony and contributed to its unhinging. It is against this background that, in the 1970s and 1980s, contemporary Islamic thinkers took up again the questions of *nahda*, modernity and authenticity.

This chapter looks at some of the key issues addressed in Islamic political thought from the turn of the twentieth century to the present. 'Islamic thought', as used here, covers writings by thinkers who work from within Islamic traditions and engage with Islamic concepts and categories. The use of this criterion for selecting writings and thinkers has excluded any in-depth examination of secular Muslim thinkers. Instead, their ideas and arguments are glimpsed through their dialogue with Islamic thinkers. It should be noted that many of the writings selected for examination do not address political questions in the narrow sense. However, in dealing with issues of philosophy, culture and history, these writings embody debates on the basis of community, the sources of knowledge and the normative standards that should guide society.

The first awakening: Islam and modernity

The construction of the *problématique* of 'awakening' in Islamic thought is grounded in the search for the elements behind the progress of the West (the Other) and the retardation of the Muslims (the Self) and how to create the conditions for a new Islamic civilisation. The *problématique* was thus constructed on the basis of a reading of the encounter with the West as taking place between unequal forces. In this context, the 'lesser' side attempted to remove the charge of inferiority. The relationship between Islam and progress was conceived of in terms of compatibility by those attempting reform from within. Others advocated a complete break with tradition. For example, Malcom Khan of Iran called for a wholesale adoption of Western customs (Mirsepassi 2000, p. 63). Our concern, here, is with thinkers who grounded themselves in Islamic traditions while attempting to engage with the challenge of Western modernity. The outcome of these efforts is conventionally referred to as 'Islamic modernism', whose main representatives were Muhammad Abduh and his disciple Rashid Rida.[4]

For Muhammad Abduh, the principles of reform were to be derived from religion. The sources of innovation could be found in the Shari'a (laws derived from the Qur'an and tradition). To deal with the issues arising from modern conditions, Muslims should draw on the dynamic principles of the Shari'a. In doing so, reason should be the guiding principle and should negate the body of classical interpretations. In elevating reason above tradition in the sense of imitation (*taqlid*), Abduh advanced the classical Islamic principle of *maslaha* (utility or interest of the community) as the overriding ethical and normative concern behind legislation and rules. Bypassing the shackles of tradition, reason was freed to deal with the questions of the time. In this task, reason is aided by revelation. Although Abduh saw reason and revelation as compatible, in the final analysis, revelation assumes a guiding role. Thus, reason, while capable of identifying right and wrong

4. The following discussion of Abduh and Rida draws extensively on Kerr (1966).

independently of revelation, may err as a result of contextual constraints. In this respect, reason should defer to revelation (Kerr 1966, pp. 107–8).

In Abduh's thought, order, stability and progress were tied to ethical rules. Influenced by the Western natural law ideas of his time, Abduh held that norms were inherent in nature and recognisable by human faculties. Religious sanction of behaviour is set in the light of the norms of nature. All the same, he appeared to establish an identity between religious ethics and the norms of nature. At the individual level, religious sanction informs ethical choices and behaviour. At the societal level, Islam's rationality provides for progress by confirming the principle of utility that directs collective actions and choices, and by revealing the general principles that should guide society. These principles are the equivalent of the laws of nature. Islam, as a rational religion, contains the norms of social action and provides the foundation of a modern society. As Aziz al-Azmeh succinctly puts it, in Abduh's thought Islam is 'transformed into a natural religion, and the reform of society is seen to reside in ridding it of the debris of history, and reviving the general sense of its original texts so they could have contemporary relevance, in such a manner that Islamic law would become a particular variant of natural law' (al-Azmeh 1993, p. 53). Utilitarian, naturalistic and rationalist, Abduh's reformed Islam is dissociated from historical Islam, retaining a form whose content is determined by reason and the interests of the time. It is this strand in Abduh's thought that is said to have carried the day among his followers, evolving into secular modernism (Hourani 1983, pp. 144–5).

Ideas about the reconciliation of Islam and modernity addressed issues of government. For instance, Muhammad Abduh affirmed the parallels between democratic forms of government and certain Islamic principles such as *shura* (consultation) which was viewed as equivalent to popular consultation through parliament. As demonstrated by Malcolm Kerr, Rashid Rida like Abduh reworked medieval doctrines with the aim of laying down the principles of reform. The main issues concerned the nature of authority, the basis and sources of legislation and the agency in charge of its application. In the first instance, the question posed was whether authority was spiritual or temporal and, by extension, whether rule was theocratic or secular.

Rida, who advocated a revival of the caliphate, viewed political authority as temporal, but subject to religious sanction. This formulation holds much of the tension that runs through modern Islamist political thought. Most present-day advocates of some form of Islamic government assert that their objective is not to establish theocratic rule. The ruler is not to be chosen on the basis of his religious or spiritual authority. Rather, it is the application of the law that invests the state with its Islamic character. In other words, legislation is the sphere in which the Islamic nature of government is actualised. At the same time, Rida, much like present-day advocates of the Islamic state, faced the problem of the relevance of the law to modern conditions. His resolution, which continues to inspire many, was to affirm that while rules must be developed to meet the imperatives of society at a given time, they must also remain within the framework of the Shari'a, which Rida argued offered general principles for governing social transactions. Another caveat to the principle of the all-encompassing Shari'a was the view that the spheres of administration and politics were the subject of the discretion of the ruler and the community (Kerr 1966, p. 189). Thus, in addition to the view that Shari'a rules in the social sphere are of a general nature and permit adaptability in line with society's interests, there also seem to be areas where it is not and cannot be operative. What, then, ensures the Islamicity of rule?

Aware of this dilemma, Rida sought mechanisms that would set constraints on the abuse of power and deviation from the general principles of the Shari'a. These constraints arise from the necessity of framing laws within the workings of *ijma'* (consensus) of the representatives of the community (*ahl al-hal wa al-aqd*: literally those who loosen and bind). Rida allowed that the field of *maslaha* is covered by a broad interpretation of current social needs and not by a literal reading of texts and Hadith (sayings of the prophet) (Kerr 1966, p. 199). Error in judgement and interpretation is avoided by consensus and by referring back to the Qur'an and the Sunna as sources of legislation which, when interpreted, would not result in disagreement. This resolution, however, is unsatisfactory. It entails a shift from the empirical level of interpretation to the ideal level of divine revelation, failing to address the question of the absence of immediacy between text and context and the fact that interpretation remains, ultimately, the work of human beings (Kerr 1966, p. 203).

On procedural matters of government, Rida deals with the question of authority and legitimacy within medieval Islamic political thought. As such, he fails to provide resolutions to the problems of checks on power, the means of ensuring legitimate government and the terms of achieving redress in cases of the abuse of power and authority. For, while Rida identifies the ruler as the one most qualified to serve, as determined by the community (*ahl al-hal wa al-'aqd*), he neglects to specify the criteria for membership in the community, the process by which the qualifications are determined and the means of withdrawing legitimacy once trust is deemed to be broken (Kerr 1966, pp. 159–64).

The relationship between religion and politics has been subject to intense debate during the latter part of the twentieth century, with the rise of movements that contest the legitimacy of secular government and call for an Islamic government. In the earlier part of the century, a religious scholar responding to different imperatives denied the existence of an Islamic form of government. Ali Abd al-Raziq, writing at the time of the abolition of the caliphate (1924) affirmed the secular nature of government in Islam. In his *Islam and the Fundamentals of Rule* (1925), he set out to demonstrate that the institution of the caliphate had no basis in Islam (Hourani 1983, pp. 185–6). Further, the form of political authority was not an essential principle of Islam. Consequently, it is a mistake to believe that there was, necessarily, no separation between religion and politics. Abd al-Raziq posited a fundamental distinction between the religious mission of the Prophet Muhammad and the polity he founded.

Abd al-Raziq's views on the caliphate were taken up again in the 1980s and 1990s in response to the Islamist claims. For instance, Muhammad Said al-Ashmawi and Faraj Fuda undertook a rereading of the early Islamic period with the aim of demonstrating the profanity of government (al-Ashmawi 1996; Fuda 1988). However, before proceeding to the contemporary debates, we should look at some important transmutations in the functionalisation of religion in the modern period and in the conceptualisation of the role of religion in politics and society. These transmutations were closely linked to historical developments such as the emergence of nationalist politics and indigenous articulations of the project of modernity.

Nationalism and the challenge of modernity were important in shaping modernist accounts of Islam, of its early history and the life of its founder. A body of literature known as the Islamiyat produced by literary figures and thinkers in Egypt during the 1930s and 1940s became a vehicle for articulating religion with modernity (Dajani 1990; Sabanegh n.d.). This is a period characterised by liberal ideas and institutions. The authors themselves were part of a liberal trend. The rationale for their endeavour may be found in the context of the writing, marked by the rise of a religio-political movement (the Muslim Brotherhood Organisation), continued British occupation, and the factionalisation of politics and Western missionary attacks.[5] These conditions propelled the authors to undertake the task of defending Islam and authenticating Muslim claims to civilisation

5. The question of how to situate these writings in Egyptian, Arab and Islamic intellectual history is subject to scholarly debate. See Smith (1999) and Gershoni and Jankowski (1997).

by producing a rationalist humanist foundation. Their endeavour resulted in the production of several biographies of the life of Muhammad and his companions. One important feature of these biographical writings is their claim to be scientific. Like Abduh, the Islamiyat authors wanted to prove that there was nothing in Islam that was inherently incompatible with science. A leading religious figure of the time, in a review of one of the biographies, pointed out that the work's author subjected all documents to the workings of reason and nothing was taken a priori (Sabanegh n.d.).

The central objective of these accounts was to assert the rationality of religion and to prove that its social moral ethos is compatible with the ethico-humanism of modern times (Sabanegh n.d.). Thus, early Islamic history was rewritten in terms of modern values and invested with a normative framework that was seen as compatible with Western values and principles (Sabanegh n.d.; Smith 1973). This mode of authenticating rationality and liberalism was integrated into national projects of development. A somewhat different path was pursued by the revolutionary forces which seized the apparatus of the state and took on the mantle of anti-imperialism and nationalism. More often than not, socialism, populism and etatism were the interpellating principles of the ruling ideology. Islamic traditions were drawn on to serve these new directions. Hence, Islamic socialism was asserted (Enayat 1982, pp. 138–50).

The politics of authenticity and identity: Islam and revolutionary action

Islamic modernism, as represented by Abduh, aimed to resolve the practical difficulties and problems that Muslims confronted in their positioning vis-à-vis the West. The resolutions were framed by a teleological view of history that incorporated modern ideas of progress and development. Yet, the implications of integrating the Self into this proposed universal movement were not worked out. Abduh argued that the Shari'a had answers for the questions of the time and that these answers corresponded to the spirit of the age in which they were posed. But given that the age was that of Western dominance and that its narrative was that of Western triumph, the answers were built on the premises this dominance put forward. It is precisely these premises and their implications that were the subject of discussion by thinkers who turned to the questions of identity and authenticity. This entailed probing the relationship between religion and reason, between religious knowledge and scientific knowledge, and between the vision of the movement of history and individual responsibility. Islamic thinkers approached these issues from different positions, drawing on various traditions of thought. As such, they offered a variety of resolutions. For the purpose of simplification, two trends may be identified. One privileged action as the expression of authenticity, the other gave primacy to self-knowledge. The first trend is associated with the revolutionary politics of militant Islamism, the second with the critical reconstruction of the Islamic heritage. These approaches are not mutually exclusive, however. Rather, they share common concerns and aims, such as seeking self-liberation and interrogating the heritage for responses to the problems of the day. This may not be sufficient to bridge the gap between the two positions, yet the overlapping interests guiding them remain. In this respect, it is interesting to consider the position of Muhammad Iqbal who raised the banner of identity much earlier in the century and who is credited with having laid the foundation for the establishment of Pakistan as an Islamic nationalist state. It is in Iqbal's insistence on the necessity of self-knowledge that we may locate the shared ground between the action-oriented thinkers and the critical thought of the heritage renewalists.[6]

Engaging with the Western project of modernity and with the decadence of the East, Muhammad Iqbal articulated a critique of both East and West and sketched out the ways of resolving the tensions arising out of their encounter. Iqbal faulted the West for rejecting religion in favour of science and for propagating a dehumanising materialism. He reproached the East for abandoning inductive reason and privileging religion as an exclusive mode of understanding to the detriment of science and philosophy. Iqbal finds the answers to the tensions between these two modes of being, which both deviate from truth, in a concept of the Self as the essence of being. The path charted by Iqbal rests on the vision of the Self as motivated by a quest for self-knowledge that is achieved in communion with the divine. The Muslim's true Self is achieved in *tawhid* ('unity', here understood as asserting oneness with the divine). The resolutions offered by Iqbal develop around the politics of authenticity in the sense of asserting an identity that is relevant to the present. Reflecting on the cultural conditions of Muslims, Iqbal argued for the need to preserve identity in the face of the corrosive effects of copying the West. To combat these effects, Iqbal proposed 'Return to the Self' as the path to truth. The idea of return to the past or to one's

6. This discussion of Iqbal's ideas is indebted to Robert D. Lee's exposition of Iqbal's thought in Lee (1997, pp. 57–82).

roots as essential for being an authentic Self and hence for Self-realisation can be found in both revolutionary Islamist writings and critical studies of the heritage. It articulates the desire to recover the unity of the Self and hence the unity of history.

The articulation of a clear line of Islamist politics occurred in the context of secular modernity adopted in Muslim countries such as Turkey, Iran and Egypt. The critique of Westernism is an important element of the shift to Islamism. An elaborate critique of Westernisation took shape in the 1960s, best represented in Jalal al Ahmad's *Gharbazadjeh*, a diagnosis of the ills that have befallen Iran in the modern period (Gheissari 1998; Borourjerdi 1996; Mirsepassi 2000). 'Westoxication' or 'occidentosis' is the malady he saw afflicting his country. Its cause was the abandonment of the traditional heritage and the adoption of Western ways in a superficial manner. The critique of Westernism points to alienation from one's roots and true identity. The imitation of the West accentuates this alienation and underscores the inauthenticity of the imitators.

The themes of alienation and the necessity of being true to the Self are articulated in Islamist writings that rejected the separation of Islam and politics and that projected a political role for religion. Islam, in this line of thought, appears as an ideology and a tradition that provides the basis of revolutionary action. Thinkers like Sayyid Qutb, Ali Shariati and Ayatollah Khomeini presented a reading of Islamic traditions that posited action as an element of faith. In essence, this reading was developed in relation to conditions of authoritarianism, and abuse of power by the existing rulers. It sought to lay down the basis for activism and engagement on the part of the Muslim. In this respect, it appealed to popular action, although, in some ways, it retained elitist visions of leadership.

The earlier systematic articulation of Islam as political is found in the writings of Sayyid Abu al-Ala al-Mawdudi. Mawdudi put forward a programme of reform based on a particular vision of Islam, emphasising the social dimension of faith. The relation between man and God is thought of as one of submission and sovereignty and is actualised in the social world. This formulation strikes a rather different tone on the concept of *tawhid* (God's unity or oneness). In contrast to Iqbal's idea of unity as knowledge of the divine, Mawdudi's unity denotes acknowledgement of the absolute sovereignty of the divine. God's sovereignty is attained in the application of divine rules and it follows that submission to God entails the establishment of an Islamic order that embodies the spirit of *tawhid*. The Islamic state constitutes an important condition of actualising the faith. Religion is not only concerned with knowledge of God, it also organises its adherents and inspires them to act (Nasr 1996, p. 57).

Mawdudi's political conceptualisation of religion becomes central in the works of radical Islamist thinkers, in particular Sayyid Qutb. However, Islamist political engagement emerged in and was shaped by different socio-historical contexts. Sunni Islamist activism has its origins in the Muslim Brotherhood Organisation and the ideas of its founder Hasan al-Banna. Al-Banna advocated a greater role for religion in regulating social relations and organising society at large. His perspective emphasised ethics and conservative morality as the foundation of society. In Sayyid Qutb's thought, the ethical and moral issues formulated by al-Banna were given a profound elaboration and articulated with a pragmatic vision of society and means of change. Qutb used the concept of *jahiliya* (state of ignorance before the advent of Islam) to describe contemporary Muslim societies (Qutb 1989).

Qutb's writings unfold as a commentary on contemporary society, expressing disenchantment with the modern way of life and a rejection of forms of organisation that deviate from the ideal set by Islam. At the foundation of Qutb's thought is the idea that Islam is not merely a religion, but a system of life. This signals the unity of the spiritual and the temporal and the absence of separation between religion and politics. This view is based on the concept of unity as embodying the relationship between man and God – a relationship understood in terms of divine sovereignty and human submission. This sense of unity is faithful to Mawdudi's and stands apart from Iqbal's. For Qutb, God's oneness is acknowledged in applying the law. This has important consequences as it leads to a notion of the Muslim as a juridical subject: one who obeys God's law.

In his earlier writings, Qutb's concern was with issues of social justice, corruption and political power. He put forward the idea that the legitimacy of rule rests on the application of the law and not the spiritual authority of the government. Qutb's commentary progresses toward the articulation of Islamist activism inspired by a metaphysical vision of society in history. In his view, knowledge of God is actualised through lived revelation. The believing community has the obligation to submit to the divine plan of history by living revelation (Abu Rabi' 1996). In the present age, characterised as *jahiliya*, the community of believers represents the vanguard struggling against distortion and alienation. Qutb identified alienation with deviation from the principle of *tawhid* caused by modern conditions. This entailed the subjugation of the individual to other human beings or to material pursuits

(Abu Rabi' 1996, p. 141). At the heart of Qutb's critique of modernity was the view that it elevated reason to the status of ultimate referential authority. Yet, for him, divine truths do not need to submit to reason. Qutb drew on Western writings to articulate this critique, finding a validation in the expressions of disenchantment with modernity by thinkers such as Bertrand Russell.[7]

Central to Qutb's view of the realisation of the Islamic way of life is the concept of *'aqidah* (doctrine), understood not just as a set of beliefs and values, but as a mode of being and of realising the individual's liberation from subjugation to other human beings (Abu Rabi' 1996, p. 141). *'Aqidah* is a dynamic way of relating to the world and asserting one's submission to God, which is simultaneously one's emancipation and freedom. As a dynamic process of understanding and interpreting the text, *'aqidah* ensures the continued relevance of the universal principles of revelation (Abu Rabi' 1996, p. 187). However, it should be noted that this evolutionary and emancipatory vision of the text exists in tension with Qutb's scripturalism (Akhavi 1997). On the one hand, Qutb asserted that meanings are fixed and inherent in texts. On the other, he opted to bypass the body of interpretations existing in the tradition. He provided his own 'inspired' reading of the Qur'an and sought to develop an interactive method of reading (Islamic envisioning). The resolution of this tension seems to lie in an enlightened interpreter, but this opens the way to claims based on visionary access to truth.

Now, this conception of *'aqidah* encompasses all aspects of the individual's life and is particularly important in the political realm. As a dynamic mode of being, it positions the Muslim in a space of resistance against oppression, corruption and abuse of power. It also necessitates activism on the part of the Muslim. This obligation was to be accorded a central place in the ideology of militant Islamists from the 1970s on. Integral to this understanding of *'aqidah*, then, is a notion of activism that is incumbent on the Muslim, a responsibility to install God's sovereignty (*hakimiya*) and to dismantle present-day *jahiliya*. This responsibility or obligation is denoted by the concept of *jihad* (struggle). *'Aqidah* in light of Qutb's reading of contemporary society places the responsibility of *jihad* on believers. They must fight against the usurpation of God's sovereignty by present-day rulers. In the context of the contemporary *jahiliya*, the task of *jihad* falls on the vanguard, the few

7. Qutb drew on Western critics of modernity, in particular Alexis Carrel. On Carrel's influence on Qutb see Choueiri (1997). An interesting exploration of the parallels between Qutb's disenchantment with modernity and critiques of modernity by contemporary Western thinkers such as Alasdair MacIntyre and Charles Taylor can be found in Euben (1999).

believers who recognise the transgression against God's sovereignty. Qutb modelled the struggle after the Meccan experience, counselling withdrawal from *jahili* society in preparation for confrontation.

The idea of struggle as forming the foundation of religion is also put forward by the Iranian thinker, Ali Shariati. Like Qutb, he delineated the framework for a militant Islamist activism. In quoting the motto of the third Shi'i Imam Husayn 'Life is verily faith (*aqidah*) and struggle (*jihad*)', the echoes of Qutb's radicalism can be heard. Once again, the fusion of theory and praxis is explained as the expression of the principle of God's oneness (*tawhid*) as guiding the Muslim's position in the world (Enayat 1982, p. 155). God's oneness translates as the unity of the universe. Conflict, contradiction and division in the social, political and economic spheres are thus incompatible with the unity of the universe. Struggles against these contradictions are carried out until the principles of *tawhid* are enshrined in society (Enayat 1982, p. 156; Akhavi 1983, p. 128). Religion, as such, constitutes a radical ideology with an emancipatory capacity, empowering Muslims to fight against oppression and Western economic and cultural hegemony (Gheissari 1998, p. 101). While Qutb, a Sunni, roots the strategy of struggle in the early period of foundation, the Meccan and Medinan experience, Shariati locates it in the early history of Shi'ism.

Shariati invests the common religious motif of the struggle between good and evil with social revolutionary meanings. In both a spiritual and a social sense, the struggle achieves the move from a lower state of self towards a higher one (Gheissari 1998, p. 105). The doctrine in its actualisation of the revolutionary potential of the individual enters into the process of self-reconstruction. Shariati conceived transformation as taking place within an organisational framework in which 'enlightened thinkers' assume vanguard positions (Borourjerdi 1996, p. 111). Parallel to Qutb's vanguard, Shariati held that Islam as ideology/doctrine constitutes and mobilises warriors and intellectuals (Borourjerdi 1998, p. 111; Shariati 1986, pp. 29–70). Similar to Qutb's vanguard, Shariati's warrior intellectuals are invested with the capacity to reinterpret texts and chart the path of transformation. Indeed, Shariati's notion of Islam as an ideology carries the same import as Qutb's *'aqidah*. Ideology guides the individual mode of action and terms of engagement (Gheissari 1998, p. 102). Shariati's image of Islam is intensely political, presenting a revolutionary ideology for mobilising the people. This is backed up by a revolutionary interpretation of the Qur'an and early Shi'i history. At the same time, religious authority is put into question and held responsible for continued oppression and absolutist rule.

Writing from the position of a third world thinker, Shariati turned to the relations of power between the West and non-Western countries (Shariati 1986). He saw in the imposition of modernity the tools of assimilation through the obliteration of indigenous culture and the destruction of traditional and moral values (Gheissari 1998, p. 100). In response, he asserted the necessity of return to the self (Shariati 1986, p. 62 and note 22). In contrast to Frantz Fanon, however, Shariati upholds the religious component of identity as essential in resisting the cultural onslaught of the West. Reassertion of identity is proposed as a resolution of alienation and liberation from Western hegemony and domination.

Reading a revolutionary message into Islamic traditions characterises the theoretical, theological and ideological contributions of a number of Shi'i and Sunni thinkers. Shi'i radicalism, with an emphasis on the role of the *ulama* as leaders of reform and guardians of rule, crystallised in Ayatollah Khomeini's doctrine of *wilayat al-faqih* (the guardianship of the jurist).[8] In the context of Shi'i thought, Khomeini sought a resolution to the problem of government posed by the absence of the Imam (the twelfth Imam being in occultation since the tenth century).[9] Rather than leaving government to corrupt rulers like the Shah, Khomeini upheld the necessity of Islamic government by investing the means of rule in the jurist. While traditional Shi'i doctrine discouraged the entanglement of jurists in political authority, it left room for activism (Rose 1983, pp. 166–88). The *ulama* and, more specifically, the *mujtahids* (experts in the interpretation of Islamic law) were given sole rights to interpret the law by the Usuli school (established in the mid-eighteenth century and dominant since the mid-nineteenth century). Prominent *mujtahids* provided believers with interpretations relating to basic practice (Mottahedeh 1995, p. 321).

Khomeini's innovation was in conferring responsibility for government on the jurist. This responsibility is acquired by virtue of knowledge of the sacred law. This he established by reference to various traditions and to the Qur'an (Bayat 1989, p. 351; Rose 1983). The jurists as such are not mere experts of religious law, but designates of God and the Imams in political as well as religious affairs (Bayat 1989, p. 352). Khomeini was critical of the

8. The doctrine is elaborated in Khomeini's *Hukumat- i Islami*, translated as 'Islamic Government'. For the full text see Khomeini (1981).
9. According to Shi'i belief, the twelfth Imam, Muhammad al-Mahdi, became absent from the physical world, but communicated with the community through a succession of four appointed deputies. This lasted for seventy years and is known as the Lesser Occultation. Following the death of the fourth appointee, no further appointment was made. This is referred to as the Greater Occultation and dates to AD 941.

ulama for being subservient to the rulers and for betraying their trust as successors to the Imams. This allows that a single jurist, possessing knowledge and moral rectitude, would rise to be a supreme jurist, holding authority over the people (Mottahedeh 1995, p. 321). Further, other *mujtahids* should submit to him. The idea of guardianship of the jurist was enshrined in Articles 5 and 107 of the 1979 Iranian constitution, but later revised in 1989 (Arjomand 1993, pp. 88–109). In practice, under Khomeini, the supreme jurist acquired absolutist powers. The new constitution (1989) dropped the qualification that the jurist be a 'source of emulation' (*marji' taqlid*), thus abandoning the requirement that the guardian be a supreme jurist.

Critical Islamic thought: history and reason as grounds of authenticity

In the latter part of the twentieth century, a new trend of Islamic thinking emerged: one that may be qualified as critical Islamic thought. The writings within this trend share a concern with the foundations of knowledge, in particular with an epistemology of knowledge as both relevant to the present and liberating of the Self. The features of this trend, the questions it poses and the modes of inquiry it follows are examined here through the works of Iranian and Arab Islamic thinkers.

The question of the relationship between religion and politics acquired new dimensions in the context of the Islamic Republic of Iran. Religious lay and clerical thinkers reflected on the theoretical implications of the innovation introduced by *wilayat al-faqih*. These post-revolutionary discourses tackle questions of self-knowledge, the foundations of knowledge and freedom as entry points into rethinking questions of action, and the nature and form of the political community.

For some, this rethinking is guided by hermeneutics as an approach to rereading and reinterpreting the text. Representing this trend among the clerics is Mojtahed-Shabestari, who uses the notion of human understanding of the Islamic sacred texts to point out that interpretation is limited by the knowledge tools available at a given historical period (Vahdat 2000, pp. 31–53). In other words, knowledge, and hence interpretation and understanding, is formed by the epistemic resources of a particular era. These resources mediate human understanding of revelation. As such, understanding and interpretation cannot have fixed value (Vahdat 2000, p. 36). Only broad and general principles are fixed, while specific precepts belong to the realm of change. It is interesting to note that according to Mojtahed-Shabestari forms of government fall under the specific (Vahdat 2000, p. 38). Human sciences such as sociology and anthropology are essential to the horizon of knowledge that should inform new interpretations (Vahdat 2000, p. 39). For Mojtahed-Shabestari, the relation of man and God does not negate human subjectivity. Rather, the relation involves dialogical interaction between the divine and human reason, ultimately confirming the human (Vahdat 2000, p. 41). This is tied to the affirmation of the individuality of faith, in the sense that each individual is free to develop his or her conception of God, the Prophet and the doctrine (Vahdat 2000, p. 44). This view has radical implications for the concept of religious authority when carried to its conclusion: there could not be an ultimate or final authority on questions of faith, let alone on practical matters of government and administration.

Discussions of the questions of religious knowledge and its scope of relevance engage with the idea of the guardianship of the jurist. In this regard, the ideas articulated by lay religious intellectual Abdolkarim Soroush have radical implications for thinking out the issues of government and the individual's position in the context of the Islamic Republic.[10] Soroush contrasts two views of the Shari'a: the view that the Shari'a is an established tradition, preserving the essence of a true and final Islam, and the view that the essence of the Shari'a cannot be captured in interpretations found in theological treaties or pronounced by *mujtahids* (Borourjerdi 1996, p. 173). The first view asserts the immutability of laws, while the second draws a distinction between the fixed and the changeable. The second view informs Soroush's work and his theory of 'the theoretical contraction and expansion of the Shari'a'.[11] It is premised on a number of interrelated postulates, the most fundamental being an epistemology of religious knowledge. Soroush advances the distinction between religion and religious knowledge: religion is fixed, religious knowledge is changing. Religious knowledge is the realm of human interpretations of the divine. These interpretations are historical and temporal, i.e. not sacred. In other words, Soroush is upholding the view that religious knowledge, by definition, is secular. This approximates the position held by secularists who argue that divine revelation ceases to be divine once it becomes the subject of human interpretation and understanding (Zakariya 1986, pp. 5–26).

Soroush's secularising impulse emerges in his recognition of the secular character of many aspects of social and political life. A related point is that

10. See Soroush (2000). For a succinct treatment of the political implications of Soroush's thought see Matin-asgari (1997).

11. This work was published as a series of articles in the leading Iranian cultural journal, *Keyhan-e Farhanghi* (Borourjerdi 1996, pp. 166–7, and Matin-asgari 1997, p. 105).

ijtihad is limited in its field of applicability to legal matters of jurisprudence. Problems of the economy, for example, do not fall within the scope of religious law. Nonetheless, religious knowledge is not excluded from addressing issues emerging in other (i.e. non-religious) fields. Dynamic *fiqh* as opposed to traditional *fiqh* aims to deal with contemporary social and non-esoteric questions (Borourjerdi 1996, p. 166). Finally, religious knowledge is tied with other fields of knowledge, once more asserting its historical character (Borourjerdi 1996, p. 170). Taking a hermeneutic view of interpretation, Soroush concludes that no interpretation is definitive (Matin-asgari 1996, p. 105).

Of the political implications of Soroush's ideas, the most challenging is the rejection of an exclusive politico-religious knowledge. From this perspective, an official understanding of religion proffered by an official group becomes untenable. Like Mojtahed-Shabestari, Soroush posits freedom as a condition of belief. Religion as an ideology undermines freedom. At the same time, religion has a place in the public sphere, allowing that the clergy represent one group, but not the ruling group.

In Arab countries, debates on the role of religion in politics and society have taken place in the context of a perceived generalised crisis reaching all domains of life. The failure of the national state and the challenge posed by the Islamists are the two most important elements of this crisis. In this context, the relation to the past and to tradition has emerged as the subject of much rethinking that takes the shape of intellectual projects by a number of Islamic thinkers. Before proceeding to an overview of the key ideas and concepts put forward in these projects, it is important to highlight the parameters delimiting the various positions from the past. On one side, secularists and liberal leftists proposed the idea of rupture as capturing the relationship to the past (Zakariya 1987). From a progressivist view of history, it was argued that Islam should undergo reformation similar to the Christian European experience (Amin 1989). Further, Marxist critiques of religious reason presented an indictment of religion, laying the blame for defeats, authoritarianism and retardation on religious thought (al-Azm 1969; Laroui 1976). In this vein, Abdallah Laroui argued for the need to acknowledge the rupture with the past and its modes of thinking, and for the imperative of joining in the march of civilisation. The underlying premise of these positions is the idea of the universality of civilisation. The objective is to situate Arab–Islamic history within a world history. This stands in contrast to the position held by the advocates of cultural specificity who insist on the particularism of the characteristics that define Islamic society and history. A distinct position is represented in the attempt to transcend the opposition between universality and specificity and provide a critical perspective on the heritage. Heritage renewal projects are guided by varying perspectives on history. However, they all aim at defining what history is and how it constitutes the pathway to knowledge of the Self and the Other.

Rather than bypassing or forgoing the past, Islamic thinkers working on the grounds of the heritage pursue excavation for the purposes of setting down new foundations and for reconstruction.[12] Towards this end, Egyptian philosopher Hasan Hanafi embarked on a massive study of the heritage.[13] Hanafi's objective, like that of other heritage excavationists, is historicising the heritage. In his case, this means reading it in light of the needs of the present. Hanafi, adopting a phenomenological perspective on the heritage, asserts that it represents the psychological storage inherited from the past. His project of heritage renewal entails mapping out the storehouse of consciousness (co-terminous with the heritage) as its ideas continue to guide behaviour in the present. Renewal for Hanafi is the task of the revolutionary. *Turath* (heritage) renewal is also integral to the search for self-identity that may come from identifying the relationship between the Self and the Other (Hanafi 1981). Renewal of the heritage is capable of doing this because it means discovering the Self, authenticating it, and freeing it from invading cultures, beliefs and methods (Hanafi 1981).

Renewal is a twofold process: a description of the behaviour and its transformation for the purpose of social action (Hanafi 1981, p. 16). This description is akin to psychoanalysis, exorcising the ghosts of the past. Hanafi's description is not static, consisting of a mere outline of accumulations of representations throughout history. On the contrary, the description aims to reveal the dynamics of relations between the present and the past in consciousness (Hanafi 1981, p. 16). This dynamic view of the heritage necessitates a study of the social dimension of the inherited, that is, placing the tradition in the historical context of its production and tracing its reproduction in relation to the social conditions of the present.

Hanafi's renewal of the heritage is anchored in a number of epistemological principles that one may argue undermine his objective of historicising the heritage. The process of renewal of the sciences, particularly the rational

12. Other heritage studies have included projects aimed at authenticating a revolutionary socialist tradition in Islamic history. For example, see Muruwah (1978).

13. The discussion here pertains to the project as outlined in his introductory work (Hanafi 1981). The project remains in progress and has resulted so far in a multi-volume oeuvre entitled *Min al-'Aqidah Ila Thawra* (From Doctrine to Revolution).

religious sciences, begins with deconstructive steps to be followed by reconstruction. A first step involves description of how each science emerged out of the intuitive understanding of the text, and how the interpretations of the text evolved in relation to the needs of the age (this step is identified as the logic of revelation). Second was a description of the cognitive processes which determined the nature of intellectual phenomena and which are behind the constitution of science. These are unified cognitive operations which emerge in every civilisation from one central given: revelation. By knowing them, the interpreter can reconstitute the science in the context of the present age (the logic of phenomena). Third was to determine the positive and negative phenomena in each science. By this Hanafi means the theoretical basis of science as it either reflects the logic of revelation or deviates from it. The final step is a reconstruction in which the preceding theoretical construct is set on new foundations, linguistically and analytically (Hanafi 1981, p. 127).

Hanafi holds the development of a theory of interpretation grounded in revelation to be the key to social transformation. However, in his methodology Hanafi moves from a phenomenological hermeneutical approach to reading the sciences toward a transcendental phenomenology. Although Hanafi's first step aims to uncover the historical interpretation of the text, taking into account the historical conditions which contextualise the understanding itself, he goes on to posit the cognitive operations that enter into the constitution of the religious sciences as an emanation of revelation. Further, he attributes deviation from the logic of revelation to the workings of history. History appears as an accessory existing outside the framework of revelation and thus external to truth. In effect, Hanafi ends up invoking a transcendental consciousness, sacrificing both the historical imperatives of the present and the historicity of revelation.

Others working on the same grounds of the Arab–Islamic heritage have assumed the task of restoring its historical dimension. They have produced studies that attempt to distil forms of cultural production that came to constitute the foundations of knowledge. At work also is the classification and periodisation of these forms. A common periodisation divides Islamic history into the age of flourishing and the age of decadence, or in Mohammed Arkoun's terms, the age of heritage production and the age of heritage consumption. In some of the works, continuity with the heritage emerges as an imperative, although different senses of continuity can be detected. This concern is evident in Muhammad Abid al-Jabiri's archaeology of the

Arab–Islamic heritage.[14] Though his analysis pays close attention to discontinuities and ruptures, the notions of tradition and continuity do not vanish amid the chronicles of breaks and interruptions.

The questions raised by al-Jabiri in reference to the Arab–Islamic heritage summarise the issues at stake (al-Jabiri 1985). These are stated as follows: what is the relationship between the heritage and the present? How can the relationship with the heritage be renewed? How can it be present in the Self's intellectual life? According to al-Jabiri, understanding of the heritage guides the uses that are made of it. So, what is left of Arab–Islamic philosophy? Al-Jabiri argues that the question is not what to take or what to leave out, but how to invest the heritage in the present. Al-Jabiri's answer is that the heritage must be deconstructed to understand its historical currents and struggles and then excavated for what could be developed now.

Al-Jabiri's answers arise out of a reading of history as it emerges in the Arab–Islamic encounter with the West. As such, he contends that recovering reason (the motor of universal development) cannot take place by adopting a European cultural frame of reference as early Muslim liberals did, but by absorbing and reviving the Arab–Islamic heritage in present consciousness. Al-Jabiri's revival of the heritage is not wholesale. Rather, what he is interested in reviving is the liberal and the rationalist dimensions. Al-Jabiri analyses the constitutive epistemological principles of the Arab mind – principles that constitute modes of Islamic reasoning. As noted by Abu Rabi', this interest in constitutive cognitive principles is motivated by an inquiry into the relationship between knowledge and power, or cognition and ideology (Abu Rabi' 1996, p. 28). Al-Jabiri demonstrates that the Arab mind is a constituted reason: that is, a set of principles governing the production of knowledge. This epistemology had its roots in *jahiliya* (the pre-Islamic period) and found its elaboration in the Islamic period. An example of the elements of the constitutive system continuing to govern knowledge is the Arabic language. Al-Jabiri sees this as setting constraints on knowledge as it froze the linguistic tools and forms, shackling the ability to think freely.

Al-Jabiri's archaeology of the Arab mind posits the dominance of the *bayan* cognitive system: that is, reason that relies on the text and tradition for presenting evidence and developing arguments. This contrasts with the *burhan* tradition, where knowledge is produced through reflection and experimentation (rationalism). *Bayan* is framed within Qur'anic discourse and

14. For an English-language introduction to al-Jabiri's work see al-Jabiri (1999).

its dialectic of reason and unreason, the universe and its order, the Qur'an and its proof, all constituting the sole reference for reason in the Qur'an. Within this cognitive system, analogical reason emerged as the main principle governing knowledge production. Text, tradition, *ijma* and *qiyas* are all referential authorities in the service of religious doctrine and setting constraints on reason in the sense of *burhan*.

Al-Jabiri's deconstruction of the history of reason in Arab–Islamic thought is central to his project of authenticating reason in the heritage. This he does by identifying the rational elements that continue to be of relevance to the present. These are the basis of his Andalusian project. The project provides the outlines for a new 'age of recording' (i.e. foundational age) and is presented as evolving and continuous. Al-Jabiri's rationalism finds its model in the critical rational discourse of Ibn Rushd (Averroës) (1126–98), as the crowning moment of the critical trend of thought in *fiqh*, theology and philosophy. The moment of Ibn Rushd is the highest point of development in the Islamic heritage and remains relevant to the present. Ibn Rushd's moment is the stage of rupture with gnosticism and the fusion of religion and philosophy attempted by Ibn Sina (Avicenna). It is also the rupture with the theologians' fusion of science and religion (al-Jabiri 1985, pp. 40–50). Ibn Rushd presented an alternative in the separation of religion and philosophy as distinct fields of knowledge which should be dealt with from within (al-Jabiri 1985, p. 51). For al-Jabiri, Ibn Rushd's approach to religion and philosophy is the one which should be adopted to achieve authenticity and contemporaneity. It is the method upon which interaction with the Other and research in the heritage should be based. In tracing the movement of philosophy from Ibn Sina to Ibn Rushd, al-Jabiri is not interested only in grounding rational thought in Islamic history, but also in reconstructing a foundation for secular rationalism in Ibn Rushd's separation of philosophy and religion. Authenticity as theorised by al-Jabiri is the *problématique* of secular rationalism as conceived from within the Arab–Islamic heritage, in opposition to religious rationality or rationalism within the *problématique* of Enlightenment thinking (al-Jabiri 1986, p. 71).

Of the various heritage projects proposed by Arab and Islamic thinkers, Mohammed Arkoun's offers a radical historicisation of the heritage (Arkoun 1987a).[15] This means situating the text and the tradition in their historical context, tracing the mechanisms of producing orthodoxy, and uncovering the role of myth in shaping the religious and social imaginary. Arkoun

15. For an English-language presentation of Arkoun's ideas see Arkoun (1987b).

problematises the claims to truth associated with the tradition, stripping them of their self-evidentness. Arkoun's project of establishing a science of applied Islamology proposes methodological principles and conceptual categories that should guide the study of Islamic history and particularly the development of Islamic reason. Integral to this project is a rereading of the founding period of Islam. Priority is given to the Qur'an and the Medinan experience, the generation of the companions, the struggle for the caliphate/imamate, tradition and orthodoxy (Arkoun 1987a, p. 16).

In Arkoun's project, the interaction between the Qur'an and Muhammad's experience and the materiality of society should constitute the subject of investigation (Arkoun 1987a, p. 17). This undertaking aims to recover the historicity of the text. According to this approach, the meanings and interpretations of the text must be understood in relation to the lived context in the time of revelation. Arkoun clearly aims to identify the meanings that were later projected onto the text and which invested in subsequent readings the idea of the transcendence of meaning. In the same vein, he is interested in the process that resulted in the mythologisation of the companions and their production as idealised model characters (Arkoun 1987a, p. 18). In all of this, he suggests paying attention to the role of myth in consolidating the 'real' or 'true' foundational information that constitutes the Islamic heritage.

Arkoun's own reading of the heritage brings into focus the process of producing orthodoxy and the epistemology that guided this production. His objective here is to demonstrate the historicity of Islamic reason by underlining how the claims to knowledge and truth intertwined with power struggles (Arkoun 1987a, p. 50). Orthodoxy is the product of classical Islamology in the founding period taken up by scholastic Islamology. The features of this epistemology were the predominance of particular theological tenets (*Ash'ari*) and the fixing of jurisprudential principles by Shafi'i. While in the period of production orthodoxy was relevant to its context and expressed power struggles, it became a mere act of repetition divorced from its sociological reality in the later periods (Arkoun 1987a, pp. 66–78). Yet by virtue of claims to transcendental truth, it dominates the intellect, establishing transcendental authority and closing the door of reason. In classical orthodoxy reasoning is anchored in the supreme sovereignty and legitimacy of verses and Hadith, the method through which theological forms and formulae spread and were generalised and in turn were supported by the jurisprudential discourse in particular during the scholastic period. The methods of jurisprudence established the idea of the transparency of the text, hence ruling out semiotic analysis (Arkoun 1987a, p. 79). They also work to fix the historicity of society by imposing 'God's rule' in all conditions – reason deduces the rule following the devised methods, thus forbidding innovation.

The methodological and conceptual recommendations made by Arkoun for rereading the heritage, and for Muslim repositioning from it, can be seen at work in historical revisionist writings and in the critical re-evaluation of Islamic knowledge. In recent years, some authors have undertaken to provide a corrective to the contemporary Islamists' idealised and mythologised image of the original Islamic community. In this respect, Mahmud Sayyid al-Qimani and Khalil Abd al-Karim attempted to reconstruct the socio-economic, political and intellectual context of the rise of Islam (al-Qimani 1996; Abd al-Karim 1997). Their objective is to institute a historical perspective on Muhammad's message and the community/state he founded. Establishing the historicity of revelation is thus conceived as an important step towards the secularisation of Islamic identity. Revisionist writings offer Muslims a new approach for dealing with and positioning themselves vis-à-vis the foundational period of the religion. This approach does not reject the heritage or deny it but affirms it in its historicity. It follows that if the heritage is to inspire or guide the Muslim in his/her present, it will do so in the light of an understanding of the historical context in which it developed and with a critical mind as to how this can link up with the present. Other revisionists, some less radical, but nonetheless endeavouring to respond to the Islamist claims and to the challenge of authenticity, are working to ground a liberal Islamic tradition or inaugurate an age of Islamic reformation.[16]

Conclusion

From the above presentation we can identify certain mechanisms of Islamic thought in the twentieth century which can characterise it as foundational or epistemological. From Muhammad Abduh's attempt to reconcile reason and revelation to Mohammed Arkoun's critique of Islamic reason, the overriding concern takes the form of epistemic questioning on the grounds of knowledge. This foundational quest appears motivated by the desire to

16. I have in mind here liberal Islamic thinkers such as Husayn Ahmad Amin and revisionist thinkers such as Hamid Nasr Abu Zayd (a critic of religious discourse) and Muhammad Shahrur (hailed by some as the 'new Luther').

reinterpret and reconstruct tradition as a liberating force. In contrast to secular thinkers who advise abandoning the heritage and starting anew, Islamic thinkers offer the retrieval of the potentialities in the heritage as a means of resolving the tensions that arise out of modern conditions.

At the turn of the century Islamic thinkers attempted to prove the compatibility of Islam and modernity. At times this effort entailed adopting the premises of the Western experience of modernity and the narrative articulating it. On the heels of Islamic modernism and in the context of state authoritarianism and repression, Islamic thinkers articulated a challenge to the presumed universality of Western modernity. This challenge emerged in relation to modern conditions and particular experiences of modernity. It confirmed that the Western narrative is an assertion of its dominance and is imbricated in relations of power and domination at the local level. The discourse of 'the Return to the Self' offered terms of disengagement from these relations, not by recreating the past but by confronting the conditions of cultural hegemony. Though seeking to provide a dynamic view of tradition and deploy it as a springboard for action, revolutionary conceptions of Islam as a mobilising doctrine are based on ontological premises that, in some respects, undermine conditions of freedom. In viewing revelation as the ultimate source of knowledge, questions of interpretation, of how to adjudicate claims to truth, and how to safeguard individual autonomy were compromised. These are precisely the issues that preoccupy critical Islamic thinkers. To ground reason and rationalism in Islamic history underlies projects of deconstruction and reconstruction of the heritage. An important objective in these intellectual enterprises is establishing the historicity of the heritage and of knowledge. Ultimately, the main objective of these thinkers is to provide the terms through which Muslims can own their past without being imprisoned by it.

EPILOGUE
The grand dichotomy of the twentieth century

STEVEN LUKES

> At the end of this century it has for the first time become possible to see what a world may be like in which the past, including the past in the present, has lost its role, in which the old maps and charts which guided human beings, singly and collectively, through life no longer represent the landscape through which we move, the sea on which we sail (Hobsbawm 1994, p. 16).

In this concluding chapter I ask what story can be told about the overall framework of political thought across the twentieth century. I shall explore Hobsbawm's suggestion, cited in the epigraph above, by applying it to politics and asking how political issues and conflicts over them were thought about in the course of the century. In particular, I shall focus on the idea, or metaphor, of political space as divided between left and right, examine its formal features, trace its history over the span of the last century and ask whether, and if so when and why, the old left–right maps and charts have lost their applicability.

A preliminary word should be said about Hobsbawm's cartographic analogy. 'Maps and charts' do not, of course, relate to our singular and collective lives as geographical maps and nautical charts relate to landscapes and seas. They enter and partly shape such lives. We live and act by them: they partly constitute what they map and chart. Furthermore, 'left' and 'right' are classifications that are both cognitive and symbolic: they promise understanding by interpreting and simplifying the complexities of political life and they stimulate emotions, awaken collective memories and induce loyalties and enmities. They are current among actors – whether politically active or not – though understood differently and to different degrees by different actors, and are thus indispensable to observers. They are, in short, Durkheimian *représentations collectives*. So the question, more precisely formulated, becomes: whether, or better to what extent, when and why did 'left–right' ways of representing politics cease to make sense of the practice of politics in the course of the twentieth century.

A final preliminary observation: the claim that the left–right opposition has had its day is neither new nor politically neutral. It has been made repeatedly in the course of the century in various quarters and typically with political intent. In 1931 the French radical philosopher Alain responded to a questionnaire launched by the monarchist publicist Beau de Lomenie entitled *Qu'appelez-vous droite et gauche?* with his famous aphorism:

> When someone asks me whether the split between parties of the right and parties of the left, between men of the right and men of the left still makes sense, the first idea that strikes me is that the man asking this question is certainly not a man of the left (Beau de Lomenie 1931, p. 64).

In 1988 Timothy Garton Ash wrote in an essay on 'Reform and Revolution':

> If asked 'How do you recognize a leftist oppositional intellectual in East Central Europe today?' the unkind answer might be: 'The leftist intellectual is the one who says that the categories left and right no longer have any significance in East Central Europe.' The right does not say that (Garton Ash 1989, p. 237).

Yet Anthony Giddens, author of *Beyond Left and Right* (Giddens 1994) and promoter of the 'third way' politics of Blair and Schroeder, asserted in 2000 that:

> the division between left and right certainly won't disappear, but the division between them has less compelling power than it used to do. In the absence of a redemptive model, to be on the left is indeed primarily a matter of values . . . third way politics is unequivocally a politics of the left (Giddens 2000, pp. 38, 39).

These three quotations suggest a possible narrative whose plausibility we must consider. The first two passages suggest that the half-century separating them saw a decline from the left's intellectually confident self-assertion in the France of the 1930s to a defensive disavowal of its own identity in the last days of communism. The third exhibits a further retreat: the left may survive as 'a matter of values' but it is no longer distinguished from the right in offering alternative analyses or the promise of an alternative institutional design for the economy that is both feasible and superior to what exists. Yet the authors of all three passages employ the distinction and thus share the assumption that, despite claims to the contrary, what is left and what is right were and remain recognisable.

As for the major social and political movements of the century, their amenability to classification in left–right terms is by no means self-evident, and yet the distinction is helpful in enabling one to make this very point. Thus Zeev Sternhell's classic study of fascist ideology in France is entitled *Neither Right nor Left*. At the end of the nineteenth century, he argues, there was born a 'particularistic and organicist tradition, often dominated by a local variant of cultural nationalism that was sometimes, but not always, of a biological or racial character, very close to the *volkisch* tradition in Germany' which 'launched an all-out attack on liberal democracy, its philosophical foundations, its principles and their application. It was not only the institutional structures of the Republic that were questioned, but the whole heritage of the Enlightenment.' Subsequently, 'intellectual dissidents and rebels, of both the new right and the new left . . . together forged that brilliant and seductive ideology of revolt that the historian identifies as fascism' (Sternhell 1996 [1986], pp. x, 302). As for the Marxist tradition in its historically conquering form of Leninist and then Stalinist communism, this too was inhospitable to the categories of left and right. Marxist and communist parties and groups might be viewed as on the left in parliamentary democracies, but the continuing significance and prospective survival of left and right formed no part of communism's self-understanding, which was essentially Jacobin and aimed at the total occupation of political space (an affinity especially marked within French Marxism, as Professor Khilnani observes). Indeed, where the term 'left' was used, it was used pejoratively, as in Lenin's pamphlet, *'Left-Wing' Childishness and the Petty-Bourgeois Mentality* (Lenin 1969 [1918]). As for nationalism, its numerous twentieth-century incarnations across the world, examined from different angles by Professors Mayall and Parekh, span the range from (right-wing) dominant, virulent expansionist powers to (left-wing) national liberation struggles. Yet all, to different degrees, exhibit nationalism's 'janus-like' character, embodying, on the one hand, Enlightenment-based ideas of popular sovereignty, mass democracy, the rights of citizens, elite-driven modernisation and independence of external controlling power; and, on the other, narrow cultural or ethnically based particularism, the 'invention of tradition', collectivist myth-making and mass manipulation, a predisposition to conflict with other nations and oppressive discrimination against internal minorities in the name of some 'imagined community'.

Left and right: formal features

Yet this spatial representation of political life is remarkably durable and pervasive. It has lasted two centuries, from the French Revolution to the aftermath of communism, spreading from France via Italy to the rest of the world and surviving successive political movements, parties and ideologies. It is also remarkably adaptable, apparently making sense in utterly diverse political contexts in different societies at different stages of development. Politics, it has been observed, is said to have its left and right in China as in Lebanon, in Russia as in Switzerland. The churches have their left and right in the United States as well as in France and so do the universities in their academic debates whether in Norway or Brazil (Laponce 1981, p. 28).

And it is general in a way that other political classifications are not. Being 'visual and spatial . . . it is immediately understandable and easily translatable across cultures' (Laponce 1981, p. 27). 'Liberal and conservative', 'progressive and reactionary', 'red and white' are all more context-specific; whereas 'left and right' can be used both to identify particular political divisions and to relate them to divisions in a wider range of other contexts, both past and present, within and across different societies, and to recognisable historical traditions.[1]

It is also a remarkably versatile spatial metaphor, for it allows for several possibilities. Left and right may dichotomise political space, or constitute opposite regions along a continuum or spectrum, or flank a centre. (And, as Norberto Bobbio has argued, that centre may, in turn, be seen as 'included', as a distinctive alternative that separates the other two, or as 'inclusive', promising to supersede them by incorporating them in a 'higher synthesis' such as a 'third way': Bobbio 1996, p. 7). Indeed, it allows one to move easily from one of these to the other, or to think of them all at once. We use this versatile metaphor (which has lost its quality as a live metaphor and has become everyday political common sense) in all these ways to map familiar political positions and to place unfamiliar ones. The journalist stepping off the aeroplane on a new assignment finds it indispensable. As Professor Lipset wrote long ago, 'at any given period and place it is usually possible to locate parties on a left to right continuum' (Lipset 1960, p. 223). Even fascists, as

1. Moreover, as we shall see, these other contrasts do not map on to that between left and right, either because, like liberal/conservative, they address different issues or because, like red/white, they are more narrowly tied to historical context.

Professor Payne observes, can be grouped into left, right and centre schools of economic thought.

It is not, however, necessary, though it seems natural. Before September 1789 it was unknown and it only caught on from the 1820s. Before that other spatial metaphors were present in the iconography of political space: notably verticality, signifying hierarchy and concentricity, as with the 'Sun King'. The perception of politics as a laterally organised conflict between forces that are opposed and themselves internally divided in left and right segments was (accidentally) invented at a particular time and place and has its own history, which, in principle, could and perhaps will or should come to an end.

Its pre-twentieth-century history can be briefly told. Its birth and sporadic use during the French Revolution were a false start because, although it distinguished opposed political groupings in the legislatures (initially those for and against the king's suspensive veto), the predominant preoccupation during this period was to abolish all political divisions. Its true birth dates from the restoration of the French monarchy following the defeat of Napoleon, and in particular from the parliamentary session of 1819–20 when it entered 'into customary practice in a coherent and regular form' in the division between liberals and ultras, deriving from the memory of 1789 and 'opposing old and new France' (Gauchet 1997). By the late 1820s the question of forming alliances capable of achieving a parliamentary majority was already framed in left–right terms between liberals and royalists, but it was with the achievement of universal manhood suffrage in France in 1848 that left and right entered mass politics, applying not merely to the topography of parliamentary chambers but now as categories of political identity, spreading rapidly across the parliamentary systems of the world.

Its role within representative democracies has a further feature: left and right entail one another. Without a left there is no right and vice versa. Moreover, laterality suggests that left and right, and points between, are on the same level. So the metaphor neatly corresponds to Gauchet's observation that the symbolism of left and right can provide flags for 'extreme passions in politics' while also being 'the emblem of moderation' (Gauchet 1997, p. 2585). The acceptance of left and right symbolises 'consent to discord' – the acceptance, that is, of political pluralism in one of its several senses: of permanent, irreducible, institutionalised conflict as inseparable from democracy and a rejection of the idea that such conflict is a pathological deviation blocking the path to a unified, reconciled society. In short, we could say that the left–right division embodies what we might call the *principle of parity*:

that implicit in the symbolism of laterality is the idea that alternative political positions – left, right and points between – co-exist on the same level, and that political alternatives are legitimately equal contenders for the support of citizens.

But of course we know that parity does not exist between left and right, either in the real world or the world of symbolism. As Laponce has remarked, 'Left and right linked politics, at the level of the cosmos, with other symbolic systems, social and religious in particular, that had already been used to explain man, society and the transcendental' (Laponce 1981, p. 68). Yet in such symbolic systems the pre-eminence of the right is virtually a cultural universal (see Hertz 1973 [1928]; Needham 1973). Consider the evidence of Indo-European languages, such as the connotations of 'sinister', 'gauche', 'linkisch' and 'maladroit' and by contrast those of 'right' and 'rectitude', 'droit' and 'droite', 'diritto' and 'Recht' (Arabic, apparently, displays a similar bias). The words for right connote dexterity, uprightness, what is customarily, morally and juridically correct, and the words for left their opposites.

Or consider the history of religions and the results of comparative ethnography, the evidence of which was summed up by Robert Hertz as follows:

> Thus the opposition between right and left has the same meaning and application as the series of contrasts, very different yet reducible to common principles, presented by the universe. Sacred power, source of life, truth, beauty, virtue, the rising sun, the male sex, and – I can add, the right side; all these terms, like their contraries, are interchangeable... from one end of the world to the other of humanity, in the sacred places where the worshipper meets his god, in the cursed places where devilish pacts are made, on the throne as well as in the witness box, on the battlefield and in the peaceful workroom of the weaver, everywhere one unchangeable law governs the functions of the two hands... The supremacy of the right hand is at once an effect and a necessary condition of the order which governs and maintains the universe (Hertz 1973 [1928], pp. 14, 19, 20).

Virtually everywhere the right symbolically prevails. God made Eve out of Adam's left side, and the forces of evil are on the left in medieval Judaism. According to the New Testament, the Son of Man 'shall set the sheep on his right hand, but the goats on his left': to the former he shall say 'Come ye, blessed of my Father, inherit the kingdom prepared for you from the beginning of the world' but to the latter 'Depart from me, ye cursed, into everlasting fire, prepared for the devil and his angels' and the Son of Man shall sit 'on the right hand of power'. Qur'anic theology displays the same bias. Tribal cultures show the same pattern. And in all these societies the right also prevails in ceremonial customs and social etiquette – in taking oaths, saluting, concluding marriages and other contracts, in greetings and the expression of respect and friendship.

In the politics of representative democracies, however, the symbolism of left and right can be seen as signifying a rejection of this pre-eminence or dominance. Left and right are *représentations collectives* which embody the principle of parity: that in representative democracies each has equal standing. It was, however, in the course of the nineteenth century that the left succeeded in establishing this principle, in France and elsewhere, and the right which for long opposed it. This perhaps explains what Louis Dumont calls the 'ideological predominance' that the left has enjoyed (Dumont 1990). It is perhaps why in political matters it has usually been the left that has been most forthright in drawing the distinction and proclaiming its own identity and why the right, as Alain noted, often denied the distinction and why it tended to acknowledge its identity with some reluctance and even embarrassment. Yet enemies of parity can certainly be found in both directions. It is not only reactionaries or religious 'fundamentalists' or nationalists who regard conflicts between left and right as pathological symptoms to be overcome in some future imagined unity. The Marxist tradition too placed no intrinsic value upon parity in either capitalist or 'real socialist' societies and envisaged communism as a community of political and moral convergence. There was a considerable Marxist and Marxisant presence on the left in some countries, above all France, as Professor Khilnani's chapter amply shows, but 'left 'and 'right' were never, as we have seen, part of the classical Marxist lexicon, and indeed 'leftist' was used as a term of abuse. Where they came into power, communist parties systematically destroyed the possibility of parity: hence the ideological reversal noted by Garton Ash.

From this brief discussion we can draw a single overall conclusion: that perceiving political divisions in left–right terms has both reflected and constituted the politics of representative democracies by means of a natural-seeming but historically contingent spatial metaphor that is durable, pervasive, adaptable, general and exceptionally versatile, and which embodies the principle of endemic and legitimate conflict between alternatives of equal standing.

But, having considered these formal features, we must now examine the *content* of the left–right model of political life. What, in the course of the twentieth century, has distinguished the left from the right? By what features can parties, movements and ideologies of the left and the right be recognised, in familiar and unfamiliar contexts?

What divides left from right?

At the turn of the new century this question is not just an analytical one, of interest to scholars. With the fall of communism and the so-called crisis of social democracy, those parties and intellectuals who continue to identify themselves with the left seek to know what they are identifying themselves with. As left parties increasingly accept a capitalist framework and left intellectuals accept market principles and the logic of profit, and even question the principle of redistribution and social transfers, it becomes important to know whether the left denotes socialism or social democracy in all their variety, or whether it names a longer tradition and history of which these have been the latest incumbents but which can be thought of as surviving the abandonment of some of their essential commitments.

In trying to answer the question posed, we should avoid several dead ends. One is the politically motivated temptation to respond to the crisis of identity on the left by devising a 'sanitised' conception of the left, for present consumption, with the unacceptable assumptions and beliefs of the past removed: a true or pure or sensible left from which the errors and excesses of the past are seen as deviations. A second dead end is reductionism: that is, seeking to identify left and right by reference to their social, psychological or policy-related correlates. Thus sociologists have focused on the social bases of voting, such as class; psychologists on attitudes or personality traits; and political scientists on orientations towards policy, such as governmental intervention in the economy. But such approaches fail to address the central issue at hand, namely, what (if anything) at the level of political thought (if not theory) can account for such choices, attitudes and orientations: what entitles us to classify them as left or right? A third dead end is essentialism: the supposition that we can arrive at cut-and-dried definitions based on mutually exclusive principles expressed in alternative conceptual vocabularies that distinguish mutually exclusive political moralities or world views. Such an approach is a non-starter, if only because all political thought is framed throughout in terms of essentially contested concepts (such as 'liberty', 'equality' and 'democracy') whose interpretation is at issue across the left–right spectrum. And a fourth dead end is the opposite of this – a thoroughgoing nominalism suggesting that the answer is always local and context-specific: that what is left and right is simply a matter of local nomenclature and can vary indefinitely across time and space. In seeking an answer, it is best to respect, as far as possible, the variety of left and right movements, parties and thinkers while presuming that they are respectively united by more than words: by common origins, intersecting histories, shared, if contested, identities and distinct, identifiable traditions.

Louis Dumont has suggested that the French left has been characterised by a principled commitment to individualism: as a pure ideal repeatedly invoked as fresh as ever in its perfection and gradually and incompletely realised, transforming political and in some measure social institutions. Thus he cites the centrality of the 'Rights of Man' to the Dreyfus affair and the remark of Jaurès that 'the human individual is the measure of all things', and he refers to Karl Polanyi's view of socialism as the end product of Christian individualism (Dumont 1990). Is individualism, as Dumont suggests, at the core of the left, while 'holism', valuing the global society above and against the individual, is to be found on the right? The trouble with this view, as Gauchet remarks, is that it implies too 'unilateral a view of both right and left, greatly underestimating the internal contradictions of each' (Gauchet 1997, p. 2589). Such an account might fit the liberals of the Restoration, but, as part II of this volume amply shows, the various twentieth-century lefts have not lacked awareness of the imperatives of political mobilisation, organisation and collective discipline, repeatedly proclaiming and implementing policies of planning and law and order, and invoking patriotism and the common good. Conversely, the right has always, in France as elsewhere, been split between attachment to a hierarchical, organic collectivism, whether traditional or, as with fascism, revolutionary, and to an entrepreneurial, free-market capitalism that proclaims equal property rights and equality of opportunity. In this connection, the role of nationalism, discussed by Professor Mayall, is interesting. For instance, it migrated from left to right in the course of the nineteenth century in France; only to migrate once more leftwards by the time of the Algerian War, when the anti-colonialist left sided with third world nationalists. In short, left and right, in France and elsewhere, have distinctive ways of being both individualist and collectivist.

Nor does it appear much more persuasive to distinguish left from right, as various authors have, by reference to their fundamental attitudes towards tradition (cited in Bobbio 1996). Is the right concerned above all to safeguard tradition whereas the left's purpose is liberation from the chains imposed by the privileges of race, status, class and so on? Or is the distinction based on attitudes to power, the right seeing it as a principle of cohesion, the left as a source of discrimination? But there are ingrained traditions of the left and indeed, in face of neo-liberalism in recent times, the left has often appeared as the guardian of tradition; and there are left-wing and right-wing ways of interpreting what counts as cohesion, discrimination and indeed power itself. Nor, as Bobbio has effectively shown, is it helpful to equate the left–right distinction with that between moderation and extremism. What extremism of the left and of the right share is hostility to democracy. This 'brings them together, not because of their position on the political spectrum, but because they occupy the two extreme points of that spectrum. The extremes meet' (Bobbio 1996, p. 21). (This is an effective riposte to Professor O'Sullivan's suggestion that 'the influential spectrum analysis of politics' is 'misleading' in bracketing conservatism with fascism on the right end of the spectrum.)

Perhaps a clue to the answer we are seeking lies in the symbolic reversal of left and right referred to above. Perhaps what unifies the left as a tradition across time and space is its very rejection of the symbolic hierarchy and the inevitability of the inequalities it sanctifies. What this suggests is that the left denotes a tradition and a project, which found its first clear expression in the Enlightenment[2] which puts in question sacred principles of social order, contests unjustifiable but remediable inequalities of status, rights, powers and condition and seeks to eliminate them through political action. Its distinctive core commitment is to a demanding answer to the question of what equality means and implies. It envisions a society of equals and takes this vision to require a searching diagnosis, on the widest scale, of sources of unjustifiable discrimination and dependency and a practical programme to abolish or diminish them. It starts from the basic humanist idea of equality: the *moral* principle that all human beings are equally deserving of concern and respect, that they should treat one another as ends not means, as having dignity, not price, and so on – a principle commonly accepted, in modern times, across the political spectrum. The tradition of the left interprets this idea as requiring both a political and social ideal: the *political* ideal of equal citizenship, where all have equal civil rights that are independent of their capacities, achievements, circumstances and ascribed identities, so that

2. Perhaps the most succinct statement of it is that of Condorcet who wrote of 'real equality' as 'the final end of the social art, in which even the effects of the natural differences between men will be mitigated and the only kind of inequality to persist will be that which is in the interests of all and which favours the progress of civilization, of education and of industry, without entailing either poverty, humiliation or dependence'. Under such conditions, Condorcet believed, people would 'approach a condition in which everyone will have the knowledge necessary to conduct himself in the ordinary affairs of life, according to the light of his own reason, to preserve his mind free from prejudice, to understand his rights and to exercise them in accordance with his conscience and his creed; in which everyone will become able, through the development of his faculties, to find the means of providing for his needs; and in which at last misery and folly will be the exception, and no longer the habitual lot of a section of society' (Condorcet, 1955 [1795], p. 174).

government represents their interests on an equal basis; and the *social* ideal of conceiving 'society', including the economy, as a cooperative order in which all are treated as equals, with equal standing or status. It is distrustful of the idea that markets and, in general, unregulated competition exemplify such cooperation, since they naturally generate inequalities of reward and condition, which, as they become excessive and cumulative, corrupt and nullify relations of social equality.

The left is, on this account, a critical, strongly egalitarian project[3] which, however, allows for successive and varying interpretations and reinterpretations of what unjustified inequalities consist in and of how – through what methods and programmes – they can be reduced or eliminated. Often, throughout the history of the left, that project has been abandoned or betrayed by those claiming to pursue it. What I here seek to identify is an ideal-typical left, an account that displays what its adherents can acknowledge as its most defensible rationale: the essential elements by virtue of which abandonment and betrayal can be identified as such. My suggestion, in a word, is that the left is defined by its commitment to what we may call the *principle of rectification* and the right by opposition to it.[4]

In making this suggestion, I seek to avoid essentialism. The varieties of the left are, clearly, related one to another by family resemblance. What counts as equality is essentially contestable: it has many faces and wears many masks. But the point is that the family of the left is a strongly egalitarian family, committed to rectification, whether radical or reformist, and it has a family history. The project of rectification can be expressed in a variety of ways – in the language of rights or of class conflict, as a story of expanding citizenship, or justice or democracy, or as a continuing struggle against exploitation and oppression; it can take any number of organisational forms, based on parties or movements, it can be elitist or democratic, statist or syndicalist or insurrectionary, it can be reformist or revolutionary, consensus-seeking or militant, integrative or sectarian, and its constituencies can be narrowly or broadly based. But whatever its language, form and following, it makes the assumption that there are unjustified inequalities which those on the right see as sacred or inviolable or natural or inevitable and that these should be reduced or abolished.

3. By 'egalitarian' I mean to include concern for those who are disadvantaged relative to others, with respect to well-being, resources, opportunities or capabilities, etc. This view is sometimes labelled 'prioritarian' (signifying weighted beneficence), since it is not directly concerned with equality as such.

4. By 'rectification' I mean to suggest not only the putting to rights of past injustices but also the correction of present and the averting of future ones.

It might be objected that few theories today challenge the basic humanist idea of moral equality. In the course of the twentieth century doctrines which rejected this very basic idea lost ground. Racist doctrines lost scientific credibility; fascism and Nazism were defeated. As Tocqueville had foreseen, the *idea* of equality had, by mid-century, prevailed across the political spectrum, and increasingly across the globe. Even apologists for South Africa's apartheid spoke not of race-based inequality but of 'separate development'. Does it also go for the various schools of twentieth-century Islamic political thought surveyed by Professor Ismail? To what extent have these various attempts to 'reinterpret and reconstruct tradition' by thinkers confronting 'the presumed universality of Western modernity' succeeded in de-emphasising and contextualising theologically Shari'a-based positions concerning gender inequality and the subordinate ethical status of non-Muslims? (And to what extent are their voices actually and potentially influential among believing Muslims?) Is it true that 'the ethical outlook of the Qu'ran . . . is uncompromisingly universalistic and inclusive' (Othman 1999, p. 182)? These questions are all the more pressing after 11 September, given the urgency of the topic of Islam's relationship to modernity and the perceived threat of so-called 'fundamentalism' whose purpose, as Professor Parekh observes, is to 'close the doors of *ijtihad* or interpretation' (chapter 26, p. 573). And what of Hinduism, whose very principle of caste hierarchy denies the core idea of moral equality, but which has responded to modernity in the various alternative ways outlined by Parekh in the world's largest liberal democracy? It may be that these doctrines do represent outposts of the language of inequality. Yet increasingly they must contend with the fact that virtually everywhere governments and intellectuals speak the language of human rights – even those that proclaim the specificity of 'Asian values' (see Bauer and Bell 1999).

By the century's end, therefore, Professor Sen could write that 'every normative theory of social arrangement that has at all stood the test of time seems to demand equality of *something*' (Sen 1992, p. 12), as alternative ways of implementing the basic idea across the surviving political spectrum. So, for instance, all the various political philosophers discussed by Miller and Dagger, including (equal) rights-based 'libertarians' such as Robert Nozick, seek equality, as Sen puts it, 'in some space'. The same goes for all utilitarians, for the market-favouring liberalism of Hayek and the monetarist and public choice theorists discussed by Professor Parsons, and for all the various conservative and Christian democratic schools of thought surveyed by Professors O'Sullivan and Caciagli.

What distinguishes left-wing thinkers (and the left wings of right-wing schools and movements) is, in the first place, their thicker rather than thinner interpretations of the political and social ideals of equality and their redistributive and other implications for present action and policy. Thus the 'coming of the welfare state', charted by Professor Freeden, was fuelled, especially in Britain and France, by thinkers and politicians who saw themselves as applying classical liberal principles to the ever more demanding 'social question' – avoiding unrest and even revolution, promoting stability and cohesion through social justice, and, after 1917, responding to the challenge of the apparent solution of really existing socialism with solutions that would both sustain and transform capitalism. In Britain it was the social or New Liberals (whose thought reached back to John Stuart Mill's 'Chapters on Socialism' and T. H. Green's idea that freedom meant actual opportunities and capacities, not mere absence of restraints) who thought this way, and it is indeed striking that the post-war British welfare state largely originated in the Liberal governments of Asquith and Lloyd George and the theories and programmes of Beveridge and Keynes, who, in Skidelsky's words, 'talked right and left at the same time' and whose liberalism was qualified, as Professor Parsons rightly emphasises, by intellectual elitism and conservatism and a disinclination directly to use public policy to generate more equality.

Others saw less opposition between liberal assumptions and socialist conclusions. Thus L. T. Hobhouse's classic statement of social liberalism had claimed that 'individualism, when it grapples with the facts, is driven no small distance along Socialist lines' (Hobhouse 1964 [1911], p. 54), echoing the Fabian socialist Sydney Olivier's view that 'Socialism is merely individualism rationalised, organised, clothed, and in its right mind' (Shaw 1889, p. 105). The same confluence of ideas can be seen elsewhere, for example in early twentieth-century France, where solidarism fed into Jaurèsian and other contemporary streams of socialism, and even in the United States, where socialism remained stillborn, in the thinking of John Dewey and the proponents of the New Deal. There, as Professor O'Sullivan reminds us, 'liberalism' since the 1930s came to mean what Europeans understand as social democracy (though, one must add, in a much diluted form). And indeed, as Miller and Dagger's chapter brings out, it is largely from the United States that, within the academic world, so-called 'egalitarian' left-liberal theories have achieved their most extensive elaboration at the hands, among many others, of John Rawls (above all), Ronald Dworkin, Michael Walzer and Amartya Sen (whose notion of equalising 'capabilities' returns the discussion to T. H. Green). Ironically, these advanced developments of egalitarian theory have coincided with an unprecedented and accelerating growth of inequalities at home, abroad and on a world scale.

'Socialism' was always supposed to be, and was seen by its adherents as, a more robust and forthright world view, contrasting with both 'capitalism' and 'individualism'. It promised social transformation into a new social order, even a 'new civilisation' transcending both capitalism and liberal democracy. But here socialists faced a crux. What did their more radical interpretation of the social ideal of equality imply for the political ideal of civil equality? In other words, is socialism compatible with democracy? More specifically still, can it be achieved by pursuing a democratic, parliamentary path? The answer to this question – the 'dilemma of democratic socialism', as Peter Gay named it (Gay 1962) – was, as Professor Geary's and Professor Harding's chapters demonstrate, what essentially divided the Second and Third Internationals. But the truth is that the Marxist socialist tradition, unlike liberalism, never had a principled commitment to the political ideal of equal civil rights or to limited and representative government. The Bolsheviks came to power without any theory of governance and, as Harding shows, there could be no discussion throughout the Soviet period of 'how to control, limit and hold power-holders accountable', let alone 'politics as contestation, the open canvassing of alternative political or economic strategies, or public appeal to particular constituencies' (chapter 11, p. 265). Moreover Marxism's ethical core was the attainment of emancipation from the class oppression and exploitation of capitalism, but its goal of social equality under communism was not a subject for reflection, and nor were issues of distributive justice. In his *Critique of the Gotha Programme*, Marx had called the discussion of such matters 'obsolete verbal rubbish' and 'ideological nonsense' and Engels had similarly disparaged talk of equality, which he saw as 'a historical product' and having no 'eternal truth'. In short, the Marxist conception of social equality was not a distinctive scheme of social cooperation governed by distinctive principles of distribution to be applied to the critique of present arrangements, but rather the vision of a world freed from the circumstances (scarcity, conflicting interests, human irrationality and conflicting values and ideals) that render rights and justice necessary – a world in which 'all the springs of cooperative wealth flow more abundantly' and 'the narrow horizon of bourgeois right' has been 'crossed in its entirety' and on whose banner is inscribed the principle 'From each according to his ability, to each according to his needs'. This radically utopian vision of social equality could indeed inspire revolutionary ardour and loyalty to the communist cause, but it had nothing to offer anyone seeking to rectify injustices this side of the coming revolution.

The expansive socio-political ideal of equality underlying the principle of rectification has several large implications: first, that there is a standard of rightness or a counter-factual ideal against which existing disadvantages and inequalities can be seen as unjustified or standing in need of rectification – an implicit or explicit theory of justice that embodies a vision of equality; second, that the scope of egalitarian concern embraces these unjustifiable disadvantages and inequalities that are systematically or structurally caused by features of the political or economic or social system as well as those that are random, idiosyncratic, biologically determined or the unintended consequences of uncontrollable processes; third, that one seek to ascertain their causes through systematic, scientific inquiry; and, fourth, that wherever possible they should be diminished, eliminated or compensated through human intervention resulting from political will.

What all this means is that the left is committed to a belief in the importance of seeking coherence in both understanding the world and acting within it. So it is committed to a vision of the larger picture, to relating private troubles to public issues, to seeking generally applicable explanatory principles that account for social mechanisms and to a conception of social justice that is not merely local. This last may see justice as a set of unitary and all-embracing principles (as in Rawls 1971) or as occupying plural spheres of social life, but even in the latter case social injustice consists in cumulative inequalities, the domination of one sphere over others, as when 'wealth is seized by the strong, honour by the wellborn, office by the well-educated' (Walzer 1983, p. 12). Often the left also sees coherence over time, viewing its project as part of some larger story of actual or at least potential progress: an overall narrative of cumulative conquests and setbacks, sometimes expressed in military metaphors (as in Hobsbawm 1981). At the very least, it believes, progress in rectification is everywhere better than regress.

The left's project also embodies the practice of social criticism, since it is committed to putting institutions and practices, and the beliefs that sustain them, to the test of justificatory, discursive discussion. It is thus universalistic in several ways. Its commitment to social criticism commits it to advancing reasons that anyone, on due reflection, can accept, as opposed to merely advancing its constituents' interests or reinforcing their commitments – reasons which citizens can publicly offer one another and acknowledge as compelling independently of their particular interests and commitments.

Second, the standpoint from which the criticism is made is external: a critique of what some of us do in terms of a wider 'we'. Third, the dynamic of the rectification principle is essentially boundary-crossing, in two ways: it moves naturally from, say, political to economic to educational to cultural inequalities and from, say, status to class to race to gender as their basis, but it is also implicitly cosmopolitan, moving from inequalities within the nation state to those on a global scale. If rectification is to take place within the nation state, what possible justification can there be for the maldistribution of the world's resources?

The conception of the left here advanced has been criticised on the ground that it 'suggests its own limits'. It allegedly 'requires no general theory of an alternative society, and accepts the need for a right as a perpetual counterweight to itself'. The values of left and right are, on this view, 'always relative' and 'a "left" could survive within an all-capitalist system that was to the right of anything now considered in the centre'. And it gives 'involuntary hostage to the enemy': in 'such a conception, the social fabric is always woven to the right: the left does no more than stretch or mend it' (Anderson 1994, p. 17).[5]

But the limits indicated are, if they exist, imposed by reality, not internal to the conception. One question is whether or not there is a known alternative to capitalism that is both feasible and viable and promises greater equality than the most egalitarian feasible capitalist society. If so, then the left, or part of it, as here conceived, would have a theory of it and strive to bring it into being. A second question is whether the left needs the counter-weight of the right. Here the evidence of history suggests that rectification requires parity: that where the left occupies the whole of political space, it subverts its own project. A third question is whether the future left may not lie to the right of the present centre. But, on the conception proposed, where it lies will depend not on the idea of rectification but on the possibilities of rectification that the future holds.

I have focused here on the meaning of the left on the assumption that the history of the right can be seen in part as reactive: that it is 'most helpfully conceived as a variety of responses to the left' (Eatwell and O'Sullivan 1989, p. 63). More precisely, we can, consistently with the interpretation proposed, identify a series of lefts and corresponding rights over the course of the nineteenth and twentieth centuries.

5. This criticism is in response to Lukes (1992).

What is left?

As Hobsbawm has suggested, one can broadly distinguish three lefts. The first left was moderate though willing to mobilise the masses in pursuit of its political ends: it fought 'to overcome monarchical, absolutist and aristocratic governments in favour of the bourgeois institutions of liberal and constitutional government' and was in general the party of 'change and progress' (Hobsbawm 2000, pp. 96, 98). The second left turned to the class struggle and formed around workers' movements and socialist parties in the nineteenth century, initially in alliance with the first left, incorporating its objectives and struggling for civil rights and political democracy but becoming increasingly independent of it, and fighting for public ownership and the planning of the economy, the rights of all to work and for social rights (though in the United States, where there was no independent working-class movement, it remained largely undeveloped and internal to the Democratic Party). This second left was split asunder by the Russian Revolution. As social democracy it succeeded throughout most of Europe in completing the first left's agenda, not least universal suffrage, and winning social rights and the establishment of welfare systems, most extensively in Scandinavia (though in some countries these also derived from liberal and Catholic movements and parties). This moderate reformist left believed in what C. A. R. Crosland called *The Future of Socialism* (Crosland 1956): 'socialism' named 'the idea of a post-capitalist society through an ill-defined belief that public ownership and management would in time develop into something more and something new' (Hobsbawm 2000, p. 101). Its 'golden age', between 1945 and the 1970s, saw dramatic and widely, if unevenly, spread successes in achieving, through public ownership, fiscal and monetary means and corporatist economic policies, extensive redistribution, provision of welfare and public services and full employment – all of it sustained by underlying conditions favourable to economic growth.

The end of this phase was heralded by the 1973 oil crisis, which signalled the gathering impact of the globalised economy in narrowing social democracy's scope of action within national borders. The most successful social democratic countries, notably Sweden and Norway, were markedly less successful from the mid-1980s. No less important was the increasingly acknowledged impossibility of command socialism and the eventual collapse in ruins of the entire Soviet communist system, depriving the world of even a failed alternative to capitalism. Lacking the model of a feasibly successful such alternative, and faced with the wave of political and economic neo-liberalism that swept across the world in the century's last decades and a widely perceived reluctance of taxpayers to finance redistribution and public goods, the second left became a weakened conservative force defending past social democratic gains against both intellectual and electoral tides.

Hobsbawm perceives a third left dating from the 1960s, but it is a left that is bereft of an electoral base and a single project. It is, in effect, the topic of this volume's part IV: a series of single-issue movements, such as the women's, anti-racist and environmental movements, social movements belonging to what came to be called 'identity politics', and various internationally focused movements from anti-nuclear campaigns and the anti-Vietnam War movement to a burgeoning variety of movements and organisations campaigning for human rights and, at the century's end, against 'globalisation'. All of this activity belongs, in Hobsbawm's view, to 'what could be called the Left continuum'. This third left, Hobsbawm dismissively writes, 'is not very important politically, and its profile has mainly been raised by the crisis of the traditional political Left' (Hobsbawm 2000, p. 103). Is Hobsbawm right?

There has certainly been a collapse of coherence, although we may well ask to what extent the coherence we see in the past is a retrospective illusion. To what extent was it clear that the social movements of the past would unite in the early days? Is there not a story to tell of the suppression and subordination of their contradictory agendas within hierarchical and exclusionary structures? Nevertheless, the left has fragmented. There is no longer any political movement or party, national or international, which integrates recognisably left-wing issues and campaigns within an overarching framework of ideas. Indeed, this situation is often seen as desirable. The contemporary left, it is said, requires a pluralistic agenda, embodied in different movements, and a network form of organisation that promises more equal and democratic forms of participation than the old hierarchical forms, enabling different, single-issue and geographically dispersed movements to fight for greater equality locally and globally.

The fragmentation is, so to speak, both horizontal across issue areas and vertical across time. It is no longer plausible to see the various left-wing causes as subsumed within a larger, encompassing socio-political project. For one thing, some of the issues in question, most obviously those central to green politics, are, as Professor Ball's chapter shows, orthogonal to the anthropocentric left–right spectrum. Furthermore, the different policies and programmes of the new social movements can lead to trade-offs and dilemmas, as when environment-friendly policies would impoverish disadvantaged people or when identity-based positive discrimination violates meritocratic selection or when respecting patriarchal religions or ethnic communities conflicts with gender equality. In the face of such conflicts there is no shared discourse of political priorities to resolve them. On the other hand, this was the very point of the third left's challenge to the second left, which it criticised for its hierarchical, patriarchal and materialist outlook, pointing to unjustified inequalities that it ignored or underplayed, of gender, race, ethnicity and so on. In this sense, the crisis of the second left was in part created by the third.

And in the dimension of time it is no longer plausible to view such movements as fitting into some larger story of social and political progress – whether it be a Marxist or Marxisant story of class struggle leading to a future classless world or a social democratic story of expanding citizenship that runs in cumulative fashion from civil to political to ever-deepening and widening social and economic rights (see Marshall 1963). Hence we see the widespread development, discussed by Professor Bellamy, of new social and protest movements increasingly disaffected and detached from party politics, in which citizens take less and less interest. And the postmodernist theorising described by Peter Dews has both expressed and encouraged, in the century's last decades, a widespread scepticism about the 'grand narratives' embodied in the left-wing party-based politics of the past – 'grand schemas of historical progress stemming from the Enlightenment'. Sometimes the exponents of these particular movements are disposed to adopt particularistic, even relativist views – a development postmodernism encourages. Such adherents of identity politics abandon the search for what Professor Tully calls 'agreement on norms of intersubjective recognition' on the basis of public, commonly acceptable or 'shared' reasons, maintaining that all reasons are 'internal' to cultures in contention and that the very notion of universalism is ethnocentric. For reasons suggested above, this kind of thinking is inimical to the very idea of the left. By embracing incoherence of thought, it can only encourage the process of fragmentation.

Does all this mean that the new social movements are 'not very important politically'? In the first place, many of them are not so new. Twentieth-century feminism, as Susan James admirably shows, is a long story that, beginning with campaigns against women's subordination within liberal institutions and within marriage and the family, led to the wider questioning of gender relations and the causes of women's oppression and thence to the focusing on the diversity of women's lives across different circumstances and experiences. Likewise, Professor Ceadel illuminatingly traces back the roots of absolutist and reformist anti-war movements to the origins of pacifism and *pacificism* and recounts their subsequent fates, and Professor Ball's account of green politics goes back to Rousseau and the early Marx. But, second, no assessment of the 'third left's' importance can dispense with some stocktaking of its achievements. Looking back over the course of the twentieth century, feminists and anti-racists, in both the developed and parts of the developing world, can observe immense progress in normative commitment (what it is respectable to say), in legislative enactments, and in the widening availability of real opportunities both of career and life-style – alongside areas of regression and failure and a huge uncompleted agenda for the future. Ecologists' ideas have been influential in the public domain only in the century's last decades, but they too can chalk up a considerable impact upon public awareness of the interconnected crises listed by Professor Ball, awareness that has mobilised activists and entered into the calculations of both public and private policy-making to an ever-increasing extent. The successes of identity politics are less straightforward to assess, in part because of the diversity of identities in question, in part because what counts as success may be contestable (is every claim to group recognition equally justified and meeting it therefore just?). Certainly discrimination on the basis of sexual orientation has declined significantly in several Western countries at the normative, legislative and behavioural levels. As for the recognition of the claims of national minorities and ethnic groups, the story is mixed. Historically, the liberal tradition has accommodated minority rights, and views within that tradition varied from 'strong support to deep anxiety' while the socialist tradition has been hostile to them (Kymlicka 1995, p. 68). Yet until its very end, the twentieth century was not lacking in ethnically based persecution and oppression across the globe. In the increasingly multicultural societies of the Western type, which have experienced waves of mass immigration, social norms, legislation and behaviour have adapted to this ever more visible challenge to the principle of rectification in different ways and with different degrees of success. The rising fortunes of the extreme right in much of Europe register the relative failures of the left in this domain.

But at the century's end it is the internationally oriented movements that have constituted the most dynamic segment of the third left. Its achievements lie at different levels: the remarkable pervasiveness across the globe of the discourse of human rights, developments in international criminal law, including the setting up and successful functioning of international war crimes courts, the multiplication of campaigning non-governmental organisations in this area, and the increasing audibility of protest movements that call attention to global inequalities and third world poverty and debt and their causes. It is too early to call such achievements successes, but they exemplify the rectification principle at work as does the rest of the foregoing catalogue, which it is hard to see as 'not very important politically'.

What is right?

The successive phases of the right can be seen as responding to and interacting with these developments on the left. Eatwell and O'Sullivan (1989) have helpfully discerned five such incarnations of the right (sketched in Professor O'Sullivan's chapter) in a way that dovetails with the analysis offered here.

The first, the 'reactionary right', consisted in the genuine reactionaries and their followers who, literally, reacted to the French Revolution and its aftermath. Inspired by theocratic and authoritarian thinkers such as Joseph de Maistre and Louis de Bonald, this right condemned individualism and markets and Enlightenment-inspired notions of reason as dangerously anarchic and sought to return to an idealised past of hierarchy and order. It survived in ever-diminishing strength through the nineteenth and early twentieth centuries, in thinkers such as Hippolyte Taine and Charles Maurras (though, as Sternhell shows, it was one source of fascism), and it still survives in currents within the Catholic church. The second, 'moderate' right has been far more long-lasting and internally complex. Its ancestor is Edmund Burke but also such liberals as Benjamin Constant and Alexis de Tocqueville: its watchwords are 'limited government', 'balance', 'pragmatism' and a generalised suspicion of abstract principles in politics. Its more authoritarian side is seen in what Professor Payne calls the 'moderate authoritarian right of early twentieth-century Europe' and is described in Professor Caciagli's chapter: its twin sources lay in 'the search for a more controlled, elitist and authoritarian liberalism and in Catholic corporatism'. This kind of right resists, in Roger Scruton's words,

> those collective goals – liberty, equality and fraternity – whose specious clarity derives from their abstraction, and which can never be translated into reality without destroying the fruits of historic compromise. The right is suspicious, too, of projects which require the massive intervention of the state, but because it values society more. It respects those institutions, such as property, religion and law, which arise spontaneously from the social impulse, and in which responsibility, deference and authority take root (Scruton 1992).

But, true to its pragmatism, it has responded to the challenges of the first and second lefts by selective absorption, eventually accepting their achievements and implementing, though seeking to moderate, counteract and where possible reverse the impact of their policies while contesting their programmes and principles.

The rise of the third, 'radical' right at the beginning of the twentieth century, and also referred to in Professor Payne's chapter, marks the moment when the right became an activist movement of change, responding to the rise of socialism by seeking salvation through politics to implement an 'aggressive and romantic vision of nationalism' (Eatwell and O'Sullivan 1989, p. 69). Influenced by thinkers such as Georges Sorel and Ernst Jünger, it constituted another source of fascism, but there were also forms of right-wing radicalism, as Payne observes, that were quite distinct from the revolutionary thrust and cultural modernism of fascism in their social elitism, commitment to existing hierarchies and grounding in religion. Their heyday was between the wars and they were eclipsed by the defeat of Nazism. The fourth category of 'extreme' right denotes the political movements and parties, hostile to both the left and conservative centre parties, and nationalist, sometimes localist, and anti-immigration and (incipiently if rarely explicitly) racist in ideology. Loosely linked to such organisations are the intellectuals of the *nouvelle droite* in France and the *nuova destra* in Italy, described by Professor O'Sullivan as 'post-Second World War radical conservatives'. Though largely ostracised by fellow intellectuals, this kind of politics grew considerably in influence and electoral appeal throughout much of Europe, especially in Austria, Denmark, Belgium, Germany, France, Switzerland and Italy in the last decades of the century. Driven more by political propaganda than intellectual reflection, this branch of the right became an integral part of late twentieth-century politics in those countries and has achieved governmental office in several.

Finally, there is the new, proactive and utopian 'neo-liberal' right whose increasingly hegemonic ideology gripped the world in the latter part of the century with the ascendancy of Ronald Reagan and Margaret Thatcher and changed the parameters within which all governments, including those claimed to be of the centre-left, operate. It represents the culmination of the right's transformation into a movement promoting innovative social transformation, through extensive marketisation, the commercialisation of public services, de-regulation and privatisation, while retaining other more traditional attachments of the right, notably to patriotism, elitism and a strong commitment to law and order. Unlike the third left, this latest, and most dynamic, version of the right succeeded to a remarkable extent in combining various contradictory agendas within an overarching neo-liberal framework of ideas. Its intellectual inspiration derives from Austrian economics and libertarian philosophers and social scientists, who maintain, against all left projects of rectifying inequalities, that these are doomed to be either futile or counter-productive or destructive of other cherished values (see Hirschman 1991).

Questions

So has this newest right prevailed? By the end of the century, acute, endemic disadvantage and deprivation were evident along several dimensions, within both the developed and developing worlds, and between them. In the United States 11.5 per cent of the population, some thirty-two million people, including 20 per cent of all children, lived in absolute poverty and some forty million people were without health insurance. There were already some twenty million people out of work in Western Europe alone, with no prospect of a return to full employment, while increasing poverty, marginalisation and social exclusion for more and more categories of people seemed to be inseparable from liberal capitalist societies. Moreover, it was widely believed that tax aversion and a so-called 'culture of contentment', on the part of a majority of those who vote, had largely robbed fiscal policy of its progressive or egalitarian potential, both in the United States and increasingly throughout Western Europe. As for global inequality, Bobbio's comment suffices: 'One has only to shift one's attention from the social questions within individual states which gave rise to socialism in the last century to the international social question in order to realise that the left has not only not completed its task, it has hardly commenced it' (Bobbio 1996, p. 82).[6]

At the same time, various arguments were increasingly advanced for the discarding of the old maps and charts. Thus Francis Fukayama, announcing 'the end of history', proclaimed liberal democracy ('the best possible solution to the human problem') to be the framework of our 'post-historical world' in which 'the major issues will be economic ones like promoting competitiveness and innovation, managing internal and external deficits,

6. According to James K. Galbraith, 'During the decades that happen to coincide with the rise of neoliberal ideology, with the breakdown of national sovereignties, and with the end of Keynesian policies in the global debt crisis of the early 1980s, inequality rose worldwide' (Galbraith 2002, p. 22).

maintaining full employment, dealing co-operatively with grave environmental problems, and the like'. On this view, if the 'left' survives, it will not be as an integral part of that system, but as a relatively minor threat to it, in the form of claims to recognition. Liberal capitalist societies are, it seems, increasingly, through various 'equalising processes', eliminating all inequalities not attributable to nature or the economically necessary division of labour: those that remain will be necessary and ineradicable, 'due to the nature of things rather than the will of man' (Fukayama 1992, pp. 338, 283, 291). Others argued that sheer social complexity was rendering old-style politics anachronistic: we are seeing an ever-greater paralysis of 'the political market, marginalising all non-conforming expectations, and emptying competition between the parties of all its potential for innovation in the face of a growing complexity and mobility in the social environment'. On this view, the political system cannot perform any function other than reducing insecurity through the management of social risks, and strategies for greater equality are beyond its scope (Zolo 1992, p. 123). And many, in the last decades of the century, came to focus on globalisation as the greatest problem:

> the emergence of a global economic system which stretches beyond the control of any single state (even of dominant states); the expansion of networks of transnational relations and communications over which particular states have limited influence; the enormous growth in international organisations and regimes which can limit the scope for action of the most powerful states, and the development of global military order, and the build-up of the means of 'total' warfare as an enduring feature of the contemporary world, which can reduce the range of policies available to governments and their citizens (Held 1993, p. 38).

So is there, as Hobsbawm suggests, no longer a coherent left-wing project of rectifying inequalities, but rather only a continuum of uncoordinated and sometimes contradictory single-issue movements and campaigns? Or is Giddens persuasive in seeing the left, or at least the centre-left, as occupied by a coherent rectifying project informed by distinctive values that constitutes the only feasible alternative to that of the neo-liberal right? Is 'socialism' the appropriate name for the left segment of the political spectrum? Can it still be used to mean a feasible and viable socio-economic system that is an alternative to capitalism and has a prospect of replacing it?

Or is capitalism sufficiently versatile to render this supposition unnecessary? Was Keynes after all right in thinking, in Professor Parsons' words, that liberal democracy and capitalism 'contained many *possibilities*' and is any approximation to socialism among them? Is private ownership combined with market allocation incompatible with egalitarian ideals? Where are markets and privatisation appropriate and where do they conflict with the requirements of social citizenship? Have we exhausted the possibilities of combining these principles? Even if Professor Goodin is right that 'the traditional universalistic cradle-to-grave welfare state' is 'politically dead for the foreseeable future', there are, as he documents, several ways of rethinking social insurance, social assistance and substantial redistribution to be found in contemporary, new-style welfare states. In Scandinavia the social democratic model was during its heyday (and since) remarkably successful at rectification along several dimensions (to cite only one, almost no-one was poor after taxes and transfers). That model began to fail in the 1980s with the end of centralised bargaining and of social democratic government. Is social democracy, then, over, in any recognisable form?[7] Was it weakened primarily by intrinsic internal deficiencies (such as excessive and inefficient regulation and government intervention, unsustainable universalistic welfare programmes, high marginal tax rates leading to capital flight and wage drift undermining the centralised wage bargains) or by external factors (the changing class structure, notably the decline of manual labour, and the impact of increasing international competition)? To what extent are these insurmountable? Does social democracy still have a future, in an appropriately modified form, despite the manifold constraints of globalisation, perhaps within contexts larger, or smaller, than the nation state? By the end of the century none of these questions was decisively answered or even answerable.

7. For a valuable discussion of this question, and of larger questions raised in this chapter, see Przeworski (1985 and 1993).

Biographies

ABDUH, MUHAMMAD
(1849–1905) was born in Tanta, Egypt. Educated at al-Azhar University in Cairo, Abduh rose to become the leading religious reformer of his time. He was a student and, later, an associate of Sayyid Jamal al-Din al-Afghani (1839–97), a major figure in the reform movement of the second half of the nineteenth century. During his sojourn in Paris in 1894, Abduh and al-Afghani published a short-lived journal, *al-'Urwa al-Wathqa* (*The Indissoluble Link*). During the early part of his intellectual career, Abduh was engaged in the movement for political change and resistance against British rule in Egypt. He later shifted his focus onto social transformation through education. Abduh was exiled from Egypt between 1882 and 1888, a period in which he came into closer contact with Western thought and with circles of Arab and Muslim thinkers. Abduh's thought was influenced by Enlightenment ideas. He visited Herbert Spencer in Great Britain and translated his *Education* into Arabic. Other influences included Rousseau and Comte. Like al-Afghani, he engaged in debates with Orientalist writers. His best-known work is *Risalat al-Tawhid* (*Treatise on Unity*, 1897). In 1899, Abduh was appointed to the position of Grand Mufti (the highest religious authority over matters of interpretation).

ADLER, ALFRED
(1870–1937) was a Viennese physician who pioneered in the study of the social sources of psychological distress. For this 'deviation' Freud expelled Adler and his Viennese followers from the Vienna Psychoanalytic Society. Adler went on to found a school of 'individual psychology', one that later had a direct impact on the psychological reasoning in the American Supreme Court's 1954 decision desegregating public schools, as well as on modern feminism. An anthology of Adler's writings is *The Individual Psychology of Alfred Adler*, ed. Ansbacher and Ansbacher (1964).

ADORNO, THEODOR
(1903–69). Born in Frankfurt, Adorno was one of the most prominent members of the Frankfurt school. He was awarded his doctorate in 1924 for a study of Husserl and then studied music, in particular the piano. In 1931 he began teaching philosophy at the University of Frankfurt but, with the rise of Nazism, he moved to England and eventually the United States. It was here that he co-authored *The Authoritarian Personality* (1950) and, with Horkheimer, an influential critique of the Enlightenment. He returned to Frankfurt in 1950 and held a chair of philosophy there. He published his *Negative Dialectics* in 1966 as well as a considerable body of work in aesthetics and musicology during the preceding years.

ALLEN, CLIFFORD (LATER LORD ALLEN OF HURTWOOD)
(1889–1939). Converted from Anglicanism and conservatism to socialism and secularism while at Cambridge in 1909, Allen became a journalist and ILP activist. During the First World War he became one of the most respected and courageous absolutist conscientious objectors, though he soon came to realise that individualistic protest of that kind had a negligible effect on the war effort when compared with political efforts such as the Russian Revolutions of 1917. Although somewhat confusingly still claiming to be a pacifist in his personal beliefs, he came in the early 1930s (by which time he had been given a peerage by Ramsay MacDonald) to advocate some kind of international air force as a protection for states which agreed to abolish their own national forces, and thus found himself disagreeing with most pacifists. In the mid-1930s he tried to balance support for collective security against aggression with the advocacy of peaceful change; but by the time of his death he had given priority to the appeasement of Germany. His health had been wrecked by his periods of imprisonment during the First World War and he died prematurely, only days before Hitler's entry into Prague undermined the cause to which he had latterly devoted himself.

ALTHUSSER, LOUIS
(1918–90). Born in Algiers, Althusser studied philosophy at the Ecole Normale Supérieure (where he also later taught), and joined the Communist Party in 1948. He remained a member of the party all his active life, but managed also to author a theory and philosophy of Marxism that appeared far removed from party orthodoxy. In collaboration with some of his brilliant students – including Etienne Balibar and Jacques Rancière – in the mid-1960s Althusser conducted a seminar on Marx's philosophy, which culminated in a series of massively influential books and articles: most notably *For Marx* (1965) and *Reading Capital* (1968). Drawing upon structuralist literary and anthropological theory, as well as on psychoanalysis, Althusser developed a complex theoretical apparatus which claimed to uncover the scientific core of Marxism – which was to be found, he insisted, not in the Hegelian heritage and the young Marx's work, but in *Capital*. The failure of the 1968 student revolt prompted him to publish *Lenin and Philosophy* (1969) whose central essay tried to develop a theory of ideology. Althusser's intellectual career ended in 1980 when, during a bout of mental illness, he killed his wife. For the last decade of his life he was confined to an institution.

APOLLINAIRE, GUILLAUME (WILHELM APOLLINARIS DE KOSTROWITSKY)
(1880–1918). Born in Rome of an Italian father and a Polish mother, Apollinaire is best known as a French poet, especially for his *Alcools* (1913) and *Calligrammes* (1918). Beginning in 1902, he was the foremost critical voice in Parisian modernism, editing avant-garde journals from *Le Festin d'Esope* (1903) to *Les Soirées de Paris* (1912–14) and authoring *Les peintures cubistes* (1913). He enlisted in 1914 and became a second lieutenant in the French infantry, but he suffered a serious head wound in 1916 and returned to Paris. Weakened by his war wound, he died two days before the armistice as one of the war's millions of influenza victims.

ARENDT, HANNAH
(1906–75) was a German-Jewish scholar who studied philosophy in Germany with Martin Heidegger and Karl Jaspers, fled Germany after the rise of Hitler, and in the United States established herself as one of the most influential political theorists of the twentieth century. Her most famous books include *Origins of Totalitarianism* (1951), *The Human Condition*

(1958), *On Revolution* (1963) and *Eichmann in Jerusalem* (1963). Arendt was an iconoclastic critic of all forms of doctrinaire thought and political authoritarianism, and her political writings extolled the virtues of extraordinary moments of spontaneous and voluntary political activity.

ARKOUN, MOHAMMED

(1928–). Born in a village of Kabilya, Algeria, Arkoun studied and taught in France. He was professor of Islamic thought at the Sorbonne, Paris-III. Trained in medieval Islamic thought, Arkoun edited two treatises by the humanist Islamic thinker, Miskawiya. Drawing on developments in French literary criticism, particularly in semiotics, he set out to provide a re-reading of Islamic legal and philosophical traditions. He demonstrated the contribution of critical literary theory and social science methods to new understandings and readings of the sacred text in his *Lectures du Coran* (1982). In *Pour une critique de la raison islamique* (1984), he identifies the analytical tools needed to undertake a critical reinterpretation of Islamic legal and religious traditions. Translations of Arkoun's work into Arabic began to appear in the 1980s. His unconventional approach to Islamic history and his use of concepts such as 'legend' and 'myth' drew criticism from the conservative religious establishment and from some lay intellectuals as well.

ARON, RAYMOND

(1905–83). Aron studied with Sartre at the Ecole Normale Supérieure and in Germany. Attracted to German philosophy, albeit to Kantian and neo-Kantian thought rather than the Hegelian tradition, and to sociological rather than philosophical themes, after 1945 Aron became the most important critic of Marxist and leftist theories in France. He wrote on a broad range of subjects, including international relations, military strategy and the sociology of industrial societies, modern ideologies and political systems, and apart from his scholarly work was prolific in his journalistic writings. In 1955 he published a powerful attack on Marxism (*The Opium of the Intellectuals*), and shortly before his death he published his *Mémoires* (1983), which provides an interesting insight into the intellectual and political life of his generation.

BAHRO, RUDOLF

(1935–97) was in his youth a loyal member of the East German Communist Party. Becoming increasingly critical of the hierarchical, authoritarian and closed character of the party, he wrote *Die Alternative: zur Kritik des real existierenden Sozialismus* (1977; English trans. *The Alternative in Eastern Europe*, 1978), smuggling the manuscript to West Germany, where it was published. Bahro was arrested and sentenced to eight years in prison. After serving two years he was released and allowed to emigrate to West Germany in 1980. Making the move (as he described it) 'from Red to Green', he became a founding member and leading theorist of die Grünen, the West German Green Party. Bahro wanted the German Greens to be less a party than a movement dedicated to the overthrow of the industrial system. A leader of the *fundi* (or 'fundamentalist') faction, he became ever more disillusioned, as the *realos* (or 'realists') gained ascendancy within the Green Party. He resigned from the German Greens in 1985. His other books include *Building the Green Movement* (1986) and *Avoiding Social and Ecological Disaster: The Politics of World Transformation* (1994).

AL-BANNA, HASAN

(1906–49) was born near Alexandria in Egypt and trained as a teacher. He worked as a correspondent for several Muslim youth magazines and participated in the movement for religious revival. He founded the Muslim Brotherhood, a militant organisation, became its *murshid* (guide) and helped set up its branches in the Sudan, Iraq, Syria and other Arab countries. When a military decree dissolved the Brotherhood, the prime minister responsible for it was assassinated. Banna was the prime suspect, and was murdered by the secret police. In his theological and political writings, he stressed the religious basis of life and the infallibility of the Qur'an, of which he offered a modernist and socialist interpretation.

BARRY, BRIAN

(1936–). Barry studied at Oxford as both an undergraduate and a graduate. His D.Phil. thesis, however, later published as *Political Argument* (1965), displayed the influence of transatlantic thought, and Barry's subsequent career has alternated between professorships in the USA and Britain. Barry has written widely on liberalism, on democratic theory and on the theory of justice. An early critical reaction to Rawls (*The Liberal Theory of Justice*, 1973) gave way to a more sympathetic appraisal in his *Treatise on Social Justice*, of which two volumes have so far appeared: *Theories of Justice* (1989) and *Justice as Impartiality* (1995). Barry's work has been characterised by analytical rigour, a firm defence of left-liberal values, and uncompromising criticism of those with whom he disagrees.

BAUDELAIRE, CHARLES

(1821–67). Born in Paris, Baudelaire was the greatest French poet of his day. Most famous for *Les fleurs du mal* (1857), which caused him to be tried and convicted for obscenity, he also wrote highly innovative prose poems, many of which are collected in *Le spleen de Paris* (1869). Baudelaire was also the foremost early theorist of aesthetic modernity, and is especially known for his essay, 'The Painter of Modern Life' (1863). He also translated the works of Edgar Allan Poe, with whom he strongly identified. The last years of his life were difficult, and he died in poverty and relative obscurity.

BAUER, OTTO

(1881–1938). Born in Vienna, Bauer was the author of *The Nationalities Question and Social Democracy* (1907), which argued that national cultural differences would increase after the social revolution but that in the shorter term national autonomy within Austria-Hungary rather than separatist ambitions best suited the needs of the proletariat. After the Austrian Revolution of 1918 he was foreign minister for a short time and subsequently became one of the strongest critics of the Bolshevik regime, which he saw as oppressing the working class, a claim defended in *Bolshevism or Social Democracy* (1920).

BEAUVOIR, SIMONE DE

(1908–86) was a leading philosopher and novelist. The partner of Jean-Paul Sartre and a friend of Maurice Merleau-Ponty, her ethical writings – *Pyrrhus and Cinéas* (1944) and *Pour une morale de l'ambiguité* (1947) – drew on and extended the phenomenological and existentialist traditions. *Le deuxième sexe*, her most influential and original philosophical work, was published in 1949. Beauvoir also wrote several novels, including *L'invitée* (1943) and *Les mandarins* (1954), and three autobiographical volumes: *Mémoires d'une jeune fille rangée* (1958), *La force de l'âge* (1960) and *La force des choses* (1963). Some of her last works – *Une mort très douce* (1964) and *La vieillesse* (1970) – explore the themes of ageing and death.

BENJAMIN, WALTER

(1892–1940). Born in Berlin, Benjamin possessed one of most fertile philosophical and critical imaginations of the inter-war generation in Europe. Poised between the Jewish messianism he shared with Gershom Scholem and the Marxism he shared with Bertolt Brecht, he had close relations with many figures of the Frankfurt school, especially Theodor Adorno. Fleeing occupied France to join Adorno and Max Horkheimer in New York, he committed suicide near the Spanish border when he believed he was about to be captured by the Gestapo. He never completed his major intellectual project on Baudelaire and the origins of modernity in the Paris arcades. Two collections of his best-known essays, translated into English, are *Illuminations* and *Reflections*. He is buried in Port Bou.

BERGSON, HENRI
(1859–1941). Born in Paris to Jewish parents and showing early mathematical genius, Bergson developed a philosophy of vitality and process which challenged the traditional metaphysical dualities. So controversial were his views that the Catholic church placed his books on the Index in 1914. His 1889 essay on *The Immediate Data of Consciousness* stressed its temporality and used the 'intuition of duration' to develop new accounts of experience, knowledge and the self. Bergson's ideas were interpreted by many as a mystical celebration of myth over reason, although in his last major work he opposed dynamic and open religions to closed, static myths. Bergson occupied a chair at the Collège de France from 1900 to 1921, where his prestige was such that he was sent by the French government to try to persuade America to enter the First World War. He died in January 1941, having refused an offer of exemption from the anti-Semitic legislation then current in France.

BERLIN, ISAIAH
(1909–98) was born at Riga, in Russia, to a prosperous Jewish merchant family, was educated in England, and began to teach philosophy in Oxford before the Second World War interrupted his academic career. Berlin worked in British embassies as a press agent during the war, first in New York and Washington, and finally in Moscow. He was appointed to the Chichele chair of social and political theory in 1957; his inaugural lecture, 'Two Concepts of Liberty', remains his most celebrated contribution to political theory. Berlin wrote extensively in the history of ideas, where he revealed himself to be a sympathetic interpreter of the nineteenth-century Romantics and others whose political outlook was far removed from his own deeply held liberalism.

BERNSTEIN, EDUARD
(1850–1932) was born in Berlin, and together with Karl Kautsky became a major propagandist of Marxism within the SPD in the 1880s, when he lived in exile in London and was in close contact with Engels, whose *Anti-Dühring* influenced him profoundly. In the mid-1890s, however, Bernstein began to question the main premises of Marxism in a series of articles, *Problems of Socialism* (1896–8), in *Die Neue Zeit* and subsequently in his major 'revisionist text', *The Preconditions of Socialism* (1899). He rejected the theories of surplus value, immiseration, class polarisation and economic collapse, calling for the SPD to pursue a strategy of gradual reforms in alliance with liberalism. His views were rejected decisively by the SPD membership, though he remained in the party and in fact became active in opposition to war, together with his old friend Karl Kautsky, from 1915. He also wrote an insightful study of the Berlin labour movement and a seminal analysis of the English Civil War.

BERRY, WENDELL
(1934–). Born in Kentucky, Berry is a farmer, poet, novelist, essayist, conservationist and prominent American advocate of environmental stewardship and 'sustainable agriculture'. His recurring themes – love of the land, of place or region, and the responsibility to care for them – appear in his poems, novels and essays. Many modern farming practices, as he

argues in *The Unsettling of America* (1977), *The Gift of Good Land* (1981) and elsewhere, deplete the soil, despoil the natural environment and deny the value of careful husbandry. A truly sustainable agriculture, as Berry notes, 'would deplete neither soil, nor people, nor communities'.

BEVERIDGE, WILLIAM HENRY
(1879–1963) was a British social reformer and policy-maker. After studying at Oxford, Beveridge developed an interest in social policy. He published *Unemployment: A Problem of Industry* (1909), and became leader writer for the conservative *Morning Post*. As a civil servant from 1908, Beveridge helped draw up parts of the Liberal social legislation programme between 1909 and 1911. From 1919 to 1937 he was director of the London School of Economics, and built up its reputation in the social sciences. In 1937 he became Master of University College, Oxford. Beveridge is best known for his anti-poverty report *Social Insurance and Allied Services* (1942), which laid the basis for a post-war national plan for a social insurance, a National Health Service, family allowances and full employment.

BLOCH, ERNST
(1885–1977). Born in Ludwigshafen in Germany, Bloch became a Marxist under the impact of the First World War. From *The Spirit of Utopia*, published in 1918, to *The Principle of Hope*, which appeared in three volumes in the late 1950s, Bloch's allusive and unsystematic thought has been imbued by a secularised Judaic messianism where redemption is always possible in the here and now. The advent of Nazism forced Bloch to move to the USA. After the war he moved to the German Democratic Republic, but his unorthodox Marxism meant an uneasy relationship with the authorities there. In 1961, he left to take up a post in Tübingen where he remained for the rest of his life.

BOBBIO, NORBERTO
(1909–). Born in Turin, Bobbio's education and entry into academia took place under fascism. His family belonged to the relatively wealthy professional middle class, his father being a surgeon. He characterised their sympathies as 'filo-fascist' and although he knew many prominent anti-fascists from school, he only went into open opposition to the regime following the fall of Mussolini in 1943. He took degrees in both philosophy and jurisprudence at Turin, and taught the latter at the University of Camerino and then at Siena, before being appointed to a chair at Padua in 1940. In 1948 he became professor of legal philosophy in Turin, a position he held until 1972, when he moved to a chair in politics at the same university, only retiring in 1984. His output is vast. His early academic studies were devoted, amongst other things, to developing Hans Kelsen's legal positivism and researching the Italian positivist political science tradition of both Mosca and Pareto. He also wrote important studies on Hobbes and Locke. At the same time, he was actively involved in politics. A socialist, he became a leading critical interlocutor with the Italian Communist Party, which he sought to convince of the necessity of adhering to liberal democratic values. During the 1970s he was also a prominent member of the peace movement and an opponent of nuclear weapons, a commitment that led him to write a number of pioneering studies in the field of international political theory. He was made a life senator in 1984. His main publications include: *A Theory of Judicial Norms* (1958), *A Theory of the Legal Order* (1960), *Which Socialism?* (1976), *The Future of Democracy: A Defence of the Rules of the Game* (1984), *State, Government and Society* (1985), *The Age of Rights* (1990), and *Left and Right* (1994).

LE BON, GUSTAVE
(1841–1931). Born in Nogent-le-Routrou, a farming community near Chartres, to a local middle-class family with a tradition of administrative service, he left – never to return – to study medicine in Paris in 1860, receiving his licence to practise six years later. Le Bon was the pre-eminent scientific populariser of his generation. An author from 1862, he carried on writing until the day he died, producing some forty volumes, many of which went through several editions, and around 250 articles in major periodicals. A positivist and materialist, Le Bon also engaged in independent scientific experiments, inventing and manufacturing technical scientific equipment. In spite of his huge popular following and his claims to have made original discoveries, including disputing with Einstein the discovery of relativity, he never achieved official recognition from the scientific community and failed to gain admission to the Academy of Sciences. However, he was fêted by politicians and, in 1929, became a Grand Commander in the Legion of Honour. Although he wrote on a wide range of subjects, from spontaneous generation to uniformitarian geology, his main contribution was to social psychology, and his principal work, the *Psychologie des foules* (1895), has gone through over forty-five French editions and has been translated into at least sixteen other languages. He applied its findings to a wide range of topics, from the analysis of criminal behaviour and the working of democracy, to the activity of the military – most notably during the First World War. Though he influenced thinkers as diverse as Sigmund Freud, Graham Wallas, Robert Michels and Georges Sorel, he was personally on the political right, becoming increasingly associated with extreme nationalism and racism – doctrines for which he attempted to offer pseudo-scientific support.

BOOTH, CHARLES
(1840–1916) was a British social investigator and reformer. With his brother Alfred, Booth founded a shipping company, and later became chairman of his own company until 1912. Though not a radical in politics, he developed an interest in working-class conditions. He also became aware of social issues through his contacts with positivist disciples of Auguste Comte. From the 1880s Booth embarked on a series of studies of social and industrial life in London that culminated in his authoritative and vastly influential work, *Life and Labour of the People in London* (1891–1903). It constituted both a crucial source on poverty for social reformers and a major example of statistically based research. Booth was also instrumental in advocating the successful establishment of old-age pensions.

BOURGEOIS, LÉON
(1851–1925) was a French politician, jurist and social theorist. After practising law, Bourgeois held a range of public offices, rising to become chief commissioner of the Paris police in 1887. As member of the Radical Party he assumed a number of cabinet posts, instigating educational reforms. Bourgeois was prime minister in 1895–6 on the basis of a programme of social reform. His most notable book, a contribution to French solidarist thought, was *Solidarité*. He was delegate to the first and second Hague Peace Conferences in 1899 and 1907. Before the First World War Bourgeois served as minister of foreign affairs and of public works. He was later instrumental in forming the League of Nations and was awarded the Nobel peace prize in 1920.

BRETON, ANDRÉ
(1896–1966). Born at Tinchebray in Orne, northern France, Breton was first a dadaist and a co-founder of the avant-garde journal *Littérature* (1919). After 1920 he separated from dada and was the main founder of French surrealism which, influenced by Freudian theory, dedicated itself to a 'pure psychic automatism' in which thought was freed from

every rational and moral constraint. Author of the movement's two principal manifestos (1924 and 1929) and two important surrealist novels, *Nadja* (1928) and *L'amour fou* (1937), he allied the movement with French communism, then broke with the party in 1935, and spent the end of the 1930s in Mexico with Leon Trotsky. During the German occupation of France he lived in the United States, returning home in 1946.

BUKHARIN, NIKOLAI IVANOVICH
(1888–1938) was arguably the most original theorist of Marxism in the twentieth century. His *World Economy of Imperialism* (1915) defined a new epoch of militant and monopolistic capitalism that had long since ceased to be progressive. His 'Towards a Theory of the Imperialist State' (1916) concluded that monopoly capitalism and its monolithic and oppressive state formation were so intertwined that to eliminate the one entailed destroying the other. He provided Lenin with much of the theoretical justification for the Bolshevik Revolution of October 1917, following which he assumed the editorship of *Pravda*. In 1920 his *Economics and Politics of the Transformation Period* provided an acute analysis of the costs of revolution and the consequent need for a rigorous dictatorship of the proletariat exercised by the Communist Party, with the goal of maximising production. By spring 1921, however, he had been converted to Lenin's more gradualist programme of the New Economic Policy whose leading ideas were the mixed economy and the proletarian/peasant alliance. When Stalin's 1928–9 programme of forced collectivisation of agriculture and rapid industrialisation decisively broke with the New Economic Policy, Bukharin was targeted as his principal 'right' opponent. He was denounced and was removed from his official posts and then, in 1937, from the party. He was tried for treason and executed in 1938.

BUTLER, JOSEPHINE
(1828–1906) was an exceptionally dedicated reformer who fought for several women's causes. She was a prominent member of the North of England Council for Promoting the Higher Education of Women, and published *The Education and Employment of Women* in 1868. A devout Christian, Butler set up a refuge for prostitutes in Liverpool, and in 1869 was a founder member of the Ladies' National Association for the Repeal of the Contagious Diseases Act. As part of her international campaign against the Act she published *The Constitution Violated* (1871). *The Voice of One Crying in the Wilderness* (1875) appeared in French and was translated into several languages. Once the Contagious Diseases Act was repealed, Butler set out to reform the British government's practice of supplying prostitutes for its soldiers in India.

CABRAL, AMILCAR
(1924–73) was born in Befata in the Portuguese colony of Guinea. Having initially relied on the trade union struggle to secure national independence, he helped organise the African Party of Independence (the PAI) to launch an armed struggle based on the mobilisation of the peasantry. The struggle was successful in liberating large areas in the countryside. In his few but highly influential writings, Cabral argued for a radical revitalisation of the traditional culture of the African masses, and making it, rather than the pseudo-Westernised culture of the native elite, the basis of the independent state. He was murdered by agents of the Portuguese government.

CAMUS, ALBERT
(1913–60) was an Algerian-born French philosophical novelist and essayist who rose to fame during the 1940s because of his work as an editor and writer for the French Resistance

newspaper *Combat*. His best-known writings include the novel *The Stranger* (1942) and his book-length essay *The Myth of Sisyphus* (1943), which explored the notion of 'the absurd' and addressed themes prevalent in the literature of French existentialism. In his later writing Camus developed the theme of rebellion and of the refusal of despair in his novel *The Plague* (1947) and his long political essay *The Rebel* (1951). Camus was a public intellectual whose political essays condemned the totalitarianisms of the left and the right. His anti-communism led to a bitter polemic with his sometime friend and associate Jean-Paul Sartre. His essays on the Algerian crisis generated much controversy, and also much grief, causing him to reflect sceptically about the difficulties of political engagement in an era of loud and melodramatic ideological controversies.

CARSON, RACHEL

(1907–64). Born in Scarsdale, Pennsylvania, Carson was trained as a zoologist at Johns Hopkins University and later joined the US Fish and Wildlife Service. Her growing interest in marine biology led her to spend summers doing research at the Woods Hole Marine Biological Laboratory in Massachusetts. Out of her studies came *The Sea Around Us* (1951) and *The Edge of the Sea* (1955), but she became best known for her controversial *Silent Spring* (1962), now regarded as a classic of modern environmentalism. She showed how pesticides and other agricultural chemicals get into food chains and poison not only insects, but birds, predator species and human beings. Her book is credited with providing much of the inspiration for the modern environmental movement.

CASTORIADIS, CORNELIUS

(1922–97). Born in Constantinople, Castoriadis grew up in Athens, joined the Greek communist movement at a young age, and became involved in a splinter Trotskyist group. His Trotskyist links continued after he fled to France in 1945 to escape the civil war in Greece, and they inspired his early critique of Stalinism. In 1948 he severed his Trotskyist connections and with Claude Lefort and others founded Socialism ou Barbarie. In 1949 a journal by that name was launched, and its pages kept up a sustained critique of communism and of fellow-travelling intellectuals such as Sartre. *Socialisme ou Barbarie* had a tiny readership, but its trenchant anti-statism, as well as its ideas and analyses – which encompassed bureaucracy, workers' councils and the idea of revolution – percolated far beyond, and played a very large part in shaping *gauchiste* currents of the late 1960s. Apart from his political career, Castoriadis was employed by the OECD as an economist, and from 1974 he also practised as a psychoanalyst – a subject that increasingly became the focus of his work in later years. In 1974 he published his major philosophical work, *The Imaginary Institution of Society*, and selections of his writings have been published in English (*Political and Social Writings*, 1988).

CATLIN, GEORGE E. G.

(1896–1979). Educated at Oxford and Cornell, Catlin was known for his vigorous advocacy of a scientific approach to politics that would aid in planning and world peace. *The Science and Method of Politics* (1927), his most striking piece of advocacy, announced that 'no such thing as political science in more than a barren name' had existed before. This and its successor volume, *A Study of the Principles of Politics* (1930), proceeded to outline an empirical science of politics based on the analysis of power, the exclusion of values, the collection of data, the design of experiments and the formulation of generalisations. Such a science was to be placed in the service of politicians and policy-makers, as well as serve the humanitarian ideals of international cooperation. He put his vision into practice as an adviser to the Fabian Society and the British Labour Party, as well as the US presidential campaign of Wendell Wilkie. During the Second World War, Catlin proposed the formation of an Anglo-American Atlantic Community, and drafted the British declaration supporting dominon status for India. He also wrote passionately on the need for democracy to propagandise on behalf of its own ideals. Catlin taught widely in North American universities, including Yale, Berkeley and McGill, and was knighted in 1970 by the British government for services to Anglo-American and Atlantic community relations. Catlin's life and works are remembered in *For God's Sake, Go! An Autobiography* (1972) and in a memoir by his feminist and pacifist wife, Vera Brittain, *Testament of Experience* (1957).

CHAMBERLAIN, HOUSTON STEWART

(1855–1927) was born into an upper-class British family. He first visited Germany in 1870 and later became an ardent devotee of the music and philosophy of Richard Wagner. Convinced of German superiority, he later married Wagner's daughter and settled permanently in Germany. In 1899 he published *Die Grundlagen des neunzehnten Jahrhunderts* (*The Foundations of the Nineteenth Century*, 2 vols., 1911), the most elaborate exposition of Aryan superiority and racism ever written. Chamberlain subsequently published other works on German culture and philosophy, and on Aryan racism, and died in Bayreuth. Adolf Hitler later acknowledged his importance and influence.

COHEN, G. A.

(1941–). Cohen's work as a scholar of Marxism, and more recently as a fierce defender of egalitarianism, finds its roots in his upbringing in a working-class communist family in Montreal. Trained in philosophy at McGill and Oxford, Cohen taught at University College, London for over twenty years. His major work of this period was his analytical reconstruction of historical materialism, *Karl Marx's Theory of History: A Defence* (1978). Cohen was awarded the Chichele chair of social and political theory at Oxford in 1985, and alongside further work on Marxism (published as *History, Labour and Freedom*, 1988), he began a critical engagement with the work of liberal political philosophers, especially Rawls and Nozick, the first fruits of which appeared in *Self-Ownership, Freedom and Equality* (1995).

CROCE, BENEDETTO

(1866–1952). Born at Peccasseroli in Apulia, Croce was the major Italian philosopher of his day. Together with Giovanni Gentile, he spearheaded the revival of the native idealist tradition. His copious writings on aesthetics, literature, history and ethics were intended to constitute a complete humanist philosophy, which he championed through his cultural journal *La Critica* and his influence over the Laterza publishing house. He became a senator in 1910 and a minister of education under Giolitti 1920–1. A conservative liberal, he did not immediately oppose Mussolini. However, he ultimately became one of the major intellectual critics of the Fascist regime and the figurehead of the liberal opposition. Protected by his fame and private fortune, he was not forced out of his Neapolitan home or prevented from publishing until the Allied invasion.

DE GASPERI, ALCIDE

(1881–1954). Born in a province (Trento) still belonging to the Austrian Empire, he participated in the Catholic movement in his town (agricultural cooperatives, rural trusts, associations, newspapers), and was a member of the Vienna parliament from 1911 to 1918. During the post-war period, he was one of the founding fathers of the Partito Popolare Italiano, and in 1921 he became a member of the Rome parliament. In 1923 he became secretary of the PPI. He remained in office until the Fascist regime dissolved the party in 1926 and imprisoned him in 1927. In 1928 he sought refuge in the Vatican, where he prepared for the reorganisation of the Catholic party, which he recreated in 1942 under the name of Democrazia Cristiana. He became secretary of the new party in 1944. From 1944 to 1953 De Gasperi took part in every Italian government, first as minister for foreign affairs, and then from 1945 to 1953 as prime minister. Indeed, he was the premier who led the reconstruction of Italy, who chose to be part of NATO, and who participated in the creation of the European Community. Some historians call that period of Italian history 'the age of De Gasperi'.

DERRIDA, JACQUES
(1930–). Derrida was born in El-Biar, Algeria, in 1930, into a family of Sephardic Jewish descent. In 1952 he began his philosophical studies at the Ecole Normale Supérieure in Paris. In 1957 he married Marguerite Aucouturier, with whom he has two children. From 1960 to 1964 Derrida taught at the Sorbonne, and from 1965 to 1984 in the philosophy department at the Ecole Normale Supérieure. Since the early 1970s he has divided much of his time between the United States, where he has taught at such universities as Yale, Johns Hopkins and the University of California at Irvine, and Paris, where he teaches at the Ecole des Hautes Etudes en Sciences Sociales. Derrida made a major impact on the intellectual world with the trilogy of books which he published in 1967, *Writing and Difference, Speech and Phenomena* and *Of Grammatology*. These were followed in 1972 by three further publications, *Margins of Philosophy*, *Dissemination* and *Positions* (a collection of highly structured interviews), which firmly established his reputation as one of the world's leading philosophers. His conception of 'deconstruction', an approach to texts and other phenomena which emphasises constitutive internal inconsistencies, has been taken up by thinkers in a wide range of disciplines in the social sciences and humanities. It has also been influential in art and architecture, and in recent years Derrida himself has collaborated with the architect Peter Eisenman. Over the years he has also been active in support of a variety of political causes, including the rights of Algerian immigrants in France and the rights of the Czech Charter 77 dissidents (on one occasion being imprisoned briefly on trumped-up drugs charges during a support visit to Prague). His award of an honorary doctorate by the University of Cambridge in 1992 caused much controversy, turning on what some anglophone academics attacked as the 'cognitive nihilism' of his philosophical views.

DEWEY, JOHN
(1859–1952) was public sage of the United States for an astonishingly long time, marrying pragmatist philosophy to democratic politics and education in a fruitful synthesis. As a graduate student at Johns Hopkins University he was deeply influenced by Hegel as well as Kant, and though he would later reject their idealism in favour of what he liked to call 'experimentalism', he retained their ambition of providing a unified account of human progress. But his account involved humans as problem-solvers, forming habits through social interaction and using knowledge to direct processes of change. From 1894 Dewey taught at the University of Chicago, where he founded the University Elementary School (known as the 'Lab school'), and then at Columbia from where he retired in 1930 although he kept teaching as an emeritus professor until 1939. In 1937 he chaired a commission of inquiry which vindicated Trotsky against Stalin, exciting enormous controversy; this was only one of his many public campaigns and popular publications, which poured out alongside his voluminous academic work.

DILTHEY, WILHELM
(1833–1911) was one of the founders of hermeneutics, a theory of interpretation which emphasised the historicity of texts and the role of language in the human sciences. Having studied theology at Heidelberg and Berlin, where he wrote on Schleiermacher's hermeneutics and ethics, Dilthey taught at various universities before being appointed in 1882 to the Berlin chair of philosophy which had once been Hegel's. In 1883 he published a major introduction to the human sciences, the first of two projected volumes, in which he emphasised the context of will, reflection and action from which all interpretation and understanding emerge. Dilthey's emphasis on immediate reflexive awareness led him to sketch a new science of psychology which would study lived experience, though he later renounced the idea of psychology as a fundamental science in returning to deepen his account of hermeneutics in his last works. Dilthey pioneered the focus on the meaningfulness and intentionality of consciousness which united so many of the philosophical responses to positivism; after the turn of the century he was impressed by Husserl's phenomenology, which he saw as a related enterprise.

DOSSETTI, GIUSEPPE
(1913–96). A scholar who specialised in canon law, Dossetti became involved in politics during the war, and also participated in the Resistance. In 1945 he became vice-secretary of the Italian Christian Democrat Party. His sympathy for the Republic and his ideas about the reform of both the state and economic and social policy led to an immediate split with Alcide De Gasperi and the moderate sections of the party. He was an important figure within the Constituent Assembly, which between 1946 and 1947 approved the constitution of the Italian Republic. He was also the inspiration behind the journal *Cronache Sociali* (1947–51). He promoted both a series of social reforms and the concept of Italy as a neutral country (he was opposed to NATO). In 1952, once the battles within the party had been lost, he retired from active politics, and subsequently entered the priesthood.

DURKHEIM, EMILE
(1858–1917). Born in Epinal in France to a rabbinical family, Durkheim turned his philosophical training to the exploration of the moral and religious social forms of modern society, becoming one of the founders of sociology and an ardent defender of the French Third Republic. He studied philosophy at the Ecole Normale Supérieure under Renouvier and Boutroux, and after some years teaching at *lycées* in Paris, was called to Bordeaux where in 1887 he gave the first university course in sociology and later founded *L'année sociologique*. From 1902 until his death he taught at the Sorbonne. He died greatly saddened by the death of his son and of many friends in the First World War.

DWORKIN, RONALD
(1931–). Trained both in philosophy and law, Dworkin entered legal practice for a brief period before taking up professorships in law at the universities of Yale and Oxford. Important early essays in jurisprudence, critical of legal positivism, were collected in *Taking Rights Seriously* (1978). Subsequently Dworkin has made a number of contributions to liberal political theory, most notably his analysis of rights and his attempt to develop a liberal theory of equality (see *Sovereign Virtue: The Theory and Practice of Equality*, 2002). He has also written on many aspects of public policy, including affirmative action, health care and the problems of abortion and euthanasia (see *Life's Dominion*, 1993).

D'EAUBONNE, FRANÇOISE
(1920–) is a French feminist theorist who coined the term 'eco-feminisme' in her *Feminisme ou la mort* (1974). She argued that women are biologically constituted to have a special,

indeed intimate, connection with the natural world. She further expanded her views about women and nature in *Féminisme-Ecologie: révolution ou mutation* (1978) which has influenced the thinking of feminists in Europe and elsewhere.

ERIKSON, ERIK H.
(1902–94) was a child analyst, trained under Anna Freud, who also did anthropological field work. Erikson's most influential book remains his *Childhood and Society*, along with his biographies of Luther and Gandhi. Erikson's version of ego psychology was designed to correct the negativism implicit in earlier psychoanalysis; through major biographical studies Erikson sought both to bring psychoanalysis into the social sciences and to expand the horizons of clinicians.

FANON, FRANTZ
(1925–61) was born in the French colony of Martinique. He joined the Free French movement and fought in the West Indies, North Africa and Europe, winning a medal for bravery. He later trained as a psychiatrist and practised in an Algerian hospital. He was later expelled from Algeria for his sympathy for that country's struggle for independence. In his few but extremely influential writings, he explored with great sensitivity the moral and psychological damage caused by colonial rule and racial humiliation and the problems involved in reconstituting fractured selves and fragmented national cultures.

FOUCAULT, MICHEL
(1926–84) was born in Poitiers, France, where his father was an eminent local surgeon. After graduating from Saint-Stanislas school, Foucault entered the prestigious Lycée Henri-IV in Paris, and in 1946 he was admitted to the Ecole Normale Supérieure as the fourth-highest ranked student. He received his *licence* in philosophy in 1948 and in psychology in 1950, and in 1952 he was awarded a diploma in psychopathology. In the early 1950s he was briefly a member of the French Communist Party. From 1954 to 1958 Foucault taught French at the University of Uppsala in Sweden, and then spent two years as a cultural attaché in Warsaw and Hamburg. In 1960 he became head of the philosophy department at the University of Clermont-Ferrand, where he published his first major work, *Madness and Civilization* (1961). When Foucault's partner, the sociologist Daniel Defert, went to Tunisia to fulfil his volunteer service requirements, Foucault followed him and spent 1966–8 teaching there. He returned to Paris to head the philosophy department at the University of Paris-VIII at Vincennes, and in 1970 he was elected to a chair in the history of systems of thought at the Collège de France. In the late 1960s and 1970s Foucault was involved in various kinds of left-wing activism, especially around the issue of prisoners and the prison system, to which he devoted one of his best-known books, *Discipline and Punish* (1975). He also spent an increasing amount of time in the United States, often on visiting academic appointments. During the last decade of his life he devoted himself to *The History of Sexuality* (1976–84), a monumental but unfinished project of which three volumes appeared before his death. Foucault was a restless experimenter, not only in his thinking and writing, but with drugs, with his body, and with his sexuality. He was one of the first prominent people to die of AIDS.

FOUILLÉE, ALFRED
(1838–1912) was a French philosopher and social evolutionary thinker. Durkheim described the largely self-educated Fouillée as being faithful to the 'method of conciliation'. Notions of determinism and freedom, idealism and naturalism, individualism and solidarity were to be reconciled into a new metaphysical synthesis in which the force of ideas

and ideals (*idées-forces*) was accorded a central place. Like other French progressive thinkers of the period, Fouillée sought a path between liberalism and socialism in which individualism was to be accommodated with the common good, and balance struck between self-interest and principles of solidarity. Like Durkheim, he emphasised the role of education in resolving social conflict, a project in which a (social) scientific approach was also to play a vital part. His works include *La propriété sociale et la démocratie* (1884), of which Durkheim wrote a highly critical review, *L'enseignement au point de vue national* (1891) and *La psychologie des idées-forces* (1893).

FREUD, SIGMUND
(1856–1939) Both Freud's parents were Jews, part of a small local minority in a town now located in the Czech Republic; in 1859, when he was a small child, his immediate family moved to Vienna. Although the Habsburg monarchy was overwhelmingly Roman Catholic, Jews had full rights of citizenship, and by the turn of the twentieth century Vienna had the largest Jewish population of any city in Western Europe. For a time Freud had believed that his patients' troubles arose from their having been sexually abused in early childhood; starting in 1897, however, Freud abandoned this seduction theory, concluding that neurosis arose from patients' longings and wishes of an infantile sexual nature. At the end of 1899 Freud published *The Interpretation of Dreams*; for the rest of his life he thought that this ranked as his most enduring contribution. In 1902, by which time Freud had attained his nominal standing as a professor at the University of Vienna, he started to assemble a professional following by holding weekly meetings at his apartment. The various intellectual difficulties he encountered were central to Freud's biography, since, as he wrote in 1935, 'psychoanalysis came to be the whole content of my life and... no personal experiences of mine are of any interest in comparison with my relations with that science'. Freud finally died in exile in London in 1939, and although it was contrary to Jewish custom, his remains were cremated and put in an ancient Greek vase.

FROMM, ERICH
(1900–80). Born in Frankfurt, Fromm studied law there and then sociology, psychology and philosophy in Heidelberg. In 1924 he embarked on a course of psychoanalysis and became, for the rest of his life, a practising psychoanalyst. In 1930 he began his collaboration with the Frankfurt school and wrote on the relationship of psychoanalysis to Marxism. Forced to emigrate to the United States in 1933, he drifted away from the Frankfurt school. The last decades of his life were devoted to studies of contemporary society, with particular reference to the roots of aggression and to the development of a socialist humanism.

FURET, FRANÇOIS
(1927–97). Born in Paris, Furet studied history at the Sorbonne, part of a cohort of brilliant young historians all of whom became members of the Communist Party. Furet himself joined the party, but even as a young man he was critical of the 'pope' of French revolutionary studies, Albert Soboul. He left the party in 1956, and his subsequent work, on eighteenth- and nineteenth-century France was guided by a desire to explain what he saw as the failure of Marxism and communism. In 1978 he published *Interpreting the French Revolution*, a critique of Jacobin and Marxist views of the revolution, and a defence of a liberal interpretation which he associated with Alexis de Tocqueville. The book had an impact well beyond the confines of French revolutionary historiography and established

him as the foremost historian of the revolution and as the most important liberal intellectual in France since Raymond Aron. To commemorate the bicentennial he published (with Mona Ozouf) a huge *Critical Dictionary of the French Revolution* (1988): this canonised his interpretation of the revolution, which saw it as the product not of economic class struggle but of ideological and political struggle, and which refused to see it as an indivisible 'bloc', but distinguished between its 'liberal' and 'totalitarian' moments. Furet was elected to the Académie Française shortly before his death.

GANDHI, MAHATMA [MOHANDAS K.]
(1869–1948) was born in Gujarat, India. Mohandas Gandhi, called Mahatma (great soul) because of his moral stature, was trained as a lawyer in London. After nearly twenty-two years in South Africa, first as a lawyer and then as a political activist, he returned to India to become the most prominent leader of the Indian independence movement. He successfully persuaded his countrymen that *satyagraha* or non-violent resistance was the only morally acceptable way to fight against injustices, including the British rule in India. In his copious writings and speeches, he advocated a simple life of minimum needs, economic and political decentralisation, and a non-violent state with minimum reliance on the police, prison and the armed forces. Soon after independence he was assassinated by a militant Hindu for his alleged partiality to Muslims.

GENTILE, GIOVANNI
(1875–1944). A Sicilian, Gentile held chairs of philosophy in several Italian universities and by 1920 had become the country's second most prestigious philosopher, surpassed only by Benedetto Croce. Gentile developed his own system of idealist philosophy known as 'Actualism'. Becoming a member of the Fascist Party, he was recognised as its most prestigious intellectual. Gentile served briefly as minister of education and for many years as president of the National Fascist Institute of Culture, as well as director of the *Enciclopedia Italiana*. Gentile developed the concept of the totalitarian 'ethical state' that would achieve a new level of pedagogy. He wrote the article on Fascist doctrine signed by Mussolini for the *Enciclopedia* in 1932 and remained loyal to the Duce to the end. He was assassinated by the Resistance in Florence in 1944. He is the only Fascist thinker whose works are still published and studied by professional scholars of philosophy and political science. These include *Genesi e struttura della società* (*Genesis and Structure of Society* 1946) and *Fondamenti della filosofia del diritto* (*Fundamentals of the Philosophy of Law* 1915).

GOLDMAN, EMMA
(1869–1940) was born in Russia, but emigrated to America in 1886 where she soon became an active anarchist. In 1892, she and her partner Alexander Berkman attempted to assassinate the steel magnate Henry Clay Frick, and by 1893 she was known as 'Red Emma'. In 1917 she was imprisoned for her outspoken opposition to the war, and was deported to Russia where she was deeply disappointed by the revolutionary regime. She left in 1921 and after several years in Europe went to Spain at the start of the civil war. She died in Canada, attempting to raise money for the Spanish cause. Her works include *Anarchism and Other Essays* (1910), *The Social Significance of the Modern Drama* (1914), *My Disillusionment with Russia* (1923 and 1924) and *Living my Life* (1931).

GOMPERS, SAMUEL
(1850–1924) was an American labour leader. Born in London, Gompers and his family emigrated to the USA in 1863. Active in the cigar-makers' union, he assisted in forming

the Federation of Organized Trades and Labor Unions of the United States and Canada in 1881, becoming its president, and in 1886 he participated in reorganising it as the American Federation of Labor as its first elected president. Gompers retained that post until his death, with the exception of 1895. He was instrumental in promoting labour legislation, steering the unions towards cooperation with employers. He resisted tendencies to socialism or greater radicalism, and focused on wage increases and other material benefits. During the First World War Gompers successfully channelled organised labour towards supporting the government.

GRAMSCI, ANTONIO
(1891–1937). Born in Sardinia, Gramsci won a scholarship to the University of Turin in 1911, and joined the Italian Socialist Party in 1913. Inspired by the Bolshevik Revolution and the ensuing political ferment among the Turin workers, Gramsci founded a new socialist weekly *L'Ordine Nuovo* in 1919 and became a founder member of the Italian Communist Party in 1921. For the next three years he worked for the Comintern in Moscow and returned to Italy in 1924 to become his party's leader. In 1926 he was arrested and remained in prison until his death in 1937. It was here that he produced his voluminous *Prison Notebooks* whose socio-historical breadth and insight have made it one of the most influential works in Western Marxism.

GREEN, THOMAS HILL
(1836–82). Born in Birkin, Yorkshire, Green was educated by his clergyman father and at Rugby and Balliol. He remained at Oxford for the rest of his short life, from 1860 as a Fellow of Balliol, where he became increasingly involved in college politics and university reforms under Benjamin Jowett's mastership. In 1878 he was elected Whyte's professor of moral philosophy at Oxford. A democrat, liberal and evangelical Anglican, Green inspired students to devote themselves to social service and was himself the first university don to be elected a city councillor for the town, not the university, of Oxford. Green attacked the reductive views of human nature and the state he found in utilitarianism and Hobbesianism, building a rival account from Plato, Kant and Hegel of political community as aiming at the realisation of a common good and of the development of the moral powers of all citizens. Many of his lectures were published posthumously.

HABERMAS, JÜRGEN
(1929–). Born in Düsseldorf, Habermas is perhaps the most influential social theorist of the late twentieth century. After studying philosophy, history and psychology in Göttingen, he earned his doctorate in Bonn and became Adorno's assistant in Frankfurt in 1956, publishing *Structural Transformation of the Public Sphere* in 1962. He became professor of philosophy and sociology in Frankfurt in 1964 where he was sympathetic to the student-led protests of the late 1960s. Habermas left Frankfurt in 1971 to become director of the Max Planck Institute in Starnberg, Bavaria. Here he continued his prolific reconstruction of historical materialism, publishing his two-volume *Theory of Communicative Action* in 1981 before returning to a chair in sociology and philosophy in Frankfurt in 1984.

HAECKEL, ERNST
(1834–1919) was a German naturalist and early ecologist born in Potsdam and educated at Wurzburg, Vienna and Berlin. An outspoken liberal non-conformist and early supporter of Charles Darwin, Haeckel was a controversial figure in a conservative era. In 1869 Haeckel coined the term *Oecologie* – translated as 'ecology' in his *The Wonders of Life* (1904) – which he defined as 'the body of knowledge concerning the economy of nature – the

investigation of the total relationship of the animal both to its organic and its inorganic environment . . . Ecology is the study of all those complex interrelations referred to by Darwin as the conditions for the struggle of existence.' A prolific and popular author in his own day, Haeckel is today considered the founder of ecology whose thinking has had an important influence on the modern environmental movement.

HANAFI, HASAN

(1935–) studied at the Sorbonne in Paris, earning a doctorate in philosophy in 1966. He is now professor of philosophy at Cairo University. Hanafi's early essays are informed by his view that a resolution of the problems facing Arab societies can be found in the reconciliation of nationalist and Islamic political ideals. His resolution took the form of the Islamic Left project which materialised as a short-lived periodical in 1981. Hanafi sees his role as that of a *faqih* (jurist-interpreter) and activist. His major work is *Heritage and Renewal* (1981), a project consisting of three planks: Our Position from the Old Heritage, Our Position from Western Heritage and Our Position from Reality. Under the first plank, he has completed five volumes. Written under the second plank, his *Introduction to the Science of Occidentalism* (1992) offers a critical reading of Western culture and thought. In 1997, following a public lecture, Hanafi became the target of radical Islamist denunciation.

HARDIN, GARRETT

(1915–) is an American ecologist and environmentalist born in Texas and educated at the University of Chicago and Stanford University. Hardin has been an outspoken advocate of population control and other controversial policies. He holds that famine relief and other aid programmes should be tied to limitations on population growth. His essay 'The Tragedy of the Commons' (1968) shows how and why unrestricted public access to and use of common land (or any other resource, including the oceans) leads inevitably and tragically to the exceeding of its 'carrying capacity', that is, its ability to support and sustain those who use it. The remedy for overfishing, overgrazing and other sorts of environmental degradation can come only through 'mutual coercion, mutually agreed upon by a majority of the people affected'. Hardin's major works include *Exploring New Ethics for Survival* (1972), *The Limits of Altruism* (1977) and *Filters against Folly* (1985).

HART, H. L. A.

(1907–92). Herbert Hart was educated at New College, Oxford, and practised law for eight years before working in military intelligence during the Second World War. Returning to Oxford, first as a tutor in philosophy and then as professor of jurisprudence, Hart introduced the analytical techniques pioneered by J. L. Austin and Gilbert Ryle into the study of legal theory. An early work, *Causation in the Law* (with A. M. Honoré, 1959), was followed by his major work in jurisprudence, *The Concept of Law* (1961), arguments against 'morals' legislation (*Law, Liberty, and Morality*, 1963), and several studies in the theory of punishment published as *Punishment and Responsibility* (1968). Hart resigned his chair in 1967 and was elected principal of Brasenose College, Oxford, in 1972.

HAYEK, FRIEDRICH

(1899–1992). Born in Vienna, Hayek became the best-known member of the Austrian school of economics. The central theme of his political thought, which is a sustained attack on planning and collectivism, first won attention in *The Road to Serfdom* (1944), in which he extended his critique of totalitarianism to social democracy (which he characterised as the road to serfdom). During the 1960s and 1970s, when Keynesian interventionist orthodoxy dominated Western politics, he was largely neglected. During the 1970s and

1980s, however, he won international renown by reacting against state planning developed in Britain and America. In 1974 he was awarded the Nobel prize in economics. In the 1980s, his anti-interventionist teaching was adopted by Ronald Reagan in the USA and by Margaret Thatcher in Britain. He died in Freiburg, having lived to see the collapse of the Soviet Union and the spread of free-market ideology throughout much of the world.

HEIDEGGER, MARTIN
(1889–1976). Heidegger was born in the small town of Messkirch in south-west Germany, where his father was the cellarman and sexton of the local church. In 1903 he went as a boarder to the high school in Konstanz, on a scholarship. His intention at this time was to train for the priesthood, and in 1906 he moved to the high school in Freiburg, where he was supported by the Catholic church. In 1909 he became a Jesuit novice, but was soon discharged, ostensibly because of a heart condition, and entered the University of Freiburg. He broke off his training for the priesthood entirely in 1911, and turned towards the study of philosophy. In 1917 he married the Protestant Elfriede Petri, and a year later became Edmund Husserl's assistant in Freiburg. He moved to an associate professorship in Marburg in 1923, and there had a passionate affair with one of his students, Hannah Arendt. His masterpiece, *Being and Time*, was published in 1927, and in 1929 he succeeded Edmund Husserl to the chair of philosophy in Freiburg. In April 1933 Heidegger was elected rector of Freiburg University, and on 1 May he joined the Nazi Party. For the next year he made enthusiastic speeches in favour of the regime, and generally promoted its academic policies, whilst seeking to mitigate some of their cruder features. He resigned as rector in April 1934, continuing to lecture at Freiburg, but publishing little until after the Second World War. In 1946 he was subjected to a teaching ban, imposed by the De-Nazification Committee of the French occupying forces, and was granted emeritus status by the university. In his later years Heidegger continued to write and to lecture extensively, travelling abroad several times to France and Greece. He died in 1976, having spent his final days helping to prepare a complete edition of his works, the *Gesamtausgabe* which is still in progress. He was buried in the churchyard in Messkirch.

HILFERDING, RUDOLF
(1877–1943) became the most significant Marxist economist of his age. In 1904, in *Marx-Studien*, he defended the theory of surplus value against Böhm-Bawerk, and six years later, having moved to Germany, produced his masterpiece, *Finance Capital* (1910), a study of capitalism in the age of imperialism which was hugely influential. He later became the social democratic Reich finance minister in 1923 and again in 1928. He was caught in France during the Second World War by the Nazi police and either died in the Buchenwald concentration camp or committed suicide.

HITLER, ADOLF
(1889–1945) was born an Austrian citizen, and son of a civil servant. Hitler moved to Germany in 1913 and served in the German army throughout the First World War, joining the Nazi Party in 1919. After his unsuccessful 'beer hall putsch' of 1923 and during his subsequent imprisonment he began writing *Mein Kampf* (My Battle, 1925), in which he set out the fundamental tenets of National Socialist ideology. Hitler soon became the party's unquestioned leader and subsequently led it to electoral triumphs in 1930 and 1932. He became constitutional chancellor of Germany in January 1933 and was voted powers to exercise a four-year dictatorship, which he subsequently made permanent, becoming president and head of state in August 1934. Hitler launched major rearmament in 1936, occupying Austria and part of Czechoslovakia two years later. He began the Second World

War in Europe with the invasion of Poland in 1939, followed by that of France and other western countries in 1940, and of Greece, Yugoslavia and the Soviet Union in 1941. His 'Final Solution' for the liquidation of European Jews was initiated in December 1941. He committed suicide in Berlin in April 1945.

HOBHOUSE, LEONARD TRELAWNY
(1864–1929) was a British social philosopher and journalist. As a young Oxford philosophy don, Hobhouse became interested in an evolutionary holism that could be empirically demonstrated. This influenced his social liberal views, which found their keenest expression in his now classic book *Liberalism* (1911), and his influence on the nascent new liberalism was considerable. Hobson was intermittently a leader-writer and journalist for the *Manchester Guardian*, though he wrote for other liberal publications such as *The Nation*. In 1908 he was appointed to the first chair in sociology at the London School of Economics and Political Science, further pursuing his studies of comparative social development, which focused on human reason and cooperation. Initially sympathetic to philosophical idealism, he reacted against German Hegelianism as a result of the First World War.

HOBSON, JOHN ATKINSON
(1858–1940) was a British social theorist, economist and journalist. Hobson developed a theory of under-consumptionism, later acknowledged by Keynes, and a critique of imperialism as an outlet for illegitimately owned surpluses and finance capitalism. These social disorders called for ethical as well as economic solutions through the redistribution of wealth. Hobson's brand of liberal organicism was decisive in shifting British new liberal thought towards a concern with social reform and welfare, utilising insights from economics, political theory, sociology and psychology. He was active in many radical reform groups including the Rainbow Circle, the South Place Ethical Society and the Union of Democratic Control. A prolific writer, Hobson produced over fifty books and pamphlets and hundreds of articles, many published in *The Nation* and *The Manchester Guardian*.

HO CHI MINH OR 'ENLIGHTENER' (real name NGUYEN TAT THANH)
(1890–1969), was a Vietnamese Communist leader and president of North Vietnam 1954–69. He was born in the village of Kimlien, Annam (central Vietnam), the son of an official who had resigned in protest against French domination of his country. After travelling the world for several years doing menial jobs, Ho ended up in Paris where he became a founding member of the French Communist Party. Trained in Moscow in late 1924, he was sent to China (1925–7) where he organised the Communist Party of Indochina (later the Vietnamese Communist Party) amongst Vietnamese exiles. In the 1930s he moved between Moscow and China, including a period in prison in Hong Kong (1931–3), but returned to Vietnam after Japan invaded in 1941 and helped organise the Vietnamese independence movement (Viet Minh). In 1945 Ho officially proclaimed the Democratic Republic of North Vietnam and directed its anti-colonial drive against the French, who were finally defeated in the battle of Dien Bien Phu of 1954. However, the country was divided at the seventeenth parallel after negotiations in Geneva. As president, Ho consolidated the Communist regime in the North, but in the 1960s conflict resumed with the South which, backed by the United States, had refused to hold the elections projected by the Geneva accord. Ho promoted a guerrilla movement in the South, the National Liberation Front or Viet Cong, to win South Vietnam from the various US-supported governments there. He died of heart failure in Hanoi on 3 September 1969.

Saigon was renamed Ho Chi Min City in his honour after the Communist conquest of the South in 1975. Aptly called 'the Saint-Just of the twentieth century', Ho displayed his great organisational talent in exploiting nationalist sentiment and peasant grievances. Although he became something of a legend among the student left in the late 1960s, he remained an activist rather than a theorist. His most important writings are early: his pamphlet on European and American racism entitled *Black Race* (1924) and *Le procès de la colonisation française* (1926).

HORKHEIMER, MAX
(1895–1973). Born in Stuttgart, Horkheimer was the originator of what became known as the Frankfurt school. Initially a student of psychology, he turned to philosophy and completed his doctorate on Kant in 1924. He became the influential director of the Institute for Social Research in Frankfurt in 1930, was the instigator of its development of a critical social theory, and held it together during its exile in the United States. He published several influential essays on critical theory in the 1930s and, with Adorno, wrote *Dialectic of the Enlightenment* in 1947. Horkheimer returned to Germany after the Second World War and continued to publish prolifically, though from a much more conservative perspective, on contemporary culture and politics.

IQBAL, MUHAMMAD
(1873–1938) was born in the Punjab. Iqbal is considered the poet-philosopher of Pakistan. He received higher education at the Government College in Lahore, earning a master's degree in philosophy in 1899. He was appointed reader in Arabic at the University Oriental College of Lahore. Iqbal pursued further studies in Germany and Britain. He received a doctorate in philosophy in 1907 from Munich University and qualified for the bar in Britain. He also studied philosophy at Cambridge University's Trinity College. In 1908, Iqbal began his involvement with the British Committee of All-India Muslim League. Through the League, he expressed his concerns about the political and cultural conditions of Muslims in the Indian subcontinent. In his 1930 presidential address to the League, he presented his concept of two nations in India. This address laid down the conceptual foundation of Pakistan. The Muslim nation was conceived by Iqbal in the Indian context as a requirement for the self-determination and cultural unification of Muslims. Iqbal's thought provided the ideological basis for the demand for a separate Muslim state and was adopted by the Muslim League under Muhammad Ali Jinnah's leadership in 1940. Iqbal's notion of the Self and his vision of East and West were expressed in his poetry, including *Secrets of the Self* (1915). In *The Reconstruction of Religious Thought in Islam*, Iqbal articulated the principles of a renewed approach to religion.

AL-JABIRI, MUHAMMAD ABID
(1936–) was born in south-eastern Morocco and studied philosophy at the University of Rabat. He completed a Ph.D. in 1970 on the thought of Ibn Khaldun. He is currently professor of philosophy at the University of Muhammad V in Rabat. He began publishing on Islamic thought in the 1970s. In 1980 a collection of his writings on Islamic philosophy was published under the title *Nahnu wa al-Turath*. In 1982, he published *al-Khitab al-'Arabi al-Mu'asir* in which he presented a critical reading of Arab thought in the modern period. His work shows the influence of structuralist and post-structuralist thought. His *Critique of Arab Reason* (1986), a three-volume work, is informed by Foucault's archaeology of systems of knowledge. Over the last decade, his writings have addressed issues of democracy, civil society and human rights in the Arab world.

JAMES, WILLIAM
(1842–1910). Older brother of the novelist Henry James and member of an illustrious American family, James became an enormously influential philosopher of pragmatism as well as a pioneering psychologist. Having studied at Harvard and earned an MD, he taught there throughout his career, advancing to professor of psychology. In the early 1870s James set up the first psychological laboratory in America. He saw the mind as essentially active and thought that this exploded most previous philosophical controversies and beliefs which presupposed a passive, reflecting mind. James was fascinated by religion and sought to defend and explain the possibility of moral action in experiential, naturalistic terms. A friend of C.S. Peirce, he popularised pragmatism as a theory of meaning and a theory of truth, but always stressed the context of action, habit and will in which the identification of truths took place. He sought to establish objective values as the most inclusive values of a caring and interactive community.

JAURÈS, JEAN
(1859–1914) was born in Castres in the south of France, studied at the Ecole Normale Supérieure and became a philosophy teacher. Subsequently elected to the Chamber of Deputies as a republican, he began to see socialism as a natural extension of the republican and revolutionary tradition. Influenced by Marx, committed to international working-class solidarity but at home with middle-class liberals, eclectic, brilliant and open-minded, his socialism differed markedly from the schematic Marxism of Jules Guesde. His fervent anti-war campaigning dominated the last years of his life and he was shot dead by a nationalist on 31 July 1914, only hours before the outbreak of war.

JUNG, CARL G. USTAV
(1875–1961) Swiss psychiatrist, his father was a clergyman whose loss of faith and contrast with his extrovert and warm mother had a profound influence on his later interest in religion. Though he had developed his ideas before they met, he worked with Freud in Vienna for seven years, becoming for a time his "crown prince" and acting for four years as President of the International Psychoanalytical Association. However, he split from him in 1914 and founded the movement known as "analytical psychology." Jung took a more positive view of the unconscious than Freud, which meant being less suspicious of both dreams and symptoms. The role of psychoanalysis became to make the individual conscious of the unconscious, explicating the meaning of dreams and fantasies through the use of association and analogy. Jung believed that certain unconscious fantasies or 'archetypes' were universal, being part of a collective unconscious, and could appear in any age in the same form. He drew heavily on the scientific analysis of his own dreams and also applied this approach to the study of religious imagery and mythology. Jung's international following today remains smaller than Freud's, but it is still considerable. His main publications include Psychology of the Unconscious (1912), Psychological Types (1921), Psychology and Religion (1938) and the semi-autobiographical Memories, Dreams. Reflections (1965).

JÜNGER, ERNST
(1895–1998). Born in Heidelberg, the son of a pharmacist and inventor, Jünger became a national hero after being wounded fourteen times during the First World War and receiving many decorations, including the Iron Cross First Class and the highest award of all, the 'Blue Max' (*Pour le mérite*). Jünger's war record, nationalism and anti-democratic 'action' philosophy gained him the admiration of the Nazis, but Jünger always kept them at arm's length and never joined their party. In 1939 he rejoined the army as a captain, but

he was dishonourably discharged in 1944, after becoming indirectly associated with the plot against Hitler earlier in that year. Some years previously Jünger had already incurred the disapprobation of the regime by the publication of a satire on dictatorship, *Auf den Marmorklippen* (*On the Marble Cliffs*, 1939), which was banned in 1940. His post-war rehabilitation was completed in the aftermath of German reunification, being symbolised by the personal visits paid to him on his hundredth birthday by the chancellor, Helmut Kohl, and the president, Roman Herzog, as well as by a congratulatory message he received from the French president, François Mitterrand. Somewhat ironically for a thinker who has been termed 'the last Nietzschean', Jünger's rehabilitation was partly due to the German Greens, who sympathised with his life-long preference for the natural world (he was an enthusiastic entomologist, with a collection of 40,000 beetles) over the society of men.

KANDINSKY, WASSILY

(1866–1944). Born in Moscow, Kandinsky decided in 1896 to pursue an artistic career in Munich, where he founded the Blaue Reiter movement in 1911. Though he returned to Russia from 1914 to 1921, the lack of artistic freedom sent him back to Germany, where he joined the Bauhaus school of design. He moved to France in 1933, soon becoming a naturalised citizen. Generally recognised, along with Piet Mondrian, as one of the greatest innovators in early abstract painting, he is especially famous for his ten 'compositions' (1910 to 1939), seven of which survive. Among his most important treatises on modernism are *Über das Geistige in der Kunst* (1911) and *Der Blaue Reiter* (1912), which he co-edited with Franz Marc.

KAUTSKY, KARL

(1854–1938) was born in Prague and went on to become the chief ideologue of German social democracy and of the Second International. More than any other single individual he defined Marxism for the generation after Marx through the magazine he founded and edited, *Die Neue Zeit*, and a host of books and articles, including *The Economic Doctrines of Karl Marx* (1887), his commentary on the *Erfurt Programme* (1892) and his writings against Eduard Bernstein on the right and Rosa Luxemburg on the left. His *Road to Power* (1909), which predicted an age of class conflict, imperial rivalry, colonial revolts and war, had a huge impact on Lenin, as his study of the *Agrarian Question* (1899) had a decade earlier. Subsequently Kautsky came to doubt that imperialism would lead to war; and he later became one of the most bitter opponents of the Bolshevik regime, especially in *The Dictatorship of the Proletariat* (1918). After 1918 his influence declined dramatically.

KELLY, PETRA

(1947–1992) was a German ecofeminist and one of the theoreticians and founders of die Grünen, the German Green Party, in 1979. Kelly was born in Bavaria of a German mother and an American father. She was educated in the United States and returned to Europe for graduate studies at the University of Amsterdam. Returning to Germany in the mid-1970s she became active in the student and feminist movements and was a founding member of die Grünen. In 1982 she was one of twenty-seven Greens elected to the German Bundestag or parliament. Although re-elected four years later, she became increasingly disillusioned with the willingness of her party to compromise on matters of principle. Her own principles are set out in several books, including *Thinking Green! Essays on Environmentalism, Feminism and Nonviolence* (1994). This pacifist and advocate of non-violence was herself murdered in 1992.

KELSEN, HANS
(1881–1973). Born into a Jewish family from Galicia, Kelsen studied law at the University of Vienna, where he was later a professor from 1911 to 1930. He then moved to Cologne, leaving in 1933, following Hitler's rise to power, when he moved to Prague, where he remained until 1938, then to Geneva and, finally, to the United States, where he taught at Berkeley for the remaining three decades of his life. The most influential modern theorist of legal positivism, he endeavoured to articulate the *Grundnorm* or basic norm presupposed by any legal system which was the source of its authority and obligatory character. His many books include the *General Theory of Law and State* (1945), *The Pure Theory of Law* (1967), *The Communist Theory of Law* (1955) and *Law and Peace in International Relations* (1942).

KETTELER, WILHELM EMMANUEL VON
(1811–77). As a young parish priest Ketteler worked with the poor and the sick in the Società of San Vincenzo, where in 1948 he first became aware of 'the social question'. From 1850 he was bishop of Mainz, where he promoted the creation of associations for religious and professional groups. From 1863 he analysed the 'workers' question' in his writings. Along with the other founders of Zentrum he was elected as a member of the Reichstag, where he drafted social legislation.

KEYNES, JOHN MAYNARD
(1883–1946) was born in Cambridge, England. While a student of philosophy and mathematics at King's College, Cambridge, he was greatly influenced by the philosopher G. E. Moore. He had a short-lived career in the civil service and returned to Cambridge as Alfred Marshall's protégé. He later joined the Treasury team at the Versailles Peace Conference. Disillusioned with the settlement, he resigned and wrote *The Economic Consequences of the Peace* (1919). In the period between the world wars Keynes was a severe critic of the ruling economic orthodoxy which held that government should not interfere in the market economy to counteract the effects of the trade cycle. This culminated in the publication of the *General Theory of Employment, Interest and Money* (1936). Keynes took a leading role in war finance and in the development of a system of national income accounts and he was responsible for negotiating an American loan. He was also a leading figure in the creation of the post-war monetary order agreed at Bretton Woods (1944). Critics such as Friedrich von Hayek and Milton Friedman blamed his theories for the growth of big government and the high levels of inflation and unemployment in the 1970s and 1980s.

KHOMEINI, RUHOLLAH AL-MUSAVI
(1902–89). A religious scholar and a leading jurist, Khomeini rose in the ranks of the *ulama* to become an eminent *mujtahid*. He studied philosophy and was influenced by mystic traditions in Islam. He wrote a number of commentaries on classical works in Islamic mysticism. Khomeini managed to fuse his interest in intuitive knowledge with a legalistic approach to religion. The latter was expressed in his public statements and his main religio-political work (*Wilayat al-Faqih*). His involvement in political opposition against the Shah of Iran began in the 1960s. Khomeini opposed policies introduced by the Shah and denounced the granting of extra-territorial rights to the USA in 1964. As a result, he was forced into exile. In exile, he developed links with anti-Shah movements abroad. He articulated his revolutionary rhetoric on audio-tapes which were widely circulated in Iran in the 1970s, contributing to the mobilisation of the public against the Shah. He returned to Iran in 1979 to become the ruling jurist of the revolutionary regime.

KIRK, RUSSELL
(1918–94). The son of a railway engineer, Kirk grew up in rural Michigan where he came at an early stage to dislike the impersonal world of modern technology symbolised for him by the progress of the motor industry in his home state under the leadership of Henry Ford. After graduating from Michigan State College, which he entered in 1936, this hostility found intellectual expression in a master's thesis which Kirk wrote on the Virginian aristocrat John Randolph whilst studying history in the postgraduate school of Duke University. Kirk's work on Randolph, whom he regarded as the American Burke, was subsequently to be published as *Randolph of Roanoke* (1931). Politically, Kirk's thought crystallised in dislike of what he considered to be the Leviathan state created by the New Deal, a dislike further intensified by his experience of military service after being drafted into the army in 1942. After the war Kirk studied for his doctorate at St Andrews University in Scotland, becoming even more deeply enchanted with the British conservative tradition in the process. The outcome of his experience and reflections was *The Conservative Mind* (1953). Although the reactionary character of Kirk's thought meant that his influence on the post-war American conservative movement was only temporary, and that he soon found himself marginalised, his enormously successful book not only made conservatism intellectually respectable in America but also gave a coherent (albeit tentative) identity to the renascent post-war conservative movement.

KOESTLER, ARTHUR
(1905–83) was an influential and controversial novelist and essayist best known for his critiques of communism. Koestler was born in Hungary and, as he recounts in his autobiographical essay in *The God that Failed* (1949), he was drawn to communism as a student in Vienna. He served as a journalist during the Spanish Civil War and was imprisoned by the fascists, an experience recounted in his *Spanish Testament* (1937). His experience of the war contributed to his disaffection with communism, which he came to see as opportunistic and totalitarian. His most famous novel, *Darkness at Noon* (1940), gives voice to this sentiment, telling the story of Rubashov, an old-guard Bolshevik who is persecuted during the Stalinist show trials of the 1930s, and is so intoxicated with communist ideology that he is incapable of refuting the claims of his own 'objective guilt' as a 'class enemy' of the revolution. Koestler furthered his critique of communism in *The Yogi and the Commissar* (1945) and in his famous contribution to Richard Crossman's anthology *The God that Failed* (1949). During the Cold War period Koestler came increasingly to be associated with extreme anti-communist sentiments. In his later years he suffered multiple illnesses, and in 1983 he committed suicide along with his wife Cynthia.

KOJÈVE, ALEXANDRE
(1902–68). Born in Russia and educated in Berlin, Kojève was a crucial conduit for German philosophical ideas into France. Between 1933 and 1938 he lectured in Paris on Hegel's *Phenomenology of Spirit* and his audience included Jean-Paul Sartre, Raymond Aron, Maurice Merleau-Ponty and Georges Bataille. These lectures (later published as *An Introduction to the Reading of Hegel*, 1947), focused on the master–slave dialectic as the key to Hegel's philosophy of history, and were greatly to influence an entire generation's understanding of Hegel. After the end of the Second World War, Kojève held a post in the French Ministry of Economic Affairs.

KOLLONTAI, ALEXANDRA
(1872–1952) was a Russian feminist who joined the Bolsheviks in 1914 and was a member of the party's Central Committee by 1917. After the October Revolution she became

the Commissar for Women in Lenin's revolutionary government. In 1920 she joined the workers' opposition within the party and was condemned by Lenin and by Stalin. She escaped Stalin's purges and became Soviet ambassador to Sweden in 1930. Among her published works are *The Social Basis of the Woman Question* (1909), *Towards a History of the Working Women's Movement in Russia* (1920), *The Labour of Women in the Evolution of the Economy* (1923), a collection of stories entitled *Love of the Worker Bees* (1923) and *Autobiography of a Sexually Emancipated Woman* (1926).

KORSCH, KARL
(1886–1961). Born in Hamburg, Korsch studied law, economics and philosophy. He became a member of the Fabian Society during his pre-war stay in England. After the war he moved rapidly leftwards and became a leading member of the Communist Party of Germany, participating actively in the workers' councils movement. During this period he published his most influential book *Marxism and Philosophy* which, like the work of the early Lukács, stressed the activist, self-reflexive element in Marxism. Korsch was expelled from the Communist Party in 1926 and, in exile in the United States from 1938 onwards, moved away from Marxism.

LABRIOLA, ANTONIO
(1843–1904) was born in Cassino, studied at the University of Naples, was for a time a school teacher, and was finally appointed to a chair at Rome University, where he continued to work as an academic philosopher. Initially influenced by Hegel, he was gradually converted to Marxism, a conversion which culminated in *On Socialism* (1889) and *Essays on the Materialist Conception of History* (1896). Open to Kant and suspicious of historical schematisation, Labriola nonetheless embraced the cause of proletarian solidarity and rejected 'revisionism'. He played much the same role of Marxist populariser as did Kautsky in Germany and Plekhanov in Russia.

LAMENNAIS, FÉLICITÉ-ROBERT DE
(1782–1854) was in the priesthood from 1816, and found himself in conflict with the Gallican religious authorities due to his strict adherence to Roman orthodoxy. After the revolution of 1830, he turned to liberal Catholicism, of which the journal *Avenir*, founded in 1831, became a symbol. After demonstrating on more than one occasion his subjection to the church, Lamennais left it in order to become a philosopher and to fight for democracy. The *Livre du peuple*, published in 1838, led to his imprisonment for twelve months due to his criticism of the monarchy. After the revolution of 1848, he became a member of parliament and a member of the Constituent Council. However, in 1851 he retired from political life a disillusioned man.

LAROQUE, PIERRE
(1907–97) was a French social administrator. He was involved in the early 1930s in implementing social insurance legislation. During the Second World War he joined the Free French forces in London. After the war he was invited to draw up plans for a French social security system. He was director general of social security from 1944 to 1951 during which time the foundations of the modern French welfare state were laid. He became a member of the Conseil d'Etat in 1951 and between 1964 and 1980 he held the presidency of its social section. In addition he was active in various roles relating to savings, old-age and population issues. He wrote extensively on the legal aspects of social security and taught on the subject.

LASSWELL, HAROLD DWIGHT

(1902–78). Born into a religious and teaching family in rural Illinois, Lasswell was a pioneer in the disciplinary study of politics. At sixteen, he went to study at the University of Chicago, completing a Ph.D. there under Charles Merriam in 1926 and staying on the faculty until 1938. His principal interests centred on the interdisciplinary relationships between psychology, psychiatry, political science and international relations, as evident especially in *Psychopathology and Politics* (1930) and *World Politics and Personal Insecurity* (1935). The title of his most famous text – *Politics: Who Gets What, When, How* (1936) – helped define a power-and-interest-oriented science of politics, just as his later emphases on behaviour and public policy proved central to the development of behaviouralism and the policy sciences. His early work (beginning with a dissertation) on propaganda and the method of content analysis provided him with the credentials to serve as the director of the Experimental Division for the Study of War-Time Communications at the Library of Congress during the Second World War. After the war, and until his retirement, he taught in the law school at Yale University and had a private practice in psychoanalysis in New York.

LEFEBVRE, HENRI

(1901–91). Born in south-west France, Lefebvre studied philosophy in Paris and, along with Paul Nizan, Georges Politzer and Georges Friedmann, formed part of the first generation of philosophers to be drawn to Marxism and the Communist Party during the 1920s and 1930s. He joined the party in 1928 and remained a member until his expulsion in 1958. He translated Marx's early writings into French and published them in 1933, and in 1940 he published perhaps his most influential book, *Dialectical Materialism*, which took issue with Stalin's own interpretation of Marxian theory. Involved in the Resistance during the war, after its end Lefebvre published a series of popularising works on Marxism – centred on the concept of alienation found in Marx's early writings. Drawing increasingly upon sociological themes and the critique of bureaucracy, after his expulsion from the party he aligned himself with revisionist currents, contributed to the journal *Arguments*, and enjoyed renown in the late 1960s and 1970s. Surprisingly, in the late 1970s he renewed his links with the French Communist Party, putting faith perhaps in the brief thaw associated with 'Euro-Communism'.

LENIN (VLADIMIR ILICH ULYANOV)

(1870–1924). Unquestionably the most influential political leader and theorist of Marxism in the twentieth century, Lenin revitalised its theory of revolution in elaborating a theory of imperialism or monopoly state capitalism (1916), and by presenting the Russian soviets as the contemporary vehicles of the participatory unmediated democracy recommended by Marx in his accounts of the Paris Commune (1917). He led the Bolsheviks in the October Revolution of 1917 and became chairman of the Council of People's Commissars. By late 1922, illness forced his effective retirement and his remaining energies were devoted to criticising distortions in the party and soviet administrative systems and to ineffective efforts to remove Stalin from the positions of power into which he had placed him. Lenin's theory of imperialism postulated a new and final phase in the development of capitalism in which it had become monopolistic, parasitic upon colonial exploitation and identified with a militarist and politically monolithic state. It had, however, globalised the contradictions of capitalism and prepared the way for the fusion of national democratic revolutions in the colonies and socialist revolutions in the capitalist heartlands. It had concentrated capital in the banks and production in trusts and cartels so that the task of bringing the economy under social control had been greatly simplified. The international war created by imperialism could only be ended by international revolution and Russia as the weakest link in the imperialist chain could begin it. The libertarian tone of Lenin's writings altered after the Bolshevik seizure of power and the dictatorship of the proletariat exercised by the Communist Party was held to be necessary to the survival of socialism in Russia, given the succession of internal and external crises it faced. Under his direction the regime became increasingly intolerant and centralised, though economic concessions and a mixed economy were introduced in 1921. His principal writings include: *The Development of Capitalism in Russia* (1899), *What Is To Be Done?* (1902), *Materialism and Empiriocriticism* (1908), *Imperialism: The Highest Stage of Capitalism* (1916), *The State and Revolution* (1917), *The Proletarian Revolution and the Renegade Kautsky* (1918), and *How We Should Reorganise the Workers' and Peasants' Inspection* (1923).

LEO XIII (VINCENZO GIOACCHINO PECCI)
(1810–1903) was elected Pope in 1878, and demonstrated immediately that he was open to the evolution of contemporary society, in contrast to the intransigence exhibited by his predecessor Pius IX. He was both able to develop a less polemical relationship with the Italian state and to close down the *Kulturkampf* in Germany. He also managed to promote a reconciliation (*ralliement*) between French Catholics and the Republic. As far as doctrine was concerned, he promoted the revival of the Thomist theological tradition. His works on contemporary social problems were crucial, the best example of which was the encyclical *Rerum novarum*.

LEOPOLD, ALDO
(1887–1948) was a pioneering American ecologist and author born in Iowa and educated at Yale University. His early career was spent in the US Forestry Service in the American south-west, where he advocated and practised 'game management', that is, the systematic killing of predators so that human hunters could kill more deer, elk and other animal species. He repudiated that view after he saw 'a fierce green fire' dying in the eyes of a she-wolf he had shot. He came round to the view that all animals, including predators, perform valuable functions for the complexly interdependent 'biotic community' to which they and human beings belong. His views are elegantly presented in his posthumously published *A Sand County Almanac* (1949), widely considered to be a classic of the modern environmental movement.

LEVINAS, EMMANUEL
(1906–95). Levinas was born in Kaunas, Lithuania, of Jewish parents who spoke both Yiddish and Russian at home. After graduating from the Russian-language Jewish Lyceum in Kaunas, Levinas went to France to study at the University of Strasbourg. In 1928–9 he studied with Husserl and Heidegger in Freiburg. Over the next few years his early publications played a pioneering role in introducing the ideas of these two thinkers into France. After earning his doctorate, Levinas taught at the Ecole Normale Israélite Orientale in Paris, a school for Jewish students, many from traditional backgrounds. During the Second World War he served as an officer in the French army, and was interned by the Germans in a prisoner-of-war camp. His family in Lithuania died in the Holocaust, while his wife and daughter hid in a French monastery. After the war Levinas acted as director of the Ecole Normale Israélite Orientale, and frequented the avant-garde philosophical circles of Jean Wahl and Gabriel Marcel. In 1961 he took a position at the University of Poitiers, moving to the Nanterre branch of the University of Paris in 1967, and finally to the Sorbonne in 1973. Levinas has been termed a 'man of four cultures': Jewish, Russian,

German and French. His most important works of philosophy are *Totality and Infinity* (1961) and *Otherwise than Being* (1974), but he also published many occasional pieces, in reviews and periodicals, on Judaism, philosophy, politics and contemporary culture, as well as three volumes of Talmudic commentary. He continued to write prolifically after his retirement in 1979, by which time the advocacy of prominent thinkers such as Jacques Derrida had brought his innovative phenomenology of ethical experience international recognition.

LIPPMANN, WALTER

(1889–1974). Born in New York to German-Jewish parents, Lippmann was a famous journalist, author and critic. Educated at Harvard under Graham Wallas and George Santayana, he began his career as a liberal critic of popular opinion with his first book, *Preface to Politics* (1913). He helped found *The New Republic* in 1914, and went on to become a writer and editor for New York City newspapers, especially the *Herald-Tribune*. President Woodrow Wilson called for his assistance in formulating the Fourteen Points and envisioning the League of Nations. Lippmann served on the Committee for Public Information during the First World War, and was sent as a delegate to the peace negotiations for the Treaty of Versailles. His two most famous works of political theory – *Public Opinion* (1922) and *The Phantom Public* (1925) – criticised the democratic ideal of the 'omnicompetent citizen'. They proved influential on the subsequent course of opinion research, and prompted a sustained response from John Dewey in *The Public and its Problems* (1927). In later writings, especially *The Good Society* (1937) and *The Cold War* (1947), Lippmann took a decidedly conservative turn, criticising the collectivist tendencies of the age. He received a special Pulitzer prize for his varied contributions in 1958.

LIST, FRIEDRICH

(1789–1846) was born in Württemberg and became a deputy in the state Chamber but was expelled in 1802. After a spell in prison, he emigrated to America, returning to Europe in 1832. His major work, *The National System of Political Economy* (1840) attacked but borrowed from the writings of Adam Smith. It expounded a theory of historical stages: (1) pastoralism; (2) agriculture; (3) agriculture united with manufacturing; and (4) agriculture, manufacturing and commerce combined. In the second and fourth stages he believed free trade to be the optimal policy, but argued strongly for national protection in the third stage. It was this aspect of his argument – and his support for the *Zollverein* – that most influenced nationalist thought.

LUKÁCS, GEORG

(1885–1971). Born in Budapest, Lukács became, from the 1920s onwards, the most prominent Marxist philosopher in the West. He studied in Germany and published widely in literary theory. In 1918, he joined the Communist Party and in the following year became People's Commissar for Education and Culture in the short-lived Hungarian Commune. In 1923 Lukács published his *History and Class Consciousness* which, although condemned by the Comintern, proved hugely influential. With the rise of fascism in Europe, Lukács moved to Moscow where he returned to his former interest in aesthetics and literary theory. After the war he moved back to Hungary where he continued to be as active in politics as the regime allowed. In addition to more work on aesthetics, he produced a massive social ontology which continued his lifelong project of re-evaluating the Hegelian roots of Marxism.

LUXEMBURG, ROSA
(1870–1919) was born of Polish-Jewish parents in Zamosc. Involved in an illegal socialist youth group, she fled to Switzerland, studied at Zurich University, then moved to Berlin in 1898, where she made an immediate impact on the left of the SPD by her biting critique of Bernstein. Subsequently she criticised both Bolshevism and Kautsky's passivity, advocating the mass strike in an age of revolution and arguing that the working class developed its capacities not through sterile organisation but action, a view decisively influenced by the time she spent in Polish Russia during the 1905/6 Revolution. Luxemburg was a founding member of the Spartacist League in Germany during the First World War, which it opposed, was imprisoned for her views and later, in a revolutionary uprising in Berlin in January 1919, was murdered by the reactionary Free Corps. Luxemburg also made important contributions to Marxist writing on the national question and on economic theory, especially in *The Accumulation of Capital* (1910).

MACINTYRE, ALASDAIR
(1929–). Born in Scotland and educated in England, MacIntyre has taught philosophy at a number of universities in Britain and the USA. Initially trained in the analytical school, but with Marxist political sympathies, MacIntyre has since developed an approach to the history of ethics which traces the social contexts in which ethical theories rise and fall, and which has led some to describe him as a communitarian. Major landmarks in this development have been *A Short History of Ethics* (1966), *After Virtue* (1981) and *Whose Justice? Which Rationality?* (1988). Although MacIntyre's political outlook has shifted over his career, he has consistently been a critic of liberal political philosophy in the style of Rawls and Nozick.

MALLARMÉ, STÉPHANE
(1842–98). Born in Paris, Mallarmé led the symbolist movement in French poetry. The celebrated 'Tuesday evenings' he hosted at his house on the rue de Rome in the 1880s and 1890s were attended by the most important writers and artists of those years including André Gide, Paul Claudel and Stefan George. Among his best-known works are *L'après-midi d'un faune* (1876), which inspired the orchestral prelude by Claude Debussy (1894), and *Un coup de dés jamais n'abolira le hasard*, which was composed in 1897 but lay unpublished until 1914. His essay, 'The Crisis in Poetry', parts of which appeared from 1886 to 1895 in avant-garde journals such as the *Revue Blanche*, is an important symbolist statement.

MAO ZEDONG
(1893–1976), the Chinese Communist leader, was born in Shaoshan, Hunan Province, China. Son of a poor peasant, who became relatively rich trading in grain, Mao was one of the founding members of the Chinese Communist Party in 1921 and quickly became the party's recognised expert on the peasantry. He emerged as undisputed leader of the party during the civil war with the Kuomintang in 1935, and of China as a whole with the founding of the People's Republic of China in 1945, a position in which he remained until his death. Mao's importance as an innovative practitioner of Marxism is undeniable. His theoretical contribution consists in his attribution to the peasantry of an initiative and role more prominent than in orthodox Marxism. Together with this went an approach to dialectics where the emphasis on practice over theory implied a flexibility which in turn reflected the difficulty of applying Marxism in a society where its traditional categories had little purchase. Mao's original visionary view of the peasantry can be found in his *Report on the Peasant Movement in Hunan* (1927) and his approach to dialectics is best exemplified

in his essay *On Contradiction* (1937). His attitude to the Cultural Revolution can be found in the revealing collection of interviews *Mao Tse-tung Unrehearsed* (1974).

MARCUSE, HERBERT
(1898–1979). Born in Berlin, Marcuse was a leading member of the Frankfurt school and the most influential thinker behind the radical student movement in the late 1960s. After studying philosophy with Heidegger and Husserl, Marcuse joined the Institute for Social Research in Frankfurt in 1933. Forced into exile by Nazism, Marcuse settled in the United States where he published influential studies of Hegel, of the relationship of Marx to Freud, a critical study of Soviet Marxism and an attack on modern industrial capitalism as a form of all-embracing domination. His book *One-Dimensional Man*, turned Marcuse into the most prominent theorist of the New Left and he remained committed to radical political activity.

MARINETTI, FILIPPO TOMMASO
(1876–1944). Born in Alexandria, Egypt, to a Milanese business family, and educated in France, Italy and Switzerland, Marinetti achieved international celebrity when he published his *Manifeste du futurisme* in *Le Figaro* (20 February 1909). Many of Europe's most important writers and artists were attracted to futurism, especially between 1910 and 1914, and it became the most international of all avant-garde movements. A journalist during the Libyan and Balkan wars of 1911–12, Marinetti eagerly participated in the First World War, the Italian campaign in Ethiopia (1935–6), and, at the age of sixty-five, the Russian front during the Second World War. He also enthusiastically supported early fascism and was dismayed by its conservative turn in 1920, but nonetheless dutifully played the role of intellectual figurehead during the regime.

MARITAIN, JACQUES
(1882–1973). A disciple of Henri Bergson, Maritain converted to Catholicism at the age of twenty-four. He was educated according to neo-Thomist principles, and was one of the most important figures in the intellectual and spiritual renewal of Catholicism, both in France and beyond, in the inter-war period. After the Second World War, he became the French ambassador to the Vatican, which increased his influence on one section of the Italian Christian Democrats. He taught in a number of American universities before retiring to Toulouse.

MARSHALL, THOMAS HUMPHREY
(1893–1981) was a British sociologist and social theorist. Trained in economic history, he lectured at the London School of Economics from 1925 to 1956, and was appointed to the Martin White chair in sociology in 1954. He participated in founding the *British Journal of Sociology*, served between 1949 and 1950 as educational adviser to the British High Commission in Germany and from 1956 to 1960 was director of the social sciences department of UNESCO. His most influential book was *Citizenship and Social Class* (1950), which transformed the historical and theoretical understanding of citizenship. In other writings, such as *Social Policy in the Twentieth Century* (1965), he established an opus of thinking on welfare, social rights and social policy.

MAURRAS, CHARLES
(1868–1952) was the leader of the nationalist Action Française movement and editor of the journal *L'Action Française*, which became a daily newspaper in 1908. Despite the small membership of the Action Française movement, it – and in particular Maurras's writings on its behalf – had a great impact on political and literary life in Italy, Spain, Belgium and

Eastern Europe. Following his election to the Académie Française in 1939, Maurras lent his intellectual support to the Vichy regime, pursuing a militantly anti-Semitic campaign on its behalf and advocating racial legislation. After the liberation of France he was sentenced to life imprisonment for collaboration with the enemy.

MAWDUDI, SAYYID ABU AL-ALA
(1903–79) was born in the Deccan into a family of notable religious lineage which had an important influence on his intellectual life. Following a period of interest and engagement in the Indian independence movement, he became more involved in Islamic intellectual circles. With a growing interest in Muslim politics, he began to write on Muslim community affairs. In the wake of the abolition of the caliphate, he began to articulate ideas of revivalism, writing a treatise on *jihad* in Islam. As part of his intellectual output, he outlined a politicisation of religion, emphasising the importance of Islamic institutions and structures for Muslim progress. His numerous writings on religion and political issues include *Islamic Way of Life* and *Islamic Law*. In 1941 he helped to establish the Jama'at -i-Islami (Islamic Party). After the partition of India, the party set up an independent unit in Pakistan. Mawdudi moved to Lahore and became active in the political developments of Pakistan. He was imprisoned on several occasions and his political vision of religion had an important impact on generations of Islamists.

MERLEAU-PONTY, MAURICE
(1908–61). Merleau-Ponty studied philosophy at the Ecole Normale Supérieure in Paris, and like many of his generation became interested in German philosophy, especially Hegel, Husserl and Heidegger. In 1945 he published his major philosophical work, *The Phenomenology of Perception*, and became a founder member of *Les Temps Modernes*. He wrote numerous essays on Marxist themes and on communist politics, and he maintained close links with the journal and with Sartre until 1952 – the year Sartre published *The Communists and Peace* and also the year Merleau-Ponty was elected to a chair in philosophy at the Collège de France. After breaking with Sartre, Merleau-Ponty developed a profound critique of Marxism, both as a philosophy of history and as a practical politics (published as *Adventures of the Dialectic*, 1955): he urged the creation of a 'revisionist' radical politics – a path that was to be pursued by his students, notably Claude Lefort. In his later writings, before his unexpected death in 1961, he returned to themes in phenomenological and linguistic philosophy.

MERRIAM, CHARLES EDWARD
(1874–1953). Born in Iowa into a politically active religious family, Merriam became a leading figure in the development of the social sciences in the United States. Educated at Columbia University, and spending his entire career at the University of Chicago from 1901 to 1940, he set out research agendas into American government, politics, and behaviour that his students and colleagues took up in increasingly sophisticated ways. He was especially influential in his manifesto calling for new methods of inquiry, *New Aspects of Politics* (1925). He helped create the Social Science Research Council in 1923 and organised large collaborative projects into public opinion and civic education. Merriam's academic interests were guided in part by his involvement in Progressive politics in Chicago, twice as alderman and once as candidate for mayor. Robert LaFollette dubbed him 'the Woodrow Wilson of the West' for the intellectual tone he set in pursuit of these activities. Merriam also served on the Committee for Public Information during the First World War, taking from it an interest in propaganda that he passed on to his premier student, Harold D. Lasswell. Later, he served on the National Resources Planning Board, confirming by his

participation his belief that the social sciences find their principal justification in their contribution to public policy.

MEYER, FRANK S.
(1909–72) was born in Newark, New Jersey. Best known for his intellectual contribution to the establishment of post-Second World War American conservatism, Meyer's path to conservatism was unusual: after graduating from Princeton he went to Oxford University, where he became a secret member of the Communist Party. He continued his communist affiliation when, after receiving a BA from Oxford (1932), he moved to the London School of Economics (1932–4) and to the University of Chicago (1934–8). He finally broke with communism in 1945, as a result of reading F. A. Hayek's *The Road to Serfdom*. In 1955 he joined the staff of the newly established conservative journal *National Review*. Under the influence of Eric Voegelin in particular, he moved away from Hayek's emphasis on economic freedom to a concern more specifically directed to promoting the conditions for virtue, amongst which he regarded liberty as the most important. A Jew, he took the unusual step of converting to Catholicism on the day of his death. His central idea, which was the need to base American conservatism on a 'fusionist' doctrine which would combine traditional conservatism with libertarianism, made him a stimulating but controversial figure in conservative circles.

MICHELS, ROBERT
(1876–1936). Born in Cologne to an upper-bourgeois Catholic manufacturing family of Italian–French origin, Michels obtained a doctorate in history with J. G. Droysen and subsequently studied extensively in France and Italy, where he made contact with syndicalist thinkers such as Georges Sorel and Antonio Labriola. In 1900 he joined the Italian Socialist Party and then the German Social Democratic Party (SDP), becoming actively involved in Marburg with a group of socialist intellectuals inclined towards anarcho-syndicalism. He criticised the SDP for its lack of radicalism, notwithstanding its revolutionary rhetoric, and advocated a syndicalist alternative that emphasised extra-parliamentary action. Turned down for his *Habilitation* (qualification for university teaching) at both Marburg and Jena because of his membership of the SDP, he emigrated to Turin in 1907 where he habilitated with Achille Loria. At Turin he came into contact with the elite theorist Gaetano Mosca and later met Vilfredo Pareto. Influenced by their views, he was to find in elitism an explanation for the SDP's moderation. Michels had for some time been working on a study of socialist politics, publishing an article on 'German Social Democracy' in the *Archiv für Sozialwissenschaft und Sozialpolitik* in 1906. Encouraged by Max Weber – with whom he had been in correspondence – he elaborated these studies into a book, *Zur Soziologie des Parteiwesens in der modernen Demokratie* (trans. *Political Parties*, 1915), published in German in 1911 and subsequently translated into many languages. He later applied and developed this argument in studies of the Italian socialist movement and the rise of fascism. In later writings, Michels came to view elitism not only as inevitable but also as desirable, arguing in the *Corso di sociologia politica* (1927) (trans. *First Lectures in Political Sociology*, 1949) that only charismatic leadership could overcome organisational conservatism and galvanise the masses. In 1928 he accepted Mussolini's offer of a chair in the pro-fascist faculty of political science at the University of Perugia.

MISES, LUDWIG HEINRICH EDLER VON
(1881–1973). Born in Lemburg, Austria-Hungary (later Lvov, Ukraine) and educated at the University of Vienna, Mises became an American citizen in 1946. His economic

education was based on the teachings of the 'Austrian school'. Mises had considerable influence via his private seminars (1929–34), not least on the young F. A. Hayek. His book *Die Gemeinwirtschaft* (1922) demonstrated the impossibility of socialism as an economic system and predicted the failure of the communist experiment. Later work attacked the methodological foundations of mainstream economics by showing how intellectually deficient and socially dangerous were positivist approaches to the social sciences. His opposition to positivism and his profound anti-statism meant that his ideas remained unfashionable for the greater part of his life. With the demise of the 'Keynesian era' in the 1970s his writings attracted more interest and support, especially from the 'New Right'.

MOJTAHED-SHABESTARI, MOHAMMAD
(1936–). An important figure among the critical clerics in contemporary Iran, Shabestari studied for eight years at the Qom seminary. During the pre-revolution period, he was director of the Islamic Centre of Hamburg. In the post-revolution period, he occupied the post of professor of theology at Tehran University and published an Islamic thought periodical. He is a member of the Institute for Political and International Studies of the Foreign Affairs Ministry. In a series of essays, he critiqued religious curricula and argued for the importance of rethinking approaches to religious knowledge drawing on theoretical developments in modern social sciences. His writings show the influence of German thought, as evidenced by the Gadamarian-hermeneutical resonance of his ideas concerning the horizon of religious knowledge.

MOORE, GEORGE EDWARD
(1873–1958). Born in Upper Norwood, England, and educated at Trinity College, Cambridge, Moore was a lecturer in moral science at Cambridge (1911–25) and later professor of philosophy (1925–39). He was also the editor of the journal *Mind* (1921–7). Moore, with Bertrand Russell, was at the forefront of attacking idealism and subverting the influence of Hegel and Kant on British philosophy. *Principia Ethica* (1903) inspired the likes of John Maynard Keynes and his fellow members of 'Bloomsbury' such as Virginia Woolf and provided them with a new 'religion' (*sic*). In providing a critique of the 'naturalistic fallacy', and arguing that the good was knowable by direct apprehension, Moore showed the importance of human intuition in ethics.

MOSCA, GAETANO
(1858–1941). Born in Palermo to a professional middle-class family, Mosca studied at the local university and graduated in 1882. While an unsalaried lecturer at Palermo in constitutional law and political theory, he wrote his first book – *Sulla teorica dei governi e sul governo parlamentare* (1884) – in which the first version of his theory of the ruling class appears. He moved to the University of Rome in 1887, publishing the first edition of the *Elementi di scienza politica* in 1896, by which time he had moved to Turin as professor of constitutional law. He remained there until 1923, when he published the second edition of the *Elementi* and went to Rome as professor of political theory, a post he held until 1931. In 1933 he published his lectures on the *Storia delle dottrine politiche*. Meanwhile, Mosca had also been active in politics. An editor of the journal of the Chamber of Deputies from 1887 to 1895, he was a deputy from 1908 to 1918, serving as under-secretary for the colonies under Salandra from 1914 to 1916. In 1918, he was appointed senator for life. A liberal conservative, he opposed both socialism and fascism, the second edition of the *Elementi* being a defence of liberal democracy. The two editions of the *Elementi* were translated into English as *The Ruling Class* in 1939.

MOUNIER, EMMANUEL
(1905–50). After studying medicine and philosophy (he was a student of Charles Péguy), Mounier committed himself to a renewal of traditional Christianity. In 1932 he founded the journal *Esprit*, which became an instrument for the promotion of his doctrine of personalism. In 1941 the journal was closed down. However, it re-emerged in 1945, still under his direction, and became one of the central elements in French culture after the war.

MÜLLER-ARMACK, ALFRED
(1901–78). Under the influence of Walter Eucken and the group of economists and legal experts of the so-called 'Freiburg school', Müller-Armack had already developed, in the last few years of Nazism and the immediate post-war period, a programme of liberal and social political economy. In 1947 he formulated the concept of a 'social market economy'. After 1949, he was minister of state for economic affairs in various Christian Democratic governments. He worked closely with the prime minister, Ludwig Erhard, and applied his model to the German economy, using it as a blueprint for the development of the Federal Republic.

MURRI, ROMOLO
(1870–1944) was a priest who, after studying at the Gregorian University in his native Marche, was a student of the Marxist Antonio Labriola at the University of Rome. As a result, he became aware of both the materialist conception of history and the proletarian question. He founded the magazine *Cultura sociale* (1898–1906) and from 1900 he worked tirelessly throughout Italy for the creation of Christian Democratic groups within the framework of the Italian Catholic movement. However, strong opposition from both the conservative and the Catholic hierarchy led to the dissolution of all Catholic organisations in 1904. In 1906, Murri founded the Lega Democratica Nazionale and proposed the inclusion of Catholics in the institutions of the Italian state. In 1907 he was suspended *a divinis* due to his commitment to modernism. In 1909, he was excommunicated after his election as a left-wing member of parliament. At the outbreak of the First World War, he was in favour of Italy's participation in the war, and was later attracted to fascism. Shortly before his death he re-entered the church.

MUSSOLINI, BENITO
(1883–1945). The son of a blacksmith and innkeeper, Mussolini became a noted socialist journalist and leader of the revolutionary wing of the Italian Socialist Party. He was expelled late in 1914 for urging Italian entry into the First World War, was wounded while serving in the Italian army and was the founding leader of the Fascist movement in 1919. Mussolini became constitutional prime minister in 1922, gained a parliamentary majority in 1924 and imposed political dictatorship in January 1925. He was called 'Duce' (leader) and 'capo del governo' (head of government), since King Victor Emmanuel III remained head of state. After 1925 Mussolini imposed the institutions of the 'corporate state', later defended in *Lo stato corporativo* (1938). He conquered Ethiopia in 1935–6 and became a formal military ally of Hitler in May 1939. Italy entered the Second World War in June 1940, but encountered defeat after defeat. Mussolini was deposed by his own Fascist Grand Council in July 1943 but was subsequently rescued by Nazi commandos. He then formed a puppet 'Italian Social Republic' in northern Italy and was executed by communist partisans in April 1945.

MYRDAL, GUNNAR

(1898–1987) was a Swedish welfare theorist, economist and politician. As an academic, Myrdal engaged in empirical research on poverty and social disadvantage. In 1934 he was elected to the Swedish Senate as a member of the Social Democratic Party. He consolidated his reputation through a study of racial discrimination against blacks in the USA, *An American Dilemma* (1944). From 1945 to 1947 Myrdal served as Swedish minister of commerce, and between 1947 and 1957 he was executive secretary of the United Nations Economic Commission for Europe. Further research on poverty in Asia culminated in his book *Asian Drama* (1968). In 1974 Myrdal was awarded the Nobel prize in economics. Myrdal was married to Alva Myrdal, a notable researcher in her own right and Nobel peace laureate in 1982.

NAESS, ARNE

(1912–) is a Norwegian philosopher and mountaineer born in Oslo and educated in Paris, Vienna, Berkeley and Oslo. His early interest in language and logic drew him to the Vienna Circle. His earliest books are inquiries into 'empirical semantics', that is, into how non-philosophers communicate. During the Nazi occupation of Norway during the Second World War Naess joined the Resistance. An avid and pioneering mountaineer, Naess has had a lifelong interest in the natural world. He draws a distinction between 'shallow' environmentalism meant mainly to benefit humans and 'deep ecology' (he coined the term) that places the interests of animals and ecosystems alongside human interests. He has attempted to construct an 'ecosophy' – that is, an ecologically centred philosophy – in which the interests of nature and her myriad creatures are recognised and valued. The most succinct statement of his views can be found in his *Ecology, Community and Lifestyle: Outline of an Ecosophy* (1989).

NEHRU, JAWAHARLAL

(1889–1964) was born in Allahabad, India, and educated in England, and was one of the most prominent leaders of the Indian independence movement. Imprisoned on nine different occasions for his part in the nationalist struggle, he used his forced leisure to write and reflect on Indian and world history as well as on problems facing contemporary India. He was independent India's first and longest-serving prime minister and laid the foundations of a secular and democratic republic wedded to social democratic ideas. He is the only prime minister in history to be succeeded first by his daughter and then by his grandson. In his writings he advocated a humanist philosophy grounded in a liberal view of history.

NIETZSCHE, FRIEDRICH

(1844–1900). Nietzsche was born at Rücken in Prussian Saxony. His father, who was a Lutheran pastor, died in 1849, and Nietzsche was then brought up by his mother, sister and other female relatives. From 1854 to 1858 he studied at the local *Gymnasium*, and then attended the celebrated boarding school in Pforta. In 1864 he went to the University of Bonn, and subsequently studied in Leipzig under Friedrich Ritschl. During this time he discovered the thought of Schopenhauer, an important influence, both positive and negative, on his own philosophy. A brilliant student, Nietzsche became a professor of philology at the University of Basel in 1869, without even taking his doctorate. He served in the ambulance corps during the Franco-Prussian war of 1870, but illness forced him to quit. He was promoted to full professor in 1871. In the early 1870s Nietzsche was also friendly with Wagner, whom he often visited at his villa on Lake Lucerne, and was an enthusiastic supporter of his music. However, the friendship soured, and Nietzsche later became a fierce critic of Wagner's work. Nietzsche's first book, *The Birth of Tragedy* (1872), was regarded as unscholarly, even scandalous, by his academic colleagues, and in 1879 he resigned his chair at the University of Basel, because of ill health and personal dissatisfaction. He spent the next ten years leading a nomadic existence. Supported by his university pension, he lived in various places in Italy and Switzerland, notably Sils Maria in the Swiss Alps, where he had his ecstatic vision of the 'Eternal Return of the Same'. It was during this itinerant period that Nietzsche wrote his most revolutionary works of philosophy and cultural criticism, including *Thus Spake Zarathustra* (1883–5), *Beyond Good and Evil* (1886) and *On the Genealogy of Morals*. In 1889 Nietzsche suffered a nervous breakdown, collapsing in the street in Turin. He spent the rest of his life in a state of mental incapacity, living first with his mother, and then with his sister, until his death in 1900.

NOZICK, ROBERT
(1938–2002). Born in Brooklyn and educated at Columbia and Princeton universities, Nozick spent most of his life as professor of philosophy at Harvard. His philosophical interests were wide-ranging, and he described his best-known book, *Anarchy, State and Utopia* (1974), as an 'accident'. Nevertheless this defence of the minimal state and wide-ranging critique of political philosophies of the left has been hailed as the most sophisticated statement of a libertarian position in the twentieth century. Nozick did not subsequently return to political philosophy, except to qualify aspects of his libertarianism in *The Examined Life* (1989).

NYERERE, JULIUS
(1922–96) was born in Butiama in Tanganyika and educated at the universities of Makerere and Edinburgh. He became the first prime minister of his country in 1961, and the first president of the United Republic of Tanzania in 1964. He declined to accept any of the grandiose titles popular among post-colonial African leaders and retired voluntarily as the president of his country. He was the author of the influential Arusha Declaration which advocated the doctrine of socialism and self-reliance for newly independent African countries. In his writings, he stressed the importance of African unity, economic and political decentralisation, and an African form of socialism based on the traditional idea of *ujamma* or familiality.

OAKESHOTT, MICHAEL
(1901–1990). The son of a civil servant and a vicar's daughter, Oakeshott attempted to join the navy just before the First World War but was rejected on the grounds of colour blindness. After the war (in 1919) he read history at Gonville and Caius College, Cambridge. Whilst at Cambridge he studied with the idealist philosopher J. M. E. McTaggart. After graduating, Oakeshott twice visited (during the 1920s) the universities of Marburg and Tübingen in order to pursue his interest in theology. In 1927 he became a Fellow of his old college. In 1939 Oakeshott joined the army and eventually commanded 'Phantom', a freelance intelligence-gathering force stationed in Holland. He returned to academic life after the war, moving in 1951 to the chair of political science at the London School of Economics, from which he retired in 1968. An essentially private, intensely individualistic and modest man who withdrew to the solitude of his cottage in Dorset when not in London, Oakeshott disdained to play the role of either a philosophical or political guru, regarding schools and parties alike as equally alien. The central concept of his political theory, which is that of civil association, was embodied in the unpretentious but exacting ideals of civility, conversation and friendship that marked his own life. It is the liberal education which he

believed was required in order to maintain civility in all its forms, rather than any narrowly political vision, that Oakeshott offered to his students and continues to offer to his readers.

ORWELL, GEORGE (ERIC BLAIR)
(1903–50) was one of the most important and influential critics of totalitarianism in the middle part of the twentieth century. He achieved prominence in the late 1940s as the author of two satirical critiques of totalitarianism – *Animal Farm* (1945), an allegory of the Bolshevik betrayal of the Russian Revolution, and *Nineteen Eighty-Four* (1949), a dystopian novel about the nihilism of totalitarian rule. These books, along with numerous critical essays, established Orwell as one of the most important and influential voices of the century. The author of such personal chronicles as *Down and Out in Paris and London* (1933) and *Homage to Catalonia* (1938), the latter a withering critique of communist machinations during the Spanish Civil War, Orwell was a public intellectual whose moral authority derived as much from his own willingness to go into the trenches as from his literary skill.

OSTROGORSKI, MOISEI
(1854–1919). Born in Grodno to a professional middle-class Jewish family, Ostrogorski graduated in law from St Petersburg and entered the civil service, where he rose to director general in the Ministry of Justice. A publicist and writer of popular histories, he left Russia in 1881 to escape the repressive climate following the attempted assassination of Tsar Alexander III and enrolled in the Ecoles Libres des Sciences Politiques in Paris, where he studied with Emile Boutmy. Here he worked on a study of women and public law that was published in 1892 and translated into numerous languages. In 1892 he also wrote a study of American political parties and in 1890 he came to Britain where he met James Bryce, whose *The American Commonwealth* had also been published in 1889. Partly encouraged by Bryce, he undertook a parallel study of parties in England. Written in French, his *Democracy and the Organisation of Political Parties* appeared in English in 1902 and in French later the same year (although bearing the date 1903). He refused an offer to teach in the USA and in 1904 returned to Russia. In 1906 he was elected on the Jewish list to the Duma as part of the Grodno electoral college. Little is known of his subsequent career.

PARETO, VILFREDO
(1848–1923). Born in Paris of an Italian father, a civil engineer from an aristocratic family exiled for his republican sympathies, and a French mother, Pareto was educated in Turin, where his father returned in 1855. An outstanding mathematician, he followed his father's profession and graduated in 1870 as a civil engineer at the Turin Polytechnic. He entered business as a director of the Rome Railway Company, moving to Florence in 1874 as managing director of the Società Ferriere d'Italia. At this time, he started to write journalistic pieces from a radical liberal perspective, attacking the protectionist and interventionist policies of the Italian state and sympathetic to the plight of the poor. In 1882 he unsuccessfully stood as an opposition candidate in Florence. His father died the same year and his mother in 1889, when he married, gave up his job for a consultancy, and entered into a series of anti-government polemics – publishing 167 articles between 1889 and 1893. At this time he became acquainted with various free-trade economists, especially Maffeo Pantaleoni and Leon Walras, whose mathematically expressed equilibrium system he now developed. In 1893 he succeeded Walras to the chair of political economy at Lausanne, publishing the two-volume *Cours d'économie politique* in 1896. Though he remained a regular commentator on events in Italy, his sympathies gradually changed and by 1900 he had

become an anti-democrat. Still an anti-statist libertarian, he now argued that the right of the labouring classes to organise had simply allowed them to replace bourgeois privileges with working-class ones. He now turned to social psychology to explain the appeal of socialist ideas, publishing *Les systèmes socialistes* in 1901–2 and developing a whole theory of sociology that was ultimately published as the *Trattato di sociologia generale* in 1916 and translated into English as *The Mind and Society* in 1935. He saw fascism as a confirmation of his theories – though he abhorred Mussolini's policies – collecting his analysis of the crisis of Italian liberal democracy in *Trasformazione della democrazia* in 1921.

PEIRCE, CHARLES SANDERS

(1839–1914). Born in Cambridge, Massachusetts, to an intellectual Harvard family, Peirce became one of the founders of philosophical pragmatism and one of the most influential philosophers of his day, despite the fact that his academic career as a lecturer in logic at Johns Hopkins University collapsed in the 1880s and he ended his days living in rural poverty. He attended Harvard College as an undergraduate and began lecturing and publishing philosophical papers while working as an aide to the coast survey. Peirce's early work attacked Descartes, offering the methods of scientific experiment and observation in place of Cartesian introspection. His view of how to clarify concepts, and his definition of the truth as that on which educated persons will eventually come to agree, were extremely influential on his friend William James, who became the standard bearer for pragmatism; Peirce preferred to call his own view 'pragmaticism'. He also wrote extensively on logic and mathematics.

PITKIN, HANNA FENICHEL

(1931–). Pitkin was born in Germany and as a young girl emigrated with her family to the United States to escape Nazi persecution. She earned her doctorate in political science at the University of California at Berkeley. After a brief career at the University of Wisconsin she returned to Berkeley, where she remained until her retirement in 2000. She is author of *The Concept of Representation* (1967), *Wittgenstein and Justice* (1972), *Fortune is a Woman: Gender and Politics in the Thought of Niccolò Machiavelli* (1984), and *Attack of the Blob: Hannah Arendt's Concept of the Social* (1998). Her work combines psychoanalytic theory, feminist theory and ordinary-language analysis in a provocative and often original way.

PLEKHANOV, GYORGY

(1856–1918) was born in central Russia and went through the early stages of a military career. Leaving this and later the Mining Institute, he read the works of Russian radicals such as Chernyshevsky and became friends with some of the revolutionaries. He became involved in anti-tsarist, populist politics until he was forced into exile to avoid imprisonment. He did not return to Russia again until 1917, living instead in the exiled community of Geneva. Here, however, he came to Marxism; and he became the catechist-in-chief of its message in Russia. He believed that the future of Russia now led to proletarian, socialist revolution but through a bourgeois, capitalist phase. His insistence on this intermediate phase and his underestimation of the revolutionary potential of the Russian peasantry soon brought him into conflict with Lenin and the Bolsheviks. Yet he it was who had been their original mentor.

QUTB, SAYYID

(1906–1966) was born in Asyut, Egypt, and received his early education in a religious school. Later, he went on to study educational sciences and art history. He began his public career as a literary critic and journalist. He also worked in the field of education.

His religious writings are conventionally divided into social and political phases, making a distinction between his radical writings of the later phases and his engagement with social issues during the earlier phases. However, there are threads of continuity in his thought and signs of progression from works such as *Islam and Social Justice* and *The Battle of Islam and Capitalism* to *Milestones*. His critique of Western materialism was supported by his own sojourn in the USA between 1948 and 1951. He joined the Muslim Brotherhood in 1951 and was in charge of organisational and strategic planning. He was imprisoned by the Egyptian authorities in 1954, and again in 1965 on charges of plotting against the Nasser regime. He was executed in 1966. His writings have influenced generations of Islamist activists.

RAWLS, JOHN

(1921–2002). Born into a wealthy Baltimore family, Rawls entered Princeton University in 1939, where, under the influence of Norman Malcolm, he developed an interest in philosophy. On leaving university he joined the army and saw active service in the Pacific. Rawls returned to Princeton to write a doctorate in moral philosophy, moving to Cornell and then to MIT before becoming a professor of philosophy at Harvard in 1962. The theory of justice as fairness he developed during these years received its fullest exposition in *A Theory of Justice* (1971), which many regard as the most influential work of political philosophy in the twentieth century. Later work refined the theory: *Political Liberalism* (1993) argued that Rawls' principles of justice could be endorsed by people holding a wide range of contrasting religious and philosophical views, and *The Law of Peoples* (1999) extended the theory to global society.

ABD AL-RAZIQ, ALI

(1888–1966) was trained at al-Azhar and Oxford universities. He worked as a judge in Shari'a courts. His main work is *Islam and the Fundamentals of Rule*. Following its publication, he was subjected to severe criticism from the religious establishment. The book was embroiled in the political divisions of the time, finding support among members of the Liberal Constitutional Party opposing the idea of a revival of the caliphate, with the Egyptian king as caliph. Other parties took a critical stance. Political pressure was exerted to have Abd al-Raziq expelled from the ranks of *ulama* and to have him removed from his position. He was reinstated later, but the episode seems to have discouraged him from engaging further in the intellectual life of his time.

REICH, WILHELM

(1897–1957) was a Viennese psychiatrist who introduced novel ideas in psychoanalytic technique. He developed political psychology as a bridge between Freudianism and Marxism, but was finally excluded from both psychoanalytic and communist organisations. After inventing his 'Orgone Box' and peddling it as a medical device, he ran foul of the US Food and Drug Administration, which brought charges against him. He failed to rebut the charges and died in a federal prison. His writings, presenting the advantages of sexual liberation, have continued to have considerable popular appeal.

RIDA, RASHID

(1865–1935) was born in Syria and received his education in both religious and secular institutions. In 1897 he moved to Cairo and became a disciple of Muhammad Abduh. He was influenced by classical theology, in particular Ghazali's *Ihya 'Ulum al-Din*. He was involved in publishing the periodical *al-Manar* and in propagating and elaborating

Abduh's ideas. Rida's elaboration privileged conservatism in the social sphere as evidenced in the position he took on the question of women's rights in the public discussion initiated by Egyptian intellectual Qasim Amin. He also rejected Ali Abd al-Raziq's views on the separation of Islam and politics. His main work is *The Caliphate or the Supreme Imamate*.

RITCHIE, DAVID GEORGE
(1853–1903) was a British philosopher born to a family of Scottish academics and clerics. He studied classics at Edinburgh University and then at Balliol College, Oxford, and was a Fellow of Jesus College from 1878, teaching Greats for Jesus and Balliol, influenced by both T. H. Green and Arnold Toynbee. In a series of books Ritchie synthesised the school of philosophical idealism with evolutionary theory and with a reworking of utilitarianism to support state intervention in moralising citizens. In 1894 Ritchie was appointed professor of logic and metaphysics at St Andrews University. His major books were *Darwinism and Politics* (1889), *The Principles of State Interference* (1891), *Darwin and Hegel* (1893) and *Natural Rights* (1895), all of which influenced the new liberalism.

ROCCO, ALFREDO
(1875–1935). A professor of law successively in various Italian universities, by 1914 Rocco had become the chief ideologue of the right-radical Italian Nationalist Association, propounding the goal of the authoritarian and imperialist 'corporate state'. The Association merged with the Fascist Party in 1923, and Rocco became one of the principal ideologues of fascism. Serving as minister of justice from 1925 to 1932, he was the chief author of the *leggi fascistissimi*, the 'ultra-fascist laws' imposed between 1925 and 1928 to create the institutions of the Fascist corporate state as outlined in his *La trasformazione dello stato* (*The Transformation of the State*, 1927).

ROSENBERG, ALFRED
(1890–1945). Rosenberg came from a lower-middle-class German family in Reval (Estonia), at that time part of the Tsarist empire. He was best known as the author of *Der Mythus des zwanzigsten Jahrhunderts* (*The Myth of the Twentieth Century*, 1933), which attempted a full-scale philosophical exposition of National Socialist doctrine and, thanks to party support, eventually sold more than a million copies. Hitler briefly placed him in charge of the party in 1923–4, but privately derided Rosenberg's ideological writing as fanciful and sometimes absurd. Rosenberg also posed as a specialist on Eastern Europe and administered, quite ineffectively, the German ministry for the occupied east from 1941 to 1944. He was sentenced to death by the Nuremberg Tribunal.

ROWNTREE, BENJAMIN SEEBOHM
(1871–1954) was a British social reformer, philanthropist and social investigator. An active member of the family chocolate manufacturing firm of Rowntrees, as well as a Quaker, Rowntree followed the family tradition of concern for the welfare of their workers and the establishing of various charitable trusts. Rowntree's interest in fostering good labour relations was accompanied by a broader dedication to exploring the conditions of the poor and the nature of poverty, under Charles Booth's influence. The result was a classic study of York entitled *Poverty. A Study of Town Life* (1901), with follow-up surveys published in 1941 and 1951. Rowntree was also involved in post-First World War reconstruction planning, wrote on the scientific management of labour, and promoted the development of industrial psychology.

ROY, M. N.
(1887–1954) was born in Bengal, India, and became a political radical and a militant nationalist at a very early age. He travelled to Japan and China in search of arms and political support for the cause of the Indian independence movement and, using various names and disguises, reached Mexico where he founded the Communist Party. At Lenin's invitation he went to Moscow and rapidly rose to high positions in the Comintern. Fearing for his life after Lenin's death, he returned to India where he was arrested and imprisoned for his nationalist activities. In his many works, written mainly in prison, he critically commented on Marxism, liberalism, nationalism and fascism and advocated materialist humanism and decentralised social democracy.

RUSSELL, BERTRAND (later THIRD EARL RUSSELL)
(1872–1970) was an eminent British philosopher and mathematical logician who also became a controversial writer and activist on political and social issues. The grandson of the Victorian prime minister Lord John Russell (later first Earl Russell), and educated privately and at Trinity College, Cambridge, Russell opposed British entry into the First World War and campaigned on behalf of conscientious objectors, losing his lectureship at Trinity in consequence and suffering imprisonment for writing an article that was deemed to be seditious. Though sympathetic to the peace movement in the 1920s, he did not espouse pacifism until 1935. He published *Which Way to Peace?* the following year but never allowed it to be reprinted, since by 1940, when he recanted his pacifism, he had come to believe that his espousal of so absolutist a viewpoint had from the outset been unconsciously insincere. After 1945 he briefly advocated the threat of nuclear war to compel the Soviet Union to accept a confederation of nations, but later became a leading campaigner against British nuclear weapons, practising civil disobedience through the Committee of 100, a direct-action offshoot of the Campaign for Nuclear Disarmament, and was again imprisoned briefly in 1961.

SANDEL, MICHAEL
(1953–). A leading exponent of 'communitarian' political theory, Sandel was educated at Brandeis University before taking up a Rhodes scholarship to study at Balliol College, Oxford. There he wrote the thesis that was later published as *Liberalism and the Limits of Justice* (1982), a critical appraisal of liberal political theory, especially the work of John Rawls. Returning to the United States to teach, Sandel moved to the government department at Harvard after a year at Brandeis. He published *Democracy's Discontent* (1996), a reappropriation of the Republican tradition in American political thought, while also serving as a contributing editor for *The New Republic*.

SANGNIER, MARC
(1873–1950). In 1898 Sangnier abandoned his career in the military in order to become a preacher of social Christian principles. He possessed excellent organisational skills (involving study groups for the young and for workers, bulletins and various journals and magazines, conferences and a series of lectures), and he became the leader of the movement for mass education called Sillon. Due to both his activism and his democratic principles, he found himself in conflict with the Roman Catholic church on several occasions. His book *Ligue de la jeune république* criticised the French right, in particular the Action Française led by Charles Maurras. From 1919, he was a member of parliament. Initially he was a pacifist, but he was later to participate in the Resistance against the Nazis. In 1945 he was re-elected to parliament and was also elected president of the Mouvement Républicaine Populaire.

SARTRE, JEAN-PAUL
(1905–80). Born in Paris, Sartre was one of the most prominent French intellectuals of the twentieth century, and a dominating figure in French left-wing thought. He studied at the elite Ecole Normale Supérieure in Paris, and later in Germany, where he attended the lectures given by Heidegger and Husserl. Known primarily as a literary writer and philosopher of existentialism during the inter-war years, after the end of the Second World War he threw himself into political causes with the launch of the journal *Les Temps Modernes* in 1945 (of which he was the first editor; his colleagues included Simone de Beauvoir, Maurice Merleau-Ponty and Raymond Aron). Although never a member of the Communist Party, he supported it from the outside, and had close relations with it until the mid-1950s. But the French Communists' reactions to events in Hungary and to the Algerian War, as well as the party's doctrinal rigidity, forced him away from it, and in the late 1950s he was associated with 'revisionism' in French Marxism. In 1960 he published the first volume of *Critique of Dialectical Reason*, an ambitious and ultimately flawed effort to reconcile Marxist themes with existentialist commitments. After abandoning this project, he continued to write (mainly on aesthetic and literary subjects), became a rallying point for anti-communist *gauchistes* in 1968 and after, and suffered a long and slow decline of his physical and mental capacities in the last decade of his life.

SCHMITT, CARL
(1888–1985). Born in Plettenberg, Schmitt was the son of a Catholic Franco-German family from the German Rhineland. The strong dislike of liberalism and socialism that prevailed in the Catholic milieu in which he grew up was reflected in the subsequent development of his political thought, and in particular in his belief that political ideas always derive from a deeper underlying religious outlook. In the years before the First World War Schmitt pursued legal studies at the University of Berlin (from which he graduated in 1907), and also at those of Munich and Strasbourg. After the war, he taught law from 1922 to 1928 at the preponderantly Catholic University of Bonn. During this period he also acted as an adviser to the Centre Party in the Rhineland and was a confidant to the Catholic parliamentarian Heinrich Brüning, whom President von Hindenburg appointed chancellor in December 1929. Although initially popular with Nazi supporters because his 'decisionist' philosophy could be used to support the Nazi *Führerprinzip*, he soon lost popularity with them because the legal emphasis of his thought had no necessary connection with the crude Nazi ideology of blood and soil. Neglected for many years in the post-war world because of his entanglement with Nazism, it is ironic that the revival of interest in Schmitt's thought since the 1980s owed much to radical left-wing thinkers who found in him inspiration for their critique of liberal democracy.

SCHOPENHAUER, ARTHUR
(1788–1860). Born in Danzig to a wealthy merchant family, Schopenhauer failed to gain the academic career which his early brilliance had promised. In the 1820s he offered lectures at Berlin at the same hour as those of Hegel and, attracting no students, he eventually retired to a solitary existence in Frankfurt from 1833 until his death. Schopenhauer was greatly influenced by Kant, Plato and first Hindu, then Buddhist, religion. His major work, *Die Welt als Wille und Vorstellung* (*The World as Will and Representation*), was first published in 1818, with a supplementary volume in 1844. Here he argued that while Kant was right to emphasise the importance of rationality, he had failed to appreciate the power of the irrational and egotistical will which in most humans wreaks havoc with their cognitive control. One could aspire only to moments of will-less experience in which one could,

like the artistic genius, see clearly and reflect on the eternal ideas at the basis of reality. Otherwise compassion was, against Kant, the only hope for ethics.

SEN, AMARTYA

(1933–). Born in Bengal and educated at Calcutta and Cambridge universities, Sen is best known for his work in welfare economics. An early study of social choice theory, *Collective Choice and Social Welfare* (1970), was followed by numerous essays and books on the related topics of inequality and poverty, including *On Economic Inequality* (1973) and *Inequality Reexamined* (1992). Some of this work was motivated by Sen's own early experiences in the Bengal famine of 1943, reflected in *Poverty and Famines* (1981). Sen has taught economics at Delhi, Oxford and Harvard, and is currently Master of Trinity College, Cambridge. He was awarded the Nobel prize for economics in 1998.

SHARIATI, ALI

(1933–77) was born in the Khurasan province of north-eastern Iran. He received his early education in the city of Mashhad and went on to complete a doctorate in medieval Islamic studies at the Sorbonne. In Paris he became familiar with the ideas of Jean-Paul Sartre, Georges Gurevich and Jacques Berque. He was involved in liberation movements, contributing in particular to the Algerian resistance movement newspaper. He also participated in the movement that opposed the rule of the Shah in Iran. After his return to Iran in 1966, he began to lecture at Mashhad University. His lectures were popular among students because of their radical content, but they aroused government concern and he was soon dismissed from his post. He joined the Husayniyah-yi Irshad in Tehran, an institute of learning focused on religious subjects. His talks and lessons attracted large numbers of youth. He was influenced by Marxist writings, while being critical of Marxism for its views on religion. His critique is elaborated in his book *Marxism and other Western Fallacies*. Shariati was imprisoned a number of times by the Shah's regime. In 1977 he was allowed to leave Iran for the UK. He died after arrival and it is widely believed that Savak (the Iranian secret service) was behind his death. His intellectual legacy was marginalised by the Islamic revolutionary regime, but his ideas continue to resonate among intellectually engaged Iranians.

SHEPPARD, H. R. L. ('DICK')

(1880–1937) was Britain's leading pacifist of the 1930s. The son of a minor canon in the royal chapel at Windsor, and educated at Marlborough and Cambridge, Sheppard was a well-connected and fashionable Anglican clergyman in London's West End, who became nationally famous when his services at St Martin-in-the-Fields were the first to be broadcast by the infant BBC. Possessed of extraordinary personal magnetism but troubled by acute asthma and an unhappy marriage, he declared himself a pacifist in 1926 though he did not issue his call for 'peace pledges' until 1934. He published *We Say 'No'* in 1935 and established the Peace Pledge Union the following year. He died suddenly in 1937, shortly after being elected by the students of Glasgow University as their rector.

SHIVA, VANDANA

(1952–) is an Indian forest ecologist and ecofeminist theorist. She is director of the Research Foundation for Science, Technology and Natural Resource Policy, which sponsors research on sustainable agriculture and third world development, and serves also as ecology adviser to the Third World Network which advocates active involvement of people (more particularly women) in the third world in issues of development, agriculture and a more equitable distribution of the world's resources. Dr Shiva is also active in the Indian ecofeminist Chipko movement which involves women in direct-action confrontations with loggers and others who seek to extract resources in exploitative and non-sustainable ways. She is the author of fourteen books, including *Staying Alive: Women, Ecology and Development in India* (1988) and *The Violence of the Green Revolution* (1991).

SIMMEL, GEORG
(1858–1918), a sociologist and philosopher, was born into a wealthy Jewish family. He spent his childhood at the heart of Berlin (the corner of Leipziger Strasse and Friedrichstrasse) at a period of the city's explosive growth into a major commercial and urban centre. After studying philosophy and history at the University of Berlin, Simmel became a *Privatdozent* and, after 1901, associate professor there. As a Jew and a liberal, Simmel, although enjoying the support of Max Weber, remained an outsider in German academic life. His material well-being was assured through an inheritance, but his academic ambitions were frustrated despite his considerable fame. Only in 1914 did he finally succeed in gaining a full chair at the provincial University of Strasbourg. Simmel's work covers a wide range, from close analysis of Kant, through to aesthetics and the philosophy of social science, and on to sociological investigations of the nature of the modern urbanised and commercialised money economy. One central theme that unites his philosophical and sociological work is his concern with the relationship and tensions between individualism and 'sociation' (*Vergesellschaftung*). His best-known work is the *Philosophy of Money* published in 1900, but he was also the author of a number of highly influential essays such as 'Metropolis and Mental Life' (which has had a lasting impact upon urban sociology). The influence of his formal sociology extends across philosophy (via Husserl and Heidegger) and into mainstream sociology (e.g. through the work of Erving Goffman). He was a co-founder (along with Ferdinand Tönnies and Max Weber) of the German Society for Sociology. Simmel died of liver cancer in 1918.

SOREL, GEORGES
(1847–1922). Born in Cherbourg, France, Sorel was a sceptical scientist and passionate moralist who defended working-class syndicalism against the dominant socialist parties, which he saw as complacently corrupt. Sorel was educated as an engineer at the Ecole Polytechnique and worked for the French government until 1893, when he retired to devote himself to writing, publishing and agitation. He pursued an ethics of socialism which could inspire the passions and the will, influenced by Bergson and then by Nietzsche's idea of the transvaluation of all values. Disgusted with the reformism of the left, Sorel flirted with the fascist Action Française, but when war broke out he was equally disgusted by the right and returned to his anarcho-syndicalist advocacy of direct proletarian action. Sorel's emphasis on the passions and ethics of socialism influenced thinkers of many different intellectual and political bents.

SOROUSH, ABDOLKARIM
(1945–). Born in Tehran, Soroush received a doctorate in pharmacology from the University of Tehran. He also studied at the University of London. In his early career Soroush contributed to the ideological development of the Islamic Republic. He was appointed to the Advisory Council on the Cultural Revolution, a position from which he later resigned. In the 1990s, he emerged as one of the most outspoken critics of the regime. His public lectures continue to attract large audiences in Iran but also draw fierce opposition from extremist groups such as Anasr-e Hezbollah. His writings include the *Non-Scientific Philosophy of History* (1978), *Lectures on Ethics and Human Sciences* (1987), *and Intellectualism*

and Religious Conviction (1988). His main work is *The Hermeneutical Expansion and Contraction of the Theory of Shari'ah* which offers a reassessment of knowledge of the Shari'a in the light of developments in the history of ideas, hermeneutics and the sociology of knowledge.

STALIN, JOSEPH (IOSIF VISSARIONOVICH DZHUGASHVILI)
(1879–1953). One of the few pre-revolutionary Bolshevik leaders to be born to a poor family, Stalin studied for the priesthood but was expelled for revolutionary activities in 1899. He became a professional revolutionary, siding with Lenin after the split in the Russian Social Democratic Labour Party in 1903, and in 1912 he became editor of *Pravda*. He was appointed Commissar for Nationalities in 1917 and from 1922 Secretary of the Communist Party of the Soviet Union, holding the post until his death. He was appointed to the Politburo of the party and was made Commissar of the Workers' and Peasants' Inspectorate, but was bitterly criticised by Lenin in his testament (1923). Stalin used his administrative powers to isolate rivals for the party's top leadership after Lenin's death, eliminating both left (Trotsky) and right (Bukharin). He then launched the Great Purge of the 1930s while contemporaneously collectivising agriculture and forcing through rapid industrialisation – at huge costs to peasants and workers. Generalissimo of the successful Soviet army in the Second World War, Stalin was credited with orchestrating communist takeovers in Eastern Europe and China. He was a symbol of the Cold War and was subsequently denounced as a paranoid and cruel dictator. His major writings include: *Marxism and the National and Colonial Question* (1912), *Problems of Leninism* (1926), *On Dialectics and Historical Materialism* (1938) and *Economic Problems of Socialism in the USSR* (1952).

STRAUSS, LEO
(1899–1986) grew up in what he described as 'a conservative, even orthodox Jewish home somewhere in a rural district of Germany'. He received his doctorate from Hamburg University in 1921, and in 1938 he left Germany in order to escape from the Nazi regime, emigrating to the USA, where he taught political science and philosophy at the New School for Social Research. In 1949 he moved to the University of Chicago, where he subsequently became Robert Maynard Hutchins Distinguished Service Professor. He retired from Chicago in 1968. Thereafter he held teaching positions at Claremont Men's College in California and at St John's College in Maryland, remaining at the latter institution until his death. A gifted lecturer and teacher, Strauss exerted a profound influence over such thinkers as Walter Berns, John Porter East, Dante Germino, Harry V. Jaffa, Willmoore Kendall and William F. Buckley Jr.

STURZO, LUIGI
(1871–1959) was a priest who devoted himself to social causes following the publication of *Rerum novarum* (1891) and the outbreak of rioting among peasant and sulphur miners in his native region of Sicily. He participated in Catholic organisations of Christian Democratic origin (peasants' associations, rural banks and cooperatives) from an early age and was also mayor in his home town of Caltagirone from 1905 to 1920. In 1919 he founded the Partito Popolare Italiano as a 'non-doctrinal and lay party of Catholics', of which he was party secretary until 1923, when, as a result of his opposition to Mussolini, the Vatican forced him to resign. His anti-fascism led to his enforced exile between 1925 and 1946, first in London and then in the USA. Once back in Italy, he resumed active politics but outside the Christian Democratic Party. In 1952 he made an unsuccessful attempt to form a centre-right coalition during the council elections in Rome.

SUN YAT-SEN
(1866–1925) was born in China and led the revolution of 1911 which overthrew the Qing dynasty and founded a republic. An ardent patriot, he sought to unite the Chinese people, whom he once called 'a sheet of loose sand', into a nation capable of standing up to the great European powers that had long sought to dominate his country. In his writings he stressed the 'three principles of the people', namely nationalism, democracy and socialism (which he later replaced with the non-ideological 'livelihood for all' under the influence of Chiang Kai-Shek). Although not a communist, he is regarded by both communists and non-communists as one of the founding fathers of modern China.

TAGORE, RABINDRANATH
(1861–1941) was born in Calcutta, India. He studied law in England and managed his family estates for nearly two decades. In 1901 he founded Shantiniketan, a residential school blending Indian, Eastern and Western cultural traditions, to which he later added the Vishwa Bharati University. He was a gifted poet, novelist, artist and musician, and exercised an enormous influence on Indian literature. He was awarded the Nobel prize for literature in 1913, the first Asian to be so honoured. In his philosophical and literary works, he propounded an aesthetically embedded, spiritually oriented, and ecologically sensitive view of life. He has the unique distinction of being the author of the national anthems of both India and Bangladesh.

TAWNEY, RICHARD HENRY
(1880–1962) was a British social theorist, historian and socialist. He read classics at Oxford and became a Fellow of Balliol. He published in early modern economic and agrarian history, while active in social reform and particularly in workers' adult education. He served on the Coal Industry Commission (1919), through which he advanced the trade union view, and later became involved in Labour Party politics. His socialism was strongly ethical and Christian, focusing on problems of social and material inequality in influential works such as *The Acquisitive Society* (1921) and *Equality* (1931). He also advanced his ideas through frequent writing for the progressive press. His best-known historical study was *Religion and the Rise of Capitalism* (1926).

TAYLOR, CHARLES
(1931–). Born in Montreal, Taylor studied at McGill University and at Oxford, and moved between these two universities throughout his career. His early interest in the philosophy of the social sciences was reflected in *The Explanation of Behaviour* (1964) and 'Interpretation and the Sciences of Man' (1971) in which he defended interpretative as against causal explanations of human action and laid some of the groundwork for later communitarian political philosophy. During the 1960s Taylor pursued an active political career in Canada's leftist New Democratic Party, standing unsuccessfully on four occasions in federal elections between 1962 and 1968. He has continued to be an influential public figure in debates on Quebec and the constitutional future of Canada. His later philosophical work includes *Hegel* (1975) and *Sources of the Self* (1989), an ambitious attempt to trace the origins of the modern Western conception of the self and its associated moral outlook.

TITMUSS, RICHARD MORRIS
(1907–73). A British social theorist and social policy-maker, Titmuss worked initially for an insurance company, and took an early interest in population statistics, publishing *Poverty and Population* in 1938. He acquired an international reputation through one of the official histories of the Second World War, entitled *Problems of Social Policy* (1950).

Despite having no academic qualifications, Titmuss was appointed to the chair of social administration at the LSE from 1950. His subsequent writings contributed to the theory and practice of the welfare state and to British social democratic thinking, in particular his pleas for altruism and for free choice alongside communal responsibilities. This received special expression in his *The Gift Relationship: From Human Blood to Social Policy* (1970).

TOLSTOY (or TOLSTOI), COUNT LEO (or LEV)
(1828–1910) was a Russian novelist turned moralist who became the world's most influential pacifist writer at the end of the nineteenth century. An aristocratic playboy in his youth who became an army officer and served at Sebastopol during the Crimean War, he developed into a major novelist, celebrated for his masterpieces *War and Peace* and *Anna Karenina*. However, at the end of the 1870s he espoused a perfectionist version of Christianity, which included an ultra-absolutist commitment to no-force pacifism, as expounded in *What I Believe* and *The Kingdom of God Is Within You*.

TONIOLO, GIUSEPPE
(1845–1918) was born and raised in the Veneto in the home of moderate liberal scholars but also in an environment with a strong religious tradition. He started to teach at the University of Padua, where he had also been a student. As professor of economics at the university between 1879 and 1917, he was one of the most influential intellectuals within the Italian Catholic movement at the turn of the century. In 1889 he founded the Unione Cattolica per gli Studi Sociali. In 1906 he became president of the Unione Popolare, the embryo of a Catholic party. Due to his great interest in both social and scholarly activities, rather than in direct political activity, he demonstrated a great interest in sociology. The *Rivista internazionale di scienze sociali*, founded in 1893, is one of the main sources of Catholic-inspired sociology.

TREITSCHKE, HEINRICH VON
(1834–96) was a German historian and editor of the *Prussian Year-Book*. Born in Dresden, von Treitschke studied history, constitutional law and economics in Bonn, Leipzig, Tübingen and Heidelberg. Between 1859 and 1863 he taught at the University of Leipzig, then at Freiburg, before taking up a chair at the University of Kiel in 1866, only to move to a chair in Heidelberg one year later, and thence to Berlin in 1873, where he succeeded Leopold von Ranke as the official historian of the Prussian state in 1886. Both in his historical and political work (he was a member of the Reichstag from 1871 until 1884), the once-liberal von Treitschke adopted an increasingly trenchant German nationalist and anti-socialist position. In opposition to the British liberal tradition in which liberty was conceptualised as freedom *from* the state, von Treitschke sought a specifically German notion of liberty as freedom *within* the state. In the 1870s and 1880s he became a vehement proponent of German imperialism and his anti-Semitic statements – e.g. 'the Jews are our misfortune' – sparked off a heated controversy. His major work was a five-volume history of nineteenth-century Germany.

TROTSKY, LEON (LEV DAVIDOVICH BRONSTEIN)
(1879–1940). Born in the Ukraine to prosperous Jewish parents, Bronstein became a revolutionary social democrat at the age of eighteen, taking Trotsky as his *nom de guerre*. Two years later, in 1898, he was arrested and sent to Siberia. In 1902 he escaped to London where he met Lenin. Three years later he returned to Russia to take a leading role in the failed 1905 Revolution. Arrested again, he escaped in 1907 to Europe, where he spent ten years in exile as a revolutionary writer and theorist. On hearing of the ousting of

the tsar in 1917 he returned to Russia to help organise the Bolsheviks' seizure of state power in the November Revolution. During the 'White' counter-revolution of 1918–20 he organised and commanded the 'Red' army. A brilliant theorist, organiser and orator, he quickly incurred the wrath of Joseph Stalin, his chief rival as V. I. Lenin's successor. Outmanoeuvred by Stalin, Trotsky was expelled from the Communist Party in 1927 and subsequently exiled to Soviet Central Asia, from where he escaped to live in Turkey, Norway and Mexico. An ultra-leftist advocate of 'permanent revolution' – as opposed to Stalin's programme of 'socialism in one country' – Trotsky was an outspoken critic of Stalin, whom he accused of 'betraying' the Russian Revolution and deviating from the Marxist-Leninist path. Trotsky was brutally murdered in Mexico City in 1940 by one of Stalin's secret agents wielding a pickaxe. Trotsky's major works include *Our Political Tasks* (1904), *Our Revolution* (1018), *Terrorism and Communism* (1920), *Lenin* (1924), *Permanent Revolution* (1930), *History of the Russian Revolution* (1931–3), *The Revolution Betrayed* (1937) and an autobiography, *My Life* (1929).

TZARA, TRISTAN

(1896–1963). Born at Moinesti in Rumania, Tzara was the principal force in the tumultuous and nihilistic 'dada' movement that arose in Zurich during the First World War. In 1920 he took his act to Paris, briefly challenged André Breton's surrealism for avant-garde leadership, then became a surrealist himself in 1929. In addition to various dada manifestos, he wrote poetry, most importantly *25 poèmes* (1918) and *L'homme approximatif* (1930). He was among those who worked hardest for the alliance between surrealism and the French Communist Party, which he joined in 1936. After the war he wrote several more volumes of poems. He is buried near Baudelaire in Montparnasse Cemetery in Paris.

VOEGELIN, ERIC

(1901–85). Born in Cologne, Voegelin was educated in Vienna and emigrated to the USA in 1938, following the *Anschluss*. Thereafter he spent most of his life in the USA. He returned, however, to Munich as professor of political science between 1958 and 1966. Although Voegelin drew on metaphysical and phenomenological traditions of thought more influential on the continent than in Anglo-American intellectual life, his influence on a select circle of US scholars (notable amongst whom are Frank Meyer and Ellis Sandoz) has been great. His critics, by contrast, regard his attempt to present the ideological mentality of the modern Western world as a secularised version of the Gnostic heresy which dominated Western life in the early centuries of the Christian era as at best over-simplistic or, at worst, wholly implausible. All, however, have acknowledged the extraordinary depth and range of his historical and philosophical scholarship. He died in Stanford, California in 1985.

WALLAS, GRAHAM

(1858–1932). Born into a clerical household in Durham, England, Wallas was a significant academic figure known for his psychological studies of politics. Educated at Oxford and influenced by John Ruskin, he gravitated to Fabian socialism and was a member of the inner circle of Fabians from 1886 to 1904. By then he was on the staff at the London School of Economics, becoming its first professor of political science in 1914. His major work – *Human Nature in Politics* (1908) – brought scientific and political realism, informed by associationist psychology, to the prospects for industrial democracy. It drew upon the American pragmatist William James in order to criticise the calculative rationalism of nineteenth-century political theorists, notably Jeremy Bentham, and to shift attention to the irrational, instinctive and non-cognitive elements in politics. The work became a manifesto for such

American political scientists as Charles Merriam who sought a 'behavioural' science of politics, as well as critics of the classical ideals of democratic citizenship like his student Walter Lippmann. A subsequent work – *The Great Society* (1914) – sought a restoration of rationality to aid in the conscious reorganisation of society. Wallas's complex views of current and possible political arrangements were informed by his active political life, especially on the London City Council and the London School Board.

WALZER, MICHAEL
(1935–). Educated at Brandeis University and at Harvard, Walzer held academic posts at Princeton and at Harvard before becoming professor of government at the Institute for Advanced Studies, Princeton. Throughout his life he has been politically involved with movements of the left, especially with the civil rights and anti-war movements of the 1960s and with the Israeli peace movement Shalom Akhshav. He is co-editor of the democratic socialist magazine *Dissent*, to which he has contributed since the 1960s. His best-known books are *Just and Unjust Wars* (1977) and *Spheres of Justice* (1983) – the latter developing a controversial interpretation of justice as made up of a plurality of contextually specific principles. Walzer has pursued these themes in his later work, alongside a growing interest in the history of Jewish political thought.

WEBB, BEATRICE
(1858–1943) was a social reformer and political activist. Initially influenced by Herbert Spencer and Joseph Chamberlain, she assisted Charles Booth with research into London living conditions and published a book on the cooperative movement in 1891. She married Sidney Webb in 1891 and they embarked on a series of collaborative projects that lasted throughout their lives. Her outspoken diary is a unique record of the times, as well as providing insight into her character and life. In 1905 she was appointed to serve on the Royal Commission on the Poor Laws and produced with Sidney in 1909 a minority report which was a milestone in practical social reform, based on identifying categories of distress. Webb was a member of a number of post-war reconstruction and planning committees.

WEBB, SIDNEY JAMES
(1859–1947) was a socialist reformer and politician. Initially a civil servant, he became from 1885 a leading light of the Fabian Society, contributing to the famous *Fabian Essays in Socialism* (1889) and writing many of its tracts, which inaugurated mass British political proselytising. Webb was instrumental in transforming British socialism into a gradualist, efficient, collectivist, empirically oriented yet widespread political movement. Webb served as an MP from 1892 to 1910, and was active in spearheading progressivism in London. He wrote important histories of trade unionism and local government in a unique intellectual partnership with his wife Beatrice and also founded the *New Statesman*. After the First World War, Webb participated in drafting the policy and new constitution of the Labour Party and served again as a Labour MP and in Labour governments.

WEBER, MAX (KARL EMIL MAXIMILIAN)
(1864–1920). Born in Erfurt, Germany, to a high-bourgeois family active in politics, Weber was one of the founders of sociology, emphasising the role of ideas and the clash of values against a background of modern rationalisation. He was an ardent German nationalist although also a liberal, and after Germany's defeat in the First World War he became a committed if grim defender of the nascent Weimar Republic. Having researched Italian trade, Roman agrarian history and its legal implications, and agriculture in East Prussia, Weber taught as professor at Freiburg, Heidelberg and, after a sick leave of fifteen years,

at Vienna. He promoted research on the cultural implications of economic change as well as on the sociology of world religions, combining these in his important thesis about the influence of the Protestant ethic in the rise of capitalism. Despite the fact that he distinguished sharply between his academic work and his own political views and values, Weber was a charismatic voice in German political life and is still regarded as a touchstone for a disillusioned liberalism.

WIGFORSS, ERNST
(1881–1977) was a Swedish politician, welfare state theorist and philologist. Initially a scholar of Swedish dialects and lecturer at Lund University from 1913–18, he was elected to parliament in 1919 and was a member of either the first or second chamber until 1953. He was minister of finance in 1925–6 and from 1932 to 1949. His approach to unemployment was influenced by Keynesianism. Throughout he was one of the leaders of the Social Democrats and a major architect of the Swedish welfare state and of its economic policies. In his writings Wigforss adapted Marxism to Swedish circumstances, moving towards gradualism while inspired by early twentieth-century British socialist thinking and its combination of social justice and liberty.

WILSON, THOMAS WOODROW
(1856–1924) was a reforming liberal and convinced internationalist, who entered office as the twenty-eighth president of the United States in 1913. His influence on international relations was inspirational rather than effective. He failed to keep America out of the war, to broker 'a peace without victory', or to secure US participation in the League of Nations, on which his plans for a new international order were based. Yet his speech, outlining fourteen points necessary for a just and lasting peace, was accepted by all sides as the basis for the Versailles Peace Conference. Wilson also established the ideas of democracy, national self-determination and collective security at the centre of the liberal international agenda, where they remained.

Bibliography

Part I: The changing fortunes of liberal democracy

Primary sources

Arendt, Hannah (1951). *Origins of Totalitarianism*, New York.

Aron, Raymond (1957 [1955]). *The Opium of the Intellectuals*, trans. Terence Kilmartin, New York.

(1972). *The Imperial Republic, the United States and the World 1945–1973*, London.

Bachrach, P. and Baratz, M. S. (1962). 'The Two Faces of Power', *American Political Science Review* 56: 947–52.

Barrès, M. (1925). *Scènes et doctrines du nationalisme*, 2 vols., Paris.

Barry, Brian (1988). *Theories of Justice*, Berkeley, Calif.

Beitz, C. (1979). *Political Theory and International Relations*, Princeton, N.J.

Bell, Daniel (1979). *Cultural Contradictions of Capitalism*, London.

Benoist, A. de (1980). *Les idées à l'endroit*, Paris.

Beran, H. (1987). *The Theory of Political Obligation*, London.

Berelson, B. *et al.* (1954). *Voting*, Chicago.

Berlin, Isaiah (1979). 'Nationalism: A Neglected Concept', in *Against the Current: Essays in the History of Ideas*, London.

Beveridge, William (1942). *Social Insurance and Allied Services*, Cmd. 6404, London.

(1945). *Full Employment in a Free Society*, London.

(1948). *Voluntary Action*, London.

Biddiss, Michael (1970) (ed.). *Gobineau: Selected Political Writings*, New York and London.

Blake, Lord, and Patten, J. (1976) (eds.). *The Conservative Opportunity*, London.

Le Bon. G. (1926 [1895]). *The Crowd: A Study of the Popular Mind*, London.

Bonald, vicomte de (1864). *Oeuvres politiques*, in *Oeuvres complètes*, ed. M. L'Abbé Migne, 3 vols., Paris.

Bottai, Giovanni (1949). *Vent'anni e un giorno*, Naviglio.

Boutros-Ghali, Boutros (1992). *Agenda for Peace*, New York.

Bryce, J. (1888). *The American Commonwealth*, 2 vols., London.

Buchanan, A. (1991). *Secession: The Morality of Political Divorce from Fort Sumter to Lithuania and Quebec*, Oxford.

Buchanan, J. M. (1975). *The Limits of Liberty*, Chicago.

Buchanan, J. M. and Wagner, E. E. (1977). *Democracy in Deficit: The Political Legacy of Lord Keynes*, New York.

Buchanan, J. M., Burton, J. and Wagner, R. E. (1978). *The Consequences of Mr Keynes*, London.

Buckley, William F. Jr. (1958). *Up from Liberalism*, New York.

Camus, Albert (1956 [1951]). *The Rebel*, New York.

Canetti, E. (1978 [1960]). *Crowds and Power*, New York.

Carr, E. H. (1945). *Nationalism and After*, London.

Castillo Velasco, Jaime (1963). *Las fuentes de la democracia cristiana*, Santiago de Chile.

Churchill, Winston S. (1909). *Liberalism and the Social Problem*, London.

Connor, W. (1978). 'A Nation is a Nation, is a State, is an Ethnic Group, is a . . .', *Ethnic and Racial Studies* 1(4): 379–88.

Croly, Herbert (1909). *The Promise of American Life*, New York.

(1915). *Progressive Democracy*, New York.

Dahl, R. A. (1956) *A Preface to Democratic Theory*, New Haven, Conn.

(1961). *Who Governs? Democracy and Power in an American City*, New Haven, Conn.

De Gasperi, Alcide (1955). *I cattolici dall' opposizione al governo*, Bari.

Dewey, John (1935). *Liberalism and Social Action*, New York.

Dossetti, Giuseppe (1994). *La ricerca costituente, 1945–1952*, Bologna.

(1995). *Scritti politici*, Genoa.

Drumont, Edouard (1886). *La France juive*, Paris.

Duncan, G. and Lukes, S. (1963). 'The New Democracy', *Political Studies* 11: 156–77.

Durkheim, Emile (1984 [1893]). *The Division of Labour in Society*, trans. W. D. Halls, Basingstoke.

(1992 [1950]). *Professional Ethics and Civic Morals*, trans. C. Brookfield, London.

Eliot, T. S. (1928). 'The Action Française, Mr. Maurras and Mr. Ward', *The Criterion*, 7(3): 195–203.

(1928–9). 'The Literature of Fascism', *The Criterion* 8(3): 280–90.

(1939). *The Idea of a Christian Society*, London.

Fanon, F. (1965). *The Wretched of the Earth*, London.

Fouillée, A. (1880). *La science sociale contemporaine*, Paris.

Fournial, H. (1892). *Essai sur la psychologie des foules: considérations médico-judiciaires sur les responsibilités collectives*, Lyon.

Freud, S. (1953–74 [1921]). *Group Psychology and the Analysis of the Ego*, the standard edition of *The Complete Psychological Works of Sigmund Freud*, ed. James Stratchey, London.

Friedman, M. (1962). *Capitalism and Freedom*, London.

(1978). 'Keynes's Political Legacy', in J. M. Buchanan, J. Burton and R. E. Wagner, *The Consequences of Mr Keynes*, London.

Friedrich, C. J. (1955). 'The Political Thought of Neo-Liberalism', *American Political Science Review* 69: 509–25.

Gentile, Giovanni (1915). *Fondamenti della filosofia del diritto*, Florence.

(1946). *Genesi e struttura della società*, Florence.

Gilmour, I. (1977). *Inside Right: A Study of Conservatism*, London.

Girault, A. (1903). *Principes de colonisation et de législation coloniales*, Paris.

Gramsci, Antonio (1971). *Selections from the Prison Notebooks*, trans. and ed. Quentin Hoare and Geoffrey Nowell-Smith, New York.

(1977). *Quaderni del carcere*, ed. V Gerratana, 4 vols., Turin.

Green, T. H. (1941 [1886]). *Principles of Political Obligation*, London.

Gumplowicz, Ludwig (1883). *Der Rassenkampf*, Innsbruck.

Hamilton, A. (1961–79 [1791]). 'Report on Manufactures', in vol. IV of *The Papers of Alexander Hamilton*, ed. Harold C. Syriett and Jacob E. Cooke, 26 vols., New York.

Havel, Vaclav (1992). 'The Power of the Powerless', in *Open Letters: Selected Writings, 1965–1990*, New York.

Hayek, F. A. (1944). *The Road to Serfdom*, London.

(1945). 'The Use of Knowledge in Society', *American Economic Review* 35(4): 519–30.
(1948). *Individualism and the Economic Order*, Chicago.
(1956). 'In Honour of Professor Mises', reprinted in Hayek (1992), pp. 129–32.
(1960). *The Constitution of Liberty*, London and Henley.
(1975). *Full Employment at Any Price?*, London.
(1976). *Denationalisation of Money*, London.
(1977). 'The Road from Serfdom', interview with T. W. Hazlett, *Reason Online*: www.reasonmag.cpm/hayekint.html.
(1978). *New Studies in Philosophy, Politics, Economics and the History of Ideas*, Chicago.
(1979). *Law, Legislation and Liberty*, 3 vols., Chicago.
(1992). *The Fortunes of Liberalism*, ed. P. G. Klein, *The Collected Works of F. A. Hayek*, vol. IV, Chicago.
Hegel, G. W. F. (1979 [1821]). *Philosophy of Right*, trans. with notes T. M. Knox, Oxford.
Hitler, Adolf (1952 [1925]). *Mein Kampf*, New Brunswick.
Hobhouse, L. T. (1899). 'The Foreign Policy of Collectivism', *Economic Review* 9: 197–220.
(1911). *Liberalism*, London.
Hobson, J. A. (1901). *The Social Problem*, London.
(1909). *The Crisis of Liberalism*, London.
(1914). *Work and Wealth: A Human Valuation*, London.
(1929). *Wealth and Life*, London.
(1988 [1902]). *Imperialism: A Study*, London.
Horkheimer, Max (1978 [1940]). 'The Authoritarian State', reprinted in Andrew Arato and Eike Gebhardt (eds.) *The Essential Frankfurt School Reader*, New York.
Jennings, W. I. (1956). *The Approach to Self-Government*, Cambridge.
Jünger, Ernst (1981 [1932]). *Der Arbeiter*, Stuttgart.
Ketteler, Wilhelm Emmanuel von (1864). *Die Arbeiterfrage und das Christentum*, Mainz.
(1871). *Die Katholiken im Deutschen Reich*, Mainz.
Keynes J. M. (1934). 'National Self-sufficiency', *Yale Review* 22: 755–69.
(1971–89). *The Collected Writings*, ed. D. E. Moggeridge, 30 vols., London.
Kirk, R. (1953). *The Conservative Mind: From Burke to Santayana*, Chicago.
Kohn, H. (1935). 'Communist and Fascist Dictatorship: A Comparative Study', in Guy Stanton Ford (ed.) *Dictatorship in the Modern World*, Minneapolis.
(1944). *The Idea of Nationalism*, New York.
Kornhauser, W. (1959). *The Politics of Mass Society*, Glencoe, Ill.
Krebs, Pierre (1982). *Die europäische Wiederburt*, Tübingen.
Kristol, Irving (1970). 'When Virtue Loses all her Loveliness – Some Reflections on Capitalism and "The Free Society" ', *The Public Interest*, Fall: 3–15.
(1978). *Two Cheers for Capitalism*, New York.
(1996). 'The Right Stuff', *Prospect* 12, October: 27–32.
Kropotkin, P. A. (1972 [1902]). *Mutual Aid: A Factor of Evolution*, London.
Lamennais, Félicité-Robert de (1946). *Oeuvres*, Geneva.
Laroque, Pierre (1953). *Refléxions sur le problème social*, Paris.
Lenin, V. I. (1920 [1916]). *Imperialism: The Highest Stage of Capitalism*, Moscow.
(1963 [1902]). *What Is To Be Done?*, trans. S. V. and P. Utechin, Oxford.
Leroy-Beaulieu, P. (1891). *The Modern State in Relation to Society and the Individual*, London.
Lichteim, G. (1971). *Imperialism*, London.
Lippmann, W. (1956). *The Public Philosophy*, New York.
(1965 [1922]). *Public Opinion*, New York.
List, F. (1904 [1840]). *The National System of Political Economy*, London.
Lugard, Lord (1965 [1922]). *The Dual Mandate*, London.

Maistre, J. de (1884). *Oeuvres complètes*, vols. I, II and IV, Lyon.

Mannheim, Karl (1940). *Man and Society in an Age of Reconstruction*, New York.

(1943). *Diagnosis of our Time*, London.

Marcuse, Herbert (1964). *One-Dimensional Man*, Boston.

(1968 [1934]). 'The Struggle Against Liberalism in the Totalitarian View of the State', reprinted in *Negations*, Boston.

Maritain, Jacques (1986–95). *Oeuvres complètes*, Paris and Freiburg.

Marshall, T. H. (1965 [1949]). *Class, Citizenship, and Social Development*, New York.

Marx, K. and Engels, F. (1959 [1853]). *On Colonialism*, Moscow.

Maurras, C. (1954). *Essais politiques*, in *Oeuvres capitales*, vol. II, Paris.

Mazzini, G. (1924 [1907]). *The Duties of Man and other Essays*, London.

Meinecke, F. (1922). *Weltbürgertum und Nationaalstaat. Studien zur Genesis des deutschen Nationalstaates*, Munich.

Merleau-Ponty, Maurice (1969). *Humanism and Terror: An Essay on the Communist Problem*, Boston.

(1973 [1955]). *Adventures of the Dialectic*, Evanston, Ill.

Meyer, Frank S. (1964). *What is Conservatism?*, New York.

(1996). *In Defense of Freedom and Related Essays*, Indianapolis.

Michels, R. (1927). *Corso di sociologia politica*, Milan.

(1959 [1911]). *Political Parties: A Sociological Study of the Oligarchical Tendencies of Modern Democracy*, New York.

Mill, J. S. (1972). *Utilitarianism, Liberty and Representative Government*, ed. A. D. Lindsay, London.

(1977 [1836]). 'Civilization', in *Essays on Politics and Society*, ed. J. M. Robson, Toronto and Buffalo.

(1991a [1861]). *Representative Government*, London.

(1991b [1859]). *On Liberty*, in *On Liberty and Other Essays*, ed. J. Gray, Oxford.

Miller, D. (1995). *On Nationality*, London.

Milosz, Czeslaw (1953 [1951]). *The Captive Mind*, New York.

Mises, L. von (1983 [1919]). *Nation, State and Economy: Contributions to the History of our Time*, trans. Leland B. Yeager, New York.

Moeller van den Bruck, A. (1971 [1923]). *Germany's Third Empire*, New York.

Montherlant, H. de (1927). *The Bullfighters*, New York.

(1960). *Selected Essays*, ed. Peter Quennell, London.

Mosca, G. (1939 [1896 and 1923]). *The Ruling Class* (Elementi di scienza politica), ed. A. Livingstone, trans. H. D. Kahn, New York.

(1958 [1884]). *Sulla teorica dei governi e sul governo rappresentativo*, in *Ciò che la storia possa insegnare: scritti di scienza politica*, Milan.

Mounier, Emmanuel (1934). *La révolution personnaliste et communautaire*, Paris.

(1936). *Manifeste au service du personnalisme*, Paris.

Müller-Armack, Alfred (1956). *Wirtschaftsordnung und Wirtschaftspolitik*, Freiburg.

Murray, Charles (1984). *Losing Ground*, New York.

Murri, Romolo (1901–4). *Battaglie d'oggi: Il programma politico della democrazia*, Rome.

Mussolini, Benito (1951–63). *Opera omnia di Benito Mussolini*, ed. E. and D. Susmel, 36 vols., Florence.

Myrdal, A. and Myrdal, G. (1941). *Nation and Family: The Swedish Experiment in Democratic Family and Population Policy*, New York.

Nehru, J. (1962). *India's Freedom*, London.

Neuhaus, Richard John (1996). Symposium on 'The End of Democracy?', *First Things*, no. 57.

Nisbet, Robert A. (1953). *The Quest for Community*, New York.
Nodia, G. (1992). 'Nationalism and Democracy', *Journal of Democracy* 3(4): 3–31.
Nordau, Max (1993 [1892]). *Degeneration*, Lincoln, Nebr.
Nozick, R. (1974). *Anarchy, State and Utopia*, Oxford.
Oakeshott, M. (1975). *On Human Conduct*, Oxford.
(1991 [1962]). *Rationalism in Politics*, Indianapolis.
Ortega y Gasset, J. (1963 [1930]). *The Revolt of the Masses*, London.
(1968 [1925]). *The Dehumanization of Art*, Princeton, N.J.
Orwell, George (1968a). 'Review: Russia Under Soviet Rule, by N. de Basily', in *The Collected Essays, Journalism, and Letters of George Orwell*, vol. I: *An Age Like This, 1920–1940*, ed. Sonia Orwell and Ian Angus, New York.
(1968b). *The Collected Essays, Journalism, and Letters of George Orwell*, vol. II: *My Country Right or Left, 1940–1943*, ed. Sonia Orwell and Ian Angus, New York.
(1980). *Homage To Catalonia*, New York.
Ostrogorski, M. (1902). *Democracy and the Organisation of Political Parties*, 2 vols., trans. F. Clarke with a preface by James Bryce, London.
Pareto, V. (1902). *Les systèmes socialistes*, 2 vols., Paris.
(1916). *Trattato di sociologia generale*, 3 vols., Florence.
(1966 [1893]). 'Introduction', to K. Marx, *Le capital*, extraits faits par P. Larfargue in *Marxisme et économie pure*, Lausanne, pp. 33–70.
(1974 [1891]). 'Socialismo e libertà', *Il Pensiero Italiano*, Feb.: 227–37, in *Ecrits politiques*, ed. G. Busino, 2 vols., Geneva, vol. I, pp. 376–409.
(1975 [1922]). Letter to Lello Gangemi, 13 Nov. 1922, in *Correspondence 1890–1923*, ed. G. Busino, 2 vols., Geneva.
(1980 [1921]). 'La trasformazione della democrazia', in *Ecrits sociologiques mineurs*, ed. G. Busino, Geneva, pp. 917–1060.
Perham, M. (1963). *The Colonial Reckoning*, London.
Plamenatz, J. (1960). *On Alien Rule and Self Government*, London.
Le Play, F. (1982). *On Family, Work, and Social Change*, ed. C. B. Silver, Chicago.
Polanyi, K. (1957 [1944]). *The Great Transformation: the Political and Economic Origins of our Time*, Boston.
Pollock, Friedrich (1941). 'State Capitalism: Its Possibilities and Limitations', *Studies in Philosophy and Social Science* 9 (2).
Primo de Rivera, José Antonio (1953). *Obras completes*, Madrid.
Rand, Ayn (1961). *For the New Intellectual*, New York.
Rauschning, Hermann (1939). *The Revolution of Nihilism: Warning to the West*, New York.
(1941). *The Beast from the Abyss*, London.
Rawls, J. (1971). *A Theory of Justice*, Cambridge, Mass.
Renan, E. (1882). *Qu'est-ce qu'une nation?*, trans. I. M. Snyder, Paris.
Ritchie, David G. (1887). *The Moral Function of the State*, London.
(1893). *Darwin and Hegel*, London.
(1895). *Natural Rights*, London.
Rosenberg, Alfred (1933). *Der Mythus der zwanzigsten Jahrhunderts*, Munich.
Rossiter, Clinton (1955). *Conservatism in America*, New York.
Rowntree, B. Seebohm (1919). *The Human Needs of Labour*, London; revised edn, 1937.
Rubinow, I. M. (1916). *Social Insurance, with Special Reference to American Conditions*, New York.
Sakharov, Andrei (1990). *Memoirs*, New York.
Sangnier, Marc (1905). *L'esprit démocratique*, Paris.
Sarraut, A. (1931). *Grandeur et servitude coloniales*, Paris.

Schmitt, C. (1976 [1927]). *The Concept of the Political*, trans. G. Schwab, New Brunswick, N.J.

(1985 [1923]). *The Crisis of Parliamentary Democracy*, trans. E. Kennedy, Cambridge, Mass.

Schumpeter, J. A. (1976 [1942]). *Capitalism, Socialism and Democracy*, London.

Scruton, R. (1990). 'In Defence of the Nation', in J. C. D Clark (ed.) *Ideas and Politics in Modern Britain*, London, pp. 53–86.

Sighele, S. (1892 [1891]). *La foule criminelle*, trans. P. Vigney, Paris.

Smith, A. (1923 [1776]). *Wealth of Nations*, 2 vols., Oxford.

Smith, A. D. (1991). *National Identity*, London.

Sorel, Georges (1908). *Réflexions sur la violence*, Paris.

Spencer, Herbert (1969 [1884]). *The Man Versus the State*, Harmondsworth.

Spengler, O. (1926 [1919]). *The Decline of the West*, vol. I, trans. C. F. Atkinson, London.

Stalin, J. (1973). 'The Nation', in *The Essential Stalin: Major Theoretical Writings 1905–1952*, ed. B. Franklin, London.

Strauss, Leo (1989). *Liberalism Ancient and Modern*, Chicago.

Sturzo, Luigi (1979). *Il pensiero politico*, Rome.

Sumner, W. G. (1883). *What Social Classes Owe to Each Other*, New York.

(1914). *The Challenge of Facts and Other Essays*, ed. A. G. Keller, New Haven, Conn.

Taine, H. (1962 [1887–8]). *The Origins of Contemporary France*, trans. Durand, 6 vols., Boston.

Tarde, G. (1890). *Les lois de l'imitation*, Paris.

(1892). 'Les crimes des foules', *Archives de l'Anthropologie Criminelle* 7: 353–86.

(1912 [1890]). *Penal Philosophy*, trans. Rapelije Howell, Boston.

Tawney, R. H. (1945 [1921]). *The Acquisitive Society*, London.

Titmuss, Richard M. (1950). *Problems of Social Policy*, Official Civil History of the Second World War, London.

(1955). 'The Social Division of Welfare: Some Reflections on the Search for Equity', reprinted in Titmuss (1987), pp. 39–59.

(1958). *Essays on 'the Welfare State'*, London.

(1967). 'Universal and Selective Social Services', reprinted in Titmuss (1987), pp. 128–40.

(1971). 'Welfare "Rights", Law and Discretion', *Political Quarterly* 42: 113–32.

(1973). *The Gift Relationship*, Harmondsworth.

(1974). *Social Policy*, London.

(1976). *Commitment to Welfare*, London.

(1987). *The Philosophy of Welfare: Selected Writings of Richard M. Titmuss*, ed. Brian Abel-Smith and Kay Titmuss, London.

Toniolo, Giuseppe (1980). *Saggi politici*, Rome.

Tönnies, F. (2001 [1887]). *Community and Civil Society*, ed. J. Harris, Cambridge.

Trotsky, Leon (1937). *The Revolution Betrayed*, New York.

Van Parijs, Philippe (1991). 'Why Surfers Should be Fed: The Liberal Case for an Unconditional Basic Income', *Philosophy and Public Affairs* 20: 101–31.

Viereck, Peter (1949). *Conservatism Revisited*, New York.

Voegelin, E. (1952). *The New Science of Politics*, Chicago.

(1986). *Political Religions*, Lewiston, N.Y.

Wallas, G. (1908). *Human Nature in Politics*, London.

Walzer, M. (1985). 'The Moral Standing of States: A Response to Four Critics', in C. R. Beitz, M. Cohen, T. Scanlon and A. J. Simmons (eds.) *International Ethics, A Philosophy and Public Affairs Reader*, Princeton, N.J.

Weaver, R. (1948). *Ideas Have Consequences*, Chicago.

Webb, Beatrice (1948). *Our Partnership*, London.

Webb, Sidney and Beatrice (1909a) (eds.). *The Break-up of the Poor Law: Being Part One of the Minority Report of the Poor Law Commission*, London.
(1909b) (eds.). *The Public Organisation of the Labour Market: Being Part Two of the Minority Report of the Poor Law Commission*, London.
Weber, M. (1948). 'The Nation', in *From Max Weber: Essays in Sociology*, trans. and ed. H. H. Gerth and C. Wright Mills, London.
(1949 [1917]). 'The Meaning of "Ethical Neutrality" in Sociology and Economics', in E. Shils and H. Finch (eds.) *Max Weber on the Methodology of the Social Sciences*, New York.
(1978a). *Economy and Society*, ed. G. Roth and C Wittich, 2 vols., Berkeley.
(1978b [1918]). 'Parliament and Government in a Reconstructed Germany', in *Economy and Society*, ed. G. Roth and C. Wittich, 2 vols., Berkeley, appendix 2, vol. II, pp. 1381–469.
(1994a [1917]). 'Suffrage and Democracy in Germany', in *Political Writings*, ed. P. Lassman and R. Speirs, trans. R. Speirs, Cambridge, pp. 80–129.
(1994b [1918]). 'Socialism', in *Political Writings*, ed. P. Lassman and R. Speirs, trans. R. Speirs, Cambridge, pp. 272–303.
(1994c [1919]). 'The Profession and Vocation of Politics', in *Political Writings*, ed. P. Lassman and R. Speirs, trans. R. Speirs, Cambridge, pp. 309–69.
Weil, Simone (1946). 'Words and War', *Politics* 70 (March).
Whitaker, W. (1982) (ed.). *The New Right Papers*, New York.
Willetts, D. (1994). *Civic Conservatism*, London.

Secondary sources.

Ackermann, Jürgen (1970). *Heinrich Himmler als Ideologe*, Göttingen.
Ambler, John S. (1991) (ed.). *The French Welfare State*, New York.
Anderson, B. (1983). *Imagined Communities: Reflections on the Origin and Spread of Nationalism*, London.
Armstrong, John A. (1961). *The Politics of Totalitarianism*, New York.
Aron, Raymond (1955). *The Century of Total War*, Boston.
Aschheim, Steven E. (1992). *The Nietzsche Legacy in Germany. 1890–1990*, Berkeley, Calif.
Ashford, Douglas E. (1986). *The Emergence of the Welfare States*, Oxford.
(1991). 'Advantages of Complexity: Social Insurance in France', in John S. Ambler (ed.) *The French Welfare State*, New York, pp. 32–57.
Atkinson, A. B. (1995). *Incomes and the Welfare State*, Cambridge.
(1996). 'The Case for a Participation Income', *Political Quarterly* 67: 67–70.
(1999). *The Economic Consequences of Rolling Back the Welfare State*. Cambridge, Mass.
Austin, D. A. (1988). *The Commonwealth and Britain*, London.
(1998). 'In Memoriam: Legacies of Empire', *Round Table*, no. 348.
Babyonshev, Alexander (1982) (ed.). *On Sakharov*, New York.
Bachrach, P. (1967). *The Theory of Democratic Elitism*, Boston.
Bachrach, P. and Baratz, M. S. (1962). 'The Two Faces of Power', *American Political Science Review* 56: 947–52.
Baehr, P. (1990). 'The "Masses" in Weber's Political Sociology', *Economy and Society* 19: 242–65.
Baget-Bozzo, Gianni (1974). *Il partito cristiano al potere. La DC di De Gasperi e di Dossetti 1945–1954*, Florence.
Bainton, Michael (1985). *The Idea of Race and Race Theory*, Cambridge.

Ball, Terence (1989). 'Party', in T. Ball, J. Farr and R. L. Hanson (eds.) *Political Innovation and Conceptual Change*, Cambridge.

(1993). 'American Political Science in its Postwar Context', in James Farr and Raymond Seidelman (eds.) *Discipline and History: Political Science in the United States*, Ann Arbor, Mich.

Bane, Mary Jo and Ellwood, David T. (1994). *Welfare Realities*, Cambridge, Mass.

Bardeche, Maurice (1961). *Qu'est-ce que le fascisme?*, Paris.

Barker, R. and Howard-Johnston, X. (1975). 'The Politics and Political Ideas of Mosei Ostrogorski', *Political Studies* 23: 415–29.

Barr, Nicholas (1987). *The Economics of the Welfare State*, London.

(1989). 'Social Insurance as an Efficiency Device', *Journal of Public Policy* 9: 59–82.

Barrows, S. (1981). *Distorting Mirrors: Visions of the Crowd in Late Nineteenth-Century France*, New Haven, Conn.

Bars, H. (1961). *La politique selon Jacques Maritain*, Paris.

Bateman, B. W. and Davis, J. B. (1991) (eds.). *Keynes and Philosophy: Essays on the Origin of Keynes's Thought*, Aldershot.

Bauer, Raymond and Inkeles, Alex (1961). *The Soviet Citizen: Daily Life in a Totalitarian Society*, Cambridge, Mass.

Beales, D. (1966). 'Mazzini and Revolutionary Nationalism', in D. Thomson, *Political Ideas*, London.

Beetham, D. (1977a). 'From Socialism to Fascism: The Relation between Theory and Practice in the Work of Robert Michels. I. From Marxist Revolutionary to Political Sociologist', *Political Studies* 25: 3–24.

(1977b). 'From Socialism to Fascism: The Relation between Theory and Practice in the Work of Robert Michels. II. The Fascist Ideologue', *Political Studies* 25: 161–81.

(1981). 'Michels and his Critics', *Archives Européennes de Sociologie* 22: 81–99.

(1985). *Max Weber and the Theory of Modern Politics*, 2nd edn., Cambridge.

(1987). 'Mosca, Pareto and Weber: A Historical Comparison', in W. Mommsen and J. Osterhammel (eds.) *Max Weber and his Contemporaries*, London, pp. 139–58.

Bellamy, R. (1987). *Modern Italian Social Theory: Ideology and Politics from Pareto to the Present*, Cambridge.

(1990). 'From Ethical to Economic Liberalism: The Sociology of Pareto's Politics', *Economy and Society* 19: 431–55.

(1992). *Liberalism and Modern Society: An Historical Argument*, Cambridge.

(2000). *Rethinking Liberalism*, London.

Bellamy, R. and Schecter, D. (1993). *Gramsci and the Italian State*, Manchester.

Bentley, M. (1977). *The Liberal Mind 1914–1929*, Cambridge.

Berkowitz, Edward D. (1991). *America's Welfare State: From Roosevelt to Reagan*, Baltimore.

Berkowitz, Edward D. and McQuaid, Kim (1992). *Creating the Welfare State*, Lawrence, Kans.

Berlin, I. (1976). *Vico and Herder. Two Studies in the History of Ideas*, London.

Bessel, Richard (1996) (ed.). *Fascist Italy and Nazi Germany: Comparisons and Contrasts*, Cambridge.

Beyme, Klaus von (1983). *Parteien in Westlichen Demokratien*, Munich.

Bialer, Seweryn (1980). *Stalin's Successors: Leadership, Stability, and Change in the Soviet Union*, Cambridge.

Biddiss, Michael (1970). *Father of Racist Ideology: The Social and Political Thought of Count Gobineau*, New York.

Birken, Lawrence (1995). *Hitler as Philosophe: Remnants of the Enlightenment in National Socialism*, Westport, Conn.

Blaug, M. (1991). 'Introduction', in *John Maynard Keynes (1983–1946)*, ed. M. Blaug, 2 vols., Aldershot.
Block, Fred, Cloward, Richard A., Ehrenreich, Barbara and Piven, Frances Fox (1987). *The Mean Season: The Attack on the Welfare State*, New York.
Bloom, Allan (1989). Foreword to Leo Strauss, *Liberalism Ancient and Modern*, Chicago.
Booth, A. (1983). 'The Keynesian Revolution in Economic Policy-Making', *Economic History Review*, 36 (1): 103–23.
(1985). 'The Keynesian Revolution and Economic Policy-Making – A Reply, *Economic History Review* 38 (1): 101–6.
Borkenau, Franz (1940). *The Totalitarian Enemy*, London.
Boyer, R. (1981). *Actualité d'Emmanuel Mounier*, Paris.
Bracher, K. D. (1981). 'The Disputed Concept of Totalitarianism', in Ernest A. Menze (ed.) *Totalitarianism Reconsidered*, New York.
(1982). *The Age of Ideologies*, London.
Bradley, I. (1980). *The Optimists: Themes and Personalities in Victorian Liberalism*, London.
Bramson, L. (1961). *The Political Context of Sociology*, Princeton, N.J.
Braybrooke, David (1987). *Meeting Needs*, Princeton, N.J.
Bremmer, I. (1993). 'Reassessing Soviet Nationalities Policy', in I. Bremmer and R. Taras (eds.) *Nations and Politics in the Soviet Successor States*, Cambridge.
Briggs, Asa (1961). 'The Welfare State in Historical Perspective', *Archives Européennes de Sociologie* 2: 221–58.
(1979). 'The Language of "Mass" and "Masses" in Nineteenth-Century England', in D. E. Martin and D. Rubinstein (eds.) *Ideology and the Labour Movement*, London.
Brinkley, Alan (1996). *The End of Reform: New Deal Liberalism in Recession and War*, New York.
Brown, G. (2001). 'The Conditions for High and Stable Growth and Employment', *Economic Journal* 111, May: C30–C44).
Brzezinski, Zbigniew (1956). *The Permanent Purge: Politics in Soviet Totalitarianism*, Cambridge, Mass.
Brzezinski, Zbigniew and Friedrich, Carl (1956). *Totalitarian Dictatorship and Autocracy*, Cambridge, Mass.
Brzezinski, Zbigniew and Huntington, Samuel P. (1964). *Political Power: USA/USSR*, New York.
Buchanan, J. M., Tollison, R. D. and Tullock, G. (1980) (eds.). *Towards a Theory of the Rent-Seeking Society*, College Station, Tex.
Bullock, A. and Shock, M. (1966) (eds.). *The Liberal Tradition from Fox to Keynes*, London.
Burleigh, Michael and Wipperman, Wolfgang (1991). *The Racial State: Germany. 1933–1945*, New York.
Burnham, James (1941). *The Managerial Revolution*, Bloomington, Ind.
Burton, J. (1986) (ed.). *Keynes's General Theory Fifty Years On: Its Relevance and Irrelevance to Modern Times*, London.
Butler, D. (1958). *The Study of Political Behaviour*, London.
Caldwell, B. J. and Hayek, F. A. (1995). *Contra Keynes and Cambridge*, London.
Carabelli, A. (1988). *On Keynes's Method*, London.
(1991). 'The Methodology of the Critique of the Classical Theory: Keynes on Organic Interdependence', in B. W. Bateman and J. B. Davis (eds.) *Keynes and Philosophy: Essays on the Origin of Keynes's Thought*, Aldershot.
Caron, Jacques (1967). *Le 'Sillon' et la démocratie chrétienne*, Paris.
Castles, Francis G. (1985). *The Working Class and the Welfare State: Welfare in Australia and New Zealand*, Sydney.

Ceicel, Robert (1972). *The Myth of the Master Race: Alfred Rosenberg and Nazi Ideology*, London.
Chick, V. (1992). 'John Maynard (1st Baron) Keynes', in P. Arestis and M. Sawyer (eds.) *A Biographical Dictionary of Dissenting Economists*, Aldershot.
Ciliga, Anton (1940). *The Russian Enigma*, London.
Clarke, P. (1978). *Liberals and Social Democrats*, Cambridge.
(1983). 'The Politics of Keynesian Economics 1924–1931', in M. Bentley and J. Stevenson (eds.) *High and Low Politics in Modern Britain*, Oxford.
Clarke, T. N. and Rempel, M. (1997). *Citizen Politics in Post-Industrial Societies: Interest Groups Transformed*, Boulder, Colo.
Cobban, A. (1945). *National Self-Determination*, London.
(1969). *Nationalism and National Self-Determination*, London.
Cohen, G. A. (1981). 'Freedom, Justice and Capitalism', *New Left Review* 126: 3–16.
Cohen, Stephen F. (1971). *Bukharin and the Bolshevik Revolution*, New York.
Colquhoun, Robert (1986). *Raymond Aron*, vol. I: *The Philosopher in History, 1905–1955*, Beverly Hills, Calif.
Connor, W. (1984). *The National Question in Marxist and Leninist Theory and Strategy*, Princeton, N.J.
Conquest, Robert (1961). *Power and Policy in the USSR*, New York.
Coser, Louis A. and Howe, Irving (1976) (eds.). *The New Conservatives: A Critique from the Left*, New York.
Crabtree, D. and Thirwall, A. P. (1980) (eds.). *Keynes and the Bloomsbury Group: The Fourth Keynes Seminar held at the University of Kent at Canterbury, 1978*, London.
Cranston, M. (1978). 'Keynes: His Political Ideas and their Influence', in A. P. Thirwall (ed.) *Keynes and Laissez-Faire: The Third Keynes Seminar held at the University of Kent at Canterbury, 1976*, London.
Crew, David F. (1998). *Germans on Welfare: From Weimar to Hitler*, New York.
Crozier, M., Huntington, S. P. and Watanuki, J. (1975). *The Crisis of Democracy: Report on the Governability of Democracies to the Trilateral Commission*, New York.
Curtis, M. (1959). *Three Against the Republic: Sorel, Barrès and Maurras*, Princeton, N.J.
(1969). 'Retreat from Totalitarianism', in Carl J. Friedrich, Michael Curtis and Benjamin R. Barber, *Totalitarianism in Perspective: Three Views*, New York.
Cutright, Phillips (1965). 'Political Structure, Economic Development and National Social Security Programs', *American Journal of Sociology* 70: 537–50.
Dalton, R. J. (1996). *Citizen Politics: Public Opinion and Political Parties in Advanced Western Democracies*, Chatham, N.J.
(1999). 'Political Support in Advanced Industrial Democracies', in P. Norris (ed.) *Critical Citizens: Global Support for Democratic Government*, Oxford.
Dalton, R. J. and Küchler, M. (1990) (eds.). *Challenging the Political Order: New Social and Political Movements in Western Democracies*, Cambridge.
Danziger, Sheldon, Haveman, Robert and Plotnick, Robert (1981). 'How Income Transfer Programs Affect Work, Savings and Income Distribution', *Journal of Economic Literature* 19: 975–1028.
Davidson, P. (1981). 'Post-Keynesian Economics', in D. Bell and I. Kristol (eds.) *The Crisis in Economic Theory*, New York.
(2000). 'Keynes, You Should be Alive this Hour', *Guardian*, 18 September.
Davies, Stephen (1997). 'Two Conceptions of Welfare: Voluntarism and Incorporationism', *Social Philosophy and Policy* 14: 39–68.
Dawson, W. H. (1912). *Social Insurance in Germany 1883–1911*, London.
Day, Patricia and Klein, Rudolph (1987). *Accountabilities: Five Public Services*, London.

Deacon, A. (1996). 'The Dilemmas of Welfare: Titmuss, Murray and Mead', in S. J. D. Green and R. C. Whiting (eds.) *The Boundaries of the State in Modern Britain*, Cambridge.

De Felice, Renzo (1966). *Mussolini il fascista*, 2 vols., Turin.

(1977). *Interpretations of Fascism*, Cambridge, Mass.

De Rosa, Gabriele (1977). *Luigi Sturzo*, Turin.

Djilas, Milovan (1957). *The New Class: An Analysis of the Communist System*, New York.

Downs, Anthony (1960). 'Why the Government Budget is too Small in a Democracy', *World Politics* 12: 541–63.

Doyal, Len and Gough, Ian (1991). *A Theory of Human Need*, Houndmills, Basingstoke.

Duncan, Greg J. (1984). *Years of Poverty, Years of Plenty*, Ann Arbor, Mich.

Duncan, Greg J., Hill, Martha S. and Hoffman, Saul D. (1988). 'Welfare Dependence Within and Across Generations', *Science* 239: 467–71.

Dunleavy, Patrick (1991). *Democracy, Bureaucracy and Public Choice*, Hemel Hempstead.

Dunn, C. W. and Woodard, J. D. (1996) (eds.). *The Conservative Tradition in America*, Lanham, Md.

Durand, Jean (1995). *L'Europe de la démocratie chrétienne*, Paris.

Earle, E. M. (1986). 'Adam Smith, Alexander Hamilton, Friederich List: The Economic Foundations of Military Power', in P. Paret (ed.) *Makers of Modern Strategy, from Machiavelli to the Nuclear Age*, Oxford.

East, John P. (1988). 'Leo Strauss and the American Conservatism', in George A. Panichas (ed.) *Modern Age: The First Twenty-Five Years*, Indianapolis.

Eatwell, R. (1996). *Fascism: A History*, London.

The Economist (2001). 'A Stimulating Debate', 27 October.

Elliot, L. (2000). 'Brown and Co Trim Keynes for the 21st Century', *Guardian*, 31 July.

Ellwood, W. (2001). *The No-nonsense Guide to Globalization*, London.

Emerson, R. (1962). *From Empire to Nation: The Rise to Self-Assertion of African Peoples*, Boston.

Esping-Andersen, Gøsta (1990). *The Three Worlds of Welfare Capitalism*, Oxford.

Ewald, François (1986). *L'état providence*, Paris.

Fainsod, Merle (1953). *How Russia is Ruled*, Cambridge, Mass.

Fattorini, Emma (1997). *I Cattolici tedeschi. dall'intransigenza alla modernità (1870–1953)*, Brescia.

Faulkner, Harold U. (1931). *The Quest for Social Justice 1898–1914*, New York.

Feher, Ferenc and Heller, Agnes (1987). *Eastern Left, Western Left: Totalitarianism, Freedom and Democracy*, Atlantic Highlands, N.J.

(1990). *From Yalta to Glasnost: The Dismantling of Stalin's Empire*, Cambridge, Mass.

Feldstein, Martin and Pellechio, Anthony (1979). 'Social Security and Household Wealth Accumulation: New Micro Econometric Evidence', *Review of Economics and Statistics* 61: 361–8.

Femia, J. V. (2001). *Against the Masses: Varieties of Anti-Democratic Thought since the French Revolution*, Oxford.

Field, G. G. (1981). *Evangelist of Race: The Germanic Vision of Houston Stewart Chamberlain*, New York.

Fine, Sidney (1956). *Laissez-Faire and the General Welfare State: A Study of Conflict in American Thought, 1865–1901*, Ann Arbor, Mich.

Fitzgibbons, A. (1988). *Keynes's Vision: A New Political Economy*, Oxford.

Flora, Peter (1986) (ed.). *Growth to Limits*, 4 vols., Berlin.

Flora, Peter and Heidenheimer, Arnold J. (1981) (eds.). *The Development of Welfare States in Europe and America*, New Brunswick, N.J.

Fraenkel, Ernst (1941). *The Dual State: A Contribution to the Theory of Dictatorship*, London.

Fraser, Derek (1973). *The Evolution of the British Welfare State*, London.

Fraser, Nancy (1994). 'After the Family Wage: Gender Equity and the Welfare State', *Political Theory* 22: 591–618.

Fraser, Nancy and Gordon, Linda (1994). ' "Dependency" Demystified: Inscriptions of Power in a Keyword of the Welfare State', *Social Politics* 1: 4–31.

Freeden, Michael (1978). *The New Liberalism: An Ideology of Social Reform*, Oxford.

(1979). 'Eugenics and Progressive Thought: A Study in Ideological Affinity', *Historical Journal* 22: 645–71.

(1986). *Liberalism Divided: A Study in British Political Thought 1914–1939*, Oxford.

(1990). 'Rights, Needs and Community: The Emergence of British Welfare Thought', in Alan Ware and Robert E. Goodin (eds.) *Needs and Welfare*, London, pp. 54–72.

(1996). *Ideologies and Political Theory: A Conceptual Approach*, Oxford.

Friedman, Milton and Friedman, Rose (1980). *Free to Choose*, Harmondsworth.

Galbraith, J. K. (1975). 'How Keynes Came to America', in M. Keynes (ed.) *Essays on John Maynard Keynes*, Cambridge.

Gamble, A. (1996). *Hayek: The Iron Cage of Liberty*, Cambridge.

Gamble, A. *et al.* (1989). *Ideas, Interests and Consequences*, London.

Gardener, R. N. (1980 [1956]). *Sterling-Dollar Diplomacy*, republished with a new introduction, New York.

Garton Ash, Timothy (1990). *The Uses of Adversity: Essays on the Fate of Central Europe*, New York.

(1995). 'Prague: Intellectuals and Politicians', *New York Review of Books*, 12 January.

Geiger, R. L. (1977). 'Democracy and the Crowd: The Social History of an Idea in France and Italy, 1890–1914', *Societas* 7: 47–71.

Gellner, E. (1983). *Nations and Nationalism*, Oxford.

(1994). *Civil Society and its Rivals*, London.

(1997). *Nationalism*, London.

Gentile, Emilio (1975). *Le origini dell'ideologia fascista*, Bari.

(1989). *Storia del partito fascista, 1919–1922*, Bari.

(1996). *The Sacralization of Politics in Fascist Italy*, Cambridge, Mass. and London.

Giovagnoli, Agostino (1991). *La cultura democristiana*, Rome and Bari.

Gleason, Abbott (1995). *Totalitarianism: The Inner History of the Cold War*, Oxford.

Glennerster, Howard (1995). *British Social Policy since 1945*, Oxford.

Goldfarb, Jeffrey C. (1989). *Beyond Glasnost: The Post-Totalitarian Mind*, Chicago.

Goodin, Robert E. (1982). 'Rational Politicians and Rational Bureaucrats in Washington and Whitehall', *Public Administration* 60: 23–41.

(1988). *Reasons for Welfare*, Princeton, N.J.

(1990). 'Stabilizing Expectations: The Role of Earnings-Related Benefits in Social Welfare Policy', *Ethics* 100: 530–53.

(1997). 'Social Welfare as a Collective Social Responsibility', in David Schmidtz and Robert E. Goodin, *Social Welfare and Individual Responsibility: For and Against*, Cambridge.

Goodin, Robert E. and Dryzek, John (1986). 'Risk-Sharing and Social Justice: the Motivational Foundations of the Post-War Welfare State', *British Journal of Political Science* 16: 1–34.

Goodin, Robert E., Headey, Bruce, Muffels, Ruud and Dirven, Henk-Jan (1999). *The Real Worlds of Welfare Capitalism*, Cambridge.

Gottfried, Paul (1993). *The Conservative Movement*, New York.

Gough, Ian (1979). *The Political Economy of the Welfare State*, London.

Gourevitch, P. A. (1984). 'Breaking with Orthodoxy: The Politics of Economic Responses to the Depression of the 1930s', *International Organization* 38, Winter: 95–130.

(1986). *Politics in Hard Times*, Ithaca, N.Y.
Gray, J. (1984). *Hayek on Liberty*, London.
(1989). *Limited Government: A Positive Agenda*, London.
(1993). in 'Hayek as a Conservative', *Post-Liberalism*, London, ch. 3.
(1995). in 'After the New Liberalism', *Enlightenment's Wake*, London, ch. 8.
Gregor, A. James (1969). *The Ideology of Fascism*, New York.
(1974). *The Fascist Persuasion in Radical Politics*, Princeton, N.J.
(1979). *Young Mussolini and the Intellectual Origins of Fascism*, Berkeley, Calif.
Greiffeuhagen, Martin (1981). 'The Concept of Totalitarianism in Political Theory', in Ernest A. Menze (ed.) *Totalitarianism Reconsidered*, New York.
Griffin, R. (1991). *The Nature of Fascism*, London.
(1995). *Fascism*, Oxford.
Griffin, R. (1998) (ed.). *International Fascism: Theories, Causes, and the New Consensus*, London.
Grimal, H. (1965). *Decolonisation: The British, French, Dutch and Belgian Empires 1919 to 1963*, London.
Haber, W. and Cohen, Wilbur J. (1948) (eds.). *Readings in Social Security*, New York.
Halévy, Elie (1966). 'The Era of Tyrannies', in *The Era of Tyrannies*, New York.
Hall, P. A. (1989a). 'Conclusions: The Politics of Ideas', in Hall (ed.) *The Political Power of Economic Ideas: Keynesianism across Nations*, Princeton, N.J.
Hall, P. A. (1989b) (ed.). *The Political Power of Economic Ideas: Keynesianism across Nations*, Princeton, N.J.
Hamilton, A. (1971). *The Appeal of Fascism*, London.
Hamminga, Bert (1995). 'Demoralizing the Labor Market', *Journal of Political Philosophy* 3: 23–35.
Hanley, D. (1994) (ed.). *Christian Democracy in Europe. A Comparative Perspective*, London.
Harris, Jose (1977). *William Beveridge: A Biography*, Oxford.
(1981). 'Some Aspects of Social Policy in Britain During the Second World War', in Wolfgang J. Mommsen (ed.) *The Emergence of the Welfare State in Britain and Germany 1850–1950*, London, pp. 247–62.
(1992). 'Political Thought and the Welfare State 1870–1940: An Intellectual Framework for British Social Policy', *Past and Present* 135: 116–41.
Harrod, R. F. (1966). *The Life of John Maynard Keynes*, London.
Hartz, Louis (1955). *The Liberal Tradition in America*, New York.
Harvie, C. (1990). 'Gladstonianism, the Provinces and Popular Political Culture 1860–1906', in R. Bellamy (ed.) *Victorian Liberalism: Nineteenth Century Political Thought and Practice*, London, pp. 152–74.
Hatzfeld, H. (1971). *Du paupérisme à la sécurité sociale 1850–1940*, Paris.
Hawthorn, G. (1976). *Enlightenment and Despair*, Cambridge.
Hay, J. R. (1981). 'The British Business Community, Social Insurance and the German Example', in Wolfgang J. Mommsen (ed.) *The Emergence of the Welfare State in Britain and Germany 1850–1950*, London, pp. 107–32.
Hayward, J. E. S. (1961). 'The Official Social Philosophy of the French Third Republic: Léon Bourgeois and Solidarism', *International Review of Social History* 6: 19–48.
(1963). ' "Solidarity" and the Reformist Sociology of Alfred Fouillée, I', *American Journal of Economics and Sociology* 22: 205–22.
Hazareesingh, Sudhir (1994). *Political Traditions in Modern France*, Oxford.
(1997). 'A Jacobin, Liberal, Socialist, and Republican Synthesis: The Original Political Thought of Charles Dupont-White (1807–1878)', *History of European Ideas* 23: 145–71.
Heald, David (1983). *Public Expenditure: Its Defence and Reform*, Oxford.

Heclo, Hugh (1974). *Modern Social Politics in Britain and Sweden*, New Haven, Conn. and London.
Heinen, Armin (1986). *Die Legion 'Erzengel Michael' in Rumanien*, Munich.
Helburn, S. (1991). 'Burke and Keynes', in B. W. Bateman and J. B. Davis (eds.) *Keynes and Philosophy: Essays on the Origin of Keynes's Thought*, Aldershot.
Heller, W. W. (1966). *New Dimensions of Political Economy*, Cambridge, Mass.
Hennock, E. P. (1986). *British Social Reform and German Precedents*, Oxford.
Hession, C. H. (1984). *John Maynard Keynes: A Personal Biography of the Man who Revolutionized Capitalism and the Way we Live*, New York.
Hilferding, Rudolf (1947). 'State Capitalism or Totalitarian State Economy', *Modern Review* I.
Hill, P. and Keynes, R. (1989) (eds.). *Lydia and Maynard: The Letters of John Maynard Keynes and Lydia Lopokova*, New York.
Hills, John (1993) (ed.). *The Future of Welfare*, York.
(1995). 'Funding the Welfare State', *Oxford Review of Economic Policy* 11 (3): 27–43.
Himmelfarb, Gertrude (1994). *The De-Moralization of Society: From Victorian Values to Modern Values*, New York.
Hirchman, A. O. (1989). 'How the Keynesian Revolution was Exported from the United States, and Other Comments', in P. A. Hall (ed.) *The Political Power of Economic Ideas: Keynesianism across Nations*, Princeton, N.J.
Hirsch, F. (1977). *The Social Limits to Growth*, London.
Hobsbawn, E. (1990). *Nations and Nationalism since 1780. Programme, Myth, Reality*, Cambridge.
Hofstadter, Richard (1948). *The American Political Tradition and the Men Who Made It*, New York.
(1955a). *The Age of Reform*, New York.
(1955b). *Social Darwinism in American Thought*, Boston.
Holmes, Stephen (1988). 'Liberal Guilt: Some Theoretical Origins of the Welfare State', in J. Donald Moon (ed.) *Responsibility, Rights, and Welfare: The Theory of the Welfare State*, Boulder, Colo. and London, pp. 77–106.
Hood, Christopher and Wright, Maurice (1981) (eds.). *Big Government in Hard Times*, Oxford.
Hook, Sidney (1967). ' "Welfare State" – A Debate that Isn't', in Charles I. Schottland (ed.) *The Welfare State*, New York, pp. 164–71.
(1987). *Out of Step*, New York.
Horowitz, David (1972). *The Free World Colossus*, New York.
Hough, Jerry (1972). 'The Soviet System: Petrification or Pluralism?', *Problems of Communism* (March–April).
Howe, Irving (1983) (ed.). *1984 Revisited: Totalitarianism in Our Century*, New York.
Howson, S. (1975). *Domestic Monetary Management in Britain, 1919–1938*, Cambridge.
Howson, S. and Winch, D. (1977). *The Economic Advisory Council, 1930–1939*. Cambridge.
Hughes, H. Stuart (1958). *Consciousness and Society: The Reorientation of European Social Thought*, New York.
Huntington, S. P. (1975). 'The Democratic Distemper', *Public Interest* 41: 9–38.
Hutchison, T. W. (1978). *Revolutions and Progress in Economic Knowledge*, Cambridge.
Hutton, W. (1986). *The Revolution That Never Was: An Assessment of Keynesian Economics*, London.
(1995). *The State We're In*, London.
Irving, R. E. M. (1979). *The Christian Democratic Parties of Western Europe*, London.
Isaac, Jeffrey C. (1996). 'The Meanings of 1989', *Social Research* 63 (2): 291–344.
(1998). *Democracy in Dark Times*, Ithaca, N. Y.

Isserman, Maurice (1987). *If I Had a Hammer: The Death of the Old Left and the Birth of the New*, New York.
Jackson Preece, J. (1998). *National Minorities and the European States System*, Oxford.
Jaeckel, Eberhard (1972). *Hitler's Weltanschauung*, Middletown, Conn.
Jay, Martin (1973). *The Dialectical Imagination*, Boston.
(1984). *Marxism and Totality*, Berkeley, Calif.
Johnson, D. (1995). 'The New Right in France', in L. Cheles *et al.* (eds.) *The Far Right in Western and Eastern Europe*, London.
Johnson, H. (1978). 'The Keynesian Revolution and the Monetarist Counter-Revolution', in H. Johnson and E. Johnson (eds.) *In the Shadow of Keynes*, Oxford.
Kahn, Lord (1974). 'On Re-Reading Keynes', Fourth Keynes Lecture in Economics, in *Proceedings of the British Academy*, vol. LX, Oxford.
Kalyvas, Stathis N. (1996). *From Pulpit to Party. The Rise of Christian Democracy in Europe*, Ithaca and London.
Kassof, Allen (1964). 'The Administered Society: Totalitarianism Without Terror', *World Politics* (July).
Kedourie, E. (1960). *Nationalism*, London.
(1995). *Hegel and Marx*, Oxford.
Kelley, Alfred (1981). *The Descent of Darwin: The Popularization of Darwinism in Germany. 1860–1914*, Chapel Hill, N.C.
Kershaw, Ian (1985). *The Nazi Dictatorship: Problems and Perspectives of Interpretation*, London.
(1987). *The 'Hitler Myth'*, Oxford.
(1998–2001). *Hitler*, 2 vols., New York and London.
Keynes, M. (1975) (ed.). *Essays on John Maynard Keynes*, Cambridge.
Kidd, Alan J. (1996). 'The State and Moral Progress: The Webbs' Case for Social Reform, c. 1905 to 1940', *Twentieth Century British History* 7: 189–205.
King, Desmond (1987). *The New Right: Politics, Markets and Citizenship*, London.
(1995). *Actively Seeking Work? The Politics of Unemployment and Welfare Policy in the United States and Great Britain*, Chicago.
(1999). *In the Name of Liberalism*, Oxford.
King, Desmond S. and Rothstein, Bo (1993). 'Institutional Choices and Labor Market Policy: A British–Swedish Comparison', *Comparative Political Studies* 26: 147–77.
Kirkpatrick, Jeanne (1982). *Dictatorships and Double Standards: Rationalism and Reason in Politics*, Washington, D.C.
Klein, Rudolf (1993). 'O'Goffe's Tale: Or What Can We Learn from the Successes of the Capitalist Welfare States?', in Catherine Jones (ed.) *New Perspectives on the Welfare State in Europe*, London, pp. 7–17.
Klingemann, H.-D. and Fuchs, D. (1995) (eds.). *Citizens and the State*, Oxford.
Kolakowski, Leszek (1985). *Main Currents of Marxism*, Oxford.
Konrad, George (1984). *Antipolitics*, New York.
(1992). 'What is the Charter?', *East European Reporter* (January/February).
(1995). *The Melancholy of Rebirth: Essays from Post-Communist Central Europe, 1989–1994*, New York.
Konrad, George and Szelenyi, Ivan (1979). *The Intellectuals on the Road to Class Power*, New York.
Kornhauser, W. (1959). *The Politics of Mass Society*, Glencoe, Ill.
Korpi, Walter (1995). 'The Position of the Elderly in the Welfare State: Comparative Perspectives on Old-Age Care in Sweden', *Social Service Review* 69: 242–73.
Koselleck, Reinhart (1972). 'Enleitung', in Otto Brunner, Werner Conze and Reinhart Koselleck (eds.) *Geschichtliche Grundbegriffe*, Stuttgart, vol. I, pp. xiii–xxvii.

Krugman, P. (2000). *The Return of Depression Economics*, Harmondsworth.
Land, Hilary (1994). 'The Demise of the Male Breadwinner – In Practice but not in Theory: A Challenge for Social Security Systems', in Sally Baldwin and Jane Falkingham (eds.) *Social Security and Social Change*, New York, pp. 100–15.
Langewiesche, D. (1990). 'German Liberalism in the Second Empire, 1871–1914' in K. H. Jarauch and L. E. Jones (eds.) *In Search of a Liberal Germany*, New York, Oxford and Munich, pp. 217–35.
Lederer, Emil (1940). *State of the Masses: The Threat of a Classless Society*, New York.
Le Grand, Julian (1982). *The Strategy of Equality*, London.
(1991). 'Quasi-markets and Social Policy', *Economic Journal* 101: 1256–67.
Leonhard, Wolfgang (1974). *Three Faces of Marxism*, New York.
Levy, Bernard-Henri (1979). *Barbarism with a Human Face*, New York.
Lewis, Jane (1992). 'Gender and the Development of Welfare Regimes', *Journal of European Social Policy* 2: 159–73.
Liebich, André (1987). 'Marxism and Totalitarianism: Rudolf Hilferding and the Mensheviks', *Dissent* (Spring).
Lieven, D. (2000). *Empire, The Russian Empire and its Rivals*, London.
Lindbeck, Assar, Molander, Per, Persson, Torsten, Petersson, Olof, Sandmo, Agnar, Swedenborg, Birgitta and Thygesen, Niels (1994). *Turning Sweden Around*, Cambridge, Mass.
Linz, Juan J. (1975). 'Totalitarian and Authoritarian Regimes', in Fred I. Greenstein and Nelson W. Polsby (eds.) *Handbook of Political Science: Macropolitical Theory*, vol. III, Reading, Mass.
(2000). *Totalitarian and Authoritarian Regimes*, Boulder, Colo. and London.
Lipset, S. M. (1960). *Political Man*, Glencoe, Ill.
(1964). 'Ostrogorski and the Analytical Approach to the Comparative Study of Political Parties', in M. Ostrogorski, *Democracy and the Organisation of Political Parties*, ed. and abridged S. Lipset, Chicago, vol. I, pp. ix–lxv.
Lively, J. (1965) (ed.). *The Works of Joseph de Maistre*, London.
Logue, William (1983). *From Philosophy to Sociology: The Evolution of French Liberalism, 1890–1914*, DeKalb, Ill.
Long, D. (1996). *Towards a New Liberal Internationalism: The International Theory of J. A. Hobson*, Cambridge.
Lönne, K. E. (1986). *Politischer Katholizismus im 19 und 20 Jahrhundert*, Frankfurt am Main.
Luhmann, Niklas (1990). *Political Theory in the Welfare State*, Berlin.
Lukes, Steven (1973). *Emile Durkheim: His Life and Work*, Harmondsworth.
(1985). *Marxism and Morality*, Oxford.
Lyttelton, Adrian (1973). *The Seizure of Power: Fascism in Italy, 1919–1929*, New York.
McBriar, A. M. (1962). *Fabian Socialism and English Politics 1884–1918*, Cambridge.
(1987). *An Edwardian Mixed Doubles*, Oxford.
McClelland, J. S. (1970) (ed.). *The French Right*, London.
(1989). *The Crowd and the Mob: From Homer to Canetti*, London.
McCormick, B. (1992). *Hayek and the Keynesian Avalanche*, London.
Macdonald, Dwight (1946). 'The Root is Man', *Politics* (April and July): 97–115, 194–214.
Maier, Hans (1973). *Revolution und Kirche. Studien zur Frühgeschichte der Christlichen Demokratie (1789–1901)*, Freiburg.
Malgeri, Francesco (1993). *Luigi Sturzo*, Cinisello Balsamo, Milan.
Mayall, J. (1990). *Nationalism and International Society*, Cambridge.
(1999). 'Sovereignty, Nationalism and Self-Determination', in Robert Jackson (ed.) *Sovereignty at the Millennium*, Oxford.

Mayeur, Jean-Marie (1980). *Des partis catholiques à la démocratie chrétienne*, Paris.
Mayo, Henry (1960). *An Introduction to Democratic Theory*, Ann Arbor, Mich.
Mead, James E. (1995). *Full Employment Regained?* Cambridge.
Mead, Lawrence M. (1997). 'Citizenship and Social Policy: T. H. Marshall and Poverty', *Social Philosophy and Policy* 14: 197–230.
Menczer, Béla (1952) (ed.). *Catholic Political Thought 1789–1848*, London.
Merrien, François-Xavier (1994). 'Divergences Franco-Britanniques', in François-Xavier Merrien (ed.) *Face à la pauvreté*, Paris.
(1997). *L'état-providence*, Paris.
Michnik, Adam (1985). *Letters from Prison and Other Essays*, trans. Maya Latynski, Berkeley, Calif.
(1992). *The Church and the Left*, ed. and trans. David Ost, Chicago.
Middleton, R. (1982). 'The Treasury in the 1930s', *Oxford Economic Papers* 34: 48–77.
Miller, Gary (1992). *Managerial Dilemmas*, Cambridge.
Miller, S. and Potthoff, H. (1986). *A History of German Social Democracy from 1848 to the Present*, Leamington Spa.
Milza, Pierre (1987). *Le fascisme français*, Paris.
(1999). *Mussolini*, Paris.
Mini, P. V. (1991). *Keynes, Bloomsbury and the General Theory*, London.
(1994). *John Maynard Keynes: A Study in the Psychology of Original Work*, London.
Mises, Ludwig von (1944). *Omnipotent Government: The Rise of the Total State and Total War*, New Haven, Conn.
(1981). *Socialism*, trans. J. Kahane, Indianapolis.
Mitchell, Allan (1991). *The Divided Path: The German Influence on Social Reform in France after 1870*, Chapel Hill, N.C.
Moffitt, Robert (1992). 'Incentive Effects of the US Welfare System: A Review', *Journal of Economic Literature* 30: 1–61.
Moggeridge, D. E. (1992). *Maynard Keynes: An Economist's Biography*, London.
Mommsen, H. (1981). 'The Concept of Totalitarian Dictatorship vs. the Comparative Theory of Fascism: The Case of National Socialism', in Ernest A. Menze (ed.) *Totalitarianism Reconsidered*, New York, pp. 146–66.
Mommsen, W. (1967). *Max Weber and German Politics 1890–1920*, New York.
(1981) (ed.). *The Emergence of the Welfare State in Britain and Germany 1850–1950*, London.
(1989). *The Political and Social Theory of Max Weber*, Cambridge.
Morsey, Robert (1977). 'Bischof Ketteler und der politischer Katholizismus', in *Jahres- und Tagungsbericht der Görres-Gesellschaft*, Cologne.
Mosse, George L. (1964). *The Crisis of German Ideology: Intellectual Origins of the Third Reich*, New York.
(1978). *Toward the Final Solution: A History of European Racism*, New York.
Murray, Charles (1984). *Losing Ground: American Social Policy, 1950–80*, New York.
Myrdal, Gunnar (1965). *Beyond the Welfare State*, London.
Nagy-Talavera, Nicholas M. (2001). *The Green Shirts and the Others*, Iasi, Oxford and Portland.
Nash, George H. (1976). *The Conservative Intellectual Movement in America since 1945*, New York.
Nelson, Barbara J. (1990). 'The Origins of the Two-Channel Welfare State: Workmen's Compensation and Mothers' Aid', in *Women, the State and Welfare*, ed. Linda Gordon, Madison, Wis., pp. 123–51.
Neumann, Franz (1942). *Behemoth: The Structure and Practice of National Socialism*, London.
Neumann, Sigmund (1942). *Permanent Revolution: The Total State in a World at War*, New York.

Niskanen, W. A. (1971). *Bureaucracy and Representative Government*, Chicago.
(1977). *Bureaucracy: Servant or Master?*, London.
Nolte, Ernst (1966). *Three Faces of Fascism*, New York.
Nye, Robert A. (1975). *The Origins of Crowd Psychology: Gustave Le Bon and the Crisis of Mass Democracy in the Third Republic*, London.
O'Brien, Martin and Penna, Sue (1998). *Theorising Welfare: Enlightenment and Modern Society*, London.
O'Connor, James R. (1973). *The Fiscal Crisis of the State*, New York.
O'Connor, Julia S., Orloff, Ann S. and Shaver, Sheila (1999). *States, Markets, Families: Gender and Social Policy in Australia, Canada, Great Britain and the United States*, Cambridge.
O'Donnell, R. (1989). *Keynes: Philosophy, Economics and Politics: The Philosophical Foundations of Keynes's Thought and their Influence on his Economics and Politics*, London.
Offe, Claus (1984). *Contradictions of the Welfare State*, Cambridge, Mass.
(1987). 'Challenging the Boundaries of Institutional Politics: Social Movements since the 1960s', in C. Maier (ed.) *Changing the Boundaries of the Political*, Cambridge.
(1992). 'A Non-Productivist Design for Social Policies', in Philippe Van Parijs (ed.) *Arguing for Basic Income*, London, pp. 61–80.
Olson, Mancur Jr. (1965). *The Logic of Collective Action*, Cambridge, Mass.
Organisation for Economic Co-operation and Development (OECD) (1981). *The Welfare State in Crisis*, Paris.
(1994). *New Orientations for Social Policy*, Paris.
Orloff, Ann Shola (1993). 'Gender and the Social Rights of Citizenship: The Comparative Analysis of Gender Relations and Welfare States', *American Sociological Review* 58: 303–28.
Osborne, David and Gaebler, Ted (1993). *Reinventing Government*, New York.
Owen, N. (1999). 'Critics of Empire in Britain', in Judith Brown and Wm. Roger Louis (eds.) *The Oxford History of the British Empire*, vol. IV, Oxford.
Pangle, T. L. (1992). *The Ennoblement of Democracy: The Challenge of the Postmodern Age*, Baltimore, Md.
Paradowska, Janina (1991). 'The Three Cards Game: An Interview with Adam Michnik', *Telos* (Summer).
Parker, Julia (1998). *Citizenship, Work and Welfare: Searching for the Good Society*, London.
Parry, G. (1969). *Political Elites*, London.
Parsons, W. (1983). 'Keynes and the Politics of Ideas', *History of Political Thought* 4 (2): 367–92.
(1985). 'Was Keynes Kuhnian?: Keynes and the Idea of Theoretical Revolutions', *British Journal of Political Science* 15: 451–71.
(1997). *Keynes and the Quest for a Moral Science*, Cheltenham.
Patterson, James T. (1994). *America's Struggle against Poverty 1900–1994*, Cambridge, Mass.
Payne, Stanley G. (1987). *The Franco Regime. 1936–1975*, Madison, Wis.
(1995). *A History of Fascism. 1914–1945*, Madison, Wis.
(1999). *Fascism in Spain, 1923–1975*, Madison, Wis.
Peacock, A. and Willgerodt, H. (1989) (eds.). *German Neo-Liberals and the Social Market Economy*, London.
Peden, G. C. (1980). 'Keynes, the Treasury and Unemployment in the Later Nineteen-Thirties', *Oxford Economic Papers* 32: 1–8.
(1983). 'Sir Richard Hopkins and the "Keynesian Revolution" in Employment Policy, 1929–1945', *Economic History Review* 36: 281–96.
Peltzman, Sam (1980). 'The Growth of Government', *Journal of Law and Economics* 23: 209–87.
Pick, D. (1989). *Faces of Degeneration: A European Disorder c. 1848–1918*, Cambridge.

Pierson, Paul (1994). *Dismantling the Welfare State: Reagan, Thatcher and the Politics of Retrenchment*, Cambridge.
Pigou, A. C. (1949). 'The Economist', in *John Maynard Keynes 1883–1946*, Cambridge.
Piven, Frances Fox and Cloward, Richard A. (1971). *Regulating the Poor*, New York.
(1979). *Poor People's Movements: Why They Succeed, How They Fail*, New York.
Plamenatz, J. (1958). 'Electoral Studies and Democratic Theory', *Political Studies* 6: 1–9.
Plant, Raymond (1988). 'Needs, Agency, and Welfare Rights', in J. Donald Moon (ed.) *Responsibility, Rights and Welfare*, Boulder, Colo., pp. 55–75.
Podhoretz, N. (1996). 'Neoconservatism: A Eulogy', *Commentary* 101 (3): 26.
Poliakov, Leon (1971). *The Aryan Myth*, New York.
Polsby, N. W. (1963). *Community Power and Political Theory*, New Haven, Conn.
Pombeni, P. (1994a). *Partiti e sistemi politici nella storia contemporanea*, 3rd edn, Bologna.
(1994b). 'Starting in Reason, Ending in Passion. Bryce, Lowell, Ostrogorski and the Problem of Democracy', *Historical Journal* 37: 319–41.
Power, Michael (1994). *The Audit Explosion*, London.
Prinz, Michael and Zitelmann, Rainer (1991) (eds.). *Nationalsozialismus und Modernisierung*, Darmstadt.
Przeworski, A. (1984). *Capitalism and Social Democracy*, Cambridge.
Putnam, R. D. (2000). *Bowling Alone: The Collapse and Revival of American Community*, New York.
Quagliariello, G. (1996). *Politics Without Parties: Moisei Ostrogorski and the Debate on Political Parties on the Eve of the Twentieth Century*, Aldershot.
Rassem, Mohammed (1992). 'Wohlfahrt, Wohltat, Wohltätigkeit, Caritas', in Otto Brunner, Werner Conze and Reinhart Koselleck (eds.) *Geschichtliche Grundbegriffe*, Stuttgart, vol. VII, pp. 595–636.
Reimann, Guenther (1941). *The Myth of the Total State*, New York.
Revel, Jean-François (1977). *The Totalitarian Temptation*, New York.
Rhoads, Steven E. (1985). *The Economist's View of the World: Government, Markets and Public Policy*, Cambridge.
Rimlinger, G. V. (1971). *Welfare Policy and Industrialization in Europe, America and Russia*, New York.
Ringen, Stein (1987). *The Possibility of Politics*, Oxford.
Ritter, Emil (1956). *Die Katholisch-Soziale Bewegung Deutschlands im XIX Jahrhundert und der Volksverein*, Cologne.
Roberts, David D. (1979). *The Syndicalist Tradition and Italian Fascism*, Chapel Hill, N.C.
Robinson, J. (1975). 'What has Become of the Keynesian Revolution?', in M. Keynes (ed.) *Essays on John Maynard Keynes*, Cambridge.
Rodgers, Daniel T. (1998). *Atlantic Crossings: Social Politics in a Progressive Age*, Cambridge, Mass.
Rollings, N. (1985). 'The Keynesian Revolution in Economic Policy-Making: A Comment', *Economic History Review* 36 (1): 95–100.
Röpke, W. (1960 [1958]). *A Humane Economy*, London.
Rosanvallon, Pierre (1990). *L'état en France de 1789 à nos jours*, Paris.
(1992). *La crise de l'état-providence*, Paris.
(2000). *The New Social Question: Rethinking the Welfare State*, Princeton, N.J.
Rose, Richard and Peters, B. Guy (1979). *Can Government Go Bankrupt?*, London.
Rothstein, Bo (1998). *Just Institutions Matter*, Cambridge.
Rowbotham, M. (2000). *Goodbye America: Globalisation, Debt and the Dollar Empire*, Charbury.
Rudé, G. (1981 [1964]). *The Crowd in History, 1730–1848*, London.

Runciman, W. G. (1963). *Social Science and Political Theory*, Cambridge.
Sainsbury, Diane (1996). *Gender, Equality and Welfare States*, Cambridge.
Saint-Jours, Yves (1982). 'France', in P. A. Köhler and H. F. Zacher (eds.) *The Evolution of Social Insurance 1881–1981*, London, pp. 93–149.
Sartori, Giovanni (1962). *Democratic Theory*, New York.
Scaff, L. (1981). 'Max Weber and Robert Michels', *American Journal of Sociology* 86: 1269–86.
Schactman, Max (1962). *The Bureaucratic Revolution: The Rise of the Stalinist State*, New York.
Schapiro, Leonard (1959). *The Communist Party of the Soviet Union*, New York.
(1972). *Totalitarianism*, New York.
Scheuerman, William E. (1994). *Between the Norm and the Exception: The Frankfurt School and the Rule of Law*, Cambridge, Mass.
Schleunes, Karl A. (1970). *The Twisted Road to Auschwitz*, Urbana, Ill.
Schottland, Charles I. (1967) (ed.). *The Welfare State*, New York.
Scoppola, Pietro (1972). 'La democrazia nel pensiero cattolico del novecento', in Luigi Firpo (ed.) *Storia delle idee politiche economiche e sociali, vol. VI: Il secolo ventesimo*, Turin.
(1986). 'Chiesa e società negli anni della modernizzazione', in A. Riccardi (ed.) *Le chiese di Pio XII*, Rome and Bari.
Scott, J. A. (1951). *Republican Ideas and the Liberal Tradition in France*, New York.
Seideman, David (1986). *The New Republic: A Voice of Modern Liberalism*, New York.
Self, Peter (1993). *Government by the Market?*, London.
Serge, Victor (1937a). *From Lenin to Stalin*, New York.
(1937b). *Russia: Twenty Years After*, New York.
Shapiro, Daniel (1997). 'Can Old-Age Social Insurance be Justified?', *Social Philosophy and Policy* 14: 116–44.
Shorter, E. and Tilly, C. (1974). *Strikes in France, 1830–1968*, Cambridge.
Skidelsky, R. (1975). 'The Reception of the Keynesian Revolution', in M. Keynes (ed.) *Essays on John Maynard Keynes*, Cambridge.
(1977) (ed.). *The End of the Keynesian Era*, London.
(1983). *John Maynard Keynes: Hopes Betrayed, 1883–1920*, London.
(1992). *John Maynard Keynes: The Economist as Saviour, 1920–1937*, London.
(1996). *Keynes*, Oxford.
(1997). 'Bring Back Keynes', *Prospect*, May.
(2000). *John Maynard Keynes: Fighting For Britain 1937–1946*, London.
(2001). 'Keynes Lives', *Financial Times*, 15 August.
Skilling, H. Gordon (1981). *Charter 77 and Human Rights in Czechoslovakia*, London.
(1989). *Samizdat and an Independent Society in Central and Eastern Europe*, Oxford.
Skilling, H. Gordon and Griffiths, Franklyn (1971) (eds.). *Interest Groups in Soviet Politics*, Princeton, N.J.
Skilling, H. Gordon and Wilson, Paul (1991) (eds.). *Civic Freedom in Central Europe: Voices from Czechoslovakia*, New York.
Skocpol, Theda (1992). *Protecting Soldiers and Mothers: The Political Origins of Social Policy in the United States*, Cambridge, Mass.
(1995). *Social Policy in the United States*, Princeton, N.J.
Souvarine, Boris (1939). *Stalin: A Critical Survey of Bolshevism*, New York.
Spiro, Herbert J. and Barber, Benjamin R. (1970). 'Counter-Ideological Uses of "Totalitarianism"', *Politics and Society* I(1) (November).
Sprawson, C. (1992). *Haunts of the Black Masseur: The Swimmer as Hero*, London.
Stein, H. (1969). *The Fiscal Revolution in America*, Chicago.
Sternhell, Zeev (1978). *La droite révolutionnaire. 1885–1914: les origines françaises du fascisme*, Paris.

Sternhell, Zeev, Sznajder, M. and Asheri, M. (1994). *The Birth of Fascist Ideology*, Princeton, N.J.

Stewart, M. (1967). *Keynes and After*, Harmondsworth.

Stigler, George J. (1970). 'Director's Law of Public Income Redistribution', *Journal of Law and Economics* 13: 1–10.

(1988) (ed.). *Chicago Studies in Political Economy*, Chicago.

Stone, J. F. (1985). *The Search for Social Peace: Reform Legislation in France 1890–1914*, Albany, N.Y.

Szöllösi-Janze, Margit (1989). *Die Pfeilkreuzlerbewegung in Ungarn*, Munich.

Talmon, Jacob (1970 [1952]). *The Origins of Totalitarian Democracy*, New York.

Taylor, M. W. (1992). *Men Versus the State*, Oxford.

tenBroek, Jacobus and Wilson, Richard B. (1954). 'Public Assistance and Social Insurance – A Normative Evaluation', *UCLA Law Review* 1: 237–302.

Thompson, E. P. (1971). 'The Moral Economy of the English Crowd in the Eighteenth Century', *Past and Present* 50: 76–136.

Thornton A. P. (1959). *The Imperial Idea and its Enemies: A Study in British Power*, London.

Tilly, C. (1979). 'Collective Violence in European Perspective', in H. D. Graham and T. R. Gurr (eds.) *Violence in America: Historical and Comparative Perspectives*, London.

Tilton, Timothy A. (1990). *The Political Theory of Swedish Social Democracy*, Oxford.

Tismaneanu, Vladimir (1992). *Reinventing Politics: Eastern Europe from Stalin to Havel*, New York.

(1994). 'NYR, TLS and the Velvet Counterrevolution', *Common Knowledge* 3 (Spring).

Tomlinson, J. (1981). 'Why Was There Never a "Keynesian Revolution" in Economic Policy?', *Economy and Society* 10 (1): 72–87.

Townsend, Peter (1962). 'The Meaning of Poverty', *British Journal of Sociology* 13: 210–27.

(1979). *Poverty in the United Kingdom*, Harmondsworth.

Tullock, G. (1965). *The Politics of Bureaucracy*, Washington, D.C.

(1976). *The Vote Motive: An Essay in the Economics of Politics with Applications to the British Economy*, London.

Ungari, Paolo (1963). *Alfredo Rocco e l'ideologia giuridica del fascismo*, Brescia.

Ungerson, Clare (1987). *Policy is Personal: Sex, Gender and Informal Care*, London.

Van Dormael, A. (1978). *Bretton Woods – The Birth of an International Monetary System*, London.

Van Parijs, Philippe (1992) (ed.). *Arguing for Basic Income*, London.

Vecchio, Giorgio (1997). *Luigi Sturzo. Il prete che portò i cattolici alla politica*, Milan.

Vincent, J. R. (1966). *The Formation of the British Liberal Party 1857–68*, London.

Wald, Alan (1987). *The New York Intellectuals: The Rise and Decline of the Anti-Stalinist Left from the 1930s to the* 1980s, Chapel Hill, N.C.

Walzer, Michael (1988). *The Company of Critics: Social Criticism and Political Commitment in the Twentieth Century*, New York.

Weber, Eugen (1962). *Action Française*, Stanford, Calif.

Weill, G. (1979). *Histoire du catholicisme liberal en France, 1828–1908*, Paris and Geneva.

Weir, M. and Skocpol, T. (1985). 'State Structures and the Possibilities for "Keynesian" Responses to the Great Depression in Sweden, Britain, and the United States', in P. Evans, D. Rueschemeyer and T. Skocpol (eds.) *Bringing the State Back In*, Cambridge.

Weisbrod, B. (1981). 'The Crisis of German Unemployment Insurance in 1928/1929 and its Political Repercussions', in Wolfgang J. Mommsen, *The Emergence of the Welfare State in Britain and Germany 1850–1950*, London, pp. 188–204.

Weiss, J. H. (1983). 'Origins of the French Welfare State: Poor Relief in the Third Republic, 1871–1914', *French Historical Studies* 13: 47–77.

White, Stuart (2000). 'Social Rights and the Social Contract – Political Theory and the New Welfare Politics', *British Journal of Political Science* 30: 507–32.
Whiteside, Kerry H. (1988). *Merleau-Ponty and the Foundations of an Existential Politics*, Princeton, N.J.
Wilensky, Harold and Lebeaux, C. N. (1958). *Industrial Society and Social Welfare*, New York.
Wilkinson, James D. (1981). *The Intellectual Resistance in Europe*, Cambridge, Mass.
Williams, R. (1971 [1958]). *Culture and Society 1780–1950*, Harmondsworth.
Winch, D. (1969). *Economics and Policy: A Historical Survey*, London.
Wippermann, Wolfgang (1989). *Faschismustheorien*, Darmstadt.
Wolf, Charles Jr. (1988). *Markets or Governments*, Cambridge, Mass.
Wolfe, Bertram D. (1961). 'The Durability of Soviet Totalitarianism', in Alex Inkeles and Kent Geiger (eds.) *Soviet Society*, Boston.
Wolin, Richard (1992). 'Carl Schmitt – The Conservative Revolutionary: Habitus and Aesthetics of Horror', *Political Theory* 20(3).
Woltermann, C. (1993). 'What is Paleoconservatism?', *Telos* 97: 9–18.
World Bank (1994). *Averting the Old Age Crisis: Policies to Protect the Old and Promote Growth*, New York.
Worswick, D. N and Trevithick, J. (1984) (eds.). *Keynes and the Modern World*, Cambridge.
Young, James P. (1996). *Reconsidering American Liberalism: The Troubled Odyssey of the Liberal Idea*, Boulder, Colo.
Zanfarino, Antonio (1994). *Il pensiero politico contemporaneo*, Naples.
Zaslavsky, V. (1992). 'Success and Collapse: Traditional Soviet Nationality Policy', in I. Bremmer and R. Taras, *Nations and Politics in the Soviet Successor States*, Cambridge.
Zitelmann, Rainer (1987). *Hitler: Selbstverständnis eines Revolutionärs*, Hamburg.
Zöllner, D. (1982). 'Germany', in P. A. Köhler and H. F. Zacher (eds.) *The Evolution of Social Insurance 1881–1981*, London, pp. 1–92.

Part II: Varieties of Marxism

Primary sources

Adorno, Theodor (1973 [1966]). *Negative Dialectics*, New York.
Adorno, Theodor *et al.* (1950). *The Authoritarian Personality*, New York.
Althusser, Louis (1971 [1969]). *Lenin and Philosophy*, London.
(1977 [1965]). *For Marx*, London.
Althusser, Louis and Balibar, Etienne (1970 [1968]). *Reading Capital*, London.
Aron, Raymond (1957 [1955]). *The Opium of the Intellectuals*, London.
(1983). *Mémoires: 50 ans de réflexions politiques*, Paris.
Ascher, O. (1976). *The Mensheviks in the Russian Revolution*, London.
Bachelard, Gaston (1938). *La formation de l'esprit scientifique*, Paris.
Bauer, Otto (1907). *Die Nationalitätenfrage und die Sozialdemokratie*, Vienna.
Beauvoir, Simone de (1953 [1949]). *The Second Sex*, London.
(1965 [1963]). *Force of Circumstance*, London.
(1977 [1972]). *All Said and Done*, London.
(1985 [1981]). *Adieux: A Farewell to Sartre*, London.
Benjamin, Walter (1973 [1968]). *Illuminations*, New York.
(1977 [1963]). *The Origins of German Tragic Drama*, London.
Bernstein, Eduard (1899). *Die Vorraussetzungen des Sozialismus*, Stuttgart.
(1901). *Wie ist wissenschaftlicher Sozialismus möglich?*, Berlin.
(1993). *The Preconditions of Socialism*, ed. Henry Tudor, Cambridge.

Bloch, Ernst (1964 [1918]). *Geist der Utopie*, Munich.
(1972). *Atheism in Christianity*, trans. J. T. Swann New York.
(1986 [1954–9]). *The Principle of Hope*, trans. N. Plaice, S. Plaice and P. Knight, 3 vols., Oxford.
Bukharin, N. I. (1925). *'K.teorii imperialisticheskogo gosudarstva' Revoliutsiia Prava*, Moscow.
(1971). *Economics of the Transformation Period*, New York.
(1972). *Imperialism and the Accumulation of Capital*, ed. J. Tarbuck, London.
Canguilhem, Georges (1979). *Etudes d'histoire et de philosophie des sciences*, Paris.
Castoriadis, Cornelius, (1987 [1974]). *The Imaginary Institution of Society*, Cambridge.
(1988). *Social And Political Writings*, 2 vols., Minneapolis.
Fetscher, Iring (1965). *Der Marxismus. Seine Geschichte in Dokumenten*, vol. III, Munich.
Foucault, Michel (1977). *Language, Counter-Memory, Practice*, Oxford.
Fromm, Erich (1971). *The Crisis of Psychoanalysis: Essays on Freud, Marx and Social Psychology*, New York.
Furet, François (1981 [1978]). *Interpreting the French Revolution*, Cambridge.
Furet, François and Ozouf, Mona (1988 [1989]) (eds.). *A Critical Dictionary of the French Revolution*, Cambridge, Mass. and London.
Garaudy, Roger (1945). *Le communisme et la morale*, Paris.
Glucksmann, André (1975). *La cuisinière et le mangeur d'hommes*, Paris.
Goldmann, Lucien (1959). *Recherches dialectiques*, Paris.
(1964 [1959]). *The Hidden God: A Study of Tragic Vision in the Pensées of Pascal and the Tragedies of Racine*, New York.
Gorz, André (1982 [1980]). *Farewell to the Working Class: An Essay on Post-Industrial Society*, London.
Gramsci, Antonio (1971). *Selections from the Prison Notebooks*, ed. Quintin Hoare and Geoffrey Nowell-Smith, New York.
(1977) *Quaderni del carcere*, ed. V. Gerratana, 4 vols., Turin.
Harding, Neil and Taylor, Richard (1983) (eds.). *Marxism in Russia. Key Documents, 1879–1906*, Cambridge.
Hilferding, Rudolf (1910). *Das Finanzkapital*, Vienna.
Horkheimer, Max (1972 [1968]). *Critical Theory*, New York.
Horkheimer, Max and Adorno, Theodor (1972 [1947]). *Dialectic of Enlightenment*, New York.
Jaurès, Jean (1933). *Oeuvres*, Paris.
Kanapa, Jean (1947). *L'existentialisme n'est pas un humanisme*, Paris.
Kautsky, Karl (1893). *Der Parlamentarismus, die Volksgesetzgebung und die Sozialdemokratie*, Stuttgart.
(1899a). *Die Agrarfrage*, Stuttgart.
(1899b). *Bernstein und das sozialdemokratische Programm*, Stuttgart.
(1905) 'Vorwart', in H. Roland-Holst, *Generalstreik und Sozialdemokratie*, Dresden.
(1907). *Sozialismus und Kolonialpolitik*, Berlin.
(1909). *Der Weg zur Macht*, Hamburg.
(1914). *Der politische Massenstreik*, Berlin.
(1925). *Die Internationale und Sowjetrussland*, Berlin.
(1927). *Die materialistische Geschichtsauffassung*, Berlin.
(1934). *Grenzen der Gewalt*, Karlsbad.
(1965 [1918]). *The Dictatorship of the Proletariat*, Ann Arbor, Mich.
(1986). *Selected Political Writings*, ed. Patrick Goode, Cambridge.
Kojève, Alexandre (1969 [1947]). *An Introduction to the Reading of Hegel: Lectures on the Phenomenology of Spirit*, ed. Allan Bloom, Ithaca and London.
Korsch, Karl (1970 [1923]). *Marxism and Philosophy*, New York.

Labriola, Antonio (1966). *Essays on the Materialist Conception of History*, London.

Lefebvre, Henri (1968 [1940]). *Dialectical Materialism*, London.

Lefebvre, Henri and Guterman, Norbert (1934). *Introduction aux morceaux choisis de Karl Marx*, Paris.

Lenin, V. I. (1950). *Selected Works*, 2 vols., Moscow.

(1960–70). *Collected Works*, 45 vols., Moscow.

Lévi-Strauss, Claude (1966 [1962]). *The Savage Mind*, London.

(1967 [1958]). *Structural Anthropology*, vol. I, London.

Lukács, Georg (1971 [1923]). *History and Class Consciousness*, London.

Luxemburg, Rosa (1902). *Sozialreform oder Revolution?*, Leipzig.

(1906). *Massenstreik, Partei und Gewerkschaften*, Berlin.

(1951). *The Accumulation of Capital*, London.

(1961). *Leninism or Marxism: The Russian Revolution*, Ann Arbor, Mich.

(1969). *Politische Schriften*, Leipzig.

(1975). *Selected Political Writings*, ed. Robert Look, London.

Mao Zedong (1965–77). *Selected Works*, 5 vols., Beijing.

Marcuse, Herbert (1955a [1941]). *Reason and Revolution: Hegel and the Rise of Social Theory*, New York.

(1955b). *Eros and Civilization: A Philosophical Enquiry into Freud*, Boston.

(1958). *Soviet Marxism*, Boston.

(1964). *One-Dimensional Man*, Boston.

Marx, K. (1970 [1871]). *The Civil War in France*, Peking.

(1977). *Selected Writings*, ed. D. McLellan, Oxford.

(1995 [1848]). *Capital*, ed. D. McLellan, Oxford.

Marx, K. and Engels, F. (1962). *Selected Works*, 2 vols., Moscow.

(1975–86). *Collected Works*, 50 vols., London.

Merleau-Ponty, Maurice (1962 [1945]). *The Phenomenology of Perception*, London.

(1969 [1947]). *Humanism and Terror*, Boston.

(1973 [1955]). *Adventures of the Dialectic*, Evanston, Ill.

Nizan, Paul (1971 [1960]). *The Watchdogs: Philosophers and the Established Order*, New York and London.

Plekhanov, G. V. (1961–8). *Selected Philosophical Works*, 5 vols., Moscow.

Protokolle der Kongresse der 2. Internationale (1900, 1904, 1907), Stuttgart.

Protokolle der Kongresse der SPD (1891–1914), Berlin.

Rançiere, Jacques (1974). *La leçon d'Althusser*, Paris.

Sartre, Jean-Paul (1947–76). *Situations*, vols. I–X, Paris.

(1966 [1942]). *Being and Nothingness: An Essay on Phenomenological Ontology*, London.

(1968 [1960]). *Search for a Method*, New York.

(1969a [1952–4]). *The Communists and Peace*, London.

(1969b [1965]). *The Spectre of Stalin*, London.

(1970). *Between Existentialism and Marxism*, London.

(1985). *Critique de la raison dialectique*, vol. II, Paris.

(1991 [1960]). *Critique of Dialectical Reason*, vol. I, London.

Saussure, Ferdinand (1959 [1916]). *Course in General Linguistics*, New York.

Sorel, Georges (1919). *Matériaux d'une théorie du prolétariat*, Paris.

Sozialistische Monatshefte (1900–14), Berlin.

Stalin, J. (1953–5). *Works*, 13 vols., Moscow.

Sukhanov, N. N. (1955). *The Russian Revolution of 1917*, London.

Trotsky, Leon (1961). *Terrorism and Communism*, Ann Arbor, Mich.

(1962). *Permanent Revolution and Results and Prospects*, London.

(1964). *Basic Writings*, ed. Irving Howe, London.
Tudor H. and J. M. (1993) (eds.). *Marxism and Social Democracy: The Revisionist Debate, 1896–1898*, Cambridge.

Secondary sources

Aidit, D. N. (1958). *Indonesian Society and the Indonesian Revolution*, Jakarta.
(1964). *The Indonesian Revolution and the Immediate Tasks of the Communist Party of Indonesia*, Peking.
Anderson, Perry (1976). *Considerations on Western Marxism*, London.
(1983). *In the Tracks of Historical Materialism*, London.
Anweiler, O. (1974). *The Soviets*, New York.
Baron, Samuel H. (1963). *Plekhanov. The Father of Russian Marxism*, London.
Blackburn, R. (1977) (ed.). *Revolution and Class Struggle*, London.
Carsten, Francis Ludwig (1993). *Eduard Bernstein, 1850–1932*, Munich.
Caute, David (1964). *Communism and the French Intellectuals 1914–1960*, London.
Chandra, N. K. (1988). *The Retarded Economies*, Bombay.
d'Encausse, H. Carrere and Schram, Stuart (1969). *Marxism and Asia*, London.
Derfler, Leslie (1991). *Paul Lafargue and the Founding of French Marxism*, Cambridge, Mass.
Descombes, Vincent (1980 [1979]). *Modern French Philosophy*, Cambridge.
Deutscher, Isaac (1954–63). *Trotsky*, 3 vols., London.
Donald, Moira (1993). *Marxism and Revolution. Karl Kautsky and the Russian Marxists*, New Haven, Conn. and London.
Duan, Z. (1996). *Marx's Theory of Social Formation*, Aldershot.
Elliot, Gregory (1987). *Althusser: The Detour of Theory*, London.
Feher, F., Heller, A. and Markus, G. (1983). *Dictatorship over Needs: An Analysis of Soviet Societies*, Oxford.
Femia, Joseph (1981). *Gramsci's Political Thought: Hegemony, Consciousness and the Revolutionary Process*, New York.
Figes, O. (1997). *A People's Tragedy. The Russian Revolution 1891–1924*, London.
Friedrich, C. (1954). *Totalitarianism*, London.
Gay, Peter (1962). *The Dilemma of Democratic Socialism*, London.
Geary, Dick (1987). *Karl Kautsky*, Manchester.
Geras, Norman (1976). *The Legacy of Rosa Luxemburg*, London.
Gilcher-Holtey, Ingrid (1986). *Das Mandat des Intellektuellen. Karl Kautsky und die Sozial Demokratie*, Berlin.
Gupta, B. S. (1972). *Communism in Indian Politics*, New York.
(1980). *The Comintern, India and the Colonial Question*, Calcutta.
Haimson, L. H. (1955). *The Russian Marxists and the Origins of Bolshevism*, Cambridge, Mass.
Harding, N. (1984). *The State in Socialist Society*, London.
(1996). *Leninism*, London.
Haupt, Georges (1972). *Socialism and the Great War*, Oxford.
Hayek, F. A. (1976). *The Road to Serfdom*, London.
Held, David (1980). *Introduction to Critical Theory: Horkheimer to Habermas*, Berkeley, Calif.
Heller, Agnes (1983) (ed.). *Lukács Revalued*, New York.
Hosking, G. (1985). *A History of the Soviet Union*, London.
Hühnlich, Reinhold (1981). *Karl Kautsky und der Marxismus der II. Internationale*. Marburg.
Hussain, Athar and Tribe, Keith (1981). *Marxism and the Agrarian Question*, 2 vols., London.
Itoh, M. (1988). *The Basic Theory of Capitalism*, London.
Jacoby, Russell (1981). *Dialectic of Defeat: Contours of Western Marxism*, New York.

Jay, Martin (1973). *The Dialectical Imagination: A History of the Frankfurt School and the Institute of Social Research 1923–1950*, Boston.
(1984). *Marxism and Totality*, Cambridge.
Joll, James (1955). *The Second International*, London.
Judt, Tony (1986). *Marxism and the French Left*, Oxford.
(1992). *Past Imperfect: French Intellectuals, 1944–1956*, Berkeley, Calif.
Kautsky, John H. (1993). *Karl Kautsky, Revolution and Democracy*, New Brunswick.
Kelly, Michael (1982). *Modern French Marxism*, Oxford.
Khanh, Huynh Kim (1982). *Vietnamese Communism 1925–1945*, Ithaca, N.Y.
Khilnani, Sunil (1993). *Arguing Revolution: The Intellectual Left in Postwar France*, New Haven, Conn. and London.
Kindersley, Richard (1962). *The First Russian Marxists*, Oxford.
Knight, N. (1990) (ed.). *Mao Zedong on Dialectical Materialism*, New York.
Kolakowski, Leszek (1978). *Main Currents of Marxism*, 3 vols., Oxford.
Konrad, G. and Szelenyi, I. (1979). *The Intellectuals on the Road to Class Power*, Brighton.
Lichtheim, George (1964). *Marxism. A Historical and Critical Study*, London.
(1966). *Marxism in Modern France*, New York.
Luk, M. (1990). *The Origins of Chinese Bolshevism: An Ideology in the Making, 1920–1928*, Oxford.
Lukács, G. (1970). *Lenin, A Study of the Unity of his Thought*, London.
McCarthy, Thomas (1978). *The Critical Theory of Jürgen Habermas*, Cambridge, Mass.
MacFarquhar, R. and Fairbank, J. (1991) (eds.). *The Cambridge History of China*, 15 vols., Cambridge.
Mackerras, C. and Knight, N. (1985). *Marxism in Asia*, London.
McLellan, David (1979). *Marxism after Marx*, London.
Melotti, U. (1977). *Marx and the Third World*, London.
Merquior, J. G. (1986). *Western Marxism*, London.
Mortimer, Rex (1979). *Indonesian Communism under Sukarno: Ideology and Politics 1959–1965*, Ithaca, N.Y.
Nettl, J. P. (1966). *Rosa Luxemburg*, 2 vols., Oxford.
Nove, A. (1992). *An Economic History of the USSR 1917–1991*, London.
Outhwaite, William (1994). *Habermas: A Critical Introduction*, Cambridge.
Patnaik, U. (1989) (ed.). *Agrarian Relations and Accumulation: The Mode of Production Debate*, Bombay.
Popper, K. (1980 [1945]). *The Open Society and its Enemies*, 2 vols., London.
Poster, Mark (1975). *Existential Marxism in Postwar France: From Sartre to Althusser*, Princeton, N.J.
Ram, M. (1971). *Maoism in India*, Delhi.
Roth, Michael (1988). *Knowing and History: Appropriations of Hegel in Twentieth Century France*, Ithaca, N.Y. and London.
Salvadori, Massimo (1979). *Karl Kautsky and the Social Revolution*, London.
Sassoon, Anne Showstack (1980). *Gramsci's Politics*, New York.
Scalapino, Robert and Lee, Chong-Sik (1972). *Communism in Korea*, 2 vols., Berkeley, Calif.
Schapiro, L. S. (1972). *Totalitarianism*, London.
Schram, S. (1974) (ed.). *Mao Tse-tung Unrehearsed*, Harmondsworth.
Schröder, Hans-Christoph (1968). *Sozialismus und Imperialismus*, Hanover.
Stafford, David (1971). *From Anarchism to Reformism: Paul Brousse*, Toronto.
Steenson, Gary P. (1978). *Karl Kautsky, 1854–1938*, Pittsburg.
Steinberg, Hans-Josef (1969). *Sozialismus und Sozialdemokratie*, Hanover.
Talmon, J. (1961). *The Origins of Totalitarian Democracy*, London.

Tang Tsou (1986). *The Cultural Revolution and Post-Mao Reforms: A Historical Perspective*, Chicago.
Trager, F. (1959) (ed.). *Marxism in Southeast Asia*, Stanford, Calif.
Ulam, Adam B. (1969). *Lenin and the Bolsheviks*, London.
Uno, K. (1980). *Principles of Political Economy: Theory of a Purely Capitalist Society*, Brighton.
Vickery, Michael (1984). *Cambodia 1975–1982*, Sydney.
Walicki, A. (1995). *Marxism and the Leap to the Kingdom of Freedom*, Stanford, Calif.
White, Stephen (1995) (ed.). *The Cambridge Companion to Habermas*, Cambridge.
Wiggershaus, Rolf (1994 [1986]). *The Frankfurt School: Its History, Theories and Political Significance*, Cambridge.
Wilson, D. (1977) (ed.). *Mao Tse-tung in the Scales of History*, Cambridge.
Wolfe, B. D. (1956). *Three Who Made a Revolution*, London.
Zeman, Z. A. B. and Scharlau, W. B. (1965). *The Merchant of Revolution: Parvus*, London.

Part III: Science, modernism and politics

Primary sources

Adorno, T. W. *et al.* (1969). *Der Positivismusstreit in der deutschen Soziologie*, Neuwied, trans. Glyn Adey and David Frisby as *The Positivismusstreit in German Sociology*, London, 1976.
Almond, Gabriel A. (1950). *The American People and Foreign Policy*, New York.
(1954). *The Appeals of Communism*, Princeton, N.J.
Almond, Gabriel A. and Verba, Sidney (1963). *The Civic Culture: Politics, Attitudes, and Democracy in Five Nations*, Princeton, N.J.
Ansbacher, Heinz L. and Ansbacher, Rowena R. (1956) (eds.). *The Individual Psychology of Alfred Adler: A Systematic Presentation in Selections from his Writings*, New York.
Apollinaire, Guillaume (1972a [1912]). 'Reality, Pure Painting', in *Apollinaire on Art: Essays and Reviews 1902–1918*, ed. Leroy C. Breunig, trans. Susan Suleiman, New York, pp. 262–5.
(1972b [1913]). 'Modern Painting', in *Apollinaire on Art: Essays and Reviews 1902–1918*, ed. Leroy C. Breunig, trans. Susan Suleiman, New York, pp. 267–71.
Arendt, Hannah (1958). *The Human Condition*, Chicago.
Ayer, A. J. (1967). 'Man as a Subject for Science', in Peter Laslett and W. G. Runciman (eds.) *Philosophy, Politics, and Society*, 3rd series, Oxford, pp. 6–24.
Baudelaire, Charles (1964 [1863]). *The Painter of Modern Life and Other Essays*, ed. and trans. Jonathan Maine, New York.
(1975 [1887]). 'Journaux intimes', in *Oeuvres complètes*, Paris, vol. I, pp. 649–70.
(1991 [1861–9]). *The Flowers of Evil and Paris Spleen*, trans. William H. Crosby, Brockport, N.Y.
(1992 [1846]). 'The Salon of 1846', in *Selected Writings on Art and Literature*, trans. P. E. Charvet, London, pp. 47–107.
Baudrillard, Jean (1994 [1981]). *Simulacra and Simulation*, trans. Sheila Faria Glaser, Ann Arbor, Mich.
Benda, Julien (1927). *Le trahison des clercs*, Paris; trans. Richard Aldington as *The Treason of the Intellectuals*, New York and London, 1969.
Benjamin, Walter (1978a [1929]). 'Surrealism', in *Reflections*, ed. Peter Demetz, trans. Edmund Jephcott, New York and London, pp. 177–92.
(1978b [1936]). 'The Work of Art in the Age of Mechanical Reproduction', in *Illuminations*, ed. Hannah Arendt, trans. Harry Zohn, New York, pp. 217–51.

(1978c [1939]). 'On Some Motifs in Baudelaire', in *Illuminations*, ed. Hannah Arendt, trans. Harry Zohn, New York, pp. 155–200.

(1983 [1938]). 'The Paris of the Second Empire in Baudelaire', in *Charles Baudelaire: Lyric Poet in the Era of High Capitalism*, trans. Harry Zohn, pp. 9–106.

Benn, S. I. and Peters, R. S. (1959). *Social Principles and the Democratic State*, London.

Berelson, Bernard (1952). *Content Analysis in Communications Research*, Glencoe, Ill.

Berelson, Bernard, Lazarsfeld, Paul F. and McPhee, William N. (1954). *Voting: A Study of Opinion Formation in a Presidential Campaign*, Chicago.

Bergson, Henri (1910 [1889]). *Time and Free Will: An Essay on the Immediate Data of Consciousness*, trans. F. L. Pogson, London.

(1911 [1907]). *Creative Evolution*, trans. Arthur Mitchell, London.

(1931). *An Introduction to Metaphysics*, trans. T. E. Hulme, London.

(1935 [1932]). *The Two Sources of Morality and Religion*, trans. R. A. Audra and C. Brereton London.

Berlin, Isaiah (1962). 'Does Political Theory Still Exist?', in P. Laslett and W. G. Runciman (eds.) *Philosophy, Politics and Society*, 2nd series, Oxford, pp. 1–33.

(1969). 'Two Concepts of Liberty', in I. Berlin, *Four Essays on Liberty*, Oxford.

Bernays, Edward L. (1923). *Crystallizing Public Opinion*, New York.

(1928). *Propaganda*, New York.

Bobbio, N. (1987 [1984]). *The Future of Democracy: A Defence of the Rules of the Game*, ed. Richard Bellamy, trans. R. Griffen, Cambridge.

(1993 [1958, 1960]). *Teoria generale del diritto*, Turin.

(1995 [1990]). *The Age of Rights*, trans. A. Cameron, Cambridge.

Bradley, F. H. (1877). *Mr Sidgwick's Hedonism*, London.

(1902 [1893]). *Appearance and Reality*, London.

(1969 [1874]). *The Presuppositions of Critical History*, Don Mills, Ontario.

Breton, André (1981 [1924]). 'Three Dada Manifestos', in Robert Motherwell (ed.) *The Dada Painters and Poets: An Anthology*, Cambridge, Mass., pp. 197–206.

Buchanan, J. (1975). *The Limits of Liberty*, Chicago.

Buckle, Henry Thomas (1882). *History of Civilisation in England*, 3 vols., London.

Bury, J. B. (1920). *The Idea of Progress: An Inquiry into its Origins and Grounds*, London.

Catlin, George E. G. (1927). *The Science and Methods of Politics*, London.

(1930). *A Study of the Principles of Politics*, London.

(1936). 'Propaganda as a Function of Democratic Government', in Harwood L. Childs (ed.) *Propaganda and Dictatorship*, Princeton, N.J., pp. 125–45.

Cendrars, Blaise (1922 [1917]). 'Profound Today', *Broom* 1: 265–7.

Cohen, G. A. (1978). *Karl Marx's Theory of History: A Defense*, Princeton, N.J.

(1988). *History, Labour and Freedom: Themes from Marx*, Oxford.

(1989). 'On the Currency of Egalitarian Justice', *Ethics* 99: 906–44.

(1995). *Self-Ownership, Freedom and Equality*. Cambridge.

Comte, Auguste (1975 [1830–42]). *Cours de philosophie positive*, reprinted as *Philosophie première: Cours de philosophie positive, LeHons 1 B 45*, ed. Michel Serres, François Dagognet and Albul Simceur; and *Physique sociale: Cours de philosophie positive, LeHons 46 B 60*, ed. Jean-Paul Enthoven, Paris.

Crespigny, A. de and Wertheimer, A. (1970) (eds.). *Contemporary Political Theory*, New York.

Croce, Benedetto (1909). *Logica come scienza del concetto puro*, 2nd edn, Bari.

(1917). *Teoria e storia della storiografia*, Bari.

(1927 [1917]). *An Autobiography*, trans. R. G. Collingwood, with preface by J. A. Smith, Oxford.

(1945 [1924]). *Politics and Morals*, trans. Salvatore J. Castiglione, New York.

Bibliography

Dahl, Robert A. (1956). *A Preface to Democratic Theory*, Chicago.
(1961). 'The Behavioral Approach in Political Science: Epitaph for a Monument to a Successful Protest', *American Political Science Review* 55: 763–72.
Deleuze, Gilles and Guattari, Felix (1984). *Anti-Oedipus: Capitalism and Schizophrenia*, trans. Robert Hurley, Mark Seem and Helen R. Lane, London.
Derrida, Jacques (1973 [1967]). *Speech and Phenomena*, trans. David B. Allison, Evanston, Ill.
(1974 [1967]). *Of Grammatology*, trans. Gayatri Spivak, Baltimore, Md.
(1978 [1967]). *Writing and Difference*, trans. Alan Bass, London.
(1981a [1972]). *Dissemination*, trans. Barbara Johnson, London.
(1981b [1967]). *Positions*, trans. Alan Bass, London.
(1982 [1972]). *Margins of Philosophy*, trans. Alan Bass, Hemel Hempstead.
(1992). 'Force of Law', in Drucilla Cornell and Michael Rosenfeld (eds.) *Deconstruction and the Possibility of Justice*, New York and London, pp. 3–67.
(1994). *Specters of Marx*, trans. Peggy Kamuf, New York.
Deutsch, Helene (1944–5). *The Psychology of Women*, 2 vols., New York.
(1991 [1925]). *Psychoanalysis of the Sexual Functions of Women*, ed. Paul Roazen, trans. Eric Mosbacher, London.
Dewey, John (1903). *Studies in Logical Theory*, with members and Fellows of the University of Chicago Department of Philosophy, Chicago.
(1928). *The Public and its Problems*, London.
Dilthey, Wilhelm (1989 [1883]). *Introduction to the Human Sciences* (vol. I of *Wilhelm Dilthey: Selected Works*), trans. and ed. Rudolf A. Makkreel and Frithjof Rodi, Princeton, N.J.
Doob, Leonard W. (1935). *Propaganda: Its Psychology and Technique*, New York.
Durkheim, Emile (1885). 'Review of Fouillée's *La propriété sociale et la démocratie*', in A. Giddens (1986) (ed.) *Durkheim on Politics and the State*, Cambridge, pp. 86–96.
(1887). 'Review of Labriola's *Essais sur la conception matérialiste de l'histoire*', in A. Giddens (1986) (ed.) *Durkheim on Politics and the State*, Cambridge, pp. 128–36.
(1897). 'Review of Merlino's *Formes et essence du socialisme*', in A. Giddens (1986) (ed.) *Durkheim on Politics and the State*, Cambridge, pp. 136–45.
(1912). *Formes élémentaires de la vie religieuse*, Paris.
(1915). *Germany Above All: German Mentality and the War*, Paris.
(1957). *Professional Ethics and Civic Morals*, trans. C. Brookfield, London.
(1960). 'Pragmatism and Sociology', in K. H. Wolff (ed.) *Emile Durkheim, 1858–1917*, Columbus, Ohio, pp. 386–436.
(1969 [1898]). 'Individualism and the Intellectuals', *Political Studies* 17: 19–30.
(1971 [1928]) *Le socialisme*, intro. M. Mauss, 2nd edn, Paris.
(1976 [1930]) *Le suicide: étude de sociologie*, 2nd edn, Paris; trans. John A. Spaulding and George Simpson as *Suicide: A Study in Sociology*, 1951.
(1983 [1913]). *Pragmatism and Sociology*, ed. John B. Allcock, trans. J. C. Whitehouse, Cambridge, 1983.
(1984 [1893/1902]). *The Division of Labour in Society*, trans. W. D. Halls, London.
Dworkin, R. (1977). *Taking Rights Seriously*, London.
(1981). 'What is Equality? Part 2: Equality of Resources', *Philosophy and Public Affairs* 10: 283–345.
(1986). *Law's Empire*, Cambridge, Mass.
(1992). 'Liberal Community', in S. Avineri and A. de-Shalit (eds.) *Communitarianism and Individualism*, Oxford.
(1993). *Life's Dominion: An Argument about Abortion, Euthanasia, and Individual Freedom*, New York.
Easton, David (1953). *The Political System: An Inquiry into the State of Political Science*, Chicago.

(1969). 'The New Revolution in Political Science', *American Political Science Review* 63: 1051–61.
Erikson, Erik H. (1950). *Childhood and Society*, New York.
(1958). *Young Man Luther: A Study in Psychoanalysis and History*, New York.
(1968). *Identity: Youth and Crisis*, New York.
(1969). *Gandhi's Truth: On the Origins of Militant Nonviolence*, New York.
Eulau, Heinz (1963). *The Behavioral Persuasion in Politics*, New York.
Foucault, Michel (1967 [1961]). *Madness and Civilisation: A History of Insanity in the Age of Reason*, London.
(1970 [1966]). *The Order of Things: An Archaeology of the Human Sciences*, trans. Alan Sheridan, London.
(1972 [1969]). *The Archaeology of Knowledge*, trans. Alan Sheridan, London.
(1973 [1964]). *The Birth of the Clinic*, trans. Alan Sheridan, London.
(1979 [1975]). *Discipline and Punish*, trans. Alan Sheridan, Harmondsworth.
(1981 [1976]). *History of Sexuality*, vol. I: *An Introduction*, trans. Robert Hurley, Harmondsworth.
(1982). 'Afterword: The Subject and Power', in Hubert L. Dreyfus and Paul Rabinow, *Michel Foucault: Beyond Structuralism and Hermeneutics*, Brighton, pp. 206–26.
(1991 [1978]). *Remarks on Marx: Conversations with Duccio Trombadori*, trans. R. James Goldstein and James Cascaito, New York.
Freud, Sigmund (1900). *The Interpretation of Dreams,* in *The Standard Edition of the Complete Psychological Works of Sigmund Freud*, vols. IV–V, ed. James Strachey, London, 1953–74.
(1901). *The Psychopathology of Everyday Life,* in *The Standard Edition of the Complete Psychological Works of Sigmund Freud*, vol. VI, ed. James Strachey, London, 1953–74.
(1921). *Group Psychology and the Analysis of the Ego,* in *The Standard Edition of the Complete Psychological Works of Sigmund Freud*, vol. XVIII, ed. James Strachey, London, 1953–74.
(1927). *The Future of an Illusion*, in *The Standard Edition of the Complete Psychological Works of Sigmund Freud*, vol. XXI, ed. James Strachey, London, 1953–74.
(1930). *Civilization and its Discontents*, in *The Standard Edition of the Complete Psychological Works of Sigmund Freud*, vol. XXI, ed. James Strachey, London, 1953–74.
Fromm, Erich (1941). *Escape from Freedom*, New York.
(1947). *Man for Himself: An Inquiry into the Psychology of Ethics*, New York.
(1956). *The Sane Society*, London.
(1958 [1955]). 'The Human Implications of Instinctivistic "Radicalism": A Reply to Herbert Marcuse', in *Voices of Dissent*, ed. Irving Howe, New York.
Fuller, Lon L. (1969). *The Morality of Law*, New Haven, Conn.
Gallie, W. B. (1966). *Philosophy and the Historical Understanding*, New York.
George, Alexander L. (1959). *Propaganda Analysis: A Study of Inferences Made from Nazi Propaganda in World War II*, Evanston, Ill.
Giddens, Anthony (1985). *The Nation-State and Violence*, vol. II of *A Contemporary Critique of Historical Materialism*, Cambridge.
(1986) (ed.). *Durkheim on Politics and the State*, trans. W. D. Hall, Cambridge.
Goldstein, Joseph, Solnit, Albert J., Goldstein, Sonja and Freud, Anna (1996). *The Best Interests of the Child: The Least Detrimental Alternative*, New York.
Green, T. H. (1888a [1881]). 'Liberal Legislation and Freedom of Contract', in T. H. Green, *Works*, ed. R. L. Nettleship, London, vol. III, pp. 365–86.
(1888b [1886]). 'Lectures on the Principles of Political Obligation', in T. H. Green, *Works*, ed. R. L. Nettleship, London, vol. II, pp. 335–553.

Habermas, Jürgen (1969a [1963]). 'Analytische Wissenschaftstheorie und Dialektik', in Adorno *et al. Der Positivismusstreit in der deutschen Soziologie*, Neuwied, pp. 155–92.

(1969b [1964]). 'Gegen einen positivisch halbierten Rationalismus', in Adorno *et al. Der Positivismusstreit in der deutschen Soziologie*, Neuwied, pp. 235–66.

(1971). 'Discussion on "Value Freedom and Objectivity" ', in O. Stammer (ed.) *Max Weber and Sociology Today*, trans. Kathleen Morris, Oxford.

(1982) *The Theory of Communicative Action*, 2 vols., trans. Thomas McCarthy Boston and London, 1984.

(1987a). *The Philosophical Discourse of Modernity*, trans. Frederick Lawrence Cambridge, Mass.

(1987b [1981]). *The Theory of Communicative Action*, Vol. II: *Lifeworld and System*, trans. Thomas McCarthy, Cambridge.

(1992 [1962]). *The Structural Transformation of the Public Sphere: An Inquiry into a Category of Bourgeois Society*, trans. Thomas Burger, Cambridge, Mass.

(1993 [1981]). 'Modernity – an Incomplete Project', in Thomas Docherty (ed.) *Postmodernism: A Reader*, Hemel Hempstead, pp. 98–109.

(1996). 'The European Nation-State – Its Achievements and its Limits: On the Past and Future of Sovereignty and Citizenship', in G. Balakrishnan (ed.) *Mapping the Nation*, London.

Hamilton, Alexander, Madison, James, and Jay, John (2003 [1787–8]). *The Federalist*, ed. Terence Ball, Cambridge.

Hare, R. (1963). *Freedom and Reason*, Oxford.

(1981). *Moral Thinking: Its Levels, Method and Point*, Oxford.

Hart, H. L. A. (1955). 'Are There Any Natural Rights?', *Philosophical Review* 64: 175–91.

(1961). *The Concept of Law*, Oxford.

(1963). *Law, Liberty*, and *Morality*, Stanford, Calif.

(1968). *Punishment and Responsibility: Essays in the Philosophy of Law*, Oxford.

(1973). 'Rawls on Liberty and its Priority', *University of Chicago Law Review* 40: 534–55.

Hart, H. L. A. and Honoré, A. M. (1959). *Causation in the Law*, Oxford.

Heidegger, Martin (1962 [1927]). *Being and Time*, trans. John Macquarrie and Edward Robinson, Oxford.

(1975–). *Gesamtausgabe*, Frankfurt am Main.

(1976). 'Only a God Can Save Us: Der Spiegel's Interview with Martin Heidegger', *Philosophy Today* 20 (4/4): 267–84.

(1979–87 [1961]). *Nietzsche*, 4 vols., trans. Joan Stambaugh, David Farrell Krell and Frank A. Capuzzi, San Francisco.

(1993). 'The Question Concerning Technology', in David Farrell Krell (ed.) *Basic Writings*, New York revised edn, pp. 311–41.

(1995). *The Fundamental Concepts of Metaphysics*, trans. William McNeill and Nicholas Walker, Bloomington, Ind.

(1999a). *Ontology – The Hermeneutics of Facticity*, trans. John van Buren, Bloomington, Ind.

(1999b). *Contributions to Philosophy: From Enowning*, trans. Parvis Emad and Kenneth Maly, Bloomington, Ind.

Hempel, Carl G. (1965). *Aspects of Scientific Explanation*, New York and London.

Hobbes, T. (1968 [1651]). *Leviathan*, ed. C. B. Macpherson, Harmondsworth.

Hobhouse, Leonard (1906). *Morals in Evolution: A Study in Comparative Ethics*, 2 vols., London.

(1913). *Development and Purpose: An Essay towards a Philosophy of Evolution*, London.

Horney, Karen (1937). *The Neurotic Personality of our Time*, London.

(1967). *Feminine Psychology*, New York.

Horkheimer, Max and Adorno, Theodor (1972 [1944]). *Dialectic of Enlightenment*, trans. J. Cumming, New York.
Irigaray, Luce (1985a [1974]). *Speculum of the Other Woman*, Ithaca, N.Y.
(1985b [1977]). *This Sex which is not One*, Ithaca, N.Y.
James, William (1891). *The Principles of Psychology*, 2 vols., London.
(1902). *The Varieties of Religious Experience*, London.
(1976 [1907]). *Pragmatism*, New York.
Jung, Carl J. (1966 [1953]). *Two Essays on Analytical Psychology*, in *The Collected Works of C. G. Jung*, ed. Herbert Read, Michael Fordham and Gerhard Adler, 2nd edn, Princeton, N.J.
Kandinsky, Wassily (1977 [1911]). *Concerning the Spiritual in Art*, trans. M. T. H. Sadler, New York.
Kelsen, H. (1945). *General Theory of Law and State*, trans. A. Wedberg, Cambridge, Mass.
Kuhn, Thomas (1963). *The Structure of Scientific Revolutions*, Chicago.
Laslett, Peter (1956) (ed.). *Philosophy, Politics, and Society*, 1st series, Oxford.
Lassman, Peter and Speirs, Ronald (1994) (eds.). *Weber: Political Writings*, Cambridge.
Lasswell, Harold D. (1927a). *Propaganda Technique in the World War*, New York.
(1927b). 'The Theory of Political Propaganda', *American Political Science Review* 21: 627–31.
(1928). 'The Function of the Propagandist', *International Journal of Ethics* 38: 258–68.
(1934). 'Propaganda', in *Encyclopedia of the Social Sciences*, London and New York, vol. XII, pp. 521–7.
(1935a). *World Politics and Personal Insecurity*, New York.
(1935b). 'The Person: Subject and Object of Propaganda', *Annals of the American Academy of Political and Social Science* 179: 189–93.
(1936). 'The Scope of Research on Propaganda and Dictatorship', in Harwood L. Childs (ed.) *Propaganda and Dictatorship*, Princeton, N.J., pp. 104–21.
(1941). *Democracy through Public Opinion*, Menasha, Wisc.
(1942). 'The Developing Science of Democracy', in Leonard D. White (ed.) *The Future of Government in the United States: Essays in Honor of Charles E. Merriam*, Chicago, pp. 25–48.
Lasswell, Harold D. and Blumenstock, Dorothy (1939). *World Revolutionary Propaganda: A Chicago Study*, Chicago.
Lasswell, Harold D. and Leites, Nathan (1949). *Language of Politics: Studies in Quantitative Semantics*, New York.
Lasswell, Harold D., Casey, Ralph D. and Smith, Bruce Lannes (1935). *Propaganda and Promotional Activities: An Annotated Bibliography*, Minneapolis.
Leites, Nathan (1953). *A Study of Bolshevism*, Glencoe, Ill.
Levinas, Emmanuel (1969 [1961]). *Totality and Infinity*, trans. Alphonso Lingis, London and The Hague.
(1981 [1974]). *Otherwise than Being, or, Beyond Essence*, trans. Alphonso Lingis, London and The Hague.
(1990 [1961]). 'Heidegger, Gargarin and Us', in *Difficult Freedom: Essays on Judaism*, trans. Seán Hand, London, pp. 231–4.
(1996 [1964]). 'Meaning and Sense', in R. Bernasconi, S. Critchley and A. Peperzaak (eds.) *Emmanuel Levinas: Basic Philosophical Writings*, Bloomington, Ind. pp. 34–64.
Lippmann, Walter (1913). *Preface to Politics*, New York.
(1922). *Public Opinion*, New York.
(1955). *The Public Philosophy*, Boston.
Lipset, Seymour Martin (1959). *Political Man*, New York.
Locke, J. (1963 [1689–90]). *Two Treatises of Government*, ed. P. Laslett, Cambridge.

(1975 [1690]). *An Essay on Human Understanding*, ed. P. H. Nidditch, Oxford.
Lowell, A. Lawrence (1921 [1913]). *Public Opinion and Popular Government*, New York.
Lucas, J. (1980). *On Justice*, Oxford.
Lyotard, Jean-François (1984 [1979]). *The Postmodern Condition: A Report on Knowledge*, Manchester.
(1993 [1974]). *Libidinal Economy*, trans. Iain Hamilton Grant, London.
Macdonald, M. (1951). 'The Language of Political Theory', in A. Flew (ed.) *Logic and Language*, 1st series, Oxford.
Mach, Ernst (1914 [1886]). *The Analysis of the Sensations*, trans. from first German edn C. M. Williams, revised and supplemented Sydney Waterlow, Chicago and London.
MacIntyre, A. (1966). *A Short History of Ethics*, New York.
(1973). 'The Essential Contestability of Some Social Concepts', *Ethics* 84: 1–9.
(1981). *After Virtue: A Study in Moral Theory*, Notre Dame, Ind.; 2nd edn 1984.
(1988). *Whose Justice? Which Rationality?*, Notre Dame, Ind. and London.
Macke, August (1974 [1912]). 'Masks', in Wassily Kandinsky and Franz Marc (eds.) *The Blaue Reiter Almanac*, ed. Klaus Lankheit, New York, pp. 81–9.
McPherson, T. (1967). *Political Obligation*, London.
Macy, Jesse (1917). 'The Scientific Spirit in Politics', *American Political Science Review* 11: 1–11.
Mallarmé, Stéphane (1956a [1886–95]). 'Crisis in Poetry', in *Selected Prose Poems, Essays, and Letters*, trans. Bradford Cook, Baltimore, Md., pp. 34–43.
(1956b [1894]). 'Mystery in Literature', in *Selected Prose Poems, Essays, and Letters*, trans. Bradford Cook, Baltimore, Md., pp. 29–34.
Marcuse, Herbert (1955). *Eros and Civilization*, Boston.
Marinetti, F. T. (1983a [1913]). 'Distruzione della sintassi, immaginazione senza fili, parole in libertà', in *Teoria e invenzione futurista*, ed. Luciano De Maria, Milan, pp. 65–80.
(1983b [1919]). 'Democrazia futurista', in *Teoria e invenzione futurista*, ed. Luciano De Maria, Milan, pp. 343–469.
Martin, R. (1993). *A System of Rights*, Oxford.
Merriam, Charles E. (1919). 'American Publicity in Italy', *American Political Science Review* 13: 541–55.
(1921). 'The Present State of the Study of Politics', *American Political Science Review* 15: 173–85.
(1931). *The Making of Citizens: A Comparative Study of Methods of Civic Training*, Chicago.
(1934). *Civic Education in the United States*, New York.
(1970 [1925]). *New Aspects of Politics*, Chicago.
Mill, John Stuart (1961 [1865]). *Auguste Comte and Positivism*, Ann Arbor, Mich.
(1974 [1859]). *On Liberty*, ed. Gertrude Himmelfarb, New York.
(1987 [1872]). *The Logic of the Moral Sciences*, reprint of *A System of Logic*, book VI, 8th edn, intro. A. J. Ayer, London.
Miller, James G. (1956). 'Toward a General Theory for the Behavioral Sciences', in Leonard D. White (ed.) *The State of the Social Sciences*, Chicago, pp. 29–65.
Moréas, Jean (1992 [1886]). 'A Literary Manifesto', in Eugen Weber (ed.) *Movements, Currents, Trends: Aspects of European Thought in the Nineteenth and Twentieth Centuries*, Lexington, Mass. and Toronto, pp. 222–7.
Munro, William B. (1927). *The Invisible Government*, New York.
Nettleship, R. L. (1888). 'Memoir', in T. H. Green, *Works*, ed. R. L. Nettleship, London, vol. III, pp. xi–clxi.
Nietzsche, Friedrich (1969 [1883–5]). *Thus Spoke Zarathustra*, trans. R. J. Hollingdale, Harmondsworth.

(1973 [1886]). *Beyond Good and Evil*, trans. R. J. Hollingdale, Harmondsworth.
(1979). *Philosophy and Truth: Selections from Nietzsche's Notebooks from the Early 1870s*, ed. and trans. Daniel Breazeale, Atlantic Highlands, N.J.
(1996) [1887]. *On the Genealogy of Morals*, trans. Douglas Smith, Oxford.
(1999 [1872]). *The Birth of Tragedy and Other Writings*, trans. Ronald Speirs, Cambridge.
Nozick, R. (1974). *Anarchy, State, and Utopia*, Oxford.
(1989). *The Examined Life: Philosophical Meditations*, New York.
Nunberg, Herman and Federn, Ernst (1962–75). *Minutes of the Vienna Psychoanalytic Society*, vols. I–IV, trans. by M. Nunberg, New York.
Parekh, B. (1996). 'Political Theory: Traditions in Political Philosophy', in R. E. Goodin and H.-D. Klingemann (eds.) *A New Handbook of Political Science*, Oxford.
Pareto, Vilfredo (1902). *Les systèmes socialistes*, Paris.
(1923 [1916]). *Trattato di sociologia generale*, 2nd edn, Florence.
(1982 [1896]). *Cours d'économie politique*, in *Oeuvres complètes*, ed. Giovanni Busino, vol. XXIV, Geneva.
Parsons, Talcott (1947 [1937]). *The Structure of Social Action*, New York.
Peirce, Charles S. (1986 [1878]). 'How to Make Our Ideas Clear', in *Writings of Charles S. Peirce: A Chronological Edition*, ed. Christian J. W. Kloegel, Bloomington, Ind., vol. III, pp. 257–76.
Popper, Karl (1945). *The Open Society and its Enemies*, 2 vols., London.
Rawls, J. (1955). 'Two Concepts of Rules', *Philosophical Review* 64: 3–32.
(1958). 'Justice as Fairness', *Philosophical Review* 67: 164–94.
(1964). 'Legal Obligation and the Duty of Fair Play', in S. Hook (ed.) *Law and Philosophy*, New York.
(1971). *A Theory of Justice*, Cambridge, Mass.
(1993). *Political Liberalism*, New York.
(1999). *The Law of Peoples; with 'The Idea of Public Reason Revisited'*, Cambridge, Mass.
Reich, Wilhelm (1970 [1935]). *The Mass Psychology of Fascism*, New York.
Rickert, Heinrich (1962 [1898]). *Science and History: A Critique of Epistemology*, ed. Arthur Goddard, trans. George Reisman, Princeton, N.J.
Rorty, Richard (1980). *Philosophy and the Mirror of Nature*, Oxford.
Sandel, M. (1982). *Liberalism and the Limits of Justice*, Cambridge; 2nd edn 1998.
(1996). *Democracy's Discontent: America in Search of a Public Philosophy*, Cambridge, Mass.
Scanlon, T. M. (1982). 'Contractualism and Utilitarianism', in A. Sen and B. A. O. Williams (eds.) *Utilitarianism and Beyond*, Cambridge.
(1998). *What We Owe to Each Other*, Cambridge, Mass.
Sorel, Georges (1936 [1908]). *Reflections on Violence*, ed. E. A. Shils, trans. T. E. Hulme and J. Roth, London.
Spencer, Herbert (1865). *First Principles of a New System of Philosophy*, New York.
(1904). *Autobiography*, 2 vols., New York.
(1966 [1892]). *The Man versus the State*, 2nd edn, Osnabrück.
Strauss, Leo (1962). 'An Epilogue', in Herbert J. Storing (ed.) *Essays on the Scientific Study of Politics*, New York, pp. 305–27.
Sullivan, Harry Stack (1953). *Conceptions of Modern Psychiatry*, New York.
Sumner, William Graham (1925 [1883]). *What Social Classes Owe to Each Other*, New Haven, Conn.
Taine, Hippolyte (1863). *Histoire de la littérature anglaise*, Paris.
Taylor, Charles (1964). *The Explanation of Behaviour*, London.
(1975). *Hegel*, Cambridge.
(1985). *Philosophical Papers*, vol. II: *Philosophy and the Human Sciences*, Cambridge.

(1989). *Sources of the Self: The Making of the Modern Identity*, Cambridge, Mass.
Truman, David (1955). 'The Impact on Political Science of the Revolution in the Behavioral Sciences', in S. K. Bailey (ed.) *Research Frontiers in Politics and Government*, Washington, D.C.
Tzara, Tristan (1981a [1918]). 'Dada Manifesto 1918', in R. Motherwell (ed.) *Dada Painters and Poets*, Cambridge, Mass., pp. 76–82.
(1981b [1920]). 'Manifesto on Feeble Love and Bitter Love', in R. Motherwell (ed.), *Dada Painters and Poets*, Cambridge, Mass., pp. 86–97.
Voegelin, Eric (1952). *The New Science of Politics*, Chicago.
Wallas, Graham (1948 [1908]). *Human Nature in Politics*, London.
Walzer, M. (1977). *Just and Unjust Wars: A Moral Argument with Historical Illustrations*, New York.
(1983). *Spheres of Justice: A Defence of Pluralism and Equality*, Oxford.
Ward, L. F. (1898). *Dynamic Sociology*, 2nd edn, 2 vols., New York.
(1903). *Pure Sociology*, New York.
Watson, John B. (1925). *Behaviourism*, London.
Weber, Max (1895). 'The Nation State and Economic Policy (Inaugural Lecture)', in P. Lassman and R. Speirs (eds.) *Weber: Political Writings*, Cambridge, 1994, pp. 1–28.
(1910). 'Diskussionsrede dortselbst zu dem Vortrag von A. Ploetz über "Die Begriffe Rasse und Gesellschaft" ', in *Gesammelte Aufsätze zur Soziologie und Sozialpolitik*, ed. Marianne Weber, Tübingen.
(1917). 'Suffrage and Democracy in German', in P. Lassman and R. Speirs (eds.) *Weber: Political Writings*, Cambridge, 1994, pp. 80–129.
(1918a). 'Parliament and Government in Germany under a New Political Order', in P. Lassman and R. Speirs (eds.) *Weber: Political Writings*, Cambridge, 1994, pp. 130–271.
(1918b). 'Socialism', in P. Lassman and R. Speirs (eds.) *Weber: Political Writings*, Cambridge, 1994, pp. 272–303.
(1919a). 'The Profession and Vocation of Politics', in P. Lassman and R. Speirs (eds.) *Weber: Political Writings*, Cambridge, 1994, pp. 309–69.
(1919b). 'The President of the Reich', in P. Lassman and R. Speirs (eds.) *Weber: Political Writings*, Cambridge, 1994, pp. 304–9.
(1922). *Wirtschaft und Gesellschaft*, Tübingen.
(1930 [1904/5]). *The Protestant Ethic and the Spirit of Capitalism*, trans. T. Parsons, London.
(1948). *From Max Weber. Essays in Sociology*, trans. and ed. Hans Gerth and C. Wright Mills, London.
(1978 [1917–19]). *Gesammelte Politische Schriften*, ed. J. Winckelmann, including 'Der Reichspräsident' (February 1919), pp. 498–501; 'Politik als Beruf' (October 1919), pp. 505–60; 'Parlament und Regierung im neugeordneten Deutschland' (May 1918), pp. 306–443; 'Wahlrecht und Demokratie in Deutschland' (December 1917), pp. 245–91.
(1984 [1918]) 'Der Sozialismus', in W. Mommsen and G. Hubinger (eds.) *Gesamtausgabe*, vol. XV: *Zur Politik im Weltkrieg*, pp. 599–633.
(1989 [1894]). 'Developmental Tendencies in the Situation of East Elbian Rural Workers', in Keith Tribe (ed.) *Reading Weber*, London.
Weldon, T. D. (1953). *The Vocabulary of Politics*, Harmondsworth.
White, Leonard D. (1950). 'Political Science, Mid-Century', *Journal of Politics* 12: 13–19.
Winch, Peter (1958). *The Idea of a Social Science*, London.
Windelband, Wilhelm (1919). *Lehrbuch der Geschichte der Philosophie*, Tübingen.
Zola, Emile (1992 [1883]). *The Ladies' Paradise*, trans. H. Vizetelly, Berkeley and Los Angeles, Calif.

Bibliography

Secondary sources

Adamson, Walter L. (1993). *Avant-garde Florence: From Modernism to Fascism*, Cambridge, Mass.

(1997). 'Futurism, Mass Culture, and Women: The Reshaping of the Artistic Vocation, 1909–1920', *Modernism/Modernity* 4: 89–114.

Adorno, Theodor W. (1984 [1970]). *Aesthetic Theory*, trans. Christian Lenhardt, London and New York.

(1991). *The Culture Industry: Selected Essays on Mass Culture*, ed. J. M. Bernstein, London.

Allen, A. L. and Regan, M. C. (1998) (eds.). *Debating Democracy's Discontent: Essays on American Politics, Law, and Public Philosophy*, New York.

Anderson, Perry (1974). *Lineages of the Absolutist State*, London.

(1998). *The Origins of Postmodernity*, London.

Ankersmit, F. R. (1996). *Aesthetic Politics: Political Philosophy Beyond Fact and Value*, Stanford, Calif.

Annan, Noël (1959). *The Curious Strength of Positivism in English Political Thought*, London.

(1991). *Our Age: The Generation that Made Post-War Britain*, 2nd edn, London.

Antliff, Mark (1993). *Inventing Bergson: Cultural Politics and the Parisian Avant-garde*, Princeton, N.J.

Arendt, Hannah (1951). *The Origins of Totalitarianism*, New York.

Arneson, R. (1982). 'The Principle of Fairness and Free-Rider Problems', *Ethics* 92: 616–33.

Arrow, K. (1973). 'Some Ordinalist-Utilitarian Notes on Rawls's Theory of Justice', *Journal of Philosophy* 70: 245–63.

Asendorf, Christoph (1993). *Batteries of Life: On the History of Things and their Perception in Modernity*, trans. Don Reneau, Berkeley and Los Angeles, Calif.

Avineri, S. and de-Shalit, A. (1992) (eds.). *Communitarianism and Individualism*, Oxford.

Ayer, A. J. (1968). *The Origins of Pragmatism*, London, Melbourne and Toronto.

Badiou, Alain (2000). *Ethics: An Essay on the Understanding of Evil*, trans. Peter Hallward, London.

Ball, Terence (1984). 'Marxian Science and Positivist Politics', in Terence Ball and James Farr (eds.) *After Marx*, Cambridge, pp. 235–60.

(1988). *Transforming Political Discourse: Political Theory and Critical Conceptual History*, Oxford.

Ball, T., Farr, J. and Hanson, R. (1989) (eds.). *Political Innovation and Conceptual Change*, Cambridge.

Barry, Brian (1965). *Political Argument*. London; 2nd edn 1990, Berkeley, Calif.

(1973). *The Liberal Theory of Justice*, Oxford.

(1995). *Justice as Impartiality*, Oxford.

(1998). 'International Society from a Cosmopolitan Perspective', in D. R. Mapel and T. Nardin (eds.) *International Society: Diverse Ethical Perspectives*, Princeton, N.J.

(1989). *Theories of Justice*, Berkeley and Los Angeles, Calif.

Basu, K., Pattanaik, P. and Suzumura, K. (1995) (eds.). *Choice, Welfare, and Development: A Festschrift in Honour of Amartya K. Sen*, Oxford.

Bauman, Zygmunt (1989). *Modernity and the Holocaust*, Cambridge.

Bayles, M. D. (1992). *Hart's Legal Philosophy: An Examination*, Dordrecht.

Beetham, David (1974). *Max Weber and the Theory of Modern Politics*, London.

Bellamy, Richard (1987). *Modern Italian Social Theory*, Cambridge.

(1992). *Liberalism and Modern Society: An Historical Argument*, Cambridge.

Bendix, Reinhard (1977). *Nation Building and Citizenship*, Berkeley, Calif.

Bibliography

Beran, H. (1987). *The Consent Theory of Political Obligation*, London.

Bersani, Leo (1990). *The Culture of Redemption*, Cambridge, Mass.

Birnbach, Norman (1961). *Neo-Freudian Social Philosophy*, Stanford, Calif.

Bourdieu, Pierre (1991). *The Political Ontology of Martin Heidegger*, trans. Peter Collier, Cambridge.

(1992b). *Les règles de l'art: genèse et structure du champ littéraire*, Paris.

Brandt, R. B. (1959). *Ethical Theory*. Englewood Cliffs, N.J.

(1992a). *Morality, Utilitarianism, and Rights*, Cambridge.

Browning, Don (1973). *Generative Man: Psychoanalytic Perspectives*, Philadelphia.

Brownmiller, Susan (1975). *Against Our Will: Men, Women and Rape*, New York.

Bürger, Peter (2000). *Der Ursprung des Postmodernen Denkens*, Weilerswist.

Burston, Daniel (1991). *The Legacy of Erich Fromm*, Cambridge, Mass.

Burtt, S. (1993). 'The Politics of Virtue Today: A Critique and a Proposal', *American Political Science Review* 87: 360–8.

Butler, Judith (1990). *Gender Trouble: Feminism and the Subversion of Identity*, New York and London.

Callinicos, Alex (1989). *Against Postmodernism*, Cambridge.

Cassirer, Ernst (1950). *The Problem of Knowledge: Philosophy, Science and History since Hegel*, trans. William H. Woglom and Charles W. Hendel, New Haven, Conn.

Charlesworth, James S. (1962) (ed.). *The Limits of Behavioralism in Political Science*, Philadelphia.

Charlton, D. G. (1959). *Positivist Thought in France during the Second Empire, 1852–1870*, Oxford.

Charney, Leo and Schwartz, Vanessa R. (1995) (eds.). *Cinema and the Invention of Modern Life*, Berkeley, Los Angeles and London.

Cladis, Mark S. (1992). *A Communitarian Defense of Liberalism: Emile Durkheim and Contemporary Social Theory*, Stanford, Calif.

Clark, Ronald (1980). *Freud: The Man and the Cause*, New York.

Clarke, Peter (1981 [1978]). *Liberals and Social Democrats*, Cambridge.

Cocks, Geoffrey (1997 [1985]). *Psychotherapy in the Third Reich*, New York.

Cohen, Marshall (1983) (ed.). *Ronald Dworkin and Contemporary Jurisprudence*, Totowa, N.J.

Coles, Robert (1970). *Erik H. Erikson: The Growth of his Work*, Boston.

Collingwood, R. B. (1946). *The Idea of History*, Oxford.

Collini, Stefan (1979). *Liberalism and Sociology: L. T. Hobhouse and Political Argument in England, 1880–1914*, Cambridge.

Collini, Stefan, Winch, Donald and Burrow, John (1983). *That Noble Science of Politics: Studies in Nineteenth Century Intellectual History*, Cambridge.

Connolly, William E. (1969) (ed.). *The Bias of Pluralism*, New York.

(1991). *Identity/Difference: Democratic Negotiations of Political Paradox*, Ithaca, N.Y. and London.

Crick, Bernard (1959). *The American Science of Politics: Its Origins and* Conditions, Berkeley, Calif. and London.

Dagger, R. (1997). *Civic Virtues: Rights, Citizenship, and Republican Liberalism*, New York.

Daly, Mary (1978). *Gyn/Ecology: The Metaphysics of Radical Feminism*, Boston.

Daniels, N. (1975) (ed.). *Reading Rawls: Critical Studies of A Theory of Justice*, New York.

Davison, Ned (1966). *The Concept of Modernism in Hispanic Criticism*, Boulder, Colo.

Dietz, Mary G. and Farr, James (1998). '"Politics Would Undoubtedly Unwoman Her": Gender, Suffrage, and American Political Science', in Helene Silverberg (ed.) *Gender and American Social Science: The Formative Years*, Princeton, N.J., pp. 61–85.

Donnelly, J. (1985). *The Concept of Human Rights*, New York.

Downs, Anthony (1957). *The Economic Theory of Democracy*, New York.

Drake, Richard (1981). 'The Theory and Practice of Italian Nationalism, 1900–1906', *Journal of Modern History* 51: 213–41.
Drucker, Johanna (1994). *The Visible Word: Experimental Typography and Modern Art, 1909–1923*, Chicago and London.
Edmundson, W. A. (1999) (ed.). *The Duty to Obey the Law: Selected Philosophical Readings*, Lanham, Md.
Ellenberger, Henri (1970). *The Discovery of the Unconscious: The History and Evolution of Dynamic Psychiatry*, New York.
Elster, J. (1985). *Making Sense of Marx*, Cambridge.
Etzioni, A. (1995) (ed.). *New Communitarian Thinking: Persons, Virtues, Institutions, and Communities*, Charlottesville, Va.
(1997) (ed.). *The New Golden Rule: Community and Morality in a Democratic Society*, New York.
Farr, James (1984). 'Marx and Positivism', in Terence Ball and James Farr (eds.) *After Marx*, Cambridge, pp. 217–34.
(2004). 'Political Science', in Theodore M. Porter and Dorothy Ross (eds.) *The Cambridge History of Science: The Social and Behavioral Sciences*, vol. VII, Cambridge.
Feigl, Herbert (1969). 'The Wiener Kreis in America', in Donald Fleming and Bernard Bailyn (eds.) *The Intellectual Migration: Europe and America, 1930–1960*, Cambridge, Mass.
Ferry, Luc and Renault, Alain (1990). *Heidegger and Modernity*, trans. Franklin Philip, Chicago and London.
FitzGerald, Michael C. (1995). *Making Modernism: Picasso and the Creation of the Market for Twentieth-Century Art*, New York.
Flathman, R. (1973) (ed.). *Concepts in Social and Political Philosophy*, New York.
Foster, Hal (1993). *Compulsive Beauty*, Cambridge, Mass.
Freeden, Michael (1978). *The New Liberalism: An Ideology of Social Reform*, Oxford.
Friedman, Leonard J. (1999). *Identity's Architect: A Biography of Erik H. Erikson*, New York.
Friedman, M. (1992). 'Feminism and Modern Friendship: Dislocating the Community', in S. Avineri and A. de-Shalit (eds.) *Communitarianism and Individualism*, Oxford.
Galipeau, C. (1994). *Isaiah Berlin's Liberalism*, Oxford.
Galston, W. (1991). *Liberal Purposes: Goods, Virtues, and Diversity in the Liberal State*, Cambridge.
Gane, Mike (1984). 'Institutional Socialism and the Sociological Critique of Communism', *Economy and Society* 13: 304–30.
Gauthier, D. (1986). *Morals by Agreement*, Oxford.
Gavison, R. (1987) (ed.). *Issues in Contemporary Legal Philosophy: The Influence of H. L. A. Hart*, Oxford.
Gay, Peter (1968). *Weimar Culture: The Outsider as Insider*, New York.
Gellner, Ernest (1983). *Nations and Nationalism*, Oxford.
Gewirth, A. (1978). *Reason and Morality*, Chicago.
(1982). *Human Rights: Justification and Applications*, Chicago.
(1996). *The Community of Rights*, Chicago.
Girard, René (1980 [1961]). '"Triangular" Desire', in *Desire, Deceit, and the Novel: Self and Other in Literary Studies*, trans. Yvonne Freccero, Baltimore, Md., and London, pp. 1–52.
Gleizes, Albert (1981 [1920]). 'The Dada Case', in R. Motherwell (ed.) *Dada Painters and Poets*, Cambridge, Mass., pp. 298–303.
Gleizes, Albert and Metzinger, Jean (1964 [1912]). 'Cubism', in Robert L. Herbert (ed.) *Modern Artists on Art*, Englewood Cliffs, N.J., pp. 1–18.
Goodin, Robert (1995). *Utilitarianism as a Public Philosophy*, Cambridge.
Gray, J. (1995). *Isaiah Berlin*, London.

Green, L. (1988). *The Authority of the State*, Oxford.
Greenberg, Clement (1992 [1961]). 'Modernist Painting', in Charles Harrison and Paul Wood (eds.) *Art in Theory 1900–1990*, Oxford and Cambridge, Mass., pp. 754–60.
Grogin, R. C. (1988). *The Bergsonian Controversy in France, 1900–1914*, Calgary, Alberta.
Guest, S. (1992). *Ronald Dworkin*, Edinburgh.
Gunnell, John G. (1993). *The Descent of Political Theory: The Genealogy of an American Vocation*, Chicago.
Gutmann, A. (1992). 'The Communitarian Critics of Liberalism', in S. Avineri and A. de-Shalit (eds.) *Communitarianism and Individualism*, Oxford.
Hampshire, S. (1978) (ed.). *Public and Private Morality*, Cambridge.
Handlin, Oscar (1963). 'The Modern City as a Field of Historical Study', in Oscar Handlin and John Burchard (eds.) *The Historian and the City*, Cambridge, Mass., pp. 1–26.
Hardin, R. (1988). *Morality within the Limits of Reason*, Chicago.
Harsanyi, J. (1982). 'Morality and the Theory of Rational Behaviour', in A. Sen and B. A. O. Williams (eds.) *Utilitarianism and Beyond*, Cambridge.
Harvey, David (1989). *The Condition of Postmodernity*, Oxford.
Held, David (1993). 'From City-States to a Cosmopolitan Order?', in David Held (ed.) *Prospects for Democracy*, Cambridge.
Hennis, Wilhelm (2000). *Max Weber's Central Questions*, 2nd edn of *Max Weber, Essays in Reconstruction* (1988), trans. K. Tribe, Newbury.
Hirst, Paul Q. (1994). *Associative Democracy: New Forms of Economic and Social Governance*, Cambridge.
(1997). *From Statism to Pluralism*, London.
Hirst, Paul Q. and Thompson, Grahame (1999). *Globalization in Question*, 2nd edn, Cambridge.
Hobsbawm, Eric (1994). *The Age of Extremes: A History of the World, 1914–1991*, New York.
Hoffman, Edward (1994). *The Drive for Self: Alfred Adler and the Founding of Individual Psychology*, Reading, Mass.
Hofstadter, Richard (1944). *Social Darwinism in American Thought, 1860–1915*, Philadelphia and London.
Horton, J. (1992). *Political Obligation*, London.
Horton, J. and Mendus, S. (1994) (eds.). *After MacIntyre: Critical Perspectives*, Cambridge.
Hughes, H. Stuart (1979 [1958]). *Consciousness and Society: The Reorientation of European Social Thought 1890–1930*, 2nd edn, New York.
Hunt, A. (1992). *Reading Dworkin Critically*, New York.
Hylton, Peter (1990). *Russell, Idealism, and the Emergence of Analytic Philosophy*, Oxford.
Ignatieff, M. (1998). *Isaiah Berlin: A Life*, New York.
Jacoby, Russell (1975). *Social Amnesia: A Critique of Conformist Psychology from Adler to Laing*, Boston.
Jameson, Fredric (1991). *Postmodernism, or, The Cultural Logic of Late Capitalism*, Durham, N.C.
Jay, Martin (1973). *The Dialectical Imagination: A History of the Frankfurt School and the Institute of Social Research 1923–50*, Boston.
(1992). '"The Aesthetic Ideology" as Ideology; or, What Does it Mean to Aestheticize Politics?', *Cultural Critique* 9: 41–61.
Jencks, Charles (1991 [1978]). *The Language of Post-modern Architecture*, revised and enlarged edn, London.
Jensen, Robert (1992). 'Selling Martyrdom', *Art in America* 80: 139–45.
(1994). *Marketing Modernism in Fin-de-Siècle Europe*, Princeton, N.J.
Joas, Hans (1993). 'Durkheim's Intellectual Development: The Problem of the Emergence of the New Morality and New Institutions as a Leitmotif in Durkheim's Oeuvre', in

Stephen P. Turner (ed.) *Emile Durkheim: Sociologist and Moralist*, London and New York, pp. 229–45.
Johnston, William M. (1972). *The Austrian Mind: An Intellectual and Social History*, Berkeley and Los Angeles.
Jones, Ernest (1953–7). *The Life and Work of Sigmund Freud*, vols. I–III, New York.
Jones, P. (1994). *Rights*, London.
Karl, Barry S. (1974). *Charles E. Merriam and the Study of Politics*, Chicago.
Kavka, G. (1986). *Hobbesian Moral and Political Philosophy*, Princeton, N.J.
Kelly, P. J. (1990). *Utilitarianism and Distributive Justice: Jeremy Bentham and the Civil Law*, Oxford.
Kern, Stephen (1983). *The Culture of Time and Space 1880–1918*, Cambridge, Mass.
King, Richard (1972). *The Party of Eros: Radical Social Thought and the Realm of Freedom*, Chapel Hill, N.C.
Klein, Naomi (2001). 'Reclaiming the Commons', *New Left Review* 9: 81–9.
Klosko, G. (1991). 'Reformist Consent and Political Obligation', *Political Studies* 39: 676–90.
(1992). *The Principle of Fairness and Political Obligation*, Lanham, Md.
Kukathas, C. and Pettit, P. (1990) (eds.). *Rawls' A Theory of Justice and its Critics*, Cambridge.
Kymlicka, W. (1989). *Liberalism, Community, and Culture*, Oxford.
Laborde, Cécile (2000). *Pluralist Thought and the State in Britain and France, 1900–25*, Oxford.
Lacoue-Labarthe, Philippe and Nancy, Jean-Luc (1988 [1978]). *The Literary Absolute: The Theory of Literature in German Romanticism*, trans. Philip Bernard and Cheryl Lester, Albany, N.Y.
Levine, Donald (1995). *Visions of the Sociological Tradition*, Chicago.
Lloyd, Jill (1991). *German Expressionism: Primitivism and Modernity*, New Haven, Conn. and London.
Lockwood, David (1992). *Solidarity and Schism*, Oxford.
Lowi, Theodore J. (1969). *The End of Liberalism*, New York.
Lukács, Georg (1964 [1955]). 'The Ideology of Modernism', in his *Realism in Our Time*, trans. John and Necke Mander, New York, pp. 17–46.
Lukes, Steven (1973). *Emile Durkheim: His Life and Work*, London.
MacCormick, N. (1981). *H. L. A. Hart*, Stanford, Calif.
(1995). 'Sovereignty, Democracy and Subsidiarity', in Richard Bellamy, Vittorio Bufacchi and Dario Castiglione (eds.) *Democracy and Constitutional Culture in the Union of Europe*, London.
McCoy, Charles and Playford, John (1967) (eds.). *Apolitical Politics*, New York.
McLeod, C. (1998). *Liberalism, Justice, and Markets: A Critique of Liberal Equality*, Oxford.
McMylor, P. (1994). *Alisdair MacIntyre: Critic of Modernity*, London.
Mandel, Ernest (1975). *Late Capitalism*, revised edn, trans. Joris de Bres, London.
Mann, Michael (1993). *The Sources of Social Power*, vol. II: *The Rise of Classes and Nation-States, 1760–1914*, Cambridge.
Manuel, Frank E. (1956). *The New World of Henri Saint-Simon*, Cambridge, Mass.
(1962). *The Prophets of Paris*, Cambridge, Mass.
Mapel, D. R. and Nardin, T. (1998) (eds.). *International Society from a Cosmopolitan Perspective*, Princeton, N.J.
Martin, M. (1987). *The Legal Philosophy of H. L. A. Hart: A Critical Appraisal*, Philadelphia.
Mayer, Arno (1981). *The Persistence of the Old Regime: Europe to the Great War*, New York.
Miller, D. (1983). 'Linguistic Philosophy and Political Theory', in D. Miller and L. Siedentop (eds.) *The Nature of Political Theory*, Oxford.
(1999). *Principles of Social Justice*, Cambridge, Mass.
Miller, D. and Walzer, M. (1995) (eds.). *Pluralism, Justice, and Equality*, Oxford.

Moore, Barrington Jr. (1969). *Social Origins of Dictatorship and Democracy*, London.
Muirhead, J. H. (1931). *The Platonic Tradition in Anglo-Saxon Philosophy*, London.
Mulhall, S. and Swift, A. (1996). *Liberals and Communitarians*, 2nd edn, Oxford.
Nicholls, Peter (1995). *Modernisms*, Berkeley and Los Angeles, Calif.
Oppenheim, Felix E. (1975 [1968]). *Moral Principles in Political Philosophy*, New York.
Ott, Hugo (1993). *Martin Heidegger, a Political Life*, trans. Allan Blunden, London.
Owen, David (1994). *Maturity and Modernity: Nietzsche, Weber, Foucault*, London.
Paul, J. (1981) (ed.). *Reading Nozick: Essays on Anarchy, State, and Utopia*, Totowa, N.J.
Pettit, P. (1997). *Republicanism: A Theory of Freedom and Government*, Oxford.
Peukert, Detlef (1989). *Max Webers Diagnose der Moderne*, Göttingen.
Pickering, Mary (1993). *Auguste Comte: An Intellectual Biography*, vol. I, Cambridge.
Pilkington, A. E. (1976). *Bergson and his Influence: A Reassessment*, Cambridge.
Pitkin, Hanna F. (1965–6). 'Obligation and Consent', *American Political Science Review* 59: 990–9 and 60: 39–52.
(1967). *The Concept of Representation*, Berkeley and Los Angeles, Calif.
Plamenatz, J. P. (1938). *Consent, Freedom and Political Obligation*, Oxford; 2nd edn 1968.
Plant, R., Lesser, H. and Taylor-Gooby, P. (1980). *Political Philosophy and Social Welfare*, London.
Plantinga, Theodore (1992). *Historical Understanding in the Thought of Wilhelm Dilthey*, Lewiston, Queenston and Lampeter.
Poggi, Gianfranco (1990). *The State: Its Nature, Development and Prospects*, Cambridge.
Prager, Jeffery (1981). 'Moral Integration and Political Inclusion: A Comparison of Durkheim's and Weber's Theories of Democracy', *Social Forces*, 59(4): 918–50.
Quinton, A. (1967) (ed.). *Political Philosophy*, Oxford.
Rabinbach, Anson (1992). *The Human Motor: Energy, Fatigue and the Origins of Modernity*, Berkeley and Los Angeles, Calif.
Raz, J. (1986). *The Morality of Freedom*, Oxford.
Rescher, N. (1966). *Distributive Justice: A Constructive Critique of the Utilitarian Theory of Distribution*, Indianapolis, Ind. and New York.
Ricci, David M. (1984). *The Tragedy of Political Science: Politics, Scholarship, and Democracy*, New Haven, Conn.
Richter, Melvin (1983 [1964]). *The Politics of Conscience: T. H. Green and his Age*, Lanham, Md.
Rieff, Philip (1959). *Freud: The Mind of the Moralist*, London.
(1966). *The Triumph of the Therapeutic: Uses of Faith After Freud*, New York.
Ringer, Fritz (forthcoming). *Reading Max Weber*, Chicago.
Roazen, Paul (1990). *Encountering Freud: The Politics and Histories of Psychoanalysis*, New Brunswick, N.J.
(1992a [1975]). *Freud and his Followers*, New York.
(1992b [1985]). *Helene Deutsch: A Psychoanalyst's Life*, New York.
(1997 [1976]). *Erik H. Erikson: The Power and Limits of a Vision*, New York.
(1999 [1968]). *Freud: Political and Social Thought*, New Brunswick, N.J.
(2001a). *The Historiography of Psychoanalysis*, New Brunswick, N.J.
(2001b). 'The Exclusion of Erich Fromm from the IPA', *Contemporary Psychoanalysis* 37(1): 5–42.
Robinson, Paul (1969). *The Freudian Left*, New York.
Roemer, J. (1986) (ed.). *Analytical Marxism*, Cambridge.
Rorty, Richard (1993 [1983]). 'Postmodernist Bourgeois Liberalism', in Thomas Docherty (ed.) *Postmodernism: A Reader*, Hemel Hempstead, pp. 323–8.
Rosenberg, Justin (2000). *The Follies of Globalisation Theory*, London.

Ross, Dorothy (1991). *The Origins of American Social Science*, Cambridge.
Ryan, Alan (1995). *John Dewey and the High Tide of American Liberalism*, New York and London.
Schaar, John (1961). *Escape From Authority: The Perspectives of Erich Fromm*, New York.
Schivelbusch, Wolfgang (1986 [1977]). *The Railway Journey: The Industrialization of Time and Space in the Nineteenth Century*, Berkeley and Los Angeles, Calif.
(1995 [1983]). *Disenchanted Night: The Industrialization of Light in the Nineteenth Century*, trans. Angela Davies, Berkeley, Los Angeles and London.
Schmidtz, D. (1990). 'Justifying the State', *Ethics* 101: 89–102.
Schmitt, Carl (1928). *Verfassungslehre*, Berlin.
Schorske, Carl (1979). *Fin-de-Siècle Vienna: Politics and Culture*, New York.
Schumpeter, Joseph (1943). *Capitalism, Socialism and Democracy*, London.
Scott, Alan (2000). 'Capitalism, Weber and Democracy', *Max Weber Studies*, 1(1): 31–53.
Seel, Martin (1989). 'Heidegger und die Ethik des Spiels', in Siegfried Blasche (ed.) *Martin Heidegger: Innen und Aussenansichten*, Forum für Philosophie Bad Homburg, Frankfurt am Main, pp. 244–72.
Seidelman, Raymond with Edward J. Harpham (1985). *Disenchanted Realists: Political Science and the American Crisis, 1884–1984*, Albany, N.Y.
Sen, A. K. (1970). *Collective Choice and Social Welfare*, San Francisco.
(1973). *On Economic Inequality*, New York.
(1982). 'Equality of What?', in A. Sen, *Choice, Welfare, and Measurement*, Oxford.
(1992). *Inequality Reexamined*, Oxford.
Sen, A. K. and Williams, B. A. O. (1982) (eds.). *Utilitarianism and Beyond*, Cambridge.
Sharaf, Myron (1983). *Fury on Earth: A Biography of Wilhelm Reich*, New York.
Shepsle, Kenneth A. (1989). 'Studying Institutions: Some Lessons from the Rational Choice Approach', *Journal of Theoretical Politics* 1: 131–48.
Sher, G. (1987). *Desert*, Princeton, N.J.
Shklar, J. N. (1957). *After Utopia*, Princeton, N.J.
Shue, H. (1980). *Basic Rights: Subsistence, Affluence and U.S. Foreign Policy*, Princeton, N.J.
Sidgwick, Henry (1874). *The Methods of Ethics*, London.
Simmons, A. J. (1979). *Moral Principles and Political Obligations*, Princeton, N.J.
(1996). 'Associative Political Obligations', *Ethics* 106: 247–73.
Simon, W. M. (1963). *European Positivism in the Nineteenth Century: An Essay in Intellectual History*, Ithaca, N. Y.
Simpson, Christopher (1994). *The Science of Coercion: Communication Research and Psychological Warfare, 1945–1960*, Oxford.
Singer, P. (1979). *Practical Ethics*, Cambridge; 2nd ed., 1993.
Skinner, Quentin (1990). *The Return of Grand Theory in the Human Sciences*, Cambridge.
Skocpol, Theda (1979). *States and Social Revolutions: A Comparative Analysis of France, Russia, and China*, Cambridge.
Smart, J. J. C. (1973). 'An Outline of a System of Utilitarian Ethics', in J. J. C. Smart and B. A. O. Williams, *Utilitarianism: For and Against*, Cambridge.
Smith, Bruce Lannes (1969). 'The Mystifying Intellectual History of Harold D. Lasswell', in Arnold A. Rogow (ed.) *Politics, Personality, and Social Science in the Twentieth Century: Essays in Honor of Harold D. Lasswell*, Chicago, pp. 41–105.
Smith, Laurence D. (1986). *Behaviorism and Logical Positivism: A Reassessment of the Alliance*, Stanford, Calif.
Somit, Albert and Tanenhaus, Joseph (1967). *The Development of American Political Science: From Burgess to Behavioralism*, Boston.
Sperber, Manes (1974). *Masks of Loneliness: Alfred Adler in Perspective*, New York.

Spragens, T. A. Jr. (1995). 'Communitarian Liberalism', in A. Etzioni (ed.) *New Communitarian Thinking*, Charlottesville, Va.

Sproule, J. Michael (1997). *Propaganda and Democracy: The American Experience of Media and Mass Persuasion*, Cambridge.

Steel, Ronald (1980). *Walter Lippmann and the American Century*, Boston.

Steiner, H. (1994). *An Essay on Rights*, Oxford.

Sultan, Stanley (1987). *Eliot, Joyce and Company*, New York.

Tam, H. (1998). *Communitarianism: A New Agenda for Politics and Citizenship*, London.

Taruskin, Richard (1982). 'From Firebird to The Rite: Folk Elements in Stravinsky's Scores', *Ballet Review* 10: 72–87.

Taylor, Seth (1990). *Left-wing Nietzscheans: The Politics of German Expressionism 1910–1920*, Berlin and New York.

Thompson, Clara (1950). *Psychoanalysis: Evolution and Development*, New York.

Tilly, Charles (1992). *Coercion, Capital, and the European States, AD 990–1992*, Oxford.

Tiryakian, Edward. A. (1965). 'A Problem for the Sociology of Knowledge: The Mutual Unawareness of Emile Durkheim and Max Weber', *European Journal of Sociology* 7(2): 330–6.

Tully, J. with Weinstock, D. M. (1994) (eds.). *Philosophy in an Age of Pluralism: The Philosophy of Charles Taylor in Question*, Cambridge.

Waldron, J. (1984). *Theories of Rights*, Oxford.

Waxman, Chaim (1968) (ed.). *The End of Ideology Debate*, New York.

Weindling, Paul Julian (1991). *Darwinism and Social Darwinism in Imperial Germany: The Contribution of the Cell Biologist Oscar Hertwig (1849–1922)*, Stuttgart and New York.

Wellman, C. H. (1997). 'Associative Allegiances and Political Obligations', *Social Theory and Practice* 23: 181–204.

Williams, B. A. O. (1973). 'A Critique of Utilitarianism' in J. C. C. Smart and B. A. O. Williams, *Utilitarianism: For and Against*, Cambridge.

Wohl, Robert (1994). *A Passion for Wings: Aviation and the Western Imagination 1908–1918*, New Haven, Conn. and London.

Wolfe, Alan and Surkin, Martin (1970) (eds.). *An End to Political Science*, New York.

Wolff, J. (1991). *Robert Nozick: Property, Justice and the Minimal State*, Oxford.

Wolff, R. P. (1970). *In Defense of Anarchism*, New York; 3rd edn Berkeley, Calif., 1998.

(1977). *Understanding Rawls: A Reconstruction and Critique of A Theory of Justice*, Princeton, N.J.

Wolin, Sheldon S. (1960). *Politics and Vision: Continuity and Innovation in Western Political Thought*, London.

Woodward, Ralph Lee Jr. (1971). *Positivism in Latin America, 1850–1900*, Lexington, Mass., Toronto and London.

Worringer, Wilhelm (1953 [1908]). *Abstraction and Empathy: A Contribution to the Psychology of Style*, trans. Michael Bullock, London.

Young, Iris Marion (1990). *Justice and the Politics of Difference*, Princeton, N.J. and Oxford.

Zweig, Stefan (1953). *The World of Yesterday*, London.

Part IV: New social movements and the politics of difference

Alberti, Johanna (1989). *Beyond Suffrage: Feminists in War and Peace 1914–28*, Basingstoke.

Amos, Valerie and Parmar, Pratibha (1984). 'Challenging Imperial Feminism', *Feminist Review* 17: 3–19.

Ang, Ien (1995). 'I'm a feminist but... "Other" Women and Postnational Feminism', in Barbara Caine and Rosemary Pringle (eds.) *Transitions: New Australian Feminisms*, New York, pp. 57–73.

Bibliography

Angell, Norman (1909a). *Europe's Optical Illusion*, London.

(1909b). *The Great Illusion*, London.

Angus, H. F. (1937). *The Problem of Peaceful Change in the Pacific Area*, London.

Bahro, Rudolf (1986). *Building the Green Movement*, trans. Mary Tyler, London.

Baier, Annette (1994). 'The Need for More than Justice', in *Moral Prejudices*, Cambridge, Mass.

Ball, Terence (2001). 'New Ethics for Old? Or, How (Not) to Think About Future Generations', in Mathew Humphrey (ed.) *Political Theory and the Environment*, London, pp. 89–110.

Ballard, Frank (1915). *The Mistakes of Pacifism, or Why a Christian Can Have Anything to Do with War*, London.

Banks, Olive (1981). *Faces of Feminism. A Study of Feminism as a Social Movement*, New York.

Barrett, Michele (1980). *Women's Oppression Today. Problems in Marxist Feminist Analysis*, London.

Barry, Brian (1989). *Democracy, Power, and Justice*, Oxford.

(2000). *Culture and Equality*, Cambridge.

Barry, Brian and Sikora, R. I. (1978) (eds.). *Obligations to Future Generations*, Philadelphia.

Bartky, Sandra Lee (1990). *Femininity and Domination. Studies in the Phenomenology of Oppression*, London.

Beauvoir, Simone de (1972). *The Second Sex*, trans. and ed. H. M. Parshley, Harmondsworth.

Bellamy, Richard (1999). *Liberalism and Pluralism: Towards a Politics of Compromise*, London.

Benhabib, Seyla (1982). 'The Generalised and the Concrete Other', in *Situating the Self*, Cambridge, pp. 148–77.

(1996) (ed.). *Democracy and Difference: Contesting the Boundaries of the Political*, Princeton, N.J.

Benhabib, Seyla, Butler, Judith, Cornell, Drucilla and Fraser, Nancy (1995). *Feminist Contributions*, London.

Benjamin, Jessica (1990). *The Bonds of Love: Psychoanalysis, Feminism and the Problem of Domination*, London.

Berry, Wendell (1981). *The Gift of Good Land*, San Francisco.

Bhabha, Homi (1994). *The Location of Culture*, London.

Bhavnani, Kum Kum (2001). *Feminism and Race*, Oxford.

Bloch, I. S. (1899). *Is War Now Impossible?*, London (a translation of the last of the six volumes of *The War of the Future*, which had appeared in Russian and French the previous year).

Bock, Gisela and Thane, Pat (1991). *Maternity and Gender Politics. Women and the Rise of the European Welfare State, 1880s–1950s*, London.

Bolt, Christine (1993). *The Women's Movements in the United States and Britain from the 1870s to the 1920s*, Hemel Hempstead.

Le Bon, Gustave (1895). *Psychologie des foules*, Paris.

Bookchin, Murray (1990). *Remaking Society: Pathways to a Green Future*, Boston.

Bordo, Susan (1987). 'The Cartesian Masculinisation of Thought', in Sandra Harding and Jean O'Barr (eds.) *Sex and Scientific Enquiry*, Chicago, pp. 247–64.

(1993). *Unbearable Weight: Feminism, Western Culture and the Body*, Berkeley, Calif.

Bradshaw, David (1996), 'The Flight from Gaza: Aldous Huxley's Involvement in the Peace Pledge Union in the Context of His Overall Intellectual Development', in B. Nugel (ed.) *Now More Than Ever: Proceedings of the Aldous Huxley Centenary Symposium, Münster 1994*, Berlin, pp. 9–27.

Braidotti, Rosi (1991). *Patterns of Dissonance. A Study of Women in Contemporary Philosophy*, Cambridge.

Brailsford, H. N. (1914). *The War of Steel and Gold: A Study of the Armed Peace*, London.

Bramwell, Anna (1989). *Ecology in the 20th Century: A History*, New Haven, Conn.
Brennan, Teresa (1989) (ed.). *Between Feminism and Psychoanalysis*, London.
(1993). *History after Lacan*, London.
Brinton, Henry (1935) (ed.). *Does Capitalism Cause War?*, London.
Brown, Wendy (1995). *States of Injury*, Princeton, N.J.
Brownmiller, Susan (1976). *Against Our Will: Men, Women and Rape*, London.
(1984). *Femininity*, London.
Bubeck, Diemut (1995). *Care, Gender and Justice*, Oxford.
Burke, C., Schor, Naomi and Whitford, Margaret (1994). *Engaging with Irigaray: Feminist Philosophy and Modern European Thought*, New York.
Butler, Judith (1989). 'Gendering the Body. Beauvoir's Philosophical Contribution', in A. Garry and M. Pearsall (eds.) *Women, Knowledge and Reality*, Boston, pp. 253–62.
(1990). *Gender Trouble: Feminism and the Subversion of Identity*, London.
Caine, Barbara (1997). *English Feminism 1780–1980*, Oxford.
Caldwell, Lynton K. (1972). *In Defense of Earth: International Protection of the Biosphere*, Bloomington, Ind.
Callicott, J. Baird (1989). *In Defense of the Land Ethic*, Albany, N.Y.
Canovan, Margaret (1977). *The Political Thought of Hannah Arendt*, London.
(1987). 'Rousseau's Two Concepts of Citizenship', in Ellen Kennedy and Susan Mendus (eds.) *Women in Western Political Theory*, Brighton.
Card, Claudia (2002). *The Cambridge Companion to Simone de Beauvoir*, Cambridge.
Cardy, Maren Lockwood (1974). *The New Feminist Movement*, New York.
Carens, Joseph (2000). *Culture, Citizenship and Community: A Contextual Exploration of Justice as Evenhandedness*, Oxford.
Carr, E. H. (1936). 'Public Opinion as a Safeguard of Peace', *International Affairs* 15: 846–62.
(1939). *The Twenty Years' Crisis 1919–1939: An Introduction to the Study of International Relations*, London.
Carson, Rachel (1962). *Silent Spring*, New York.
Carter, April (1973). *Direct Action and Liberal Democracy*, London.
Carter, April, Hoggett, David and Roberts, Adam (1970). *Non-Violent Action. A Selected Bibliography*, revised and enlarged edn, London and Haverford, Penn.
Catton, William R. (1980). *Overshoot: The Ecological Basis of Revolutionary Change*, Urbana, Ill.
Ceadel, Martin (1980). *Pacifism in Britain 1914–1945: The Defining of a Faith*, Oxford.
(1987). *Thinking about Peace and War*, Oxford.
(1991). 'Supranationalism in the British Peace Movement During the Early Twentieth Century', in Andrea Bosco (ed.) *The Federal Idea*, vol. I: *The History of Federalism from the Enlightenment to 1945*, pp. 169–91.
(1996). *The Origins of War Prevention: The British Peace Movement and International Relations, 1730–1854*, Oxford.
(2000). *Semi-Detached Idealists: The British Peace Movement and International Relations, 1854–1945*, Oxford.
Chanter, Tina (1995). *Ethics of Eros. Irigaray's Reading of the Philosophers*, London.
Chatfield, Charles (1971). *For Peace and Justice: Pacifism in America 1914–1941*, Knoxville, Tenn.
Chodorow, Nancy (1978). *The Reproduction of Mothering*, Berkeley, Calif.
Clements, Barbara Evans (1979). *Bolshevik Feminist: The Life of Alexandra Kollontai*, Bloomington, Ind.
Code, Lorraine (1987). *Epistemic Responsibility*, Hanover, N.H.
Commoner, Barry (1971). *The Closing Circle*, New York.

Connolly, William (1991). *Identity/Difference*, Ithaca, N.Y.
(1995). *The Ethos of Pluralization*, Minneapolis, Minn.
Cooper, Sandi (1991). *Patriotic Pacifism: Waging War on War in Europe, 1815–1914*, New York.
Cornell, Drucilla (1992). 'Gender, Sex and Equivalent Rights', in Judith Butler and Joan W. Scott (eds.) *Feminists Theorise the Political*, London.
(1995). *The Imaginary Domain: Abortion, Pornography and Sexual Harassment*, London.
(2000) (ed.). *Feminism and Pornography*, Oxford.
Crook, Paul (1994). *Darwinism, War and History: The Debate Over the Biology of War from the 'Origin of Species' to the First World War*, Cambridge.
Cruttwell, C. R. M. F. (1937). *A History of Peaceful Change in the Modern World*, London.
Dagger, Richard (2003). 'Stopping Sprawl for the Good of All: The Case for Civic Environmentalism', *Journal of Social Philosophy* 34: 28–43.
de Jong van Beek en Donk, B. (1917). *Neutral Europe and the League of Nations*, The Hague.
Delphy, Christine (1977). *The Main Enemy*, London.
Delphy, Christine and Leonard, Diana (1992). *Familiar Exploitation: A New Analysis of Marriage in Contemporary Western Societies*, Cambridge.
Derrida, Jacques (1992). *The Other Heading: Reflections on Today's Europe*, trans. Pascale-Anne Brault and Michael Naas, Bloomington, Ind.
de-Shalit, Avner (1995). *Why Posterity Matters: Environmental Policies and Future Generations*, London.
Devall, Bill and Sessions, George (1985). *Deep Ecology: Living as if Nature Mattered*, Salt Lake City.
Deveaux, Monique (2000). *Cultural Pluralism and the Dilemmas of Justice*, Ithaca, N.Y.
Dickinson, G. Lowes (1915). *After the War*, London.
(1916). *The European Anarchy*, London.
(1917). *The Choice Before Us*, London.
(1926). *The International Anarchy 1904–1914*, London.
Dietz, Mary G. (1985). 'Citizenship with a Feminist Face: The Trouble with Maternal Thinking', *Political Theory* 13: 19–37.
(1998). 'Context is All: Feminism and Theories of Citizenship', in Anne Phillips (ed.) *Feminism and Politics*, Oxford, pp. 378–400.
Dobson, Andrew (1995). *Green Political Thought*, 2nd edn, London.
(1998). *Justice and the Environment*, Oxford.
Doyle, Michael W. (1983). 'Kant, Liberal Legacies and Foreign Affairs', *Philosophy and Public Affairs* 12: 205–35.
Dryzek, John (1997). *The Politics of the Earth: Environmental Discourses*, Oxford.
(2000). *Deliberative Democracy and Beyond: Liberals, Critics, Contestations*, Oxford.
Dryzek, John and Schlosberg, David (1998) (eds.). *Debating the Earth*, Oxford.
DuCille, Ann (1994). 'The Occult of True Black Womanhood: Critical Demeanour and Black Feminist Studies', *Signs. Journal of Women in Culture and Society* 19: 591–629.
Dworkin, Andrea (1981). *Pornography: Men Possessing Women*, London.
Eaubonne, Françoise d' (1974). *Féminisme ou la mort*, Paris.
(1978). *Féminisme-Ecologie: révolution ou mutation*, Paris.
Ehrenfeld, David (1978). *The Arrogance of Humanism*, New York.
Ehrlich, Paul R. (1969). *The Population Bomb*, San Francisco.
Eisenstein, Zillah R. (1979). *Capitalist Patriarchy and the Case for Socialist Feminism*, New York.
(1981). *The Radical Future of Liberal Feminism*, New York.
(1982). 'The Sexual Politics of the New Right: Understanding the "Crisis of Liberalism" for the 1980's', *Signs. Journal of Women in Culture and Society* 7: 567–88.
(1988). *The Female Body and the Law*, Berkeley, Calif.

Elshtain, Jean (1981). *Public Man, Private Woman: Women in Social and Political Thought*, Princeton, N.J.

Engels, Friedrich (1985). *The Origin of the Family, Private Property and the State*, Harmondsworth.

Etzioni, Amitai (1962). *The Hard Way to Peace: A New Strategy*, New York.

(1964). *Winning Without War*, New York.

Evans, Richard (1977). *The Feminists. Women's Emancipation Movements in Europe, America and Australia, 1840–1920*, London.

(1987). *Comrades and Sisters. Feminism, Socialism and Pacifism in Europe, 1870–1945*, Brighton.

Evans, Ruth (1998). *Simone de Beauvoir's 'The Second Sex': New Interdisciplinary Essays*, Manchester.

Evans, Sara (1979). *Personal Politics: The Roots of Women's Liberation in the Civil Rights Movement and the New Left*, New York.

Fanon, Frantz (1963). *The Wretched of the Earth*, trans. C. Farrington, New York.

Farnsworth, Beatrice (1980). *Aleksandra Kollontai: Socialism, Feminism and the Bolshevik Revolution*, Stanford, Calif.

Ferry, Luc (1995). *The New Ecological Order*, trans. Carol Volk, Chicago.

Finnis, John, Boyle, Joseph and Grisez, Germain (1987). *Nuclear Deterrence, Morality and Realism*, Oxford.

Firestone, Shulamith (1970). *The Dialectic of Sex. The Case for Feminist Revolution*, New York.

Flax, Jane (1983). 'Political Philosophy and the Patriarchal Unconscious: A Psychoanalytic Perspective on Epistemology and Metaphysics', in Sandra Harding and Merrill Hintikka (eds.) *Discovering Reality*, Dordrecht, pp. 245–81.

(1990). *Thinking Fragments: Psychoanalysis, Feminism and Postmodernism in the Contemporary West*, Berkeley Calif.

Foreman, Dave (1991). *Confessions of an Eco-Warrior*, New York.

Foucault, Michel (1982). 'The Subject and Power', in H. L. Dreyfus and P. Rabinow (eds.) *Michel Foucault: Beyond Structuralism and Hermeneutics*, Chicago, pp. 208–26.

Frye, Marilyn (1983). *The Politics of Reality*, Trumansburg, N.Y.

Gagnon, A.-G. and Tully James (2001) (eds.). *Multinational Democracies*, Cambridge.

Gallop, Jane (1982). *Between Feminism and Psychoanalysis*, London.

Galtung, Johan (1969). 'Violence, Peace, and Peace Research', *Journal of Peace Research* 6: 167–91.

Gatens, Moira (1991). *Feminism and Philosophy: Perspectives on Difference and Equality*, Cambridge.

(1996). *Imaginary Bodies: Ethics, Power and Corporeality*, London.

Gatens, Moira and Lloyd, Genevieve (1999). *Collective Imaginings*, London.

Gilligan, Carol (1982). *In a Different Voice: Psychological Theory and Women's Development*, Cambridge, Mass.

Goldman, Emma (1972). *Red Emma Speaks. Selected Speeches and Writings of the Anarchist and Feminist Emma Goldman*, ed. A. Kates, New York.

(1987). *Living my Life*, vol. I, London.

Goldsmith, Edward *et al.* (1972). 'A Blueprint for Survival', *The Ecologist* 2(1): 1–44.

Goodin, Robert E. (1992). *Green Political Theory*, Cambridge.

Gregg, Richard B. (1936 [1934]), *The Power of Non-Violence*, London.

Grosz, Elizabeth (1989). *Sexual Subversions. Three French Feminists*, Sydney.

Grundmann, Reiner (1991). *Marxism and Ecology*, Oxford.

Die Grünen (1983). *Programme of the German Green Party*, trans. Hans Fernbach, London.

Gutmann, Amy (1994) (ed.). *Multiculturalism*, Princeton, N.J.

Haaland, Bonnie (1993). *Emma Goldman: Sexuality and the Impurity of the State*, Montreal.

Habermas, Jürgen (1994). 'Discourse Ethics: Notes on a Program of Philosophical Justification', in *Moral Consciousness and Communicative Action*, trans. Christian Lenhardt and S. W. Nicholsen, Cambridge, Mass, pp. 43–115.

(1995). 'Reconciliation Through the Use of Public Reason', *Journal of Philosophy*, 92(3): 109–31.

(1996). *Between Facts and Norms*, trans. William Rehg, Cambridge, Mass.

Haeckel, Ernst (1904). *The Wonders of Life*, London.

Hampton, Jean (1993). 'Feminist Contractarianism', in Louise M. Anthony and Charlotte Witt (eds.) *A Mind of One's Own. Feminist Essays on Reason and Objectivity*, Boulder, Colo.

Hardin, Garrett (1968). 'The Tragedy of the Commons', *Science* 162: 1243–8.

Harrison, Brian (1987). *Prudent Revolutionaries: Portraits of British Feminists between the Wars*, Oxford.

Hartman, Heidi (1981a). 'The Unhappy Marriage of Marxism and Feminism: Towards a More Progressive Union', in Lydia Sargent (ed.) *Women and Revolution*, London.

(1981b). 'The Family as the Locus of Gender, Class and Political Struggle. The Example of Housework', *in Signs: Journal of Women in Culture and Society* 6: 109–34.

Hartsock, Nancy C. M. (1979). 'Feminist Theory and the Development of Revolutionary Consciousness', in Zillah R. Eisenstein, *Capitalist Patriarchy and the Case for Socialist Feminism*, New York.

Havemann, Paul (1999) (ed.). *Indigenous Peoples' Rights in Australia, Canada and New Zealand*, Oxford.

Heilbroner, Robert L. (1980). *An Inquiry into the Human Prospect*, New York.

Hobson, J. A. (1901). *The Psychology of Jingoism*, London.

(1902). *Imperialism: A Study*, London.

Holroyd, Michael (1967). *Lytton Strachey: A Critical Biography*, 2 vols., London.

Honig, Bonnie (1993). *Political Theory and the Displacement of Politics*, Ithaca, N.Y.

(1995). *Feminist Interpretations of Hannah Arendt*, University Park, Penn.

Honneth, Axel (1995). *The Struggle for Recognition: The Moral Grammar of Social Conflicts*, trans. J. Anderson, Cambridge.

hooks, bell (1984). *Feminist Theory from Margin to Center*, Boston.

Hughes, Jonathan (2000). *Ecology and Historical Materialism*, Cambridge.

Huxley, Aldous (1936), *What Are You Going To Do About It? The Case for Constructive Peace*, London.

(1937). *Ends and Means: An Inquiry into the Nature of Ideals and into the Methods Employed for their Realisation*, London.

Hyatt, John (1972). *Pacifism: A Selected Bibliography*, London.

Irigaray, Luce (1993). *Je, Tu, Nous: Towards a Culture of Difference*, trans. Alison Martin, London.

Ivison, Duncan, Patton, Paul and Sanders, Douglas (2000) (eds.). *Political Theory and the Rights of Indigenous Peoples*, Melbourne.

Jaggar, Alison (1983). *Feminist Politics and Human Nature*, Totowa, N.J.

James, Susan (1992). 'The Good Enough Citizen: Citizenship and Independence', in Gisela Bock and Susan James (eds.) *Beyond Equality and Difference. Citizenship, Feminist Politics and Female Subjectivity*, London, pp. 48–65.

Johnson, James Turner (1975). *Ideology, Reason, and the Limitation of War: Religious and Secular Concepts, 1200–1740*, Princeton, N.J.

(1981). *Just War Tradition and the Restraint of War: A Moral and Historical Inquiry*, Princeton, N.J.

(1984). *Can Modern War Be Just?*, New Haven, Conn.

Johnson, Lawrence E. (1991). *A Morally Deep World: An Essay on Moral Significance and Environmental Ethics*, Cambridge.

Jones, Kathleen B. (1993). *Compassionate Authority: Democracy and the Representation of Women*, London.

Jordan, Jane (2001). *Josephine Butler*, London.

Kant, Immanuel (1903 [1795]). *Perpetual Peace: A Philosophical Essay*, trans. with intro. and notes M. Campbell-Smith, London.

Katz, Eric, Light, Andrew and Rothenberg, David (2000) (eds.). *Beneath the Surface: Critical Essays in the Philosophy of Deep Ecology*, Cambridge, Mass.

Kelly, Paul and Held, David (2002) (eds.). *Multiculturalism Reconsidered*, Cambridge.

Kelly, Petra (1994). *Thinking Green! Essays on Environmentalism, Feminism and Nonviolence*, Berkeley, Calif.

Kent, Susan Kingsley (1990). *Sex and Suffrage in Britain, 1860–1914*, London.

(1993). *Making Peace: The Reconstruction of Gender in Interwar Britain*, Princeton, N.J.

Keohane, Robert O. and Nye, Joseph S. (1971) (eds.). *Transnational Relations and World Politics*, Cambridge, Mass.

(1977). *Power and Interdependence*, Boston, Mass.

Kiss, Elizabeth (1997). 'Alchemy or Fool's Gold. Assessing Feminist Doubts about Rights', in Mary Lyndon Shanley and Uma Narayan (eds.) *Reconstructing Political Theory*, Cambridge.

Kollontai, Alexandra (1977). *Selected Writings*, trans and ed. A. Holt, London.

(1984a). *Communism and the Family*, London.

(1984b). *Sexual Relations and the Class Struggle*, London.

Kraus, Peter (2000). 'Political Unity and Linguistic Diversity in Europe', *Archives Européennes de Sociologie* 41(1): 137–62.

Kymlicka, Will (1991). *Liberalism, Community, and Culture*, Oxford.

(1995). *Multicultural Citizenship*, Oxford.

(1999). *Finding Our Way: Rethinking Ethnocultural Relations in Canada*, Oxford.

Kymlicka, Will and Norman Wayne (2000) (eds.). *Citizenship in Diverse Societies*, Oxford.

Lacey, Nicola (1998). *Unspeakable Subjects: Feminist Essays in Legal and Social Theory*, Oxford.

Laden, Anthony (2001). *Reasonably Radical: Deliberative Liberalism and the Politics of Identity*, Ithaca, N.Y.

Landes, Joan (1998) (ed.). *Feminism, the Public and the Private*, Oxford.

Lane, Ralph [Norman Angell] (1903). *Patriotism under Three Flags: A Plea for Rationalism in Politics*, London.

Leiss, William (1972). *The Domination of Nature*, New York.

Leopold, Aldo (1949). *A Sand County Almanac*, Oxford and New York.

Lewis, Jane (1984). *Women in England, 1870–1950: Sexual Divisions and Social Change*, Brighton.

Lewy, Guenther (1988). *Peace or Revolution: The Moral Crisis of American Pacifism*, Grand Rapids, Mich.

Light, Andrew (2001). 'The Urban Blind Spot in Environmental Ethics', in Mathew Humphrey (ed.) *Political Theory and the Environment*, London, pp. 7–35.

List, Peter C. (1993) (ed.). *Radical Environmentalism: Philosophy and Tactics*, Belmont, Calif.

Lloyd, Genevieve (1984). *The Man of Reason: 'Male' and 'Female' in Western Philosophy*, London.

Locke, John (1992 [1690]). *Two Treatises of Government*, Cambridge.

Lugones, Maria (1996). 'Playfulness, World Travelling and Loving Perception', in Ann Garry and Marilyn Pearsall (eds.) *Women, Knowledge and Reality*, London, pp. 419–33.

Mackay, Louis and Fernbach, David (1983) (eds.). *Nuclear-Free Defence*, London.

Mackenzie, Catriona (1998). 'A Certain Lack of Symmetry: Beauvoir on Autonomous Agency and Women's Embodiment', in Ruth Evans (ed.) *Simone de Beauvoir's 'The Second Sex'*, Manchester.
MacKinnon, Catherine A. (1989). *Towards a Feminist Theory of the State*, Cambridge, Mass.
McKinnon, Catriona and Hampsher-Monk Iain (2000). 'Introduction', in C. McKinnon and I. Hampsher-Monk (eds.) *The Demands of Citizenship*, London and New York.
Manning, C. A. W. (1937) (ed.). *Peaceful Change: An International Problem*, London.
Mansbridge, Jane (1993). 'Feminism and Democratic Community', in John W. Chapman and Ian Shapiro (eds.) *Democratic Community*, NOMOS vol. XXXV, New York.
Mappen, Ellen F. (1986). 'Strategists for Change: Socialist Feminist Approaches to the Problem of Women's Work', in Angela V. John (ed.) *Unequal Opportunities: Women's Employment in England 1800–1918*, Oxford.
Maynard, Mary (1994). 'Race, Gender and the Concept of Difference in Feminist Thought', in H. Afsha and M. Maynard (eds.) *The Dynamics of Race and Gender*, London, pp. 9–25.
Meehan, Elizabeth (1990). 'British Feminism from the 1960s to the 1980s', in Harold L. Smith (ed.) *British Feminism in the Twentieth Century*, Aldershot, pp. 189–204.
Miller, David (1995). *On Nationality*, Oxford.
Millett, Kate (1977). *Sexual Politics*, London.
Minow, Martha (1990). *Making all the Difference*, Ithaca, N.Y.
Mitchell, Juliet (1971). *Women's Estate*, Harmondsworth.
(1974). *Psychoanalysis and Feminism*, Harmondsworth.
Moi, Toril (1987). *French Feminist Thought. A Reader*, Oxford.
Morgenthau, Hans J. (1949). *Politics Among Nations: The Struggle for Power and Peace*, New York.
Murry, John Middleton (1937). *The Necessity of Pacifism*, London.
(1938). *The Pledge of Peace*, London.
Muste, A. J. (1947). *Not By Might. Christianity: The Way to Human Decency*, New York.
Naess, Arne (1989). *Ecology, Community and Lifestyle: Outline of an Ecosophy*, trans. and ed. David Rothenberg, Cambridge.
Nash, Roderick Frazier (1989). *The Rights of Nature: A History of Environmental Ethics*, Madison, Wis.
Nicholson, Linda (1987). 'Feminism and Marx: Integrating Kinship with the Economic', in Seyla Benhabib and Drucilla Cornell (eds.) *Feminism as Critique*, Cambridge, pp. 16–30.
(1990). *Feminism/Postmodernism*, London.
Noddings, Nel (1984). *Caring: A Feminine Approach to Ethics and Moral Education*, Berkeley, Calif.
Novicow, Jacques (1893). *Les luttes entre sociétés humaines et leurs phases successives*, Paris.
(1912), *War and its Alleged Benefits*, London.
Nussbaum, Martha (1999). 'The Professor of Parody: The Hip Defeatist Feminism of Judith Butler', *New Republic* 22 February: 37–45.
O'Brien, Mary (1979). 'Reproducing Marxist Man', in Lorenne M. G. Clark and Lynda Lange (eds.) *The Sexism of Social and Political Theory: Women and Reproduction from Plato to Nietzsche*, Toronto, pp. 99–116.
Oelschlaeger, Max (1991). *The Age of Ecology: From Prehistory to the Age of Ecology*, New Haven, Conn.
Okin, Susan (1989). *Justice, Gender and the Family*, New York.
(1991). 'Gender, the Public and the Private', in David Held (ed.) *Political Theory Today*, Cambridge, pp. 67–90.
O'Neill, John (1993). *Ecology, Policy and Politics: Human Well-Being and the Natural World*, London

O'Neill, Michael and Austin Dennis (2000) (eds.). 'Democracy and Cultural Diversity', special edition of *Parliamentary Affairs* 53(1).

Ong, Aihwa (1988). 'Colonialism and Modernity: Feminist Re-presentations of Women in Non-Western Societies', *Inscriptions* 3(4): 79–93.

Ophuls, William (1977). *Ecology and the Politics of Scarcity: Prologue to a Theory of the Steady State*, San Francisco.

Ortner, Sherry (1974). 'Is Female to Male as Nature is to Culture?', in Michelle Z. Rosaldo and Louise Lampere (eds.) *Woman, Culture and Society*, Stanford, Calif.

Ostrom, Elinor (1991). *Governing the Commons*, Cambridge.

Parekh, Bhikhu (2000). *Rethinking Multiculturalism: Cultural Diversity and Political Theory*, Cambridge, Mass.

Parsons, Howard (1977) (ed.). *Marx and Engels on Ecology*, Westport, Conn.

Partridge, Ernest (1981) (ed.). *Responsibilities to Future Generations*, Buffalo, N.Y.

Passmore, John (1980). *Man's Responsibility for Nature*, 2nd edn, London.

Pateman, Carol (1988). *The Sexual Contract*, Cambridge.

(1989). *The Disorder of Women*, Cambridge.

Pateman, Carole and Gross, Elizabeth (1986). *Feminist Challenges. Social and Political Theory*, Sydney.

Phillips, Anne (1987) (ed.). Introduction to *Feminism and Equality*, Oxford.

(1995). *The Politics of Presence*, Oxford.

(2002). 'Feminism and the Politics of Difference, Or Where Have All the Women Gone?', in S. James and S. Palmer (eds.) *Visible Women*, Oxford, pp. 11–28.

Plumwood, Val (1993). *Feminism and the Mastery of Nature*, London.

Pois, Robert A. (1986). *National Socialism and the Religion of Nature*, London.

Ponsonby, Arthur (1925). *Now is the Time: An Appeal for Peace*, London.

Poole, Ross (1999). *Nation and Identity*, London and New York.

Porritt, Jonathon (1984). *Seeing Green: The Politics of Ecology Explained*, London.

Porter, Cathy (1980). *Alexandra Kollontai: A Biography*, London.

Porter, Roy (1997). *The Greatest Benefit to Mankind: A Medical History of Humanity from Antiquity to the Present*, London.

Proceedings of the 10th Universal Peace Congress (1901). Glasgow.

Ramsey, Paul (1961). *War and the Christian Conscience: How Shall Modern War Be Conducted Justly?*, Durham, N.C.

(1988). *Speak up for Just War or Pacifism*, University Park, Penn.

Rawls, John (1971). *A Theory of Justice*, Cambridge Mass.

(1993). *Political Liberalism*, New York.

(1995). 'Reply to Habermas', *Journal of Philosophy*, 92(3): 132–80.

(1998). *Collected Papers*, Cambridge, Mass.

Rendall, Jane (1985). *The Origins of Modern Feminism: Women in Britain, France and the United States 1780–1860*, Basingstoke.

Rhode, Deborah (1992). 'The Politics of Paradigms: Gender Difference and Gender Disadvantage', in G. Bock and S. James (eds.) *Beyond Equality and Difference: Citizenship, Feminist Politics and Female Subjectivity*, London.

Rich, Adrienne (1987). *Blood, Bread and Poetry: Selected Prose 1979–1985*, London.

Richmond, Sarah (2000). 'Feminism and Psychoanalysis: Using Melanie Klein', in Miranda Fricker and Jennifer Hornsby (eds.) *The Cambridge Companion to Feminism in Philosophy*, Cambridge.

Roberts, Adam (1915). 'The Question of Christian Duty in Wartime', in Joan M. Fry (ed.) *Christ and Peace: A Discussion of some Fundamental Issues Raised by the War*, London, pp. 17–33.

Roberts, Adam (1967) (ed.). *The Strategy of Civilian Defence*, London.
Rowbotham, Sheila (1992). *Women in Movement: Feminism and Social Action*, London.
Ruddick, Sara (1989). *Maternal Thinking: Towards a Politics of Peace*, London.
Russell, Bertrand (1936). *Which Way to Peace?*, London.
Sagoff, Mark (1988). *The Economy of the Earth: Philosophy, Law, and the Environment*, Cambridge.
Said, Edward W. (1993). *Culture and Imperialism*, New York.
Salleh, Ariel (1997). *Ecofeminism as Politics*, London.
Sapiro, Virginia (1981). 'When are Interests Interesting? The Problem of Political Representation of Women', *American Political Science Review* 75: 701–16.
Sarah, Elizabeth (1983). 'Christabel Pankhurst. Reclaiming her Power', in Dale Spender (ed.) *Feminist Theorists: Three Centuries of Key Women Thinkers*, New York.
Schumacher, E. F. (1973). *Small is Beautiful: Economics as if People Mattered*, New York.
Scott, Joan Wallach (1996). 'Gender: A Useful Category of Historical Analysis', in *Feminism and History*, Oxford.
Sessions, George (1995) (ed.). *Ecology for the 21st Century*, Boston.
Sevenhuijsen, Selma (1998). *Citizenship and the Ethics of Care. Feminist Considerations on Justice, Morality and Politics*, London.
Shapiro, Judith (2001). *Mao's War Against Nature: Politics and the Environment in Revolutionary China*, Cambridge.
Sharp, Gene (1973). *The Politics of Nonviolent Action*, Boston.
Shaw, Jo (1999). 'Postnational Constitutionalism in the European Union', *Journal of European Public Policy*, special issue 6(4): 579–97.
Shiva, Vandana (1988). *Staying Alive: Women, Ecology and Development in India*, London.
Simon, Julian and Kahn, Herman (1984) (eds.). *The Resourceful Earth*, New York.
Skinner, Quentin (1996). *Reason and Rhetoric in the Philosophy of Hobbes*, Cambridge.
Smith, Harold L. (1981). 'The Problem of Equal Pay for Equal Work in Great Britain during World War II', *Journal of Modern History* 53: 652–72.
Spelman, Elizabeth (1988). *Inessential Woman: Problems of Exclusion in Feminist Thought*, Boston.
Squires, Judith (2000). 'The State in (and of) Feminist Visions of Political Citizenship', in Catriona McKinnon and Iain Hampsher-Monk (eds.) *The Demands of Citizenship*, London.
Stannard, David E. (1992). *American Holocaust: Columbus and the Conquest of the New World*, Oxford.
Stites, Richard (1978). *The Women's Liberation Movement in Russia. Feminism, Nihilism and Bolshevism 1860–1930*, Princeton, N.J.
(1981). 'Alexandra Kollontai and the Russian Revolution', in Jane Slaughter and Robert Kern (eds.) *European Women on the Left. Socialism, Feminism and the Problems Faced by Political Women, 1880 to the Present*, Westport, Conn., pp. 101–23.
Strachey, John (1940). *Federalism or Socialism?*, London.
Strathern, Marilyn (1987). 'An Awkward Relationship: The Case of Feminism and Anthropology', *Signs* 12(2): 276–92.
Taylor, A. J. P. (1957). *The Trouble Makers: Dissent over Foreign Policy 1792–1939*, London.
Taylor, Charles (1994). 'The Politics of Recognition', in A. Gutmann (ed.) *Multiculturalism*, Princeton, N.J., pp. 25–74.
Taylor, Paul W. (1986). *Respect for Nature: A Theory of Environmental Ethics*, Princeton, N.J.
Thomas, Keith (1984). *Man and the Natural World: Changing Attitudes in England 1500–1800*, London.
Thompson, E. P. (1980). 'Notes on Exterminism, the Last Stage of Civilisation', *New Left Review* 121: 3–31.

(1982). *Zero Option*, London.
Tolstoy, Leo (1885). *What I Believe*, trans. C. Popoff, London.
(1894). *The Kingdom of God Is Within You*, trans. A. Delano, London.
Tully, James (1995). *Strange Multiplicity: Constitutionalism in an Age of Diversity*, Cambridge.
(2000). 'The Challenge of Reimagining Citizenship and Belonging in Multicultural and Multinational Societies', in C. McKinnon and I. Hampsher-Monk (eds.) *The Demands of Citizenship*, London and New York, pp. 212–34.
Voet, Rian (1998). *Feminism and Citizenship*, London.
Walby, Sylvia (1990). *Theorising Patriarchy*, Oxford.
Waldron, Jeremy (1992). 'Minority Cultures and the Cosmopolitan Alternative', *University of Michigan Journal of Law Reform* 25(3): 751–93.
Walzer, Kenneth (1977). *Just and Unjust Wars: A Moral Argument with Historical Illustrations*, New York.
Wexler, Alice (1989). *Emma Goldman in Exile*, Boston, Mass.
White, Lynn, Jr (1968). 'The Historical Roots of Our Ecologic Crisis', in *Machina ex Deo: Essays in the Dynamism of Western Culture*, Cambridge, Mass.
Whitford, Margaret (1991a). 'Irigaray's Body Symbolic', *Hypatia* 6: 97–110.
(1991b). *Luce Irigaray. Philosophy in the Feminine*, London.
Wilkie, Wendell L. (1943). *One World*, New York.
Williams, Beryl (1986). 'Kollontai and After: Women in the Russian Revolution', in Sian Reynolds (ed.) *Women, State and Revolution. Essays on Power and Gender in Europe since 1789*, Brighton, pp. 60–80.
Williams, Patricia (1991). *The Alchemy of Race and Rights*, Cambridge, Mass.
Wittig, Monique (1988a). 'One is not Born a Woman', in Sarah L. Hoagland and Julia Penelope (eds.) *For Lesbians Only: A Separatist Anthology*, London, pp. 439–48.
(1988b). 'The Straight Mind', in Sarah L. Hoagland and Julia Penelope (eds.) *For Lesbians Only: A Separatist Anthology*, London, pp. 431–39.
Worster, Donald (1994). *Nature's Economy: A History of Ecological Ideas*, 2nd edn, Cambridge.
Wright, Cyril and Augarde, Tony (1990) (eds.). *Peace is the Way: A Guide to Pacifist Views and Action*, Cambridge.
Yeatman, Anna (1994). *Postmodern Revisionings of the Political*, London.
Yoder, John (1976). *Nevertheless*, 2nd edn, Scottdale, Penn.
Young, Iris Marion (1981). 'Beyond the Unhappy Marriage of Marxism and Feminism: A Critique of the Dual Systems Theory', in Lydia Sargent (ed.) *Women and Revolution*, London, pp. 43–69.
(1990a). *Justice and the Politics of Difference*, Princeton, N.J.
(1990b). 'Throwing Like a Girl: A Phenomenology of Feminine Body Comportment, Motility and Spatiality', in *Throwing Like a Girl and Other Essays in Feminist Philosophy and Social Theory*, Bloomington, Ind., pp. 141–59.
(2000). *Democracy and Inclusion*, Oxford.

Part V: Beyond Western political thought

Primary sources

Abduh, Muhammad (1965). *Risalat al-Tawhid* (Treatise on Unity), Cairo.
Amin, Samir (1989). 'al-Ijtihad wa al-Ibda' fi al-Thaqafa al-'Arabiya wa Amam al-Tahadi al-Hadari' (Ijtihad and Innovation in Arab Culture in the Face of Civilisational Challenge), *Qadaya Fikriya* 8: 295–305.
Arkoun, Mohammed (1982). *Lectures du Coran*, Paris.

(1984). *Pour une critique de la raison islamique*, Paris.
(1987a). *Tarikhiyat al-Fikr al-'Arabi al-Islami* (The Historicity of Arab Islamic Thought), Beirut.
(1987b). *Rethinking Islam Today*, Washington D.C.
al-Ashmawi, Muhammad Said (1996). *al-Khilafa al-Islamiyya* (The Islamic Caliphate) 3rd edn, Cairo.
al-Azm, Sadiq Jalal (1969). *Naqd al-Fikr al-Dini* (A Critique of Religious Thought), Beirut.
Fanon, F. (1967). *The Wretched of the Earth*, Harmondsworth.
(1970). *Black Skin, White Masks*, London.
Fuda, Faraj (1988). *al-Haqiqa al-Gha'iba* (The Missing Truth), Cairo.
Hanafi, Hasan (1981). *Al-Turath wa al-Tajdid* (Heritage and Renewal), Beirut.
(1992). *Muqadimah fi 'Ilm al-Istighrab* (Introduction to the Science of Orientalism), Beirut.
Iqbal, Muhammad (1940). *Secrets of the Self (Asrar-I Khudi) a Philosophical Poem*, 2nd edn, trans. from the original Persian with introductory notes by Reynold A Nicholson, Lahore.
(1954). *The Reconstruction of Religious Thought in Islam*, Lahore.
al-Jabiri, Muhammad Abid (1982). *Al-Khitab al-Arabi al-Mu'asir* (Contemporary Arab Discourse), Beirut.
(1985). *Nahnu wa al-Turath* (We and the Heritage), Beirut.
(1986). *Naqd al-Aql al-Arabi: Binyat al-'Aql al-'Arabi, Dirasa Tahliliya li Nuzum al-Mi'rifa fi al-Thaqafa al-'Arabiya* (Critique of Arab Reason, the Structure of Arab Reason: An Analytical Study of the Systems of Knowledge in Arab Culture), Beirut.
(1999). *Arab-Islamic Philosophy: A Contemporary Critique*, trans. from the French by Aziz Abbassi, Austin, Tex.
Abd al-Karim, Khalil (1997). *Quraysh min al-Qabila ila al-Dawla* (Quraysh from Tribe to Central State), Cairo.
Khomeini, Ruhollah al-Musavi (1981). 'Islamic Government', in *Islam and Revolution: Writings and Declarations of Imam Khomeini*, trans. and annotated Hamid Algar, Berkeley, Calif.
Laroui, Abdallah (1976). *The Crisis of the Arab Intellectual: Traditionalism or Historicism?*, trans. Diarmid Cammell, Berkeley, Calif.
Mawdudi, Sayyid Abu al-Ala (1955). *Islamic Law*, trans. Ahmad Khurshid, Karachi.
(1979). *Islamic Way of Life*, trans. and ed. Khurshid Ahmad, 11th edn, Lahore.
Muruwah, Husayn (1978). *al-Naza'at al-Madiya fi al-Falsafah al-'Arabiya al-Islamiya* (Materialist Tendencies in Arab Islamic Philosophy), Beirut.
Nyerere, J. (1967). *Freedom and Unity*, Oxford.
(1968). *Freedom and Socialism*, Oxford.
al-Qimani, Mahmud Sayyid (1996). *Al-Hizb al-Hashimi wa Ta'sis al-Dawla al-Islamiya* (The Hashemite Faction and the Foundation of the Islamic State), Cairo.
Qutb, Sayyid (1987). *Ma' rakat al-Islam wa al-Ra'smaliya* (The Battle of Islam and Capitalism), 10th edn, Cairo.
(1989). *Ma'alim fi al-Tariq* (Milestones), 13th edn, Cairo.
Abd al-Raziq, Ali (1925). *al-Islam wa Usul al-Hukm* (Islam and the Fundamentals of Rule), Cairo.
Rida, Rashid (n.d.). *al-Khilafa aw al-Imama al-Uzma* (The Caliphate or the Supreme Imamate), Cairo.
Shari'ati, Ali (1980). *Marxism and Other Fallacies: An Islamic Critique*, trans. R. Campbell, Berkeley, Calif.
(1986). 'What Is To Be Done', in *What Is To Be Done: The Enlightened Thinkers and an Islamic Renaissance*, ed. and annotated Farhang Rajaee, Houston, Tex., pp. 29–70.

Soroush, Abdolkarim (2000). *Reason, Freedom and Democracy in Islam, Essential Writings of Abdolkarim Soroush*, trans., ed. and with a critical introduction by Mahmoud Sadri and Ahmad Sadri, Cambridge.

Tagore, Rabindranath (1917). *Nationalism*, London.

Zakariya, Fu'ad (1986). 'al-Muslim al Mu'asir wa al-Bahth 'an al-Yaqin' (The Contemporary Muslim and the Search for Certainty), in *al-Haqiqa wa al-Wahm fi al-Sahwa al-Islamiya al-Mu'asira* (Reality and Illusion in the Contemporary Islamist Resurgence), Cairo, pp. 5–26.

(1987). 'al-Takhaluf al-fikri wa Ab'adahu al-Hadariya' (Intellectual Retardation and its Civilisational Dimensions), in *al-Sahwa al-Islamiya fir Mizan in al-'Aql* (Islamic Resurgence in the Scale of Reason), Cairo, pp. 37–62.

Secondary sources

Abdo, Geneive (1998). *No God But God: Egypt and the Triumph of Islam*, Oxford.

Abu Rabi', Ibrahim M. (1996). *Intellectual Origins of Islamic Resurgence in the Modern Arab World*, New York.

Akhavi, Shahrough (1983). 'Shariati's Social Thought', in Nikki R. Keddie (ed.) *Religion and Politics in Iran*, New Haven, Conn., pp. 125–44.

(1997). 'The Dialectic in Contemporary Egyptian Social Thought: The Scripturalist and Modernist Discourses of Sayyid Qutb and Hasan Hanafi', *International Journal of Middle East Studies* 29: 377–401.

Algar, Hamid (1985) (ed.). *Imam Khomeini: Islam and Revolution*, London.

Arjomand, Said Amir (1993). 'Shi'ite Jurisprudence and Constitution Making in the Islamic Republic of Iran', in Martin E. Marty and R. Scott Appelby (eds.) *Fundamentalisms and the State*, Chicago, pp. 88–109.

al-Azmeh, Aziz (1993). *Islams and Modernities*, London.

Bayat, Mangol (1989). 'Ayatollah Sayyid Ruhullah Musawi Khumayni', in *Expectation of the Millennium: Shi'ism in History*, ed. and annotated Seyyed Hossein Nasr, Hamid Dabashi and Seyyed Vali Reza Nasr, Albany, N.Y.

Borourjerdi, Mehrzad (1996). *Iranian Intellectuals and the West: The Tormented Triumph of Nativism*, New York.

Brown, Daniel (1999). *Rethinking Tradition in Modern Islamic Thought*, Cambridge.

Choueiri, Youssef (1990). *Islamic Fundamentalism*, Boston.

(1997). *Islamic Fundamentalism*, rev. edn. London.

Coetzee, P. H. and Roux, A. J. P. (1998) (eds.). *The African Philosophy Reader*, London.

Constantino, R. (1985). *Synthetic Culture and Development*, Quezon City, Philippines.

Dajani, Zahia Ragheb (1990). *Egypt and the Crisis of Islam*, New York.

Enayat, Hamid (1982). *Modern Islamic Political Thought*, Austin, Tex.

Escobar, A. (1995). *Encountering Development: The Making and Unmaking of the Third World*, Princeton, N.J.

Esposito, John (1983) (ed.). *Voices of Resurgent Islam*, New York.

(1998). *Islam: The Straight Path*, New York.

Euben, Roxanne L. (1999). *Enemy in the Mirror: Islamic Fundamentalism and the Limits of Modern Rationalism*, Princeton, N.J.

Fairbank, John (1992). *China: A New History*, Cambridge.

Gernet, Jacques (1996). *A History of Chinese Civilisation*, Cambridge.

Gershoni, Israel and Jankowski, James (1997). *Redefining the Egyptian Nation, 1930–1945*, Cambridge.

Gheissari, Ali (1998). *Iranian Intellectuals in the 20th Century*, Austin, Tex.
Hourani, Albert (1983). *Arabic Thought in the Liberal Age*, Cambridge.
Kerr, Malcolm (1966). *Islamic Reform: The Political and Legal Theories of Muhammad Abduh and Rashid Rida*, Berkeley, Calif.
LaGuerre, John (1982). *Enemies of Empire*, St Augustine, Fla.
Lee, Robert D. (1997). *Overcoming Tradition and Modernity: The Search for Authenticity*, Boulder, Colo.
Levenson, J. (1958). *Confucian China and its Modern Fate*, Berkeley, Calif.
Mardin, Serif (1962). *The Genesis of Young Ottoman Thought, A Study of the Modernization of Turkish Political Ideas*, Princeton, N.J.
Matin-asgari, Afshin (1997). 'Abdolkarim Sorush and the Secularization of Islamic Thought in Iran', *Iranian Studies* 30(1–2): 95–115.
Miller, C. L. (1990). *Theories of Africans: Francophone Literature and Anthropology in Africa*, Chicago.
Mirsepassi, Ali (2000). *Intellectual Discourse and the Politics of Modernization: Negotiating Modernity in Iran*, Cambridge.
Mottahedeh, Roy P. (1995). 'Wilayat al-Faqih', in *The Oxford Encyclopedia of the Modern Islamic World*, vol. IV, ed. John L. Esposito, New York.
Mphale, Ezekiel (1962). *The African Image*, New York.
Nandy, Ashis (1988). *Science, Hegemony and Violence: A Requiem for Modernity*, Delhi.
(1994). *The Illegitimacy of Nationalism*, Delhi.
Nasr, Seyyed Vali Reza (1996). *Mawdudi and the Making of Islamic Revivalism*, New York and Oxford.
Parekh, Bhikhu (1989). *Gandhi's Political Philosophy*, London.
(1992). 'The Poverty of Indian Political Theory', *History of Political Thought* 13: 535–60.
(1994). 'The Concept of Fundamentalism', in A. Shtromas (ed.) *The End of 'Isms'?*, London, pp. 105–26.
(1999). *Colonialism Tradition and Reform*, Delhi.
Rose, Gregory (1983). 'Velayat al-Faqih and the Recovery of Islamic Identity in the Thought of Ayatollah Khomeini', in Nikki R. Keddie (ed.) *Religion and Politics in Iran*, New Haven, Conn., pp. 166–88.
Roucek, Joseph (1946) (ed.). *Twentieth Century Political Thought*, New York.
Sabanegh, E. S. (n.d.). *Muhammad, le Prophète: portraits contemporains, Egypte 1930–50*, Paris.
Samson, G. B. (1984). *The Western World of Japan*, Tokyo.
Senghor, L. (1965). *On African Socialism*, Stanford, Calif.
(1967). *Negritude or Servitude*, Yaounde, Cameroon.
Smith, Charles (1973). 'The Crisis of Orientation: The Shift of Egyptian Intellectuals to Islamic Subjects in the 1930s', *International Journal of Middle Eastern Studies* 4: 382–410.
(1999). 'Cultural Constructs and Other Fantasies: Imagined Narratives in *Imagined Communities*; Surrejoinder to Gershoni and Jankowski's "Print Culture, Social Change and the Process of Redefining Imagined Communities in Egypt" ', *International Journal of Middle East Studies* 31 (1): 95–102.
Tan, Chester (1971). *Chinese Political Thought in the Twentieth Century*, New York.
Vahdat, Farzin (2000). 'Post-Revolutionary Discourse of Mohammad Mojtahed Shabestari and Mohsen Kadivar: Reconciling the Terms of Mediated Subjectivity, Part I: Mojtahed Shabestari', *Critique* 16: 31–53.
Wiredu, Kwasi (1966). *Cultural Universals and Particulars: An African Perspective*, Bloomington, Ind.
Worsley, Peter (1967). *The Third World*, London.

Epilogue: The grand dichotomy of the twentieth century

Anderson, P. (1994). 'Introduction', in P. Anderson and P. Camiller (eds.) *Mapping the West European Left*, London.

Bauer, J. and Bell, D. A. (1999) (eds.). *The East Asian Challenge for Human Rights*, Cambridge.

Beau de Lomenie, E. (1931). *Qu'appelez-vous droite et gauche?*, Paris.

Bobbio, N. (1996). *Left and Right: The Significance of a Political Distinction*, Cambridge.

Condorcet, M. J. A. N. de (1955 [1795]). *Sketch for a Historical Picture of the Progress of the Human Mind*, London.

Crosland, C. A. R. (1956). *The Future of Socialism*, London.

Dumont, L. (1990). 'Sur l'idéologie politique française: une perspective comparative', *Le Débat* 58: 128–58.

Eatwell, R. and O'Sullivan, N. (1989) (eds.). *The Nature of the Right: American and European Politics and Political Thought since 1789*, London.

Finocchiaro, M. A. (1999). *Beyond Right and Left: Democratic Elitism in Mosca and Gramsci*, New Haven, Conn.

Fukayama, F. (1992). *The End of History and the Last Man*, London.

Galbraith, J. K. (2002). 'A Perfect Crime: Inequality in the Age of Globalisation', *Daedalus* 131(1): 11–25.

Garton Ash, T. (1989). *The Uses of Adversity*, Cambridge.

Gauchet, M. (1997). 'La droite et la gauche', in P. Nora (ed.) *Les lieux de mémoire*, Paris, vol. II, pp. 2533–601.

Gay, P. (1962). *The Dilemma of Democratic Socialism*, London.

Giddens, A. (1994). *Beyond Left and Right: The Future of Radical Politics*, Cambridge.

(2000). *The Third Way and its Critics*, Cambridge.

Held, D. (1993). 'Democracy: from City-States to a Cosmopolitan Order?', in D. Held (ed.) *Prospects for Democracy: North, South, East, West*, Cambridge, pp. 13–52.

Hertz, R. (1973 [1928]). 'The Pre-eminence of the Right Hand: A Study in Religious Polarity', in R. Needham (ed.) *Right and Left: Essays on Dual Symbolic Classification*, Chicago and London, pp. 3–31.

Hirschman, A. O. (1991). *The Rhetoric of Reaction: Perversity, Futility, Jeopardy*, Cambridge, Mass.

Hobhouse, L. T. (1964 [1911]). *Liberalism*, New York.

Hobsbawm, E. (1981). *The Forward March of Labour Halted*, London.

(1994). *Age of Extremes: The Short Twentieth Century 1914–1991*, London.

Hobsbawm, E. with A. Pollito (2000). *The New Century*, London.

Kymlicka, W. (1995). *Multicultural Citizenship*, Oxford.

Laponce, J. A. (1981). *Left and Right: The Topography of Political Perceptions*, Toronto.

Lenin, V. I. (1969 [1918]). *'Left-Wing Childishness' and the Petty-Bourgeois Mentality*, in V. I. Lenin, *Selected Works*, London.

Lipset, S. M. (1960). *Political Man: The Social Bases of Politics*, London.

Lukes, S. (1992). 'What Is Left?', *Times Literary Supplement*, 27 March.

Marshall, T. H. (1963). 'Citizenship and Social Class', in T. H. Marshall, *Sociology at the Crossroads*, London.

Needham, R. (1973) (ed.). *Right and Left: Essays on Dual Symbolic Classification*, Chicago and London.

Othman, N. (1999). 'Grounding Human Rights Arguments in Non-Western Culture: Shari'a and the Citizenship Rights of Women in a Modern Islamic State', in J. Bauer and D. A. Bell (eds.) *The East Asian Challenge for Human Rights*, Cambridge, pp. 169–92.

Przeworski, A. (1985). *Capitalism and Social Democracy*, Cambridge.

(1993). 'Socialism and Social Democracy', in J. Krieger (ed.) *The Oxford Companion to the Politics of the World*, New York and Oxford.
Rawls, J. (1971). *A Theory of Justice*, Cambridge, Mass.
Scruton, R. (1992). 'What is Right? A Reply to Steven Lukes', *Times Literary Supplement*, 3 April.
Sen, A. (1992). *Inequality Re-Examined*, New York and Cambridge, Mass.
Shaw, G. B. (1889) (ed.). *Fabian Essays in Socialism*, London.
Sternhell, Z. (1996 [1986]). *Neither Right nor Left: Fascist Ideology in France*, Princeton, N.J.
Walzer, M. (1983). *Spheres of Justice: A Defence of Pluralism and Equality*, New York and Oxford.
Zolo, D. (1992). *Democracy and Complexity: A Realist Approach*, University Park, Penn.

Subject index

Subject index

Subject index

Subject index

Name index